CHINA
FACTS & FIGURES
ANNUAL

Please turn to the Questionnaire found on page x of this volume.

HOW TO SUBSCRIBE TO

CHINA FACTS & FIGURES ANNUAL

Institutions—Send Purchase Order for Volume 1 (1978) and following as available and published (Standing Order) for automatic shipping on account.

Individuals and Booksellers—Request pro forma invoice for subscriptions or for volumes desired.

Separate volumes—Available if not out of print.

Editions—CHIFFA appears in limited editions oriented to subscriptions. Order now to reserve your copy.

Contents—Each volume of CHIFFA contains masses of information not found in other volumes of the series.

Send orders to Academic International Press, POB 1111, Gulf Breeze FL 32561 USA

CHINA
FACTS & FIGURES
ANNUAL

Edited by
John L. Scherer

VOLUME 9, 1986

Academic International Press
1986

CHINA FACTS & FIGURES ANNUAL
Volume 9

ISBN: 0-87569-093-9

Title page by King & Queen Press
Composition by Jayne Berndsen, Mary Virginia McDaris
and Penelope Ann Wilkes

By direct subscription from the publisher.

*A list of Academic International Press publications
is found at the end of this volume.*

ACADEMIC INTERNATIONAL PRESS
Box 1111 Gulf Breeze FL 32561 USA

CONTENTS

vi CONTENTS

QUESTIONNAIRE

The purpose of this questionnaire is to learn better who is using CHIFFA, and where, how well CHIFFA is meeting the needs of users, what shortcomings need to be corrected, and what improvements are necessary. All responses will be treated confidentially.

DO NOT TEAR OUT THE QUESTIONNAIRE. LEAVE IT FOR OTHERS TO USE.

INSTRUCTIONS. (1) Answer the questions by number on a separate sheet of lined paper. There is no need to write the questions. (2) Use as much detail in your responses as you wish. The more the better. Please be frank. Your responses will have an impact. (3) Leave a blank line between questions. (4) Type or print or write very clearly—we must be able to read what you write. (5) Return to Academic International Press, POB 1111, Gulf Breeze FL 32561.

(1)   Today's date.
(2)   Which volume are you using?
(3)   Where are you using this volume?
(4)   Have you used other volumes of CHIFFA?
(5)   If yes, which volumes have you used?
(6)   If yes, where have you used these volumes?
(7)   When did you learn about CHIFFA?
(8)   How did you learn about CHIFFA?
(9)   Where did you learn about CHIFFA?
(10)   Do you have regular access to CHIFFA?
(11)   How do you have access (personal copy, institutional library, other)?
(12)   If an institutional library or other, please identify.
(13)   How frequently do you use CHIFFA?
(14)   Why are you using this volume?
(15)   Have you found what you want in CHIFFA?
(16)   If yes, what were you looking for?
(17)   If not, what were you looking for?
(18)   Which section(s) of CHIFFA is most useful to you? Explain.
(19)   Which section(s) of CHIFFA is least useful to you? Explain.
(20)   Which section(s) of CHIFFA is strongest? Why?
(21)   What section(s) of CHIFFA is weakest? Why?
(22)   As a whole, what is strong about CHIFFA?
(23)   As a whole, what are CHIFFA's shortcomings?
(24)   Please rank the sections of CHIFFA (Government, Party, Demography, etc.) according to their interest to you.
(25)   What additional features would you like to see in CHIFFA?
(26)   Which sections, if any, should be modified? Explain.
(27)   Which sections, if any, should be dropped? Explain.
(28)   Would you say that the quality and coverage of CHIFFA have been rising, falling, or unchanged, over recent years? Please comment.
(29)   What do your colleagues say about CHIFFA?
(30)   How much xeroxing do you do from CHIFFA and for what purpose?
(31)   Do you use CHIFFA or xeroxes for instructional purposes? Explain.
(32)   Do you have expertise suitable for publication in CHIFFA? Explain.
(33)   Please make any comments or suggestions.
(34)   Names and addresses of others who should know about CHIFFA.
(35)   Your name and address, if desired.

Thank You!

OPPOSITION TO REFORM

1985 seemed to be the year that observers discovered Deng Xiaoping's reforms might not last. 1) There was popular opposition to retail price hikes in the spring, and hoarding prior to the increases. Between May and September, the price index in cities rose 11 percent, the most serious inflation since 1949. The current subsidy of $2.19 per month paid to every urban resident to offset the rise in food prices will be raised in 1986, probably increasing inflation once again.

2) Reversing policy of the previous year, officials began to discourage consumer spending. The campaign to promote consumer purchases to develop domestic industries had resulted in sizeable consumer imports, and an expanding trade deficit of $14.9 billion in 1985. The deficit with Japan, for example, reached $2.3 billion by mid-1985. Foreign reserves have been reduced from $17 to $7 billion.

3) Urban residents have continued to resent the disproportionate gains in rural income since 1978. Deng's economic program to increase productivity is based on the unequal distribution of wealth, linking wages and bonuses to output, to encourage enterprise and effort. The reforms were begun in the countryside, where they substantially raised the per capita income of many peasants, and have recently been introduced in the cities.

4) For several years, Party leaders have been concerned about the loss of power to localities and to the emerging rich peasantry.

5) Chen Yun, who is said to have compared China's economy to a bird which must be kept in a cage, has opposed Deng's Open Door Policy, which, he believes, has allowed Western culture and materialistic goals to corrupt Chinese youth. Chen has spoken of "some cadres' children" who engage in profiteering. Pornographic videotapes and prostitution in China were also mentioned for the first time in an October 1985 meeting of the Central Disciplinary Commission.

6) Between 1981 and 1984 the grain harvest rose from 326 million tons to the world record of 407 million tons. Peasants currently receive guaranteed prices for about 40 percent of their agricultural output. Subsidies have forced the government to divert money from energy projects to pay the farmers. A wet spring and summer in the northeast provinces of Liaoning, Heilongjiang, and Jilin reduced crops 10-12 million tons. An autumn drought in Hebei, Hunan and Sichuan, which account for 10 percent of the grain harvest, and a reduction in sown area were expected to cut the grain harvest to 395-400 million tons in 1985. Nevertheless, this would still be the third largest grain harvest in 36 years. Farmers have reduced the area planted to cotton and wheat in favor of cash crops, such as sugar, tobacco, hemp, or oil-bearing crops. Grain acreage decreased from 78.3 percent of the total crop acreage in 1984 to 75.6 percent in 1985. Chen Yun has foreseen a mass migration from the farms to the cities, and the resulting grain shortages provoking social unrest. It is believed that 50 million have already shifted from farming to rural industry. The sociologist Fei Xiaotong has warned, "If our people rush to the cities, we will sink into the ocean."

7) Price increases and inflation have discouraged foreign investors, who are uncertain about the costs of domestic labor and goods. A number of investors are displeased by the joint-venture boards, on which five of the nine representatives are Chinese, including the chairman. They are said to be forums for the Chinese to make speeches and extreme proposals to gain a bargaining advantage. Enormous problems remain for foreign businessmen converting yuan to foreign currency.

8) Capital investment has continued to grow too rapidly, straining the energy and transportation sectors. Between January and July 1985 investment in capital construction grew 44.9 percent over the corresponding period in 1984. The availability rate of projects dropped from 24.4 percent to 15.6 percent. The number of large and medium-sized projects completed and commissioned decreased from 14 during this period in 1984 to 10 in 1985. By summer, officials were expressing confidence that local and central capital investment had been brought under control. The excessive increase in capital construction has been attributed to: a) projects undertaken without adequate feasibility studies; b) insufficient attention to preliminary budgets, with cost overruns; c) poor investment planning, worked out year-by-year, without mid- and long-term plans; d) the paramount interest of construction companies

to arrange new contracts rather than finish old projects; and e) specialized banks competing with one another to grant credits for capital construction.

9) Late in 1985 students demonstrated in Beijing against what they perceive as growing Japanese influence, against nuclear testing in Lop Nor, and against housing military units on a university campus. Protests brought out 4-10,000 students in Urumqi. The anti-Japanese demonstrations appeared to have been organized by Deng's opponents to criticize his Open Door Policy of importing foreign technology and culture. Deng responded by organizing other demonstrations, with student speakers favoring his policies.

10) There was opposition to the rise of the "princes' party," with student leaders publishing the names of the children of senior cadres appointed to important posts. That number has actually remained small, just over 10, according to a Party official. Nonetheless, the children of senior officials have managed to travel abroad, join the PLA, enroll in universities, and set up lucrative businesses using family names and connections.

Ever since Deng took power, the media has revealed opposition to his programs. Leftist influences obviously remain: 1) In 1985, grass-roots cadres were criticized for taking class struggle as the key link; 2) Certain people continued to believe that "large in size and collective in nature" was superior; 3) Obstacles to rehabilitating victims of the Cultural Revolution have endured; 4) Some people have hesitated to negate the influences of the Cultural Revolution; 5) Some have not diversified in agriculture, and still take grain as the key link; 6) Part of the masses continue to think it is glorious to be poor and disgraceful to be rich, and do not work hard to become wealthier; and 7) The fear of criticism has inhibited tradesmen and specialists from fully utilizing their talents to develop the economy.

RESPONSES

Much of the opposition reported by Western analysts may be exaggerated. The Chinese press may report some opposition to justify harsher measures and to rally the population behind the reforms. Deng still seems very much in control. Many observers interpreted his 1985 reference to the Shenzhen Special Economic Zone being only an "experiment" as an indication that opposition had increased. The SEZs, whose development strategy was designated by Zhao Ziyang in November 1984 as "two fan sectors and one pivot" (one fan radiating inwardly and one outwardly to earn foreign exchange, with the SEZ acting as the pivot), have failed to balance foreign exchange income and expenses. Their factory products have not been sufficiently competitive on the international market, and a large share of output has been sold domestically, without providing the desired foreign exchange. An investigation in March 1985 revealed that two-thirds of the companies dealing in imports and exports in the Shenzhen SEZ had violated the foreign currency control system.

In this and other matters, one should expect some reversals and shifts in direction. Deng has basically succeeded in implementing his reforms in the countryside, and the second phase is currently being introduced with difficulties into China's cities. Some economic innovations have seemed vague. Many experiments simply will not work. There have been moves to decentralize decisions, particularly with foreign trade and banking, then attempts to reassert central controls; decisions to increase, then control, capital investment; to import Western technology, then reduce purchases; to encourage consumer spending, then restrain consumption for savings. Hu Yaobang has compared the shifts to driving a car: "As you go forward, you turn the wheel to the left and right, adjusting as you go, but you don't turn around. It's not a reversal."

There should be no question, however, most of the reforms have been successful. The banking system has been decentralized; a partial market mechanism introduced; a new tax system developed based on cash payments; urban and rural trade fairs (free markets) restored; both foreign and domestic joint ventures and foreign capital investment encouraged; the communes have been replaced by townships and the administrative and economic functions of localities separated; an infrastructure of ports, railways, and roads developed; and foreign trade system reorganized. Deng and his proteges have renewed the traditional Chinese respect for education, and stressed science and technology. A "responsibility system" introduced in the countryside has allowed households to market any surplus agricultural production at higher prices to the state or at free markets. The second stage of reforms in the cities was announced in August 1984. It expanded the autonomy of enterprises (begun on an experimental basis in Sichuan in 1978) with 10 regulations concerning their decision-making powers, set Chongqing up as a model, and increased the economic authority of provinces and municipalities (initially begun in 1983).

The Chinese media reported numerous cases of corruption and profiteering in 1985, especially in Hainan Island. This, like many other problems, should have been anticipated. Officials there imported some 75,000 Japanese vehicles worth $600-$900 million, then sold them to buyers on the Mainland at three to four times the original price. Party and government cadres have established at least 16,000 unsanctioned and illegal businesses, and reportedly have reaped "staggering profits." The government has tried to end these businesses, and it also has promised to fire administrators who fail to allow enterprises more autonomy. Nevertheless, supervisory bodies have been reluctant to relinquish their power to the factories, particularly at Guangzhou and in Guangdong province, thereby reducing the efficiency and initiative expected from the 1984 enterprise reforms. These are extremely complicated economic and political issues, and many Chinese are dealing with unfamiliar territory.

In 1985, Deng identified a "third echelon" of Party leaders. General Secretary Hu Yaobang and Premier Zhao Ziyang form a "second tier" of administrators. The "third" is dominated by Hu Qili, referred to as a "permanent Secretary" of the Central Committee, where he is in charge of daily affairs, and who is expected to succeed Hu Yaobang, and by Li Peng, a Vice-Premier, and the likely successor to Zhao. At a special Party conference attended by some 1,000 persons in September, Deng named 64 newcomers to the Central Committee, 29 full members and 35 alternates. Their average age was over 50, and 76 percent had college educations. Just 4 percent of the Party's 42 million members have college degrees. Ten of the 24 Politburo members were retired, including Ye Jianying, 88, Deng Yingchao, Xu Xianqian, Nie Rongzhen, Ulanhu, Wang Zhen, Wei Guoqing, Li Desheng, Song Renqiong, and Zhang Tingfa. Fifty-six new members were appointed to the Central Advisory Commission, and 31 to the Central Discipline Inspection Commission. Deng apparently felt he could not wait until the regular Party Congress convened in 1987, and used the occasion to remove some aged leaders.

Several adversaries of Deng have also remained in office, such as Chen Yun, 83, who is said to resent the fact that "one person alone has the say;" Hu Qiaomu, 73; Peng Zhen, 83, the Chairman of the National People's Congress; and Deng Liqun, who launched the drive against "spiritual pollution" in the autumn of 1984, but was subsequently removed as Director of the Propaganda Department of the Central Committee. Deng Liqun also has lost his position as the Director of the Secretariat's Institute for Policy Studies to Wang Zhaoguo, the head of the General Office of the Central Committee and recently appointed a member of the Secretariat. In 1985, however, Deng Liqun's views frequently appeared in the press. This may indicate Deng Xiaoping's inability to eliminate the opposition, or more likely, Deng gradually removes people who do not support his policies. He does not humiliate adversaries, or eliminate them in a single stroke, but subtly, in several stages. Deng has appointed opponents to new administrative positions, moved them around in the bureaucracy, often from their provincial strongholds to the center in Beijing, or eliminated them through his rejuvenation campaign, which seeks younger and more educated leaders for China. Deng started reshuffling the central bureaucracy in 1982 and had reached the sub-provincial level by mid-1983. He changed the leadership of the Armed Forces, reducing the number of Military Regions from 11 to seven in June 1985. Personnel also have been removed or reshuffled in the Chinese media. Since 1982, two purges have replaced nearly all of the managers of the 3,000 largest state enterprises.

The growth of private enterprises has been another victory for Deng. The main hope is in collective enterprises in the PRC. Some 100 million work in 1.7 million collectives. The 85,000 state-owned factories continue to produce about 80 percent of China's industrial output. The most notable change during the last few years, however, has been the growth of private businesses and services. There were 10.6 million registered private businesses with total sales of $8 billion, employing 15 million workers, or 4.5 percent of the non-farm work force.

Deng has emphasized productive forces ("leading an ox by the reins") rather than differentiating between "the enemy, ourselves, and friends," and has spoken about developing a "second civilization," requiring political and ideological education as well as the development of socialist education, science and technology, and culture. For the most part, he has succeeded beyond anybody's expectations. China's economy has sustained phenomenal rates of growth. Total agricultural and industrial output value increased about 15 percent and national income 13.9 percent in 1984. Both rates were expected to exceed 13 percent in 1985. Industrial output value grew 18 percent, and the value of agricultural production rose 10 percent. Energy production has grown from virtually nothing a few years ago to about 8 percent annually. Consumption levels increased 7 percent a year during 1981-85. State revenue rose 20 percent in 1985, allowing the budget to be balanced and eliminating deficit spending for the first time in the 1980s. Production by township enterprises rose 35 percent. The Seventh Five Year Plan, however, envisages significantly lower annual growth rates, about 7 percent for national income, for the gross value of industrial and agricultural output and for industrial production. Agricultural output is to increase about 6 percent a year during 1986-90, and the production of goods and services in rural areas by approximately 8.4 percent annually.

THE MILITARY

The Armed Forces remain the least important of the Four modernizations. It was announced in June 1985 that the PLA would cut its personnel by one million over the next two years. It appears that some 800,000 troops actually will return to civilian life in 1986, but recent reductions simply have moved personnel from military to civilian jurisdiction. PLA strength has fallen below 4 million by shifting its internal security functions to the Ministry of Public Security in 1983, and by transferring the Railway Engineer Corps to the Ministry of Railways and placing the Capital Construction Engineering Corps under civilian control in 1984. The militia has also been reorganized, and China has started to purchase weapons from the US and other nations after many years of looking without buying.

Deng removed General Li Desheng as Commander of the Shenyang Military Region in June, and then from the Politburo in September 1985. The number of regional commands has been reduced from 11 to seven, with younger, educated cadres filling the posts.

FOREIGN TRADE

China's foreign trade has grown from $29.3 billion in 1979 to $49.7 billion in 1984. Direct foreign trade investments during the past five years totaled $1.7 billion. The most significant factor in foreign trade in 1985 may have been the deficit with Japan. Turnover with the USSR has soared since 1983. Beijing also began to trade with Indonesia for the first time since 1965.

While disagreement continued with Washington about textile quotas, and bumper grain harvests precluded major grain purchases, a nuclear technology agreement went into effect. Despite pledges that China will not divert the technology for military uses, a nuclear weapon was prepared for testing in Xinjiang for Pakistan. Basically, the market for nuclear technology was considered too lucrative to ignore, with sales estimated between $3 billion and $7 billion. The guarantees that the technology will not be diverted are, in any case, unenforceable. Most experts predict, however, that a nuclear power reactor cannot become operational for at least 10 years. President Reagan also vetoed a trade protectionist bill which would have cut American imports of Chinese textiles, shoes, and copper.

SINO-SOVIET RELATIONS

During March and October 1985, China and the USSR exchanged parliamentary delegations for the first time in years, and Deputy Premier Yao Yilin visited Moscow in July. Trade has risen sharply since 1983, totaling 4.6 billion Swiss francs in 1985, the highest turnover in 25 years. The singer Hu Xiaoping was in the USSR in February and March. A protocol on education was signed in April 1985, and for the first time in many years, trade union and women's delegations were exchanged. The USSR-China Friendship Society sent a delegation to China in April, reciprocating for a Chinese visit in 1984. A cultural agreement was signed in June. The Soviets exhibited books in Beijing in July, and participated in the Fourth International Fair of Asian and Pacific Countries in Beijing in November. The PRC took part in the 14th International Film Festival in Moscow, Chinese ballerinas performed in the Fifth International Ballet Contest there, and the Gansu Dance Ensemble toured the Soviet Union. The Moscow Classical Ballet Ensemble visited the PRC in October, and the Opera Troupe of the PLA General Political Department performed a Soviet work. The Belorussian State

Academic People's Choir was in the PRC in December. The Chinese observed the jubilees of many Soviet writers, such as Chekhov, Sholokov, and Lev Tolstoi. A Beijing radio station started to broadcast Russian language lessons in August for the first time in 25 years.

THE FUTURE

There have been rumors that Deng is seriously ill. Within five years of Deng's death, many of his reforms will probably be modified or reversed. The changes in China since 1978 have been fascinating, and certainly as successful as social changes anywhere in the world since World War II. A significant number of people inevitably will be left behind by the reforms, and rural equality and social services probably will be reemphasized by his successors. Foreign contacts could be curtailed, and presumably, Deng will be criticized for insufficient planning and ideological laxity. Even if Deng's proteges and the "third echelon" manage to retain power, the new leaders will want to leave their own mark on China. It is unlikely that they could increase the rates of economic growth more rapidly than Deng, and presumably, they will go in the other direction, and stress planning and greater central direction of the economy. There should be less foreign cultural influence, and a narrower choice of subjects and forms of expression for artists and writers.

In the near future, the pace of replacing officials and purging the Party and state bureaucracies should slow. This has gone on for several years now, and most serious political opposition to Deng has been removed, demoted, or silenced by his demands for younger, more educated leaders. There is no use for a permanent purge in China.

Political relations between the PRC and the Soviet Union are stalled. There is no way, nor really any need, to improve political relations without a sizeable withdrawal of Soviet troops near the Chinese border and from Afghanistan, and reduced Soviet aid to the Vietnamese in Cambodia. On the other hand, cultural contacts and trade should continue to grow significantly.

While trade between the US and China will increase more slowly, American agricultural exports to the PRC should remain low. They have fallen precipitously since 1982 as a result of record Chinese harvests. Trade turnover amounted to almost $8.5 billion in 1985.

The PRC will have to reduce Japanese imports after running up large trade deficits. One expects that Japan will continue to play the primary role in the economic development of China, but the purchase of whole plants and the use of Japanese credits must be tempered.

Finally, the state has to become even more active in developing the energy and transportation sectors. The average annual percentage increase in hydropower capacity has dropped from 10.7 percent during 1965-79 to 5.8 percent during 1979-84. China's largest inland oil fields have peaked. Offshore resources need to be developed and new inland resources exploited. Doubling natural gas production by 2000 will primarily depend on the speed of extracting gas from the Sichuan Basin and from new fields at Zhongyuan and Hainan Island. To achieve targets for coal production by 2000, China will have to increase output by some 40 million tons annually. This seems unlikely, even though coal production increased 45 million tons in both 1983 and 1984. Energy targets are simply too high.

Not only does China depend on higher energy output for industrial growth, but the export of petrochemical products accounted for 20 percent of the value of its total foreign trade turnover and 25 percent of its exports in 1985. China must produce oil to sell abroad in order to purchase foreign technology.

Exploiting energy resources also will require greater investment in the transportation sector, particularly railroads. In the past few years, regional railroads and airlines have formed. At the end of 1985, there were some 1,300 private or collectively-owned transport services and joint ventures. New private taxi services, for example, should relieve some urban transport problems, but developing the infrastructure of the Chinese economy is an immense task, and as in other areas, one requiring central organization, planning, and investment.

Readers are urged to consult previous volumes of CHIFFA for different statistical tables and information. Each volume of CHIFFA is virtually a different book. FBIS-CHI refers to the US Foreign Broadcast Information Service daily reports on China. XNB is the Xinhua News Bulletin. A considerable amount of information on China may be found in *USSR Facts & Figures Annual*, also published by Academic International Press. CHIFFA uses the Stanford format. Comments, suggestions and information for CHIFFA may be sent to the Editor, c/o Academic International Press, Box 1111, Gulf Breeze, Florida 32561. All subscription orders should be sent to the publisher at the above address.

John L. Scherer

II SUMMARY OF INDUSTRIAL AND AGRICULTURAL PRODUCTION, 1985

		Increase Over 1984 (percent)
Total industrial output value (bn yuan)	875.9	18.0
Including the output value of industry run by villages (bn yuan)	969.4	21.4
Total output value of light industry (bn yuan)	408.9	18.1
Total output value of heavy industry (bn yuan)	467.0	17.9
Primary energy output (mn tons of std coal)	839.0	7.8
Total output value of agriculture, including		
industry run by villages (bn yuan)	451.0	13.0
excluding industry run by villages (bn yuan)	357.5	3.0

MAJOR PRODUCTS OF HEAVY INDUSTRY:

Coal	850 million metric tons	7.7
Crude Oil	125 million metric tons	8.9
Electricity	407.3 billion kwh	8.0
of which hydroelectricity	91 billion kwh	4.8
Steel	46.66 million million metric tons	7.3
Rolled Steel	36.79 million metric tons	9.1
Timber	63.1 million cubic meters	-1.2
Cement	142.46 million metric tons	15.8
Sulfuric Acid	6.69 million metric tons	-18.2
Soda Ash	2 million metric tons	6.5
Chemical Fertilizers	13.35 million metric tons	-8.6
Chemical Insecticides	205,000 metric tons	-31.3
Power-generating equipment	5.61 million kw	20.1
Machine tools	155,000	15.7
Motor vehicles	439,000	38.7
Tractors (over 20 hp)	44,600	12.3
Locomotives	746	13.4
Steel ships for civilian use	1.66 million metric tons	0.6

MAJOR PRODUCTS OF LIGHT INDUSTRY:

Cotton yarn	3,510,000 tons	9.1
Cloth	14.3 billion meters	4.2
Wool fabrics	210 million meters	16.8
Machine-made paper and paper board	8,260,000 tons	9.3
Sugar	4,450,000 tons	17.1
Cigarettes	23.51 million boxes	10.3
Chemical pharmaceuticals	57,000 tons	9.6
Bicycles	32,350,000	13.0
Sewing machines	9,860,000	9.8
Wrist watches	41,730,000	9.6
TV sets	16,220,000	61.6
of which Color sets	4,100,000	206.0
Cassette recorders	12,710,000	63.7
Cameras	1,800,000	42.4
Household washing machines	8,830,000	52.8
Household refrigerators	1,390,000	154.0

MAJOR FARM PRODUCTS:

Grain	378,980,000 tons	-7.0
Cotton	4,150,000 tons	-33.7
Oil-bearing crops	15,780,000 tons	32.5
Sugar cane	51,470,000 tons	30.2
Beet root	8,910,000 tons	7.6
Jute, ambary hemp	3,400,000 tons	128.1
Flue-cured tobacco	2,080,000 tons	34.5
Silkworm cocoons	370,000 tons	4.8
Tea	440,000 tons	6.8

OUTPUT OF MAJOR ANIMAL BY-PRODUCTS AND NUMBERS OF LIVESTOCK:

Output of pork, beef, and mutton	17,550,000 tons	13.9
Milk	2,500,000 tons	14.2
Sheep wool and goat hair	180,000 tons	-3.3
Hogs slaughtered	238,950,000 head	8.4
Large animals at year end	113,820,000 head	5.0
Pigs at year end	331,480,000 head	8.0
Sheep and goats at year end	156,160,000 head	-1.4

FBIS-CHI 41 (3 Mar 1986), K4/6.

III GOVERNMENT

PRESIDENT, VICE-PRESIDENT, AND COUNCIL OF MINISTERS OF THE PEOPLE'S REPUBLIC OF CHINA

President	Li Xiannian
Vice President	Ulanhu
Premier, State Council	Zhao Ziyang
Vice Premier, State Council	Li Peng
Vice Premier, State Council	Tian Jiyun
Vice Premier, State Council	Wan Li
Vice Premier, State Council	Yao Yilin
State Councilor, State Council	Chen Muhua
State Councilor, State Council	Fang Yi
State Councilor, State Council	Gu Mu
State Councilor, State Council	Ji Pengfei
State Councilor, State Council	Kang Shi'en
State Councilor, State Council	Song Ping
State Councilor, State Council	Wang Bingqian
State Councilor, State Council	Wu Xueqian
State Councilor, State Council	Zhang Aiping
State Councilor, State Council	Zhang Jingfu
Secretary General	Tian Jiyun
Auditor General of Auditing Admin.	Lu Peijian
Chmn., Central Military Comn.	Deng Xiaoping
Min. in Charge of National Defense Sci., Tech., & Industry Comn.	Ding Henggao
Min. in Charge of State Economic Comn.	Lu Dong
Min. in Charge of State Education Comn.	Li Peng
Min. in Charge of State Family Planning Comn.	Wang Wei
Min. in Charge of State Nationalities Affairs Comn.	Yang Jingren
Min. in Charge of State Physical Culture & Sports Comn.	Li Menghua
Min. in Charge of State Planning Comn.	Song Ping
Min. in Charge of State Restructuring of Economic System Comn.	Zhao Ziyang
Min. in Charge of State Sci. & Tech. Comn.	Song Jian
Min. of Aeronautics	Mo Wenxiang
Min. of Agriculture, Animal Husbandry, & Fishery	He Kang
Min. of Astronautics	Li Xu'e
Min. of Chemical Industry	Qin Zhongda
Min. of Civil Affairs	Cui Naifu
Min. of Coal Industry	Yu Hongen
Min. of Commerce	Liu Yi
Min. of Communications	Qian Yongchang
Min. of Culture.	Zhu Muzhi
Min. of Electronics Industry	Li Tieying

continued . . .

PRESIDENT, VICE-PRESIDENT, AND COUNCIL OF MINISTERS OF THE PEOPLE'S REPUBLIC OF CHINA (continued)

Min. of Finance	Wang Bingqian
Min. of Foreign Affairs	Wu Xueqian
Min. of Foreign Economic Relations & Trade	Zheng Tuobin
Min. of Forestry	Yang Zhong
Min. of Geology & Mineral Resources	Zhu Xun
Min. of Justice	Zou Yu
Min. of Labor & Personnel	Zhao Dongwan
Min. of Light Industry	Yang Bo
Min. of Machine-Building Industry	Zhou Jiannan
Min. of Metallurgical Industry	Qi Yuanjing
Min. of National Defense	Zhang Aiping
Min. of Nuclear Industry	Jiang Xinxiong
Min. of Ordnance Industry	Zou Jiahua
Min. of Petroleum Industry	Wang Tao
Min. of Posts & Telecommunications	Yang Taifang
Min. of Public Health	Cui Yueli
Min. of Public Security	Ruan Chongwu
Min. of Radio & Television	Ai Zhisheng
Min. of Railways	Ding Guangen
Min. of State Security	Jia Chunwang
Min. of Textile Industry	Wu Wenying
Min. of Urban & Rural Construction & Environmental Protection	
Min. of Water Resources & Electric Power	Qian Zhengying
Pres., People's Bank of China	Chen Muhua

CIA, *Chiefs of State and Cabinet Members of Foreign Governments* (Nov-Dec 1985), 18-20.

GOVERNMENT NEWS, 1985

Townships—Efforts to dismantle 56,000 rural communes as the basic units of state government have been completed after five years. Some 92,000 townships have been established in their place. The move sought to decentralize government, reduce interference by commune officials in village life, and provide better-educated, younger administrators. Township officials are an average of four to five years younger than former commune officials. *Beijing Review,* 24 (17 Jun 1985), 8.

Court Decisions to be Published—The Supreme People's Court began to publish its decisions in May, 1985. This is the first time in 35 years that the Court has published communiques. Some decisions by the Court's Judicial Committee and provincial people's courts will also be published. *China Daily* (26 May 1985), 1.

Lunch—Beijing civil servants will have an hour-and-a-half lunch break during the summer. The break had been reduced from two hours to one in January, 1985. New York *Times* (7 Jul 1985), 4.

Last of the Communes—China's 56,000 communes from the Great Leap Forward have been completely replaced by 92,000 townships. The administrative and economic functions of the townships are separated. Directly elected villagers committees, currently numbering 820,000, have also replaced production brigades. *Asian Wall Street Journal Weekly* (10 Jun 1985), 13.

continued . . .

GOVERNMENT NEWS, 1985 (continued)

Chen Yonggui—*Wen Wei Po* (Hong Kong, 23 and 24 Apr 1985) carries an interview with Chen Yonggui, 71, former leader of the Dazhai brigade. Chen left Dazhai several years ago and has worked as an adviser at the Beijing Eastern Suburbs State Farm.

Educational Level of Cadres—The level of education of cadres is:

	Million	Percent
Total	22+	100
Higher education	4.8	22
Secondary or specialized	6.2	29
Senior middle-school	3	14
Junior middle-school or primary	8	37

Of the more than 9 million professional and technical cadres, 1.3 million are senior or medium-level technological personnel. China will need an estimated 8.53 million senior and middle-level personnel trained in the six specialities of economic planning, statistics, finance and trade, monetary affairs, management engineering, and technological and economic management by the year 2000. It currently has just over 710,000 such people. FBIS-CHI 24 (5 Feb 1985), K1. In 1983 there were 8,423 Party and cadre schools and institutions of higher learning and secondary schools training cadres. That year about 788,000 cadres completed their studies (p. K5).

Vietnam—Robert Shaplen reports that Le Duc Tho may have met secretly with the Chinese in Paris while attending the French Communist Party Congress in February 1985. Vietnamese Foreign Minister Nguyen Co Thac has written a conciliatory letter to Chinese Foreign Minister Wu Xueqian thanking the PRC for all the assistance given Hanoi in the past and proposing "secret talks in order to restore our old friendship." See the *New Yorker* (29 April 1985), 114.

Administrative Expenses—The State Council has ordered a 10-percent reduction in administrative expenses. Administrative costs in 1984 reached 12 billion yuan ($4.18 billion), or 44 percent more than was budgeted. *Asian Wall Street Journal Weekly* (15 Jul 1985), 6. No public money is to be used to buy motorcycles, sofas, carpets, or cars. London *Financial Times* (8 Jul 1985), 3.

Streamlining—William deB. Mills summarizes the reductions in Party and state provincial leadership bodies in 1983 in "Leadership Change in China's Provinces," *Problems of Communism*, XXXIV, 3 (May-Jun 1985), 24-40. He describes the techniques of central reformers in dealing with bureaucrats in Hunan and Shanxi provinces.

CPPCC's—The *China News Analysis*, 1285 (15 May 1985) deals with the revitalized Chinese People's Political Consultative Conferences. At the end of June 1984, there were 2,645 in the PRC with 281,000 members. They perform a "democratic supervisory role," soliciting opinion, engaging in fact-finding, and discussing general issues.

TOWNSHIP GOVERNMENTS, yearend 1984

Township governments	84,340
Villagers' committees	822,000+
Ethnic minority townships	2,700+
New towns established in 1984	4,680
Total towns	7,280

Renmin Ribao (23 Jan 1985). These township governments have been established since 1983 to replace people's communes.

PARTY SECRETARIES, CHAIRMEN OF PEOPLE'S CONGRESSES STANDING COMMITTEES, GOVERNORS, AND CHAIRMEN OF THE CHINESE PEOPLE'S POLITICAL CONSULTATIVE CONFERENCES OF PROVINCES, MUNICIPALITIES, AND AUTONOMOUS REGIONS

Provinces, Municipalities, Autonomous Regions	CPC Secretary of Provinces, Municipalities, and Autonomous Regions	Chairman of People's Congress Standing Committee	Provincial Governor, Mayor (Chairman)	CPPCC Chairman
Beijing	Li Ximing	Zhao Pengfei	Chen Xitong	[no name as published]
Tianjin	Ni Zhifu (concurrently)	Zhang Zaiwang	Li Ruihuan	Chen Bing
Hebei	Xing Chongzhi	Sun Guozhi	Zhang Shuguang	Yin Zhe
Shanxi	Li Ligong	Ruan Bosheng	Wang Senhao	Li Xiuren
Nei Monggol	Zhou Hui	Batu Bagen (Mongolian)	Buhe (Mongolian)	Shi Shengrong
Liaoning	Li Guixian	Zhang Zhengde	Quan Shuren	Xu Shaofu
Jilin	Gao Di	Zhao Xiu	Gao Dezhan	Liu Jingzhi
Heilongjiang	Sun Weiben	Li Jianbai	Hou Jie	Wang Zhao
Shanghai	Rui Xingwen	Hu Lijiao	Jiang Zemin	Li Guohao
Jiangsu	Han Peixin	Chu Jiang	Gu Xiulian (female)	Qian Zhonghan
Zhejiang	Wang Fang	Li Fengping	Xue Ju	Wang Jiayang
Anhui	Huang Huang	Wang Guangyu	Wang Yuzhao	Yang Haibo
Fujian	Xiang Nan	Cheng Xu	Hu Ping	Yuan Gai
Jiangxi	Wan Shaofen (female)	Wang Shufeng	Ni Xiance	Wu Ping
Shandong	Liang Buting	Li Zhen	Li Changan	Li Zichao
Henan	Yang Xizong	Zhang Shude	He Zhukang	Song Yuxi
Hubei	Guan Guangfu	Han Ningfu	Huang Zhizhen	Li Wei
Hunan	Mao Zhiyong	Jiao Linyi	Xiong Qingquan	Cheng Xingling
Guangdong	Lin Ruo	Luo Tian	Ye Xuanping	Wu Nansheng
Guangxi	Chen Huiguang	Gan Ku (Zhuang)	Wei Chunshu (Zhuang)	Qin Yingji (Zhuang)
Sichuan	Yang Rudai	He Haoju	Jiang Minkuan	Feng Yuanwei (Yi)
Guizhou	Hu Jintao	Zhang Yuhuan	Wang Chaowen (Miao)	Miao Chunting
Yunnan	Pu Chaozhu	Li Guiying (female, Yi)	He Zhiqiang (Naxi)	Liang Jia
Xizang	Wu Jianghua	Ngapoi Ngawang Jigme (Zang)	Duojicairang (Zang)	Yangling Duojie (Zang)
Shaanxi	Bai Jinian	Yan Kelun	Li Qingwei	Tan Weixu
Gansu	Li Ziqi	Li Dengying	Chen Guangyi	Wang Bingxiang
Qinghai	Yin Kesheng	Song Lin	Song Ruixiang	Shen Ling
Ningxia	Li Xuezhi	Ma Qingnian (Hui)	Hei Boli (Hui)	Li Yunhe
Xinjiang	Song Hanliang	Tomur Dawamat (Uygur)	Ismail Amat (Uygur)	Ismail Yashenof (Uygur)

FBIS-CHI 199 (15 Oct 1985), K14/15; press reports.

ADMINISTRATIVE DIVISIONS OF CHINA, yearend 1984

Provinces, autonomous regions and municipalities directly under the Central Government	Number of prefectures	Number of Cities Total	Number of Cities Prefecture level	Number of Cities County level	Number of counties	Districts under the administration of cities
Total	175	297	148	149	2,069	595
Beijing Municipality					9	10
Tianjin Municipality					5	13
Hebei Province	9	12	9	3	137	38
Shanxi	7	10	4	6	96	15
Inner Mongolia Autonomous Region	8	15	4	11	73	16
Liaoning Province		13	13		44	56
Jilin Province	3	9	4	5	38	13
Heilongjiang Province	4	16	10	6	63	64
Shanghai Municipality					10	12
Jiangsu Province		13	11	2	62	41
Zhejiang Province	4	9	6	3	67	17
Anhui Province	8	15	8	7	67	33
Fujian Province	5	10	4	6	59	14
Jiangxi Province	5	12	6	6	79	17
Shandong Province	6	18	8	10	95	31
Henan Province	8	18	9	9	110	39
Hubei Province	7	14	8	6	65	21
Hunan Province	9	18	6	12	86	25
Guangdong Province	5	16	9	7	93	25
Guangxi Zhuang Autonomous Region	8	11	5	6	76	21
Sichuan Province	12	16	6	10	179	23
Guizhou Province	7	6	2	4	77	5
Yunnan Province	15	10	2	8	116	4
Tibet Autonomous Region	7	1	1		77	1

continued . . .

ADMINISTRATIVE DIVISIONS OF CHINA, yearend 1984 (continued)

Provinces, autonomous regions and municipalities directly under the Central Government	Number of prefectures	Number of Cities				Number of counties	Districts under the administration of cities
		Total	Prefecture level	County level			
Shaanxi Province	6	8	4	4		89	13
Gansu Province	10	7	3	4		72	7
Qinghai Province	7	2	1	1		37	4
Ningxia Hui Autonomous Region	2	4	2	2		15	7
Xinjiang Uygur Autonomous Region	13	14	3	11		73	10
Taiwan Province			(not available)				

Note: The number of cities is 300, if the three municipalities directly under the Central Government are included, namely, Beijing, Tianjin and Shanghai.

State Statistical Bureau, *China: A Statistics Survey in 1985* (1985), 1.

SOVIET UNION, EAST AND SOUTH ASIA

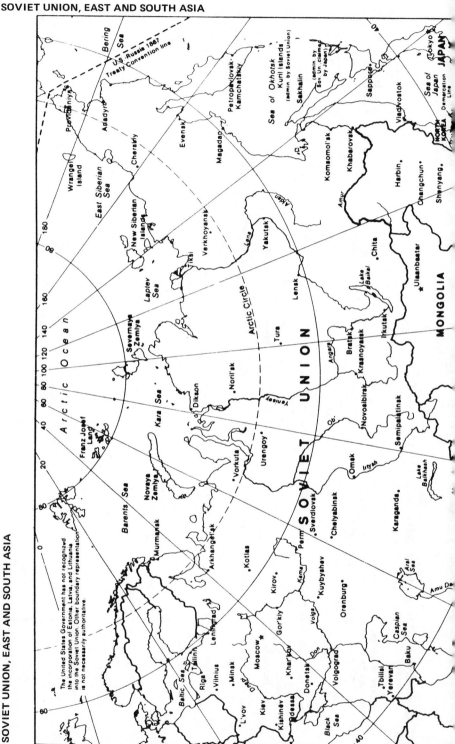

SOVIET UNION, EAST AND SOUTH ASIA

The United States Government has not recognized the incorporation of Estonia, Latvia, and Lithuania into the Soviet Union. Other boundary representation is not necessarily authoritative.

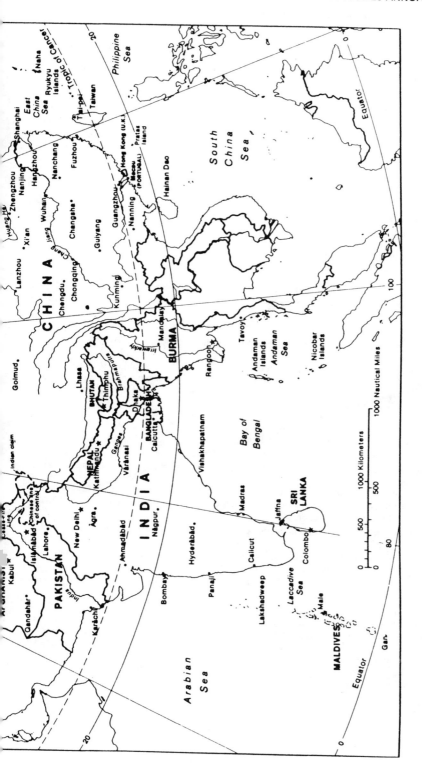

US Geological Survey Circular 934 (1984), 10.

PARTY AND GOVERNMENT REJUVENATION

	Average Age	Difference with Previous Leaders
Provincial Party Secretaries	58	-7.5 years
Provincial Governors	55.6	-3.7 years
Major Leaders of 81 Departments		
Under the State Council	56.5	-5 years
Leading Groups of the Seven Military Regions	NA	-7 years
Full Politburo Members, Oct 1985	68	-5 years
Percentage of Provincial Party Secretaries and		
Governors Currently Under:		
60 years		74.0
50 years		15.5
Percentage of Major State Council		
Leaders Under 55:		
Before reorganization		10
After reorganization		30
Percentage of Major State Council Leaders		
with College Educations:		
Before reorganization		44.5
After reorganization		71.0

Beijing Review, 38 (23 Sep 1985), 4; 41 (14 Oct 1985), 4; FBIS-CHI 172 (5 Sep 1985), K1; *China News Analysis*, 1291 (15 Aug 1985), 7-8, on the average ages of Standing Committee members.

COUNTY-LEVEL ADMINISTRATIVE CHANGES, Jul-Dec 1985

Nei Monggol Autonomous Region: Huolinguole City has been established (a county-level city). A portion of the administrative area of Jerim League's Jarud Banner is incorporated into the city, which is under the leadership of Jerim League. The seat of the city people's government is at Zhusihua.

Jilin Province: 1. Gongzhuling City was made into a county-level city, and Yitong County has been put under the jurisdiction of Siping City. 2. Meihekou City was made into a county-level city and Huinan and Liuhe Counties have been put under the jurisdiction of Tonghua City.

Zhejiang Province: 1. Zhenhai County has been abolished and its administrative area incorporated into Ningbo City's Zhenhai District. Zhengai District has been established in Ningbo City, and the administrative area of Ningbo City's Binhai District has been expanded. 2. Yuyao County has been abolished and Yuyao City established (a county-level city). The city incorporates the former county's administrative area.

Fujian Province: Licheng District is added to Quanzhou City without suburban districts attached for the time being.

Guangdong Province: Dongguang County has been abolished and Dongguan City established (a county-level city). The city incorporates the former county's administrative area.

Sichuan Province: Cangxi County in Nanchong Prefecture has been put under the jurisdiction of Guangyuan City.

Gansu Province: 1. Tianshui Prefecture has been abolished and Tianshui City upgraded to a prefectural level city. Tianshui County has been abolished and its former administrative area incorporated into Tianshui City. Qincheng and Beidao Districts have been added to Tianshui City. 2. The former Tianshui Prefecture's Qinan, Wushan, Gangu, and Qingshui Counties and Zhangjiachuan Hui Autonomous County have been put under the jurisdiction of Tianshui City. 3. The abolished Tianshui Prefecture's Huixian and Liangdang Counties have been incorporated into Longnan Prefecture.

continued . . .

COUNTY-LEVEL ADMINISTRATIVE CHANGES, Jul-Dec 1985 (continued)

Qinghai Province: 1. Minhe County has been abolished and the Minhe Hui and Tu Autonomous County established. The latter covers the former's previous administrative area. 2. Datong County has been abolished and the Datong Hui and Tu Autonomous County established. The latter incorporates the former's previous administrative area.

FBIS-CHI 22 (3 Feb 1986), K16/17.

LEGAL ASSISTANCE, 1984

Full and part-time lawyers	18,500
Law firms and legal advisory offices	2,600
Cases handled by law firms, 1984	
Criminal	120,000
Civil	31,000
Government agencies and enterprises engaging lawyers	10,000+
Economic disputes resolved, Jan-Sep 1984	145,000
Losses avoided (mn yuan)	580

XNB (14 Feb 1985), 11.

PROCLAMATION (NO. 3) OF THE PATENT OFFICE OF THE PEOPLE'S REPUBLIC OF CHINA, Jan 19, 1985

The Implementing Regulations of the Patent Law of the People's Republic of China, approved by the State Council on January 19, 1985, is hereby promulgated. The Implementing Regulations shall enter into force on April 1, 1985.

PROCLAMATION (NO. 4) OF THE PATENT OFFICE OF THE PEOPLE'S REPUBLIC OF CHINA, Jan 19, 1985

Under Article 67 of the Patent Law of the People's Republic of China, any application for a patent filed with, and any other proceedings before, the Patent Office shall be subject to the payment of a fee as prescribed. The various items of patent fees to be paid are prescribed in the first paragraph of Rule 82 of the Implementing Regulations of the Patent Law of the People's Republic of China. According to the second paragraph of the same Rule, a list of the patent fees to be charged is hereby issued as follows:

PATENT FEES

(unit: RMBY)

1.	Application fee for	
	(1) patent for invention	150
	(2) patent for utility model	100
	(3) patent for design	80
2.	Application maintenance fee for patent for invention, per year	100
3.	Examination fee for application for patent for invention	400
4.	Re-examination fee for	
	(1) application for patent for invention	200
	(2) application for patent for utility model	100
	(3) application for patent for design	80
5.	Opposition fee for	
	(1) application for patent for invention	39
	(2) application for patent for utility model	20
	(3) application for patent for design	20

continued . . .

PROCLAMATION (NO. 4) OF THE PATENT OFFICE OF THE PEOPLE'S REPUBLIC OF CHINA, Jan 19, 1985 (continued)

(unit: RMBY)

6. Renewal fee for the term of patent for utility model or design — 100
7. Handling fee for making changes in the bibliographic data — 10
8. Patent certificate fee for
   (1) patent for invention — 100
   (2) patent for utility model — 50
   (3) patent for design — 50
9. Fee for the proof of priority — 20
10. Fee for a request for invalidation of
    (1) patent for invention — 300
    (2) patent for utility model — 200
    (3) patent for design — 150
11. Fee for a request for a compulsory license for exploitation of
    (1) patent for invention — 300
    (2) patent for utility model — 200
12. Fee for a request for adjudication on exploitation fee of a compulsory license — 100
13. Annual fee for
    (1) patent for invention
    from the 1st year to the 3rd year, per year — 200
    from the 4th year to the 6th year, per year — 300
    from the 7th year to the 9th year, per year — 600
    from the 10th year to the 12th year, per year — 1200
    from the 13th year to the 15th year, per year — 2400
    (2) patent for utility model
    from the 1st year to the 3rd year, per year — 100
    from the 4th year to the 5th year, per year — 200
    from the 6th year to the 8th year, per year — 300
    (3) patent for design
    from the 1st year to the 3rd year, per year — 50
    from the 4th year to the 5th year, per year — 100
    from the 6th year to the 8th year, per year — 200

NOTES: 1. Where the applicant or the patantee is a foreigner, any of the above-listed fees shall be paid in foreign currency according to the exchange rate at the time of payment.

2. The ordinal number of years listed in Item 13 shall be counted from the filing date. The annual fee shall, beginning with the year in which the patent right was granted, be paid according to the amount prescribed for that year.

Beijing Review, 7-8 (18 Feb 1985), xiii-xiv.

RULES FOR IMPLEMENTATION OF PUNISHMENT FOR VIOLATION OF FOREIGN EXCHANGE CONTROLS, Approved by the State Council 25 Mar 1985 and Promulgated the State Administration of Foreign Exchange Control 5 Apr 1985

Article 1. This set of rules is formulated for the implementation of the provisions in Article 31 and Article 33 of the "Provisional Regulations on Foreign Exchange Control of the People's Republic of China."

Article 2. The following acts are considered as illegal procurement of foreign exchange:

1. Making payments in renminbi for imported goods or other items that should have been paid for with foreign exchange, without the approval of the State Administration of Foreign Exchange Control and its branches (hereafter referred to as exchange control agencies) or unless otherwise provided for in other state provisions;

continued . . .

RULES FOR IMPLEMENTATION OF PUNISHMENT FOR VIOLATION OF FOREIGN EXCHANGE CONTROLS (continued)

2.   Payments in renminbi made by domestic institutions for expenses of institutions operating abroad, foreign institutions in China, enterprises run with Overseas Chinese capital, enterprises run with foreign capital, Chinese-foreign joint ventures, and individuals on short visits to China in exchange for foreign exchange that should have been sold to the state;

3.   When institutions operating abroad use their renminbi in China to pay for expenses of other people in exchange for their foreign exchange;

4.   When foreign institutions in China, enterprises run with Overseas Chinese capital, enterprises run with foreign capital, Chinese-foreign joint ventures, and their personnel use renminbi to pay for expenses of other people, who then make repayments in foreign exchange or use other similar methods of repayment;

5.   When delegations and work groups stationed in foreign countries or in Hong Kong and Macao, or their personnel, use their foreign funds, or income obtained through activities in connection with their work, to buy goods or use them for other purposes and then compensate for the used amount with renminbi;

6.   When domestic institutions use their income in foreign exchange derived from exports and other sources to compensate for expenses for the importation of goods or for other payments.

Article 3. Violators in illegally procuring foreign exchange are subject to the following punishment according to the merits of each case:

1.   If the foreign exchange obtained illegally by an individual or an institution has not been used, they will be ordered to exchange it with the state within a prescribed time limit; if the foreign exchange has been used, they will be ordered to exchange an equivalent amount of foreign exchange with the state, or have a similar amount of foreign exchange deducted from them; if a procurer of illegal foreign exchange has used it and is unable to return the foreign exchange, he will be made to pay for the difference in the domestic and foreign price of the goods purchased; in addition, a fine ranging from 10 to 30 percent of the amount of illegally obtained foreign exchange may be imposed;

2.   An individual or institution that illegally sells foreign exchange will be subject to a fine ranging from 10 to 30 percent of the amount of foreign exchange depending on the seriousness of the case.

Article 4. The following acts are considered as evasion of foreign exchange:

1.   When a domestic institution privately keeps, uses, or deposits the foreign exchange it has obtained without the approval of the exchange control agencies; when foreign exchange obtained is deposited in a foreign country in violation of the provisions of the "Rules for the Implementation of Foreign Exchange Controls Relating to Enterprises Run With Overseas Chinese Capital, Enterprises Run With Foreign Capital, and Chinese-Foreign Joint Ventures;"

2.   When domestic institutions, enterprises run with Overseas Chinese capital, enterprises run with foreign capital, and Chinese-foreign joint ventures understate their foreign exchange receipts by understating the prices of export goods and commissions or overstate foreign exchange payments by overstating the prices of import goods, expenses, and commissions, and then keep the amount of foreign exchange thus obtained for private use or deposit it in foreign countries.

3.   When institutions operating overseas or Chinese investors of Chinese-foreign joint ventures established in foreign countries violate state regulations by using profits that should be repatriated to China for business operations or for other purposes in the country of residence;

4.   When delegations and work groups stationed in foreign countries or in Hong Kong and Macao, or their personnel, fail to use their foreign exchange according to the specified plan and, instead, deposit their foreign funds, or foreign exchange obtained through activities relating to their work in foreign countries, or use them for other purposes.

Article 5. Offenders in the evasion of foreign exchange are subject to the following punishment according to the merits of each case:

continued . . .

RULES FOR IMPLEMENTATION OF PUNISHMENT FOR VIOLATION OF FOREIGN EXCHANGE CONTROLS (continued)

1. In case the foreign exchange obtained through evasion has not been used, the offenders or the departments in charge of the offenders will be ordered to repatriate the foreign exchange within a prescribed time limit for compulsory conversion, or may have the entire amount or part of the foreign exchange confiscated; in addition, a fine ranging from 15 to 50 percent of the evaded amount may be imposed;

2. In case the foreign exchange obtained through evasion has been used, the offenders will be ordered to turn in an equivalent amount of foreign exchange for compulsory conversion, or may have the same amount of foreign exchange confiscated; in addition, a fine ranging from 15 to 50 percent of the evaded amount may be imposed;

3. In case the offenders have used the foreign exchange obtained through evasion and are unable to return the same amount, they will be fined an amount higher than 30 percent of the evaded amount but lower than the evaded amount, or may have the illegally obtained foreign exchange confiscated or have a punishment consisting of both a fine and confiscation imposed on them.

Article 6. The following are considered as acts of disrupting finance:

1. Dealing in foreign exchange business without the approval of the State Administration of Foreign Exchange Control, or expanding foreign exchange operations beyond the approved scope;

2. When domestic institutions, without the approval of the State Council or the organizations authorized by the State Council, issue securities that have the value of foreign exchange in China or in a foreign country and accept loans from banks and enterprises in a foreign country or in Hong Kong and Macao;

3. When domestic institutions, without the approval of the exchange control agencies, settle accounts, accept or extend loans, and make transfers and pledges with foreign exchange, or circulate and use foreign currencies;

4. Engaging in private selling and buying of foreign exchange, in selling and buying foreign exchange under disguise, in selling and buying foreign exchange at rates higher than those fixed by the State Administration of Foreign Exchange Control, or in buying and reselling foreign exchange for a profit.

Article 7. Violations listed in the preceding article are, on the merit of each case, subject to the following punishment;

1. An offender of item one, in addition to being ordered to discontinue foreign exchange business or that part of his foreign exchange business that exceeds the approved scope shall have his illegal income confiscated, be fined an amount equivalent to or less than the volume of illegal business involved, or be punished by both confiscation and fine.

2. An offender of item two, in addition to being prohibited from issuing new securities or receiving new loans, may be fined an amount less than 20 percent of the volume of illegal securities or loans involved.

3. An offender of items three and four, in addition to being ordered to convert his illegal foreign exchange, shall have his illegal income confiscated, or be fined an amount equivalent to or less than the illegal foreign exchange involved, or be punished by both confiscation and fine.

Article 8. Other violations of foreign exchange controls not specifically stipulated in article two, four and six may, on the merit of each case, be dealt with an punished according to the most closely applicable articles of this set of rules.

Article 9. An offender of foreign exchange controls, if the circumstances are not serious or the offender voluntarily confesses to his crimes to the exchange control agencies, shows true repentance, or demonstrates meritorious service by informing against other offenders, may receive mitigated punishment or even be exempted from punishment. An offender who resists in interrogation, covers up his crimes, or refuses to mend his ways despite repeated admonition shall be punished severely.

continued . . .

RULES FOR IMPLEMENTATION OF PUNISHMENT FOR VIOLATION OF FOREIGN EXCHANGE CONTROLS (continued)

Article 10. Serious cases of illegal procurement of foreign exchange, evasion of foreign exchange, and disruption of finance shall be referred to the judicial departments to be dealt with in accordance with law.

Article 11. In investigating and handling cases of violations of foreign exchange controls, the exchange control agency may notify banks to freeze the violating unit's illegal funds to prevent it from transferring its capital. The freeze period shall not exceed 2 months and shall be automatically lifted when time is due. In special cases requiring appropriate extension of the freeze period, the exchange control agency shall formally issue a renotification. The exchange control agency may order banks to deduct fines or funds to be confiscated from the account of a violating unit if it refuses to pay them.

Article 12. In handling violations of exchange control, the exchange control agency shall notify the unit or individual under investigation of its decision on punishment. A party who refuses to accept the decision may appeal to the exchange control agency at the next higher level within 15 days after he receives the notice to have the decision reconsidered. A party who refuses to accept the reconsidered decision may file a suit with the local people's court.

Article 13. Cases of violation of foreign exchange controls are under the jurisdiction of exchange control agencies; cases of illegal procurement or evasion of foreign exchange, or a smuggling nature, by way of freight, luggage, mail, and conveyances that cross national borders are under the jurisdiction of customs departments; cases of speculation and profiteering involving foreign exchange and foreign currency instruments are under the jurisdiction of industry and commerce administrative departments.

Article 14. Regulations on punishment for violation of foreign exchange controls in special economic zones shall be formulated by the Guangdong and Fujian Provincial People's Governments by reference to these rules.

Article 15. The State General Administration of Exchange Control is responsible for the interpretation of these rules.

Article 16. These rules shall go into effect on the day they are promulgated.

FBIS-CHI 76 (19 Apr 1985), K17/20.

STATE COUNCIL REGULATION STRICTLY BANNING OBSCENE MATERIAL, 17 Apr 1985

Obscene material is very harmful because it poisons people's minds and induces crime. In order to protect the physical and mental health of the general public, young people in particular, safeguard social order, and ensure that the drive for socialist modernization will continue smoothly, it is necessary to impose a strict ban on all obscene materials. For this purpose, the following rules are formulated:

1. The import, manufacture (including duplication), sale, and distribution of all obscene materials, whether or not for the purpose of making profit, will be strictly prohibited.

2. Items covered by the ban are: Videotapes, audiotapes, movies, television films, slides, pictures, illustrations, books, newspapers and magazines, and manuscripts that specifically portray sexual behavior or conspcuously publicize pornographic and lascivious images; toys and articles bearing drawings or pictures of this category; and aphrodisiacs and sex aids.

3. The work of cracking down on obscene material should be carried out firmly and seriously, but it must not go too far. Literary and art works of artistic value having obscene content and fine art works showing the beauty of the human body as well as works on physiological and medical knowledge about the human body and other natural sciences are not considered obscene material and will not be included in the ban.

continued . . .

STATE COUNCIL REGULATION STRICTLY BANNING OBSCENE MATERIAL, 17 Apr 1985 (continued)

4.   Customs should step up inspection to prevent import of the banned materials. All obscene materials carried, mailed, or smuggled in will be confiscated by customs, which may also fine the persons involved. Serious cases will be handled by the public security and judicial organs in accordance with the law.

5.   In the various localities, the work to ban obscene material should be organized and carried out, under the unified leadership of the local people's governments, by the public security, cultural, educational, and radio and television departments as well as administrations for industry and commerce according to their respective responsibilities and with better coordination efforts.

6.   For any material with obscene content imported for work purpose that needs to be retained, there must be a strict system regulating its loan for reading or use. No access to the material should be given to anyone not connected with the work. When no longer needed, the material should be turned over to a public security department for disposition.

7.   When obscene materials left by foreign visitors are found by units handling the reception of such visitors or by the transport and communications units concerned, the materials should all be collected and turned over to a public security department. No unit or individual is allowed to keep the materials, much less pass them on to any other unit or individual.

8.   All obscene materials confiscated by customs in accordance with the law will be destroyed by customs as required. Those obscene materials otherwise intercepted or discovered will be collected and turned over to the public security departments for disposition.

9.   Person or persons who smuggle, manufacture, sell, or organize the distribution of obscene materials to the extent that constitutes a crime will be prosecuted by the judicial organs in accordance with the law. Where such acts do not constitute a crime, administrative measures will be taken according to the serious of the matter.

Anyone who distributes obscene material to minors less than 18 years old, takes advantage of his work position to distribute confiscated obscene materials, or takes advantage of his functions and powers and the equipment under his control to duplicate or distribute obscene materials will be sternly punished in accordance with the law.

10.   Those who watch an obscene videotape, movie, or television film should be criticized and educated. Those who pass on pornographic publications or pictures for viewing or duplication must be criticized and educated, and the materials in their possessions must be surrendered. Those who continue such offenses despite repeated education will be subjected to administrative measures by the departments in charge.

11.   Rules for the implementation of this regulation will be formulated by the Ministry of Public Security, Ministry of Culture, Ministry of Education, Ministry of Radio and Television, State Administration for Industry and Commerce, and the General Administration of Customs.

12.   This regulation will become effective the date of its promulgation.

FBIS-CHI 77 (22 Apr 1985), K19/20.

REGULATIONS OF THE PEOPLE'S REPUBLIC OF CHINA CONCERNING RESIDENTS' IDENTIFICATION CARDS, Approved 6 Sep 1985

Article 1:   These regulations are especially formulated for identifying the status of a resident, facilitating a citizen to engage in social activities, maintaining public order, and safeguarding citizens' lawful rights.

Article 2:   A Chinese citizen residing in the People's Republic of China should apply for a PRC resident's identification card upon turning 16 years of age in accordance with these

continued . . .

REGULATIONS OF THE PEOPLE'S REPUBLIC OF CHINA CONCERNING RESIDENTS' IDENTIFICATION CARDS, Approved 6 Sep 1985 (continued)

regulations. Instead of resident's identification cards, members of the PLA and the People's Armed Police Force on active service will be issued servicemen and armed police identification documents by the PRC Central Military Commission and the Headquarters of the Chinese People's Armed Police Force.

Article 3: Information registered on a resident's identification card should include name, sex, nationality, date of birth, and address. The language used to register this information on a resident's identification card should be the one generally used in the country. Autonomous organs of the autonomous regions of national minorities may decide on using either the language of the minority nationality or one of the languages generally used in the region in accordance with the actual situation in the region.

Article 4: A resident's identification card will be valid for 10 years, 20 years, or permanently. Those between the ages of 16 and 25 will be issued a resident identification card with a 10-year period of validity; those between the ages of 26 and 45 will be issued a resident identification card with a 20-year period of validity; and those over 46 years will be issued a permanent identification card.

Article 5: Resident's identification cards are to be uniformly printed, issued, and supervised by public security organs.

Article 6: A citizen should apply for a resident's identification card at the residence registration office of the citizen's permanent domicile and complete the application procedures according to the regulations.

Article 7: An Overseas Chinese returning to settle in the country should apply for a resident's identification card when going through the procedures for registering residence.

Article 8: When a resident's identification card expires, when there is an alteration or correction to the registered information, or a resident's identification card is seriously damaged beyond recognition it is necessary to apply for a new card in accordance with the regulations. Those who have lost their document should report to the authorities and apply for a new one.

Article 9: A citizen conscripted to active military service should return resident's identification card when deregistering his residence. After retiring from active service, the resident's identification card should be returned or he should apply for a new one.

Article 10: Those who have not yet applied for the resident's identification card but have been under criminal detention, sentenced to criminal punishment with fixed-term imprisonment, sent to rehabilitation through labor, or held in custody, will not be issued a resident's identification card during his or her detention, prison term, rehabilitation, and custody. Those who have already obtained a resident's identification card, will have the card confiscated by the law enforcement organ in accordance with the regulations. After their release, the original resident's identification card will be returned to them, or they should apply in person for a new card.

Article 11: A citizen who is required to deregister his residence because of leaving the country should return his resident's identification card when going through the procedures to deregister his residence.

Article 12: The resident's identification card of a deceased citizen should be returned to the public security organ.

Article 13: In the performance of its duty, a public security organ has the right to demand checking the resident's identification card of citizens. The latter should not reject the demand. When checking a resident's identification card, the public security personnel should produce their work certificates. A public security organ should not retain the resident's identification cards of citizens, except for those who are under the compulsory measures of the "Criminal Procedure Law of the People's Republic of China."

continued . . .

REGULATIONS OF THE PEOPLE'S REPUBLIC OF CHINA CONCERNING RESIDENTS' IDENTIFICATION CARDS, Approved 6 Sep 1985 (continued)

Article 14: When handling affairs involving rights and interests in political, economic and social lives, a citizen may produce his resident's identification card to show his status. Concerned units should not retain the resident's identification card or take it as a pledge.

Article 15: Whoever commits one of the following acts will be punished according to the relevant articles in the "Regulation of the People's Republic of China Regarding Punishment in Public Security Administration:"
  1. Refusing a public security organ's demand to check his resident's identification card;
  2. Transferring the possession of or leasing his resident's identification card;
  3. Using another person's resident's identification card; and
  4. Deliberately destroying another person's resident's identification card.

Article 16: Whoever commits a serious case of forging, altering, or stealing resident's identification cards will be punished in accordance with Article 167 of the "Criminal Law of the People's Republic of China."

Article 17: A public security worker who practices favoritism or other irregularities and violates a citizen's lawful rights and interests when enforcing these regulations, should be subjected to administrative disciplinary measures; when circumstances are serious enough to constitute a crime the public security worker should be investigated for criminal responsibility.

Article 18: These regulations are not applicable to foreigners and stateless persons residing in the People's Republic of China.

Article 19: Detailed rules for implementing these regulations will be formulated by the Ministry of Public Security and put into effect after being submitted to the State Council for approval.

Article 20: These regulations come into force upon promulgation.

Appendix: A relevant article of the Criminal Law: Article 167: Whoever forges, alters, steals, forcibly seizes or destroys official documents, certificates, or seals of state organs, enterprises, institutions, or people's organizations is to be sentenced to not more than 3 years of fixed-term imprisonment, criminal detention, control or deprivation of political rights; when circumstances are serious, the sentence is to be not less than 3 years and not more than 10 years of fixed-term imprisonment.

FBIS-CHI 173 (9 Sep 1985), K13/15.

THE LAW OF THE PEOPLE'S REPUBLIC OF CHINA GOVERNING FOREIGNERS' ENTRY AND EXIT, Adopted by the 13th Session of the Standing Committee of the 6th National People's Congress 22 Nov 1985

Chapter One: General Principles

Article 1. This law is formulated for the sake of safeguarding the sovereignty, security, and social order of the People's Republic of China and promoting the development of international contacts.

This law applies to foreigners when they enter, depart, or transit the People's Republic of China, or when they want to settle or travel in China.

Article 2. Approval by competent authorities of the Chinese Government is necessary when foreigners enter, transit, or settle in China.

Article 3. Foreigners' entry, exit, or transit must be made in ports opened to them, or other designated ports, and they are subject to the frontier inspection authorities' inspection.

Foreign vehicles' entry, exit, and transit must be made at ports opened to foreigners, or at the designated ports, and they are subject to the frontier inspection authorities' inspection and guardianship.

continued . . .

THE LAW OF THE PEOPLE'S REPUBLIC OF CHINA GOVERNING FOREIGNERS' ENTRY AND EXIT, Adopted by the 13th Session of the Standing Committee of the 6th National People's Congress 22 Nov 1985 (continued)

Article 4. The legitimate rights and interests of foreigners in China are protected by the Chinese Government.

Foreigners' personal freedom shall not be violated, they shall not be arrested unless the arrest has been authorized, or decided upon, by the People's Procuratorate, or decided upon by the People's Court, and the arrest is executed by a public security organ or a state security organ.

Article 5. When in China, foreigners must abide by Chinese laws and must not endanger China's state security, harm its public interests, or undermine its social order.

Chapter Two: Entry

Article 6. To enter China, foreigners should apply for visas at Chinese diplomatic representative or consular institutions, or other institutions abroad authorized by the Ministry of Foreign Affairs. Under special circumstances, foreigners may also apply for visas at visa-issuing agencies at ports designated by competent authorities of the Chinese Government in accordance with the regulations of the State Council. Entry of personnel from countries having visa agreements with the Chinese Government will be handled according to the agreements.

In accordance with circumstances, competent authorities of the Chinese Government may take appropriate measures for foreign countries that have special regulations governing Chinese citizens' entry and transit in their countries.

Visas are not necessary for foreign transit passengers traveling by international scheduled flights and holding through tickets, if their stay in China does not exceed 24 hours and their stay is limited to the airport. Extempore requests to leave the airport must be approved by the frontier inspection authorities.

Article 7. In applying for various types of visas, foreigners must submit their valid passports, or other relevant documents whenever necessary.

Article 8. When applying for visas, foreigners hired to work in China should have proof of hiring.

Article 9. While applying for visas, foreigners coming to settle in China should have the documents confirming their settlement status. Such documents are available at public security organs in areas where the applicants want to settle.

Article 10. The competent authorities of the Chinese Government will issue appropriate visas to foreigners according to the purposes of their applications for entry.

Article 11. Upon arriving in Chinese ports, the captains and the skippers, or their agents, of aircraft or ships must provide the list of passengers' names to the frontier inspection authorities; foreign aircraft and ships must also provide lists of their crew.

Article 12. Entry shall be denied for foreigners whose stay may be considered as endangering China's security and social order.

Chapter Three: Residence

Article 13. To reside in China, foreigners must have the documents certifying their identity or residence issued by competent authorities of the Chinese Government. The length of the validity of these documents will be determined by reasons of entry. Foreigners residing in China should have their papers examined by the local public security organs within the prescribed period.

Article 14. Foreigners who need to stay in China on a long-term basis for such needs as making investment in China according to Chinese laws, or carrying out economic, scientific, technical, and cultural cooperation with Chinese enterprises or institutions, may acquire long-term or permanent residence in China after being approved by competent authorities of the Chinese Government.

continued . . .

THE LAW OF THE PEOPLE'S REPUBLIC OF CHINA GOVERNING FOREIGNERS' ENTRY AND EXIT, Adopted by the 13th Session of the Standing Committee of the 6th National People's Congress 22 Nov 1985 (continued)

Article 15. Foreigners who seek refuge in China because of political reasons will be allowed to reside in China after being approved by competent authorities of the Chinese Government.

Article 16. For foreigners who do not abide by Chinese laws, competent authorities of the Chinese Government may curtail the length of their stay in China, or revoke their residence in China.

Article 17. Foreigners in China should have their temporary residence registered according to regulations.

Article 18. In changing their residence in China, foreigners having residence permits must have the relocation formalities processed according to regulations.

Article 19. Without the approval of competent authorities of the Chinese Government, foreigners and foreign students studying in China who have yet to acquire residence status may not seek employment in China.

Chapter Four: Travel

Article 20. Foreigners with valid visas or residence permits may visit areas the Chinese Government has designated open to foreigners.

Article 21. To visit areas not open to foreigners, they must apply for travel documents from the local public security organs.

Chapter Five: Exit

Article 22. Foreigners leave the country using their valid passports or other valid documents.

Article 23. Foreigners of any one of the following categories are not allowed to leave the country: 1) who are defendants in criminal cases, or whom public security organs or the people's courts consider to be suspects; 2) who have been notified by people's courts not to leave the country because of unfinished civil lawsuits; 3) whose other violations of Chinese laws have not yet been handled and who competent authorities consider necessary to investigate.

Article 24. Frontier inspection authorities are authorized to stop the departure of, and handle according to law, foreigners of any one of the following categories: 1) who hold invalid exit documents; 2) who hold other people's exit documents; 3) who hold fabricated or altered exit documents.

Chapter Six: Administrative Organs

Article 25. Chinese Government organs abroad accepting foreigners entry or transit applications are Chinese diplomatic representative organs and consular institutions, or other institutions in foreign countries authorized by the Ministry of Foreign Affairs.

Chinese Government organs at home accepting foreigners' entry, transit, residence, and travel applications are the Ministry of Public Security, local public security organs authorized by the Ministry of Public Security, and local foreign affairs departments authorized by the Ministry of Foreign Affairs.

Article 26. Organs accepting foreigners' entry, transit, residence or travelling applications are authorized to deny visas and other documents, or revoke them, or declare them null and void.

Whenever necessary, the Ministry of Public Security and the Ministry of Foreign Affairs may change the decisions made by their authorized organs.

Article 27. For foreigners who have entered the country or obtained residence illegally, county-level public security organs and above may detain and examine them, and place their residence under surveillance, or deport them.

Article 28. While performing their duties, foreign affairs police of county-level public organs and above are authorized to check foreigners' passports and other documents. During the

continued . . .

THE LAW OF THE PEOPLE'S REPUBLIC OF CHINA GOVERNING FOREIGNERS' ENTRY AND EXIT, Adopted by the 13th Session of the Standing Committee of the 6th National People's Congress 22 Nov 1985 (continued)

check, they should show their identification cards, and institutions and individuals concerned are obliged to provide the necessary assistance.

Chapter Seven: Penalties

Article 29. For foreigners who have entered or departed the country illegally; who have resided or stayed in China illegally; who have fabricated, altered, used, or transferred other people's entry or exit permits in violation of this law, county-level public security organs and above may serve them warnings, impose fines, or detain them for a period of up to 10 days; serious cases constituting crimes shall have the criminal responsibilities investigated according to law.

If they disagree, foreigners upon whom public security organs have imposed a fine or have been detained may, within 14 days after being notified, appeal to public security organs at a higher level, who will make the final ruling. They may also take legal proceedings directly to the local People's Courts.

Article 30. For those guilty of acts mentioned in Article 29, and if the cases are serious, the Ministry of Public Security may set a time limit for them to leave the country, or expel them from the country.

Chapter Eight: Supplementary Articles

Article 31. The term foreigners mentioned in this law refers to people without Chinese nationality in the light of the "nationality law of the People's Republic of China."

Article 32. Extempore requests to enter or exit China by foreigners of countries adjacent to China, and people residing along the two countries' border areas shall be handled according to the agreements between the two countries, if there are such agreements, otherwise they will be handled according to regulations of the Chinese Government.

Article 33. The Ministry of Public Security and the Ministry of Foreign Affairs shall draw up the details of implementation according to this law and shall submit them to the State Council for approval.

Article 34. After their entry, personnel of foreign countries' diplomatic organs and consular institutions, as well as foreign nationals enjoying special privileges and immunity, shall be administered according to the relevant regulations of the State Council and its competent authorities.

Article 35. This law becomes effective on 1 February 1986.

FBIS-CHI 228 (26 Nov 1985), K2/6.

CITIZENS' EXIT AND ENTRY CONTROL LAW OF THE PEOPLE'S REPUBLIC OF CHINA, Adopted by the 13th Session of the 6th National People's Congress Standing Committee 22 Nov 1985

Chapter I: General Principle

Article 1. In order to protect the proper rights and interests of Chinese citizens, regarding exit from and entry into the territory of China, and to promote international intercourse, the above law is hereby formulated.

Article 2. A Chinese citizen may leave, or enter, the territory without visa processing by showing a valid passport, or other valid certificates, issued by the State Council's organization in charge, or its authorized organizations.

Article 3. To pass through a port, either open or designated, a Chinese citizen must be inspected by the border defense inspection organization, when leaving or entering the territory.

continued . . .

CITIZENS' EXIT AND ENTRY CONTROL LAW OF THE PEOPLE'S REPUBLIC OF CHINA, Adopted by the 13th Session of the 6th National People's Congress Standing Committee 22 Nov 1985 (continued)

Article 4. Chinese citizens are not permitted to take any actions detrimental to the motherland's security, honor, or interest after leaving the territory.

Chapter II: Exit

Article 5. Except for situations as stipulated by Article 8, all applications for exit on account of personal affairs, submitted by Chinese citizens to the city or county public security organizations in their respective localities, will be approved.

The public security organizations should decide whether or not to approve an application for exit on account of personal affairs submitted by a Chinese citizen and notify the applicant within the stipulated time.

Article 6. For the exit of Chinese citizens on account of official business, the departments sending them abroad are required to apply to the Foreign Ministry, or its authorized foreign affairs departments in the localities, for exit certificates.

Article 7. For the exit of maritime personnel on account of official tasks, the harbor affairs supervisory bureaus, or their authorized harbor affairs supervisors, are required to process the exit certificates.

Article 8. No approval will be granted for exit under any one of the following situations: 1) defendants in criminal cases and criminal suspects confirmed by public security organizations, People's Procuratorates, or People's Courts; 2) persons involved in ongoing civil cases, according to notices from the People's Courts; 3) persons who are serving sentences passed against them; 4) persons who are undergoing education through labor; or 5) persons whose exit will damage the security of the country, or result in heavy losses to the interests of the country, as deemed by the State Council's organization in charge.

Article 9. Border defense inspection organizations are authorized to stop someone from exiting and handle it according to law under any one of the following situations: 1) persons holding invalid exit certificates; 2) persons holding other people's exit certificates; or 3) persons holding forged or altered exit certificates.

Chapter III: Entry

Article 10. Chinese citizens residing abroad but requesting to return home to settle down should process their requests with the representative foreign affairs organizations stationed abroad by China, its consular organizations, or other organizations abroad authorized by the Ministry of Foreign Affairs. They may also submit their requests to the public security organizations in the provinces, autonomous regions, and central-government-controlled municipalities concerned.

Article 11. Chinese citizens who have entered the territory to settle down, or to work, should make permanent household registrations after entry in accordance with the household management regulations. Those who have entered the territory for temporary lodging should make temporary lodging registrations in accordance with the household management regulations.

Chapter IV: Controlling Organizations

Article 12. Passports for use by Chinese citizens leaving the territory on official business are issued by the Ministry of Foreign Affairs, or the local foreign affairs departments authorized by the Ministry of Foreign Affairs. Certificates for maritime personnel are issued by the harbor affairs supervisory bureaus, or the harbor affairs supervisors authorized by the harbor affairs supervisory bureaus. Passports for use by Chinese citizens leaving the territory on account of personal affairs are issued by the Ministry of Public Security, or the local public security organizations authorized by the Ministry of Public Security.

Passports and certificates applied for by Chinese citizens abroad are issued by the representative foreign affairs organizations stationed abroad by China, its consular organizations, or other organizations stationed abroad as authorized by the Ministry of Foreign Affairs.

continued . . .

CITIZENS' EXIT AND ENTRY CONTROL LAW OF THE PEOPLE'S REPUBLIC OF CHINA, Adopted by the 13th Session of the 6th National People's Congress Standing Committee 22 Nov 1985 (continued)

Article 13. The Ministry of Public Security, the Ministry of Foreign Affairs, the harbor affairs supervisory bureaus, and the original certificate-issuing organizations are authorized to revoke, or to announce nullification of, the passports and certificates they have issued or those issued by organizations they have authorized to do so.

Chapter V: Punishment

Article 14. The public security organizations may serve warnings or impose detentions for a period of 10 days or less against persons who have illegally left, or entered, the territory; who forged, or altered, their passports; who used other people's passports; or who transferred their exit, or entry, certificates to others, in violation of the stipulations of this law.

Article 15. Citizens who do not agree with the detentions imposed on them by the public security organizations may appeal to the upper-level public security organizations within 15 days after the date of receiving the notification, and the upper-level public security organizations will make the final arbitration. They may also present the lawsuits directly to the local people's courts.

Article 16. State personnel responsible for enforcing this law will be punished in accordance with the "criminal code of the People's Republic of China" and the NPC Standing Committee's "decision on severely punishing crimes that seriously damage the economy," if they use their authority to extort and receive bribes. Those who commit other acts in violation of the law or who act in dereliction of their duty with serious consequences constituting crimes will be further investigated for their criminal responsibilities in accordance with the stipulations in the criminal code of the People's Republic of China."

Chapter VI: Appendices

Article 17. Methods of controlling travels of Chinese citizens to and from Hong Kong and Macao will be formulated separately by the State Council's department concerned.

Article 18. The temporary exit and entry of Chinese citizens residing in the border areas between China and other countries will be carried out according to the agreement between the two countries, if such agreements are available; otherwise, they will be carried out according to the stipulations of the Chinese Government.

The exit and entry of crew members of international trains and civil aviation aircraft, as well as domestic railway personnel, will be carried out according to agreements and stipulations concerned.

Article 19. The Ministry of Public Security, the Ministry of Foreign Affairs, and the Ministry of Communications shall formulate implementation details according to this law and submit them to the State Council for approval and enforcement.

Article 20. This law will be enforced from 1 February 1986.

FBIS-CHI 228 (26 Nov 1985), K6/8.

CHINESE AMBASSADORS

		Credentials Presented
Afghanistan		
Albania	Xi Zhaoming	id Sep 1983
Algeria	Lu Weizhao	id Jul 1983
Angola	Zhao Zhenkui	id Nov 1984
Antigua and Barbuda	Li Xie	id Dec 1984
Argentina	Wei Baoshan	id Dec 1984
Australia	Nie Gongcheng	id Oct 1983
Austria	Wang Shu	id Jul 1980
Bangladesh		
Belgium		
Benin	Sun Zhicheng	id Nov 1982
Bolivia		
Botswana	Lu Defang	id Sep 1983
Brazil	Xu Zhongfu	id Jan 1982
Bulgaria	Wang Benzuo	id Sep 1983
Burkina Faso	Feng Zhishan	id Feb 1984
Burma	Zhou Mingji	13 Aug 1985
Burundi	Shen Lianrui	18 Apr 1985
Cameroon	Shi Nailang	id Dec 1984
Canada	Yu Zhan	id Oct 1983
Cape Verde	Liang Taosheng	26 Feb 1985
Chad		
Colombia	Tao Dazhao	id Jul 1983
Comoros		
Congo	Du Yi	id Apr 1984
Cuba	Wang Jin	id Nov 1983
Cyprus	Li Heng (f)	id Sep 1983
Czechoslovakia	Zhang Dake	18 Apr 1985
Denmark	Chen Luzhi	id Sep 1984
Djibouti	Wang Changyi	id Jun 1983
Ecuador	Pan Wenjie	id Mar 1985
Egypt	Wen Yezhan	26 Feb 1985
Equatorial Guinea	Liu Fangpu	id Aug 1984
Ethiopia		
European Communities	Liu Shan	23 Sep 1985
Fiji	Ji Chaozhu	id Sep 1985
Finland	Lin Aili (f)	id May 1985
France	Cao Keqiang	id Mar 1983
Gabon	Tian Yimin	15 Jan 1985
The Gambia	Liang Feng	id Feb 1984
German Democratic Republic	Ma Xusheng	id Aug 1984
Germany, Federal Republic	Guo Fengmin	id May 1985
Ghana	Jia Huaiji	id Mar 1980
Greece	Zhuang Yan	id May 1983
Grenada		
Guinea	Yu Huimin	id Dec 1984
Guinea-Bissau	Hu Jingrui	id Apr 1984
Guyana	Ni Zhengjian	id Nov 1984
Hungary	Zhu Ankang	17 Sep 1985
Iceland	Chen Luzhi	id Jan 1985
India	Li Lianqing	id Nov 1984
Iran	Fan Zuokai	id Apr 1983
Iraq	Zhang Junhua	id Dec 1984
Ireland	Xing Zhongxiu	id Sep 1984

continued . . .

CHINESE AMBASSADORS (continued)

		Credentials Presented
Italy		
Ivory Coast	Zhu Chengcai	id Feb 1984
Jamaica	Gao Jie	id Jul 1983
Japan	Zhang Shu	24 Sep 1985
Jordan	Huang Shixie	id Oct 1982
Kampuchea		
Kenya	Wei Yongqing	id Nov 1984
Kiribati	Ji Chaozhu	id Sep 1985
Korea, Democratic People's Republic	Zong Kewen	id Aug 1982
Kuwait	Yang Fuchang	id Feb 1984
Laos		
Lebanon	Wu Shunyu	19 Sep 1985
Lesotho	Mou Ping	id Apr 1984
Liberia	Xiang Zhongpu	id May 1985
Libya	Yang Hushan	id May 1985
Luxembourg	Zhang Shu	id Sep 1983
Madagascar	Yang Guirong	23 Apr 1985
Malaysia	Hu Gang	id Jan 1985
Maldives	Zhou Shanyan	id Oct 1984
Mali	Zhou Haiping	id Apr 1983
Malta	Hua Renqin	id May 1983
Mauritania	Sun Hao	id Jun 1982
Mauritius	Chen Tan	15 Mar 1985
Mexico	Li Chao	id Aug 1983
Mongolia	Li Juqing	id Nov 1983
Morocco	Wei Dong	28 Feb 1985
Mozambique	Wang Hao	id Dec 1982
Nepal	Tu Guowei	id Apr 1984
Netherlands	Guo Jie	id Apr 1984
New Zealand	Zhang Longhai	id Jan 1984
Niger	Xing Geng	id Sep 1985
Nigeria	Wang Yusheng	id May 1985
Norway	Zhang Yongkuan	id Aug 1983
Oman	Guan Zihuai	id May 1985
Pakistan	Wang Chuanbin	id Jun 1982
Papua New Guinea	Gao Jianzhong	8 Mar 1985
Peru	Yang Mai	id Oct 1984
Philippines	Chen Songlu	id Aug 1984
Poland	Wang Jinqing	17 Apr 1985
Portugal	Lu Jixin	id Apr 1984
Romania	Yu Hongliang	24 Apr 1985
Rwanda	An Fengshi	8 Jan 1985
San Marino		
Sao Tome and Principe	Tian Yimin	id 1985
Senegal	Liang Feng	id May 1983
Seychelles		
Sierra Leone		
Singapore		
Somalia	Wang Shikun	id Sep 1983
Spain	Cao Yuanxin	id Aug 1984
Sri Lanka	Zhou Shanyan	id Nov 1984
Sudan	Liu Hua	id Dec 1984
Suriman	Yan Hongliang	id Aug 1983
Sweden	Wu Jiagan	id Dec 1984

continued . . .

CHINESE AMBASSADORS (continued)

		Credentials Presented
Switzerland	Tian Jin	id Mar 1984
Syria	Lin Zhaonan	id Oct 1983
Tanzania	Liu Qungyou	23 Apr 1985
Thailand	Zhang Dewei	id 1985
Togo	Jin Minsheng	id May 1982
Trinidad and Tobago	Cui Mingtang	id Aug 1983
Tunisia	Xie Bangding	id Sep 1983
Turkey	Zhang Zhiliang	id Dec 1984
Uganda	Jin Boxiong	id May 1985
USSR	Li Zewang	1 Mar 1985
United Arab Emirates	Hun Changlin	id May 1985
United Kingdom	Hu Dingyi	id May 1985
United Nations		
New York	Li Luye	29 Aug 1985
Geneva	Qian Jiadong	id Aug 1983
Vienna	Cao Guisheng	id May 1985
United States	Han Xu	22 May 1985
Vanuatu	Ji Chaozhu	id Sep 1985
Venezuela	Hu Hongfan	id May 1985
Vietnam	Li Shichun	16 Sep 1985
Western Samoa	Gu Ji	id Apr 1983
Yemen Arab Republic	Li Chengren	id May 1985
Yemen, People's Democratic Republic	Tang Yong	id May 1982
Yugoslavia	Xie Li	id Nov 1983
Zaire	An Guozheng	id May 1985
Zambia	Gu Jiaji	id Mar 1985
Zimbabwe	Zheng Yaowen	16 Apr 1985

No entry for an ambassador indicates that he is being replaced. Dates credentials were presented for years prior to 1985 may be found in previous editions of CHIFFA. The PRC and Grenada established diplomatic relations 1 October 1985. Bolivia became the 131st country to establish diplomatic relations with the PRC 9 July 1984. Diplomatic relations were established with Nicaragua 7 December 1985. The USSR and PRC agreed in May 1985 to set up Consulates General at Leningrad and Shanghai and to simplify visa procedures. The Embassy of the PRC in Jakarta, Indonesia was abandoned in 1967 and has been turned into a municipal parking lot. Beijing wants any future trade mission or Embassy to be located outside Chinatown in Jakarta. China established a Consulate General at Tijuana, Mexico 15 August 1985. The Italian Consulate General at Shanghai opened 21 June 1985. A Chinese Consulate General had opened in Milan, Italy, 11 June 1985. Consulates for the PRC opened officially 4 May 1985 at Nagasaki and Fukuoka, Japan. The fourth Consulate General in the US was inaugurated at Chicago, Illinois by President Li Xiannian 26 July 1985. A Consulate General opened at Marseille, France, 19 December 1985. Xie Qimei was appointed an Undersecretary-General for Technical Cooperation for Development at the United Nations as of 1 June 1985, replacing Bi Jilong.

Compiled from press reports.

AMBASSADORS NEWLY ACCREDITED TO THE PRC, 1985

		Credentials Presented
Australia	Ross Garnaut	25 Nov
Bangladesh	A.Z.M. Enayetullah Khan	28 May
Cameroon	Jean Keutcha	14 Aug
Ethiopia	Philippos Walde-Mariam	25 May
Ghana	Osei Bonsu Amankwa	16 May
India	K.P.S. Menon	28 Mar
Lebanon	Farid Samaha	17 Aug
Libya *	Abd al Hamid az-Zintani	
New Zealand	Lindsay J. Watt	6 June
Peru	Roberto Villeran Koechlin	30 Dec
Poland	Zbigniew Dembowski	26 Jan
Portugal	Octavio Neto Valerio	17 Aug
United States	Winston Lord	19 Nov
Yugoslavia	Zvone Dragan	6 Nov
Zaire	Lombo Lo Mangamanga	14 Aug

* Bureau Secretary

Compiled from press reports.

IV PARTY

PARTY NEWS, 1985

Communist Youth League—In 1979 there were 4,863 rural production brigades without Communist Youth League branches in the PRC. The number had increased to 6,548 brigades in 1980. There were 180,000 production teams without any League members. Despite recruitment of some 26 million members between 1978 and 1982, the number of members in the Communist Youth League did not change between the 10th and 11th Party Congresses, remaining at 48 million out of a total youth population of 250 million persons 15 to 28 years old. Stanley Rosen has described problems of the League and various programs to attract youth to the Party in "Prosperity, Privatization, and China's Youth," *Problems of Communism*, XXXIV, 2 (Mar-Apr 1985), 1-28.

Family Origins—"Family origins" will no longer be considered in examining political cadres. The reason given is that exploiting classes have ceased to exist in China. FBIS-CHI 95 (16 May 1985), K9.

Party Documents—*The Annotated Edition of the Resolution on Certain Issues in the History of Our Party Since the Founding of the People's Republic of China* will be published with some 130 annotations.

Second-Stage Party Rectification—The goals of Party rectification are to achieve ideological unity, rectify work style, strengthen discipline, and purify Party organizations. The second stage of Party rectification will concentrate on rectifying unhealthy tendencies and on strengthening Party discipline and spirit. *Banyuetan*, 7 (10 Apr 1985), 11-14. Party "consolidation" is being carried out in prefectural and county organizations and at enterprises, institutions, and other units at these two levels. The second stage will continue from the winter of 1984 to the end of 1985. *Beijing Review*, 10 (11 Mar 1985), 4.

Party Ties with Moscow—Wu Xingtang, a Deputy Director of the International Liaison Committee of the Central Committee, has mentioned that Beijing still opposes the resumption of relations with the Communist Party of the USSR. New York *Times* (30 Jan 1985), 4.

Literacy—Of China's 40 million Party members, 78 percent are either illiterate or have no more than a 9th-grade education. *Business Week* (14 Jan 1985), 56. The breakdown is summarized below:

	Percent
College	4.0
Senior middle-school or polytechnical education	13.8
Primary school	42.2
Illiterate	10.1

FBIS-CHI 54 (20 Mar 1985), K29.

Hong Kong CP—Emily Lau describes the Communist Party in Hong Kong, known as the Hong Kong Macau Work Committee (HMWC), in the *Far Eastern Economic Review* (1 Aug 1985), 22-23. The Party has traditionally been headed by the Director of the Xinhua News Agency in Hong Kong, currently Xu Jiatun. The representatives of major commercial organizations belong to the HMWC, including Zhang Jianhua, the General Manager of China Resources; Jiang Wengui, head of the branch of the Bank of China in Hong Kong; and Yuan Geng, Vice-Chairman of the China Merchants Steam Navigation Company, representing the Ministry of Communications in the PRC. Yeung Kwong, a member of the HMWC and delegate to the National People's Congress, leads the 170,000-member Hong Kong Federation of Trade Unions. Li Liansheng, President of the Graziers' Union, has organized the New Territories Association of Societies, with 50,000 members. Chinese Communist Party members in Hong Kong are thought to number 2-3,000. There are some 2,000 Chinese officials working in Hong Kong, and it is assumed that most belong to the Party.

continued . . .

PARTY NEWS, 1985 (continued)

Letters– The Bureau of Written Inquiry of the Central Committee received some 202,700 letters during the first half of 1985. Almost 30 percent were complaints and 21 percent were requests for assistance of some sort, compared to the 49 and 48 percent received in these categories in 1984. The number of letters exposing crimes or scandals dropped nearly 20 percent to 8.8 percent. *China Daily* (5 Oct 1985), 3.

"Third Echelon''– Deng Xiaoping advanced a "third echelon" of Party leaders during 1985. Deng and other elder statesmen comprise the "first echelon," and Hu Yaobang and Zhao Ziyang are part of the "second." These younger leaders include Li Peng, 57, the adopted son of the late Zhou Enlai; Tian Jiyun, 56, Zhao's former financial deputy and an economist; Wang Zhaoguo, 44, the Director of the General Office of the Central Committee; Hu Qili, 56, expected to succeed Hu Yaobang as the General Secretary, and former Mayor of Tianjin; and Hao Jianxiu, 50, a factory worker who became Minister of Textiles and is an alternate member of the Party Secretariat, the only woman among the core of the "third echelon." For additional biographical information, see the *Asian Wall Street Journal Weekly* (6 May 1985), 14; *Newsweek* (15 Jul 1985), 32; Ch'i Mao-chi, "Red China's Leadership Succession Problem: An Analysis of the 'Third Echelons' Plan," *Issues & Studies*, 21, 1 (Jan 1985), 38-57, *Cheng Ming*, 93 (1 Jul 1985), 6-8. The fathers of several members of the "third echelon" are important figures in the CPC Central Committee, and they have been called the "Crown Prince Party." *Ming Pao* (30 Dec 1985), 5, has noted that children of senior cadres at and above the level of Vice-Minister account for just 2.8 percent of the 1,000 members of the third echelon at the provincial and ministerial level. Senior cadres' children account for merely 4.3 percent of the existing leaders of the 110 ministries, commissions, offices, and other departments directly subordinate to the State Council. Senior cadres' children make up 2.9 percent of all members and alternate members of the CPC Central Committee.

CHINESE POLITBURO AND SECRETARIAT, yearend 1985

Politburo Full Members (listed by age)

Peng Zhen	83	
Deng Xiaoping	81	
Chen Yun	80 or 86	
Li Xiannian	80	
Yang Shangkun	78	
Yang Dezhi	75	
Hu Qiaomu	73	
Xi Zhongxun	72	
Yu Qiuli	71	
Hu Yaobang	70	
Wan Li	69	
Fang Yi	69 or 71	
Zhao Ziyang	67	
Wu Xueqian	64	ap 24 Sep 1985
Ni Zhifu	63	
Qiao Shi	61	ap Sep 1985
Li Peng	57	ap 24 Sep 1985
Hu Qili	56	ap 24 Sep 1985
Tian Jiyun	56	ap 24 Sep 1985

Alternate Members

Qin Jiwei	75 or 81
Chen Muhua	65
Yao Yilin	68

continued . . .

CHINESE POLITBURO AND SECRETARIAT, yearend 1985 (continued)

Politburo Members Removed 16 September 1985

Ye Jianying	88
Nie Rongzhen	86
Xu Xiangqian	83
Ulanhu	81
Deng Yingchao	81
Wei Guoqing	79
Wang Zhen	77
Song Renqiong	76
Li Desheng	69
Zhang Tingfa	

Standing Committee of the Politburo

Deng Xiaoping
Hu Yaobang
Chen Yun
Li Xiannian
Zhao Ziyang
Ye Jianying was removed 16 September 1985

Secretariat Full Members

Hu Yaobang (General Secretary)		
Chen Pixian		
Deng Liqun	71	
Gu Mu *		
Hu Qili (Permanent Secretary)		
Wan Li		
Xi Zhongxun *		
Yao Yilin *		
Yu Qiuli		
Li Peng		ap 24 Sep 1985
Tian Jiyun		ap 24 Sep 1985
Hao Jianxiu (f)	50	ap 24 Sep 1985
Qiao Shi		ap 24 Sep 1985
Wang Zhaoguo	44	ap 24 Sep 1985

Central Advisory Commission

Chairman: Deng Xiaoping
162 members

Central Discipline Inspection Commission

Chairman: Chen Yun
129 members

Military Commission

Chairman: Deng Xiaoping
9 members

Central Committee

210 full members/123 alternate members

*Removed from the Secretariat 24 September 1985.

BIOGRAPHIES OF NEW POLITBURO AND SECRETARIAT MEMBERS, 24 Sep 1985

Tian Jiyun—Member of the Political Bureau and the Secretariat of the CPC Central Committee. Born in 1929; a native of Feicheng County, Shandong Province. He joined the Communist Party of China in May 1945. After 1947, he was head of a land reform work team, a confidential secretary of the financial take-over department of the Guiyang Military Control Commission, class instructor at Guiyang People's Revolutionary University and at the Guizhou provincial training center for financial cadres, head of the secretarial section under the Guizhou Provincial Department of Finance, director of its General Office, head of its planning section and of its budget division, and then deputy director of the finance department; and deputy director of the Financial and Monetary Division of the Office of Financial and Economic Affairs under the Southwest China Bureau of the CPC Central Committee. After 1969, he served in Sichuan Province successively as deputy head of the management and control section of the group in charge of finance and trade under the provincial Revolutionary Committee, deputy director and then director of the provincial Bureau of Finance and secretary of its group of leading party members, director of the provincial Department of Finance and secretary of its group of leading party members, and then became deputy secretary-general of the State Council, vice-premier of the State Council and concurrently its secretary-general. He is also a member of the 12th CPC Central Committee.

Qiao Shi—Member of the Political Bureau and the Secretariat of the CPC Central Committee. Born in 1924; a native of Dinghai County, Zhejiang Province. With a higher educational background, he joined the Communist Party of China in 1940. After 1940, he became secretary of the party branch and then of the general party branch of the Shanghai Middle School and deputy secretary of the new city district. After 1949, he served as secretary of the youth committee of the Hangzhou municipal party committee, deputy head of the United Front Work Department of the youth committee of the East China Bureau of the party Central Committee, head of the capital construction and technical section of the Anshan Iron and Steel Company, president of the designing institute and then of the research institute of the Jiuquan Iron and Steel Company. He then became a bureau director in the International Liaison Department of the CPC Central Committee and vice-head of the department. After 1983, he was appointed director of the General Office of the CPC Central Committee, head of the Organization Department of the CPC Central Committee and secretary of the Central Political Science and Law Commission, and was elected a member of the 12th CPC Central Committee and alternate member of the Secretariat of the Central Committee in 1982.

Li Peng—Member of the Political Bureau and the Secretariat of the CPC Central Committee. Born in 1928; a native of Changdu City, Sichuan Province. He had a higher educational background and joined the Communist Party of China in November 1945. After 1939, he studied at Yan an Middle School, Yan an Institute of Natural Sciences and Zhangjiakou Industrial School. After 1946, he was a technician at the Shanxi-Qahar-Hebei electric company, assistant manager and party branch secretary of the Harbin Oils and Fats Corporation. After 1948, he studied at Moscow Power Institute and was elected president of the association of the Chinese students in the U.S.S.R. After 1955, he served successively as deputy director and chief engineer of the Fengman power station in Jilin Province, deputy chief engineer of the Northeast China Electric Power Administration and director of the Fuxin power plant in Liaoning Province. After 1966, he served as acting secretary of the party committee of the Beijing Power Supply Bureau and chairman of its Revolutionary Committee; deputy director of the Beijing Electric Power Administration and deputy secretary of its party committee, and then its director and secretary of its group of leading party members. After 1979, he became vice-minister and then minister of the power industry and secretary of the group of leading party members in the ministry; and first vice-minister of water resources and electric power, and deputy secretary of its group of leading party members. After 1983, he served as vice-premier of the State Council and concurrently minister in charge of the State Education Commission. He is a member of the 12th CPC Central Committee.

Wu Xueqian—Member of the Political Bureau of the CPC Central Committee. Born in 1921; a native of Shanghai. With a higher educational background, he joined the Communist Party

continued . . .

BIOGRAPHIES OF NEW POLITBURO AND SECRETARIAT MEMBERS, 24 Sep 1985
(continued)

of China in May 1939. After 1938, he was a group leader of the Students Association for National Salvation, a front organization of the Shanghai underground party organization; member and then secretary of a committee (also under the Shanghai underground party organization) in charge of party work in middle schools; and head of the liaison office of the Urban Work Department of the Central China Bureau of the CPC Central Committee in Huainan. After 1944, he was member, deputy secretary and then secretary of the student work committee of the Shanghai underground party organization, and member of the underground Shanghai municipal party committee. After 1949, he served successively as secretary-general of the Shanghai Municipal Committee of the Communist Youth League, representative of the league's Central Committee at the World Federation of Democratic Youth, deputy director and then director of the International Liaison Department of the league's Central Committee and member of the Central Committee and of its Standing Committee, division chief and then bureau director in the International Liaison Department of the CPC Central Committee. After 1978, he became deputy head of the International Liaison Department of the CPC Central Committee, first vice-minister of foreign affairs and concurrently secretary of the group of leading party members of the ministry, and then minister of foreign affairs and secretary of the party committee of the ministry, and state councillor. He was a member of the Fifth National Committee of the Chinese People's Political Consultative Conference and elected member of the CPC 12th Central Committee in 1982.

Hu Qili—Member of the Political Bureau of the CPC Central Committee. Born in 1929; a native of Yulin County, Shaanxi Province. A graduate from the mechanics department of Beijing University, he joined the Democratic Youth League in 1947 and the Communist Party of China in 1948. While studying at Beijing University in 1948, he was chairman of the university's Engineering College and secretary of the general branch of the Youth League. After 1951, he worked successively as Standing Committee member of the Beijing University party committee and concurrently secretary of the university Youth League Committee, president of the All-China Students Federation, member of the Secretariat of the International Union of Students, alternate member of the Secretariat of the Central Committee of the Communist Youth League and vice-president of the All-China Youth Federation. After 1972, he served as deputy secretary of the Xiji County party committee in the Ningxia Hui Autonomous Region, deputy secretary of the Guyuan Prefectural party committee, director of the General Office of the Ningxia Regional party committee and vice-president of Qinghua University. After 1978, he served successively as member of the Secretariat of the Communist Youth League Central Committee, president of the All-China Youth Federation, secretary of the Tianjin Municipal party committee, mayor of Tianjin and director of the General Office of the CPC Central Committee. He was deputy to the Third and the Fifth National People's Congress and Standing Committee member of the Fifth National Committee of the Chinese People's Political Consultative Conference. He was elected a member of the 12th CPC Central Committee and member of its Secretariat in 1982.

Yao Yilin—Member of the Political Bureau of the CPC Central Committee. Born in 1917; a native of Guichi County, Anhui Province. He joined the Communist Party of China in November 1935. After 1934, he worked in the Association for Armed National Self-defense at Qinghua University and served as secretary of the group of leading party members in the Beijing Students Association, assistant in the Propaganda Department of the Northern Bureau of the CPC Central Committee and head of the Propaganda Department of the Tianjin municipal party committee. During the war of resistance against Japanese aggression (1937-1945), he became secretary of the Tianjin municipal party committee, secretary-general of the Hebei provincial party committee and head of its Propaganda Department, head of the Propaganda Department of the Hebei-Rehe-Liaoning area party committee; and secretary-general of the northern Shanxi-Qahar-Hebei sub-bureau of the CPC Central Committee and of its Shanxi-Qahar-Hebei Bureau. During the war of liberation (1946-49), he served as director of the Industrial Bureau of the Shanxi-Qahar-Hebei border area people's government and deputy

continued . . .

BIOGRAPHIES OF NEW POLITBURO AND SECRETARIAT MEMBERS, 24 Sep 1985 (continued)

director of its financial and economic office and head of the Industry and Commerce Department of the north China people's government. After the founding of the People's Republic of China in 1949, he became vice-minister of trade and then of commerce and deputy secretary of the group of leading party members in the two ministries, deputy head of the Finance and Trade Department of the CPC Central Committee, deputy director of the Office of Finance and Trade under the State Council, minister of commerce and secretary of the group of leading party members in the ministry, director of the Political Department under the CPC Central Committee for the Finance and Trade Ministries, and deputy secretary of the party committee for the Finance and Trade Ministries of the State Council. After 1973, he served as first vice-minister of foreign trade, minister of commerce and secretary of the group of leading party members in the ministry, deputy secretary-general of the CPC Central Committee, director of the General Office of the CPC Central Committee, secretary-general of the Committee of Financial and Economic Affairs under the State Council, minister in charge of the State Planning Commission and secretary of its group of leading party members and vice-premier of the State Council. He was elected an alternate member of the Eighth and the Tenth CPC Central Committee, member of the 11th and the 12th Central Committee; he became member of the Secretariat at the Fifth Plenary Session of the 11th CPC Central Committee, and alternate member of the Political Bureau of the 12th CPC Central Committee and member of its Secretariat.

Hao Jianxiu—Member of the Secretariat of the CPC Central Committee. Born in 1935; a native of Qingdao City, Shandong Province. A graduate of the East China Textile Engineering Institute, she joined the Communist Party of China in 1953. She became a worker in the Qingdao No. 6 cotton mill in 1949. After 1953, she studied and graduated from a special middle school attached to the Chinese People's University and the East China Textile Engineering Institute. After 1962, she became a technician at the Qingdao No. 6 cotton mill and later an engineer and deputy director of the Qingdao No. 8 cotton mill; she later served as deputy secretary of the Qingdao City party committee and vice-chairman of the city Revolutionary Committee. After 1977, she became a Standing Committee member of the Shandong Provincial party committee, vice-minister and then minister of textile industry and vice-president of the All-China Women's Federation. She was elected a member of the 11th and the 12th Central Committee of the CPC and an alternate member of the Secretariat of the Central Committee.

Wang Zhaoguo—Member of the Secretariat of the CPC Central Committee. Born in 1941; a native of Fengrun County, Hebei Province. He joined the Communist Party of China in December 1965. He graduated from Harbin Engineering University in 1966. While studying at the university, he was vice-chairman of a faculty students union, Standing Committee member and director of cultural affairs of the university students union. After 1968, he was a technician of the chassis division of the No. 2 motor vehicle plant. After 1973, he became secretary of the plant Communist Youth League committee, Standing Committee member of the plant party committee, deputy head of its Political Department and concurrently first secretary of the party committee of the plant's truck body division, secretary of the plant party committee and deputy director of the plant. After 1982, he served as first secretary of the Central Committee of the Communist Youth League and concurrently president of the Central Youth League School, director of the General Office of the CPC Central Committee and secretary of the party committee of the departments under the CPC Central Committee. He was elected a member of the 12th CPC Central Committee in 1982 and Standing Committee member of the Sixth National People's Congress in 1983.

FBIS-CHI 185 (24 Sep 1985), K7/11.

V ARMED FORCES

FOREIGN MILITARY DELEGATIONS TO CHINA, 1985

January
General John W. Vessey, Jr., Chairman of the US Joint Chiefs of Staff
Melvin R. Paisley, Assistant Secretary of the US Navy

February
Major General Richard Evralre, Commandant of the Canadian National Defense College

April
Lieutenant General Dr. Hans Joachim Linde, Surgeon General of the Federal German Armed Forces Medical and Health Service
Giovanni Spadolini, Italian Minister of Defense

May
Peter Corrieri, Chief of the Austrian Defense Minister's Office
Admiral John Fieldhouse, First Sea Lord of Britain and Chief of Staff of the Royal Navy
Haruo Natsume, Administrative Vice-Minister of the Japanese Defense Agency
Major General M. Abdus Samad, Chief of the General Staff of the Bangladesh Army
O Chin-u, member of the Presidium of the Politburo of the WPK Central Committee and Minister of the People's Armed Forces of the Democratic People's Republic of Korea
General Thianchai Sirisamphan, Deputy Commander-in-Chief of the Royal Thai Army

June
General Vasile Milea, First Vice-Minister of Defense and Chief of the General Staff of the Romanian Army

July
Youcef Yalaoui, member of the Central Committee of the Algerian National Liberation Front Party and General Secretary of the National Veterans Organization
General D.B. Musuguri, Chief of the Tanzanian People's Defense Force
Lieutenant General Tissa Idraka Weeratunge, Commander of Joint Operations of Sri Lanka

August
Joiah Tungamirai, Deputy Commander of the Air Force, Zimbabwe

September
General Sir Philip Bennett, Chief Commander of the Australian Defense Forces

October
Field Marshal Sir Edwin Bramall, Chief of Britain's Defence Staff
General Charles Gabriel, Chief of Staff of the US Air Force
Lieutenant-General Gheorghe Enciu, Commander of the Romanian Communication Corps

November
Lieutenant-General Fathi Abu Taleb, Chief of Staff of the Jordanian Armed Forces
General Kim Pong-yui, Vice-Minister of the People's Armed Forces, People's Democratic Republic of Korea

December
General Jacques de Barry, Secretary-General of National Defense of France

Press reports.

CHINESE MILITARY DELEGATIONS ABROAD, 1985

January
He Zhengwen, Deputy Chief PLA General Staff, to Pakistan (Dec-Jan)

continued . . .

CHINESE MILITARY DELEGATIONS ABROAD, 1985 (continued)

February
> Fu Jize, Deputy Commander PLA Navy, to Thailand (Feb-Mar)
> Zhao Guocheng, Deputy Commander-in-Chief of the first Chinese expedition teams to the Antarctic and Commander of the Navy J121 vessel, and He Chunlian, Deputy Commander of the ship, visit Bellingshausen, the Soviet survey station in the Antarctic near the Chang Cheng station

March
> Xu Xin, Deputy Chief of PLA General Staff, to Burma

May
> Zhang Tingfa, Commander-in-Chief of the Air Force, to France and Britain (May-Jun)

July
> Zhang Aiping, Minister of Defense, to Pakistan, Romania and Portugal (Jun-Jul)

August
> Han Huaizhi, Deputy Chief of the PLA General Staff, to Ecuador, Colombia, Venezuela, and Mexico (Aug-Sep) (This was the first visit to Ecuador by a Chinese military delegation since the two countries established diplomatic relations in 1980.)

October
> Yang Dezhi, Chief of the General Staff, to Italy and Turkey

November
> Admiral Liu Huaqing, Commander-in-Chief of the PLA Navy, to US and France
> A Chinese naval squadron with a guided-missile destroyer and an oil-and-water supply ship to visit Pakistan, Sri Lanka, and Bangladesh (Nov-Jan)
> He Qizong, Deputy Chief of the General Staff, to Gabon and Zaire (Nov-Dec)

Press reports.

GROUND FORCES, THE MILITIA, AND GENERAL NEWS, 1985

First PLA Post-Graduate School—The PLA's first post-graduate school was established at Changsha, Hunan in January, 1985. It is based on the University of Science and Technology for National Defense, which was itself formed from the Harbin Military Engineering Institute, the first higher educational institution of the Army. The school will offer doctorates and master's degrees to the approximately 670 students enrolled in 1985. XNB (1 Feb 1985), 27-28.

Post-Graduate Courses—Approximately 20 post-graduate students will enroll at the Chinese Military Academy in September, 1985. The Academy will offer courses in military concepts, including the development of Mao Zedong's military thinking, his ideas on the people's war and active defense, and the military strategy of the USSR; the science of campaigns, including mobile, positional, and amphibious warfare; and the history of war, including World War II and the PLA. Applicants must be officers under 37, on active duty, and have a university or intermediate military academy background or the equivalent education. Graduates will be allowed to engage in advanced teaching and research or to become senior staff officers. China now has over 100 military academies and schools. Graduates make up 87 percent of the divisional commanders and 71 percent of the regimental commanders. XNB (13 Feb 1985), 19.

Pakistani Nuclear Device—Pakistan planned to test a nuclear device in the Taklamakan Desert in Xinjiang. Its yield was to be about the same as that tested by the Chinese in 1964. FBIS-SOV 211 (31 Oct 1985), D1.

Military Institute Opens—The Modern Administration Institute has opened in Shenyang to train PLA cadres. Liu Zhenhua, the Political Commissar of the Military Region, is its President. FBIS-CHI 60 (28 Mar 1985), S1.

continued . . .

GROUND FORCES, THE MILITIA, AND GENERAL NEWS, 1985 (continued)

Liberation Army Daily Reorganized—Liu Zonghou has been removed as the Director of *Jiefangjun Bao* (*Liberation Army Daily*), and He Guyan has been fired as a Deputy Director. Qian Diqian, the Vice-President of the PLA Political Academy, will replace Liu. Hua Nan, another Deputy Director of the newspaper, has been relieved of his post as Deputy Director of the PLA General Political Department. The pretext for the changes was the charge that erotic videotapes had been played for several years in the *Jiefangjun Bao* offices. *Kuang Chiao Ching*, 150 (Hong Kong, 16 Mar 1985), 8-9.

Strategic Institute Established—The Institute for Strategic Studies, attached to the Academy of the Chinese PLA, has been organized in Beijing. It will teach global and regional military strategies, strategies of major military blocs, military theory, and other subjects. *Jiefangjun Bao* (3 Jun 1985).

Personnel Reductions—Over the next two years China will demobilize 1 million troops. The move will cut revolutionary commanders and make the PLA more combat-effective. *Beijing Review*, 24 (17 Jun 1985), 6. The Logistics Department of the PLA will cut its staff by half. The reduction will be made at headquarters and in military units, such as factories, research institutes, colleges, hospitals, and other facilities. *China Daily* (26 Jun 1985), 1.

Budgetary Share—The share of the military in the total state budget has been reduced from 16.3 percent in 1980 to 11.9 percent in 1985. FBIS-CHI 123 (26 Jun 1985), K2. Also see John Frankenstein, "Military Cuts in China," *Problems of Communism*, XXXIV, 4 (Jul-Aug 1985), 56-60.

Simulation Devices—Services of the PLA have held their first maneuvers involving simulation devices. The weapons were laser and electronic firing and receiving devices which simulated the sound of battle. The exercise played out an attack on a motorized rifle company's defensive position by a tank battalion. XNB (18 Oct 1985), 62.

Military Aid to Pakistan—The No. 5 Anti-Aircraft Gun Factory has opened at Wah, Pakistan. The plant will make 12.7-mm guns. Pakistan currently produces ammunition and weapons in 13 factories, many constructed with aid from Beijing. *China Post* (Taipei, 9 Nov 1985), 4.

Military Attaches—Forty-three countries have set up military attache offices in Beijing. *Jiefangjun Bao* (18 Dec 1985).

New Uniforms—Beginning 1 May 1985 the PLA was to adopt new uniforms. The new uniforms for cadres at and above regimental rank will be made of woolen and blended woolen materials. The new uniforms for cadres and fighters at battalion level and lower rank will still be made of cotton material. The form of the new uniforms will not be significantly different from the current uniforms. The cadres and fighters of the whole Army will wear peaked military caps (women fighters will retain their present headgear without peak), new collar insignias, and shoulder boards. The emblem on the cap will be changed from the present design to a round one with "five stars and the words 1 August" surrounded by wheat ears and cog wheels. It shows that our fighters are soldiers of the people and our Army is a symbol of unity. Chin straps for cadres' caps will be silver gray silk knitted bands and that for fighters will be black man-made leather.

The colors of the new uniforms include a palm green woolen uniform for the Army; dark blue woolen winter uniform for the Navy, white woolen jacket and dark blue woolen trousers for the Navy in summer; and palm green woolen jacket and dark blue woolen trousers for the Air Force. The colors of uniforms made of cotton materials will remain the same as the present uniforms. The jackets for cadres will have epaulets and golden color metal buttons with the design of "five stars and the words 1 August." All cadres and fighters will have additional long sleeve and short sleeve shirts designed for collar and shoulder insignias. The shirts for cadres will have epaulets with golden color metal buttons with the design of "five stars and the words 1 August," while the shirts for fighters will not have epaulets and the buttons for fighters' shirts will be made of bakelite as before. Cadres' collar badges will be made of heavy woolen cloth in red for the Army, black for the Navy, and blue for the Air Force. They will have golden edges with golden stars. The fighters' collar badges will also be made

continued . . .

GROUND FORCES, THE MILITIA, AND GENERAL NEWS, 1985 (continued)

of heavy woolen cloth with colors the same as those for cadres. The fighters' color badges will have coats of arms of services as follows: "five stars and the words 1 August" for the Army, iron anchor for sailors; and "five stars and the words 1 August" with two flying wings for the Air Force. All cadres and volunteer soldiers of the whole Army will wear semi-rigid shoulder boards. The materials for shoulder boards of the three services will be the same as for their respective winter uniforms and the signs of arms of services will be embroidered on the shoulder boards. The new-type uniforms will be distributed in groups starting 1 March.

FBIS-CHI 8 (11 Jan 1985), K2/3.

Tactical Weapons Offered for Sale—The Chinese are offering various tactical anti-aircraft and anti-ship missiles for sale and joint production. They include:

HQ-2J surface-to air missile, based on the Soviet SA2 Guideline

Length (m)	10.8
Diameter of the first of two stages (m)	0.654
Propellant of first stage	Solid
Second-stage propellant	Liquid
Weight of warhead (kg)	193
Number of fragments (th)	12
Lethal radius (m)	6

HY-2 anti-ship missile

Maximum effective range (km)	95
Length (m)	7.36
Diameter (m)	0.76
Operational range (km) at Mach 0.9	20-95
Weight (km)	2,998
Warhead weight (kg)	513
Propellant of boosters	Solid

The missile is fired from a portable land-based launcher. The HY2-G version has an active radar homing and uses a radio altimeter to cut cruise altitude. The HY-2A has passive infrared homing radar.

C601 air-launched anti-ship missile

Length (m)	7.38
Weight (at launch, kg)	2,440
Maximum range (km)	95-100
Cruise speed	Mach 0.9
Cruise altitude (m)	70-100

The missile has a monopulse terminal guidance radar. *Aviation Week & Space Technology* (17 Jun 1985), 25. An HN-5 shoulder-launched anti-aircraft missile has been demonstrated. The missile travels at 500 meters/sec against low-altitude targets.

Modernization—*The Beijing Review*, 18 (6 May 1985), 19-21, mentions that Air Force pilots must now have at least a senior middle school education. One in four pilots has graduated from college. Some 85 percent of the officers and engineering and technical staff of the Strategic Missile Corps are college graduates. Another 127,000 officers from all branches of the PLA are receiving a higher education while on active service.

The PLA is using a new-sub-machine gun and automatic rifle. The rifle has a firing rate of a sub-machine gun and can launch anti-tank grenades.

Officers Retired—China will retire 47,000 officers with long years of service during 1985-86. It is believed that the cuts will be made in heavily staffed support echelons, or possibly, in the military garrisons of major cities. Current manpower is about 4.2 million. The moves apparently are being made to increase Deng Xiaoping's control of the Armed Forces and to

continued . . .

GROUND FORCES, THE MILITIA, AND GENERAL NEWS, 1985 (continued)

reduce the financial burden on China by transferring soldiers to the civilian economy. New York *Times* (21 Apr 1985), 3. The reductions are part of the planned retirement of more than 80,000 PLA officers during the next few years. New York *Times* (31 Mar 1985), F3; *Beijing Review*, 11 (18 Mar 1985), 8.

Defense University—Zhang Zhen, former deputy Chief of the PLA General Staff, has been named the first President of the new Defense University in Beijing. FBIS-CHI 243 (18 Dec 1985), K1.

Defense Academy—Li Desheng, formerly the Commander of the Shenyang Military Region, will head the new supreme defense academy to form from several existing institutions. *China Quarterly*, 103 (Sep 1985), 564.

Atlas An atlas of the deployment of PLA divisions and fleets appears in Michael Kidron and Dan Smith, *The War Atlas* (1983), map 22.

Militia Militia training centers are to be established in each of China's over 2,000 counties. Militia units are directly subordinate to the commander of the local military district. The militia includes both men and women and is composed of two segments: one is an active reserve of persons aged 18-28 whose members train regularly with conventional weapons, the other is a reserve of people aged 29-35. *China Daily* (29 Jan 1985), 1.

Defense Magazine—*Shen Jian* (*Divine Sword*) is a new magazine dealing with issues of national defense. FBIS-CHI 39 (27 Feb 1985), K28.

Reserve Division Formed—The Beijing Infantry Reserve Service Second Division was established 1 February 1985. Renmin Ribao (2 Feb 1985).

Breakthrough—The Soviets reportedly taught the Chinese that a force ratio (troops and materiel) as high as 8:1 was necessary for offensive actions. US doctrine puts the ratio at 3:1. Alfred D. Wilhelm, Jr., "National Security—The Chinese Perspective," *China Policy for the Next Decade* (1984), 187.

Size of Construction Corps—More than 100,000 members of the PLA have participated in the construction of major projects in the past few years. These have included building highways in the Shengli oil field and digging canals to move water from the Luan He River to Tianjin. FBIS-CHI 123 (26 Jun 1985), K1/2.

Structural Changes—William T. Tow points out that organizational changes have reduced the power of the General Political Department and the Commission on Science, Technology, and Industry for National Defense in "Science and Technology in China's Defense," *Problems of Communism*, XXXIV, 4 (Jul-Aug 1985), 15-31, esp. p. 18.

Soviet Force Readiness—The International Institute for Strategic Studies reported in 1982 that the percentage of Soviet divisions east of the Urals in categories 1 and 2, the highest states of readiness with at least half their wartime complement, had fallen from 50 to 25 in three years. This percentage was apparently corrected to 35 in the 1983 edition of *The Military Balance*. Most of the category 1 divisions are located near the Sea of Okhotsk, suggesting some concessions by the Soviets along the border with China. Carl G. Jacobson, "The Far East," SAFRA/8 (1985), 250.

Modern Technology—The need for modern equipment in the PLA is stressed in the "Introduction to National Defense Modernization" in JPRS, *China Report: Political, Sociological and Military Affairs* (JPRS-CPS-85-011, 4 Feb 1985), 3-61. This is a recent translation of *Guofang Xiandaihua* (Jul 1983), 1-36, 198-224.

Military Science Prize—The Chinese Military Academy has established a foundation to award 100,000 yuan each year to outstanding teachers of military science. The Liu Bocheng Foundation is named after a founder of the PLA and a military theorist. *Beijing Review*, 38 (23 Sep 1985), 9.

Base Command Established—A base command to unify management of warehouses in the strategic rear has been established in the PLA General Logistics Department, FBIS-CHI 205 (23 Oct 1985), K18.

continued . . .

GROUND FORCES, THE MILITIA, AND GENERAL NEWS, 1985 (continued)

Development of Chinese Nuclear Weapons—Nie Rongzhen describes China's atomic weapons development program in the *Beijing Review*, 17 (29 Apr 1985), 15-18. This is an excerpt from Nie's recently published memoirs. After the Soviets decided to withhold an atomic weapon promised China, Marshal Chen Yi argued that the PRC should develop its own weapon, "even if we have to pawn our pants." Also see a summary in the New York *Times* (5 May 1985), 15.

Target Drone—China has developed a target drone which flies between 500 and 16,500 meters above sea level at 850-910 km per hour. It can turn in a radius of about 1.5 km. It was made by the Nanjing Aeronautical Engineering Institute. FBIS-CHI 100 (23 May 1985), K12. Zhongguo Xinwen She has announced that the drone flies between 500 and 18,000 meters, has a maximum speed exceeding 1,000 km per hour, and has a flight endurance of 90 minutes.

Israeli Assistance—*Sankei Shimbun* reported in January, 1985 that China's T-69 medium tanks were equipped with British 106-mm guns made under license in Israel. New York *Times* (22 Jul 1985), 1, 3.

Undersea Missile Launch—The PRC is believed to have launched a missile from a submarine 15 October 1985. China currently possesses about 50 missiles with a range of 1,800 and 60 IRBMs with a range of 5,500 km. It has also deployed some ICBMs. FBIS-CHI 220 (14 Nov 1985), K14.

Modernization, 1983-84—Major William C. Bennett mentions that progress in Ground Forces weapons has been less impressive than in the Navy and Missile Artillery, but better than in the Air Force. The PLA was able to reduce its strength below 4 million by shifting its internal security functions to the Ministry of Public Security in 1983, and by transferring the Railway Engineer Corps to the Ministry of Railways and putting the Capital Construction Engineering Corps under civil jurisdiction in 1984. See "Professionalism in the People's Liberation Army," *Military Review*, LXV, 11 (Nov 1985), 65-73. Also see John Frankenstein, "Military Cuts in China," *Problems of Communism*, XXXIV, 4 (Jul-Aug 1985), 56-60.

Military Regions Reduced to Seven—The number of Military Regions in China was reduced from 11 to seven in June, 1985. The Beijing, Guangzhou and Shenyang Regions remain, but the Hubei and new Sanxia Provincial Military Districts have been absorbed into the Guanzhou Region. The Wuhan Military Region, excluding the Hubei Provincial Military District, has merged into the Jinan Military Region. The Urumqi Region has become part of the Lanzhou Military Region; the Chengdu Military Region has absorbed the Kunming Region; and the Fuzhou Military Region is now part of the Nanjing Military Region. *China Quarterly,* 103 (Sep 1985), 564.

Nuclear Equipment for Iran—In June, 1985 officials of the PRC discussed providing nuclear equipment to Iran. Washington *Post* (14 Nov 1985), 1A, 35A.

MILITARY ORGANIZATION OF CHINA

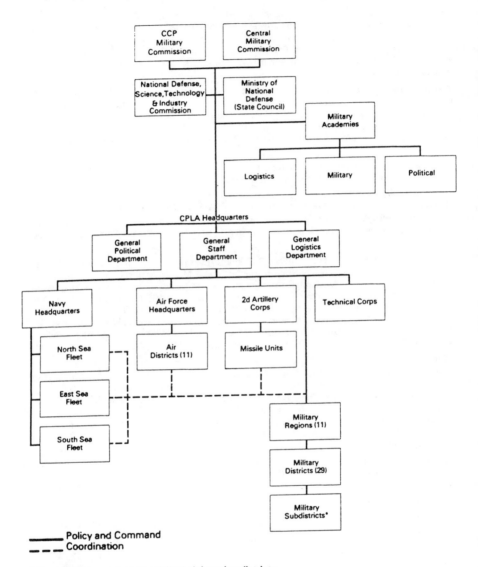

_____ Policy and Command
_ _ _ Coordination

* Boundaries correspond to civil administrative districts.

Defense Intelligence Agency, _Handbook of the Chinese People's Liberation Army_ (1985),
A-19.

PROBABLE MILITIA ORGANIZATION

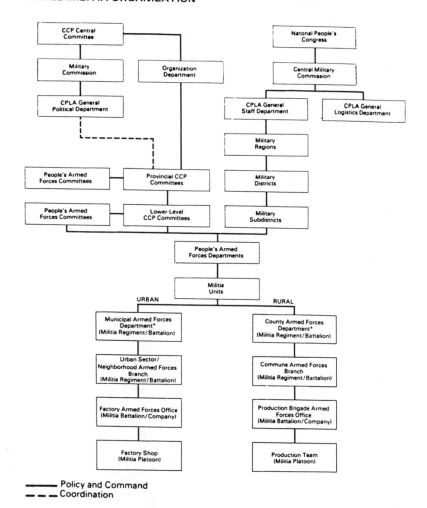

——— Policy and Command
— — — Coordination

* Militia activity is supervised by county or municipal "People's Armed Forces Department." These departments are probably shared by a mixture of regular CPLA and civilian personnel and are subject to dual control as military bodies. They are subject to the next higher military echelon, the military subdistrict; as political organs, they are subject to the county or municipal party committee, which they serve as a military staff section.

NOTE: Within the various militia units, elements of each of the three militia categories may be found. The armed and basic militia serving primarily as cadres.

Defense Intelligence Agency, *Handbook of the Chinese People's Liberation Army* (1984), A-1. Also relevant is June Teufel Dreyer, "Civil-Military Relations in the People's Republic of China," *Comparative Strategy*, 5, 1 (1985), 27-49. In line with streamlining the militia, the number of militiamen has been cut by 60 percent and the number of grass-roots militia cadres by 80 percent. The militia has been combined with the PLA reserves, so that militia organizations now supervise reserve personnel. FBIS-CHI 243 (18 Dec 1985), K12.

MILITARY ORGANIZATIONS OF THE PEOPLE'S REPUBLIC OF CHINA

Central Military Commission of the National People's Congress

The Central Military Commission was established by Article 93 of the Chinese Constitution adopted in December 1982. The Constitution states that the new commission is a State organ, subordinate to the National People's Congress, and directs the armed forces of the country.

Chairman	* Deng Xiaoping
Executive Vice Chairman	* Yang Shangkun
Vice Chairmen	Nie Rongzhen
	Xu Xiangqian
Members	Hong Xuezhi
	* Yang Dezhi
	* Yu Qiuli
	Zhang Aiping

Military Commission of the Chinese Communist Party Central Committee

The Military Commission of the Chinese Communist Party Central Committee is the traditional leadership organization of the military establishment and is subordinate to the Party.

Chairman	* Deng Xiaoping
Permanent Vice Chairman	* Yang Shangkun
Vice Chairmen	Nie Rongzhen
	Xu Xiangqian
Secretary General	* Yang Shangkun
Deputy Secretaries General	Hong Xuezhi
	* Yang Dezhi
	* Yu Qiuli
	Zhang Aiping
Advisers	Li Da
	Li Jukui

National Defense Science, Technology, and Industry Commission

The National Defense Scientific and Technological Commission merged with the National Defense Industry Office in August 1982. The primary two functions of the organization are the supervision of weapons research and development and the coordination of the military with the civilian sectors of the economy. The defense-oriented ministries of the State Council supervise the production of military hardware and supplies by diversified plants.

Chairman	Ding Henggao
Vice Chairmen	Qian Xuesen
	Shen Rongjun
	Wu Shaozu
	Xie Guang
	Ye Daming
	Zhang Yunyu
	Zhang Zhenhuan

Ministry of National Defense of the State Council

Minister	Zhang Aiping
Vice Minister	Xiao Ke
Foreign Affairs Bureau	
Director	Song Wenzhong

continued . . .

MILITARY ORGANIZATIONS OF THE PEOPLE'S REPUBLIC OF CHINA (continued)

People's Liberation Army

General Logistics Department

Director	Hong Xuezhi	
Deputy Directors	Li Yuan	Zhang Bin
	Liu Mingpu	Zhao Nanqi
	Xu Guangyi	Zong Shunliu

General Staff Department

Chief of Staff	Yang Dezhi	
Assistants to the Chief of Staff	Liu Kai	Tan Jingqiao
Deputy Chiefs of Staff	Han Huaizhi	Xu Huizi
	He Qizong	Xu Xin

General Political Department

Director	* Yu Qiuli	
Deputy Directors	Gan Weihan	Zhou Wenyuan
	Zhou Keyu	Zhu Yunqian

Service Arms

Air Force

Commander	Wang Hai
Political Commissar	Zhu Guang

Second Artillery Corps

Commander	He Jinheng
Political Commissar	Liu Lifeng

Navy

Commander	Liu Huaqing
Political Commissar	Li Yaowen

East Sea Fleet:	Commander	Nie Kuiju
	Political Commissar	Huang Zhongxue
North Sea Fleet.	Commander	Ma Zinchun
	Political Commissar	Li Changru
South Sea Fleet:	Commander	Chen Xuejiang
	Political Commissar	Zhang Haiyun

Military Regions and Districts

Beijing Military Region

Commander	** Qin Jiwei	
Political Commissars	Fu Chongbi	Yang Baibing
Hebei Military District:	Commander	Zhang Zhenchuan
	1st Political Commissar	Gao Yang
Nei Mongol Military District:	Commander	Cai Ying
	1st Political Commissar	Zhou Hui
Shanxi Military District:	Commander	Zhang Guangyou
	1st Political Commissar	Li Ligong

continued . . .

MILITARY ORGANIZATIONS OF THE PEOPLE'S REPUBLIC OF CHINA (continued)

Military Regions and Districts (continued)

Chengdu Military Region
Commander	Fu Quanyou
Political Commissar	Wang Haifeng

Guizhou Military District:
Commander	Wang Zheng
1st Political Commissar	Chi Biqing

Sichuan Military District:
Commander	Zhang Wenqing
1st Political Commissar	Yang Rudai

Xizang Military District:
Commander	Jiang Hongquan
1st Political Commissar	Yin Fatang

Yunnan Military District:
Commander	Wang Zuxin
1st Political Commissar	An Pingsheng

Guangzhou Military Region
Commander	You Taizhong
Political Commissar	Zhang Zhongxian

Guangdong Military District:
Commander	Zhang Juhui
1st Political Commissar	Ren Zhongyi

Guangxi Military District:
Commander	Li Xinliang
1st Political Commissar	Qiao Xiaoguang

Hainan Military District:
Commander	Peng Weijiang
1st Political Commissar	Yao Wenxu

Hubei Military District:
Commander	Wang Shen
1st Political Commissar	Guan Guangfu

Hunan Military District:
Commander	Jiang Jinliu
1st Political Commissar	Mao Zhiyong

Jinan Military Region
Commander	Li Jiulong
Political Commissar	Chi Haotian

Henan Military District:
Commander	Zhan Jingwu
1st Political Commissar	Liu Jie

Shandong Military District:
Commander	Liu Yude
1st Political Commissar	Su Yiran

Lanzhou Military Region
Commander	Zhao Xianshun
Political Commissar	Li Xianhua

Gansu Military District:
Commander	Zhou Yuechi
1st Political Commissar	Li Ziqi

Ningxia Military District:
Commander	Liu Xueji
1st Political Commissar	Li Xuezhi

Qinghai Military District:
Commander	Xie Quanwei
1st Political Commissar	Zhao Haifeng

Shaanxi Military District:
Commander	Ji Tingbi
1st Political Commissar	

Xinjiang Military District:
Commander	Liu Haiqing
1st Political Commissar	

continued . . .

MILITARY ORGANIZATIONS OF THE PEOPLE'S REPUBLIC OF CHINA (continued)

Military Regions and Districts (continued)

Nanjing Military Region
Commander   Xiang Shouzhi
Political Commissar   Fu Kuiqing

Anhui Military District: Commander   Jiu Dehe
1st Political Commissar   Huang Huang

Fujian Military District: Commander   Lu Fuxiang
1st Political Commissar   Xiang Nan

Jiangsu Military District   Commander   Zhen Shen
1st Political Commissar   Han Peixin

Jiangxi Military District: Commander   Wang Baotian
1st Political Commissar   Bai Dongcai

Zhejiang Military District   Commander
1st Political Commissar   Wang Fang

Shenyang Military Region
Commander   Liu Jingsong
Political Commissar   Liu Zhenhua

Heilongjiang Military District: Commander   Li Dehe
1st Political Commissar   Li Lian

Jilin Military District: Commander   Chen Tongyi
1st Political Commissar   Qiang Xiaochu

Liaoning Military District: Commander   Ding Jianrui
1st Political Commissar   Guo Feng

*   Politburo, Member
** Politburo, Alternate Member

CIA, *Military Organizations of the People's Republic of China* (Oct 1985). The number of Military Regions have been reduced from 11 to seven. *Ban Yue Tan*, 16 (25 Aug 1985), 19.

NAVAL DEVELOPMENTS, 1985

H-3- The PRC will build a 47-meter (154-foot) fast patrol boat designated the H-3 with the help of the H-3 Research and Development Group of Rancho Santa Fe, California. It will have three gas turbines, and a full-load displacement of 239 tons. The hull will be made from a marine aluminum alloy, and the recommended armament is a 75-mm Oto Melara bow gun, four McDonnell Douglas Harpoon missiles at midship, and a General Dynamics Phalanx 20-mm gun on the upper main deck. *Aviation Week & Space Technology* (11 Feb 1985), 56.

Floating College—A college has opened on the No. 105 guided-missile destroyer at Dalian. It has enrolled 182 officers and sailors for a two-year law course. Teachers from the Beijing People's University will spend a month and a half at sea with students, and courses will be conducted by correspondence the rest of the time. FBIS-CHI 95 (16 May 1985), K13.

New Commander of Fleet—Nie Kuiju has become the new Commander of the East Sea Fleet. Zhang Wenhua is the new Political Commissar. Chen Qingji has become the Chief of Staff. FBIS-CHI 200 (16 Oct 1985), K21/22.

Mutiny—Two Chinese sailors on a torpedo boat on maneuvers in the Yellow Sea mutiny 21 or 22 March, killing six officers. The mutineers apparently want political asylum in Taiwan.

continued . . .

NAVAL DEVELOPMENTS, 1985 (continued)

The boat drifts and is eventually towed into Hawangdung, South, Korea. Three PLA torpedo boats are turned back by the South Koreans when they pursue the stray vessel. Thirteen crew members are returned to the PRC 28 March. *Facts on File* (5 Apr 1985), 237F1/238; New York *Times* (24 Mar 1985), 1, 8.

Submarine Repair Vessel—China's first submarine repair ship has started operations for the Navy. *Jiegangjun Bao* (14 Jan 1985), 48.

CHINESE NAVAL ORDER OF BATTLE

Chinese Naval Forces

Submarines	
GOLF Class SSB	1
HAN Class SSN	2
MING Class SS	2
ROMEO Class SS	78
S-1 Class SS	1
WHISKEY Class SS	21
Total	105

Principal Combatants	
Destroyers	14
Frigates	19
Total	33

Minor Combatants	
Patrol Combatants	14
Amphibious Warfare Ships	35
Mine Warfare Ships	23
Coastal and Roadstead Patrol Craft	1,004
Amphibious Warfare Craft	470
Mine Warfare Craft	80
Total	1,626

Support Ships	
Underway Replenishment Ships	3
Material Support Ships	3
Fleet Support Ships	38
Other Auxiliaries	88
Yard and Service Craft	380
Total	512

Total Ship Strength	2,276

Defense Intelligence Agency, *Handbook of the Chinese People's Liberation Army* (1985), 56.

AIR FORCE DEVELOPMENTS, 1985

Chinese Aircraft Marketed in US—The Custom Associates Company of East Northport, New York is selling Chinese aricraft in the US. Prices are the following:

MIG-15	two-seat trainer	$193,000
MIG-15	one-seat fighter	$193,000
MIG-17F	Shenyang J-5	$198,000
MIG-19	F-6 fighter	$1,600,000
MIG-19	A-5 attack version	$2,600,000
MIG-21	F-7	$2,600,000
MIG-21	F-8	$5,500,000
engines		$30,000

These aircraft engines are said to have less than 10 hours of flight. Most of the earlier engines had 100-125 hours between overhauls. *Aviation Week & Space Technology* (21 Jan 1985), 25.

SAM Hits—The Air Force surface-to-air missile unit was organized in the late 1950s. Within a few years of its formation, it shot down five U-2 reconnaissance aircraft from Taiwan. The first SAM hit occurred 7 October 1959 above north China. Another was shot down in 1960. A pilotless high-altitude reconnaissance plane was hit in 1968. FBIS-CHI 47 (11 May 1985), K11/12. David C. Isby mentions in *Weapons and Tactics of the Soviet Army* (1981), 246, that China has downed four U-2s with the SA-2 surface-to-air missile. The SA-2 has two dead zones through which the missile cannot be guided. One such zone is the cone above the launcher, and the other is below the performance envelope, making it difficult to engage low-flying aircraft. The missile accelerates to full speed only at 7.63 km (25,000 feet), and is not effective against maneuverable tactical aircraft.

Air Force Modernization—The number of all-weather pilots in the PLA Air Force has increased six times since 1978. For over six years, the number of serious accidents in 10,000 hours of flying is only slightly higher than the world's best record. The PLA Air Force has opened about 14 military airfields to civilian aircraft. *Kuang Chiao Ching*, 153 (Hong Kong, 16 Jun 1985), 11-13.

F-7—The Chinese F-7 sells for just 10 percent what the French Mirage 2000 costs. *Frankfurter Allgemeine Zeitung* (4 Dec 1984), 6. The F-5 and F-7 are being upgraded to improve their radar and gunsight and add a 30-mm gun. *Asian Wall Street Journal Weekly* (17 Jun 1985), 14.

New Air Force Commander—Wang Hai, 59, replaced Zhang Tingfa, 67, as the PLA Air Force Commander in July, 1985.

ARMS DEALS

Iran—Iran will supply the PRC with 2 million tons of crude oil over two years and pay the rest of the $1.6 billion-deal in cash in exchange for 12 Shenyang F-6 fighters, 200 T-59 main battle tanks, multibarreled rocket launchers, replicas of Soviet SAM-2 and -7 missiles, and hundreds of field guns. *Asian Wall Street Journal Weekly* (1 Apr 1985), 6; (17 Jun 1985), 14.

Italy—During the first eight months of 1984, Italy exported electronics worth DM160 million for the Chinese arms industry. *Der Spiegel*, 16 (15 Apr 1985), 152.

United States—The US Pentagon has offered to sell the PRC plans and equipment for a munitions factory for 155-mm artillery shells. The deal could be worth as much as $98 million. This would be the first government-to-government weapons sale between the two countries. New York *Times* (1 Oct 1985), 5.

Brazil—Talks have been going on for over two years to enable the Chinese to obtain Brazilian military technology to produce armored personnel carriers. Brazil has not found Chinese terms acceptable. *Krasnaia zvezda* (5 Nov 1985).

continued . . .

ARMS DEALS (continued)

Helicopters—The Sikorsky Co., a division of United Technologies Corp., delivered 24 S-70C helicopters to the PLA in November 1985. Trade between the PRC and UTC companies totaled $16.3 billion in 1984. Purchases included helicopters, electronics, air-conditioning systems, aircraft motors, elevators and standard controls. *Beijing Review*, 52 (30 Dec 1985), 26-27.

Equipment Purchases—The PLA Navy has agreed to purchase American Mark 46 torpedoes, towed sonars, gas turbine engines, and Phalanx shipboard Gatling Guns for use against anti-ship missiles. It is also interested in Standard and Sparrow missiles and radars, but sale for these has not yet been approved. The Air Force wants to obtain avionics for its F-8s. *Washington Post* (12 Jan 1985), A1, A17. The Phalanx is a six-barreled, 20-mm rapid-fire gun aimed by self-contained radar. New York *Times* (13 Jan 1985), 4.

Italian Deal—Italy will sell the PRC electronics equipment, signaling and mechanization technology. The deal may include jet fighters, hydrofoils and electronic gunsights. Purchases of radar, helicopters, torpedoes, and mines have been discussed. Italy may also teach parachute jumping and mountain warfare to the Chinese. *Asian Wall Street Journal Weekly* (15 Apr 1985), 16.

ORGANIZATION OF THE PLA AIR FORCES

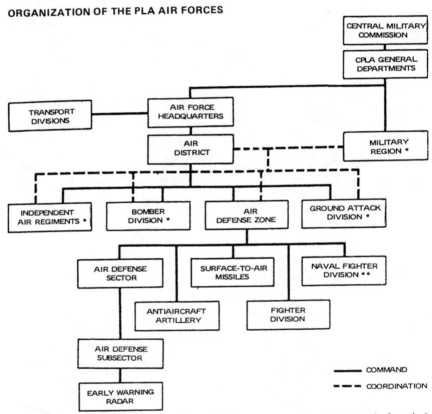

* Military Region Headquarters would probably assume operational command of tactical air units in wartime
** Navy Fighter Divisions probably are controlled by CPLAAF for air defense operations

Defense Intelligence Agency, *Handbook of the Chinese People's Liberation Army* (1985), 63.

CONSCRIPTION WORK REGULATIONS, Promulgated by the State Council and the Central Military Commission 24 Oct 1985

Chapter I: General Principles

Article 1. This set of regulations is formulated in accordance with the relevant provisions of the "Military Service Law of the People's Republic of China."

Article 2. The draft of new recruits is an important work to step up Army building and defend the socialist motherland. People's governments and military organs at all levels should make serious efforts to do this work well.

Article 3. All male citizens who are 18 years old before 31 December of the year should be drafted for active service. Anyone not drafted in the year due for conscription will remain eligible for the draft until he is 22 years old.

When needed by the military, female citizens may be called up for active service according to the provisions in the foregoing paragraph.

When needed by the military and on a voluntary basis, male and female citizens not yet 18 years old before 31 December of the year may be drafted.

A citizen may be exempted from conscription if the person has a serious physiological defect or serious deformity that makes the person unsuitable for military service. A citizen eligible for conscription may be entitled to a postponement if the person is the only able-bodied one to provide for the family or a student studying in a fulltime school.

A citizen eligible for conscription will not be drafted if the person is under investigation, indicted or on trial, or has been sentenced to imprisonment, detained, or placed under restrictions and who is serving time and has been stripped of political rights in accordance with the law.

Article 4. The number of persons to be called up and the specifications and schedules of conscriptions each year will be determined in the conscription order issued by the State Council and the Central Military Commission.

Article 5. All provinces, autonomous regions, and municipalities should arrange for conscription work in their respective localities in accordance with the conscription order issued by the State Council and the Central Military Commission.

In assigning conscription quotas, all provinces, autonomous regions, and municipalities should make overall plans for reasonable distribution by taking the number and physical condition of the citizens eligible for conscription and the production and living conditions of the people into consideration. It is also permissable to rotate conscription by prefecture or county. Conscription quotas may be reduced or canceled for prefectures or counties that have had relatively more serious natural disasters.

Article 6. All provinces, autonomous regions, and municipalities should divide the technical recruits' draft zones in a planned way in accordance with the requests of the military regions where they are located.

Article 7. The nationwide conscription work will be organized and carried out by the Ministry of National Defense under the leadership of the State Council and the Central Military Commission.

The various military regions will be responsible for the conscription work within their regions.

A provincial military district (garrison command, garrison district, military subdistrict, and the People's Armed Forces department of a county, autonomous county, city, or a district of a city (hereafter referred only as a county or city) will act concurrently as the military service organ of the people's government at the respective level. During the conscription period, the people's governments at and above the county level should organize the departments to establish a conscription office to take charge of the conscription work in their respective areas.

All offices, organizations, enterprises, and institutions and people's governments of the townships, nationality townships, and towns should carry out the conscription work for their units or localities in accordance with the arrangements and requests of the respective counties or cities.

continued . . .

CONSCRIPTION WORK REGULATIONS, Promulgated by the State Council and the Central Military Commission 24 Oct 1985 (continued)

Article 8. During the period of conscription, all units must conduct intensive education among young people in patriotism, revolutionary heroism, and performance of military service according to the law, carefully perform the ideological and political work among citizens eligible for conscription well, and encourage them to enthusiastically sign up for enlistment to defend the socialist motherland.

Chapter II: Conscription Registry

Article 9. Prior to 30 September each year, county and city conscription offices must organize basic-level units to conduct a conscription registry of all male citizens who are 18 years of age before 31 December of that year.

Article 10. According to county and city conscription offices' arrangement, offices, organizations, enterprises, and institutions and the people's governments of townships, nationality townships, and towns should organize male citizens of the proper age in their respective units and areas to register for conscription, fill in the "Conscription Registration Form," and, according to law, determine who should perform military service, who is exempt from it, and who is not qualified for it. Those who have registered and are qualified for conscription after preliminary screening are categorized as citizens eligible for conscription.

Article 11. Offices, organizations, enterprises, and institutions, and the people's governments of townships, nationality townships, and towns should, according to county and city conscription offices' arrangements and requirements, conduct visual physical examinations, review medical records, and conduct preliminary political and educational screening of the registered citizens eligible for conscription and select those who are politically and ideologically reliable, physically fit, and better educated as the targeted conscripts of the year.

Chapter III: Physical Examination

Article 12. When conscription starts, county and city conscription offices should make arrangements for the physical examination of citizens eligible for conscription in a planned way according to the conscription quotas.

Article 13. In a unified way, county and city public health departments should transfer medical personnel, organize them into a certain number of physical examination groups, establish a certain number of physical examination centers to conduct the physical examinations of citizens eligible for conscription at fixed points or by mobile groups. Counties and cities may also assign some hospitals to perform the physical examination if conditions permit.

Article 14. Offices, organizations, enterprises, and institutions, and the people's governments of townships, nationality townships, and towns should mobilize citizens eligible for conscription to undergo physical examinations at physical examination centers on time. The number of persons sent to those centers should be determined by counties and cities according to the conscription quotas assigned by the higher level and to the general physical conditions of citizens eligible for conscription in the area.

Article 15. Medical personnel responsible for the physical examination work must strictly implement the "Physical Requirements for Citizens Eligible for Conscription" promulgated by the Ministry of National Defense and related regulations, correctly master the standard, and effectively ensure the good physical quality of new recruits.

Article 16. The liver function test (including surface antigen test) and physical reexamination should be conducted among the citizens eligible for conscription about to be approved for enlistment. Physical reexamination for submarine personnel should be conducted by regions in a unified manner. Examinations for surface vessel personnel, tank crews, and paratroopers should be conducted by counties and cities. Counties and cities should conduct spot checks of ordinary soldiers' physical condition. The number of them subjected to spot checks should not be less than one-third of the number to be enlisted. If the number of those disqualified is found to be quite large during the spot check, all the new soldiers should be subjected to physical reexamination.

continued . . .

CONSCRIPTION WORK REGULATIONS, Promulgated by the State Council and the Central Military Commission 24 Oct 1985 (continued)

Chapter IV: Political Screening

Article 17. The work of carrying out political screening of citizens eligible for conscription should be done by a county or city by organizing the public security departments and basic-level units under its jurisdiction.

Article 18. On the basis of the arrangements and requirements of a county or city and in accordance with the "Rules With Regard to Political Requirements for Conscripts" set by the Ministry of Public Security, the PLA General Staff Department, and the Ministry of Public Security the PLA General Staff Department, and the PLA General Political Department, offices, organizations, enterprises and institutions, the people's governments of townships, nationality townships or towns, and local police stations should earnestly carry out the political screening of those citizens eligible for conscription who have passed their physical examinations. The principle task is to gain a clear idea of what they actually did and to help them fill out the "Registration Form for Citizens Eligible for Conscription to Join the Army."

Article 19. A county or city must review, case by case, all those citizens eligible for conscription whom it is ready to approve to serve the Army on active duty. It is necessary to strictly carry out check and to ensure that the new recruits are politically reliable. We should avoid recruiting into the Army whose who fail to meet our political requirements.

Chapter V: Screening New Recruits

Article 20. In screening new recruits, a county or city should evaluate, in an overall manner, those citizens eligible for conscription who have already passed their physical examinations and political screening. It is necessary to give higher priority to approving those who are politically sound in thinking and who have a strong physique and high cultural standards for induction as new recruits on active duty.

Article 21. Those citizens eligible for conscription who have been approved to serve in the Army on active duty should report to any county or city-level conscription organ to undergo the induction procedure and obtain a "Notice for Induction to a Citizen Eligible for Conscription." His or her dependents should bring this notice to the relevent household registration department to cancel his or her household registration, and apply for privileges as military dependents.

Article 22. If those citizens eligible for conscription who have been approved to serve in the Army on active duty are workers of a government organ, an office, organization, enterprise, or institution (including a state-owned unit), they should be issued all the wages, bonuses, and all types of allowances for that particular month by the original unit.

Chapter VI: The Handover of New Recruits

Article 23. The handover of new recruits may be conducted in one of the following ways: New recruits may be escorted to the Army units by personnel designated by the counties or cities, they may report for duty at the Army units themselves, or they may be accepted locally by personnel from the Army units.

Article 24. In case new recruits are to be escorted to the Army units by personnel designated by the counties or cities, the following work should be carried out:

1. When conscription begins, the Army units at the divisional or independent regimental level (at the corps or independent detachment level in the case of the Armed Police Force; the same below) shall dispatch liaison groups to contact the relevant county or city conscription offices and to decide together with them such related matters as the destinations, transfer, and handover of the new recruits.

2. New recruits should be concentrated in a few Army units. Generally, new recruits conscripted from the same counties or cities should not be assigned to more than three divisions or independent regiments.

continued . . .

CONSCRIPTION WORK REGULATIONS, Promulgated by the State Council and the Central Military Commission 24 Oct 1985 (continued)

3. The counties or cities should select capable cadres to escort the new recruits to the Army divisions or independent regiments. The number of escort cadres and the number of new recruits should be in the ratio of about 1 to 30.

4. After the new recruits are gathered, the counties or cities should organize them into groups by destination and number and give them the necessary education on military basics.

5. After escorting the new recruits to the Army units, the escort cadres should brief the Army units on the new recruits' political and physical condition, education, and special skills. The escort cadres should return to their counties or cities as soon as they have completed the handover procedures.

6. The Army units should warmly welcome the new recruits upon their arrival and appropriately arrange for the boarding and lodging of the new recruits and the escort cadres.

Article 25. In case the counties or cities let the new recruits report for duty at the Army units by themselves, the following work should be carried out:

1. When conscription begins, the Army units at the divisional or independent regimental level should dispatch liaison groups to contact the relevant counties and cities and to decide, together with them, on the locations at which the new recruits should report for duty, the means of contact, the acceptance procedures, and other related matters.

2. Counties and cities should organize the new recruits into groups by destination and number and should select those with organizational skills to serve as squad, platoon, or company leaders to take care of things during the new recruits' journey to their destinations.

3. Army units should set up reception groups at the train stations or piers where the new recruits are to report for duty. The reception groups shall handle the new recruits' acceptance.

Article 26. In case the Army units dispatch personnel to accept the new recruits locally, the following work should be carried out:

1. The Army units should select ideologically sound cadres with a strong sense of policy and organizational skills and medical personnel to form a small but efficient provisional new recruits acceptance office to handle the acceptance.

2. Upon their arrival at the acceptance locations, the acceptance cadres should work under the leadership of the local government and military organs and actively help the conscription office in the conscription work.

3. Military service organs at various levels should take the initiative and properly arrange for the boarding and lodging of the acceptance personnel, brief them on the conscription work, solicit their views, and decide with them matters related to the handover of the new recruits.

4. The gathering and handover of new recruits may be held at the site of the county or city people's government or at other convenient locations. The handover procedure should be completed one day before the departure of the new recruits.

Article 27. The following work must be done well in handling the procedures of handing over new soldiers:

1. Two "new soldiers' rosters" shall be prepared jointly by the counties and cities concerned. One copy shall be handed over to the Army and the other copy shall be kept by the county and city military service offices concerned.

2. When the Army is accepting new soldiers from the personnel dispatched by the counties and cities concerned, both sides must certify that the handing over of new soldiers is correct according to the "new soldiers' rosters" by affixing their signatures and seals on them. Both the records and the letters of recommendation concerning the new soldiers must be handed over to the Army.

3. If new soldiers are organized to report to the Army by themselves, they must be led by a designated company and platoon leader and the "new soldiers' rosters," records, and

continued . . .

CONSCRIPTION WORK REGULATIONS, Promulgated by the State Council and the Central Military Commission 24 Oct 1985 (continued)

letters of recommendation concerning new soldiers must be sealed. When new soldiers are handed over at the point where they are designated to report, the Army should check the number of persons according to the "new soldiers' rosters," and should also promptly notify the county and city military service offices in the conscription area of the number of soldiers received and the time of their arrival.

Article 28. The counties and cities concerned should carefully observe the newly conscripted soldiers before sending them to the Army. If anyone is discovered to have failed to meet the requirements for new soldiers due to political reasons or a change in physical conditions, he must be promptly replaced in order to avoid sending unqualified new soldiers to the Army.

Article 29. New soldiers' bedding and clothing will be provided and shipped to counties and cities by the logistics departments of military regions, provincial military districts (garrison command and garrison districts), and military subdistricts. Bedding and clothing of new soldiers of the People's Armed Police will be provided and shipped to counties and cities by the logistics departments of the Armed Police Corps of provinces, autonomous regions, and municipalities directly under the central government. The counties and cities are responsible for distributing the bedding and clothing to new soldiers before sending them to the Army.

Chapter VII: The Transport of New Soldiers

Article 30. Fifteen days before conscription is to begin, the Army shall direct various armies, independent divisions (the People's Armed Police Corps and independent units) to dispatch liaison groups to the provinces, autonomous regions, and municipalities concerned to discuss plans for transporting the new soldiers.

Article 31. On the basis of the number of new soldiers to be transported and the starting point and destination of their trip, provincial military districts (garrison commands and garrison districts) shall propose to their transport departments plans for transporting new soldiers according to the transport regulations concerned.

Article 32. Railway and transport departments shall promptly make arrangements according to plans for transporting new soldiers in order to ensure that the new soldiers reach the Army safely.

Article 33. County and city conscription offices and the military units designated to receive new recruits shall make transportation arrangements according to schedule. Prior to transportation, they should teach new soldiers how to ride in a vehicle (boat) in order to prevent accidents on the way.

Article 34. Military representative offices located at a station or a wharf should take the initiative in solving problems encountered in the transportation of new soldiers. Cadres involved in sending and receiving new soldiers and the new soldiers themselves must accept the guidance of military representatives.

Chapter VIII: Quarantine and Discharge

Article 35. New soldiers shall be quarantined after arriving at a military unit. If anyone is found to be affected by a contagious disease, he must be promptly separated from others for treatment and epidemic prevention measures must be taken, if necessary.

Article 36. During the quarantine period, if a new soldier is found to fail to meet the requirements politically and physically, thus making him unfit for military service, he may be discharged. The time limit for discharge due to failure to meet political requirements, starting from the day of arrival of a new soldier at the Army to the day his discharge is approved by the Army, shall not exceed 90 days. The time limit for discharge due to physical disqualification shall not exceed 45 days. The Army should promptly provide medical treatment to new soldiers who are afflicted with a contagious disease or other dangerous diseases. At the same time, it should notify the county and city military service offices in the conscription areas that such new soldiers will be discharged when their condition has stabilized.

continued . . .

CONSCRIPTION WORK REGULATIONS, Promulgated by the State Council and the Central Military Commission 24 Oct 1985 (continued)

In this case, the time limit for discharge will not be restricted. No replacements will be made after such discharge.

Article 37. When a recruit is discharged from the service due to failure to meet the physical requirements, an examination should be conducted and testimony given by the military hospital concerned (or by the Armed Police Corps' hospital or the prefectural or city people's hospital in the case of members of the Armed Police Force), and approval obtained from the authorities concerned at or above the divisional (Armed Police Corps) level. When a recruit is discharged from the service due to failure to meet the political qualifications, the unit concerned should, prior to the discharge, verify the case through investigation in coordination with the public security bureau and the conscription office of the county or city where the recruit was drafted, and approval should be obtained from the political department at or above the divisional (Armed Police Corps) level.

Article 38. In dealing with the discharged new recruit, the PLA unit concerned should perform good ideological work, complete the discharge procedure as required, and send a cadre to escort him to the county or city where he was drafted.

Article 39. County or city conscription offices should receive the disqualified new recruits discharged by the PLA units in accordance with the required procedures, and the public security organs should allow their settlement. If the discharged recruits were staff members or workers of government offices, organizations, enterprises, or institutions, their jobs and positions should be restored in their original units.

Chapter IX: Expenses

Article 40. Expenses for the work of conscription and registration of military service should be borne by the provinces, autonomous regions, and municipalities concerned and included as "conscription expense" in their respective local budgets.

Article 41. The definition of conscription expense and regulations governing the use and administration of such expense should be drawn up by the provincial, regional, and municipal conscription offices and financial departments in light of the actual local situation.

Article 42. Expenses for drafting new members of the Armed Police Force should be appropriated by the provincial, regional, and municipal Armed Police Corps in accordance with the local regulations for conscription expense.

Article 43. Logistics departments of the military districts concerned or the provincial, regional, and municipal Armed Police Corps concerned are responsible for reimbursement of the transportation expense for sending new recruits' bedding and clothing to counties and cities. Expenses paid by counties and cities for dispatching bedding and clothing to new recruits should be defrayed from the conscription expense.

Article 44. Expenses incurred for transportation, meals, and accommodations of new recruits traveling from the assembly centers in counties and cities to the PLA units, whether they are dispatched by the local authorities or traveling by themselves, should be reimbursed by the PLA units concerned in accordance with the prescribed procedures. In case the PLA units send representatives to receive the new recruits, the PLA units are responsible for the expenses from the date the new recruits are received.

Article 45. When a cadre escorts new recruits to the PLA unit, his per diem and traveling expenses and money spent for accommodations during the period of handing-over procedures following his arrival at the PLA unit should be reimbursed by the PLA units according to the prescribed standards. His meal subsidy during the handing-over period and per diem and traveling expenses on his return trip should be defrayed by the county or city concerned as conscription expense.

continued . . .

CONSCRIPTION WORK REGULATIONS, Promulgated by the State Council and the Central Military Commission 24 Oct 1985 (continued)

Chapter X: Supplementary Provisions

Article 46. Citizens with military service obligation but refusing or evading military service registration and citizens who are drafted but refuse or evade being recruited should be forced to fulfill their military service obligation by the grass-roots people's governments according to law, provided that education fails to make them correct their wrongdoing.

Article 47. In doing conscription work, personnel of organs of state should strictly carry out conscription orders and ensure the quality of new recruits. Those who have made remarkable achievements in conscription work should be commended and rewarded. Acts of receiving bribes, malpractices for the sake of private interests, and dereliction of duty causing a serious adverse effect on conscription work should be punished according to Article 62 of the "Military Service Law of the People's Republic of China."

Article 48. The Ministry of National Defense is responsible for the interpretation of these regulations.

Article 49. These regulations take effect from the date of promulgation.

FBIS-CHI 210 (30 Oct 1985). K18/27.

VI DEMOGRAPHY

DEMOGRAPHIC NEWS, 1985

Minority Name Change—The Benglong minority nationality in Yunnan province has been renamed the Deang nationality. This nationality, which exceeds 10,000 persons, lives primarily in the Santaishan area of Luxi County, Dehong Dai-Jingpo Autonomous Prefecture, and Zhenkang County, Lincang Prefecture. FBIS-CHI 188 (27 Sep 1985), K25.

Divorce Rate—A sample of 310,000 women between the ages of 15 and 67 in 1982 indicated the divorce rate in China was 0.3 percent. Among these women, 70 percent were married, 25.5 percent were unmarried, and 4.2 percent were widowed. XNB (17 Oct 1985), 62-63.

Exceptions to One-Child Policy—There are eight exceptions to the one-child policy. These regulations were issued by the Guangdong provincial government and Party committee 12 June 1984:

1. The first child is disabled and cannot become a member of the normal labor force;
2. A worker regularly works in a mine pit for long periods of time;
3. A peasant lives in a distant border or mountainous area with a sparse population;
4. A fisherman works on an island in the ocean;
5. A person in a rural area has given birth to a girl only and has had practical difficulty;
6. One of a remarried couple in a rural area has had only one child and the other of the couple has had no child or had had a child but the child died; a remarried couple of the nonagricultural population in an urban area whose spouse died has only one child;
7. A couple has had no child for many years after marriage but pregnancy occurs after adopting a child;
8. A single son and a single daughter get married.

FBIS-CHI 204 (22 Oct 1985), P1. People in parts of Shandong, Guangdong, Zhejiang and Guangxi are now allowed to have one more child if their first-born is a girl.

One-Child Families—China now has 35 million one-child families, or 21.2 percent of all the families with a wife of childbearing age. *Beijing Review*, 4 (28 Jan 1985), 8; 25 (24 Jan 1985), 7.

Imbalance of Sexes—On 1 July 1982 the male population in China had reached 519.43 million and the female population 488.74 million. About 30 million males, or some 5.72 percent of the total male population, will be unable to find mates. There are also about 5 percent more males than females in the population aged 1 to 4, so this imbalance of sexes will increase. *Ming Pao* (3 Jun 1985), 6. Unmarried young people above age 28 total 150,000 in Beijing and 120,000 in Shanghai. XNB (22 May 1985), 17.

Unplanned Children—A survey of women in three urban and 10 suburban districts of Beijing conducted by UNESCO, the All-China Women's Federation, and China's Research Society of Marriage and the Family found that over 16.7 percent of the rural women and 36 percent of those in cities had unplanned children. FBIS-CHI 120 (12 Jun 1985), K19/20.

Mortality and Life Expectancy—The average life span in China was 67.88 years in 1982, compared to 25-30 before 1949. Life expectancy in Shanghai was 72.5 years. There are 3,700 people over 100 in the PRC, with the oldest person 130. The mortality of lying-in women has been reduced from 15 to 0.5 per 1,000 and of infants from 200 to 34.6 per 1,000. *China Reconstructs*, XXXIV, 3 (Mar 1985), 24.

Abortion Rates Compared—Marshall Green writes that the abortion rate of 25 per 100 live births in China is lower than the rate of 42 abortions per 100 live births in the US. Washington *Post Weekly* (22 Jul 1985), 28.

Infant Mortality—The death rate for children in Beijing has dropped from 124 per thousand in the 1950s to 10 per thousand today. XNB (6 June 1985), 9. Infant mortality in border areas exceeds 100 per 1,000. It is 116.2 in the Yushu Tibetan Autonomous Prefecture in

continued . . .

DEMOGRAPHIC NEWS, 1985 (continued)

Qinhai and 146 per thousand in the Henan Mongolian Autonomous County. The figure for Beijing is given as 11.61, while the mortality rate for pregnant and postnatal women was 0.27 per thousand in 1984. The goal during the next five years is to reduce infant mortality below 10 per thousand in cities, 30 per thousand in rural areas, and 40 per thousand in remote minority areas. *Beijing Review*, 33 (19 Aug 1985), 9; *China Daily* (8 Aug 1985), 3.

Vietnamese Refugee Births—Some 30,000 children of refugees from Vietnam now living in China have been born. *Der Spiegel*, (12 Aug 1985), 113-14.

Fines for More Than One Child—Couples who sign the one-child pledge in China are given priority in housing, medical care and other benefits. Those who refuse to have an abortion are said to have lost their jobs and been fined. Fines in Yunnan province have reached $700, a family's annual income. New York*Times* (12 May 1985), 24E.

Exceptions to One-Child Policy—Couples may have two children if they are a peasant family in special difficulties; if they belong to a non-Chinese minority nationality under 10 million; if they give their second child to another couple who are childless; or if they are both only children themselves. In Guangdong province a second child is now permitted if the first was a girl. *Der Spiegel*, 31 (29 Jul 1985), 98, 100.

Adultery—There has been a sharp increase in adultery in China. During the past five years, the divorce rate has risen 70 percent to 63 per 1,000 marriages. About one-fourth of all divorces are the result of "third-party interference." It is extremely difficult to carry on an affair in China because of a housing shortage, and the provision requiring a couple to produce a marriage license and an introduction from work units before they can register at a hotel. Chinese divorce laws are strict, and adulterers receive sentences to labor camps. A women's federation has recently called for a national law against adultery. *Newsweek* (8 Apr 1985), 46.

1982 Census Statistics—Complete statistics from the 1982 census were to appear in a seven-volume *China Population Manual* early in 1985. It was to include information on the distribution of the population, ethnic groups, ages, educational levels and occupations. Figures on marriages, occupations and mortality rates were to be published for the first time. XNB (31 Jan 1985), 36.

Shanghai and Beijing—Census figures for Shanghai and Beijing on 1 July 1982 appear in *Chinese Sociology and Anthropology*, XVII, 2 (Winter 1984-85), 79-84.

One-Child Policy—The one-child policy could increase the percentage of elderly to one-third of the total population within 50 years. A typical family could consist of one child, a working-age couple, and four grandparents. The 1982 census found 3.2 million births which had not been recorded in 1981, suggesting 15 percent of the births in China are not reported. Local officials may not register some births to fulfil family-planning targets. John S. Aird in the *Asian Wall Street Journal Weekly* (24 Jun 1985), 15.

Divorce—Women file 70 percent of the divorce petitions in China. Between 1950 and 1980 divorce courts heard an average of 400,000 cases annually. About a third of the 500,000 divorces currently granted each year result from what the Chinese call the vestiges of feudalism—male dominance and the abuse of women who fail to bear sons. Approximately half of the divorce petitions are denied. The number of divorce cases in Beijing is shown below. New marriage laws in 1950 and 1981 resulted in increases in the number of petitions filed.

1949	736	1960-1966	c. 7,000
1950	1,710	1966-1976	< 7,000
1951	5,832	1979	3,845
1952	7,581	1980	4,516
1953	8,925	1981	6,581
1954	6,545	1982	7,220
1955-1958	c. 6,000	1983	7,885
1959	7,237	1984 Jan-Jun	4,404

continued . . .

DEMOGRAPHIC NEWS, 1985 (continued)

The results of divorce cases heard in people's courts in Beijing in 1983 were:

Result	Number	Percentage of of Total
Divorces allowed by court	822	10.5
Divorces not allowed by court	425	5.4
Negotiated divorces	3,035	38.6
Reconciliations after mediation	1,327	16.9
Cases handed over to other judicial bodies	67	0.8
Appeals withdrawn	2,096	26.6
Cases terminated	92	1.2
Total	7,864	100

Beijing Review, 5 (4 Feb 1985), 18-21; *Asian Wall Street Journal Weekly* (11 Feb 1985), 12.

Cremations—A February 1985 decree of the State Council has stipulated that cremation should become the standard funeral practice in urban areas. Some 85 percent of China's cities and 40 percent of its counties have crematories which handle some 1 million cremations annually. With a death rate of about 6 per 1,000 in China, some 6 million persons die every year, and 5 million are buried. Burial occurs more frequently in the countryside, with approximately 4 million each year. Fewer than 30 percent of the dead were cremated in 1983, down from 37 percent in 1978. For every 1 million burials, 667 hectares of land are used and 300,000 m³ of wood are cut for coffins. Burial remains a potential threat to water supplies. Exceptions to the decree will be made for minority nationalities, such as Tibetans who have "sky or bird burials" on mountains for vultures to devour the body, or "tree burials" where coffins are put on four tree stumps. "Water" and "wind" burials are also practiced. *Beijing Review,* 13 (1 Apr 1985), 9-10; New York *Times* (23 May 1985), 6.

Marriage Opportunities for the Elderly—China is attempting to find partners for its large number of single elderly persons. There are about 1.4 million people in Shanghai over 60 out of its 12 million inhabitants. The monthly *Modern Family* (circ. 500,000) runs ads for marriage partners. According to its statistics, two-thirds of those seeking spouses are widowed, and the rest are divorced. *Der Spiegel,* 35 (26 Aug 1985), 111, 113.

US Deletes Aid Fund—The US has withheld $10 million of the $46 million approved by Congress for the United Nations Fund for Population Activities for 1985 to protest the reported use of forced abortions in the PRC. China has said there are no forced abortions in the country, and that no US money has gone toward abortion in the PRC. New York *Times* (31 Mar 1985), 10.

First Children—Shen Guoxiang, the Deputy Director of China's State Family Planning Commission, has said that about 60 percent of all new-born babies in the PRC are first children, whereas 20 percent are third or beyond. Minneapolis *Star and Tribune* (19 May 1985), 5B.

Centenarians—The 1982 census indicated that 70.5 percent of China's centenarians were women. Of the 3,765 persons 100 or over, 2,303 were Hans, 801 Uygurs, 117 Zhuangs, 117 Tibetans, and 18 Tadzhiks. *Beijing Review,* 48 (2 Dec 1985), 29.

VITAL RATES, 1984 (per thousand) *

Birth rate	17.5
Mortality rate	6.69
Natural increase	10.81
Population, yearend (mn)	1,036.040

* According to a sample survey of 472,354 residents in 2,971 groups (villages) in 379 counties and cities in 29 provinces, autonomous regions and municipalities. *Beijing Review,* 12 (25 Mar 1985), viii.

POPULATION OF CHINA, 1949-84

	Total Population (mn)	Urban Population		Rural Population	
		Total (mn)	Percentage of Total Population (Percent)	Total (mn)	Percentage of Total Population (Percent)
1949	541.67	57.65	10.6	484.02	89.4
1950	551.96	61.69	11.2	490.27	88.8
1951	563.00	66.32	11.8	496.68	88.2
1952	574.82	71.63	12.5	503.19	87.5
1953	587.96	78.26	13.3	509.70	86.7
1954	602.66	82.49	13.7	520.17	86.3
1955	614.65	82.85	13.5	531.80	86.5
1956	628.28	91.85	14.6	536.43	85.4
1957	646.53	99.49	15.4	547.04	84.6
1958	659.94	107.21	16.2	552.73	83.8
1959	672.07	123.71	18.4	548.36	81.6
1960	662.07	130.73	19.7	531.34	80.3
1961	658.59	127.07	19.3	531.52	80.7
1962	672.95	116.59	17.3	556.36	82.7
1963	691.72	116.46	16.8	575.26	83.2
1964	704.99	129.50	18.4	575.49	81.6
1965	725.38	130.45	18.0	594.93	82.0
1966	745.42	133.13	17.9	612.29	82.1
1967	763.68	135.48	17.7	628.20	82.3
1968	785.34	138.38	17.6	646.96	82.4
1969	806.71	141.17	17.5	665.54	82.5
1970	829.92	144.24	17.4	685.68	82.6
1971	852.29	147.11	17.3	705.18	82.7
1972	851.77	149.35	71.1	722.42	82.9
1973	892.11	153.45	17.2	738.66	82.8
1974	908.59	155.95	17.2	752.64	82.8
1975	924.20	160.30	17.3	763.90	82.7
1976	937.17	163.41	17.4	773.76	82.6
1977	949.74	166.69	17.6	783.05	82.4
1978	962.59	172.45	17.9	790.14	82.1
1979	975.42	184.95	19.0	790.47	81.0
1980	987.05	191.40	19.4	795.65	80.6
1981	1,000.72	201.71	20.2	799.01	79.8
1982	1,015.41	211.54	20.8	803.87	79.2
1983	1,024.95	241.26	23.5	783.69	76.5
1984	1,034.75	330.06	38.9	704.69	68.1

Statistical Yearbook of China 1983 (HK, 1983), 103-04; press reports.

POPULATION GROWTH RATE IN CHINA AND SICHUAN (per 1,000)

PRC		Sichuan Province	
1965	28.5	1970	31.21
1974	15.7	1983	6.05
1984	10.81	1984	3.07
Target	10	Average during the past two decades	21

Sichuan is the most populous province in the PRC with about 101 million of China's 1.03 billion people. There are now some 1,200 birth-control centers and more than 200 sterility clinics in Sichuan province. *Asian Wall Street Journal Weekly* (20 May 1985), 13.

VII ECONOMY

ECONOMIC DEVELOPMENTS, 1985

Main Points of Price Reform—The 1985 price reform attempted to:

1. Rationally readjust the purchasing and marketing prices of grain and the purchasing price of cotton in the rural areas and introduce the practice of state purchase according to contract. Price controls will be gradually relaxed for other farm and sideline products by subjecting them to regulation by market mechanism so as to promote the growth of a commodity economy in the rural areas and the restructuring of agricultural production;

2. Appropriately raise charges for short-distance railway transport to facilitate the restructuring of the transportation system and make full use of highway and water transportation;

3. Properly widen price differences for products of different quality and increase regional price differences, reduce or eliminate expensive and unmarketable products of inferior quality and encourage a rapid increase in the manufacture of brand-name, high-quality products in order to facilitate rational commodity circulation; and

4. Leave basically unchanged the prices of those raw and semifinished materials, fuels, and other major means of production which are distributed according to state plan, while the prices of those marketed by the enterprises through their own channels according to specific regulations will be determined by market forces. This will help bring the means of production into the market.

Ban Yue Tan, (10 May 1985), 6-8, quoted in FBIS-CHI 110 (7 Jun 1985), K11; New York *Times* (10 May 1985), 3; *Der Spiegel*, 5 (28 Jan 1985), 120, 122. The phone number to register complaints about prices is 75 35 49.

Warranties—There are no warranties for retail merchandise sold in China. If the product is faulty—tough luck. "Trading," part 12 of "The Heart of the Dragon" (PBS, 1985).

Selection of Goods—Nanfang Daxia, the largest department store in Guangzhou, has increased the varieties of goods offered its customers from 6,000 in 1978 to more than 30,000 in 1984. New York *Times* (11 Nov 1985), 1, 6.

Renewal of Equipment—During the 8th Five Year Plan (1991-95), China hopes to renew its equipment at enterprises every 15 years. All the equipment in use by 1995 should have been manufactured after 1980. In the 9th Five Year Plan, the renewal cycle of fixed assets will be shortened to 12-13 years, and in the first Five Year Plan of the 21st century it will be maintained around 10 years. During 1981-85, the renewal cycle is being reduced to 20 years. *Jingji Ribao* (6 Nov 1985), 3.

Product Costs—The consumption of raw materials, semi-finished materials, and fuel generally accounts for 75 percent of the cost of industrial products in the PRC. *Beijing Review*, 14 (8 Apr 1985), 18.

Factory Losses—Prior to 1979, about one-third of China's industrial enterprises lost money each year. Losses ran up to 4 billion yuan. Unprofitable enterprises made up 11.6 percent of the total in 1984. Their total deficit dropped to 2.1 billion yuan. FBIS-CHI 53 (19 Mar 1985), K16/17.

Workers in the Tertiary Industries—The percentage of workers in tertiary industries has risen from 23.7 percent in 1978 to 33.4 percent in 1984. *Beijing Review*, 45 (11 Nov 1985), 4-5.

Northeast Economic Zone—An economic zone, including Liaoning, Heilongjiang, Jilin, and parts of Inner Mongolia, has been created. Its combined output value of industry and agriculture accounted for 15 percent of China's total. It amounted to 25 percent of the national iron and steel production, 60 percent of the oil extracted, and 33 percent of the output of natural gas. *Beijing Review*, 43 (28 Oct 1985), 8.

Pork Rationing—Ration coupons are required in 21 cities to purchase pork. In recent years, no limit on purchases had applied, but shortages have required coupons to be used from

continued . . .

ECONOMIC DEVELOPMENTS, 1985 (continued)

1 February 1985. Residents in Beijing, Shanghai, Tianjin, Nanjing and other large cities may buy 1.5 kg per month, while the limit is 1 kg in medium-sized cities. Rationing will not resume in Guangzhou and Chongqing. *Beijing Review*, 6 (11 Feb 1985), 7.

Educated Managers—Up to half of the managers at China's state-run enterprises have less than a junior high school education. *Asian Wall Street Journal Weekly* (11 Feb 1985), 12.

Rural Price Reform—The state monopoly and fixed-quota purchase system will change in China during 1985. The state will first gradually decontrol purchasing and selling prices of fish, poultry, eggs, vegetables, meat and other perishable foods. The prices will be regulated by market forces. The state will subsidize the costs to urban consumers according to particular local conditions. Prices will also be fixed for grain, edible oil and other major products as well as products purchased under state contracts. The purchasing and selling prices of these products are the same in the rural areas, while the selling prices are lower for urban consumers. Grain and oil-bearing crops not included in the contracts can be sold at market prices, but the state sets minimum protective prices so that the peasants will not suffer unacceptable economic losses dur to price fluctuations. *Beijing Review*, 25 (24 Jun 1985), 16-17.

Cardin—Pierre Cardin has presented a fashion show to 10,000 spectators at the Beijing Workers' Gymnasium. Three Chinese cities will manufacture Cardin cosmetics, clothing and accessories. Cardin has also started a French bakery in Beijing. In 1982 he financed Maxim's Restaurant, a copy of the Parisian establishment, and the less expensive Minim's, in the Chinese capital. He has recently brought nine Chinese models to Paris to show off his fall and winter lines. *Der Spiegel*, 22 (27 May 1985), 125; *Time* (5 Aug 1985), 56.

Growth to be Curtailed—Premier Zhao Ziyang has announced a five-point program to curtail rapid inflationary economic growth in China:

1. Wages will be paid through supervised bank accounts.

2. The People's Bank of China will begin a unified credit and monetary policy with ceilings for currency at every bank.

3. Heavy taxes will be imposed on investments which exceed norms.

4. State departments must reduce administrative costs by 10 percent and group purchases by 20 percent.

5. Consumer goods will be used to withdraw currency from circulation.

Asian Wall Street Journal Weekly (1 Apr 1985), 1, 17.

Clothing Sales—Retail sales of clothing have almost doubled from 5.6 billion yuan to 10.5 billion yuan in 1984. Over 20,000 new styles are created each year in Shanghai. The city sold 60 million garments locally and exported 70 million in 1984. *Beijing Review*, 19 (13 May 1985), 9. Clothing factories manufactured over 1.05 billion garments in 1984. Another 200+ million garments were produced by household businesses and township collectives. *Asian Wall Street Journal Weekly* (4 Feb 1985), 7.

Managerial Decisions—The manager of a large shirt factory in China now makes decisions concerning what materials to buy for shirts, how many shirts to produce, where to sell them, and who should do the sales and marketing. Employees at an Arrow shirt factory in the PRC make an average of 20 cents an hour. PBS, "Adam Smith in the New China" (1985).

Consumerism—A good idea of the emphasis on consumerism in China is depicted in Irv Drasnin's "Looking for Mao" (1985). The film was probably made in 1983 in China.

Private Ownership—Some 80 percent of China's retail stores, restaurants, and service shops are privately-owned. *US News & World Report* (4 Feb 1985), 37.

Audit—State enterprises had irregularities totaling nearly 3.4 billion yuan ($1.2 billion) in 1984, according to a government audit. National income was 548.5 billion yuan, so the irregularities were about 0.6 percent of China's economic activity. New York *Times* (17 Mar 1985), 8.

continued . . .

ECONOMIC DEVELOPMENTS, 1985 (continued)

Errors in Calculating Peasant Income—Several errors may be introduced in calculations of the annual incomes of peasants.

1. Grain, firewood, and foods produced by peasants for their own use have been calculated at current market prices. This "income" accounts for 30-50 percent of peasants' annual income.

2. Local officials estimate the grain harvested by peasants at local market prices with a deduction for the "three retentions." Some of this grain is stored and never used or sold.

3. In certain cases, peasants' income is averaged. One peasant who is well off can raise the annual incomes of several others.

4. Calculations of peasant incomes are often done a year after the autumn harvest and are based on memory.

5. Sometimes output value is equated with income.

6. Incomes are occasionally estimated, and there are arithmetical errors.

7. In several cases, cadres are cheating and falsifying reports.

Renmin Ribao (17 Aug 1985).

Fountain Pens—The PRC manufactures 150 fountain pens each year, or some six times the output in the 1960s. China ranks first in world trade in pens, with 25 million exported annually. XNB (20 May 1985), 78.

Trademark Counterfeiting—Chinese authorities are attempting to control the counterfeiting of trademarks on inferior merchandise. A factory in Jiangsu was turning out bicycles with the prestigious "Phoenix" and "Forever" trademarks, and an enterprise in Zhejiang was found to be putting "Baoshihua," "Shanghai" and "Spring Thunder" markings on their own watches. London *Financial Times* (17 Jul 1985), 3.

Employment-Between 1979 and 1985, 46 million people found employment in the PRC. Another 15 million college graduates and other persons were assigned jobs by the state. Most were recruited by urban collective or cooperative enterprises, and some became self-employed. There are 38,000 labor service companies in China. During the past five years, they trained and found jobs for 8.31 million persons and operated 210,000 collective enterprises. FBIS-CHI 170 (3 Sep 1985), K9/10.

Subsidies to Tibet—Central government subsidies to Tibet have amounted to 7.1 billion yuan since 1952. There are currently 296 factories in the region, but very little economic base. It manufactures virtually no goods fit for marketing, and 96 percent of the commodities sold in Tibet are imported from elsewhere in China and subsidized. *Far Eastern Economic Review* (11 Jul 1985), 20, 22-23.

Hongze EZ—An economic zone will be developed in the Lake Hongze area in northwest Jiangsu province starting in 1986. Hongze is the fourth largest lake in China. The province will invest 80 million yuan during the first phase of construction to build an aquatic product center. Between 1990 and 2000, Hongze will become a tourist and convalescent center. The lake covers 2,069 km^2 and connects the Huaihe River in Anhui province with the Yangtze River. FBIS-CHI 184 (23 Sep 1985), O1.

Industries Defined—The General Office of the State Council has proposed that departments and regions compile statistics of tertiary industry. The various kinds of industries in China are defined as follows:

First industry: agriculture (including forestry, animal husbandry, fishery, and so forth).

Second industry: industry (including mining and manufacturing industries; supply of running water, power, steam, hot water, and coal gas) and construction.

Tertiary industry: all other services which do not fall into the first and second categories mentioned above.

continued . . .

ECONOMIC DEVELOPMENTS, 1985 (continued)

Since tertiary industry involves many trades and covers an extensive scope, it can be divided into two major departments in the light of our country's actual situation, the circulation department and the service department; these two major departments can be subdivided into four levels:

First level: circulation departments, including communications and transport, postal and telecommunications services; catering services; commodity supply, marketing and storage services.

Second level: departments serving production and daily life, including banking, insurance, geological survey, real estate, public utilities, community services, tourism, consultative and information services, and various types of technical services.

Third level: departments set up to promote science and education and people's well-being, including educational and cultural services; radio and television broadcasting; scientific research; health care; sports; and social welfare services.

Further level: departments serving public needs, including state organs, government and party organs, and social groups, as well as the Armed Forces and police, and so forth.

Maintenance Tax—A 7-percent maintenance tax will be levied on all enterprises now paying value-added and buiness taxes. The taxes will be used for construction and renovation in cities. The monies had previously come from business profits handed over to the state, but businesses now retain after-tax profits. *Asian Wall Street Journal Weekly* (18 Feb 1985), 13.

Unemployment Insurance—Enterprises will pay 5-8 percent of their total employees' wages to an insurance fund which subsidizes people who lose their jobs. Some 20-30 percent of Chinese factories are poorly run or obsolete and should close. During 1983 over 10,000 of these enterprises lost 2.79 billion yuan. *Asian Wall Street Journal Weekly* (18 Mar 1985), 6.

Faulty Construction Projects—Nearly 3,000 of the 56,000 projects completed or under construction have been found unsafe as a result of faulty design or workmanship. Work has stopped on 721 projects, 207 will be torn down and rebuilt, and 1,516 need significant repairs. *Beijing Review*, 49 (9 Dec 1985), 9.

Retail Price Rises—Between 1950 and 1983 retail prices in China rose 55.6 percent. This amounts to an average of 1.68 percent annually. *Renmin Ribao* (3 Jul 1985), 8.

Individually-Owned Businesses—At the end of 1984 the PRC had 9.3 million individually-owned businesses, an increase of 57.4 percent. They employed over 12 million workers, up 74.3 percent from 1983. Retail sales of individual businesses amounted to 28.8 billion yuan, or 8.6 percent of the national total. Approximately 55 percent of these businesses engaged in commercial activities, while the rest were involved in catering, handicrafts, repairs, transport, small industry, etc. FBIS-CHI 53 (19 Mar 1985), K19/20.

World Bank Loans—The World Bank extended $1.04 billion in interest-free loans to China during fiscal year 1984, and another $1.09 billion during fiscal year 1985. Since 1981 the World Bank has offered $3 billion in loans. The Bank was to establish a permanent office in Beijing in July 1985. *Asian Wall Street Journal Weekly* (13 May 1985), 4.

China Ranked 16th—The standing of the PRC in world exports has jumped from 28th in 1980 to 16th in 1984. Exports have increased 44.3 percent during that time to $26.14 billion. FBIS-CHI 186 (25 Sep 1985), K6/7.

Signatures—The number of signatures an enterprise requires to get a loan approved has been reduced from 36 to 22. *Asian Wall Street Journal Weekly* (25 Mar 1985), 2.

Food Technology—The UN and Italy are cooperating with the PRC to provide about $7.7 million for a food research and technology center at Beijing. China will contribute 11,151,640 yuan in personnel and facilities. Italy and the UN will give the remaining 30 percent, including 4,332 billion lira. FBIS-CHI 73 (16 Apr 1985), A1.

continued . . .

ECONOMIC DEVELOPMENTS, 1985 (continued)

Pepsi—Pepsi-Cola International will build its second plant in China for $4 million. The factory will open in Guangzhou at the end of 1985. New York *Times* (16 Feb 1985), 23.

Duty-Free Shop—A duty-free shop opened in Beijing 30 November 1985. The shop will cater only to foreign diplomats and their families so they will not have to make special trips abroad to buy provisions. Foreign businessmen and non-diplomats will not be admitted. New York *Times* (1 Dec 1985), 13.

Growth Targets—The Chinese fear that rapid growth of the economy will result in high inflation. They hope to reduce industrial growth from 14 percent in 1984 to 8 percent in 1985 and agricultural growth from 14.5 percent to 6 percent. Combined industrial and agricultural output value increased 14.2 percent in 1984 compared to the average annual growth between 1979 and 1983 of 7.9 percent. *Asian Wall Street Journal Weekly* (1 Apr 1985), 1.

Labor Productivity—Labor productivity of workers at state enterprises rose 8.7 percent in 1984. The average output value produced by each worker was more than 14,000 yuan, but the value was 30,288 yuan in Shanghai. The most rapid rise occurred in Fujian province, where productivity increased 17 percent. XNB (23 Feb 1985), 108.

Inflation—The rate of inflation runs as high as 15 percent in China. *Beijing Review*, 32 (12 Aug 1985), 12. The Chinese have mentioned that 8 billion yuan in surplus currency was issued in 1984. Dividing this by about 50 billion yuan, the total currency in circulation, suggests the inflation rate was 16 percent, or close to this 15 percent figure.

Free Markets—More than 10 percent of China's retail trade in 1984 was in the free markets. The end of mandatory state purchases of grain, cotton, pork and other items has benefited free markets. *Asian Wall Street Journal Weekly* (13 May 1985), 4.

Lipstick—The manager of the Ruby Beauty Salon in Shanghai mentions that middle- and upper-strata women should wear light lipstick. The bride should wear the brightest color lipstick at her wedding to stand out from the other women. PBS, "Adam Smith in the New China" (1985).

Incomes and Loans—In 1984 the individual incomes of urban residents rose an average of 12.5 percent over 1983, while those of peasants increased 14.7 percent. Bank loans were up 28.9 percent. *Le Monde* (29 Mar 1985), 1, 30.

GROWTH OF NATIONAL INCOME, GROSS VALUE OF AGRICULTURAL AND INDUSTRIAL OUTPUT, 1950-84 (average annual percentage growth)

	National Income	Agricultural Output	Industrial Output
1950-2	19.3	14.1	34.8
1953-7	8.9	4.5	18.0
1958-62	−3.1	−4.3	3.8
1963-5	14.5	11.1	17.9
1966-70	8.4	3.9	11.7
1971-5	5.6	4.0	9.1
1976	−2.7	2.5	1.3
1977	7.8	1.7	14.3
1978	12.3	9.0	13.5
1979	7.0	8.6	8.5
1980	6.9	2.7	8.7
1981	3.0	5.7	4.1
1982	7.4	11.0	7.7
1983	9.0	9.5	10.5
1984	12.0	14.5	14.0

Keith Griffin, ed., *Institutional Reform and Economic Development in the Chinese Countryside* (1985), 256, to 1981, and annual state statistical reports, 1982-84.

GROWTH RATES AND PROPORTIONS

Growth rates (annual average, percent)	1953-79	1981-84
Agriculture	3.2	11.0
Light industries	9.1	10.5
Heavy industries	13.6	7.7

Proportions in total value of agricultural and industrial output (percent)

	1978	1984
Agriculture	27.8	34.8
Industry	72.2	65.2

Proportions in value of total agricultural output (percent, excluding village-run industries)

	1978	1984
Farming	76.7	70.1
Forestry, animal husbandry, and fishery	20.2	24.1

Proportions in value of total industrial output (percent)

	1978	1985 Jan-Jun
Light industry	43.1	50.1
Heavy industry	56.9	49.9

Growth rates of primary and tertiary industries (annual average, percent)

	1953-80	1981-84
Primary	2.4	11.0
Tertiary	5.3	11.5

Accumulation rates (proportion between consumption and accumulation, percent, 100 = balanced)

1980	31.5	1983	c. 100
1981	28.3	1984	up
1982	c.100		

FBIS-CHI 179 (16 Sep 1985), K18/19.

GROSS ECONOMIC INDICATORS, 1984

		Percentage Increase Over 1983
Total product of society (bn yuan) *	1,283.5	13.0
Total output value of industry and agriculture (bn yuan)	1,062.7	14.2
National income (bn yuan)	548.5	12.0
Total output value of industry (bn yuan)	701.5	14.0
Planned growth (percent)		5.0
Total output value of rural industry run by villages (brigades) (bn yuan)	55.0	
Total output value of industry:		
State-owned		11.0
Collectively-owned		21.9
Other kinds of ownership		56.8
Industry in the four Special Economic Zones (Shenzhen, Shantou, Xiamen, and Zhuhai)		51.5

continued . . .

GROSS ECONOMIC INDICATORS, 1984 (continued)

		Percentage Increase Over 1983
Total output value of agriculture (bn yuan)	361.2	14.5
Planned growth (percent)		4.0
Total output value of light industry (bn yuan)	337.4	13.9
Total output value of heavy industry (bn yuan)	364.1	14.2
Primary energy output (mn tons of standard coal)	766	7.4
Energy savings by industrial enterprises above the county level (mn tons of standard coal)	20+	

* The total product of society is the sum of the total output value of agriculture, industry, the building trade, communications and transportation, and commerce, including the supply and marketing of materials and equipment and the catering trade. National income is the sum of the net output value of the five above-mentioned material producing departments. All figures for the total product of society, total industrial output value, total agricultural output value and national income cited in the communique are calculated in terms of 1984 prices, and the rate of growth over the previous year is calculated on comparable prices.

Beijing Review, 12 (25 Mar 1985), i-iii.

INDUSTRIAL PRODUCTION, Jan-Jun 1985

		Percentage Growth Over Jan-Jun 1984
Industrial output value (bn yuan)	408.6	23.1
Heavy industry	203.9	21.0
Light industry	204.7	25.3
Energy production (mn tons of standard coal)	409	11.3
Raw coal (mn tons)	414	11.8
Crude oil (mn tons)	61.46	10.9
Electricity (bn kWh)	199.1	9.1
Commodities:		
Television sets		84.5
Color sets		240
Washing machines		70
Electric fans		96.2
Refrigerators		220
Motor vehicles		58.8
Small tractors		46.7
Diesel engines		54.8
Plywood		11.5
Cement		18.4
Plate glass		22.9

Press reports.

MAJOR HEAVY INDUSTRIAL PRODUCTS, 1984

			Increase Over 1983 (Percent)
Coal	772,000,000	tons	8.0
Crude oil	114,530,000	tons	8.0
Natural gas	12.3	billion cubic meters	1.7
Electricity	374.6	billion kwh	6.6
of which:			
Hydro-electricity	85.5	billion kwh	−1.0
Pig Iron	39,980,000	tons	7.0
Steel	43,370,000	tons	8.4
Rolled steel	33,710,000	tons	9.7
Timber	55,000,000	cubic meters	5.1
Cement	121,080,000	tons	11.8
Plate glass	47,370,000	standard cases	13.7
Sulphuric acid	8,130,000	tons	−6.5
Soda ash	1,880,000	tons	5.0
Caustic soda	2,220,000	tons	4.6
Chemical fertilizers	14,820,000	tons	7.5
of which			
Nitrogenous fertilizer	12,260,000	tons	10.5
Phosphate fertilizer	2,520,000	tons	−5.3
Chemical insecticides	310,000	tons	−6.8
Plastics	1,160,000	tons	3.2
Mining equipment	230,000	tons	13.6
Power-generating equipment	4,650,000	kw	69.8
Machine tools	131,400		8.6
Motor vehicles	131,400		31.4
Tractors	39,700		7.3
Walking tractors	670,000		34.7
Locomotives	658		11.7
Steel ships for civilian use	1,440,000	tons	11.1

Beijing Review, 12 (25 Mar 1985), iii.

MAJOR LIGHT INDUSTRIAL PRODUCTS, 1984

			Increase Over 1983 (Percent)
Cotton yarn	3,220,000	tons	−1.5
Cloth	13.4	billion meters	−10.0
of which:			
Chemical fabrics	5.8	billion meters	8.7
Chemical fibers	730,000	tons	34.2
Woollen piece goods	175	million meters	22.6
Machine-made paper and paper board	7,140,000	tons	8.0
Sugar	3,740,000	tons	0.8
Beer	2,190,000	tons	34.4
Cigarettes	53.125	packs	9.6
Chemical pharmaceuticals	52,000	tons	9.0
Detergents	810,000	tons	19.1
Bicycles	28,570,000		3.6
Sewing machines	9,320,000		−14.3
Wrist-watches	36,440,000		5.1

continued . . .

MAJOR LIGHT INDUSTRIAL PRODUCTS, 1984 (continued)

		Increase Over 1983 (Percent)
Television sets	9,960,000	45.7
of which:		
Color sets	1,290,000	140
Radios	21,860,000	9.4
Casette recorders	7,480,000	50.4
Cameras	1,270,000	37.0
Household washing machines	5,780,000	58.1
Household refrigerators	537,300	190

Beijing Review, 12 (25 Mar 1985), iii.

CAPITAL CONSTRUCTION, 1984

		Percentage Increase Over 1983
Total investment in fixed assets for state-owned enterprises (bn yuan)	116.0	21.8
To capital construction (bn yuan)	73.5	23.8
State plan, 1984 (bn yuan)	65.0	
Adjusted state plan, 1984 (bn yuan)	70.6	
Capital construction by sectors:		
Energy (bn yuan)	15.8	25.1
Transportation, posts and telecommunications	10.5	34.2
Investment in 123 large and medium-sized top-priority projects (bn yuan)	17.6	
Over planned investment (bn yuan)	0.9	
Investment in the four Special Economic Zones (Shenzhen, Zhuhai, Shantou, and Xiamen) (bn yuan)	2.2	77.6
Projects put into operation, 1984:		
Large and medium-sized projects	102	
Single items attached to large and medium-sized projects	132	
Percentage of planned large, medium-sized projects and single items put into operation	88	
Percentage of capital construction projects finished and put into operation		
1983	53.2	
1984	48.0	
Percentage of housing completed		
1983	52.3	
1984	49.0	

These projects included the Baishan hydroelectric power station in Jilin Province, with a total generating capacity of 900,000 kw; Liaoning Province's Jinzhou power plant, with a total capacity of 600,000 kw; a 3-million-ton-a-year open-cast coal mine in Inner Mongolia's Huolinhe mining area; the 3-million-ton-a-year Xiqupingtong coal mine in Shanxi's Gujiao mining area; the Dongpang coal washing plant in Hebei's Xingtai mining area, with an annual capacity of washing 1.8 million tons of coal; a 540-km-long railway from the city of Wuhu in Anhui Province to Guixi in Jiangxi Province; the 218-km Handan-Changzhi railway; the 683-km Hairag-Golmud railway on the Qinhai-Tibet line; the 476-km Turpan-Korla railway in southern Xinjiang; the Jidong Cement Factory in Hebei, with an annual capacity of 1.55 million tons; Guangxi Province's Nanning plate glass factory, with an annual production capacity of 1.2 million standard cases, and Shandong Province's Yantai Synthetic Leather Factory, which is capable of producing 3 million square meters of synthetic leather.

continued . . .

CAPITAL CONSTRUCTION (continued)

		Percentage Increase Over 1983
Production capacities added:		
Coal (mn tons)	18.13	
Crude oil (mn tons)	13.1	
Power-generating capacity (mn kW)	3.5	
Railways (km):		
New	1,247	
Double-tracked railways already in use	584	
Electrified	695	
Post cargo handling capacity (mn tons)	9.18	
Chemical fibers (th)	25	
Sugar (mn tons)	385	
Timber (th cu m)	530	
Cement (mn tons)	4.7	
Newly verified geological reserves:		
Coal (bn tons)	24	
Iron ore (mn tons)	880	
Tunneling footage completed (mn m)		
1983	9.5	
1984	11.07	
Total investment by state-owned enterprises in equipment replacement, technical modernization, and other purposes (bn yuan)	42.5	18.8
Invested in energy conservation projects (bn yuan)	10.0	33.0
Invested to increase the variety of products and to raise their quality (bn yuan)	4.5	25.0
Investment in equipment replacement and technical modernization (bn yuan)	30.4	

Beijing Review, 12 (25 Mar 1985), iv-v.

RETAIL TRADE, 1984

		Percentage Increase Over 1983
Value of retail sales (bn yuan)	335.7	17.8
Percentage growth when price increases are considered		14.6
Increase in sales of consumer goods		18.7
Increase in sales of farming materials and equipment		12.7
Increase in retail sales:		
Grain		19.5
Edible oils		18.1
Pork		3.0
Eggs		16.1
Sugar		9.7
Cotton-chemical fiber blended fabrics		4.9
Chemical fabrics		13.3
Cotton cloth		-3.3
Woolen piece goods		23.8
Silks and satins		19.0
Knitting wool		29.6

continued . . .

RETAIL TRADE, 1984 (continued)

	Percentage Increase Over 1983
Knitwear	5.8
Wristwatches	24.6
Bicycles	9.9
Cameras	17.7
Electric fans	54.0
Television sets	53.3
Cassette tape recorders	59.7
Washing machines	83.7
Refrigerators	130.0

Second-level industrial goods wholesale centers decontrolled by the state, yearend	489
Urban trade centers set up by the state, yearend	2,248
For industrial goods	1,254
For farm and sideline products	753
For all-purpose trading	241
Small state-owned enterprises in the retail businesses permitted self-management	58,060
Leased to collective management	46,589
Turned over to collective ownership	5,554
Leased to individuals	5,917
Number of commodity fairs (free markets) in cities and the countryside	
1983	48,000
1984	56,000

Increase in retail sales by sectors:	
Public-owned	9.7
Collective	16.4
Joint-management	110.0
Individual	76.4
Peasants to non-agricultural residents	27.8
Increase in state-controlled sales of the means of production (percent)	
Coal	6.3
Rolled steel	13.0
Timber	5.0
Cement	12.4
Of these, sales to rural areas by material departments rose	
Coal	26.0
Rolled steel	7.0
Timber	31.0
Cement	11.0
Heavy-duty trucks	28.0
Rise in average general price indices for purchases of farm and sideline products	4.0
General retail price index	2.8
Price increases (percent):	
Fresh vegetables	7.5
Meat, poultry and eggs	5.0
Aquatic products	11.0
Fruit	9.5
Preserved fruit	4.0

continued . . .

RETAIL TRADE (continued)

	Percentage Increase Over 1983
Traditional Chinese medicines	9.0
Western medicines	2.1
Farming materials and equipment	8.9
Grain, garments, cultural and recreational goods, and household electrical appliances	0
Cost of living index for workers and staff	2.7
Prices for consumer goods	2.5
Prices for service trades	5.4

Beijing Review, 12 (25 Mar 1985), v-vi.

SUMMARY OF TARGETS FOR THE 7TH FIVE YEAR PLAN (1986-90)

	Annual Percentage Increase	Output or Value by 1990	Percentage Increase 1990 Over 1985
Gross National Product	7+	1,100 bn yuan	
Total Value of Industrial and Agricultural Output	nearly 7	1,600 bn yuan	
Industry	7		
Agriculture	6		
Production:			
Electricity		550 bn kWh	
Coal		1 bn tons	
Oil		150 mn tons	
Rolled Steel		44 mn tons	
Freight-Handling Capacity			30
Trade			40-50
Average Level of Consumption			25
Average Annual Population Growth (per th)		12.5	

PRIVATE BUSINESSES, 1978-1985 (mn)

1978	0.012	1983 mid-year	4.6[1]
1980	0.660	1984 yearend	9.3-11
1982	0.920-1.5	1985 Jun	10.65[2]
		1985 yearend	11.22
			(16.69 mn people)

1. Five percent of all retail sales were in the private sector.
2. Fourteen percent of all retail sales were in the private sector. Various estimates of the number of private businesses have appeared in the Chinese press. The number of private businesses at the end of 1984 was probably closer to 9.3 million.

CHIFFA/6 (1983), 149; 7 (1984), 89; 8 (1985), 2; (New York *Times* (3 Oct 1985, 10; *Beijing Review*, 50 (30 Dec 1985), 8. By type of businesses at the end of June, 1985:

Total	10		
Private commercial	5.8	Repair shops	0.75
Food stalls and restaurants	1.0	Transport firms	0.80
Service shops and stalls	0.65	House-repair businesses	0.04

The retail trade turnover of the private sector amounted to 24.5 billion yuan during the first half of 1985, up 92.5 percent over the first half of 1984. FBIS-CHI 182 (19 Sep 1985), K13/14.

INDEX OF GROSS INDUSTRIAL AND AGRICULTURAL OUTPUT VALUE
(1960 = 100, 1978 = 100)

1960	100	1978	100
1961	68.9	1979	108.4
1962	61.9	1980	116.6
1963	67.8	1981	122
1968	100	1982	132.6

Guangming Ribao (30 Nov 1985).

ESTIMATED UNEMPLOYMENT RATES BY REGIONS AND PROVINCES,
Mid-Year 1982 (percent)

Region and Province	Both Sexes	Men	Women
Total	4.7	4.0	5.5
East	4.2	3.6	5.1
Shanghai	2.9	2.6	3.3
Jiangsu	3.6	2.9	4.4
Zhejiang	4.6	3.8	5.7
Anhui	3.3	2.6	4.2
Fujian	6.4	5.2	8.3
Jiangxi	4.8	3.9	5.9
Shandong	4.6	4.2	5.1
North	5.3	4.6	6.3
Beijing	4.5	4.2	5.0
Tianjin	5.3	4.2	6.7
Hebei	5.2	4.3	6.5
Shanxi	4.4	4.0	5.0
Neimenggu	7.3	6.6	8.5
Northeast	8.9	8.0	10.5
Liaoning	8.2	7.5	9.4
Jilin	9.5	8.5	11.3
Heilongjiang	9.3	8.1	11.5
Northwest	4.2	3.7	4.9
Shaanxi	4.5	4.2	5.0
Gansu	4.1	3.3	5.0
Qinghai	5.3	4.4	6.3
Ningxia	4.7	4.1	5.5
Xinjiang	3.0	2.5	3.7
South	3.9	3.3	4.7
Henan	3.7	2.9	4.5
Hubei	3.6	3.0	4.2
Hunan	4.6	3.7	5.8
Guangdong	4.8	3.9	5.8
Guangxi	2.4	2.3	2.6
Southwest	4.5	3.7	5.4
Sichuan	4.7	3.7	5.9
Guizhou	4.5	4.0	5.0
Yunnan	3.6	3.4	3.9
Xizang	.	.	.

Jeffrey R. Taylor, *Employment and Unemployment in China: Results from 10-Percent Sample Tabulation of 1982 Population Census* (US Bureau of the Census, 1985), 24.

DISTRIBUTION OF ESTIMATED LABOR FORCE, by Region and Province: 1982

REGIONAL DISTRIBUTION

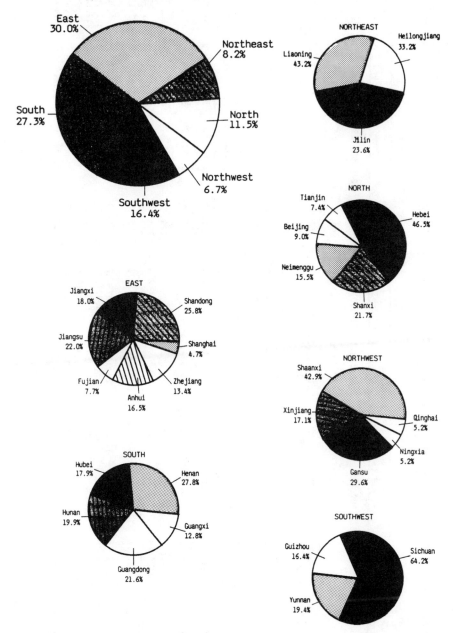

Jeffrey R. Taylor, *Employment and Unemployment in China: Results from 10-Percent Sample Tabulation of 1982 Population Census* (US Bureau of the Census, 1985), 10.

ESTIMATED LABOR FORCE BY EMPLOYMENT STATUS, SEX AND PROVINCE, Mid-Year 1982 (th)

Region and province	Both sexes			Men			Women		
	Total	Employed	Unemployed (estimated)	Total	Employed	Unemployed (estimated)	Total	Employed	Unemployed (estimated)
Total	546,015.86	520,389.79	25,626.07	305,388.17	293,038.52	12,349.65	240,627.69	227,351.27	13,276.42
East	163,603.83	156,677.64	6,926.19	91,639.43	88,349.66	3,289.77	71,964.40	68,327.98	3,636.42
Shanghai	7,697.24	7,471.70	225.54	4,065.49	3,959.46	106.03	3,631.75	3,512.24	119.51
Jiangsu	36,030.95	34,730.88	1,300.07	19,127.05	18,567.05	560.00	16,903.90	16,163.83	740.07
Zhejiang	21,889.53	20,892.08	997.45	13,273.55	12,768.01	505.54	8,615.98	8,124.07	491.91
Anhui	26,960.50	26,067.05	893.45	14,830.36	14,451.00	379.36	12,130.14	11,616.05	514.09
Fujian	12,570.02	11,760.88	809.14	7,654.61	7,253.13	401.48	4,915.41	4,507.75	407.66
Jiangxi	16,294.52	15,517.25	777.27	9,294.27	8,931.98	362.29	7,000.25	6,585.27	414.98
Shandong	42,161.07	40,237.80	1,923.27	23,394.10	22,419.03	975.07	18,766.97	17,818.77	948.20
North	62,996.65	59,649.97	3,346.68	36,893.58	35,201.67	1,691.91	26,103.07	24,448.30	1,654.77
Beijing	5,677.36	5,420.32	257.04	3,153.04	3,021.93	131.11	2,524.32	2,398.39	125.93
Tianjin	4,660.16	4,413.87	246.29	2,651.17	2,539.92	111.25	2,008.99	1,873.95	135.04
Hebei	29,281.05	27,749.13	1,531.92	17,334.75	16,584.44	750.31	11,946.30	11,164.69	781.61
Shanxi	13,641.53	13,041.81	599.72	7,880.07	7,566.17	313.90	5,761.46	5,475.64	285.82
Neimenggu	9,736.55	9,024.84	711.71	5,874.55	5,489.21	385.34	3,862.00	3,535.63	326.37
Northeast	44,639.77	40,665.59	3,974.18	28,024.46	25,794.61	2,229.85	16,615.31	14,870.98	1,744.33
Liaoning	19,302.19	17,709.85	1,592.34	11,582.34	10,717.44	864.90	7,719.85	6,992.41	727.44
Jilin	10,536.37	9,531.83	1,004.54	6,793.39	6,213.59	579.80	3,742.98	3,318.24	424.74
Heilongjiang	14,801.21	13,423.91	1,377.30	9,648.73	8,863.58	785.15	5,152.48	4,560.33	592.15
Northwest	36,479.68	34,950.39	1,529.29	20,114.16	19,379.67	734.49	16,365.52	15,570.72	794.80
Shaanxi	15,643.26	14,934.65	708.61	8,764.14	8,397.31	366.83	6,879.12	6,537.34	341.78
Gansu	10,802.50	10,362.20	440.30	5,816.14	5,623.45	192.69	4,986.36	4,738.75	247.61
Qinghai	1,913.07	1,811.93	101.14	1,029.37	984.29	45.08	883.70	827.64	56.06
Ningxia	1,892.00	1,802.65	89.35	1,030.16	988.11	42.05	861.84	814.54	47.30
Xinjiang	6,228.85	6,038.96	189.89	3,474.35	3,386.51	87.84	2,754.50	2,652.45	102.05

continued . . . .

ESTIMATED LABOR FORCE BY EMPLOYMENT STATUS, SEX AND PROVINCE, Mid-Year 1982 (th) (continued)

ESTIMATED LABOR FORCE BY EMPLOYMENT STATUS, SEX AND PROVINCE, Mid-Year 1982 (th) (continued)

Region and province	Both sexes			Men			Women		
	Total	Employed	Unemployed (estimated)	Total	Employed	Unemployed (estimated)	Total	Employed	Unemployed (estimated)
South	149,002.92	143,156.01	5,846.91	81,340.30	78,691.43	2,648.87	67,662.62	64,464.58	3,198.04
Henan	41,366.90	39,855.19	1,511.71	22,335.42	21,681.86	653.56	19,031.48	18,173.33	858.15
Hubei	26,718.55	25,769.23	949.32	14,609.30	14,165.64	443.66	12,109.25	11,603.59	505.66
Hunan	29,610.34	28,234.13	1,376.21	16,712.98	16,088.21	624.77	12,897.36	12,145.92	751.44
Guangdong	32,229.10	30,685.88	1,543.22	17,448.18	16,760.50	687.68	14,780.92	13,925.38	855.54
Guangxi	19,078.03	18,611.58	466.45	10,234.42	9,995.22	239.20	8,843.61	8,616.36	227.25
Southwest	89,293.01	85,290.19	4,002.82	47,376.24	45,621.48	1,754.76	41,916.77	39,668.71	2,248.06
Sichuan	57,341.39	54,619.94	2,721.45	30,682.96	29,539.96	1,143.00	26,658.43	25,079.98	1,578.45
Guizhou	14,611.47	13,958.54	652.93	7,634.01	7,327.29	306.72	6,977.46	6,631.25	346.21
Yunnan	17,340.15	16,711.71	628.44	9,059.27	8,754.23	305.04	8,280.88	7,957.48	323.40
Xizang	.	.	.	.			.		

Note: All data pertain to persons age 15 years and above and are drawn or calculated from Guowuyuan . . . [Ten Percent Sample Tabulation], 1983, pp. 12-17, 326-327. The 10 percent figures were scaled up by a factor of 10 to represent national totals. Unemployment is estimated as the sum of persons awaiting unified state assignment, persons waiting for jobs in cities and towns, and nonworkers of unspecified status. Labor force estimates for Xizang (Tibet) have been omitted from the table because the 10 percent sample tabulation did not have sufficiently detailed information for this province on nonworkers by economic status, meaning unemployment could not be estimated. Employment for Xizang is known, however, and is listed in the 10 percent sample tabulation as 496.70 thousand for males, 491.24 thousand for females, and 987.94 thousand for both sexes combined.

Jeffrey R. Taylor, *Employment and Unemployment in China: Results from 10-Percent Sample Tabulation of 1982 Population Census* (US Bureau of Census, 1985), 11.

EMPLOYMENT BY OCCUPATION AND SEX, 1982

Occupation	Absolute level (Thousands of persons)			Shares (Percent)		
	Both sexes	Men	Women	Both sexes	Men	Women
Total	521,377.73	293,535.22	227,842.51	100.0	56.3	43.7
Professional and technical personnel	26,442.64	16,346.99	10,095.65	100.0	61.8	38.2
Scientific research	151.42	109.41	42.01	100.0	72.3	27.7
Engineering, agriculture and forestry	2,933.93	2,419.73	514.20	100.0	82.5	17.5
Science and technology management and support staff	294.40	85.20	209.20	100.0	28.9	71.1
Airplane and shipbuilding technology	64.85	63.86	0.99	100.0	98.5	1.5
Health and medical work	4,606.42	2,414.89	2,191.53	100.0	52.4	47.6
Economic affairs	7,668.49	4,692.19	2,976.30	100.0	61.2	38.8
Legal affairs	171.26	152.11	19.15	100.0	88.8	11.2
Teaching	9,596.53	5,855.05	3,741.48	100.0	61.0	39.0
Arts and sports	521.69	354.16	167.53	100.0	67.9	32.1
Cultural activities	410.02	180.56	229.46	100.0	44.0	56.0
Religion	23.63	19.83	3.80	100.0	83.9	16.1
Heads of organizations	8,084.65	7,242.55	842.10	100.0	89.6	10.4
Government agencies and subunits	829.09	783.31	45.78	100.0	94.5	5.5
Party committees and people's organizations	1,247.40	1,053.84	193.56	100.0	84.5	15.5
Street administrative offices and rural people's communes	396.71	294.79	101.92	100.0	74.3	25.7
Enterprises, institutions and related administrative organs	5,611.45	5,110.61	500.84	100.0	91.1	8.9

continued . . .

EMPLOYMENT BY OCCUPATION AND SEX, 1982 (continued)

Occupation	Absolute level (Thousands of persons)			Shares (Percent)		
	Both sexes	Men	Women	Both sexes	Men	Women
Office clerks and related staff	6,767.14	5,113.85	1,653.29	100.0	75.6	24.4
Administrative staff	3,623.53	2,655.16	968.37	100.0	73.3	26.7
Political and security staff	2,037.29	1,769.73	267.56	100.0	86.9	13.1
Post and telecommunications staff	601.03	294.72	306.31	100.0	49.0	51.0
Other office clerks and staff	505.29	394.24	111.05	100.0	78.0	22.0
Workers engaged in commerce	9,428.32	5,084.16	4,344.16	100.0	53.9	46.1
Sales staff	7,058.68	3,030.75	4,027.93	100.0	42.9	57.1
Purchasing agents and supply and marketing staff	1,863.71	1,678.15	185.56	100.0	90.0	10.0
Procurement staff	406.30	297.23	109.07	100.0	73.2	26.8
Other workers engaged in commerce	99.63	78.03	21.60	100.0	78.3	21.7
Workers engaged in service trades	11,471.65	5,969.40	5,502.25	100.0	52.0	48.0
Attendants	7,755.54	3,578.53	4,177.01	100.0	46.1	53.9
Cooks and kitchen workers	3,044.15	1,862.45	1,181.70	100.0	61.2	38.8
Tour guides	1.87	1.15	0.72	100.0	61.5	38.5
Repairers of consumer goods	574.34	481.87	92.47	100.0	83.9	16.1
Other workers in service trades	95.75	45.40	50.35	100.0	47.4	52.6
Workers engaged in agriculture	375,499.54	199,773.89	175,725.65	100.0	53.2	46.8
Agricultural production leaders	1,739.49	1,703.54	35.95	100.0	97.9	2.1
Farmers	360,099.17	188,897.73	171,201.44	100.0	52.5	47.5
Forestry workers	3,037.32	2,098.05	939.27	100.0	69.1	30.9
Animal husbandry workers	5,835.04	2,854.14	2,980.90	100.0	48.9	51.1

continued . . .

EMPLOYMENT BY OCCUPATION AND SEX, 1982 (continued)

EMPLOYMENT BY OCCUPATION AND SEX, 1982 (continued)

Occupation	Absolute level (Thousands of persons)			Shares (Percent)		
	Both sexes	Men	Women	Both sexes	Men	Women
Fishery workers	1,739.27	1,419.69	319.58	100.0	81.6	18.4
Hunters	2.96	2.59	0.37	100.0	87.5	12.5
Agricultural machinery operators	2,323.34	2,296.44	26.90	100.0	98.8	1.2
Other agricultural workers	722.95	501.71	221.24	100.0	69.4	30.6
Production, transport and related workers	83,204.24	53,724.57	29,479.67	100.0	64.6	35.4
Mining, quarrying, exploring, well drilling and salt making	4,330.99	3,865.41	465.58	100.0	89.3	10.7
Metal smelting and processing	2,931.18	1,989.90	941.28	100.0	67.9	32.1
Chemical workers	1,482.68	830.66	652.02	100.0	56.0	44.0
Rubber and plastic products	1,263.80	383.95	879.85	100.0	30.4	69.6
Textiles, knitting and dyeing	4,902.71	1,154.13	3,748.58	100.0	23.5	76.5
Leather, fur and their products	772.65	278.36	494.29	100.0	36.0	64.0
Clothing	5,018.74	715.64	4,303.10	100.0	14.3	85.7
Food and beverages	3,284.04	2,008.95	1,275.09	100.0	61.2	38.8
Tobacco	93.12	38.77	54.35	100.0	41.6	58.4
Wood processing, wood, bamboo, hemp, cane, palm and straw products	6,968.38	5,619.25	1,349.13	100.0	80.6	19.4
Papermaking and paper products	881.57	328.21	553.36	100.0	37.2	62.8
Printing and related activities	892.64	311.35	581.29	100.0	34.9	65.1
Stone cutting and carving	364.63	333.10	31.53	100.0	91.4	8.6
Forging, manufacture of tools and installation of machine tools	6,559.19	4,471.55	2,087.64	100.0	68.2	31.8
Machine assembly and the manufacture of precision instruments	3,917.97	3,253.42	664.55	100.0	83.0	17.0

continued ...

EMPLOYMENT BY OCCUPATION AND SEX, 1982

EMPLOYMENT BY OCCUPATION AND SEX, 1982 (continued)

Occupation	Absolute level (Thousands of persons)			Shares (Percent)		
	Both sexes	Men	Women	Both sexes	Men	Women
Installation, repair and assembly of electric and electronic equipment, and related activities	4,153.66	2,991.21	1,162.45	100.0	72.0	28.0
Radio broadcasters and film projectionists	279.07	243.10	35.97	100.0	87.1	12.9
Plumbers, welders, workers for cold-working and installation of metal components	2,978.36	2,070.52	907.84	100.0	69.5	30.5
Glass, ceramics and enamel products	902.36	480.27	422.09	100.0	53.2	46.8
Painters	892.78	439.78	453.00	100.0	49.3	50.7
Other production and related workers	4,782.46	2,977.16	1,805.30	100.0	62.3	37.7
Construction workers	6,879.40	5,678.25	1,201.15	100.0	82.5	17.5
Power plant operators	1,765.09	1,397.22	367.87	100.0	79.2	20.8
Loaders and operators for loading equipment	3,630.51	2,729.77	900.74	100.0	75.2	24.8
Transport equipment operators	6,424.48	5,826.71	597.77	100.0	90.7	9.3
Workers for inspection, measuring, testing and analysis and related activities	2,077.53	743.60	1,333.93	100.0	35.8	64.2
Other production, transport and related workers	4,774.25	2,564.33	2,209.92	100.0	53.7	46.3
Other unclassified workers	479.55	279.81	199.74	100.0	58.3	41.7

Jeffrey R. Taylor, Employment and Unemployment in China: Results from 10-Percent Sample Tabulation of 1982 Population Census (US Bureau of the Census, 1985), 41-42.

AGE PYRAMID FOR EMPLOYMENT: 1982 (Percent of total employment by sex)

AGE PYRAMID FOR EMPLOYMENT: 1982 (Percent of total employment by sex)

Age group	Men	Women
65+	2.2	0.6
60–64	3.0	1.0
55–59	4.9	2.4
50–54	6.7	4.3
45–49	8.3	6.9
40–44	8.7	8.3
35–39	9.6	10.0
30–34	12.8	13.7
25–29	16.0	17.5
20–24	12.4	14.5
15–19	15.3	21.0

Jeffrey R. Taylor, *Employment and Unemployment in China: Results from 10-Percent Sample Tabulation of 1982 Population Census* (US Bureau of the Census, 1985), 21.

PERCENT DISTRIBUTION OF PERSONS WAITING FOR JOBS IN CITIES AND TOWNS, BY AGE AND SEX: 1982

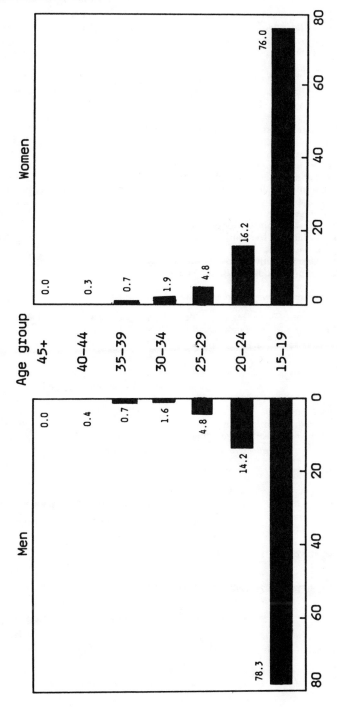

Jeffrey R. Taylor, *Employment and Unemployment in China: Results from 10-Percent Sample Tabulation of 1982 Population Census* (US Bureau of the Census, 1985), 26.

FACTORIES AND WORKERS, 1985

	Factories	Employees
Total (mn)	3.68	128
State-owned factories	0.8331	56.81
Collectively-owned factories	2.8+	70.28
Joint-venture enterprises (th)	2+	160+

Beijing Review, 20 (20 May 1985), 4.

WAGES

Average wage in state-owned or urban collective enterprise, 1985 (yuan)	1,143
Percentage increase over 1980	50
Real annual income of worker after deducting the rise in the cost of living index since 1980 (yuan)	958
Rise in the cost of living index since 1980 (percent)	25.7
Estimated total wage bill (bn yuan)	138
Percentage increase over 1980	78.5
Annual percentage wage increase, 1980-1985	12.3
Planned annual increase (percent)	4.9
Percentage increase, 1985	21.8
Estimated total wage bill with subsidy for the increase in non-staple food prices added, 1985 (bn yuan)	142
Percentage increase over 1980	83.7
Increase in real income for wage-earners, 1980-1985 (percent) *	54

* Both the national income and the total industrial and agricultural output value have grown more than 60 percent during the past five years. FBIS-CHI 172 (5 Sep 1985), K10/11.

COLLECTIVE AND INDIVIDUAL SECTORS, 1978-1983

	Collective Sector	Individual Sector
Businesses added (th)	351	
Employees added (mn)	3.059	5.826
Individual households added (mn)		4.742

Percent share of the retail market by sectors:

	Collective	Individual	State
1978	7.2	0.1	90.7
1983	16.6	6.5	72.1

Retail and service trades:

	Businesses (mn)	Employees (mn)
1978	1.255	6.078
1983	6.6046	16.676

Beijing Review, 30 (29 Jul 1985), 25-26.

ECONOMIC DISPUTES, 1979-1983

1979-1980	3,800+
1981	19,000
1983	44,000+
Value of suits (bn yuan)	2.960

Beijing Review, 11 (18 Mar 1985), 24.

PERCENTAGE CHANGES IN RETAIL SALES VOLUME *

Percentage Change in Retail Sales Volume
of Social Commodities from Previous Year:

	In Towns	In the Countryside	In the PRC
1961	−5.2	−21.5	
1962	−14.0	−12.7	
1963	−11.7	−8.4	
1979			7.4
1980			18.8
1981			9.8
1982			9.3

* Calculated in fixed prices. *Guangming Ribao* (30 Nov 1985).

DISTRIBUTION OF TOWNSHIP ENTERPRISES, 1984 (percent)

Enterprises

Industrial	71
Machinery	24
Building materials	20
Textiles	11
Food-processing	9
Chemicals	7
Coal	5
Plastic-processing	4
Metallurgy	3
Other	17
Construction	13
Commerce and service trades	8
Agricultural	4
Transport	4
Total output value (bn yuan)	170
Number of employees, including those at privately- operated enterprises (mn)	52.06

Township enterprises have increased rapidly to create new jobs in the countryside and to develop rural economies. *Beijing Review*, 25 (24 Jun 1985), 17.

KEY PROJECTS BY TYPE, 1985

		Projects	Percent
Total		169	100.0
Energy		60	35.5
Increases in capacity (mn tons):			
Coal	84.3		
Oil	31.33		
Electricity	24.3		
Transportation and communications		39	23.1
Raw materials extraction and processing		33	19.5
Education and medicine		16	9.5
National defense		8	4.7
Automotive, light and textile industries		13	7.7

XNB (8 Jan 1985), 3.

COMPARATIVE DATA, REPUBLIC OF CHINA   AND THE PEOPLE'S REPUBLIC OF CHINA

	Republic of China (Taiwan)	People's Republic of China
Controlled territory	36,000 sq. km.	9,600,000 sq. km.
Population	18,733,000 (End of 1983)	1,024,950,000 (End of 1983)
Population density	520.4 per sq. km. (End of 1983)	106.8 per sq. km. (End of 1983)
Per capita arable land	0.518 sq. km.	0.777 sq. km.
Per capita GNP	US$ 2,744 (1983)	US$ 228 (1983)
Per capita daily calories	2,720 (1983)	1,820 (1983)
Per capita annual textile consumption	53.1 meters (1982)	10 meters (1982)
Total world trade	US$ 52,415,000,000 (1984)	US$ 53,632,000,000 (1984)
Total exports	US$ 30,456,000,000 (1984)	US$ 25,962,000,000 (1984)
Total imports	US$ 21,959,000,000 (1984)	US$ 27,670,000,000 (1984)
Trade balance	(+US$ 8,497,000,000) (1984)	(- US$ 1,708,000,000) (1984)
Foreign exchange	US$ 15,664,000,000 (1984)	US$ 14,420,000,000 (1984)
Net Foreign Assets	US$ 19,555,000,000 (1984)	US$ 11,324,000,000 (September 1984)
Literacy rates	91.2 percent (1984)	75 percent (1984)
Daily newspaper circulation	16.3 per 1,000 persons (1982)	74 per 1,000 persons (1982)
Students as a percentage of the population	25.6 percent (1983)	17.9 percent (1983)
Percentage of students in secondary schools	35.1 percent (1983)	25.3 percent (1983)
Percentage of students in colleges	8.2 percent (1983)	0.6 percent (1983)
University trained scientists	28,438 (1984)	21,008 (1983)
Life expectancy at birth	70.3, male; 75.3 female (1984)	68, male/female (1984)
Physicians	7.8 per 10,000 people (1983)	1.3 per 10,000 people (1983)
Hospital beds	345 persons per bed (1982)	453 persons per bed (1982)
Death rate	4.9 per thousand (1983)	7.1 per thousand (1983)
Infant mortality	9.6 per thousand (1979)	56 per thousand (1978-79)
Per capita energy consumption	Oil-equivalent liters: 1,519 (1981)	Oil-equivalent liters: 467 (1981)
Population percentage served by electricity	99.7 percent (1983)	Basically limited to urban population
Number of telephones	1,778.2 per 10,000 persons (1980)	50 per 10,000 persons (1983)
Number of automobiles	566.3 per 10,000 persons (1983)	12 per 10,000 persons (1981)
Number of motorbikes	2,986.5 per 10,000 persons	*Pedal bicycles:* 154 per 10,000 persons (1983)
Washing machines	74.1 per 100 households (1983)	Insignificant
Refrigerators	97.1 per 100 households (1983)	Insignificant
Color television sets	90.6 per 100 households (1983)	Black & White TV: 13.0 per 100 households (1981)
Air conditioners	24.8 per 100 households (1983)	Insignificant, basically limited to tourist hotels
Military manpower	Regulars 484,000; reserves, 1,500,000 (1983)	Regulars 4,000,000; reserves, 5,000,000 (1983)
Combat aircraft	484	5,000 plus (1983)
Major surface combat ships	35 (1983)	36 (1983)
Submarines	2 (1983)	100 plus (1983)

Reprinted with permission from the *Free China Review*, 35, 9 (Sep 1985), 30-31.

PRICE INCREASES IN BEIJING, 10 May 1985 (yuan per kg)

	Old Price	New Price
Pork	2.20	2.98
Lean pork	2.92	5.00
Beef	2.00	4.40
Mutton	2.00	3.60
Hairtail fish	1.06	3.20
Eggs	2.20	2.60

All 5.5 million urban residents will receive a 7.50 yuan monthly subsidy to help them cope with price increases. Hui Muslim minority people will get a 9 yuan subsidy to buy mutton and beef. College students will also receive 9 yuan. Hui college students will be given 10.50 yuan a month. Foreign students on scholarships will get a subsidy, and foreign experts employed by the Beijing government will get a raise of 80 yuan per month. Prices for cooking gas, matches, and the public baths have increased. The prices for grain and edible oils did not change. *Beijing Review,* 20 (20 May 1985), 6-7.

RURAL INSURANCE, 1983-1984 yearend

Value of policies taken out by peasants (by yuan)

	1983	27.3*
	1984	95.7

Premiums (mn yuan)

	1983	93.9*
	1984	338

*Calculated. XNB (23 May 1985), 33-34.

PROVISIONAL REGULATIONS GOVERNING REGULATORY TAX ON WAGES IN STATE-OWNED ENTERPRISES, Promulgated by the State Council 3 Jul 1985

Article 1. The following regulations are especially formulated for facilitating reform of the wage system for staff and workers of state-owned enterprises, gradually raising the wages of staff and workers in a planned manner, and rationally controlling the growth rate of consumption funds in marcoeconomic activities.

Article 2. All state-owned enterprises, practicing the system of letting the total payroll fluctuate according to economic performance, in accordance with the State Council provisions for wage system reform in state-owned enterprises, must pay regulatory tax on wages in state-owned enterprises (hereafter called the regulatory tax on wages for short) as stipulated in these provisions.

Article 3. All enterprises, obliged to pay the regulatory tax on wages, are hereafter called the tax payer.

Article 4. The regulatory tax on wages will be levied on the increased portion of wages in excess of 7 percent of the total wages approved by the state for the preceding year.

Article 5. The regulatory tax on wages will be computed at progressive rates listed in the appended tax rate table.

Article 6. The regulatory tax on wages will be paid at the locality where the tax payer is located.

Article 7. The tax office will be responsible for collecting, and managing, the regulatory tax on wages.

Article 8. The regulatory tax on wages will be computed and levied annually, paid in installments in advance, and balanced and settled at year end.

continued . . .

PROVISIONAL REGULATIONS GOVERNING REGULATORY TAX ON WAGES IN STATE-OWNED ENTERPRISES, Promulgated by the State Council 3 Jul 1985 (continued)

Article 9. When the accumulated total of the increased portion of wages is 7 percent in excess of the total wages approved by the state for the preceding year, the tax payer should submit to the local tax office a statement of wage funds (including funds for increasing wages) and a tax report statement. After statements are reviewed and verified by the tax office, a tax payment notice will be issued to the tax payer to pay tax within a set time. Specific time limits for paying the tax will be decided by the local tax authorities.

At the end of a year, the tax payer should, regardless of whether, or how much, it has increased the wages during the year, submit the annual tax report statement and the statement of final accounts to the local tax authorities by 4 February of the following year.

Article 10. The tax office has the right to investigate the wage funds withdrawn, or deposited, by the tax payer, and its issuance of wages. The tax payer and its affiliated organizations should submit factual reports, account books, receipts, bills, vouchers, invoices, wage forms, and other relevant documents, and should never conceal these documents from the tax office. The tax office should keep the documents confidential.

Article 11. The tax office should order a tax payer who fails to honestly declare the tax and pay it on time, to pay the tax within the time limit. It may impose a fine under 5,000 yuan, according to the tax payer's circumstances. Surcharge for overdue tax payment will be added at a daily rate of 5 per 1,000 of the overdue tax payment, effective immediately.

Article 12. The tax payment, fine, and surcharge for overdue tax payment should be listed as expenditure from the funds for increased wages.

Article 13. In the case of a tax payer in arrears over tax payment, fines, or surcharges for overdue tax payment, the tax office may, after repeatedly pressing the former, notify the bank in which the tax payer has kept an account to deduct the payment from the account.

Article 14. In case of a tax payer evading, or refusing to pay, tax, the tax office should, in addition to ordering the tax payer to factually report the increased portion of wages, set a time limit on paying the tax. It may impose a fine under 100 percent of the due payment, according to the tax payer's circumstances. Personnel directly responsible for serious cases involving violation of the criminal law will be investigated by judicial organs, according to law.

Article 15. If the tax payer has a dispute with the tax authorities over tax payment, he must first pay the tax, as prescribed by the tax authorities, before applying to higher tax authorities for reconsideration. The higher tax authorities must reply within 30 days of receiving the application. If the tax payer does not accept the decision of the higher tax authorities after reconsideration, he may bring a suit in the People's Court.

Article 16. A state-run enterprise, whose total payroll does not fluctuate with its economic performance, should still pay bonus tax.

Article 17. The Ministry of Finance is responsible for interpreting these regulations, and formulating the rules for their implementation.

Article 18. These regulations are to go into effect, beginning fiscal year 1985.

Appendix: Table of Progressive Rates for the Regulatory Tax on Wages

Grade	Percentage of total wage increase in approved total wage	Percentage of tax rate	Percentage of deduction rate for speedy computation
1	under 7 percent	0	0
2	7-12 percent	30	2.1
3	12-20 percent	100	10.5
3	over 20 percent	300	50.5

continued . . .

PROVISIONAL REGULATIONS GOVERNING REGULATORY TAX ON WAGES IN STATE-OWNED ENTERPRISES, Promulgated by the State Council 3 Jul 1985 (continued)

Calculation formula: Regulatory tax on wages equals approved total wage times percentage of total wage increase in approved total wage times appropriate tax rate—deduction rate for speedy computation, or:

Total wage increase times appropriate tax rate—deduction rate for speedy computation times total approved wage.

FBIS-CHI 134 (12 Jul 1985), K8/10.

PROVISIONAL REGULATIONS GOVERNING ECONOMIC SANCTIONS AGAINST VIOLATIONS OF PRICE DISCIPLINE, Revised, Promulgated by the State Price Bureau 10 Aug 1985

To strengthen price supervision and control and enforce price discipline, the following regulations concerning questions of economic sanctions against violations of price discipline by units and individuals are hereby laid down in accordance with the State Council "Provisional Regulations Governing Price Control" and other relevant regulations.

1. Any of the following acts constitutes a violation of price discipline:

A. Exceeding one's authority to set or adjust prices for industrial and agricultural products as well as charges for transport, materials management, and things other than commodities, which are set and controlled by the state, and unauthorized alteration of pricing measures and price-difference rates stipulated by the state;

B. Exceeding one's authority to increase the number of products with floating prices and the range of floating prices stipulated by the state;

C. Failing to implement state stipulations governing prices for industrial and agricultural products as well as charges for transport, materials management, and things other than commodities, presumptuously increasing rates and raising prices, forcing down rates and prices, or wantonly collecting charges under all sorts of pretext;

D. Transferring state-priced means of industrial production out of the state plan and selling them at raised prices in violation of state stipulations;

E. Changing, without authorization, products at fair prices stipulated by the state to ones at negotiated prices and selling them at such prices;

F. Implementing, without authorization, a state notice on price readjustment earlier or later than the specified time thereby making illicit profit or causing losses to the state;

G. Industrial and commercial wholesale enterprises selling commodities to retail enterprises or individual retailers at prices higher than the wholesale prices set by the state;

H. Fraudulently purchasing products at or above the retail prices set by the state and selling such products at elevated prices in violation of state stipulations;

I. Fraudulently purchasing important means of production and durable consumer goods in short supply and profiting by selling them at increased prices in violation of state regulations on the division of work in dealing in commodities;

J. In the catering trade that sells staple and non-staple food, failing to implement state stipulations governing prices and gross profit rates;

K. Raising prices in a disguised form by passing off poor-quality products as good-quality ones, adulterating one product with another, giving short measure, making products in a rough and slipshod way, or lowering product quality;

L. Processing enterprises and catering establishments illegally reselling raw materials at elevated prices, and materials supply and marketing organizations and enterprises reselling

continued . . .

PROVISIONAL REGULATIONS GOVERNING ECONOMIC SANCTIONS AGAINST VIOLATIONS OF PRICE DISCIPLINE, Revised, Promulgated by the State Price Bureau 10 Aug 1985 (continued)

important means of production at elevated prices to make a profit in violation of stipulations on the scope of their businesses;

M. Divulging secrets about prices to seek illicit gain or causing losses to the state by doing so.

2. Violations of price discipline are divided into three types according to the amount of illicit income: general violations of price discipline; general cases of violating price discipline; and major cases of violating price discipline.

Illicit income of less than 1,000 yuan gained by enterprises, institutions, and individual industrial and commercial undertakings or the same amount of losses caused by them to the state is a general violation of price discipline; illicit income of 1,000 to 10,000 yuan or the same amount of losses caused to the state is a general case of violating price discipline; and illicit income of more than 10,000 yuan or the same amount of losses caused to the state constitutes a major case of violating price discipline. Those involved in serious cases of violating the criminal law shall be investigated by judicial organs for their criminal responsibility.

3. Measures and limits of economic sanctions. Economic sanctions against a unit or an individual that has violated price discipline include confiscating the illicit income and imposing a fine.

A. Regardless of what types of acts or cases of violations, any illicit income gained from violating price discipline shall be confiscated. When appropriate, monies should be refunded to the consumers or users, and that which should not or cannot be refunded shall be confiscated. Assessment of the amount of illicit income must be practical and rational.

B. In addition to confiscating the illicit income of the units or individual industrial and commercial undertakings that have violated price discipline, they may also be fined according to the seriousness of their cases. Fines may be waived for those whose cases are relatively inconsequential, or those who readily admit their mistakes, or those who discover the illicit acts on their own initiative; but heavy fines ahall be imposed on those who repeatedly violate price discipline, whose cases are serious, and against whom the masses have serious complaint.

With regard to fines for units and individual industrial and commercial undertakings that have violated the price discipline, a fine of up to 500 yuan shall be imposed for a general violation of price discipline; a fine of up to 5,000 yuan shall be imposed for a general case of violating price discipline, and a fine of 20 percent of the amount of illicit income—not to exceed 100,000 yuan—shall be imposed for a major case of violating price discipline.

C. An occasional price mistake that is really caused by professional unfamiliarity, and that is promptly corrected, may be handled leniently.

D. Economic sanctions against the personnel responsible for violating price discipline and the leaders of the units responsible for violating price discipline include withholding part of their bonuses or part of their salaries, or a fine of up to 100 yuan. Fines shall be collected by the price inspection departments and turned over to the national treasury, and those whose payments are overdue shall have their salaries garnisheed by their units.

Those whose cases are relatively inconsequential and who readily admit their mistakes may be exempted from economic sanctions, but party and government departments concerned shall be requested to take party or administrative disciplinary measures against those who have seriously violated price discipline.

4. Management and collection of money resulting from economic sanctions.

A. Illicit income to be returned to the original owners or to be turned over to the national treasury shall be deducted from the revenue of the enterprises or institutions that they have earned from marketing their products. The fines an enterprise must pay shall be defrayed

continued . . .

PROVISIONAL REGULATIONS GOVERNING ECONOMIC SANCTIONS AGAINST VIO-LATIONS OF PRICE DISCIPLINE, Revised, Promulgated by the State Price Bureau 10 Aug 1985 (continued)

from its own funds, such as the percentage of profits it can retain, the percentage of profits it is entitled to keep after fulfilling a contract, and the after-tax profits it can keep; such fines shall not be written off as production or distribution costs or non-operational expenses, nor shall they be deducted from the revenue to be turned over to the state. The fine an institution has to pay shall be defrayed from the money it has saved from carrying out a contractual budget, or from its non-budgetary funds, and such fines shall not be written off as part of its budget.

B. A unit that has violated price discipline should follow the decision on economic sanctions made by the price inspection department and pay its fine or the confiscated income to the bank within a prescribed period. For those that do not pay their illicit income or fines, the price inspection departments at various levels are authorized to act in accordance with the State Council's ruling and notify the banks or credit unions of these units to transfer the payments from their accounts.

Should a violator disagree with the decision of economic sanctions it has 15 days to appeal to the unit that handles its case, or to a higher-level price inspection department. The department concerned should review the case promptly and in a practical manner, and correct any mishandling. It should reassess the amount of fines in accordance with the results of the recheck.

C. All illicit income and fines collected from violations of price discipline shall be turned over to the national treasury by price inspection departments at all levels.

FBIS-CHI 177 (12 Sep 1985), K14/16.

CHINA: ECONOMIC PERFORMANCE IN 1985. A Report Presented to the Subcommittee on Economic Resources, Competitiveness, and Security Economics of the Joint Economic Committee by the Central Intelligence Agency 17 Mar 1986

China: Economic Performance in 1985

Summary—In 1985, Beijing confronted numerous problems arising from the implementation of economic reforms. Poor weather and confusion surrounding new agricultural policies caused China's grain output to fall for the first time in five years. Industrial output, spurred by greater use of economic incentives and relaxed central controls, grew more rapidly than Beijing intended—worsening longstanding bottlenecks in the economy. Inflation, as measured by China's official price indices, tripled in 1985, while its balance of trade worsened sharply and its foreign exchange reserves declined.

Despite these problems, China's economy registered some significant gains in 1985. Energy output increased by over 8 percent, largely because of enhanced production incentives, increased state investment, and technology acquisitions. According to official statistics, despite inflation, workers experienced an improvement in their standard of living. Moreover, government revenues increased over 20 percent in 1985, and Beijing claimed success in narrowing its budget deficit.

At a national conference last September, the Chinese Communist Party formally made reform its primary economic goal for the five-year period beginning in 1986. Chinese leaders, however, recently announced that no major new reforms will be implemented this year. Beijing apparently intends to improve its control of the economy—using both indirect economic levers and administrative measures—before proceeding with key price reforms.

Agricultural Performance in 1985—Mixed Results—Since the economic reforms were launched in 1979, agriculture has been the centerpiece of Beijing's effort to improve economic efficiency by introducing pragmatic, market-oriented policies into an ossified planning system.

continued . . .

CHINA: ECONOMIC PERFORMANCE IN 1985 (continued)

While agricultural reforms are still the single most important success of the reform program—agricultural output increased at an average annual rate of 11 percent from 1981 to 1984—growth rates fell in 1985. According to China's State Statistical Bureau, agricultural output—not counting the production of rural industries—increased only 3 percent last year.

After three consecutive years of record harvests, grain output fell 7 percent in 1985 (see chart on page 101)—a result of reduced acreage, flood damage, and confusion over new reforms that eliminated grain quotas and replaced them with a market-oriented contract system. Rapidly developing rural industries also pulled peasants away from less lucrative grain production. Reform leaders maintain, however, that surpluses from previous years will more than make up for the shortfall.

Notwithstanding the lower harvest, China became a net grain exporter in 1985. According to Chinese trade data, China exported over 9 million metric tons of grain last year—almost triple the level in 1984. Chinese grain imports were approximately 5.4 million metric tons—with about 800 thousand metric tons coming from the United States.

Efforts to diversify agricultural production were bolstered by officially sanctioned price hikes. Output of sugar cane, peanuts, and oilseeds each increased by more than 25 percent last year, according to Chinese statistics. Production of meat increased by 14 percent, and eggs by 23 percent. In a planned effort to reduce stockpiles, cotton production fell by more than a third.

Industrial Performance—Overly Rapid Growth—China's industrial output increased 18 percent last year, according to Chinese statistics. This continued a trend of double-digit growth in industrial production that began in 1983 and accelerated in the second half of 1984. During the first half of 1985, industrial output expanded at a 23-percent annual rate, but efforts to cool the economy reduced the growth rate to 10 percent by the end of the year (see charts on pages 102 and 103).

Rural industry was the most rapidly growing sector of China's economy in 1985. Chinese media reported that the output of rural factories shot up by 35 percent, and accounted for almost a third of total industrial production.

In light industry, buoyant consumer demand sustained a boom in the production of electrical home appliances. Output of washing machines, electric fans, and television sets increased over 50 percent, and production of refrigerators more than doubled. Output of building materials, heavy equipment, and machinery generally increased more than 15 percent during the year, while production of rolled steel increased about 9 percent.

Rapid industrial growth has been caused by skyrocketing investment spending—up by 35 percent in 1985—and a surge in wages and bonuses for industrial workers. Successful rural reforms have increased the availability of raw materials for industrial use, while boosting rural incomes and fueling consumer demand. Rapid industrial growth also has been facilitated by industrial reforms, particularly those allowing enterprises to sell overquota production at prices above the state-set levels. To a lesser extent, rapid growth last year was due to the technical modernization of some segments of Chinese industry.

Major Indicators

The mixture of strong economic growth and relaxed economic control was evident in China's principal economic indicators.

GNP—Real GNP grew approximately 11-12 percent last year, about the same as in 1984.

Inflation—Although output grew rapidly in 1985, it was not sufficient to meet the strong demand for consumer goods, equipment, and building materials, and demand pressures boosted prices. According to China's official retail price index, prices increased 8.8 percent, triple the rate in 1984.

Energy Production—China registered 8-9 percent increases in coal, oil and electrical production last year. China is the world's second largest coal producer, with output topping 850 million tons in 1985. Recent gains in production have been due to policies that eased restrictions on private and collective small-scale mining operations and that permitted state mines to sell overquota production at free market prices.

continued . . .

CHINA: ECONOMIC PERFORMANCE IN 1985 (continued)

China produced about 2.5 million barrels of oil per day, exporting a quarter of the total. Gains in oil production were due to new finds and improved recovery technologies. Increases in electric power generation largely came from completion of new coal-fired facilities and increased deliveries of coal to power plants.

Foreign Trade—Loosened central oversight of foreign trade and a surge in investment and consumer spending led to a flood of imports—up 54 percent last year according to Chinese customs data. Because of strong domestic demand, Chinese exports increased by less than 5 percent—leaving Beijing with a 1985 trade deficit of $14.9 billion. Because of the deficit, China's foreign exchange reserves fell 25 percent between September 1984 and September 1985. According to Chinese statistics, in 1985 China used $2.4 billion in foreign loans and absorbed $1.9 billion in direct foreign investment.

Government Budget—Strong industrial growth, rising prices, and increased tariffs on some exports pushed up government revenues by over 20 percent in 1985, despite media reports of widespread tax evasion. Although statistics on government spending have not yet been released, Chinese press reports indicate that Beijing believes the budget deficit was eliminated last year.

Defense Spending—Defense expenditures were budgeted to increase only 3.3 percent in nominal terms in 1985 to 18.67 billion yuan ($5.83 billion at current exchange rates)—maintaining about a 12 percent proportion of total state expenditures. Spending for national defense is presented as a single line item in China's central budget, and there has been no official explanation as to its scope—the programs that the figures represent. Since 1979, defense spending has declined as a percent of total budget expenditures, reflecting the diminished priority given the defense sector under the economic reform program (see chart on page 104).

Problems Associated with Rapid Growth

Beijing wrestled with a problem last year that, on the surface, is very unusual for a country at China's level of economic development—how to slow economic growth.

Despite the sharp increases in production of coal, oil, and electricity last year, energy supplies in China are strained. Additions to the transportation network have not kept pace with the growth in industrial output, and the system remains seriously overburdened. Chinese media report that factories still must suspend production occasionally because of shortages of electricity and delayed shipments of raw materials.

Chinese media reports also suggest that key reform goals, such as improvements in industrial efficiency and product quality, are being undermined by the rapid growth. Beijing acknowledges that high output in some cases is caused not by efficiency gains but by the use of large amounts of inputs. A Hong Kong newspaper reported that losses by state-owned enterprises were up by over 9 percent during the first nine months last year. Press reports also suggest that rapid growth is wearing out equipment at excessive rates, increasing occupational hazards in factories, and generating higher levels of environmental pollution.

High output levels have been possible, in part, because China imported large amounts of raw materials. Imports of rolled steel last year, for example, were equivalent to one-half of China's total rolled steel production, yet China's industries experienced shortages of rolled steel and other raw materials. Beijing probably recognizes that its industrial development cannot be based on imports of raw materials and equipment, and that its foreign exchange holdings cannot sustain such high rates of growth.

Beijing counts on increased competition between state-owned enterprises to spur improvements in product quality. The shortages caused by strong demands for consumer goods and construction materials, however, have actually eased pressure on firms to maintain quality standards. Press reports emphasize that low product quality remains a serious problem throughout the economy.

Beijing probably is concerned that rising prices will jeopardize popular support for economic reforms. Although large increases in wages and bonuses have cushioned the impact of higher prices for some consumers, a jump in retail food prices has caused widespread complaints among urban residents, and the rising cost of living apparently was a factor in student protests last fall.

continued . . .

CHINA: ECONOMIC PERFORMANCE IN 1985 (continued)

Measures to Slow Growth

Beijing reacted quickly to data indicating the economy was overheating. After industrial output increased at a 23-percent annual rate during the first quarter of 1985, Beijing implemented a combination of market-oriented macroeconomic adjustments and administrative controls.

China's 1985 budget, announced in April, called for narrowing the budget deficit by slowing the growth of government spending. In particular, Beijing ordered a 10-percent cut in administrative expenditures. Beijing also began pursuing a tight money policy.

** In April, Beijing raised interest rates on time deposits and on loans for working funds. In August, it boosted rates on capital construction loans and again hiked time deposit rates.

** Lacking an established secondary market for government securities, China's banking system cannot conduct open market operations. Instead, Beijing reduces the money supply by increasing sales of goods from state-run stores. To soak up excess currency, Beijing set aside $2 billion in foreign exchange reserves to be used to import scarce consumer durables, and the Ministry of Commerce was ordered to mark down prices of overstocked domestic commodities and increase sales to the public.

Many of the administrative controls were employed through China's banking system.

** China's central bank was ordered to set and enforce quarterly credit limits for its branches and the specialized banks (such as the Agricultural Bank and the Industrial and Commercial Bank).

** Banks were ordered to stop offering loans to inefficient enterprises and to firms that produce poor quality products for which there is little demand.

** Banks were prohibited from extending credit for capital construction projects whose spending exceeds the state quota or for projects not listed in the state plan.

** To prevent indiscriminate increases in wages and bonuses, enterprises were required to place wage funds in special accounts to be monitored by the banks.

Although industrial production has slowed since July 1985, recent statements by Chinese leaders suggest that Beijing remains very concerned with inflation, excessive investment spending, and its large trade deficit. Beijing probably will continue to tighten control over credit and capital construction this year.

Economic Reforms in 1985

The Third Plenum of the 12th Party Congress which met in October 1984 approved a general set of guidelines for expanding China's economic reform program to its urban areas. During the first half of 1985, Beijing announced initial steps toward price and wage reforms, while promoting increased autonomy for industrial enterprises. The first party document issued in 1985, however, signaled a new phase in China's agricultural reform program.

Second-Stage Agricultural Reforms—In 1985, Beijing implemented policies designed to broaden the influence of market forces on agriculture. Instead of setting mandatory purchase quotas for peasants to fulfill, the state now signs production contracts for grain (and cotton) with individual farmers. The contracted amounts generally are less than the previous quotas, and peasants are expected to sell surplus production on the free market. The state has dropped its former commitment to purchase all overquota production at premium prices, and will now purchase excess grain only if the free market price falls below the set procurement price. In addition, the state no longer purchases non-staple products such as vegetables, fruit, or meat—but state-owned marketing units in cities are being encouraged to sign contracts with peasants to improve supplies of non-staples in urban areas. Finally, rural industry is being promoted to absorb some of the excess labor created by increasingly efficient agricultural production.

The new policies were designed to promote the development of a diversified agricultural sector and to encourage peasants to produce better quality products and make more efficient use of their land. The policies, however, probably elicited a stronger response than

continued . . .

CHINA: ECONOMIC PERFORMANCE IN 1985 (continued)

Beijing intended. Peasants were quick to switch to more profitable crops, such as oilseeds and vegetables. Strong consumer demand and readily available funds spurred the development of rural industries, and some peasants left their land idle to take jobs in industry. Much of the decrease in grain production in 1985 probably can be attributed to the new rural policies.

In recent months, reformers have bluntly defended the 1985 agricultural reforms against unnamed domestic critics—stating that the drop in grain output will not adversely affect the economy and highlighting the gains in production of cash crops and livestock and the important role that rural enterprises are playing. Nonetheless, agricultural policies for 1986 have been adjusted to boost grain production. Beijing has announced that it will increase state investment in agriculture and make available to peasants subsidized fertilizer and fuel. Generally, 1986 will be a year of "consolidation and digestion" of policies implemented last year.

Reforms of Enterprise Management—According to Chinese media, output has increased markedly in some factories in which managers have been given enhanced decisionmaking authority. The right to market overquota production seems to have been a particularly strong lever for increased efficiency and production. Chinese press reports, however, suggest that the implementation of increased enterprise autonomy has been uneven. Apparently, party officials and higher administrative units still make the important decisions in many factories. Other press reports indicate that many managers have taken advantage of their new authority by excessively increasing capital construction and randomly expanding wages and bonuses—two of the principal sources of economic instability in 1985. Chinese reformers are aware that the grant of autonomy is still onesided—managers have more flexibility in using enterprise revenues, but their decisionmaking is not yet disciplined by market forces. Beijing still subsidizes state enterprises that lose money, and experiments with enterprise bankruptcy laws have so far been limited, in part because the present system of irrational prices makes it difficult to determine which enterprises should be closed.

Price Reform—China's price system is irrational in that prices of many goods do not reflect relative market scarcities or the costs of production. State-set prices have been changed infrequently since the 1950s, and some goods are piled up in inventories while others are in chronic shortage. Within the next five years Beijing plans to establish a more rational, three-tiered price system. Prices of key products, such as coal and steel, will still be set by the state, but at levels that better reflect relative scarcities in the economy. Prices of many other products, including most manufactures, will fluctuate in response to market conditions within bounds set by the state. Supply and demand alone will determine the prices of minor consumer goods—for instance, some clothing products, cosmetics, and vegetables—and over-quota production of most industrial goods.

Beijing took a cautious approach to price reform in 1985. The key reform implemented was the removal of controls on retail prices of vegetables, meat, and other non-staple farm products. Beijing also removed price controls on some consumer goods, and—to encourage greater use of highway transport—raised short-haul railroad rates for passengers and freight.

While Chinese media report that the reforms have prompted gains in efficiency, higher prices—particularly for food—have sparked widespread complaints. Because the planning system generally kept inflation low in the past, consumers and Chinese leaders are sensitive to price hikes. Reform leaders probably are concerned that if they relax price controls on additional products, the current excessive demands for consumer and investment goods would boost the inflation rate—so they have postponed major price reforms until after 1986. While maintaining price stability is the major goal this year, Beijing may implement some minor adjustments, such as widening price differentials for similar products of differing quality.

Wage Reforms—Chinese reformers, recognizing that Maoist egalitarianism corroded labor productivity, are encouraging enterprise managers to reward workers for superior skills and performance. Last year, some industrial enterprises, on a trial basis, were allowed to float their total wage funds upward or downward based on the amount of profits earned and the

continued . . .

CHINA: ECONOMIC PERFORMANCE IN 1985 (continued)

amount of taxes delivered to the state. In July 1985, Beijing announced a wage reform package for teachers and government workers in which wages are to be based on the employee's position, seniority, and performance.

Wage reforms ran into serious snags last year. Unauthorized across-the-board wage hikes for factory workers contributed to inflation and undermined efforts to link remuneration to performance. Wage reforms for teachers and government workers fell almost a year behind the original timetable, delayed, probably, by budget concerns and reluctance to add to inflationary pressures.

Readjustment and Consolidation

Deng Xiaoping and other top Chinese leaders remain committed to reform despite the economic dislocations in 1985. The economic problems, however, have forced Beijing to slow the pace of reforms.

In major speeches early this year, Chinese leaders called for a period of consolidation and adjustment in the reform program. Premier Zhao Ziyang stated recently that no major price reforms would be implemented in 1986, and in his speech to the national party conference in September 1985, he suggested that Beijing might need a two-year readjustment period to perfect macroeconomic control techniques. Chinese economic leaders probably realize that further price and wage reforms might be destabilizing in an inflationary economy, and that they must improve their ability to use indirect economic levers, such as taxes and interest rates, to regulate the economy. The two-year time frame mentioned by Premier Zhao probably is a guideline for the readjustment period. Beijing may move ahead with key reforms as soon as it is confident that capital construction is under control and that it has improved its economic regulatory mechanisms.

CHINA: GRAIN PRODUCTION

CHINA: GROWTH IN INDUSTRIAL OUTPUT

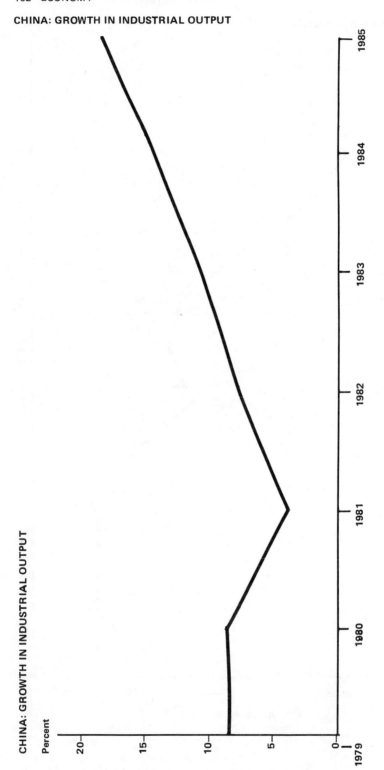

CHINA: GROWTH IN INDUSTRIAL OUTPUT

CHINA: GROWTH IN INDUSTRIAL OUTPUT BY QUARTER IN ANNUALIZED PERCENTAGE RATE

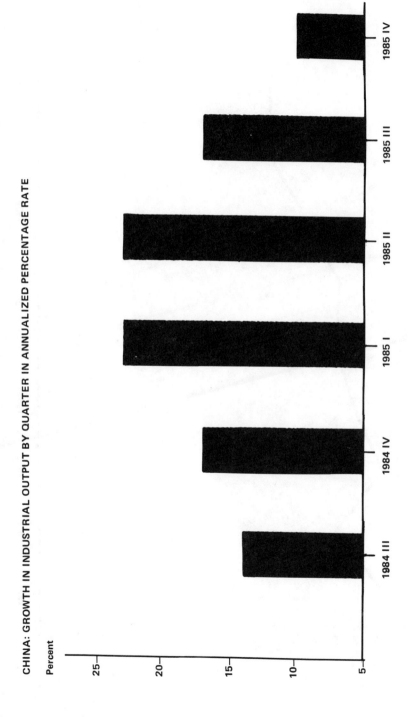

CHINA: GROWTH IN INDUSTRIAL OUTPUT BY QUARTER IN ANNUALIZED PERCENTAGE RATE

Percent

UNCLASSIFIED

ANNOUNCED CHINESE DEFENSE EXPENDITURES AS PERCENT OF CENTRAL BUDGET

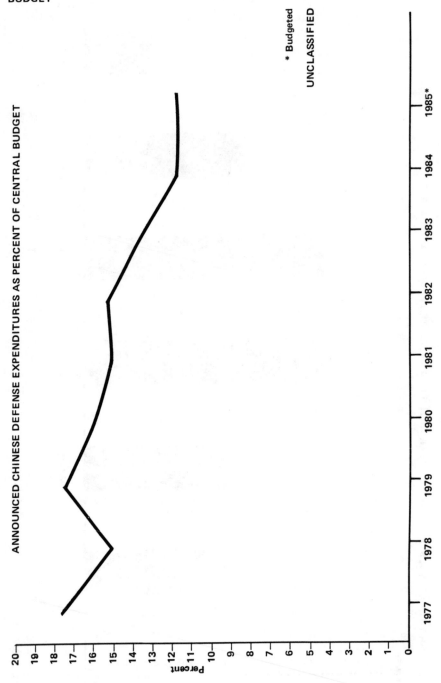

ANNOUNCED CHINESE DEFENSE EXPENDITURES AS PERCENT OF CENTRAL BUDGET

Percent

1977 1978 1979 1980 1981 1982 1983 1984 1985*

* Budgeted

UNCLASSIFIED

VIII ENERGY

ENERGY OUTPUT BY QUARTERS, 1985

Production:	Jan-Mar	Jan-Jun	Jan-Sep
Total (mn tons std. coal)			620.49
Crude oil (mn tons)	30.23	61.46	
Electricity (bn kWh)	95.7		
Raw coal (mn tons)		414	

Percentage Increase Over the Same Period in 1984	Jan-Mar	Jan-Jun	Jan-Sep
Total		11.3	10.8
Crude oil	10.28	10.9	
Electricity	7.3		
Raw coal		11.8	

Beijing Review, 14 (8 Apr 1985), 10; 31 (5 Aug 1985), 6; 44 (4 Nov 1985), 7; CHIFFA/8, 151.

TOTAL ENERGY CONSUMPTION AND ITS COMPOSITION

	Total Domestic Consumption (mn tons)	Proportion of Total Energy Consumption (percent)			
		Coal	Petroleum	Natural gas	Hydropower
1953	54.11	94.33	3.81	0.02	1.84
1957	96.44	92.32	4.59	0.08	3.01
1965	18.901	86.45	10.27	0.63	2.65
1978	57.144	70.67	22.73	3.20	3.40
1979	58.588	71.31	21.79	3.30	3.60
1980	60.275	71.81	21.05	3.14	4.00
1981	59.447	72.74	19.92	2.85	4.49
1982	61.937	73.92	18.67	2.56	4.85
1983	65.648	73.71	18.56	2.47	5.26
1984	70.732	75.12	17.66	2.34	4.88

Based on information in the State Statistical Bureau, *China: A Statistics Survey in 1985* (1985), 52.

CHINESE ENERGY SURPLUSES, 1965-83 (mn barrels per day of oil equivalent)

1965	0.036	1974	0.222	1981	0.500
1970	0.031	1975	0.420	1982	0.644
1973	0.001	1979	0.793	1983	0.709
		1980	0.418		

Calculated by subtracting consumption from production figures given in CIA, *Handbook of Economic Statistics, 1984* (1984), 126-27; *1985* (1985), 128-29.

ENERGY SAVINGS, 1985

Energy saved by China's enterprises (mn tons of standard coal)	
Target, 1985	18
Estimated actual savings, 1985	30+
Estimated savings, 1981-85	120+
Energy consumption per 100 million yuan of industrial output value, 1981-85 (th tons of standard coal)	60

XNB (29 Nov 1985), 14-15.

RURAL ENERGY

Supply of Rural Commercial Energy, 1983 (percent)

	Coal			Electricity	Oil
From local mines	From state mines	Total			
52.37	25.37	77.74		13.64	8.62

Non-Commercial Energy Consumption in Rural Areas (percent)

Straw	Firewood	Dung	Biogas	Other
50.31	46.76	2.56	0.23	0.14

Beijing Review, 21 (27 May 1985), 23. The commercial energy consumed in rural areas amounted to 139 million tons of standard coal in 1983, or 38.7 percent of all rural energy consumption and 21.4 percent of China's total commercial energy consumption. The energy used in rural production exceeded 90 million tons of standard coal that year, compared to 60 million tons in 1978.

RURAL ENERGY SHORTAGES, 1985

Rural energy demand (mn tons of standard coal)

1985	500
2000	700

Estimated supplies (mn tons of standard coal)

1985	250-300*
2000	500

Requirements for daily cooking (average kilocalories)	4,500
Supplies for daily cooking (average kilocalories)	3,500
Electricity lost from damaged power lines (percent)	20
Number of irrigation and drainage machines made in the 1950s and 1960s with low energy efficiency (mn)	5
Number of tractors made in the 1950s and 1960s with low energy efficiency (mn)	3

* Calculated. XNB (13 Jun 1985), 37-38.

PETROLEUM DEVELOPMENTS, 1985

Daqing—The first production wells are to be drilled at the Chaoyanggou oil pool in Zhaozhou, Zhaoyuan, and eastern Zhaodong County, Heilongjiang province. Reserves have been verified at 120 million tons, and the annual output of crude is expected to attain 1.5 million tons in 1985. The new oil pool is around Daqing. XNB (1 Jul 1985), 75.

Exports to Turkey—The first oil tanker from China arrived in Istanbul 12 September 1985. The PRC plans to deliver 503,000 tons of crude to Turkey in 1985. FBIS-CHI 178 (13 Sep 1985), G3.

Zhujiang Estuary—A well with daily output of 2,000 tons of crude has been drilled in Nan Hai of the Zhujiang Estuary Basin. Of seven wells drilled over the last two years in the 147,000 km^2 area, yields have ranged from 411 to 2,300 cubic meters per day. The Jiangxi 24-3-2 well drilled by Philips produced 2,345 cubic meters daily. Four oil-bearing structures (Wechang 19-1, Huizhou 33-1, Jiangxi 24-3 and Huizhou 21-1) have been located. It is believed that the oil and gas zone covers about 6,000 km^2. There are probably a total of 26 oil-bearing

continued . . .

PETROLEUM DEVELOPMENTS, 1985 (continued)

structures in seven belts. Of eight structures bored, three are believed to have commercial possibilities. The zone is 160-180 km away from Hong Kong and about 300 km from Guangzhou. FBIS-CHI 190 (1 Oct 1985), P1/2.

Equipment Deal—Heilongjiang province has awarded a $105 (HK) million order for oilfield equipment to Dyer Equipment Inc. of Alberta, Canada. *South China Morning Post* (7 Oct 1985), business, 5.

Traps—There are 400-600 possible trap structures in the 50 percent of the shelf which has been surveyed. It may require 100 wells at $8-$10 million each to determine the potential of the shelf. Drilling costs were expected to exceed $500 million by 1985, and the first 100 wells should have been drilled in the Pearl River Basin by the end of 1987. Drilling costs may reach $1-$1.5 billion by 1990 if oil is discovered, and then could total $20-$30 billion during the 1990s. Committee on Foreign Affairs, US House of Representatives, *United States-China Relations* (1984), 136-37.

Oil Refinery—China is planning a joint-venture oil refinery in the Meizhou Bay region, Fujian. First Pacific Finance Ltd., a Hong Kong bank controlled by Indonesian Chinese interests, is advising project investors. If the refinery is built, it will require $500 million and be the third largest joint venture in China. *Asian Wall Street Journal Weekly* (15 Jul 1985), 7.

Third Yellow Sea Well—Chevron-Texaco Orient Co. and the China National Offshore Oil Corp. began a third exploratory well in the South Yellow Sea 250 km north of Shanghai 16 August 1985. The Changzhou 24-1-1 well is to be 4,000 meters. No oil or gas of commercial value has been found in the South Yellow Sea, but prospects are considered good by Chinese geologists. Cluff Oil Ltd. of Britain will start drilling there early in 1986. FBIS-CHI 160 (19 Aug 1985), B2.

Areas Opened to Foreign Oil Exploration—The China National Oil Development Corp. (CNODC) has opened Jiangsu, Zhejiang, Anhui, Fujian, Hunan, Jiangxi, Yunnan, Guizhou, Guangdong and the Guangxi Zhuang Autonomous Region to foreign companies for onshore oil exploration. The provinces cover 1.83 billion km^2. Oil-bearing sedimentary structures involve some 1 million km^2. Negotiations are being conducted with about 20 foreign oil companies. *Beijing Review*, 18 (6 May 1985), 29.

Daqing—A petroleum reserve estimated at 100 million tons was found at Daqing in the northern Songhua-Liaohe River Basin of Heilongjiang province in 1984. It was the largest discovery since Daqing started operations in 1960. Daqing produced 53.5 million tons of crude in 1984, half of China's output. XNB (8 Jan 1985), 6.

Nantou—Mutual Oil of America has signed an agreement worth about $450 million to develop four projects on the Nantou Peninsula to assist offshore oil and gas development in the South China Sea. They involve the construction of an oil refinery with a capacity of 3 million tons a year; two to four deep-water berths for 50,000-ton ships; an international information center; and a 47-km railway. New York *Times* (17 May 1985), 33.

Shengli—Oil production at the Shengli field reached 23.01 million tons in 1984, up 4.64 million tons from 1983. *Beijing Review*, 30 (29 Jul 1985), 21.

Gas and Oil Exploration and Exploitation—The Shengli field may become China's second Daqing by 1989. New oil reserves have been found around Daqing. More discoveries were made in the Junggar Basin and Karamay fields in Xinjiang. Since 1956 Karamay oil has come from the earliest rock system of the Mesozoic Era, but digital seismic prospecting has proved that the Triassic limestone system has even larger reserves.

Fifteen producing wells have been drilled in the Erlian basin bordering Mongolia since 1979. North of Xilin Hot four oil-bearing structures have been located. Large-scale exploration is under way in the Taklimakan, China's largest desert.

Oil and gas bearing structures have been found in the sedimentary basins of the Bohai, Yellow and Yingge seas, the mouth of the Pearl River and Beibu Bay in the South China Sea. Since 1979, when China began her open door policy, joint efforts with foreign firms

continued . . .

PETROLEUM DEVELOPMENTS, 1985 (continued)

have located 300 reserve structures in her coastal waters. Of 49 wells drilled, 17 have struck oil and gas.

China has signed 23 joint offshore exploration contracts with companies from the United States, Britain, Japan, France, Spain, Italy, Canada, Australia and Brazil. Five of the "big seven" oil corporations—Exxon, Texaco, Chevron, BP and Shell—have such contracts.

Before 1979 China had done some surveying on her continental shelf. An experimental platform had been located in the Bohai Sea.

The first offshore oilfield, the Chengbei, jointly explored with Japan, is beginning production at an annual rate of 400,000 tons. The two countries have sunk 25 wells in the Bohai Sea in the past four years, 15 of which struck oil. Two wells in a sunken limestone stratum are especially high-yield.

In Beibu Bay, China and France's Total Company discovered another rich field. All four wells drilled are heavy yielders. This resulted in an agreement signed in May, 1984 to begin experimental production in 1986 at an annual output of 700,000 tons.

The Atlantic Richfield Company and Santa Fe Minerals (Asia) Inc. of the United States are China's partners in exploration in the Yingge Sea. Two high-yield gas wells have been brought in, one at 1.2 million and the other at 1.83 million cubic meters daily. These will ease south China's energy shortage.

In September, 1984 Esso China Inc. and Shell China Ltd. struck gas near the mouth of the Pearl River with a single well that yields 156,000 tons a year. The field is rich in oil and gas.

New discoveries have been made in the South Yellow Sea. Nine test wells drilled in the past produced nothing. But in September 1984 the first well of the BP group struck rich oil-bearing structures. *China Reconstructs*, XXXIV, 5 (May 1985), 17-18.

Costs of Oil Search—Oil companies spend an estimated $500,000 a day in China to buy equipment and goods and to pay staff and for services. It can cost as much as $750 to install a telephone, and a rig worker is paid about $800 a month. Workers at foreign enterprises in China may earn as little as $50-$100 a month. Western firms apparently plan to spend $1-$2 billion on oil exploration in the next few years. *Asian Wall Street Journal Weekly* (11 Feb 1985), 23.

Mobile Rigs—Dreco Energy Services Ltd. of Edmonton, Alberta will supply China with $6.3 million in oil rigs by June, 1985. The China National Machinery Import & Export Corp. will receive five mobile rigs. *Asian Wall Street Journal Weekly* (21 Jan 1985), 4.

Xinjiang—Two exploratory wells have started producing in a new field in the Junggar Basin of Xinjiang. One is pumping 350 barrels a day, and two other wells are being drilled there for gas. FBIS-CHI 114 (13 Jun 1985), T2.

Statoil—The Norwegian State Oil Company (Statoil) will buy 50 percent of the license of a British oil company for drilling in the Yellow Sea. Statoil will invest 60 million krones ($6 million) annually for four years. FBIS-CHI 127 (2 Jul 1985), G2.

Investment—According to Chinese statistics, direct foreign investment was approximately $1.3 billion in 1984. Over one-third went to offshore oil development. US Department of State, *Current Policy No. 725* (Jul 1985), 2.

Undersea Drilling Equipment—Vetco Southeast Asia Ltd., a unit of Combustion Engineering Inc., and Dalong Machinery Works of Shanghai will make undersea drilling equipment under a new joint venture. *Asian Wall Street Journal Weekly* (4 Mar 1985), 11.

Paraffin Wax—The China Petrochem Corp. International and the Hong Kong-based Lithcon Petroleum Ltd. have agreed to a joint venture to market Chinese paraffin wax in the US. The PRC produces about 880,000 tons of paraffin wax yearly. *Asian Wall Street Journal Weekly* (1 Apr 1985), 6.

Hainan Island—China will sign a contract with an Australian consortium led by CSR Orient Oil PTE Ltd. to explore for oil on Hainan Island. Until this contract, the PRC has allowed foreign companies to develop offshore oil and gas only. New York *Times* (28 May 1985), 38.

continued . . .

PETROLEUM DEVELOPMENTS, 1985 (continued)

Pipeline Wax—Oil deliveries have been interrupted by wax clogging the pipeline between Dandong city, Liaoning and Sinuiju city, North Korea. Chinese workers were able to clear the pipeline in September, 1984. FBIS-CHI 43 (5 Mar 1985), D4.

Changzhou 6-2—Drilling began in June, 1985 on the second exploratory oil well sunk in the South China Sea by a Chinese corporation, British Petroleum Development Ltd., and four other foreign companies. The Changzhou 6-2 is 300 km north of Shanghai, and 8.5 km from the first well drilled by BP in 1984. A small quantity of oil was found at the first well. FBIS-CHI 123 (26 Jun 1985), A3.

Oil Exports—China's exports of petroleum and products reached a record 30.8 million tons in 1984, a 40-percent increase over exports in 1983. Oil and oil products earned 25 percent of China's export-generated foreign exchange. *Asian Wall Street Journal Weekly* (11 Feb 1986), 12. The exports provided $4.2 billion in foreign exchange in 1983 and about $5 billion in 1984. *Asian Wall Street Journal Weekly* (25 Feb 1985), 16.

British Petroleum—The ninth British Petroleum well in the South China Sea has failed to find oil or gas. New York *Times* (20 Feb 1985), 47.

Bohai—Japan's Nitchu Oil Exploration Company will begin production at Bohai Bay in 1987, and it expects output to peak between 1990 and 2000. It is believed that 260 million barrels of crude can be extracted from the Bay. FBIS-CHI 59 (27 Mar 1985), K21.

Foreign Cooperation—Some 1.83 million km^2 in Jiangsu, Anhui, Zhejiang, Jiangxi, Hunan, Fujian, Guangdong, Guizhou, and Yunnan provinces and the Guangxi Zhuang Autonomous Region are open for cooperation with foreign oil companies. There are 136 sedimentary basins covering 356,000 km^2 in these areas. Seven cover more than 10,000 km^2. *China Daily* (31 Mar 1985), 1.

Offshore Estimates—A number of estimates have been made for oil reserves beneath China's vast coastal waters. More data is available for the Bohai Bay area than for others because it has been worked for several years by the Chinese, Japanese, and French.

The Chengei field in Bohai will probably produce 13,000 barrels of oil per day (bopd) with estimates of 15 million metric tons (m.t.) recoverable reserves. The Japanese, who operate a joint venture in five Bohai concession areas, have estimated Bohai reserves as high as 75 billion bbls. Based on his work in the 1960s, A.A. Meyerhoff estimated Bohai reserves at 5.6 billion bbls (747 million m.t.). Meyerhoff's estimates for other offshore areas were:

—South China Sea (including the Pearl River Basin), 8.03 billion barrels (1.1 billion m.t.);
—Yellow Sea, 5.6 billion barrels (747 million m.t.);
—East China Sea, 12.84 billion barrels (1.7 billion m.t.).

Japanese estimates for the East China Sea range as high as 112 billion barrels. Meyerhoff's total equals 32.07 billion barrels (4.3 billion m.t.). Jan-Olaf Willums of Norway estimated China's "recoverable" offshore reserves at 20 to 60 billion barrels, with 30 billion barrels (4.1 billion m.t.) a "conservative estimate." This is in line with estimates from the most recent data developed by foreign firms.

Based on the extensive seismic surveys conducted offshore China in 1980, the Vice Minister of petroleum in 1982, Zhang Wenben, claimed that the Pearl River Basin held reserves of "as much as 30 billion m.t." (or over 200 billion barrels). In comparison, the major onshore field, Daqing, has recoverable reserves of 1.7 billion m.t.

Despite these mostly high estimates of offshore reserves, the record for offshore exploration at the end of 1984—after more than $1.5 billion investment by foreign firms—is thin and expectations for large easy finds are declining. In Bohai, there have been 9 discoveries since 1980 when drilling began (50-percent success rate). However, the geologic structure of this area may well mean that these are small isolated pockets of oil, so that only a few wells may be developed commercially.

In the Pearl River Basin, clearly the centerpiece of China's offshore program, the results have been uninspiring. An Esso drill site has produced a possible commercial find, measured

continued . . .

PETROLEUM DEVELOPMENTS, 1985 (continued)

at 3,200 bopd unrestricted flow which was followed by a dry hole in delineation drilling. More recently, a consortium of Agip, Chevron, and Texaco announced a discovery in the South China Sea, which has tested at 2,589 bopd. A Phillips-Pecten strike may actually test close to 7,000 bopd.

In the Tonkin Gulf, activity has produced a sizable gas find by ARCO, although potential development will involve very expensive projects. A French firm, Total Chine, after drilling 14 exploratory wells with marginal success, plans commercial development for only one well that tested at 3,000 to 10,200 bopd. The field reportedly is located in an area contested by Vietnam.

Under the existing contracts for the 12 concession areas in the Pearl River Basin, companies have committed to drilling at least 50 wells. So far, 19 wells have been drilled with three possible commercial discoveries. China recently announced that a second round of offshore concession areas in the Pearl River Basin would be offered soon. So far, 27 foreign firms have expressed interest in participating, and the terms may be less burdensome, as China may no longer require a $1 million fee for participation. Based on seismic data, however, the prospects for the new areas are no better or worse than the first round. Contracts for the second round are not likely to be signed before the end of 1985.

The early exploration results, particularly in the Pearl River Basin, have been mixed. If these results continue, the eventual contribution of offshore resources may fall short of the early expectations. Committee on Energy and Commerce, US House of Representatives, *China's Economic Development and US Trade Interests* (1985), 21-22.

Drop in Production Increases—According to the National Council for US-China Trade, the annual growth rate of oil production has dropped from 20 percent during 1970 to 1975 to near 1 percent during 1980 to 1984. The annual change in the production of gas has fallen from 25 percent during 1970 to 1975 to -5 percent during 1980 to 1984. *Wall Street Journal* (27 Feb 1985), 38.

Fields—The *China Business Review*, 12, 1 (Jan-Feb 1985), 19-24, surveys oil and gas fields in China in detail.

Japanese Contract—The China National Offshore Oil Corp. signed a contract 8 November 1985 with three Japanese companies (Japan Petroleum Exploration Co., Huanan Oil Development co., and Nippon Mining Co.) for the joint exploration of a 5,100-km^2 area in the South China Sea. This is the first contract with foreign firms in the second round of bidding. The first round began in 1982, and 23 contracts were signed with 31 foreign companies. The second round started in November, 1984. FBIS-CHI 218 (12 Nov 1985), D2/3.

Amoco and Shell-Exxon Contracts—Amoco Orient Petroleum has signed a contract after three years of negotiations to explore for oil in the Pearl River estuary. Also in November, 1985, Royal Dutch/Shell announced that it and Exxon of the US had signed a contract with the China National Offshore Oil Corp. to look for oil in the Pearl River. The two companies will bear 50 percent of the cost. This is the second contract in the second round of bidding for offshore oil exploration rights. New York *Times* (13 Nov 1985), 3; (18 Nov 1985), 32.

Xinjiang—A new oilfield has been located at Mogui, north of the Zhunger Basin, which produces 129 tons of oil per day. Two additional wells have been found producing over 30 and 140 tons each day. FBIS-CHI 68 (9 Apr 1985), T3.

Chaheji and Banqiao—China and Canada will cooperate to improve planning and operation of the Chaheji and Banqiao oilfields, both located near Beijing. Canada will also train 42 specialists under the $6.3 million (Canadian, $4.8 million US) contract. FBIS-CHI 63 (2 Apr 1985), J2.

continued . . .

PETROLEUM DEVELOPMENTS, 1985 (continued)

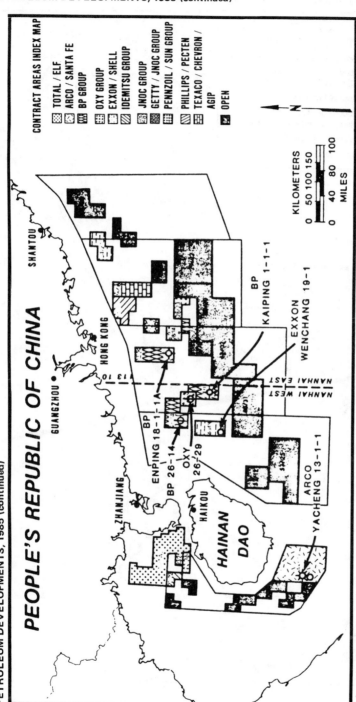

China has signed 23 contracts with 32 oil companies from 12 nations on the joint exploration and exploitation of its offshore oil. One hundred exploratory and 59 producing wells have been drilled in the Bohai Sea, South Yellow Sea Basin, the Zhujiang (Pearl) River Estuary Basin of the South China Sea, the Beibu Gulf, and the Yingge Sea. Oil and gas have been found in 21 formations. *Beijing Review*, 38 (23 Sep 1985), 29.

continued . . .

PETROLEUM DEVELOPMENTS, 1985 (continued)

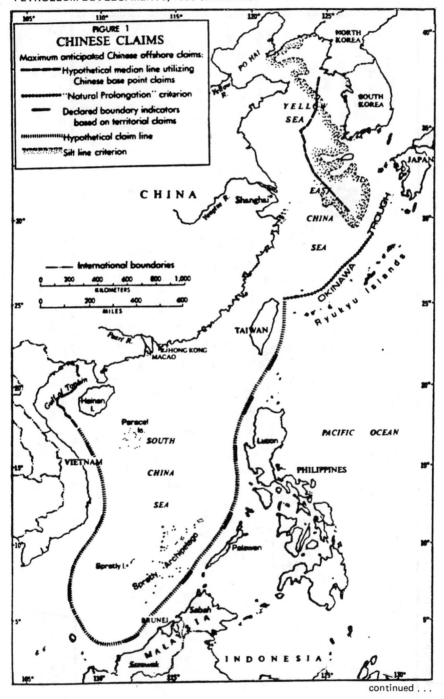

FIGURE 1

CHINESE CLAIMS

Maximum anticipated Chinese offshore claims:

━ ━ ━ Hypothetical median line utilizing Chinese base point claims

••••••••••• "Natural Prolongation" criterion

━━━ Declared boundary indicators based on territorial claims

⊞⊞⊞⊞⊞ Hypothetical claim line

▚▚▚▚▚ Silt line criterion

continued . . .

PETROLEUM DEVELOPMENTS, 1985 (continued)

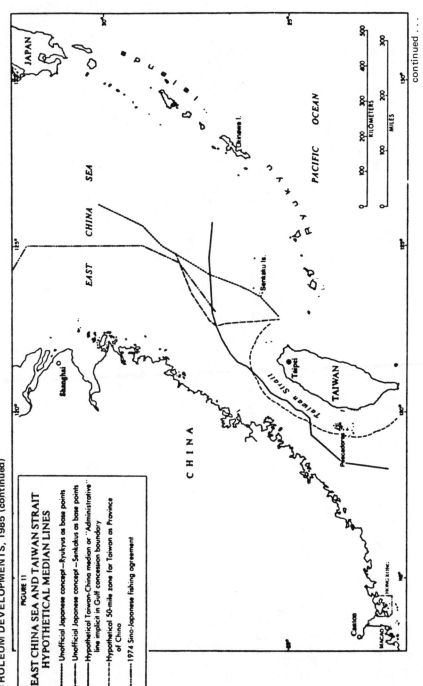

PETROLEUM DEVELOPMENTS, 1985 (continued)

FIGURE 11
EAST CHINA SEA AND TAIWAN STRAIT
HYPOTHETICAL MEDIAN LINES

——————— Unofficial Japanese concept—Ryukyus as base points

——————— Unofficial Japanese concept—Senkakus as base points

————— Hypothetical Taiwan-China median or "Administrative"
line implicit in Gulf concession boundary

– – – – – Hypothetical 50-mile zone for Taiwan as Province
of China

————→ 1974 Sino-Japanese fishing agreement

continued . . . .

PETROLEUM DEVELOPMENTS, 1985 (continued)

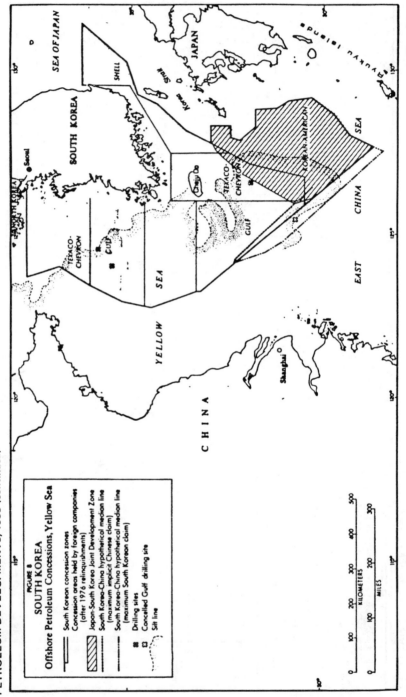

FIGURE 8
SOUTH KOREA
Offshore Petroleum Concessions, Yellow Sea

South Korean concession zones
Concession areas held by foreign companies
(after 1976 relinquishments)
Japan-South Korea Joint Development Zone
South Korea-China hypothetical median line
(maximum implicit Chinese claim)
South Korea-China hypothetical median line
(maximum South Korean claim)
Drilling sites
Cancelled Gulf drilling site
Silt line

PETROLEUM DEVELOPMENTS, 1985 (continued)

continued . . .

PETROLEUM DEVELOPMENTS, 1985 (continued)

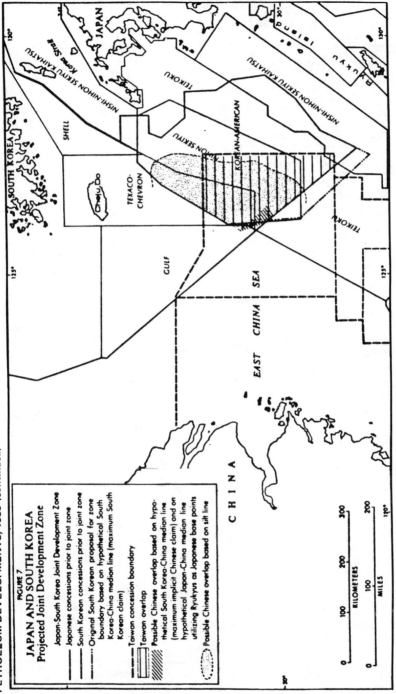

FIGURE 7

JAPAN AND SOUTH KOREA
Projected Joint Development Zone

Japan-South Korea Joint Development Zone

Japanese concessions prior to joint zone

South Korean concessions prior to joint zone

Original South Korean proposal for zone boundary based on hypothetical South Korea-China median line (maximum South Korean claim)

Taiwan concession boundary

Taiwan overlap

Possible Chinese overlap based on hypothetical South Korea-China median line (maximum implicit Chinese claim) and on hypothetical Japan-China median line utilizing Ryukyus as Japanese base points

Possible Chinese overlap based on silt line

continued . . . .

PETROLEUM DEVELOPMENTS, 1985 (continued)

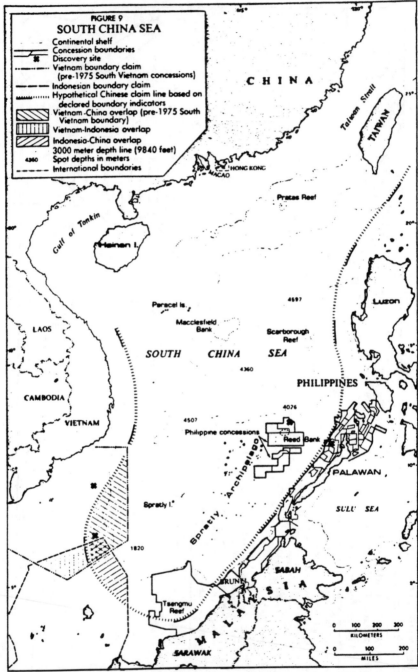

FIGURE 9
SOUTH CHINA SEA

Committee on Energy and Commerce, US House of Representatives, *China's Economic Development and US Trade Interests* (1985), 19, 24-27, 65.

PRC: CRUDE OIL PRODUCTION AND OIL EXPORTS (thousand b/d)

	1975	1976	1977	1978	1979	1980	1981	1982	1983	1984
Production	1,542	1,736	1,874	2,082	2,123	2,113	2,024	2,044	2,120	2,280
Exports [a]	194	170	182	226	267	265	277	304	300	439
Japan	157	121	132	150	147	157	178	179	185 [b]	235
Brazil	0	0	0	1	16	20	20	20	35	50
Romania	5	9	10	20	20	20	18	17	NA	NA
United States	0	0	0	0	11	2	0	18	14	44
Philippines	8	11	17	23	20	20	10	7	15	30 [b]
Other	24	29	23	32	53	46	51	63	NA	NA

[a] Excludes petroleum products.
[b] Estimated.

CIA, *International Energy Statistical Review* (26 Nov 1985), 24.

ANNUAL RATE OF GROWTH OF OIL AND GAS OUTPUT (percent)

	Oil	Gas
1970-1975	20	25
1980-1984	1	-5

Asian Wall Street Journal Weekly (25 Feb 1985), 16.

GAS DEVELOPMENTS, 1985

Shanghai Gas Works—The largest gas works in China will be constructed in Shanghai. The Shidongkou Gas Works will produce 3 million m³ per day. The city currently produces 3.6 million m³ each day. A second project, the Pudong Gas Works, with a capacity of 2 million m³ per day, will be ready by 1986. The Shanghai Coking Works is being expanded to add another 2 million m³ of daily capacity. XNB (19 Jan 1985), 48-49.

Gas Facilities—Gas facilities are provided in 98 cities, saving about 32 million tons of coal annually. Eighty percent of China's urban population still uses coal for heat and food preparation. By 1990 more than 40 percent of the urban population will be able to cook with gas. *Beijing Review*, 31 (5 Aug 1985), 9.

Shengli-Huangdao Pipeline—Novacorp International Consulting Ltd. has signed a second contract for design, automation, construction, and start-up assistance for a 155-mile oil pipeline from the Shengli field to Huangdao, Shandong. The pipeline will transport 22 million tons of waxy crude annually. *Asian Wall Street Journal Weekly* (25 Mar 1985), 4.

Henan Pipelines—A 148-km gas pipeline has started operations between the Zhongyuan oil field and Kaifeng city. It has a capacity of 110 million m³ annually. A 248-km pipeline now runs between the Zhongyuan field and Luoyang city. Its annual capacity is 2 million tons of oil. XNB (18 Feb 1985), 31.

Rolls Deal—Rolls Royce will provide 56 million yuan (16 million pounds Sterling) worth of gas turbine engines for aircraft and ships and for generating electricity at the southern Xinjiang oilfield. In 1984 the Daqing oilfield obtained similar engines. FBIS-CHI 74 (17 Apr 1985), G4.

Gas Pipeline—Arco-China Inc. and Santa Fe Minerals (Asia) Inc. signed an agreement in September, 1985 with the China National Offshore Oil Corp. to build a $500 million gas distribution network. The natural gas will move from the Yacheng field through an undersea pipeline to the south coast of Hainan Island. The line has a daily capacity of 500 million cubic feet. New York *Times* (1 Oct 1985), 36.

THE USE OF GAS BY URBAN RESIDENTS

1983 *

Cities with gas facilities	98
Percentage of total	33
Number of people using gas (mn)	21

1990 Plan

Percentage of people using gas in China's 50 major cities	60+
Percentage of people using gas in Beijing, Tianjin, and Shanghai	70

2000 Plan

Percentage of urban population using gas	70
Percentage of cities and medium-sized towns in the countryside having gas facilities	c. 100

*Based on a national survey.
China Daily (8 Mar 1985), 4.

COAL DEVELOPMENTS, 1985

Mechanization—By 1990 the percentage of mechanization will increase from 44 to 60 percent. New mines will add a capacity of 44.8 million tons. Fully mechanized, open-cast coal mines will be emphasized. They currently account for only 4-5 percent of total output. XNB (26 Jun 1985), 24-26.

continued . . .

COAL DEVELOPMENTS, 1985 (continued)

Antaibao—An agreement was finally signed in June, 1985 to develop the Antaibao coal mine in Shanxi. It will be the first Chinese mine developed with foreign cooperation. Production is to reach 15.3 million tons, with 8 million for Japan. Operations are to start in September, 1987. Occidental will hold 25 percent of the $650-million venture, the China National Coal Development Corp. will own 50 percent, and the Bank of China Trust and Consultancy Co. will have the remaining 25 percent of the shares. London *Financial Times* (17 Jul 1985), 10.

Xinglongzhuang Coal-Dressing Plant—This coal-dressing plant with a capacity of 3 million tons of raw coal annually went into operation in the Yanzhou field in July, 1985. Construction took from January, 1982 to September, 1984. The Yanzhou coal field in Shandong has four pits with a combined output of 5.25 million tons a year. Three more are under construction with a total annual capacity of 7.6 million tons. The field should produce over 30 million tons of coal and wash 24 million tons each year by the end of the century. XNB (1 Aug 1985), 59-60.

Chengzhuang and Changcun—The Federal Republic of Germany will provide China with DM4.5 million in technical assistance to conduct feasibility studies and design work of the Chengzhuang and Changcun coal mines in Shanxi province. Each mine will produce 4 million tons of coal annually. The World Bank has provided a $126 million loan for Changcun. XNB (7 Feb 1985), 23; *Beijing Review*, 30 (29 Jul 1985), 31.

Shanxi—China will encourage peasants to develop local coal mines in Shanxi province. The area has a verified reserve of 500 billion tons, or nearly 70 percent of China's total. Production is to increase over 400 million tons during the 7th Five Year Plan (1986-90), or about half of the national increase. Two-thirds of the growth in Shanxi's output will come from small mines. XNB (13 Feb 1985), 5-6.

Reserves—The PRC verified 10.2 billion tons of coal reserves in 1984. Coal reserves now total over 780 billion tons. *Guangming Ribao* (22 Jan 1985).

World Bank Project—The World Bank will provide $126 million for a mechanized underground coal mine in Shanxi. Output will be about 4.5 million tons of coal annually. The 20-year loan is at a variable rate linked to the World Bank's borrowing, currently 9.29 percent. The entire project will cost some $357 million. *Asian Wall Street Journal Weekly* (25 Mar 1985), 4.

Coal Capacity Expanded—China developed or expanded 21 major coal mines in 1984, adding over 17.9 million tons of coal capacity. New or expanded mines with capacities over 1 million tons include the second phase of the Pingdingshan No. 8 mine, Henan; the open-cut mine at Yiminhe, Inner Mongolia; the Xiaoqing mine of the Tiefa coal field, Liaoning province; the Tucheng mine, Guizhou province. XNB (2 Jan 1985), 18.

New Coalfields—Many new coalfields with reserves exceeding 100 million tons were discovered in 1984. Medium- and small-sized fields included Guangdong's Luolongyan, Hunan's Limin and Yongfeng, Hubei's Hengshi, Jiangxi's Shangrao, Fujian's Longyan and Fuling, and Guangxi's Dawan and Dali. FBIS-CHI 19 (29 Jan 1985), K22.

Xinjiang—A 147-meter-thick coal seam, the thickest in the PRC, has been found at the Shaerbu coal field in Xinjiang, about 750 km southwest of Urumqi. Estimated reserves of low-sulphur steam coal total 30 billion tons. FBIS-CHI 102 (28 May 1985), T2.

Cost of New Capacities—Building one ton of coal capacity costs an average of 175 yuan. *Beijing Review*, 21 (27 May 1985), 29.

Shanxi Coal Exports—Shanxi province will be allowed for the first time to export 600,000 tons of coal in 1985. It produced 187 million tons of coal in 1984, or about 25 percent of the national total. FBIS-CHI 133 (11 Jul 1985), R3.

Xingantai—The USSR will assist the Chinese in raising the output of the Xingantai coal mine in Heilongjiang province to 5 million tons a year. The Soviets helped develop the mine in the 1950s, bringing the design capacity to 1.5 million tons of crude coal and 1.5 million tons of

continued . . .

COAL DEVELOPMENTS, 1985 (continued)

washed coal annually. The mine's output reached 3.15 million tons of coal in 1984, and it should amount to 3.5 million in 1985. The Soviets will modernize two sets of pitshaft lifting equipment for excavation and monitoring. FBIS-CHI 137 (17 Jul 1985), C1.

Small Coal Mines—China has over 16,000 small coal mines. During the past few years, the output of small mines has grown at an annual average rate exceeding 13 percent, from 110 million tons in 1980 to 160 million in 1983. The coal supplied by these mines to rural areas has increased from 40 million to 102 million tons during this period. *Beijing Review*, 21 (27 May 1985), 25.

Hebei Coal-Dressing Plant—The Dongpang Coal-Dressing Plant has started production at Shijiazhuang, Hebei. Its annual capacity is 1.8 million tons of dressed coal for industries in north China. FBIS-CHI 106 (3 Jun 1985), R1.

Pingshuo—Occidental Petroleum signed a contract with China 29 June 1985 to develop the Pingshuo Antaibao open-cast coal mine. The designed annual capacity of the mine will be 15.33 million tons. It is the largest coal joint venture ever undertaken by China. The venture will run 30 years. Total investment amounts to $650 million. Operations should begin in September, 1987. FBIS-CHI 126 (1 Jul 1985), B1/2.

Heilongjiang—A coal field has been discovered in western Heihe of Heilongjiang province. The field covers 400 km^2 and is suitable for open-cast mining. XNB (22 Apr 1985), 30-31.

Coal Shortage—Total coal consumption in the 14 coastal cities and four Special Economic Zones open to foreign investment was 44.14 million tons in 1984. The coal shortage is estimated to amount to 14.11 million tons in 1985 and 18 million tons annually for the next five years. XNB (25 Apr 1985), 60-61.

Gujiao Mine—A coal mine is being developed in the Gujiao mining area of Shanxi province. The shafts will increase production there to 12.5 million tons annually. Japanese loans will amount to $200 million of the $322 million cost of development. The mine will produce 4 million tons of raw coal a year when fully operational in 1992. FBIS-CHI 187 (26 Sep 1985), D3.

Datong Mine—The Datong coal mine in Shanxi province produced 30.24 million tons of raw coal by 24 December 1985. This is the largest coal enterprise in the PRC. FBIS-CHI 248 (26 Dec 1985), K1/2.

Construction—China will speed the construction of 31 large coal mines during the next five years. Their planned capacity will be 74.1 million tons annually. Coal accounts for 70 percent of China's energy supply, but production has been short about 20 million tons for the past several years. Nineteen coal mines began operation during 1981-85, adding 29.64 million tons of capacity. A total of $1.51 billion in foreign funds was used for 12 underground and open-pit mines during the Sixth Five Year Plan. FBIS-CHI 249 (27 Dec 1985), K13/14.

NUCLEAR POWER DEVELOPMENTS, 1985

Changshan—A 3,000-MW nuclear power plant will be built at Changshan, Jiangsu. It will have four 900-MW reactors, two of which will be installed by 1990.

Qinshan—Mitsubishi Heavy Industry Corp. will provide the major equipment for the reactor-pressure vessel at the Qinshan, Zhejiang nuclear power plant. KSB of the Federal Republic of Germany will deliver the main coolant pump, and tubes for the steam generator will be supplied by Sweden. Qinshan is the site of China's first nuclear plant. *Asian Wall Street Journal Weekly* (4 Feb 1985), 7. It is a 300-MW plant. *Beijing Review*, 5 (4 Feb 1985), 8.

Daya Bay—The 1,800-MW nuclear power plant under construction at Daya Bay near Hong Kong will not reprocess spent fuel for at least 10 years. The PRC signed an agreement January 18 with China Light & Power Co. of Hong Kong to build the $3.5-billion plant. Some

continued . . .

NUCLEAR POWER DEVELOPMENTS, 1985 (continued)

70 percent of its electricity will go to Hong Kong. Completion is scheduled for 1991. *Asian Wall Street Journal Weekly* (21 Jan 1985), 4.

Brazil—The nuclear cooperation agreement between the PRC and Brazil of October, 1984 appears in *Folha de Sao Paulo* (12 Oct 1984), 7, and the translation in Committee on Energy and Commerce, US House of Representatives, *China's Economic Development and US Trade Interests* (1985), 94-94.

Progress Report—The progress of five nuclear projects in China (Qinshan/728, Sunan, Liaoning, Jinshanwei, Daya Bay) is reported in the *China Business Review*, 12, 4 (Jul-Aug 1985), 26-27.

Japan—The PRC and Japan planned to sign an agreement in July, 1985 concerning cooperation and the peaceful use of nuclear energy. Japanese companies will compete to help construct 10 plants in China by the year 2000. New York *Times* (7 Jul 1985), 6.

Daya Deals—China has apparently decided to buy two 900-MW nuclear reactors from Framatone for at least $1.3 billion. It has also agreed to purchase two 985-MW turbine generators worth $360 million from the GE Corp. of Britain and other equipment for the Daya Bay plant from Electricite de France. The total cost of the facility is estimated at $3.5 billion. New York *Times* (3 Dec 1985), 35; (16 Dec 1985), 6; (3 Jan 1986), 23.

Heat Supply Nuclear Reactor—Construction of the first low-temperature nuclear heat supply reactor began in November, 1985 at the Institute of Nuclear Technology at Qinghua University. This 5,000-kW reactor will be used for heating and refrigeration. Construction of 30 4,000-kW reactors would save over 10 million tons of coal annuall. Reactors are planned for Harbin and Shenyang. FBIS-CHI 234 (5 Dec 1985), K21/22.

US Agreement—The US and the PRC initialed an agreement for nuclear cooperation 30 April 1984, and not having been rejected by Congress before December 1985, it will take effect. The agreement permits the transfer of low enriched uranium (non-weapons-grade material) for power reactors for peaceful purposes. Potential US sales may range from $3-$7 billion. It will take at least 10 years before a power reactor could be operational. US General Accounting Office, *Nuclear Agreement: Cooperation Between the United States and the People's Republic of China* (1985).

ELECTRICAL POWER DEVELOPMENTS, 1985

Urumqi—A 50-MW unit was installed at the Hongyanchi Power Station in Urumqi, Xinjiang during the summer of 1985. XNB (5 Jul 1985), 49.

Power Shortages—Winter power shortages were partly responsible for the fall in electrical output from 351 billion kWh in 1983 to 320 in 1984. To achieve an annual rate of growth of 11 percent in the GNP, as expected for 1985-1990, the production of electricity must increase an estimated 11 percent per year and the output of coal about 7 percent. Investment in thermal power plants grew 35 percent in 1984 over the previous year. Requiring three years to build, they are favored over large hydropower plants, which take 10-12 years. Committee on Energy and Commerce, US House of Representatives, *China's Economic Development and US Trade Interests* (1985), 32. On the other hand, China was able to sustain an annual rate of industrial growth of 8 percent from 1978 to 1983 despite power shortages. David Denny explains this growth by 1) increases in the supply of electrical power to industry; 2) a shift in the industrial output structure from heavy to light industry, which has a value of output per kWh about four times that of heavy industry; and, 3) greater efficiency of electrical power use. See the *China Business Review*, 12, 4 (Jul-Aug 1985), 17. During the coming two years, the PRC intends to import 10,000 MW of thermal power capacity for coastal cities, perhaps worth $2 billion to foreign suppliers. See pp. 17-22.

Northeast—The Northeast—Heilongjiang, Liaoning, and Jilin provinces—has 50 medium and large thermal and hydropower stations, 200 smaller thermal plants, and 1,000 small hydroelectric power stations in rural areas. Capacity added in 1984 totaled 1,300 MW, an increase

continued . . .

ELECTRICAL POWER DEVELOPMENTS, 1985

of 13.4 percent. Three 200-MW generators were installed in 1984 at the Jinzhou Power Plant in southern Liaoning. The facility is under construction, and will eventually have six units. It will supply the Anshan Iron and Steel Complex. The Baishan Hydropower Station, the largest in the Northeast, is being built in the Changbai Mountains. Three 300-MW generators are already in place, and two more will be added. A 149-meter dam on the Sungari River has been completed at the site. A power plant with a capacity of 1,200 MW is located south of Qiqihar in western Heilongjiang. It will supply the Daqing oilfield. There are three large plants south of Harbin which produce power-generating equipment. One makes 300-MW water-turbogenerators, and is developing a 600-MW turbogenerator. A boiler plant and a steam turbine factory also plan to increase production during 1986-90. Half of China's investment in this industry will go to Harbin during the next Five Year Plan. Electrical consumption has been increasing in the Northeast an average of 7 percent a year. *China Reconstructs*, XXXIV, 6 (Jun 1985), 24-27.

Shortages—Power shortages limit Chinese industrial output to about 70 percent of capacity. The PRC invests 18 percent of its total industrial investment in the electrical power industry, resulting in annual growth of 6-7 percent. It is far behind world standards in plant design, thermal efficiencies, and the network transmission. Committee on Foreign Affairs, US House of Representatives, *United States-China Relations* (1984), 142.

Largest Power Station—Construction has begun on China's largest power station in a suburb of Shanghai. Planned capacity is 2.4 million kW. Some 960 million yuan will be invested in construction. Four generators of 300-MW will be installed during the first phase. *Izvestiia* (27 Mar 1985).

Transmission Line—China's longest high-voltage DC power transmission line will carry electricity from the Northwest Grid to northwest China in 1988. The 1,300-km line will run from Xining, Qinghai to Shijiazhuang, Hebei, and it should ease shortages in Tianjin and Beijing. *Beijing Review*, 20 (20 May 1985), 8.

Datong-Fangshan Line—A 500-kV transmission line began operations between Datong, Shanxi and the Fangshan Substation in Beijing 6 October 1985. *Beijing Review*, 51 (23 Dec 1985), 9.

Shaxikou—Kuwait will provide a loan of $30 million to construct the Shaxikou Hydropower Station in Fujian province. Annual output will reach 960 million kWh. The station is to be ready by 1988. *Asian Wall Street Journal Weekly* (14 Jan 1985), 13.

World Bank Loan—The World Bank will provide a $117 million loan to the PRC to develop power transmission in eastern areas. The project will eventually cost $283 million, and include a 680-km 500-kV transmission line between Xuzhou and Shanghai. It will be completed by mid-1988. The Chinese government will contribute $4.4 million and Chinese banks will provide another $151.4 million. The Italian government will finance the rest. The World Bank loan extends for 20 years with a variable interest rate. The current loan rate is 9.29 percent. *China Daily* (26 Feb 1985), 2.

General Electric Deal—The GE Commpany of the US has signed a co-design, co-manufacturing agreement with the Dongfang Electric Corp. of Sichuan. GE's 600-MW steam turbine technology will be transferred, and four units will initially be produced. FBIS-CHI 105 (31 May 1985), B1/2.

Hydropower Plans—By the year 2000 China will build 17 1-million-kW hydropower stations. The Longyangxia, Gezhouba, Ertan, Baishan, and Tianshengqiao stations will be operational. The installed capacity of the stations planned for the three gorges on the Changjiang River will reach 13 million kW. *Beijing Review*, 23 (10 Jun 1985), 29.

Qinghe—A 200-MW unit has been installed at the Qinghe Thermal Power Station in Liaoning province. The unit raises the station's total capacity from 1.1 to 1.3 million kW, and the annual power output from 7.5 to 8.1 billion kWh.

Power Lines—Four power lines totaling 4,680 km are under construction. They run from Shentou to Datong in Shanxi province, and from Beijing to Tianjin. Two others are in northeast China. They are part of 11 500-kV transmission lines to be built in the near future.

continued . . .

ELECTRICAL POWER DEVELOPMENTS, 1985 (continued)

Yunnan—A hydroelectric power station is planned in Yunnan province. Its generating capacity will be 1.5 million kW, and will double the current capacity in Yunnan. Another power station now under construction should eventually bring total capacity in the province to 4 million kW.

Shajiao—Hopewell Power Ltd. of Hong Kong will participate in a joint venture to build the 700-MW Shajiao Thermal Power Plant B in the Shenzhen Special Economic Zone. The venture will involve an investment of 900 million yuan. It will begin operations in 1988 and be operated jointly for 10 years. The Shajiao Plant A is under construction with a designed capacity of 600 MW.

Tongjiezi—Construction of the Tongjiezi Hydroelectric Power Station on the Dadu River in Sichuan province has begun. The station in Leshan city will have a capacity of 600 MW and generate 3.2 billion kWh annually, or 20 percent of Sichuan's current output. Completion is planned for 1993. A 700-MW station was built on the Dadu at Gongzui in 1977.

Shijingshan—The Shijingshan Power Station outside Beijing will be modernized. It will add 600 MW of capacity to the Beijing power grid. FBIS-CHI 209 (29 Oct 1985), RI.

Baishan Reservoir and Stations—The Baishan Reservoir in Fusong, Jingyu and Huadian counties of Jilin province has been completed. Its capacity is 6,812 million cubic meters. Three power units with a capacity of 900 MW are operating at the Baishan Station, and two more with a capacity of 600 MW are planned. XNB (5 Sep 1985), 53-54.

Liaoning Station—Beijing has asked for Japanese technical assistance to build the world's largest dam in Liaoning province. It would have a capacity of 13 million kW, and cost about $8 billion. New York *Times* (12 Apr 1985), 30.

Jilin—The installed capacity of small hydroelectric power stations in Jilin province has grown from 70.4 MW in 1980 to more than 131 MW in 1985. XNB (30 Dec 1985), 12.

Longyang Gorge—The Longyang Hydroelectric Power Station is under construction on the upper reaches of the Yellow River. It will be the second largest station after the Gezhouba project. The concrete dam will be 1,140 meters long and 178 meters high. When completed in 1989, the station will have a capacity of 1.28 million kW. Four hydropower stations already exist on the upper reaches of the Yellow at the Liujia, Yanguo, and Bapan Gorges in Gansu province and the Qingtong Gorge in the Ningxia Hui Autonomous Region. The PRC plans to build 15 hydropower stations on the upper reaches of the Yellow to generate 50 billion kWh a year. XNB (16 Nov 1985), 33-34.

HYDROPOWER STATIONS, 1984 yearend

Small hydropower stations in operation (th) *	78
Capacity (mn kW)	9
Electricity produced (bn kWh)	21.6
Increase over 1983 (percent)	8.41
Hydropower stations built in 1984	1,421
Increase in capacity (th KW)	470

* Each able to generate up to 12,000 kW.

China Daily (28 Feb 1985), 3.

GEZHOUBA WATER CONTROL PROJECT LAYOUT

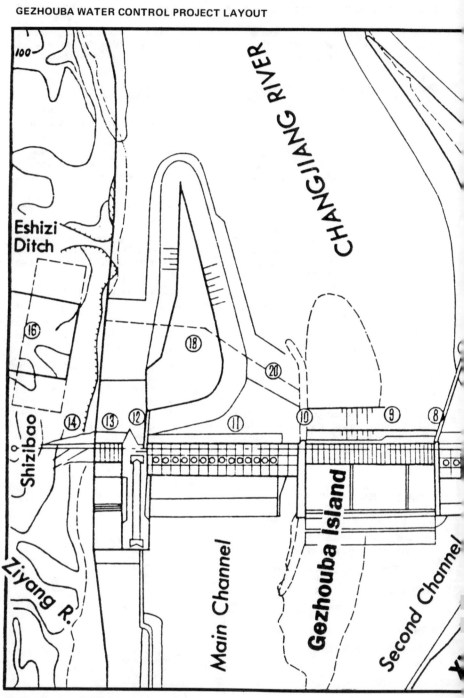

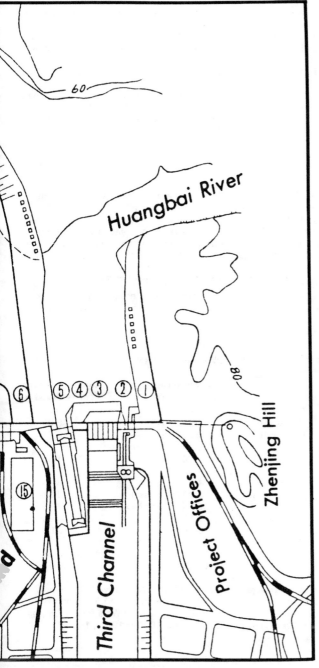

1. Left bank earth and rockfill dam
2. No. 3 ship lock
3. third channel silt-discharge gate
4. Third channel concrete dam section
5. No. 2 ship lock
6. Huangcaoba concrete dam section
7. Second channel power plant
8. Guide wall between power station and spillway
9. Second channel spillway
10. Concrete cofferdam between spillway and main channel power plant
11. Main channel power plant
12. No. 1 ship lock
13. Main channel silt-discharge gate
14. Right bank earth and rockfill dam
15. 220,000-volt switchgear station
16. 550,000-volt switchgear station
17. Third channel silt-diversion dike
18. Main channel silt-diversion dike
19. Silt-control wall
20. Silt-control wall

continued . . .

GEZHOUBA WATER CONTROL PROJECT LAYOUT (continued)

The Gezhouba Dam is situated 2.3 km downstream from Nanjinguan Pass, the mouth of the famous Three Gorges at a bend where the 6,300-km Changjiang (Yangtze) River suddenly turns south and widens from 300 to 2,200 metres. The dam, the first on the Changjiang, is built at the point where two islands once divided the river into three channels, a physical feature which facilitated the construction of the project. The project is divided into two stages. The first, completed at the end of 1980, included a 27-bay spillway, a 6-bay silt discharge gate, two ship locks and a power plant on the second and third channels of the river. The second stage was begun in early 1981 with the damming of the main channel. When completed, it will include a second power plant, another ship lock and another 6-bay silt discharge gate. The two power plants will have a combined generating capacity of 2.72 million kw. The average annual power output will be 14 billion kwh.

SOLAR POWER

Solar-Technical Station—The PRC has opened its first solar-technical station at Lanzhou, Gansu. It wil study the possible uses of solar energy. The center is subordinate to the Gansu branch of the Natural Energy Institute of the Chinese Academy of Sciences The first phase phase of construction includes nine buildings with heat-absorption materials on the roof, a a pump house, monitoring station, library and exhibition hall, and meteorology station. The UN Development Program has provided financing. FBIS-SOV 137 (17 Jul 1985), B2; XNB (24 May 1985), 37.

First Solar Station—China opened its first solar power station in Yuzhong county, Gansu 7 October 1985. Japan's Kyoto Ceramic Company financed the 10-kW installation. Accumulator cells can store electricity for six to seven days for use when the weather is overcast. XNB (8 Oct 1985), 38-39.

THE HONGSHUI RIVER HYDROELECTRIC POWER NETWORK

Station	Location	Installed capacity (mn kW)	Annual generating capacity (bn kWh)
Lubuge	Nanpan R.	0.6	3.06
Tianshengqiao upper dam	Nanpan R.	1.08	5.3
Tianshengqiao lower dam	Nanpan R.	0.88 (first phase)	8.2
		0.44 (second phase)	
Pingban	Hongshui R.	0.36	1.86
Longtan	Hongshui R.	4	18.6
Yantan	Hongshui R.	1.1	8
Dahua	Hongshui R.	0.4 (first phase)	3.6
		0.2 (second phase)	
Bailongtan	Hongshui R.	0.18	0.91
Etan	Hongshui R.	0.56	3.62
Qiaogong	Hongshui R.	0.50	3.15
Datengxia	Qianjiang	1.2	6.58
Total		11.5	62.78

Two headwater reservoirs will be constructed on the Hongshui River to drive 11 hydropower stations along its 1,100-meter drop. The stations will have a capacity of 11.5 million kW, or 46 percent of China's total in 1984. This will generate 62.78 billion kWh annually. *Beijing Review*, 26 (1 Jul 1985), 14, 16; *China Reconstructs*, XXXIV, 10 (Oct 1985), 18-23.

continued . . .

THE HONGSHUI RIVER HYDROELECTRIC POWER NETWORK (continued)

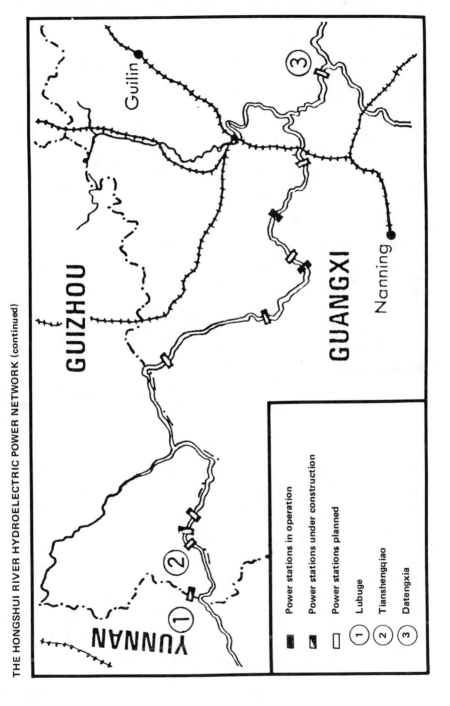

IX INDUSTRIES

IRON AND STEEL INDUSTRY

Shanxi—The three major iron and steel plants in Shanxi province will expand their capacity during the Seventh Five-Year Plan (1986-90) from 1.75 to 3 million tons of steel a year. A tar-processing plant will be built with an annual capacity of 150,000 tons, and a compound fertilizer factory with a designed capacity of 900,000 tons and an aluminum plant with a capacity of 1.5 million tons will be constructed. FBIS-CHI 95 (16 May 1985), K10/11.

Unprofitable Enterprises—In 1982 10,898 industrial enterprises lost a total of 4.2 billion yuan, averaging a loss of 390,000 yuan apiece. In 1983 losses amounted to 2.79 billion yuan. It is estimated that 20-30 percent of Chinese enterprises may never show a profit. Some units are being closed and others merged. Between 1978 and 1982, 339 small iron-smelting factories, or 72.6 percent of the total, merged with other plants. The total deficit in the industry was cut from 630 to 70 million yuan, and the cost per ton of iron decreased from 303 to 239 yuan. *Beijing Review*, 10 (11 Mar 1985), 25-26.

High-Quality Steel—The PRC will produce some 200,000 tons of cold rolled quality steel in 1985, an increase of 54 percent over output in 1984. FBIS-CHI 107 (4 Jun 1985), K12.

Small Steel Mills—In Kunming, Yunnan 22 small steel-rolling mills have been constructed or are being built. Consequently, raw materials are scarce. The Kunming Metallurgical Industrial Company produces about 100,000 tons of rolled steel annually, but as a result of a shortage of billets, output was only 56,000 tons in 1984. Scrap iron and steel are also running short. FBIS-CHI 113 (12 Jun 1985), Q1/2.

Baoshan—The first phase of the Baoshan Steel Mill, located about 50 minutes from the center of Shanghai, will have a production capacity of 3.18 million tons of steel. The capacity will rise to 6.71 million tons with the completion of the second phase. Approximately 10 percent of China's steel will be made at Baoshan. *Liberal Star*, 14, 159 (Japan, 10 Apr 1985), 4-5. Baoshan is to produce some 300,000 tons of iron and steel in 1985. After the first phase is built in September, 1985, annual production of iron and steel will be 3 million tons each and 500,000 tons of seamless steel tubing. The first phase is to cost about 12 billion yuan, and the entire project should run 30-40 billion yuan. *Asian Wall Street Journal Weekly* (1 Apr 1985), 6. Hitachi Zosen Corp. will build two continuous-casting plants at Baoshan by 1989. Each plant will have an annual capacity of 2 million tons of steel plates. The deal is worth 60 billion yen ($4.2 billion). *Asian Wall Street Journal Weekly* (22 Apr 1985), 14. The No. 1 blast furnace started up 15 September 1985. *Beijing Review*, 37 (16 Sep 1985), 30.

Panzhihua—The second phase of the Panzhihua Iron and Steel Complex has started at Chengdu, Sichuan. The $3 billion yuan project is to be ready in 10 years. A 1,350-m^3 blast furnace, a 130-m^2 sintering machine, two large coke ovens, and a continuous casting system will be installed. Annual production capacity for pig iron will reach 2.8 million tons, 2.5 million tons for steel, and 2.16 million tons for rolled steel. The first stage of construction occurred during 1965-74. Output was 2.07 million tons of pig iron, 1.75 million tons of steel, and 860,000 tons of rolled steel in 1984. XNB (12 Jun 1985), 52-53.

Handan—The Handan Iron and Steel Mill is being expanded to produce up to 1.5 million tons of pig iron, 1.1 million tons of steel, and 1 million tons of rolled steel by 1990. The cost of the expansion is 500 million yuan. XNB (9 Apr 1985), 28.

PRC—China has 13 steel plants with an annual capacity exceeding 1 million tons. The Anshan Iron and Steel Company, the largest, produced 7 million tons of steel and 6.43 million tons of pig iron in 1984. Chinese plants make some 1,000 types of special steel and rolled steel of 20,000 specifications. FBIS-CHI 23 (4 Feb 1985), K28. Major steel plants and their expansion and renovation plans are listed in the *China Business Review*, 12, 3 (May-Jun 1985), 29. Recent purchases of foreign equipment and technology for the steel industry appear on pp. 22-23.

continued . . .

IRON AND STEEL INDUSTRY (continued)

Sintering Plant—China's biggest sintering plant started production at the Baoshan Iron and Steel Complex 16 August 1985. Its annual capacity is 4.9 million tons. XNB (17 Aug 1985), 45-46.

Baoshan—Siemens AG and AEG Telefunken have been awarded a DM400 ($122.9 million) contract for electronic gear to operate the Baoshan hot-rolling steel plant. Siemens will receive about DM300 million. *Asian Wall Street Journal Weekly* (18 Feb 1985), 13.

COMPUTER INDUSTRY

US Computer Sales—Sales of American computers to China doubled between 1983 and 1984, and sales are expected to double again in 1985. *Asian Wall Street Journal Weekly* (18 Feb 1985), 13.

Tariffs on Microchips Reduced—The PRC has reduced tariffs on imported microchips and data processing equipment from 25 percent to 6-9 percent. These and other tariff reductions have been implemented to encourage the import of necessary technology. *Asian Wall Street Journal Weekly* (11 Mar 1985), 13.

Bull Computer—Bull has been awarded to $6.5 million contract for five DPS 7 mainframe computers, five DPS 6 minicomputers 320 Quester terminals, and 54 Micral 30 minicomputers starting in 1986. *Asian Wall Street Journal Weekly* (22 Apr 1985), 14.

Computerland—Computerland of the US has provided 60 computers to the new Beijing Computerland Institute. The school has 600 students. There are 400 computer clubs in Beijing with some 20,000 members and 1,300 computers. FBIS-CHI 89 (8 May 1985), B2/3. ·

Japanese Production Line—The North China Terminal Equipment Corp. in Baoding, Hebei is importing a production line from the Nippon Electric Corp. to make 16-bit microcomputers. Production is to begin in 1985. Nippon set up a software center in Beijing three years ago. FBIS-CHI 25 (6 Feb 1985), D3.

Imports—China has imported a total of 100,000 microcomputers. *South China Morning Post* (27 Mar 1985), business, 1.

Semiconductors—Dana I. Robinson describes the Chinese semiconductor industry in detail in Committee on Foreign Relations, US House of Representatives, *United States-China Relations* (1984), 154-72.

Fujian Venture—The IMI Company of the US has signed an agreement with Fujian province to provide equipment for a floppy disc production line. The line will manufacture 230 sets of Model 500H 5.25-inch full-width floppy discs every day. FBIS-CHI 89 (8 May 1985), B3.

Computer Problems—China spent at least $425 million on foreign computers in 1984. The Chinese may waste $20-$85 million within the next three years repairing computers purchased in 1984 because of improper maintenance. They do not purchase service contracts because they do not understand insurance. Personal computers tend to be switched on and off many times daily. This does not save energy, and wears down the equipment. The Chinese apparently do not use computers for a variety of new operations, but usually only for the purpose it was bought. The machines are frequently idle, and the Chinese do not buy new software to get the maximum use from computers and programs. New York *Times* (5 May 1985), F9.

Mainframes—There are only some 4,000 mainframes in the PRC. David H. Ahl, "Two Billion Armpits Waiting For a Deodorant," *Creative Computing*, 11, 1 (Jan 1985), 26. Ahl mentions the dates of various computer developments in China:

First vacuum-tube computer built	1953
First transistor computer built	1965
First IC (third generation) built	1971
First LSI built	1981

continued . . .

COMPUTER INDUSTRY (continued)

Computer Gift—Hong Kong Renful International Ltd. has given seven 1BC-400 Chinese-English computers to department of the Central Committee of the CCP and to the State Council. FBIS-CHI 75 (18 Apr 1985), E9.

Apple—Apple Computers Inc. will sell Apple II and Macintosh personal computers in China. The distributor, ACI Kaihin, will also develop software for use in Chinese schools. New York *Times* (30 May 1985), 37.

Microcomputers—Cary Lu describes the state of microcomputers in China in "China's Emerging Micro Industry," *High Technology*, 5, 3 (Mar 1985), 69-70. The biggest domestically produced RAM chip holds only 1 kilobit, whereas the US and Japan make 256-kilobit chips. Microcomputers all use imported parts for the critical components. The Baiyun State Electronics Factory in Guangzhou makes Rio PC-XTs. Another factory in Hangzhou assembles Xizi XZ-PCs, and a third in Fujian province makes the Great Wall Micro. All are based on the IBM PC. The floppy-disc version of the Rio PC costs approximately $10,400, while an authentic IBM PC-XT sells for more than $20,000. Almost everyone writes his programs in BASIC and/or FORTRAN; even programs running on mainframes serving Ministries in Beijing use BASIC. Many users lack manuals, cannot purchase spare parts, and have no maintenance and repair arrangements.

Chinese Computer Market—China has reduced foreign-exchange spending, raised import duties 100 percent, and cut domestic computer prices 23 percent. All of these moves have dampened hopes for continued direct computer sales to the PRC. US computer sales rose to $150 million in 1984, a 500-percent increase over sales in 1982. Additional computers have entered China illegally through Hong Kong, and users are finding it difficult to get them serviced. Companies are now arranging joint ventures with the Chinese for the assembly and manufacture of their computers. Hewlett-Packard formed such a venture in June, 1985 to assemble microcomputers and oscilloscopes in Beijing. The equipment will be sold in China for dollars, but Burroughs plans to charge local currency for the B20s and B25s it will assemble in southern Yunnan province. *Business Week* (8 Jul 1985), 42.

Apple—Apple signed an agreement 30 May 1985 to market computers in the PRC through an independent distributor, ACI Kaihin Co. Ltd. *Facts on File* (19 Jul 1985), 535A1.

Honeywell Contract—A 10-year agreement has been signed between Yamatake-Honeywell and the Sichuan Instrument Complex to supply China with the technology to manufacture equipment for the TDC 3000 digital process-control system. The system monitors and controls production in industries such as petroleum refining, electricity production, pulp and paper mills, and pharmaceutical manufacturing. Minneapolis *Star and Tribune* (10 Dec 1985) 5B.

Burroughs—The Burroughs Corp. has signed a contract to assemble B25 computers at a factory in Kunming, Yunnan, to distribute, and to maintain the B20 and B25 small business computers. The $20 million deal was concluded with the Yunnan Import-Export Corp., the Yunnan Electronic Equipment Factory, and the Beijing Ever Bright Industrial Corp. Hong Kong Standard (10 Jan 1985), business, 2.

Computers in Operation—Some 10,000 factories and other civilian organizations use computers for management, storage, banking, transportation and quality control. *Beijing Review,* 21 (27 May 1985), 8. With approximately 400,000 enterprises operating in China, this means that only 2.5 percent use computers.

COMPUTERS IN CHINA, 1985

Computer workers (th)	90+	Microcomputers produced (est, th)	32
Computer production factories	111	Robots in operation	c. 100
Computer service units	40	Manipulators (th)	2
Computer research establishments	8		

Beijing Review, 47 (25 Nov 1985), 8; 48 (18 Nov 1985), 17-21.

MOTORCYCLE INDUSTRY

Production (th)

1980	47*
1984 ·	520
1985 est	800
Motorcycle Manufacturing Companies	100+
Employees (th)	150

* Calculated. China plans to increase production by 20 percent during each of the next five years. The largest manufacturer in the PRC is the Jialing Machinery Factory in Chongqing, Sichuan, with an output of 180,000 motorcycles in 1984 and plans to make 250,000 in 1985. XNB (5 Jul 1985), 49.

MOTOR VEHICLE INDUSTRY

Fiat—The Nanjing Associated Automobile Manufacturing Corp. and Fiat-Eveco Company signed an agreement in March, 1985 to manufacture 100,000 Fiat light motor vehicles within the next five to six years. The Nanjing Corp. will produce 29 types of one- to three-tons trucks, twin-row-seat cars, coaches and box-type and cross-country vehicles. Nanjing will return part of its profits to Fiat. The deal is worth about 1 billion yuan ($353 million). Fiat will also build training and technical centers in Nanjing, install and test equipment. Nanjing now produces 25,000 light motor vehicles annually. FBIS-CHI 62 (1 Apr 1985), 02.

Shenyang—The Shenyang Auto Industrial Co. produced more than 10,000 vehicles in 1984, an increase of 47 percent over 1983. Output is to double in 1985 to meet the need for trucks in China. The Soviets equipped the Shenyang plant during the 1950s. Automotive factories were equipped by the Soviets (Changchun) in the 1950s and the French (Sichuan) in the 1960s, but the technology has not been modernized. The PRC manufactured more than 300,000 vehicles in 1984, up 27 percent over 1983. From now until 1990, it will import the technology to make 600,000 modern heavy-duty trucks, medium-sized and light vehicles, jeeps and cars. *Beijing Review*, 10 (11 Mar 1985), 6-7.

Lack of Planning—*Ming Pao* (25 May 1985), 5, notes that planned production of automobiles in China greatly exceeds domestic needs. Some 900,000 are believed needed by 1990, but annual output will be 2 million, including 1.04 million light vehicles, or 360 percent more than estimated needs. In 1985 25 general plants have been opened, bringing the total to over 100.

Peugeot—Automobiles Peugeot will organize a joint venture valued at $60 million to make 15,000 pickup and station wagon versions of the Peugeot 504 sedan by the end of the 1980s. The cars will be made at the Huang Pu Plant, 12 miles from Guangzhou. A second phase of the project may be negotiated to increase annual production to 25-30,000 units annually. Some 5,000 vehicles will be exported annually three years after the plant becomes operational. *Asian Wall Street Journal Weekly* (18 Mar 1985), 6; New York *Times* (14 Mar 1985), 33.

Fiat—Fiat and the Nanjing Motor Corp. agreed in March, 1985 to a licensing deal to produce 3- and 5-ton trucks. The PRC will invest $260 million and the Italian government will loan China $100 million to assist in building 17 plants and support facilities in and around Nanjing. Minneapolis *Star and Tribune* (28 Mar 1985), 9B; *Asian Wall Street Journal Weekly* (11 Mar 1985), 13.

Polish Deal—A contract has been signed for 3,000 Polish tracks, automobiles, and buses. The deal is valued near $25 million. *Beijing Review*, 31 (5 Aug 1985), 9.

continued . . .

MOTOR VEHICLE INDUSTRY (continued)

Beijing—A motor vehicle import and export corporation was established in Beijing in February, 1985. Last year the city produced 17,000 jeeps, 4,000 one-ton and 15,000 two-ton trucks, 1,200 minibuses, and 10,000 motorcycles. Output is to reach 250,000 motor vehicles and 100,000 motorcycles by 1990. The PRC produced 300,000 motor vehicles in 1984. The first vehicle was made at the Beijing Auto Works in 1958. Beijing now has four motor vehicle plants, one motorcycle factory, and over 130 parts manufacturers. Two production centers will be set up at Huairou and Shunyi counties. XNB (12 Feb 1985), 7-8.

Factory Purchased—*Der Spiegel* 8 (18 Feb 1985), 70-74, describes the purchase of the Zundapp Works in Munich by the Tianjin Bicycle Industry Company for DM16 million. About 15,000 tons of equipment to manufacture mopeds were crated and sent to Tianjin via the Trans-Siberian Railway and by sea.

Tire Line Imported—China will import a tire production line from British Dunlop International Projects Ltd. The line will be installed at the Changzheng Tire Plant at Chaoyang, Liaoning, and have an annual capacity of 150,000 steel wire meridian automobile tires. The line will begin operations in 1988. Current production is 460,000 tires a year. XNB (18 Feb 1985), 15.

Volkswagen—Volkswagenwerk AG will produce 100,000 automobiles annually at its Shanghai factory by 1990. The renovated facility, covering 500 acres and costing $960 million, will reach maximum production of 300,000 Santana and Audi sedans and 500,000 engines by 1995. *Asian Wall Street Journal Weekly* (11 Feb 1985), 12.

TELEVISION INDUSTRY

Imports of Color Television Lines—China has a production capacity of 2.3 million tv sets annually, but new contracts have been signed to import lines which will increase capacity to 4.3 million sets per year. There are estimates that the PRC will ultimately be able to manufacture 10 million sets annually if trends continue. The same lack of planning is occurring with refrigerator and washing machine production. *Ming Pao* (25 Apr 1985), 5.

Guangzhou—A color-tv frequency-tuners production line began operations at the Guangzhou Liming Electronic Accessories Plant in March, 1985. Equipment from Matsushita of Japan can produce 500,000 tuners annually. China manufactured 1,290,000 color television sets in 1984, an increase of 140 over 1983. XNB (30 Mar 1985), 25.

Color-TV Production—The PRC will produce 1 million additional color television sets in 1985. This will bring total tv output to 11.5 million. With the import of 2 million color sets, 13.5 million color and black-and-white sets will be offered for sale. In 1984 12.92 million tv sets were purchased. It is expected that by the end of 1985, 67.5 million sets will be in Chinese homes, averaging 30 per 100 households. XNB (3 Jul 1985), 26.

Integrated Circuit Line—The largest integrated circuit assembly line in the PRC went into operation in June 1985 at a radio factory in Wuxi, Jiangsu. With equipment from Japan and the US, the line can make integrated circuit chips for 5 million television sets. The first Chinese production line for 18-inch color tv picture tubes has started up at Xian, Shaanxi. It can produce 160,000 18-inch kinescopes and 1.12 million others. XNB (27 Jun 1985), 23-24.

Philips—N.V. Philips of the Netherlands will supply China with 115 million guilders ($39.3 million) in color tv sets. Within the past four months Philips has sold the PRC over 640 million guilders in contracts. *Asian Wall Street Journal Weekly* (25 Mar 1985), 4. An agreement was signed 28 May 1985 for the production of Philips color tv tubes at Nanjing, Jiangsu. When finished at the end of 1987, the joint-venture factory will be able to product 1.5 million 16- and 20-inch tubes and deflection yokes. Philips will hold 30 percent of the shares. XNB (18 Jun 1985), 9-10.

continued . . .

TELEVISION INDUSTRY (continued)

Color TV—As a result of uncontrolled price hikes for color tv sets, the state is enforcing retail prices for the following sizes:

14-inch	998 yuan
18-inch	1,330 yuan
20-inch	1,500 yuan
22-inch	1,700 yuan

FBIS-CHI 66 (5 Apr 1985), K17.

CHEMICAL AND PETROCHEMICAL INDUSTRY

Ningxia—Construction of a chemical plant has begun at Yinchuan, Ningxia. It will produce 300,000 tons of synthetic ammonia and more than 500,000 tons of urea each year. Equipment will be imported from the Federal Republic of Germany, the Netherlands, and Japan. Completion is scheduled for 1987. XNB (17 May 1985), 49.

GDR—The China National Technology Import Corp. signed a contract 4 June 1985 to import two sets of soda ash production equipment from the German Democratic Republic. This is the first complete set of equipment from Eastern Europe since the 1950s. *Beijing Review*, 33 (19 Aug 1985), 30.

Shanghai—The third phase of construction at the Shanghai Petrochemical Complex began in late June, 1985. The first phase started 13 years ago, and the second phase was finished early in 1985. The complex produces 300,000 tons of chemical fiber, 70,000 tons of plastics, and over 1 million tons of oil products and chemical raw materials. A 300,000-ton ethylene system from Japan will be installed in the third phase. Seven auxiliary systems, including a glycol system with an annual capacity of 120,000 tons, an acrylonitrile system with a capacity of 100,000 tons, and a polyethylene unit with a capacity of 70,000 tons, will be put into operation. XNB (2 Jul 1985), 30-31.

SINOPEC—Facilities of China's petrochemical industry are listed in the *China Business Review*, 12, 1 (Jan-Feb 1985), 40-41.

Fertilizer Plants—Two chemical fertilizer plants with imported equipment are being built in Shanxi and Anhui provinces. They will produce 980,000 tons of nitrophosphate and 140,000 tons of diammonium phosphate annually. Additional equipment will be placed in a dozen phosphate fertilizer factories in China, each manufacturing 10-30,000 tons of ammonium phosphate from low-grade ore every year. Output of compound fertilizer will reach 3 million tons in 1985, or 20 percent of the total fertilizer production. The PRC ranks third in world fertilizer output. XNB (12 Jan 1985), 19.

Qinhuangdao—The China National Chemical Construction Corp. has agreed with the Petrochemical Industries Company of Kuwait and the Phosphoric Acid and Fertilizer Corp. of Tunisia to establish a fertilizer company at Qinhuangdao with an annual production capacity of diammonia phosphate or 600,000 tons of compound fertilizer of nitrogen, phosphorous and potassium. FBIS-CHI 5 (8 Jan 1985), 11.

Kunming—A yellow phosphorous fertilizer plant with an annual capacity of 300,000 tons will be constructed near Kunming, Yunnan. The province currently has 25 phosphate mines with an annual production of 3.5 million tons, or 25 percent of China's total output. There are 26 phosphate fertilizer plants in Yunnan. It ranks first in phosphorous reserves in the PRC, with 1.91 billion tons verified. XNB (28 Aug 1985), 6.

Yizheng—The first phase of the Yizheng, Jiangsu Chemical Fiber Works, the largest in the PRC, has been handed over to China. Each of its six installations can produce 100 tons of polyester a day. The plant was imported from the Federal Republic of Germany. XNB (16 Nov 1985), 67.

continued . . .

CHEMICAL AND PETROCHEMICAL INDUSTRY (continued)

Synthetic Rubber Venture—Polystar Ltd. of Canada will share half interest in a synthetic rubber joint venture with the Gao Qiao Petrochemical Corp. of Shanghai. Polystar will provide the equipment to triple annual production to about 3,000 tons of carboxylated latex by 1986. The product is used primarily in the paper-coating industry. *Asian Wall Street Journal Weekly* (29 Apr 1985), 17.

Fluor—The Fluor Corp. signed a contract in 1985 to build three large petrochemical plants in the Shanghai area. Its new joint-venture construction company will employ 250-300 Chinese and up to 40 Fluor engineers on the projects. New York *Times* (4 May 1985), 22.

Urumqi—A fertilizer plant with a capacity of 820,000 tons a year began operations at Urumqi, Xinjiang 31 July 1985. It will provide 520,000 tons of carbamide annually, and with equipment from the UBE Co. of Japan can produce 300,000 tons of synthetic ammonia each year. The Urumqi General Petrochemical Works, where the plant is located, cost 583.8 million yuan. It includes an oil refinery with an annual capacity of 1.5 million tons, and will add a belt-weaving workshop from Austria built with a $45.4 million loan from the Kuwait Fund for Arab Economic Development. *Beijing Review*, 33 (19 Aug 1985), 29-30.

CHEMICAL INDUSTRY, 1984

Production (mn tons)

Chemical fertilizer	14
Synthetic ammonia	18
Caustic soda	2.21
Soda ash	1.87
Tires (mn sets)	14
Investment in key projects (bn yuan)	1.35

Capacities added (th tons)

Butadienestyrene rubber	80
Acrylic acid	25
Acrylic products	30
Neutral dyes and agents	1+

Preparatory work has been started for two soda plants at Tianjin and Lianyungang.

Contracts signed to import chemical technology for factories in Shanghai, Tianjin, Dalian and Jiangsu	104

XNB (26 Jan 1985), 32.

MINERAL INDUSTRY

Ministry of Geology and Mineral Resources—In 1984 the Ministry employed 3,660 research workers and college and technical-school graduates. The output value of factories attached to the Ministry totaled 189 million yuan, an increase of 19 percent over 1983. *China Daily* (30 Jan 1985), 1.

Asbestos Plant—An asbestos dressing plant for concentrated ore has begun operations at Mangnai, Qinghai province. Designed capacity is 12,000 tons a year. Another plant with a capacity of 5-10,000 tons a year is planned for Babao in the Qilian Mountains of northern Qinghai. FBIS-CHI 102 (28 May 1985), T2.

continued . . .

MINERAL INDUSTRY (continued)

Gold Production—There are more than 100,000 gold miners and construction workers at 100 gold mines in the PRC. Another 200,000 people work at small gold mines opened by collectives and individuals. They produce 40 percent of China's gold. The gold purchasing price has been raised from 696.64 yuan to 895.70 yuan per troy ounce to increase production and curtail gold smuggling. XNB (20 Aug 1985), 36. Gold production is to double in 1990 over 1985, and total gold output should increase 55 percent during 1986-90 over 1981-85. FBIS-CHI 199 (15 Oct 1985), K12. Gold mines and deposits and diamond mines are listed in the *China Business Review*, 12, 3 (May-Jun 1985), 12. The *Beijing Review*, 51 (23 Dec 1985), 26-27, mentioned there were some 150,000 people specializing in gold mining in China in 1984. The PRC has gold reserves of 400 tons. Shandong province produced over 80,000 ounces in 1984. Output in the PRC has increased 10 percent annually during the last decade.

Mineral Deposits—Over the past five years, Chinese geologists have discovered 629 mineral deposits, including 316 large and medium-sized mines. Another 684 mines are being explored. XNB (30 Jan 1985), 23.

Copper Mine—A copper mining center with six mines and a smelter was scheduled to begin operations in September, 1985. Production capacity is 70,000 tons each year. *Beijing Review*, 27 (8 Jul 1985), 2.

New Mineral—A new mineral, chaidamuite, has been discovered in the Qaidam Basin of Qinghai province. The geologists Li Wanmao and Chen Guoying found the non-metallic mineral in a zinc and iron mine in 1983, and their discovery has recently been approved. XNB (5 Oct 1985), 20.

Diamond Deposit—The largest diamond deposit in China has been found near Dalian, Liaoning province. XNB (29 Oct 1985), 25.

PRODUCTION OF NON-FERROUS METALS

Increase in output of 10 main non-ferrous metals, 1984 over 1983 (percent)   9

Planned annual increase, 1985-90 (percent)   10+

The Chinese plan to renovate existing plants and launch 26 projects to develop aluminum, lead, zinc, copper and nickel. The 10 main non-ferrous metals include aluminum, lead, zinc, copper, nickel, tin, antimony, titanium, mercury, and magnesium. XNB (1 Mar 1985), 9.

BREWERIES

Qingdao—The Qingdao Brewery has doubled its annual production capacity to 100 million liters. By 1990 output is to reach 5 billion liters in China, or twice the 1984 figure. XNB (6 Mar 1985), 5.

Loans—The People's Construction Bank of China will provide 800 million yuan in loans over three years to increase the production of beer. The PRC will double its present capacity of 2.2 billion liters by 1987. XNB (24 Jan 1985), 10.

Output to Double—The PRC will spend $1 billion during the next three years to double its beer output. Production has already risen 33 percent since 1980. Twenty-three breweries are planned. New York *Times* (31 May 1985), 38.

Zhujiang—The Zhujiang Brewery in Guangzhou began operations in June, 1985. Its annual capacity of 50,000 tons of beer will increase to 120,000 tons by 1986. Some 40 percent of production will be exported. This is the first Chinese brewery built in a compensation deal. France supplied equipment and Belgium provided brewing techniques. *Beijing Review*, 34 (26 Aug 1985), 34; XNB (19 Nov 1985), 49.

Ningbo—Construction of a brewery and malthouse at Ningbo, Zhejiang was to begin 1 October 1985 and end in 1987. The Sino-French joint venture will produce 50 million liters of beer and 20,000 tons of malt annually. The project will cost about 300 million French francs or some 96 million yuan. XNB (13 Jul 1985), 35.

SOFT DRINK INDUSTRY

Production (mn liters)

1980	265*
1985 est	800+
1990 est	2,000+

*Calculated. China has imported or co-produced with foreign companies more than 100 bottling lines for soft drinks. XNB (11 Oct 1985), 41.

INSURANCE INDUSTRY, yearend 1985

Life insurance policy holders (mn)	5
Families with property insurance (mn)	14+
Total value of insured family property (bn yuan)	24+
Enterprises with property insurance (th)	350+
Total value of insured property (bn yuan)	350
Amounts paid by the People's Insurance Company for losses from natural disasters, Jan-Sep 1985 (mn yuan)*	610

*The Company reopened in 1979. XNB (16 Nov 1985), 26-27.
The People's Insurance Company handled $60 billion in foreign insurance in 1985. Premiums were expected to total $230 million. Its total premium income reached $830 million, and the amount paid in claims was $410 million. Compensation recovered from other countries totaled $31 million. *Beijing Review*, 4 (27 Jan 1986), 31.

INSURANCE INDUSTRY, yearend 1984

Offices of the PICC[1]	2,100
Staff	35,000
Offices overseas	25
Types of insurance offered[2]	120+
Property policies issued to:	
Enterprises[3]	340,000
Households (mn)	13.8
Motor vehicles insured (mn)	c.2
Life insurance policy holders (mn)[4]	2.9
Premiums collected (bn yuan)[5]	5.4
Settlements paid (bn yuan)	2.4

1. The People's Insurance Company of China was revived in 1979. There are no offices in Tibet or Taiwan.
2. Including property, motor vehicle, pension, medical, crop and livestock insurance.
3. By 1984 almost all urban state-owned enterprises and 70-80 percent of the local enterprises had bought property insurance.
4. This is a six-fold increase from 500,000 policy holders in 1983.
5. In Beijing, it costs about 3.2 yuan per year for 1,000 yuan coverage of household property.

Beijing Review, 33 (19 Aug 1985), 11, 23.

ENAMEL INDUSTRY

Production (th)

1983	138*
1984	146
1985 est.	150

Number of pieces of enamel-ware owned by each resident

Urban	4.53
Rural	1.54

*Calculated.

XNB (1 Jun 1985), 17. Sales are estimated to increase 6-7 percent in 1985.

REFRIGERATOR PRODUCTION

1980	49.0*	1983	189
1981	55.6	1984	537
1982	99.9		

Number of manufacturers and dealers

1985	116
Planned reduction	41

*Calculated.

While production of refrigerators still fails to meet the demand, the State Council is trying to control the manufacture of refrigerators and limit their import. FBIS-CHI 123 (26 Jun 1985), K4; CHIFFA/8, 10.

X AGRICULTURE

AGRICULTURAL NEWS, 1985

Tea Price Rises—The cost of tea has risen 400 percent in 1985 because of an unusually cold and rainy spring, particularly in Zhejiang and Anhui. Tea purchases by state agencies dropped 60 percent in April compared to purchases in April, 1984. New York *Times* (15 May 1985), 6.

Vegetable Subsidies Resumed—Beijing has resumed vegetable subsidies at state-run stores. Cabbage will be sold for 0.4 yuan per kg, cucumbers for 0.8 yuan per kg, and tomatoes for 1.3 yuan per kg. Residents of Beijing consume about 4 million tons of vegetables annually. The acreage devoted to vegetable growing around Beijing dropped 25 percent in 1985 from 16,000 to 12,000 hectares as a result of increased construction projects and lower production. *China Daily* (4 Jun 1985), 3.

Mixed Feeds—China plans to increase the production of mixed feeds from 7 million tons in 1983 to about 50 million tons by 1990. XNB (14 Mar 1985), 30.

Fiat Tractors—Fiat Trattori of Italy has signed a contract to transfer the technology to build 50 to 100 h.p. tractors at Shanghai and Luoyang. The factories will each be able to produce 10,000 annually after starting operations in 1987. The deal is worth $90 million XNB (8 Jun 1985), 42.

Cotton Exports—China will resume cotton exports to Poland after 30 years. Exports should reach 17,000 tons in 1985, then increase to 20-30,000 tons. Poland will import cotton yarn and grey cotton cloth in addition to medium-length and long-fiber cotton. *Beijing Review*, 44 (4 Nov 1985), 30.

Description of New Grain Purchasing System—The CPC Central Committee and the State Council have decided that beginning this year (the annual year for grain begins on 1 April) planned purchase of grain will be abolished and replaced by contracted purchase of grain.

The so-called contracted purchase of grain means that the state orders grain from producers by signing contracts with them. Specifically the state works out plans for ordering grain in accordance with demand. According to the stipulations contained in the plans concerning the categories and quantity of grain to be purchased, grain departments sign contracts with peasants. The grain which is not covered by the purchase plans will be freely handled by the producers. This helps promote multichannel management of grain. The price of grain is calculated according to a "70:30" ratio (70 percent is based on previous above-quota purchase price, and 30 percent is based on previous planned purchase price). To encourage peasants to produce more high quality grain in accordance with the principle of higher prices for better quality grain and lower prices for poor quality grain, with the condition that the "70:30" ratio remain in effect, various provinces, autonomous regions, and municipalities directly under the central government may properly increase the purchase price of high-quality and marketable grain, and reduce the purchase price of the low-quality and unmarketable grain.

Grain which the state purchases includes wheat, rice, and corn. It also purchases soybeans produced by the six main-producing areas of Liaoning, Jilin, Heilongjiang, Nei Monggol, Anhui, and Henan. Other kinds of grains which are not covered by the state's plans can, in principle, be bought and sold freely. In light of the actual conditions wherein certain kinds of grain not covered by the state purchase plans are still the main staple food of some localities, to ensure sufficient supplies of such grain and non-staple foods for the cities and towns concerned, certain amounts of these kinds of grains may also be included in the state purchase plans.

The state's purchase plans for grain are implemented by localities at all levels. According to the plans, before sowing time, people's governments of counties and townships must organize grain departments to discuss with state farms, collective production units, and peasants the matter of purchasing their grain, and to sign contracts with them. The contracts should cover the categories and amount of grain set by the state, and the prices should be calculated

continued . . .

AGRICULTURAL NEWS, 1985 (continued)

according to the ratio fixed by the state. The contracts should be signed according to the requirements contained in the "law of economic contracts" and "regulations for purchase and sale of agricultural and sideline products." The signing of contracts means the embodiment of the economic activities of purchasing grain in legal form, and the specific implementation of the purchase plans. *Ban Yue Tan*, 8 (25 Apr 1985), 28-29, translated in FBIS-CHI 92 (13 May 1985), K12/13.

Chemical-Free Vegetables—China has almost 20,000 hectares of vegetables grown without chemical fertilizers or insecticides. *Beijing Review*, 19 (13 May 1985), 8.

Rat Control—Pests consume 15 million tons of grain annually. Rats are being controlled by using their skins for children's shoes or by selling live rats for food. Rats cost about 50 cents a pound in the Guangxi Zhuang Autonomous Region, or almost as much as chicken. The rat steaks are marinated and cooked with rice, bran and sesame oil. *China Daily* (11 May 1985). Peasants killed 526 million rats in 1984 in 17 provinces, municipalities and autonomous regions. XNB (29 Jan 1985), 11.

Grain Requirements for Meat Production—It requires four pounds of grain to raise one pound of pork, and eight pounds of grain for one pound of beef. Dwight Perkins on "Heart of the Dragon" (PBS, part 2, 13 May 1985).

Rice—China has over 40,000 varieties of rice. Local varieties comprise 77 percent of China's total, and rare and high-quality types account for 10 percent. XNB (9 Jan 1985), 33-34.

Pests—China suffered the worst attack of pests and diseases on its rice crop in more than a decade. Close to 1 million tons reportedly were destroyed by pestilence. The PRC was expected to export 1 million tons of rice in calendar year 1985 and 900,000 in CY 1986. US Department of Agriculture, *Foreign Agriculture Circular: Grains* (Nov 1985), 24.

Poverty Level Defined—Farmers earning less than 310 yuan a year are officially designated as poor. The PRC has 70 million poor peasants, or more than 8 percent of the rural population. In 1984, some 22 million peasants earned less than 100 yuan a year. The average worker in large cities earns approximately 1,000 yuan annually. *Asian Wall Street Journal Weekly* (14 Jan 1985), 13.

Plain Production—The plain around the Yellow, Huaihe and Haihe Rivers covers 350,000 km^2 and includes 18 million hectares of farmland. The plain provides 58 percent of China's cotton, almost 20 percent of its grain, and about 25 percent of its soybeans, peanuts and flue-cured tobacco. FBIS-CHI 100 (23 May 1985), K13.

Problems with Grain—Despite record grain production, problems remain: 1) National output averages 800 jin per person, which is still a low figure. 2) Distribution varies, and there are areas of China where people are living at a subsistence level. 3) Much of the grain is coarse and poor quality. 4) Only a small part of the grain is used to increase animal products, such as meat, milk, poultry and eggs. FBIS-CHI 53 (19 Mar 1985), K13/14.

Specialized Households—Rural specialized households have been encouraged since 1979 to develop the economy in the countryside. There were 4.256 million specialized households at the end of 1984, amounting to 2.3 percent of the total rural households. Their annual income was 4,624 yuan, 81 percent above the average income of China's peasants. According to new guidelines, rural specialized households must meet the following criteria:

1. Established on the unit of the individual household, the family's major labor force or most members of the family take part in a certain production, or embark on specialized managing activities, on which more than 60 percent of the labor time are spent.

2. The household obtains more than 60 percent of its total income from specialized production.

3. More than 80 percent of specialized products turned out by the household must be for sale. (The specialized grain-producing households, however, are at a commodity rate of more than 60 percent.)

continued . . .

AGRICULTURAL NEWS, 1985 (continued)

4. The household's income obtained from selling products (including service fees) must double the average household-income made from sales by local (taking county as a unit) non-specialized households.
Beijing Review, 49 (9 Dec 1985), 27.

Rural Industrial Growth—Chen Muhua, the new President of the People's Bank of China, has told a monetary conference that rural industry has grown too rapidly, and must now rely on its own funds for development. Bank loans for rural industries amounted to more than 50 percent of the total rural bank loans. Priority will be given projects involving building materials, small coal mines, small hydroelectric power stations, and farm and sideline processing industries. Bank loans to mechanical factories, small iron-and-steel plants, and diesel-engine power-generating factories are to be reduced. FBIS-CHI 77 (22 Apr 1985), K5.

Surplus Rural Labor—By the end of the century, rural towns are expected to provide jobs for 300 million peasants no longer needed on farms, or 40 percent of the rural population. Half of the other 60 percent will work in forestry and half will cultivate crops. *Beijing Review,* 13 (1 Apr 1985), 4.

Rural Migration—The fear and pattern of urbanization in China is considered in the Los Angeles *Times* (26 Oct 1985), 1, 24.

AGRICULTURAL OUTPUT, 1984

		Percentage Increase Over 1983
Total value of agriculture (bn yuan)	361.2	14.5
Total value of farm crops (bn yuan)	214.1	8.9
Total value of forestry products (bn yuan)	15.1	15.8
Total value of animal husbandry (bn yuan)	54.3	11.7
Total value of sideline production (bn yuan)	70.0	36.8
Total value of fishery products (bn yuan)	7.7	13.2
Total value of industrial output of rural enterprises (bn yuan)	55.0	49.5
Total value of agricultural output (total output of agricultural minus the value of industrial production of rural enterprises (bn yuan)	306.2	9.9
Total number of large and medium-sized tractors, (th)	857	1.9
Total number of small-capacity and walking tractors (mn)	3.289	19.6
Total number of trucks (th)	345	25.5
Total power capacity of farm machines (mn h.p.)	265	8.3
Total capacity of irrigation and drainage power equipment (mn h.p.)	78.281	0.0
Chemical fertilizers applied in 1984 (mn tons)	17.731	6.8
Total consumption of electricity in rural areas (bn kWh)	46.2	6.2
Output of aquatic products (mn tons)	6.06	11.0
Catch of marine products		8.7
Catch of fresh-water products		15.6
Production of forest products:		
Rubber		9.4
Tea-oil seeds		20.5
Tung-oil seeds		0.7

continued . . .

AGRICULTURAL OUTPUT, 1984 (continued)

		Percentage Increase Over 1983
Total output value of village-run sideline industries (bn yuan)	55.0	45.5
Total industrial and agricultural output value of state farms built on reclaimed wasteland (bn yuan)	13.7	8.5

MAJOR AGRICULTURAL PRODUCTS

		Percentage Increase Over 1983
Grain (mn tons)	407.120	5.1
of which:		
Rice	178.090	5.5
Wheat	87.680	7.7
Soybean	9.700	−0.7
Cotton (mn tons)	6.077	31.1
Oil-bearing crops (mn tons)	11.852	12.3
of which:		
Peanuts	4.810	21.8
Rapeseed	4.194	−2.2
Sesame	0.467	33.9
Sugar-bearing crops (mn tons)	47.946	18.9
of which:		
Sugarcane	39.662	27.4
Beetroot	8.284	−9.8
Jute, ambary hemp (mn tons)	1.489	46.1
Silkworm cocoons (mn tons)	0.357	5.0
Tea (mn tons)	0.411	2.6

MAJOR ANIMAL PRODUCTS AND LIVESTOCK

		Percentage Increase Over 1983
Output of pork, beef and mutton (mn tons)	15.250	8.8
Milk (mn tons)	2.210	19.9
Sheep wool and goat hair (mn tons)	0.190	−6.6
Hogs slaughtered (mn head)	218.700	5.8
Large animals (yearend, mn head)	108.320	4.7
Pigs (yearend, mn head)	306.090	2.5
Sheep and goats (yearend, mn head)	158.240	−5.2

Beijing Review, 12 (25 Mar 1985), i-ii.

GRAIN OUTPUT, 1978, 1984

	1978	1984	Percentage Increase
Grain production (bn jin)	609.5	814.6	33.7
Average per-mu output (jin)	337	481	42.7
Total output of rice, wheat, and soybeans (bn jin)	396.6	551.5	39.1

continued . . .

GRAIN OUTPUT, 1978, 1984 (continued)

	1978	1984	Percentage Increase
Average per-capita output of fine food grain (unprocessed food grain (unprocessed food grain) (jin)	415	536	29.2
Percentage of production:			
Coarse food grains	34.9	32.3	
Fine food grains	65.1	67.7	
Output of potatoes (bn jin)	63.5	57.0	−10.3
Average grain output per agricultural worker (jin)	2,074	2,505	20.8
Commodity grain output per agricultural worker (jin)	420	867	94.0
Commodity grain output (bn jin)	123.5	281.9	128.3
Percentage of grain for peasants' own consumption	54.0	48.7	
Percentage of commodity grain to total grain output	20.3	34.6	
Local grain used for feed (bn jin)	87.5	123.4	41.0

FBIS-CHI 191 (2 Oct 1985), K10/11.

PROVINCIAL GRAIN PRODUCTION, 1981-84 (mn tons)

	1981	1982	1983	1984
NORTHEAST				
Heilongjiang	12.50	11.50	15.49	17.50
Liaoning	11.61	11.52	14.85	14.25
Jilin	9.22	10.00	14.78	16.18
NORTH				
Shandong	23.13	23.75	27.00	30.40
Hebei	15.75	17.52	19.00	18.70
Beijing	1.81	1.86	2.02	2.18
Tianjin	1.07	1.23	1.11	1.31
Henan	23.15	22.17	29.04	29.20
Shanxi	7.25	8.25	8.06	8.72
NORTHWEST				
Shaanxi	7.50	9.25	9.65	10.24
Gansu	4.35	4.69	5.40	5.55
Nei Monggol	5.10	5.30	5.60	5.94
Ningxia	1.27	1.20	1.45	1.54
Xinjiang	3.90	4.08	4.54	4.87
Qinghai	.80	.93	.90	1.04
EAST				
Zhejiang	14.20	17.13	15.84	18.17
Jiangsu	25.12	28.56	30.53	33.06
Shanghai	1.86	2.16	2.07	2.50
Anhui	17.88	19.33	20.11	22.03
CENTRAL				
Hubei	17.07	19.96	19.88	22.50
Hunan	21.71	23.75	26.54	26.00
Jiangxi	12.69	14.09	14.61	15.49

continued . . .

PROVINCIAL GRAIN PRODUCTION, 1981-84 (mn tons) (continued)

SOUTH	1981	1982	1983	1984
Guangdong	16.56	19.43	19.61	19.60
Guangxi	11.50	13.53	13.63	13.50
Fijian	8.10	8.48	8.58	8.50
SOUTHWEST				
Sichuan	34.66	37.35	40.09	40.80
Guizhou	5.68	6.54	7.03	7.40
Yunnan	9.17	9.46	9.55	10.05
Xizang	.49	.45	.37	0.48
TOTAL (sum)	325.02	353.43	387.28	407.68
SSB TOTAL	325.02	354.50	387.28	407.12

US Department of Agriculture, *China: Outlook and Situation Report* (1985), 37.

MAJOR MANUFACTURED FARM INPUTS, 1980-84

Yearend stocks	Unit	1980	1981	1982	1983	1984
Large-medium tractors	1,000 no.	745	792	812	841	857
Hand tractors	1,000 no.	1,874	2,037	2,287	2,750	3,289
Rural trucks	1,000 no.	138	175	206	275	NA
Power irrig. & drain. equip.	1,000 hp.	74,645	74,983	76,697	78,492	78,281
Machinery production						
Large-medium tractors	1,000 no.	98	53	40	37	40
Hand tractors	1,000 no.	218	199	298	498	670
Internal combustion engines	1,000 hp.	25,390	20,840	22,960	28,990	NA
Rural electric consumption[1]	Mil. kWh.	32,080	36,990	39,690	43,520	46,200
Fertilizer output[2]	1,000 tons	12,321	12,390	12,781	13,789	14,820
Nitrogen	1,000 tons	9,993	9,857	10,219	11,094	12,260
Phosphate	1,000 tons	2,308	2,508	2,537	2,666	2,520
Potassium	1,000 tons	20	26	25	29	(40)
Fertilizer applied[2]	1,000 tons	12,694	13,349	15,134	16,598	17,731
Chemical pesticides	1,000 tons	537	484	457	331	310

( ) Indicates derived.
1. Not all for agricultural production.
2. All figures in effective nutrient weight.

US Department of Agriculture, *China: Outlook and Situation Report* (1985), 24.

PURCHASES UNDER RECENTLY COMPLETED GRAIN TRADE AGREEMENTS[1]

Country	Date signed	Delivery period	Grain	Amount Total Million tons
ARGENTINA				
Agreement:	Sep 1980	1981-1984	Wheat, corn and soybeans	1.0-1.5 yearly
Purchases:		Calendar year 1981	Wheat	.126
			Soybeans	.081
				.207[2]
		Calendar year 1982	Wheat	.094
			Corn, sorghum	.155
			Soybeans	.053
				.301[2]
		Calendar year 1983	Wheat	2.946
			Corn	.050
				2.996
		Calendar year 1984	Wheat	.001
				.001[2]
		4-year total		3.505
		Annual average		.876
AUSTRALIA				
Agreement:[3]	Nov 1981	1982-1984	Wheat	1.5-2.5 yearly
Purchases:[3]		Calendar year 1982	Wheat	2.136[2]
		Calendar year 1983	Wheat	0.416
		Calendar year 1984	Wheat	2.425
		3-year total		4.977
		Annual average		1.659
CANADA				
Agreement:[3]	May 1982	Aug 1982-Jul 1985	Wheat	10.5-2.5 yearly
Purchases:[3]		Aug 1982-Jul 1983	Wheat	4.424[2]
		Aug 1983-Jul 1984	Wheat	3.428
		Aug 1984-Jul 1985	Wheat	3.100[2,4]
		Approx. 3-year total		11.000
		Approx. annual average		3.667
FRANCE				
Agreement:[3]	Sep 1980	Aug 1980-Jul 1983	Wheat	.5-.7 yearly
Purchases:[3]		Aug 1980-Jul 1981	Wheat	.530[2]
		Aug 1981-Jul 1982	Wheat	.080
		3-year total		1.995
		Annual average		.652
UNITED STATES				
Agreement:	Oct 1980	1981-1984	Wheat, corn	6.0-8.0 yearly
		Calendar year 1981	Wheat	7.617
			Corn	.468
				8.085
		Calendar year 1982	Wheat	6.870
			Corn	1.590
				8.460
		Calendar year 1983	Wheat	2.458
			Corn	1.357
				3.815[2]
		Calendar year 1984	Wheat	4.038
				4.038[2]
		4-year total		24.371
		Annual average		6.093

1. Earlier years are available in previous issues of this report.
2. Indicates years with sales of less than annual minimums.
3. Small amounts of barley sold in addition.
4. Projected based on Canadian data through April 1985.

US Department of Agriculture, *China: Outlook and Situation Report* (1985), 39.

WORLD WHEAT EXPORTS TO CHINA

Year	Argentina	Australia	Canada	EEC	Origin (1,000 MT) Spain	Sweden	USA	USSR	Other	World
1973-74	0	1,239	1,367	26	0	0	3,190	0	9	5,831
1974-75	210	1,244	2,366	180	0	0	1,496	0	0	5,496
1975-76	0	1,126	1,204	0	0	0	0	0	0	2,330
1976-77	477	750	1,929	0	0	0	0	0	0	3,156
1977-78	373	4,603	3,321	0	0	0	225	0	0	8,522
1978-79	885	1,382	3,181	0	0	0	2,610	0	0	8,058
1979-80	465	3,575	2,621	90	0	0	1,929	0	0	8,680
1980-81	200	1,397	2,911	607	0	0	8,662	0	0	13,777
1981-82	199	1,413	2,991	116	0	0	8,504	0	0	13,223
1982-83	1,956	1,170	4,242	1,410	0	0	4,186	0	0	12,964
1983-84	1,010	1,660	3,848	137	0	0	3,131	0	0	9,786
1984-85	673	1,399	2,737	82	NA	0	2,440	NA	NA	7,331

Year	Argentina	Australia	Canada	EEC	Origin (Percent) Spain	Sweden	USA	USSR	Other	World
1973-74	0	21.2	23.4	0.4	0	0	54.7	0	0.2	100
1974-75	3.8	22.6	43	3.3	0	0	27.2	0	0	100
1975-76	0	48.3	51.7	0	0	0	0	0	0	100
1976-77	15.1	23.8	61.1	0	0	0	0	0	0	100
1977-78	4.4	54	39	0	0	0	2.6	0	0	100
1978-79	11	17.2	39.5	0	0	0	32.4	0	0	100
1979-80	5.4	41.2	30.2	1	0	0	22.2	0	0	100
1980-81	1.5	10.1	21.1	4.4	0	0	62.9	0	0	100
1981-82	1.5	10.7	22.6	0.9	0	0	64.3	0	0	100
1982-83	15.1	9	32.7	10.9	0	0	32.3	0	0	100
1983-84	10.3	17	39.3	1.4	0	0	32	0	0	100
1984-85	9.2	19.1	37.3	1.1	NA	0	33.3	NA	NA	100

continued . . . .

WORLD WHEAT EXPORTS TO CHINA (continued)

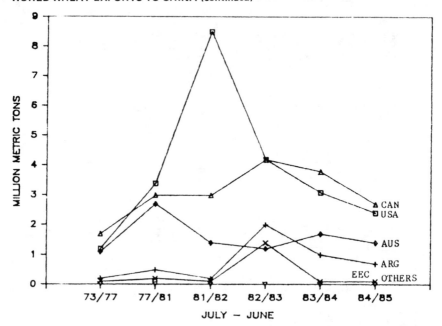

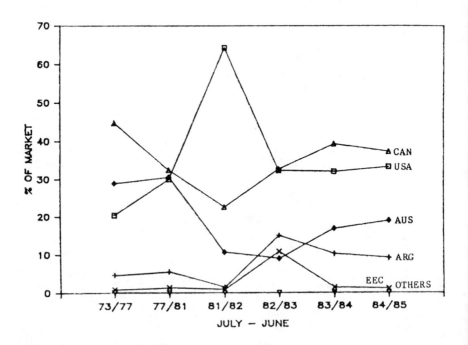

continued . . .

WORLD WHEAT EXPORTS TO CHINA (continued)

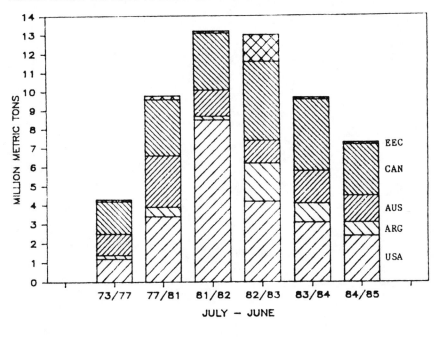

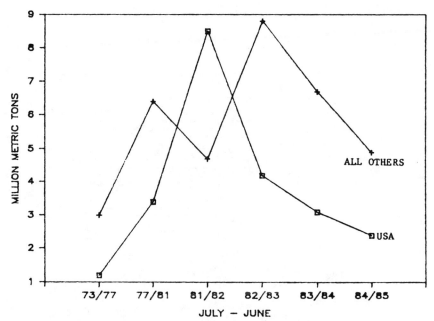

US Department of Agriculture, *Foreign Agriculture Circular: Grains* (Dec 1985), 26-27.

CHINESE TOTAL GRAIN IMPORTS FROM US AND ALL OTHER SOURCES

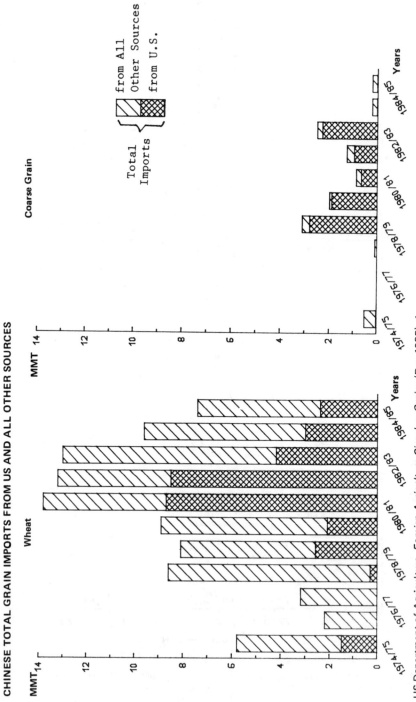

US Department of Agriculture, *Foreign Agriculture Circular: Grains* (Dec 1985), 1.

PERCENT OF TOTAL CHINESE WHEAT IMPORTS FROM ALL OTHER SOURCES

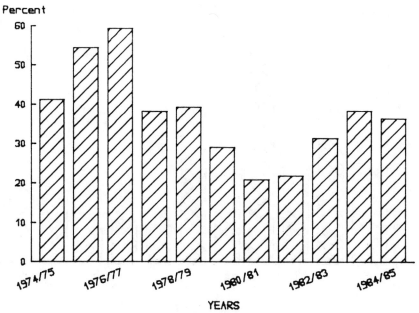

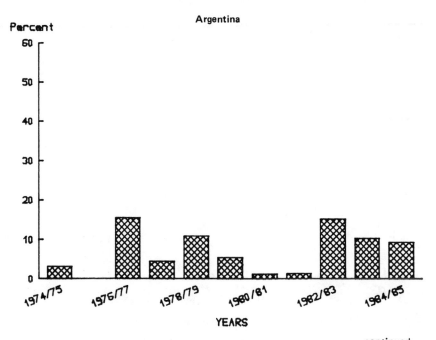

continued . . .

PERCENT OF TOTAL CHINESE WHEAT IMPORTS FROM ALL OTHER SOURCES
(continued)

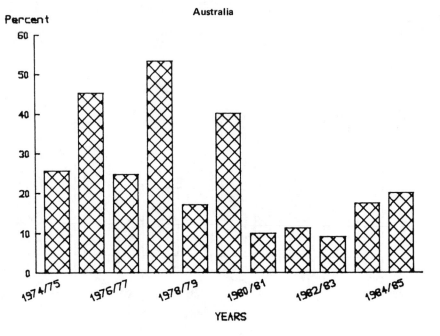

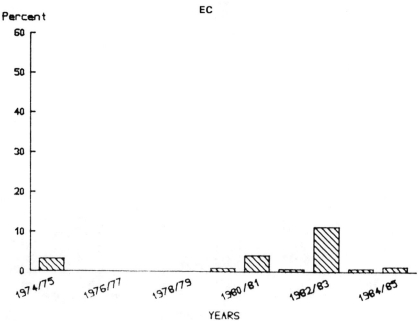

US Department of Agriculture, *Foreign Agriculture Circular: Grains* (Dec 1985), 12.

CHINESE WHEAT AND COARSE GRAIN TRADE

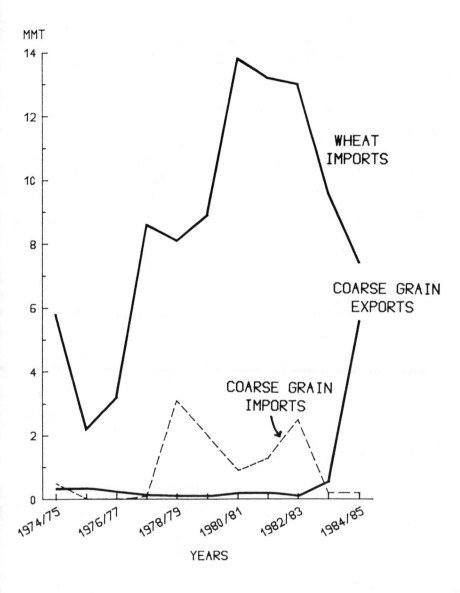

continued . . .

CHINESE WHEAT AND COARSE GRAIN TRADE (continued)

1974/75-1984/85 July/June Years

Years	Wheat Imports US	All Other Sources	Coarse Grain Imports US	All Other Sources	Total Wheat Imports	Total Coarse Grain Imports	Exports
			Million Metric Tons				
1974/75	1.5	4.3	—	0.5	5.8	0.5	0.3
1975/76	0.0	2.2	0.0	0.0	2.2	0.0	0.4
1976/77	0.0	3.2	0.0	0.0	3.2	0.0	0.2
1977/78	0.3	8.3	0.0	0.1	8.6	0.1	0.1
1978/79	2.6	5.5	2.8	0.3	8.1	3.1	0.1
1979/80	2.1	6.8	1.9	0.1	6.9	2.0	0.1
1980/81	8.7	5.1	0.7	0.2	13.8	0.9	0.2
1981/82	8.5	4.7	1.0	0.3	13.2	1.3	0.2
1982/83	4.2	8.8	2.3	0.2	13.0	2.5	0.1
1983/84	3.0	6.6	—	0.2	9.6	0.2	0.6
1984/85	2.4	5.0	—	0.2	7.4	0.2	5.6

"—" denotes less than 50,000 MT.

US Department of Agriculture, *Foreign Agriculture Circular: Grains* (Dec 1985), 13.

CHINESE TOTAL WHEAT IMPORTS: PERCENT FROM US AND ALL OTHER SOURCES

1974/75-1984/85 July/June Years

	US	Canada	Australia	Argentina	EC
			Percent		
1974/75	25.9	41.4	25.9	3.4	3.4
1975/76	0.0	54.5	45.5	0.0	0.0
1976/77	0.0	59.4	25.0	15.6	0.0
1977/78	3.5	38.4	53.5	4.7	0.0
1978/79	32.1	39.5	17.3	11.1	0.0
1979/80	23.6	29.2	40.4	5.6	1.1
1980/81	63.0	21.0	10.1	1.4	4.3
1981/82	64.4	22.0	11.4	1.5	0.8
1982/83	32.3	31.5	9.2	15.4	11.5
1983/84	31.3	38.5	17.7	10.4	1.0
1984/85	32.4	36.5	20.3	9.5	1.4

US Department of Agriculture, *Foreign Agriculture Circular: Grains* (Dec 1985), 13.

PRIVATELY-OWNED TRACTORS, 1980-84

1980	38,000	1983	2,000,000
1981	380,000	1984	3,110,000
1982	1,000,000		

China Reconstructs, XXXIV, 9 (Sep 1985), 33.

FARM MACHINERY AND PRODUCTION, 1984

		Percentage Increase Over 1983
Total power of farm machinery (mn h.p.)	265	7.6
Tractors (mn)	4.15	
Large and medium-sized	0.86	1.4
Small	3.28	19.2
Total power of farm machinery for irrigation and drainage (mn h.p.)	78.51	0.7
Combine harvesters (th)	36.6	0.4
Motor vehicles for agricultural use (th)	349	26.8
Equipment owned by peasant households or individual peasants		
Tractors (mn)	3.12	47.3
Motor vehicles for agricultural use (th)	180	100.0

			Percent of Total Area, 1984
Areas cultivated:			
Area plowed by tractors (mn mu)	570	5.4	39.0
Area sown by machine (mn mu)	190	3.3	8.6
Area of rice transplanted by machine (mn mu)	2.5	35.3	0.5
Area harvested by machine (mn mu)	71.31	3.9	3.3
Number of specialized households engaged in providing farm machinery services, 1984 (th)	930		
Tractor-plowing services	194		
Average net income of each household (yuan)	4,170		

Nongmin Ribao (13 Jun 1985), 1.

TEA PRODUCTION AND CONSUMPTION, 1984

Production (th tons)	450
Percentage increase over 1983	2.6
Percentage of rural consumption	68

Asian Wall Street Journal Weekly (25 Mar 1985), 4.

MARKET SHARES OF US FARMS EXPORTS, 1980-84 (percent)

Japan	15.8
Netherlands	7.1
Mexico	5.1
Canada	4.8
USSR	4.5
Korea	4.5
West Germany	4.2
PRC	3.6
Spain	3.3
Taiwan	3.1
Italy	2.5
United Kingdom	2.3
Rest of world	39.1

Minneapolis *Star and Tribune* (29 May 1985), 1M.

FISHING NEWS, 1985

Jiangsu Province—Some 569,000 tons of fish were caught in Jiangsu province in 1984, or 78,000 tons more than in 1983. Freshwater breeding accounted for 73 percent of the increase. XNB (27 Feb 1985), 24.

Fishing Agreements—Since 1981 40 countries have asked for fishing agreements with China. Beijing has established eight cooperative enterprises in Guinea-Bisseau, Sierra Leone, Senegal, Sri Lanka, Mauritius, Guyana, and elsewhere. An agreement allowing the Chinese to fish in Alaskan waters was recently concluded. *Beijing Review,* 26 (1 Jul 1985), 25.

New Shark Species—Two new shark species have been found in the East China Sea. They have been named Atripturus Abbreviatus and Centrothorus Robustus. More than 20,000 species of fish are known throughout the world, and some 2,000 of them are in China. XNB (17 Jun 1985), 5.

West African Fleet—China's first ocean-going fleet has started to fish off West Africa. The fleet includes 12 trawlers and an 800-ton storage vessel. All are owned by the Yantai Ocean Fishing Co., the Zhoushan Ocean Fishing Co., and the Fujian-Africa Ocean Fishing Co. Agreements have been signed with Senegal, Sierra Leone, Guinea Bissau, and Spanish Las Palmas. China produces only 5 kg of seafood per capita each year compared to the world average of 15 kg per capita. *Beijing Review,* 33 (19 Aug 1985), 8.

Alaska—Following an agreement with the US in July, 1985, the Chinese fishing fleet of three refrigerator vessels and six trawlers began to fish coastal waters off Alaska for the first time. It hoped to catch and process 30-50,000 tons of fish by the end of 1986, and eventually increase the haul to 100,000 annually. *Beijing Review,* 42 (21 Oct 1985), 28.

FISH FARMING, 1985

State-owned enterprises	c. 6,000
Employees (th)	400
Percentage of freshwater output:	
State-owned enterprises	50
Specialized fish farmers	50
Number of specialized fish farmers (mn)	4+
Area of water in China (mn ha)	16.7
Area devoted to fish farming (mn ha)	3.27
Total output (mn tons)	2.25
Percentage of total fish products	36
Number of educational institutions specializing in fishery production:	
Universities and colleges	5
Secondary schools	13
Fishery academy	1
Number of researchers at provincial, municipal, and autonomous Republic fishery research organizations (th)	14

Beijing Review, 49 (9 Dec 1985), 21-23.

AQUATIC PRODUCTS, 1984

Rural households and cooperatives specializing in fish and shrimp breeding (mn)	2.34
Peasant households engaged in fish breeding as a sideline occupation (mn)	4.9
Inland waters suitable for fish breeding (mn ha)	5.6
Percent developed	54
Coastal shallows (mn ha)	1.33
Percent utilized	14
Output of fish and shrimp at fish farms (mn tons)	2.45+
Percent of China's total output of aquatic products	33
Production at freshwater farms (mn tons)	1.85
Production at farms in coastal waters (mn tons)	0.60
Breeding area (mn ha)	3.47
Area of ponds at fish farms (th ha)	142

XNB (2 Mar 1985), 25-26; (30 May 1985), 33.

FORESTRY DEVELOPMENTS, 1985

Bamboo—Approximately 46.8 percent of the 500,000 hectares of bamboo forests have died after flowering. This has reduced the wild panda population to about 1,000. *Beijing Review*, 19 (13 May 1985), 9-10.

Foreign Cooperation—China imported $35 million in forestry equipment in 1984. The Beijing Timber Factory acquired a particleboard line with an annual output of 30,000 m^3 from the Federal Republic of Germany. The Fuzhou Timber Factory imported a heavy-density particleboard production line with an annual capacity of 50,000 m^3 from the US. A timber mill with an annual output of 50,000 m^3 of particleboard from the Federal Republic of Germany is undergoing trial production in Jilin province, and an enterprise in Shanghai has imported a heavy-density particleboard line from Sweden. The Changsha Artificial Board Factory in Hunan province used $20 million in foreign exchange in 1984 to obtain equipment to product 100,000 m^2 of wood-based paneling and 1.8 million m^2 of laminated board. Plywood factories in Harbin and Changchun in northeast China, Chengdu in Sichuan, Xian in Shaanxi, and Wuhu in Anhui have purchased equipment from Japan, and plants in Sichuan, Inner Mongolia, Heilongjiang and Yunnan have imported technology and machinery from the US, Austria, Denmark and Italy. The Huaxi Timber Industrial and Commercial Co. Ltd. is the single timber-related joint venture in the PRC. China owns 95 percent of the $2 million in capital, and Brazil owns 5 percent. *Beijing Review*, 15 (15 Apr 1985), 30-31.

Malaysia—The PRC will purchase 1.4 million Malaysian dollars ($565,000) of logs from the Sarawak Timber Industry Development Corp. in Malaysia. *Asian Wall Street Journal Weekly* (11 Feb 1985), 12.

Great Green Wall—The first stage of the Great Green Wall, involving the afforestation of 5.93 million hectares, has been completed. The Wall will eventually extend 7,000 km through the arid north. Another 6.51 million hectares will be planted in the second stage during 1986-90. The third stage will add 10,66 million hectares by the year 2000. The shelterbelt will increase forest coverage across northern China to 10.6 percent. *Beijing Review*, 21 (27 May 1985), 9.

Canadian Assistance—The Canadian International Development Agency will provide China with funds, technology and equipment to the Lanxiang Forestry Bureau in Yichun city, Heilongjiang. An experimental center and computerized network for forestry management will be set up and a timber-processing plant built. The Lanxiang Bureau manages 260,000 hectares, with trees planted on 93,000. The Canadian intensive forestry management system will be used in the area. XNB (18 Mar 1985), 14.

continued . . .

FORESTRY DEVELOPMENTS, 1985 (continued)

Jiangxi—Some 114,000 hectares of mountain slopes were seeded by air in Jiangxi province in 1985, about 2.7 times the area seeded in 1984. Another 292,000 hectares are to be planted with seedlings. The area covered by trees will be expanded from 33.3 percent to 40.7 percent in 1990 and 54.4 percent by 1000. Jiangxi currently is fifth in the percentage of area covered by trees among China's provinces. XNB (23 Apr 1985), 10-11.

Cardboard—China plans to build an industrial base for cardboard in Shanxi, Hebei, Shandong, and Henan provinces. Capacity will reach 200-300,000 tons annually by 1990, and 1 million tons by 2000. By utilizing cotton straw, which contains about 25 percent long fiber, one can save three cubic meters of wood for every ton of cardboard. These four provinces produce half of China's cotton and approximately 10 million tons of cotton straw annually. XNB (23 Apr 1985), 29-30.

Forestry Plans—The Chinese have reforested about 28 million hectares of land over the past 30 years, bringing forest cover to 12.7 percent. In 1949 it was only 8.6 percent. The current percentage is less than half the world average and 18 percent of the world average per-capita forest cover. The more than 180,000 state and collective forestry centers or tree farms in the PRC have planted over 63 million hectares with seedlings. Nonetheless, more than 80 million hectares of barren hillsides and waste lands need to be reforested. By the end of the century, forest cover is to increase to 20 percent. *Beijing Review*, 28 (15 Jul 1985), 8-9.

Sino-Japanese Research—The Sino-Japanese research project signed in October, 1984 to study timber utilization in Heilongjiang began at the end of June, 1985. It includes the technical development of shaving board, and study of the properties of timber, compound board, drying, veneer, and coating. Japan will provide 500 million yen to buy instruments, and China will invest 3.5 million yuan in laboratory construction. The agreement will last five years. One-third of China's commercial timber is cut in Heilongjiang, and processing residues amount to 5 million m^3 a year. Approximately 20 percent of these residues are used. XNB (2 Jul 1985), 17-18.

Afforestation Contracts—The *China News Analysis*, 1284 (1 May 1985), 7, describes a contract for a family engaged in afforestation. The family contracts for a minimum of 100 *mu* (6.67 ha), and receives a subsidy of 20 kilograms of grain and 16 yuan per *mu*. Each *mu* is expected to produce 15 m^3 of timber in 15 years, which, subtracting 65 yuan per m^3 for investments and production costs, should provide a net profit of some 60 yuan per *mu* per year.

Timber Harvest—China is planning to reduce its annual timber harvest of 55 million m^3 by up to 15 percent. Forests cover 115 million hectares of the PRC, and total timber resources are estimated at 9 billion m^3. China imported $35 million in equipment and lumber mills in 1984. A particleboard production line from the Federal Republic of Germany has an annual capacity of 30,000 m^3, and another from the US in Fuzhou has a yearly output capacity of 50,000 m^3 of heavy-density particleboard. *China Daily* (18 Apr 1985).

Largest Forest—The Yakeshi forest zone in the Great Hingan Mountains covers 212,000 km^2 in Heilongjiang and Inner Mongolia. Total timber reserves amount to 560 million m^3. More than 50 percent of its trees have been logged since 1952, providing over 80 million m^3 of timber. XNB (12 Aug 1985), 22-23.

XI FOREIGN TRADE

TRADE NEWS, 1985

Imported Technology—Preliminary statistics indicate that China has imported about $15.3 billion in equipment and know-how for over 1,600 projects during the past three decades. The Ministry of Foreign Economic Relations and Trade approved contracts for the transfer of technology totaling $1.87 billion between 1982 and 1984, with over half approved in 1984. That year 741 joint ventures were approved, bringing in about $1.1 billion in foreign investment. This was a 466-percent increase over 1983. Another $1.5 billion was involved in cooperative projects in 1984, a rise of 195 percent. *Beijing Review*, 17 (29 Apr 1985), 9-10. China plans to import 3,000 advanced technologies from 1983 through 1985. Deals were concluded for 1,620 items in 1984, or 2.5 times the number in 1983. They amounted to $1.56 billion in 1984, or 2.6 times the value the previous year. This means that some 2,270 items have already been imported, and the plan will be overfulfilled. FBIS-CHI 31 (14 Feb 1985), K19. The PRC could import 1,500 Western technological processes in 1985. New York *Times* (3 Feb 1985), 11. One estimate of high-technology exports from the US to China, excluding commercial aircraft but including all green line product categories (computers, computerized instruments, microcircuits, electronic instruments, recording equipment, and semiconductor equipment), indicates that their value nearly doubled to over $214 million between 1982 and 1983. These exports exceeded $300 million in 1984. The value of export licenses approved for China by the Department of Commerce (including commercial aircraft and technical data exports) rose from $523 million in 1982 to $2 billion in 1984. US Department of State, *GIST* (Mar 1985), 1-2.

Shenzhen—The Shenzhen Special Economic Zone with some 400,000 inhabitants has been ringed by an 80-km fence to keep capitalists in and Chinese black-marketeers out. The Shenzhen SEZ has become a boomtown, but still does not pay its way: in five years, it has used up $1.2 billion for infrastructure alone. *Newsweek* (22 Jul 1985), 39. It has not produced the foreign currency expected. Only 40 percent of its products are exported. New York *Times* (28 Aug 1985), 6.

Investment Protection Agreement—China and Holland signed an agreement 17 June 1985 to encourage and protect economic relations and investment. The agreement will be in force for 10 years. XNB (18 Jun 1985), 29.

Tacheng—Tacheng, Xinjiang will be opened to trade with the Soviet Union. The port has been closed to Soviet trade for 40 years. *Jiefang Ribao* (26 Jul 1985).

Four of 14 Coastal Cities Given Priority—Shanghai, Dalian, Tianjin, and Guangzhou among the 14 coastal cities opened to foreign investment in 1984 will receive priority in their development. The other 10 cities will experience slower growth. In January, 1985 Chinese officials were talking about opening even more cities to foreign investment, but the sharp fall in foreign exchange reserves has apparently caused leaders to move more cautiously. London *Financial Times* (17 Jul 1985), 3.

Foreign Capital—In 1984 China signed agreements for foreign capital totaling $4.8 billion, up 40 percent from 1983. Capital actually used amounted to $2.66 billion, an increase of 35.7 percent. Some 741 joint ventures were approved with total foreign investment of $1.1 billion. Seventy-four factories have been built in China exclusively with foreign capital, including 26 in 1984. Between 1979 and 1984, the PRC used $17.3 billion of the foreign capital, $4.03 billion of which came directly from foreign businessmen. By the end of 1984, 31 foreign oil companies had signed 23 contracts for surveys and exploration with a total investment of $1.2 billion. *China Reconstructs*, XXXIV, 6 (Jun 1985), 18-19.

Substandard Imports—Of 76,117 import shipments inspected by the Chinese in 1984, 11,165, or 15 percent, were in some way deficient. During the first quarter of 1985, 23 percent (4,683 of 40,387 shipments) were also found substandard. *Beijing Review*, 29 (22 Jul 1985), 31.

continued . . .

TRADE NEWS, 1985 (continued)

World Bank and IFC Loans to China—A list of the $1.1 billion in World Bank, International Finance Corp., International Development Association, and International Bank for Reconstruction and Development Loans to the PRC during fiscal year 1985 may be found in the *China Business Review,* 12, 4 (Jul-Aug 1985), 48.

Three Zones Opening to Foreign Investment—The PRC will open the Changjiang (Yangtze) River delta, the Zhujiang (Pearl) River delta, and the Xiamen-Zhangzhou-Quanzhou delta to foreign investment. The cities of Suzhou, Wuxi, Changzhou, Changshu, Jiaxing, Huzhou, Quanzhou, Zhangzhou, Foshan, Jiangmen and Zhongsan and their more than 50 surrounding counties and townships will be the first to allow foreign investments. The Liaodong and Jiaodong Peninsulas will also be opened gradually so that the entire east China coast will accept foreign investment. The economic zones will subsequently extend inland. *Beijing Review,* 17 (29 Apr 1985), 4.

Taxes on Foreign Firms—China has introduced a 15-percent enterprise income tax on foreign-based subsidiaries' earnings from services and consultations retroactive to 1 January 1985. It also levied a 5-percent industrial and commercial tax on Hong Kong, Macao, and other foreign enterprises from 1 June 1985. *Asian Wall Street Journal Weekly* (20 May 1985), 13. Taxable items were to include commissions, rebates and fees received for conducting market surveys and providing business information, and for liaison, consulting, and other services. Foreign enterprises with offices in various parts of China will be required to pay taxes in each locality. All foreign firms must register to do business in China. *Beijing Review,* 21 (27 May 1985), 10.

Tallest Building in Beijing—The International Mansions, Beijing's tallest building, rises 101 meters on eastern Chang An Boulevard. The 31-story structure has 47,741 m^2 of office and residential space. The building is the headquarters of the China International Trust and Investment Corp. *Beijing Review,* 23 (10 Jun 1985), 10.

Sino-Belgian Joint Venture—The Shanghai Bell Telephone Equipment Manufacturing Company, the first Sino-Belgian joint venture, will begin operations in October, 1985. It will made 30,000 channel telephone exchanges in 1985, and 70,000 more in 1986. By 1987 the firm will turn out 300,000 channel exchanges. *Beijing Review,* 20 (20 May 1985), 30.

First Tianjin Zone Joint Venture—The Jiatai Ceramics Industry Company Ltd. is the first joint venture in Tanggu, the 33-km^2 economic development zone of Tianjin. The company will produce 6,000 m^2 of glazed tiles, cutlery, and quarried stone annually. XNB (17 Jan 1985), 22.

Joint Ventures, 1984—There were 741 joint ventures in 1984, exceeding the total for the previous five years. China used $2.66 billion in foreign investment, 35.7 percent more than in 1983. Over 1,000 items of technology will be imported as a result of these contracts. FBIS-CHI 61 (29 Mar 1985), K5.

Japanese Bond Issue—The PRC will float a second bond issue worth 30 billion yen ($118.3 million in Japan. The 10-year bonds have an interest rate of 6.675 percent. The issuing price will be 99.55 percent of the face value of the bond, and the coupon rate will be 6.6 percent. The China International Trust & Investment Corp. will float the bonds. The first series was issued in Japan in November, 1984. *Asian Wall Street Journal Weekly* (4 Feb 1985), 7.

Sino-Singapore Venture—Shanghai's first joint venture with a Southeast Asian firm is a ship-repair service jointly funded by Metalock of Singapore and the Shanghai Ocean Shipping Repair Dockyard. The venture opened in Shanghai 18 May 1985. *Beijing Review,* 24 (17 Jun 1985), 33.

Dual Exchange Rates—As part of the devaluation of the yuan, the internal settlement rate introduced in 1981 is being eliminated. The rate was devised to let Chinese trading corporations convert foreign exchange at a rate more favorable than 2.8 to $1 (US). The rate is being scrapped because the official exchange rate is already below the internal settlement rate of 2.8. It is hoped that devaluation of the yuan will increase exports, cut imports to

continued . . .

TRADE NEWS, 1985 (continued)

China, and end foreign-currency transactions in the gray market. *Asian Wall Street Journal Weekly* (18 Feb 1985), 12.

Direct Equity Investment—China's first direct equity investment in a firm outside Hong Kong will involve the purchase of 8 percent of the Sunshine Australia Ltd. investment company. The price will be $8 million (Australian) or $5.3 million (US). Sunshine Australia already is participating in a $40 million venture with the PRC to manufacture printed circuit boards. *Asian Wall Street Journal Weekly* (13 May (1985), 4.

First IFC Loan—The first International Finance Corp. loan to China was announced 26 June 1985. The IFC will provide a loan of $15 million and make an equity investment of $2.02 million in the Guangzhou Peugeot Automobile Company. The company will be able to produce 50,000 pick-up trucks annually. The IFC is an affiliate of the World Bank which finances businesses in the private sector in developing countries. FBIS-CHI 125 (28 Jun 1985), A3.

Xerox—Xerox and two Shanghai companies have agreed to build manufacturing facilities and to sell various Xerox copying products in China, including 10,000 small copiers over the next 12 months. *Asian Wall Street Journal Weekly* (4 Mar 1985), 11; New York *Times* (14 Jun 1985), 31.

TRADE NEWS BY COUNTRIES, 1985

Tibet-Nepal—There are 27 trading posts along the border between Tibet and Nepal. Six Tibetan prefectures and cities can sign trade agreements directly with Nepal. Turnover was 14 million yuan in 1983. Tibet will export 700 tons of wool, 5,000 live sheep, textiles, and household articles to Nepal, and Kathmandu will provide 7,000 tons of rice, 3,000 tons of flour, 5,000 tons of cement, and steel products each year from 1985 to 1987. *Beijing Review,* 24 (17 Jun 1985), 33.

United Kingdom—Sino-British trade amounted to $1.19 billion in 1984. This was only 0.3 percent of Britain's foreign trade. Just nine of the more than 700 joint ventures arranged in 1984 were with British firms. XNB (3 Jun 1985), 34-35.

European Economic Community—Bilateral trade between China and Western Europe came to almost $7 billion in 1984. West European countries had invested $900 million in China and set up 30 joint ventures by the end of the year. Sino-EEC trade accounts for 30 percent of China's foreign trade, but just 0.4 percent of its own. Western Europe is now the PRC's second biggest trading partner after Japan. It has provided only 10 percent of China's direct foreign investment. XNB (3 Jun 1985), 36.

East Germany—China plans to triple its trade with the German Democratic Republic by 1990. A five-year agreement signed in July, 1985 is estimated to be worth $2.08 billion. East Germany will export railway cars and machinery, and the PRC will export agricultural products, textiles, and raw materials. *Asian Wall Street Journal Weekly* (22 Jul 1985), 8; New York *Times* (17 Jul 1985), 44.

Indonesia—Indirect trade between Indonesia and the PRC in 1984 amounted to about $24 million in exports to China and over $200 million in imports from the PRC. *Asian Wall Street Journal Weekly* (20 May 1985), 2. A memorandum on direct trade was signed 5 July 1985. Direct trade was suspended 18 years ago.

Philippines—Bilateral trade is to increase to $500 million annually. Trade reached $280 million in 1984, with Philippine exports totaling $60 million and imports $220 million. *Asian Wall Street Journal Weekly* (29 Apr 1985), 18.

Greece—Trade turnover between Greece and China is to reach $108 million in 1985, up from $58 million in 1984. The PRC provides tools, textiles, silk and meat, and Greece sells China fertilizer, steel, synthetic fibers and leather. *Asian Wall Street Journal Weekly* (15 Apr 1985), 16.

continued . . .

TRADE NEWS BY COUNTRIES, 1985 (continued)

Poland—Sino-Polish trade is to reach 1.3 billion Swiss francs in 1985, or 2.8 times the total in 1984. The PRC, particularly Yunnan, will provide 10,000 tons of tea to Poland, or one-third of its total tea imports. *Beijing Review,* 14 (8 Apr 1985), 29.

Sino-Soviet Border Trade—Trade between Heilongjiang province and Khabarovsk, Soviet coastal areas in the Far East, and the Amur region amounted to 18 million Swiss francs ($7 million) in 1983. Trade increased more than 70 percent in 1984. The province exports light industrial products, textiles, tinned meats, soybeans, fur hats, hog bristle brushes, thermos flasks, and various household items to the Soviet Union. Heilongjiang imports timber, cement, glass, chemicals, soda ash, motorcycles, and household electrical appliances. When border trade between the USSR and Inner Mongolia was restored in 1983, it totaled 3 million Swiss francs. It reached 15 million in 1984. *Beijing Review,* 4 (28 Jan 1985), 30-31.

Taiwan—The *Hong Kong Economic Journal* has reported that exports from the PRC to Taiwan via Hong Kong amounted to $999 million (HK) in 1984, up 43 percent from 1983. Exports from Taiwan to China via Hong Kong reached $3.327 billion (HK). Mainland exports of fish increased to $120 million (HK), a three-fold rise over the previous year, and Taiwanese exports of synthetic fibers amounted to $844 million (HK), also a three-fold increase. *Beijing Review,* 10 (11 Mar 1985), 8. A later report in the *Beijing Review,* 33 19 Aug 1985), 8, put the value of indirect trade at $560 million (US), up 15.7 percent.

Turkey—China and Turkey have agreed to increase trade from $40 million to $100 million in 1985. Turkey will import wheat, rice, soybean, raw silk, steam coal, crude oil (503,000 tons), machinery and equipment, while China will import tobacco, fertilizers, cotton, cement, and chrome ore. XNB (9 Mar 1985), 4-5; FBIS-CHI 178 (13 Sep 1985), G3.

Thailand—Sino-Thai trade from 1978 to 1984 was:

	Chinese Exports (mn dollars)	Chinese Exports (mn dollars)	Chinese Exports (mn dollars)
1978	73	86	−13
1979	77	241	−164
1980	124	416	−292
1981	131	195	−64
1982	326	157	+169
1983	106	251	−145
1984	350-400 (turnover)		

Beijing Review, 9 (4 Mar 1985), 33.

West Germany—The Federal Republic of Germany is China's biggest European trading partner. Volume totaled $2.2 billion in 1984, up 3.4 percent from 1983. China exported textiles, electrical equipment, farm and sideline products, while West Germany exported rolled steel, chemicals, machinery and various equipment and technology. XNB (5 Jun 1985), 51-52.

Malaysia—China and Malaysia have agreed to open direct trade and to protect mutual investments. Malaysia has also expressed some interest in participating in joint ventures in timber-processing. XNB (12 Jul 1985), 12.

USSR, 1986-90—A trade agreement between the USSR and PRC signed 10 July 1985 stipulates that the volume of reciprocal trade will increase to approximately 12 billion rubles during 1986-90. The total will reach 3 billion rubles by 1990, or almost twice the level in 1985. The Soviets will help reconstruct 17 enterprises in the coal, steel, machine-building, power-engineering and chemical industries. Seven new facilities will be built. *Pravda* (11 Jul 1985).

Japan—The Japanese External Trade Organization (JETRO) has estimated that bilateral trade between China and Japan reached $13.16 billion in 1984, with a $1.26 billion surplus

continued . . .

TRADE NEWS BY COUNTRIES, 1985 (continued)

for Japan. Japanese exports to the PRC totaled $7.21 billion, up 47 percent over 1983. Imports reached $5.95 billion, an increase of 17 percent. Steel accounted for 40 percent of the Japanese exports, and crude oil comprised 39 percent ($2.34 billion) of its imports. China is now Japan's third largest trading partner after the US and South Korea. *Facts on File* (15 Feb 1985), 109C3.

Taiwanese Trade with the PRC—The *China Post* (12 Apr 1985), 12, reported Taiwanese exports to Mainland China through Hong Kong, Japan, Singapore and other countries totaled $430 million (US) in 1984, and a 170-percent increase over 1983. Imports from the PRC through third countries amounted to $130 million, a 40-percent rise.

China Trade with Hong Kong—Hong Kong exported $11.283 billion (HK) worth of manufactured commodities to the PRC in 1984, an increase of 81.3 percent over 1983. Hong Kong's imports from the PRC totaled $55.753 billion (HK), a rise of 30.2 percent. Reexports to the Mainland amounted to $28.064 billion, up 130.4 percent. Chinese-made goods reexported to other countries through Hong Kong totaled $28.107 billion, an increase of 42.8 percent. The PRC has invested about $4 billion (US) in Hong Kong in the past several years, while Hong Kong's investment in China is thought to be about 60 percent of the total foreign investment. In 1984, 8,036,452 Hong Kong residents visited the PRC, or 9.7 times the number in 1974. FBIS-CHI 69 (10 Apr 1985), E7.

India—China and India signed a 1986 trade protocol 25 November 1985. Turnover will amount to a record $160 million. Trade has increased from about $2 million (25.6 million rupees) in 1984. China's major imports include metal products, shellac, iron ore, iron and steel, chromite, and various raw materials. Its exports to India include silk, industrial chemicals, non-ferrous metals, yarn and spices. *Beijing Review*, 47 (25 Nov 1985), 29.

FOREIGN TRADE SUMMARY, 1985

	Billion Dollars	Percentage Increase Over 1984
Total	59.21	19.0
Imports	33.41	31.8
Exports	25.80	5.7
By Main Trading Partners:		
Japan	16.57	30.2
Hong Kong	9.60	7.2
EEC	6.90	24.5
US	6.42	7.6
FRG	2.84	27.9
USSR	1.90	61.0
UK	1.43	20.1
Italy	0.83	25.0
France	0.79	36.2

Beijing Review, 5 (3 Feb 1986), 28-29.

CHINESE FOREIGN TRADE (mn US$)

CHINESE FOREIGN TRADE[a] (mn US$)

Year		Total Trade	Communist Countries				Non-Communist Countries		
			Total	Eastern Europe	USSR	Other[b]	Total	Developed Countries	Less Developed Countries[c]
1965	Exports	2,035	650	95	225	330	1,385	575	810
	Imports	1,680	515	110	190	215	1,165	805	360
1970	Exports	2,155	480	255	20	205	1,675	660	1,015
	Imports	2,045	390	225	25	140	1,655	1,370	285
1975	Exports	7,130	1,375	630	150	595	5,755	2,610	3,145
	Imports	6,830	1,005	595	130	280	5,825	4,985	840
1979	Exports	13,735	1,755	1,050	240	465	11,980	5,645	6,335
	Imports	14,490	1,945	1,200	270	475	12,545	10,170	2,375
1980	Exports	18,925	1,885	1,130	230	525	17,040	8,270	8,770
	Imports	19,305	1,945	1,110	295	540	17,360	13,515	3,845
1981	Exports	21,495	1,240	745	130	365	20,255	10,045	10,210
	Imports	17,940	1,270	700	115	455	16,670	12,740	3,930
1982	Exports	23,435	1,210	660	145	405	22,230	10,225	12,005
	Imports	16,690	1,670	925	165	580	15,020	10,805	4,215
1983	Exports	23,520	1,365	670	310	385	22,155	9,940	12,215
	Imports	18,340	1,650	845	340	470	16,690	11,720	4,965
1984	Exports	27,440	1,555	590	625	340	25,885	11,870	14,015
	Imports	25,100	2,075	1,050	575	455	23,025	15,440	7,585

a. Data are f.o.b. and rounded to the nearest US $5 million.
b. Including data for Albania, Cuba, Mongolia, North Korea, Vietnam, and Yugoslavia.
c. Including data for Hong Kong and Macao.

CIA, Handbook of Economic Statistics, 1985 (1985), 104.

CHINESE EXPORTS (mn US$)

CHINESE EXPORTS[a] (mn US$)	1970	1975	1979	1980	1981	1982	1983	1984
Total	2,155	7,130	13,735	18,925	21,495	23,435	23,520	27,440
Food and live animals	660	2,045	2,650	3,210	3,450	3,595	3,250	3,420
Live animals	70	215	265	340	380	395	295	305
Meat and meat preparations	105	240	305	385	375	500	425	385
Fish and fish preparations	70	190	380	400	425	385	325	350
Cereals and cereal preparations	150	615	420	485	510	495	345	355
Vegetables and fruit	170	435	775	935	1,050	1,040	1,000	1,035
Beverages and tobacco	20	80	100	120	120	140	145	165
Crude materials, excluding fuel	380	840	1,600	1,820	2,050	1,790	2,060	2,440
Oilseeds, oil nuts, and oil kernels	70	160	190	185	525	245	320	345
Textile fibers and wastes	105	245	510	545	500	550	750	940
Crude animal and vegetable materials	115	225	450	540	455	465	475	545
Mineral fuels, lubricants, and related materials	60	1,025	2,465	4,415	4,765	5,255	4,805	5,735
Petroleum and petroleum products	5	865	2,250	4,165	4,495	4,930	4,485	5,185
Animal and vegetable oils and fats	25	55	90	85	105	70	105	130
Chemicals	115	350	770	1,180	1,300	1,280	1,290	1,400
Chemical elements and compounds	25	100	270	480	550	565	540	610
Manufactured goods	590	1,650	3,515	4,410	5,140	5,005	4,930	6,010
Textile yarn, fabrics, made-up articles	390	1,035	2,285	2,765	3,080	2,920	3,180	4,135
Nonmetallic mineral manufactures	60	170	330	415	480	480	380	385
Manufactures of metal	40	110	285	390	520	565	595	665
Machinery and transport equipment	75	260	485	610	805	790	810	1,075
Miscellaneous manufactured goods	225	800	2,025	3,010	3,665	4,150	4,500	5,795
Clothing	100	355	1,055	1,665	2,095	2,435	2,740	3,475
Other	5	25	35	65	95	1,365	1,625	1,270

a. Data are f.o.b. and rounded to the nearest US $5 million.

CIA, *Handbook of Economic Statistics, 1985* (1985), 105.

CHINESE IMPORTS (mn US$)

CHINESE IMPORTS[a] (mn US$)

	1970	1975	1979	1980	1981	1982	1983	1984
Total	2,045	6,830	14,490	19,305	17,940	16,690	18,340	25,100
Food and live animals	330	815	1,775	2,860	3,080	3,495	2,380	2,420
Cereal and cereal preparations	255	540	1,305	2,225	2,340	2,475	1,625	1,560
Sugar, sugar preparations, and honey	65	155	210	300	470	650	380	315
Crude materials, excluding fuels	235	730	1,960	3,325	3,175	2,520	2,365	2,450
Rubber, crude (including synthetic and reclaimed)	95	165	315	430	215	245	230	295
Textile fibers and their waste	95	395	1,140	2,065	2,280	1,470	1,155	1,040
Mineral fuels, lubricants, and related materials	40	130	180	175	175	175	190	240
Petroleum and petroleum products	10	40	35	30	55	30	60	50
Animal and vegetable fats and oils	5	40	180	180	105	95	95	90
Chemicals	310	815	1,445	2,185	2,025	2,110	2,235	2,930
Chemical elements and compounds	175	250	410	545	470	525	575	590
Fertilizers, manufactured	65	390	595	980	755	580	570	700
Manufactured goods	690	2,190	4,710	4,575	4,000	4,195	5,715	7,200
Textile yarn, fabrics, made-up articles, and products	40	90	295	845	1,575	1,160	1,010	1,555
Iron and steel	390	1,475	3,460	2,235	1,320	1,870	3,315	4,020
Nonferrous metals	200	395	340	420	165	430	665	710
Machinery and transport equipment	405	2,010	3,845	5,350	4,595	3,280	4,260	7,910
Machinery, other than electric	190	985	1,990	2,790	2,545	1,405	1,815	3,300
Electric machinery	30	190	540	1,070	1,345	820	1,190	2,245
Transport equipment	190	835	1,310	1,490	705	1,055	1,255	2,365
Miscellaneous manufactured goods	25	75	300	485	595	670	895	1,605
Other	NEGL	25	95	170	190	145	205	255

a. Data are f.o.b. and rounded to the nearest US $5 million.

CIA, *Handbook of Economic Statistics, 1985* (1985), 106.

Holland article

78 FJ - 87
70
762 !!

CHINESE TRADE BY COMMODITY, 1982-84 (million dollars)

	Chinese Imports		
	1982	1983	1984
All Commotities	16,686.0	18,341.0	25,100.8
Food and Live Animals	3,362.6	2,291.4	2,260.0
Live Animals	2.6	2.2	3.9
Meat and Meat Preparations	3.0	3.1	4.3
Dairy Products and Eggs	45.4	13.1	25.6
Fish and Fish Preparations	4.2	9.8	8.9
Cereals and Cereal Preparations	2,449.1	1,625.2	1,561.9
Fruits and Vegetables	109.2	118.4	167.3
Sugar, Honey, and Preparations	628.6	380.9	316.5
Coffee, Tea, and Spices	67.6	75.2	119.3
Animal Feedstuffs	42.8	53.5	38.3
Miscellaneous Food Preparations	10.2	9.9	14.0
Beverages and Tobacco	77.0	88.1	159.6
Beverages	12.1	25.3	41.3
Tobacco, Tobacco Manufactures	64.9	62.8	118.3
Crude Materials	2,447.2	2,364.8	2,448.4
Hides and Skins, Undressed	24.5	15.1	34.8
Oilseeds, Oil Nuts	80.8	45.2	10.1
Crude Rubber	199.0	228.0	292.8
Wood, Lumber, and Cork	351.4	454.2	475.4
Pulp and Waste Paper	143.9	230.8	222.1
Textile Fibers	1,402.7	1,153.3	1,037.7
Crude Fertilizer and Minerals	61.9	60.8	93.2
Metalliferous Ores	98.3	103.7	189.8
Crude Animal and Vegetable Materials	84.8	73.8	92.6
Mineral Fuels and Products	180.4	189.7	240.5
Coal, Coke, and Briquettes	130.1	108.2	147.3
Petroleum and Petroleum Products	31.6	58.4	51.6
Gas, Natural and Manufactured	0.4	0.7	1.1
Electric Energy	18.4	22.4	40.6
Animal and Vegetable Oils and Fats	88.2	96.7	91.3
Animal Oils and Fats	27.1	96.7	91.3
Fixed Vegetable Oils and Fats	51.1	75.7	65.0
Processed Oils and Fats	10.0	8.0	3.2
Chemicals	2,169.9	2,235.0	2,930.6
Elements and Compounds	520.8	575.5	589.3
Mineral Tar	0.8	7.0	5.4
Dyestuffs and Paints	140.9	117.1	86.2
Medicinal and Pharmaceutical Products	34.0	43.0	61.9
Essential Oils and Soaps	22.1	39.5	50.7
Fertilizers, Manufactured	621.9	569.1	700.2
Explosives and Products	1.0	0.7	1.7
Plastic Materials and Resins	633.9	575.1	1,132.9
Chemical Materials and Products, NES.	194.6	307.8	302.4
Semi-Manufactured Goods	4,216.3	5,716.7	7,202.0
Leather and Dressed Skins	158.5	110.4	135.7
Rubber Manufactures	12.7	16.3	27.5
Wood and Cork Manufactures	48.3	34.3	41.0
Paper and Paperboard	167.3	176.6	245.5

continued . . .

CHINESE TRADE BY COMMODITY, 1982-84 (million dollars) (continued)

	1982	1983	1984
Textile Yarn and Fabrics	1,154.2	1,008.4	1,556.1
Mineral Manufactures	175.2	195.1	189.6
Iron and Steel	1,878.5	3,316.9	4,018.0
Nonferrous Metals	452.1	666.2	711.9
Metal Manufactures, NES	169.5	192.5	276.8
Machinery and Equipment	3,325.4	4,258.1	7,907.9
Non-electric Machinery	1,506.0	1,813.9	3,301.3
Electrical Machinery	801.8	1,189.4	2,244.1
Transport Equipment	1,017.6	1,254.8	2,362.5
Miscellaneous Manufactured Articles	670.8	896.7	1,607.2
Building Fixtures, Fittings	7.9	12.0	24.1
Furniture	8.5	13.9	25.7
Travel Goods, Handbags	1.2	2.1	3.5
Clothing	50.3	61.3	90.7
Footwear	1.7	2.0	3.9
Precision Instruments	315.8	406.6	707.5
Miscellaneous Manufactured Articles, NES	285.4	398.8	751.7
Other Transactions	148.1	203.7	253.2
Postal Packages	0.1	0.1	0.1
Special Transactions	145.8	201.2	251.3
Animals, NES	1.1	1.0	1.2
Military Firearms	0.3	0.2	0.1
Coins, Nonmonetary	0.9	1.3	0.5

		Chinese Exports	
	1982	1983	1984
All Commodities	22,900.3	3,248.2	27,439.8
Food and Live Animals	3,302.7	3,248.2	3,421.5
Live Animals	340.3	297.0	304.7
Meat and Meat Preparations	416.2	427.1	386.7
Dairy Products and Eggs	95.7	79.4	76.7
Fish and Fish Preparations	375.4	324.7	350.6
Cereals and Cereal Preparations	411.2	344.6	353.0
Fruits and Vegetables	990.0	999.0	1,032.8
Sugar, Honey, and Preparations	117.1	117.4	94.6
Coffee, Tea and Spices	370.7	365.5	437.3
Animal Feedstuffs	134.6	234.6	315.7
Miscellaneous Food Preparations	51.5	58.9	69.6
Beverages and Tobacco	136.6	147.2	166.0
Beverages	79.1	78.4	74.6
Tobacco, Tobacco Manufactures	57.5	68.8	91.4
Crude Materials	1,798.2	2,058.4	2,440.1
Hides and Skins, Undressed	84.5	94.4	107.3
Oilseeds, Oil Nuts	248.0	317.8	343.9
Crude Rubber	4.2	3.6	7.1
Wood, Lumber, and Cork	22.0	18.1	16.8
Pulp and Waste Paper	0.1	0.5	0.6
Textile Fibers	565.0	748.0	938.2
Crude Fertilizer and Minerals	281.5	285.8	319.4
Metalliferous Ores	130.7	115.0	162.4
Crude Animal and Vegetable Materials	462.1	475.2	544.4

continued . . .

CHINESE TRADE BY COMMODITY, 1982-84 (million dollars) (continued)

	1982	1983	1984
Mineral Fuels and Products	5,224.3	4,807.1	5,737.3
Coal, Coke, and Briquettes	327.5	319.5	551.1
Petroleum and Petroleum Products	4,896.8	4,486.5	5,184.7
Gas, Natural and Manufactured	0.0	1.0	1.5
Electric Energy	0.0	0.0	0.0
Animal and Vegetable Oils and Fats	75.4	103.9	129.8
Animal Oils & Fats	0.4	0.2	0.2
Fixed Vegetable Oils and Fats	72.6	99.9	126.2
Processed Oils and Fats	2.4	3.8	3.5
Chemicals	1,296.1	1,289.1	1,397.7
Elements and Compounds	580.6	541.3	608.4
Mineral Tar	30.9	15.9	14.5
Dyestuffs and Paints	71.1	80.9	88.8
Medicinal and Pharmaceutical Products	223.6	236.8	247.9
Essential Oils and Soaps	97.6	110.0	120.0
Fertilizers, Manufactured	2.7	2.9	0.9
Explosives and Products	109.6	112.5	122.3
Plastic Materials and Resins	43.3	54.5	57.1
Chemical Materials and Products, NES	136.7	134.3	137.8
Semi-Manufactured Goods	4,823.4	4,930.9	6,009.4
Leather and Dressed Skins	63.9	59.0	82.3
Rubber Manufactures	55.5	59.1	63.2
Wood and Cork Manufactures	55.3	51.6	52.9
Paper and Paperboard	163.7	173.0	198.2
Textile Yarn and Fabrics	2,849.3	3,182.1	4,134.0
Mineral Manufactures	379.5	380.2	383.9
Iron and Steel	482.4	263.7	263.5
Nonferrous Metals	214.6	167.3	166.6
Metal Manufactures, NES	559.1	594.8	664.6
Machinery and Equipment	768.2	809.2	1,075.3
Non-electric Machinery	332.1	303.1	344.6
Electrical Machinery	332.1	382.9	532.0
Transport Equipment	104.0	123.1	198.7
Miscellaneous Manufactured Articles	4,113.4	4,500.7	5,793.8
Building Fixtures, Fittings	69.2	63.5	69.2
Furniture	202.9	161.5	174.4
Travel Goods, Handbags	144.4	189.9	323.9
Clothing	2,419.6	2,741.0	3,475.2
Footwear	263.7	272.8	328.2
Precision Instruments	144.5	165.3	200.4
Miscellaneous Manufactured Articles, NES	869.0	906.7	1,222.5
Other Transactions	1,362.1	1,625.3	1,268.9
Postal Packages	0.9	0.8	0.8
Special Transactions	63.4	76.9	82.7
Animals, NES	4.9	4.3	6.5
Military Firearms	1,289.1	1,535.6	1,170.0
Coins, Nonmonetary	3.8	7.7	9.0

Imports and exports F.O.B.
CIA, *China: International Trade Fourth Quarter, 1984* (1985), 8-11.

CHINESE TRADE BY AREA AND COUNTRY, 1982-84 (million dollars)[1]

	Chinese Exports		
	1982	1983	1984
World	22,900.0	23,519.5	27,439.4
Non-Communist Countries	21,625.0	22,156.0	25,883.5
Developed Countries	10,224.6	9,942.3	11,868.2
East Asia and Pacific	5,442.7	5,108.1	6,011.8
Australia	319.2	230.1	313.1
North America	2,440.2	2,451.1	3,332.0
Canada	165.3	199.5	258.0
United States	2,274.9	2,251.6	3,074.0
Western Europe	2,341.7	2,383.1	2,524.4
Belgium	120.7	98.4	88.6
France	379.7	376.7	383.0
West Germany	610.1	667.7	740.0
Italy	372.1	359.8	373.9
Netherlands	167.0	155.1	145.6
Spain	86.6	73.2	99.5
Sweden	74.9	68.4	75.4
Switzerland	62.8	65.4	72.2
United Kingdom	295.0	305.5	323.4
Less Developed Countires	11,400.4	12,213.7	14,015.3
Southeast Asia	7,540.4	7,774.4	9,812.9
Hong Kong	5,430.5	5,846.5	7,130.5
Indonesia	219.9	194.3	226.8
Malaysia	263.7	256.7	284.6
Philippines	212.1	75.8	216.9
Singapore	838.6	787.7	1,282.6
Thailand	222.5	252.5	308.3
South Asia	405.6	360.1	476.9
Bangladesh	103.0	55.6	160.1
Pakistan	142.2	139.7	136.8
Sri Lanka	40.0	40.0	34.5
Middle East	2,201.9	2,646.6	2,292.8
Kuwait	127.5	147.9	172.6
Saudi Arabia	223.0	222.0	237.0
Syria	64.7	105.0	122.6
United Arab Emirates	121.8	132.1	157.1
Yemen Arab Republic	59.1	61.2	71.5
North Africa	236.4	264.8	303.6
Egypt	49.0	50.8	59.3
Tunisia	19.5	28.4	17.5
Sub-Sahara Africa	487.7	489.6	568.5
Cameroon	18.9	11.9	5.2
Nigeria	44.1	45.6	53.3
Sudan	24.8	29.7	34.6
Zambia	2.5	2.6	3.0

continued . . .

CHINESE TRADE BY AREA AND COUNTRY, 1982-84 (million dollars) (continued)

	1982	1983	1984
Latin America	528.4	678.2	560.7
Argentina	9.3	4.3	4.7
Brazil	332.7	451.6	416.8
Chile	19.7	9.0	11.3
Guatemala	.6	1.5	2.0
Mexico	58.9	11.3	12.5
Communist Countries	1,275.0	1,363.5	1,555.9
USSR	142.6	307.9	625.2
Eastern Europe	725.8	672.1	592.2
Czechoslovakia	71.6	90.1	103.8
East Germany	68.6	59.0	85.9
Hungary	25.9	25.9	27.8
Poland	177.8	163.5	100.6
Romania	341.8	289.7	222.8
Yugoslavia	18.0	16.0	18.6
Other[2]	406.6	383.5	338.5

Percent of Estimate Obtained from Trade Partner Data[3]

	1982	1983	1984
World	96.85	94.53	87.74
Developed Countries	100.00	100.00	99.49
Less Developed Countries	93.76	89.69	78.42
Communist Countries	99.22	98.03	82.10

	Chinese Imports		
	1982	1983	1984
World	16,686.0	18,341.0	25,100.9
Non-Communist Countries	14,969.6	16,688.6	23,024.2
Developed Countries	10,803.9	11,721.6	15,441.7
East Asia and Pacific	4,446.0	5,420.5	8,057.5
Australia	837.9	392.8	735.8
Japan	3,500.0	4,917.7	7,198.7
North America	3,917.2	3,362.2	3,971.8
Canada	1,005.2	1,189.1	967.5
United States	2,912.0	2,173.1	3,004.3
Western Europe	2,440.7	2,939.9	3,412.4
Belgium	203.3	213.3	272.2
France	335.8	450.0	310.2
West Germany	852.6	1,074.9	1,037.8
Italy	210.3	264.5	394.6
Netherlands	66.3	132.9	167.0
Spain	111.9	109.1	185.1
Sweden	59.7	114.5	120.9
Switzerland	128.2	124.3	123.0
United Kingdom	178.5	243.6	424.0
Less Developed Countries	4,165.7	4,967.0	7,582.5
Southeast Asia	2,996.6	3,240.7	6,024.8
Hong Kong	1,954.4	2,494.8	5,030.7
Indonesia	14.1	26.9	37.0
Malaysia	110.4	156.7	176.6

continued . . .

CHINESE TRADE BY AREA AND COUNTRY, 1982-84 (million dollars)[1] (continued)

	1982	1983	1984
Philippines	105.2	22.4	60.2
Singapore	240.4	212.8	243.0
Thailand	306.5	107.3	182.3
South Asia	213.3	219.1	121.1
Bangladesh	25.7	18.6	8.3
Pakistan	144.6	145.9	40.2
Sri Lanka	8.4	15.9	19.5
Middle East	167.6	121.6	180.1
Kuwait	.0	.0	.0
Saudi Arabia	.0	.0	.0
Syria	11.2	43.5	59.9
United Arab Emirates	.0	.0	.0
Yemen Arab Republic	.1	.1	.1
North Africa	75.2	95.2	91.9
Egypt	35.4	39.3	54.1
Tunisia	16.2	13.1	11.3
Sub-Sahara Africa	144.6	201.7	286.8
Cameroon	.0	.4	.0
Nigeria	.0	.0	.0
Sudan	25.7	57.1	78.6
Zambia	12.0	13.4	18.4
Latin America	568.4	1,088.7	877.8
Argentina	136.6	471.6	85.3
Brazil	86.2	272.4	461.1
Chile	61.9	93.7	125.3
Guatemala	15.1	.6	.0
Mexico	87.1	53.7	98.9
Communist Countries	1,716.4	1,652.4	2,076.6
USSR	165.2	339.7	574.6
Eastern Europe	975.3	845.1	1,049.3
Czechoslovakia	185.1	112.7	124.6
East Germany	134.5	186.8	131.2
Hungary	33.7	45.3	58.9
Poland	98.1	99.8	160.0
Romania	430.2	309.1	448.9
Yugoslavia	49.1	71.8	98.8
Other[2]	575.9	467.6	452.7

Percent of Estimate Obtained from Trade Partner Data[3]

World	97.90	96.82	93.13
Developed Countries	100.00	100.00	98.99
Less Developed Countries	91.60	89.91	86.69
Communist Countries	100.01	95.04	73.08

1. Country listings for any given area are not exhaustive: only major trade partners are presented.
2. Kampuchea, Cuba, Mongolia, Laos, North Korea, and Vietnam.
3. Includes quarterly data that have been interpolated from annual trade-partner data.

Imports and exports F.O.B.
CIA, *China: International Trade Fourth Quarter, 1984* (1985), 2-5.

CHINESE TRADE BALANCES BY AREA AND COUNTRY, 1982-84 (million dollars) [1]

	1982	1983	1984
World	6,214.0	5,178.5	2,338.5
Non-Communist Countries	6,655.4	5,467.4	2,859.3
Developed Countries	-579.4	-1,779.3	-3,573.5
East Asia and Pacific	996.7	-312.4	-2,045.7
Australia	-518.7	-162.7	-422.6
Japan	1,583.4	-71.5	-1,538.6
North America	-1,477.0	-911.1	-639.8
Canada	-839.9	-989.6	-709.5
United States	-637.1	78.5	69.7
Western Europe	-99.0	-555.9	-888.0
Belgium	-82.6	-114.9	-183.6
France	43.9	-73.3	72.8
West Germany	-242.5	-407.2	-297.8
Italy	161.8	95.3	-20.7
Netherlands	100.7	22.2	-21.4
Spain	-25.3	-35.9	-85.6
Sweden	16.2	-46.1	-45.5
Switzerland	-65.4	-58.9	-50.8
United Kingdom	116.5	61.9	-100.6
Less Developed Countries	7,234.7	7,246.7	6,432.8
Southeast Asia	4,543.8	4,533.7	3,788.1
Hong Kong	3,476.1	3,351.8	2,099.9
Indonesia	205.8	167.4	189.8
Malaysia	153.3	100.0	108.0
Philippines	106.9	53.4	156.8
Singapore	598.2	574.8	1,039.6
Thailand	-84.0	145.3	126.1
South Asia	192.3	141.1	355.8
Bangladesh	77.4	37.1	151.7
Pakistan	-2.4	-6.2	96.6
Sri Lanka	31.6	24.1	15.0
Middle East	2,034.3	2,525.0	2,112.7
Kuwait	127.5	147.9	172.6
Saudi Arabia	223.0	222.0	237.0
Syria	53.5	61.5	62.7
United Arab Emirates	121.8	132.1	157.1
Yemen Arab Republic	59.0	61.2	71.4
North Africa	161.2	169.7	211.6
Egypt	13.6	11.5	5.2
Tunisia	3.3	15.2	6.2
Sub-Sahara Africa	343.1	287.9	281.8
Cameroon	18.9	11.5	5.2
Nigeria	44.1	45.6	53.3
Sudan	-.9	-27.5	-44.0
Zambia	-9.5	-10.8	-15.4
Latin America	-39.9	-410.5	-317.1
Argentina	-127.2	-467.3	-80.6
Brazil	246.5	269.2	-44.3
Chile	-42.2	-84.7	-114.0
Guatemala	-14.5	-.9	2.0
Mexico	-28.2	-42.4	-86.4

continued . . .

CHINESE TRADE BALANCES BY AREA AND COUNTRY, 1982-84 (million dollars)[1]
(continued)

	1982	1983	1984
Communist Countries	-441.4	-288.9	-520.8
USSR	-22.6	-31.8	50.6
Eastern Europe	-249.5	-173.0	-457.2
Czechoslovakia	-113.5	-22.6	-20.8
East Germany	-65.9	-127.8	-45.3
Hungary	-7.8	-19.4	-31.1
Poland	79.6	63.7	-59.5
Romania	-88.4	-19.4	-226.1
Yugoslavia	31.1	-55.9	-80.2
Other[2]	-169.3	-84.1	-114.2

1. Country listings for any given area are not exhaustive; only major trade partners are presented.
2. Kampuchea, Cuba, Mongolia, Laos, North Korea, and Vietnam.

F.O.B.
CIA, *China: International Trade Fourth Quarter, 1984* (1985), 6-7.

SINO-AMERICAN TRADE (mn dollars)

	1982	1983	1984	1985*
US Exports				
Total	$2,912	$2,173	$3,004	$3,077
Agricultural	1,504	544	613	121
US Imports				
Total	$2,502	$2,477	$3,381	$3,531
Agricultural	170	143	192	191

* January-October, 1985. Note the immense decline in American agricultural exports to China since 1982. China has not renewed its long-term grain agreements with several suppliers, including the US. US Department of State, *GIST* (Jan 1986), 2.

INCREASES IN CHINESE TRADE WITH EASTERN EUROPE

Total trade with Eastern Europe, 1985 (bn dollars)   2.64

Percentage increases planned in trade agreements for 1985:

	Percent Increase Over 1984
Poland	180
Hungary	170
GDR[1]	54.5
Czechoslovakia	39.6
Bulgaria	up
Yugoslavia[2]	up

1. China and the German Democratic Republic agreed 24 December 1985 to increase trade by 33 percent in 1986.
2. Trade reached $130 million in 1984, a 65 percent increase over 1983. FBIS-CHI 249 (27 Dec 1985), H1/2.

SINO-SOVIET TRADE, 1975-84 (mn dollars)

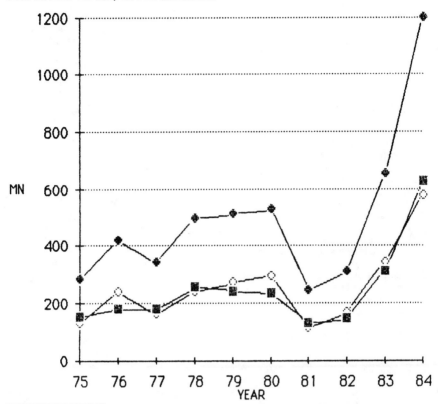

◆ Total

◇ Chinese Imports

■ Chinese Exports

CHIFFA/7, 145: CIA, *Handbook of Economic Statistics,* (1985), 104. Note how closely imports parallel exports. Yao Yilin and Ivan Arkhipov signed an agreement on trade turnover and payments during 1986-90 on 10 July 1985. Turnover will reach about 12 billion rubles during the five-year period. It will total 3 billion rubles in 1990, or almost twice the level in 1985. The Soviets will assist the Chinese in building seven new facilities and the reconstruction of 17 others in fields such as metallurgy, machine building, power engineering, transportation, the coal and chemical industries. *Pravda* (11 Jul 1985).

SINO-CANADIAN TRADE, 1981-84 (mn Canadian dollars)

	1981	1982	1983	July 1984
Canadian imports:				
Total	$220	$204	$246	$189
Textiles	33	30	30	22
Clothing, etc.	64	73	103	89
Canadian exports:				
Total	1,018	1,228	1,607	630
Wheat	687	757	970	334

Committee on Energy and Commerce, US House of Representatives, *China Economic Development and US Trade Interests* (1985), 72.

1984 FOREIGN TRADE TOTALS (bn yuan)

		Percentage Increase Over 1983
Total	120.12	39.7
Exports	58.06	32.5
Percentage increase deducting price and fluctuations in exchange rates		14.6
Imports	62.06	47.1
Percentage increase deducting fluctuations in prices and exchange rates		24.7
Trade deficit	4.0	
Exports (percent of total)		
Manufactured goods	54.4	12.6
Primary products	45.6	24.0
Imports (percent of total)		
Manufactured goods	81.0	42.6
Primary products	19.0	−10.3
Foreign funds utilized (bn dollars)	2.66	35.7
Loans	1.32	25.7
Direct foreign investment	1.34	47.3
For joint exploration and development of offshore petroleum	0.52	79.3
Contracts for overseas projects and labor services (bn dollars)		
Concluded	1.68	82.6
Fulfilled	0.55	22.0

Beijing Review, 12 (25 Mar 1985), vi-vii.

FOREIGN EXCHANGE RESERVES (bn dollars)

	Dec 1984	Mar 1985	Jun 1985	Sep 1985
Foreign exchange reserves	14.42	11.262	10.852	12.592
State reserves	8.21	7.682	5.37	3.377
Cash in the Bank of China	6.2	3.58	5.482	9.215
Borrowed from abroad	4.055	3.955	4.254	4.487

FBIS-CHI 130 (8 Jul 1985), K20; 204 (22 Oct 1985), K27; 237 (10 Dec 1985), K21/22. Gold reserves have remained at 12.67 million ounces.

CHINA'S INTERNATIONAL BALANCE OF PAYMENTS, 1982-84 (mn dollars)

	1982	1983	1984
(1) Regular Items	5,674	4,240	2,030
a) Trade	4,249	1,990	14
Exports (F.O.B.)	21,125	20,707	23,905
Imports (F.O.B.)	−16,876	−18,717	−23,891
b) Labor Service	939	1,739	1,574
Earnings	3,604	4,028	4,819
Payments	2,665	2,289	3,245
c) Transfers Gratis	486	511	442
Private	530	436	305
Government	−44	75	137

continued . . .

CHINA'S INTERNATIONAL BALANCE OF PAYMENTS, 1982-84 (mn dollars) (continued)

	1982	1983	1984
(2) Capital	338	−226	−1,003
a) Long-Term	389	49	−113
Inflow	3,312	2,702	4,128
Outflow	−2,923	−2,653	−4,241
b) Short-Term	−51	−275	−890
Inflow	224	59	223
Outflow	−295	−334	−1,113
(3) Errors and Omissions	279	−366	−932
(4) Increase or Decrease of			
Reserves	−6,291	−3,648	−95

1. Trade figures are based on customs statistics and adjusted to the terms of international revenues and expenditures.
2. Labor services include carriage and premiums on cargo, port supplies and services, tourism, investment profits, bank interest, service charges and other items.
3. Transfers gratis include free aid and donations between China and international organizations and foreign governments, overseas remittances, revenues and expenditures of residents, etc.
4. Long-term capital refers to capital with contractual payment time limits exceeding one year and capital with undefined payment time limits, such as capital stocks. It includes direct investments, stock investments, loans from international organizations and foreign countries, money borrowed by banks, departments and localities, overdue payments, overdue receiving, processing and assembling, evaluated payments for equipment, loans owed to foreign businesses in compensation trade, and other items.
5. Short-term capital refers to immediate payments and capital with contractual payment time limits of one year or less, including currency. It includes money borrowed by banks, departments and localities, overdue payments, and overdue receiving.
6. Errors and omissions are differences between regular items and capital items, and the sum of the increase and decrease of reserved assets.
7. The sum of the increase and decrease of reserved assets reflects the differences between the surplus of the present year and the previous year in China's gold reserves, reserved money supplies of fund organizations, special rights to draw money and the use of fund credits. An increase in reserved assets is indicated by a minus sign, and a decrease by no symbol.

Beijing Review, 35 (2 Sep 1985), 30-31.

TOTAL CHINESE FOREIGN EXCHANGE RESERVES (mn SDRs)

	Total Reserves with Gold at SDR 35 per Ounce	Total Reserves Minus Gold
1978	1,643	1,195
1979	2,083	1,635
1980	2,444	1,996
1981	4,790	4,346
1982	10,733	10,288
1983	14,759	14,315
1984	15,830	15,386
1985 Jun	12,050	11,605

International Monetary Fund, *International Financial Statistics* (Dec 1985), 41, 45.

INDEX OF FOREIGN TRADE, SELECTED YEARS (1959 = 100, 1978 = 100)

1959	100	1979	128
1961	60.2	1980	158.7
1962	54.1	1981	202
1978	100	1982	213

Guangming Ribao (30 Nov 1985).

DOLLAR-YUAN EXCHANGE RATES, 1971-85 (yuan per dollar)

1971	2.39	1980	1.55
1973	2.01	1981	1.49
1975	1.96	1982	1.70
1977	1.94	1983	1.98
1978	1.85	1984	2.32
1979	1.68	1985 Oct 31	3.17

CIA, *Handbook of Economic Statistics, 1985* (1985), 61; Chase Manhattan, *Foreign Exchange* (31 Oct 1985), 3, for 1985. These are average exchange rates for the year.

SPECIAL ECONOMIC ZONES, 1984*

Contracts on economic cooperation with foreign countries signed, 1984	1,400
Foreign investment involved (mn dollars)	900
Actual investment in 1984 (mn dollars)	330
Contracts on economic cooperation with foreign countries signed from date of establishment to end of 1984	4,000
Foreign investment involved (mn dollars)	4,000+
Actual investment (mn dollars)	800
Investment by four SEZs in capital construction	
(bn yuan)	2
(mn dollars)	c. 700
Increase over 1983 (percent)	73
Output value of industry and agriculture in the four SEZs (bn yuan)	3.34
(bn dollars)	c. 1.1
Increase over 1983 (percent)	62
Increase in output value of Shenzhen SEZ (percent)	100
Total revenue of four SEZs (mn yuan)	700
Increase over 1983 (percent)	40
Increase in revenue of Shenzhen SEZ (percent)	50

* Shenzhen, Zhuhai, Shantou and Xiamen SEZs.

Beijing Review, 12 (25 Mar 1985), 30.

CITIES OPEN TO FOREIGN INVESTMENT

Beihai

Basics

- Population (millions): total 0.17, urban 0.17, workforce 0.04.
- Area: 270 km².
- Climate: average temperature 22°C, mean annual rainfall 1659 mm.
- Foreign trading port since 1876.
- An important entrepot centre in southern China, close to the oil exploration areas in the Beibu Gulf.
- Resources include ilmenite and quartz sand.

Infrastructure

- A total of 123 industrial enterprises employ 14,000 workers. Main products are motors, fire crackers and shell carvings. Annual output valued at RMB¥14 million.
- An important fishing centre: exports of marine products earn US$3 million a year.
- Access point to the Guangxi Zhuang Autonomous Region and the entire southwest China.
- Workable deposits of quartz, gypsum and kaolin.
- Total exports last year reached US$41.91 million.
- Fangcheng port now has nine berths, two of them deep-water. Annual handling capacity topped 860,000 tonnes in 1983.

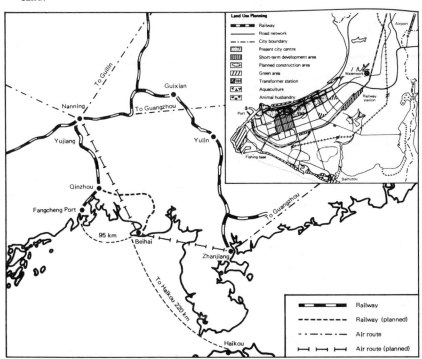

continued . . .

CITIES OPEN TO FOREIGN INVESTMENT (continued)

Beihai

- Power available off the Guangxi grid; a third high voltage transmission line to be added next year.
- Hydrofoil services between Beihai and Fangcheng.
- Rail link to Kunming, via Nanning.
- Hotel: Huachiao Hotel.

Development Zone, Focus and Plans

- No actual development zone in Beihai – the entire area is open – but plans aim to concentrate light industry and tourism around Beihai City and shipbuilding and related marine industries at the port of Fangcheng, some 50 nautical miles away.
- High technology industries and an oil refinery are ultimately projected.
- Three major hotels are in the planning or construction stage.
- New rail links are being developed with the hinterland.
- A medium-sized airport should be operating by the end of 1985.
- Priority given to petrochemicals and extractive industries.
- Tourist development planned of the 20-mile long city beach.

Foreign Investment

- At the end of May 1984, 81 initial agreements and letters of intent covering RMB¥370 million had been signed with domestic and overseas investors.

Dalian

- Projects under negotiation with businessmen from the US, France, the FRG and Southeast Asia include port and railway construction, aviation, electronics, shipbuilding, food processing, textiles, building materials, prawn and pearl breeding, fishing and sea transportation.
- Building applications yet to be approved include 63 buildings, 12-stories or higher, for residential blocks and offices.
- Two hotels planned, one with Hong Kong, one with Singapore financial backing.

Projects for Negotiation

- Total 9, Renovation 3, New 3, Expansion 3.

Investors' Data

- Beihai Economic Development Corporation
  Director: Meng Guoyan
  Address: 2 Dongerxiang, Beihai, Guangxi
  Tel: 2612
- Beihai Industry Development Committee
  Deputy Director: Liu Mengbiao
  Address: 2 Dongerxiang, Beihai, Guangxi
  Tel: 3272
  Cable: 8017
- Coordinating bank:
  Bank of Communications

Basics

- Population (millions): total 4.76, urban 1.52, workforce 1.09.
- Area: 12,500 km².
- Climate: average summer temperature 8-10°C, mean annual rainfall 600-1000 mm.
- Rich in natural resources, diamonds, limestone and silicon mining.

continued . . .

CITIES OPEN TO FOREIGN INVESTMENT (continued)

Dalian

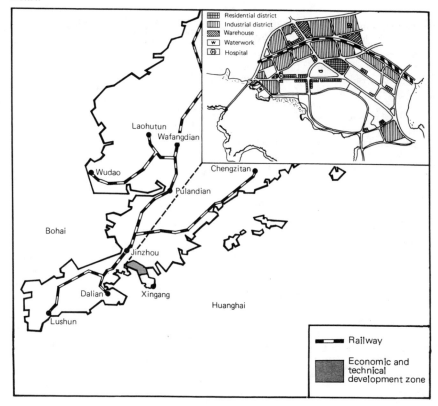

- Major fishing ground, worldwide exports of sea cucumbers, fan fish and abalone.
- More than 1,900 industrial enterprises; 59 of which produce more than 70% of the city's total output, RMB¥8,430 million in 1983. Specialist industries include shipbuilding, machinery, petrochemicals and textiles. Major apple exporting centre.

Infrastructure

- Second-largest port after Shanghai with a handling capacity of 3.5 million tonnes annually. By 1990 the planned handling capacity will have risen to 42 million tonnes.

- Zhoushuizi Airport will be expanded and international flights established to Japan and Hong Kong.
- A special rail link to Dalian harbour connects with national rail network.
- Planned improvements include a new power station and renovation of three old ones, enlargement of Dalian harbour and the long-term construction of a 100 million-tonne dock in Dayao Bay designed for the twenty-first century and scheduled to begin in 1986, construction of a 5 million-tonne capacity coal dock at Heshangdao to open in 1987, upgrading of highway to Shenyang, and telecommunications links to Japan and Hong Kong.

continued . . .

CITIES OPEN TO FOREIGN INVESTMENT (continued)

Dalian

*D*evelopment Zone, Focus and Plans

- Magiaozi Economic Development Zone in Jinxian county totals 50 km^2 with expansion planned for a 20 km^2 site. It includes areas for industry, banking and trade, science and education, sports and tourism.
  Plans focus on computer products, precision instruments, micro-electronics, marine engineering, chemicals, metallurgy, food and beverages.
- Foreign investment and advanced technology will be used to build a modern oil refinery (annual capacity 10 million tonnes) and an ethylene plant (annual capacity 300,000 tonnes).

*F*oreign Investment

- Funds and imported technology worth US$80 million were absorbed through 78 contracts in the first eight months of 1984, or 240% more than was accepted in the whole of 1983.

- More than 200 business groups had come to Dalian to discuss projects involved in the development of the open city policy by August 1984.
- Major plans for foreign investment include the renovation of 30 factories, the introduction of 300 new product items and the redesigning of a further 250 to improve quality.

*P*rojects for Negotiation

- Total 14, Renovation 9, New 3, Expansion 2.

*I*nvestors' Data

- Dalian Committee for Economic and Trade- Relations with Foreign Countries
  Officer in Charge: Wang Ruren
  Address: No.1 Stalin Square, Dalian.
  Tel: 31480
- Coordinating Banks:
  Nanyang Commercial Bank, and the China State Bank.

Fuzhou

*B*asics

- Population (millions): total 4.75, urban 1.14, workforce 0.62.
- Area: 1,043 km^2.
- Climate: average temperature 19.6°C, mean annual rainfall 1,700 mm.
- Mawei harbour is one of the oldest Chinese commercial ports. A shipyard was built there in 1886.

- More than 700,000 overseas Chinese trace their antecedents to Fuzhou.
- The city is well known for its silk, satin, handicrafts and surrounding beauty spots.

*I*nfrastructure

- A total of 2,400 industrial enterprises employ more than 270,000 people. Products include motors, machine tools, TV sets, recorders and instruments.
- Fuzhou airport serves internal Chinese destinations and Hong Kong. It will shortly be expanded to handle international flights to Bangkok, Manila and Hawaii.

continued . . .

CITIES OPEN TO FOREIGN INVESTMENT (continued)

Fuzhou

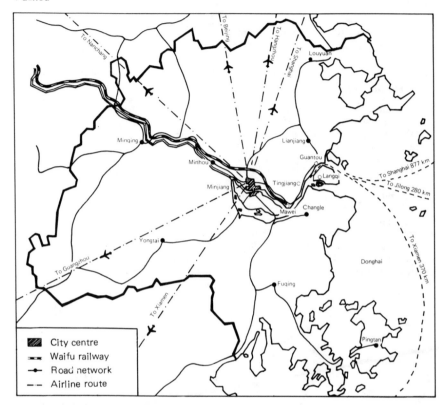

- City centre
- Waifu railway
- Road network
- Airline route

- Railways connect Fuzhou to the national network; part of the line is to be electrified.
- Industrial output in 1983 was RMB¥2.6 billion, covering 170 types of product.
- The port services shipping from Shanghai, Hong Kong, Singapore and Bangkok.
- Seven waterworks supply the city with 250,000 tonnes a day.
- There are more than 30 industrial research institutes in the area, with 8,170 technical personnel and 1,270 engineers.
- Hotels: Overseas Chinese (Tel:67603), Minjiang (Tel: 57895), West Lake (Tel: 57008).

*D*evelopment Zone, Focus and Plans

- The Mawei Development Zone covers an area of 23 km^2.
- A total of 155 projects have been earmarked this year for foreign cooperation.
- Immediate priority is given to precision machinery manufacture, glass, foodstuffs and electronics.
- Additional berths are to be constructed in Mawei harbour.
- Tourism figures prominently in Fuzhou's economic plans.
- A new telephone system is being installed linking the city to Hong Kong and the US.

continued . . .

CITIES OPEN TO FOREIGN INVESTMENT (continued)

Fuzhou

- Long term plans envisage development of the entire lower reaches of the Minjiang into a major industrial zone.

Foreign Investment

- A total of US$25.69 million has been invested in the last five years. Of this, US$13.61 million went into seven joint ventures, a further US$3.18 million in cooperative enterprises, plus around US$4 million each in compensation trade and agreements covering the processing and assembling of customer-supplied materials.
- Projects now underway include a steel rolling mill, a highway linking Fuzhou with Mawei, and housing within the zone for foreign businessmen.

Projects for Negotiation

- Total 10, Renovation 2, New 1, Expansion 7.

Investors' Data

- Fuzhou Foreign Economic Relations and Trade Commission
  Director: Sheng Hequn
  Address: 34 Wushan Road, Fuzhou, Fujian.
  Tel: 55308, 56176
- Coordinating banks:
  China Development Finance Corp., and Sin Hua Trust, Savings & Commercial Bank.

Guangzhou

Basics

- Population (millions): total 6.84, urban 3.16, workforce 1.79.
- Area: 16,000 km^2.
- Long history of industrial development going back 2,800 years.
- The leading financial centre of south China and important trading port. Export Commodities Trade Fairs held here since 1957, China's major international trade fair.
- 4,000 industrial enterprises, including textiles, electronics and pharmaceuticals. Rapidly developing petrochemical and shipbuilding activities with development of the Nanhai oilfield.

Infrastructure

- The transportation and communication hub of south China.
- Container facilities at Huangpu up to 20,000 tonnes.
- Rail links to Hong Kong. Electrification planned.
- Direct flights from Baiyun Airport throughout China, to Hong Kong and to major cities in Southeast Asia and Australia.
- Regional expressways planned to Shenzhen and Zhuhai.
- Direct telephone dialing to Hong Kong.

Development Zone, Focus and Plans

- Huangpu Economic Development Zone consists of six districts, totalling 58 km^2.
- Of this, 36 km^2 contain shipbuilding, petrochemicals and automobile plants already developed.

continued . . .

CITIES OPEN TO FOREIGN INVESTMENT (continued)

Guangzhou

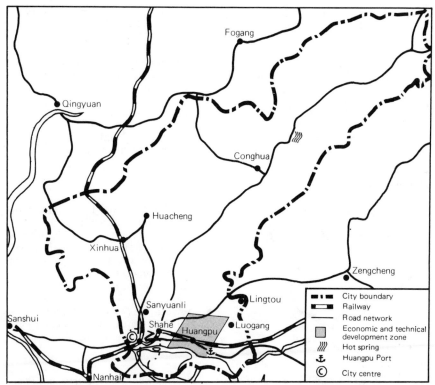

- Plans focus on high-technology development, computer software, IC's and components, as well as food processing, consumer electronics, garments, machinery and textiles.
- Construction of the zone to be completed by 1990.

Foreign Investment

- 209 contracts worth US$600 million, signed up to 30 September 1984. Of these, 12 joint ventures valued at US$43.21 million; 125 co-operative projects valued at US$540 million; and 44 compensation trade projects valued at US$45.13 million. Processing agreements also signed, totalling US$270 million.

Projects for Negotiation

- Total 9, Renovation 4, New 5.

Investors' Data

- The Commission for Economic Relations and Trade
  Director: Yang Ziyuan
  Address: Yue Xiu Hotel, Block No.4, Guangzhou.
  Tel: 35782
  Cable: 4006
- Preparatory Committee for the Canton Economic & Technical Development Zone
  Director: Zhu Senlin
  Address: Gangqian Road, Huangpu
  New Harbour Area,
  Guangzhou.

continued . . .

CITIES OPEN TO FOREIGN INVESTMENT (continued)

Guangzhou

Rms 1260 & 1262,
Dongfang Hotel,.
Guangzhou.
- Guangdong International Trust and
Investment Corp.
Address: Qiaoguang Rd., Guangzhou.
Tel: 35341, 30975
Cable: GUTIC
Telex: 44122 GUTIC CN
- Guangdong Enterprises Ltd.
Deputy General Manager:
Zheng Kangming

Address: 152-155 Connaught Rd.
Central, Hong Kong.
Tel: 5-451939 ext.221
Telex: 62103 GDEL HX
Cable: 0952 GUDOFAHK.
- Guangdong Foreign Economic
Consulting Services Centre
Director: Mai Zhaoru
Address: Rm 2260, Dongfang Hotel,
Guangzhou.
- Coordinating bank:
Kwangtung Provincial Bank

Hainan Island

- Scheduled flights from Haikou to Guangzhou and Zhanjiang.
- Rich mineral resources including one of the biggest iron ore mines in China.
- More than half a million hectares of unused, arable land.
- Roads connect all major coastal cities.
- Adjacent fishing grounds cover nearly 100,000 square nautical miles.
- Hotels: Huaqiao, Haikou.

*B*asics

- Population (millions): total 5.82, urban 0.88, workforce 0.36.
- Area: 34,000 km^2.
- Climate: average temperature 23°C, mean annual rainfall 2,300 mm.
- A total of 158 rivers, many capable of generating hydro-power.
- More than 1,200 types of tropical plants grow on the island.

*I*nfrastructure

- Important oil and natural gas finds are expected to transform the island's economy.
- Produces 66% of China's natural rubber.
- The three main ports last year handled 5.20 million tonnes of cargo.
- Construction started last year on 24 key industrial projects.

*D*evelopment Zone, Focus and Plans

- Twelve existing projects with foreign funding totalling US$100 million.
- Between January-June 1984, 46 contracts and agreements were signed with foreign firms, totalling US$52.06 million.
- A 10-year development scheme around the southern port of Sanya is being drawn up by Japanese consultants.

*F*oreign Investment

- Six distinctive and mutually complementary economic zones will eventually be formed on the island, encompassing its 18 cities and counties.

continued . . .

CITIES OPEN TO FOREIGN INVESTMENT (continued)

Hainan Island

CITIES OPEN TO FOREIGN INVESTMENT (continued)

Hainan Island

continued . . . .

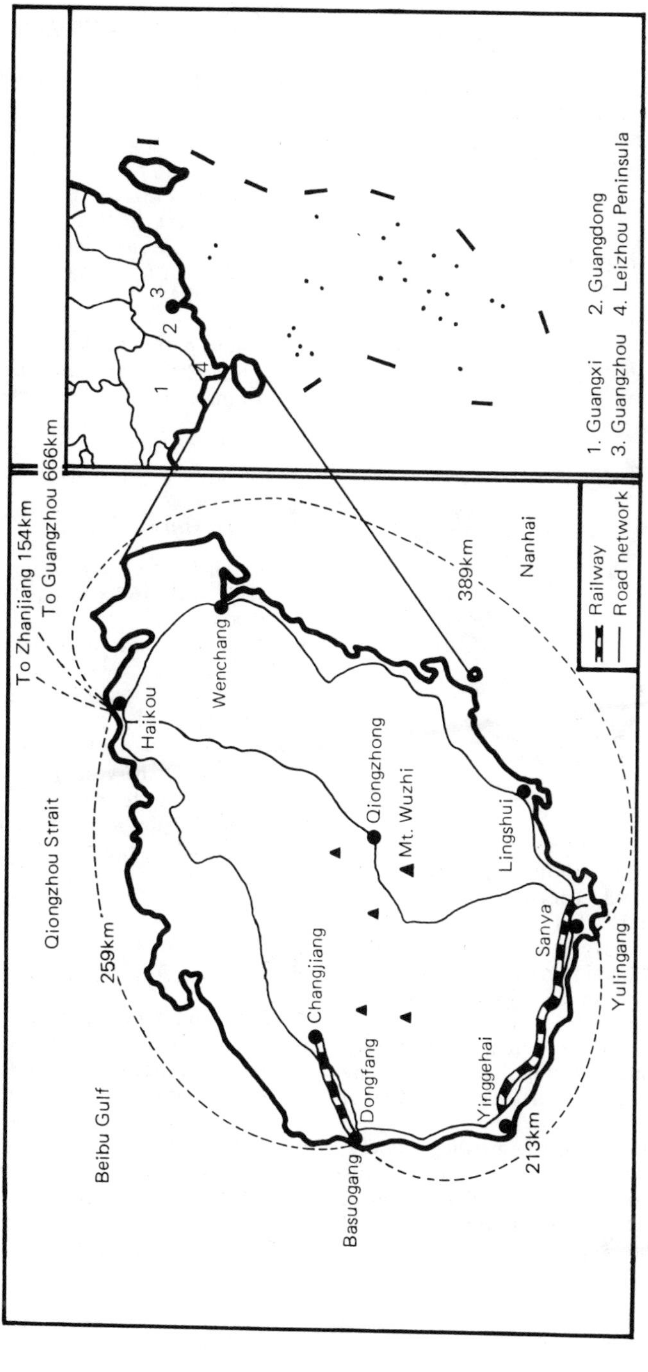

1. Guangxi   2. Guangdong
3. Guangzhou 4. Leizhou Peninsula

Railway
Road network

To Zhanjiang 154km
To Guangzhou 666km

Qiongzhou Strait

Beibu Gulf

259km

Haikou

Wenchang

Qiongzhong

Mt. Wuzhi

Lingshui

Sanya

Yulingang

Yinggehai

Dongfang

Basuogang

Changjiang

213km

389km

Nanhai

CITIES OPEN TO FOREIGN INVESTMENT (continued)

Hainan Island

- Both airports at Sanya and Haikou are being modernized. Next year, the Haikou airport will open to international traffic.
- A thermal power station generating one million kw is in the planning stage.
- A deep water harbour is being developed at Yangpu.
- Autodial telephone, telex and express mail service available within the next 12 months.
- Expansion planned for highways, harbours and electric power.

Projects for Negotiation

- Total 10, New 3, Expansion 7.

Investors' Data

- Hainan Foreign Economic Affairs Committee
  Director: Kang Xingmin
  Address: 17 Datong Road, Haikou.
  Tel: 22313
  Cable: 2611
- Coordinating banks:
  China State Bank, and the
  China and South Sea Bank

Lianyungang

Basics

- Population (millions): total 2.92, urban 0.43, workforce 0.31.
- Area: 5,881 km^2.
- Climate: average temperature 14°C, mean annual rainfall 1000 mm.
- Construction as a harbour began in 1933, reconstructed in 1973.
- A port on the Huanghai developed this century to stimulate the economy of the vast hinterlands of northwest China.
- Industry has been growing rapidly, increasing lately at a rate of 11%. Products include medicines, wine, salt, mica, canned foods and ground phosphates.

Infrastructure

- Shipping links by sea, river and canals with 167 ports in more than 50 countries.
- Inland rail links now being double-tracked.
- Civil airport will be operational next year.
- Expanding agricultural output; regional grain harvest in 1983 exceeded 17 million tonnes.
- Major distribution centre for grain, food, salt, energy, fisheries and construction materials.

Development Zone, Focus and Plans

- Zhongyun Development Zone consists of 30 km^2 divided into industrial, warehouse, residential, urban transportation and green areas. It is adjacent to the city's water supplies.
- Plans to improve 1,235 enterprises with the use of foreign funds and advanced technology. Investment up to 1990 is expected to total US$370 million.

continued . . .

CITIES OPEN TO FOREIGN INVESTMENT (continued)

Lianyungang

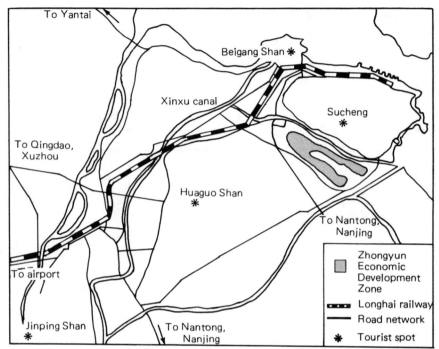

- Priority will be given to food and paper processing, household appliances, chemicals, electronics and textiles.
- The economic structure is to be diversified to include a coastal area for tourism, a scientific city, eight agricultural bases, an industrial zone, and a bulk cargo shipping terminus.

Foreign Investment

- The Jiangsu-Suntory Food Co., a Sino-Japanese joint venture, brews Huaguoshan beer.
- A packaging materials plant has been set up as a joint venture with a Hong Kong company.
- The first prawn farm was established by agreement with a Japanese firm in 1979.

Projects for Negotiation

- Total 10, Renovation 7, New 3.

Investors' Data

- Lianyungang Economic and Technical Development Company
  Deputy Manager: Jiao Haisheng
  Tel: 3023
  Telex: 34080 LETDC CN
- Lianyungang Foreign Economic Committee
  Director: Wang Qingyun
  Tel: 3263
- Coordinating bank:
  Bank of Communications

continued . . .

CITIES OPEN TO FOREIGN INVESTMENT (continued)

Nantong

*B*asics

- Population (millions): total 7.41, urban 0.40, workforce 0.65.
- Area: 120 km^2
- Climate: average temperature 15°C.
- A busy ice-free port on the north bank of the Changjiang, a major reshipment point in central China.

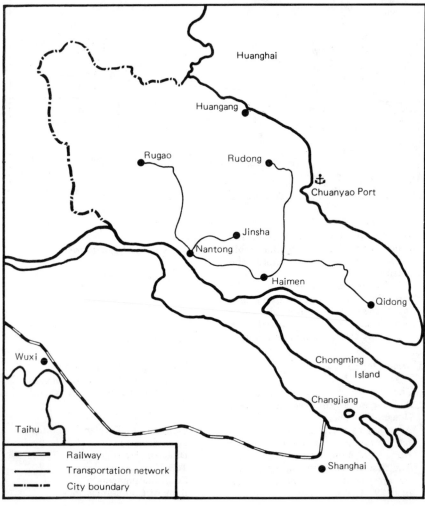

continued . . .

CITIES OPEN TO FOREIGN INVESTMENT (continued)

Nantong

- One of the oldest Chinese industrial centres; its textiles date back to the mid-19th century. Recent developments include chemicals, electronics, machinery, and shipbuilding.

*I*nfrastructure

- More than 5,000 industrial enterprises.
- Nine wharves and 11 berths handle river, coastal and ocean-going shipping.
- Industrial output during 1983 was valued at RMB¥6 billion, covering 830 varieties of product.
- More than 100 kinds of textiles were exported last year to 60 countries and regions.
- An established cotton-growing region with rich offshore fisheries.
- Educational levels are high: the Nantong region has 4,200 colleges and schools, including 40 scientific research institutes.

*D*evelopment Zone, Focus and Plans

- The Nantong Economic and Technical Development Zone covers 4.62 km^2.
- Emphasis is on technology-intensive, energy-saving and pollution-free enterprises, including micro-computers, integrated circuits, precision machinery and textiles.

Ningbo

- The first batch of 85 projects will help update 65% of the city's existing industries. A second batch is planned for the period 1998-90.
- A 10-year development plan has been drawn up to extend industry throughout the Changjiang Valley.
- Priority to light industry, electronics, especially TV set production and VCRs, household appliances, computers, chemicals and medicines.

*F*oreign Investment

- Between 1978-84 a total of 116 contracts were signed with foreign firms, 66 of which are in production.
- These include a US textiles deal worth US$143 million, a chemical fibre factory established with Federal German interests and a shoes factory jointly operated with Japan.

*P*rojects for Negotiation

- Total 10, Renovation 4, New 6.

*I*nvestors' Data

- Nantong External Opening Bureau Director: Lu Chunkang
  Address: No.1, Jian She Road,
      Nantong, Jiangsu, China
  Tel: 2759 or 6131-398
  Cable: 1413
- Coordinating bank:
  Bank of Communications

*B*asics

- Population (millions): total 4.81, urban 0.60, workforce 0.55.
- Area: 403 km^2
- Climate: subtropical, mean annual rainfall 1450 mm.
- A major Chinese port since the Song and Tang dynasties.

continued . . .

CITIES OPEN TO FOREIGN INVESTMENT (continued)

Ningbo

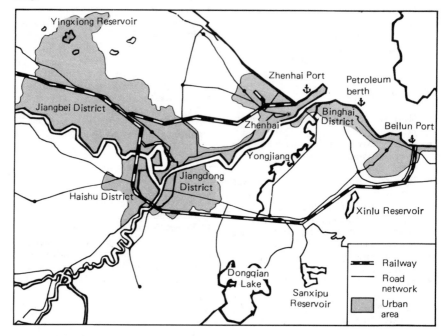

- Major economic activities are textiles, machinery construction, food and tourism.

Infrastructure

- The recently modernized port has berths for ships of up to 100,000 tonnes. Total handling capacity is more than 26 million tonnes of cargo a year, with sea links to Korea, Japan and Southeast Asia.
- When dredging work on the Xiachi channel is completed, Beicang harbour will handle ships of 150,000 tonnes.
- Ningbo is the terminal of the Xiaoyun line linking into the national rail network.
- Completion of the Hanyun canal project will eventually link the port with Beijing and Tianjin.

- Major recent installations are the Zhenhai power station, already in first-phase operation, and the Zhenhai Petrochemical Works. There are 5,400 industrial enterprises now operating in the city.
- Hotels: the Ningbo Hotel, Overseas Chinese Hotel and Ningbo Harbour Hotel.

Development Zone, Focus and Plans

- The development zone is located near Beicang harbour.
- Plans focus on expanding the existing airport, while at the same time building an international airport southwest of the city.
- Installation of expanded telephone and microwave links.
- Improved road and rail communications, plus increased power supplies.

continued . . .

CITIES OPEN TO FOREIGN INVESTMENT (continued)

Ningbo

- Airport extension will usher in servies to Hong Kong, Japan, Shanghai and Hangzhou.

Foreign Investment

- More than 360 contracts signed with Hong Kong businesses since 1980.
- Talks held this year with businessmen from 15 countries leading to signature of more than 40 contracts.
- A container wharf is being planned with 30,000 tonnes handling capacity.
- Ship repair facilities of up to 100,000 tonnes as back-up for offshore oil exploration.
- Priority to marine diesels, transformers, telephones and processed aquatic products.

Projects for Negotiation

- Total 11, Renovation 9, New 1, Expansion 1.

Investors' Data

- Ningbo General Corp. of Economic and Technological Development
  Officer in charge : Geng Dianhua
  (Mayor)
  Address: 63 Jiefang Nanlu, Ningbo, Zhejiang.
  Tel: 65593
  Cable: 0026
  Telex: 35085 NPHCM CN
- Coordinating bank:
  National Commercial Bank

Qingdao

Basics

- Population (millions): total 6.2, urban 1.21, workforce 0.86.
- Area: 1,065 km^2.
- Climate: average temperature 12°C.
- Former treaty port.
- A centre for textiles and other light industries, oceanographic research and tourism. The city's rubber industry ranks third nationwide. Its beer is marketed worldwide.

Infrastructure

- Qingdao's ice-free harbour is the fourth largest in China. The nine local harbours have a total of 36 berths, 15 of which are capable of handling ships of more than 10,000 tonnes. The total amount of goods handled in 1983 was 22 million tonnes.
- The Huanghe has been partially diverted to solve Qingdao's water supply problem; this project will be finished by 1987.

Development Zone, Focus and Plans

- The zone is located in the Huangdao district on the western shores of Jiaozhou Bay; by the year 2000 the industrial area will serve a population of 100,000 and cover 15 km^2, plus additional scientific, cultural and educational facilities.
- The first phase will concentrate on a 4 km^2 area and the setting up of 100 enterprises.
- Long-term development priorities are joint ventures and enterprises funded exclusively with foreign investment, with emphasis on electronics, marine biology, foodstuffs, textiles and chemicals.

continued . . .

CITIES OPEN TO FOREIGN INVESTMENT (continued)

Qingdao

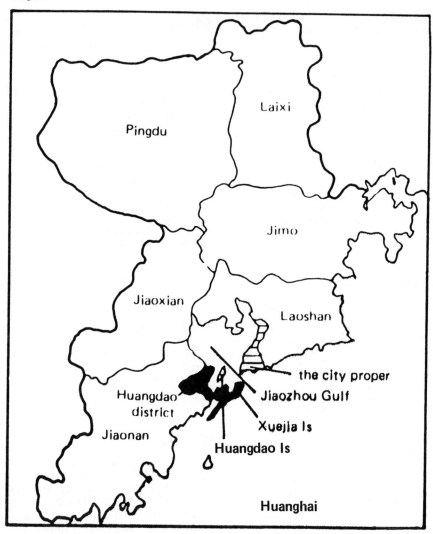

- Expansion of the Huangdao power station.
- Completion of airport expansion, including runways to handle jumbo jets, by the end of 1985.
- Double-tracking existing rail links to Jinan to be completed by 1987. A rail connection is also to be built between the harbour and the economic zone.
- Planned harbour expansion in the Qianwan area, including container area.
- Installation of new telephone and micowave links with Jinan.

continued . . .

CITIES OPEN TO FOREIGN INVESTMENT (continued)

Qingdao

- Two tourist areas will be set aside on Xuejia Island and Shilaoren, featuring an international club, conference hall and recreational facilities. The first section should be operational in time for the summer season in 1985.

*F*oreign Investment

- In the first eight months of 1984, 70 contracts involving more than US$60 million were signed. More than half were with Japanese companies and another quarter with the FRG.
- In recent years more than 170 technical renovation projects have been completed with foreign assistance. A further 440 projects are slated for completion by 1990.
- Since April 1984, 16 contracts have been signed with Hong Kong firms; 2 joint ventures, 1 cooperative agreement and 13 technology import arrangements.

*P*rojects for Negotiation

- Total 15, Renovation 10, New 1, Expansion 4.

*I*nvestors' Data

- Qingdao Foreign Capital Utilization & Technology Import Office
  Director: Song Zhaoqi
  Address: 17 Hebei Road, Qingdao, China.
  Tel: 86976
  Telex: 33246 FTOQD CN
  Cable: TFTB QINGDAO
- Coordinating banks:
  China and South Sea Bank, and the Po Sang Bank.

Qinhuangdao

*B*asics

- Population (millions): total 2.33, urban 0.41, workforce 0.26.
- Area: 7,721 km^2.
- Climate: average temperature 10.1°C, mean annual rainfall 684 mm.
- A treaty port in 1898.
- Hebei province's only port, through which coal from Shanxi and oil from Daqing are exported.

- Well developed industry including 27 glass-making enterprises.

*I*nfrastructure

- An ice-free harbour with more than 10,000 dockers and twelve large berths capable of handling 3.6 million tonnes a year, ranking third nationally. This includes 60% of China's coal exports.
- Jingqin railway recently double-tracked and electrified.

*D*evelopment Zone, Focus and Plans

- 5 km^2 between Qinhuangdao and Shanhaiguan have been designated as the first stage of the development zone. It will ultimately cover 37 km^2.

continued . . .

CITIES OPEN TO FOREIGN INVESTMENT (continued)

Qinhuangdao

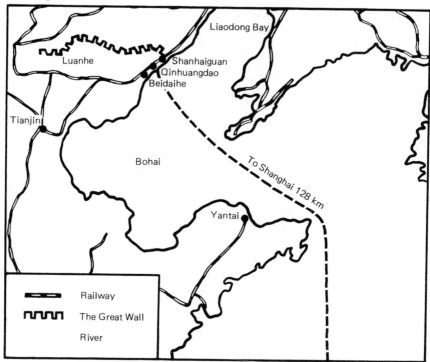

- Plans are in hand to boost port handling capacity to an annual figure of 100 million tonnes by 1992.
- The railway to Datong is being extended to facilitate the export of coal and a new 200,000 kw power station is to be constructed.
- Four large industrial schemes, now in the planning stage, include factories to make colour TV components, cement and acrylic fibre plus a brewery.
- A total of 180 projects are available for foreign cooperation representing a total investment figure of US$1.5 billion, of which US$0.7 billion will be foreign capital.

*F*oreign Investment

- More than 120 delegations from 13 countries have already visited Qinhuangdao.

- Coal berths at Qinhuangdao harbour financed by Japan.
- Glass-making factories.

*P*rojects for Negotiation

- Total 9, Renovation 1, Expansion 8.

*I*nvestors' Data

- Qinhuangdao Economic and Technical Development Corp.
  Director: Gao Zhixin
  Address: 39 Wenhua Rd,Qinhuangdao.
  Tel: 4886
  Telex: 2055
- Qingang Development Co. Ltd.
  Chairman of the Board of Directors: Wang Qi
  Address: 16 Wenhuali, Qinhuangdao.
  Tel: 4656

continued . . .

CITIES OPEN TO FOREIGN INVESTMENT (continued)

Qinhuangdao

- Director & Manager of the Hong Kong office: Lew Mon Hung Address: 50 Connaught Rd Central, Hong Kong.

- Tel: 5-455977
- Coordinating bank: Yien Yieh Commercial Bank

Shanghai

Japan, North America, Europe, Hong Kong and Southeast Asia.

*D*evelopment Zone, Focus and Plans

- Two zones managed by the Minhang-Hongqiao Development Company, a joint venture between the Hong Kong and Shanghai branches of the Bank of China.

- Minhang New Industrial Zone, 240 hectares, 30 km southwest of the city centre, established in June 1984 as a site for Sino-foreign ventures, èxclusively foreign-owned enterprises and trade centre. Minhang is Shanghai's first satellite town.

- A management centre combining banking and trade facilities will be set up. Standard factory buildings are under construction and a four-lane highway will link Minhang with Shanghai proper.

- Hongqiao New Area, 62 hectares, close to Shanghai's airport with office blocks and apartments for overseas businessmen and diplomats, complete with cultural and sports facilities.

*B*asics

- Population (millions): total 11.94, urban 6.39, workforce 4.83.
- Area: 6,185 km^2.
- Climate: average temperature 15.3°C, mean annual rainfall 1,150 mm.
- Leading industrial and financial centre in central China.
- Produces half of China's cameras, one-third of China's radios and watches, a quarter of all TV sets and a fifth of bicycles and sewing machines.
- Economic activities include heavy industry, chemicals, shipbuilding, laser technology and textiles.

*I*nfrastructure

- Seven satellite towns concentrate on specific industries and research: the shift of population concentrations to these towns is an integral part of the plan.
- Largest port in China: 100 berths, including 50 deep-water berths for ships of over 100,000 tonnes.
- Transportation hub at the mouth of the Changjiang.
- International airport with connections throughout China, as well as

*F*oreign Investment

- Ten contracts worth US$251 million signed in the first half of 1984; 14% higher than the total amount absorbed 1979-83. Total investment to the end of June 1984 came to US$788 million in 546 projects.

- 50 foreign enterprises and banks maintain branch offices in Shanghai, 37 of them Japanese, 9 American.

continued . . .

CITIES OPEN TO FOREIGN INVESTMENT (continued)

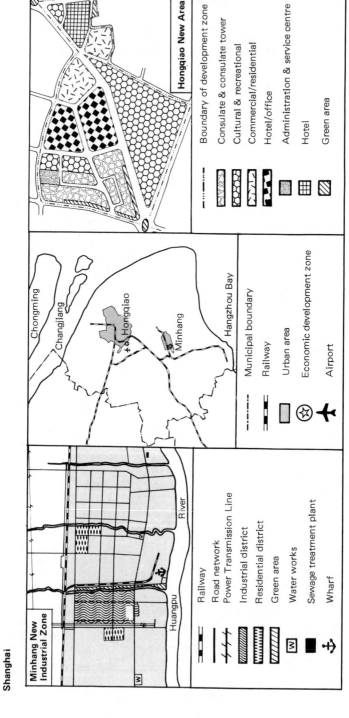

continued . . .

CITIES OPEN TO FOREIGN INVESTMENT (continued)

Shanghai

*P*rojects for Negotiation

• Total 13, Renovation 9, New 4.

*I*nvestors' Data

• Shanghai Foreign Economic Relations and Trade Committee

Directors: Yang Zhenhan,
Lu Guoxian
Address: 33, Zhongshan Rd., E.1.,
Shanghai.
Tel: 232200
• Coordinating banks:
Bank of China (HK),
and the Kincheng Banking Corp.

Shantou SEZ

• A 200,000 kw thermal power station is operational.
• Hotel: the Longhu Hotel.

*D*evelopment Zone, Focus and Plans

• The Longhu Export Processing Area, founded in 1982, remains the keystone of SEZ activity, with 200 factories providing employment for 50,000 workers. It will be expanded in three stages to cover 52.6 km^2.
• Power supplies are to be further improved with installation of an electric sub-station.
• Work is underway to install 4,000 telephone and 2,800 microwave communications lines.
• A trunk road network is planned within the industrial areas.
• The railway is to be extended 212 km to Meixian, Fengshun and Xingning.
• Current airport expansion will extend jumbo jet services from Guangzhou and Hong Kong.
• A container shipping wharf is scheduled for completion by July of next year.
• A petrochemical complex is being developed separately in the Guangao district to serve the Nanhai oilfields.
• Foreign capital is sought for the development of porcelain, polystyrene products, film, fisheries and hi-tech products.

*B*asics

• Population (millions): total 0.72, urban 0.44.
• Area: 10,346 km^2.
• Climate: subtropical, average temperature 21.3°C, mean annual rainfall 1,514 mm.
• Established as a Special Economic Zone in November 1981.
• An ancient port city, ancestral home of many overseas Chinese.

*I*nfrastructure

• Combined industrial and agricultural output last year exceeded RMB¥4 billion.
• Thriving foreign trade, closely linked with Guangzhou-Hong Kong.
• Existing industries include 370 enterprises, of which 120 are engaged in export production. Items produced include electronic instruments, light-sensitive chemicals, canned food and handicraft artifacts.

continued . . .

CITIES OPEN TO FOREIGN INVESTMENT (continued)

Shantou SEZ

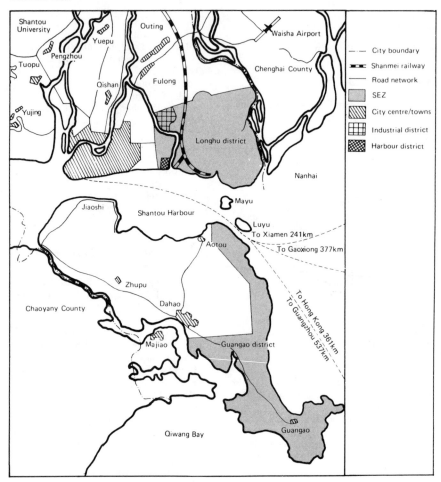

*F*oreign Investment

- By July of this year 59 contracts had been signed with foreign firms, with 26 put into effect.
- The SEZ absorbed HK$44.06 million in foreign investment during 1983. The net income from operations totalled HK$11.27 million.

*P*rojects for Negotiation

- Total 13, Renovation 3, New 10.

*I*nvestors' Data

- Shantou SEZ Development Corp.
  Address: Longhu Industrial Section,
  Shantou, Guangdong, China.
  Tel: 6544

continued . . .

CITIES OPEN TO FOREIGN INVESTMENT (continued)

Shantou SEZ

- Shantou SEZ Trust & Investment Corp.
  Address: Longhu Industrial Section, Shantou, Guangdong, China.
  Tel: 3456
- Shantou SEZ Liaison Department in HK
  Address: 7/F., Arion Commercial Centre,

2-12 Queen's Rd., W., HK.
Tel: 5-430852, 5-452679
- Shantou SEZ office in Shenzhen
  Address: 39, G/F., Hongqun Building, Shenzhen.
  Tel: 22622
  Coordinating bank:
  Hua Chiao Commercial Bank

Shenzhen SEZ

- Six tourist resorts have opened so far; four more are planned.
- The Shekou passenger-cargo port, the 10,000-tonne berth at Chiwan plus Nantou airfield have all been completed.

*B*asics

- Population (millions): total 0.3, urban 0.3, workforce 0.25.
- Area: 328 km^2.
- Climate: subtropical, average temperature 22°C, mean annual rainfall 1,948 mm.
- The largest and most advanced of the four Special Economic Zones established by the Standing Committee of the National Peoples' Congress in August 1980.

*I*nfrastructure

- Directly bordering Hong Kong with immediate sea, rail and road links.
- Capital construction projects worth RMB¥2,500 million had been completed as of June 1984.
- 29 of 35 projected highways have been completed.
- Eight sea routes connect Shenzhen with Hong Kong and Chinese coastal ports.

*D*evelopment Zone, Focus and Plans

- The Daya Bay nuclear power plant will boost generating capacity, as will a new 700,000 kw thermal power station.
- The Shenzhen Special Economic Zone is divided into 18 functional sectors.
- Deep-water berths are being built at Chiwan and Mawan.
- A container terminal is under construction at Yantian.
- Plans focus on high quality goods ranging from handicrafts to electronics.
- Wage levels are generally 45% of those prevailing in Hong Kong.
- By 1990, the population will have reached 0.45 million and the urban area expanded to 60 km^2 to create a modern city.

*F*oreign Investment

- Five Hong Kong and foreign banks have opened offices in the SEZ. These are the Nanyang Commercial Bank, the Hong Kong & Shanghai Banking Corp., Banque Nationale

continued . . .

CITIES OPEN TO FOREIGN INVESTMENT (continued)

Shenzhen SEZ

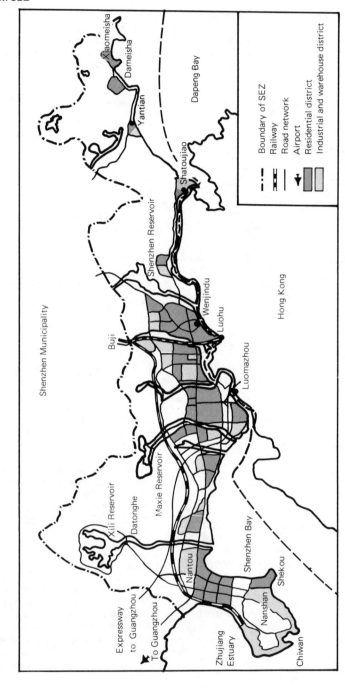

continued . . .

CITIES OPEN TO FOREIGN INVESTMENT (continued)

Shenzhen SEZ

de Paris, the Chartered Bank, and Banque de L'indochine. Others represented are Citibank, Takugin International (Asia) Ltd and Lloyd's Bank International Ltd.

- Up to the end of June 1984, 3,272 agreements had been signed with foreign firms involving a total investment of US$1,800 million. 80% of this business has been generated through Hong Kong firms, and US$500 million has been directly used in production processes. Some 30,000 pieces of equipment have been introduced into the SEZ.

Projects for Negotiation

- Total 9, New 9.

Investors' Data

- Shenzhen Municipal Industrial Development Committee
  Director: Yang Deqian
  Address: Huaqiang Lu Kou,
  Shennan Road Central,
  Shenzhen
  Tel: 38213, 38223
- Coordinating banks:
  Kincheng Banking Corporation, and the BOC (HK).

Tianjin

Basics

- Population (millions): total 7.85, urban 5.19, workforce 2.68.
- Area: 191 km^2.
- Climate: Average temperature 12°C, mean annual rainfall 500-700 mm.
- One of the most important ports in northern China. Second largest figure of national bulk cargo traffic.
- Wide range of industries.

Infrastructure

- Port with an annual handling capacity of 15 million tonnes. New container wharf able to handle 100,000 containers a year, with three more wharves coming on line in 1985.

- Planned construction of China's first expressway will run between Beijing and Tianjin port; the four-lane expressway is scheduled to take three years to complete.
- Tianjin airport is located 38 km northwest of the Tanggu Economic and Technical Development Zone.
- Expansion of telecommunications facilities proceeding as planned.
- Two international trade centres projected, with approval for the first under contract to a Hong Kong firm already agreed.

Development Zone, Focus and Plans

- Tanggu Economic and Technical Development Zone totals 70 km^2, 6 km from Tianjin port.
- Priority renovation of some 4,000 existing enterprises, specifically electronics, machinery and textile products, optical fibre communications material and food-processing equipment.

continued . . .

CITIES OPEN TO FOREIGN INVESTMENT (continued)

Tianjin

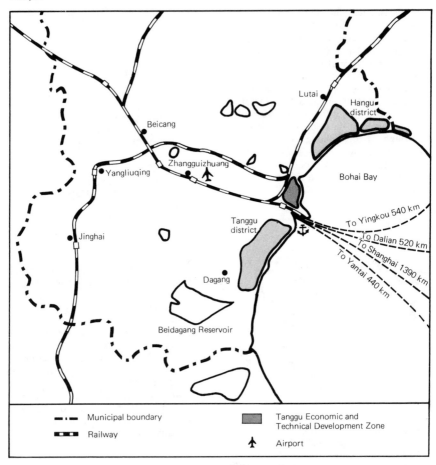

▬ ▪ ▬ Municipal boundary	▬ Tanggu Economic and Technical Development Zone
▭▭▭ Railway	✈ Airport

*F*oreign Investment

- Total amount of foreign capital utilized between 1979 and 1983 amounted to US$50 million.
- Tianjin has concluded agreements with overseas firms for 50 joint ventures. More than 50 contracts have been signed covering imports of advanced technology and equipment, 23 of which are with Hong Kong firms. A total of 10 are already in operation.

- A coal mine, coal gasification plant, joint shipbuilding and food processing are being undertaken with French capital.

*P*rojects for Negotiation

- Total 15, Renovation 8, New 6, Expansion 1.

*I*nvestors' Data

- Tianjin Commission of Foreign Economic Relations and Trade

continued . . .

CITIES OPEN TO FOREIGN INVESTMENT (continued)

Tianjin

Director: Hou Yigang
Address: 57 Hubei Road, Heping
District, Tianjin.
Tel: 3.0101
Telex: 23122 TJFET CN
Cable: 1358
• Tianjin International Trust and
Investment Corp.
Officer-in-charge of Development
Department: Li Xiaohua
Address: 36 Hubei Road, Heping
District, Tianjin.
Tel: 3.6394

Telex: 23255 TITIC CN
Cable: TITIC TIANJIN
• Tsinlien Trading Co. Ltd.
General Manager: Wang Yuchun
Address: Cammer Commercial Bldg.,
2/F., 30-32 Cameron Road,
Hong Kong.
Tel: 3-669536 , 3-7210402-7
Cable: TSINLIENTC HONG KONG
Telex: 37476 TSINS HX
• Coordinating banks:
Sin Hua Trust, Savings &
Commercial Bank, and the
Nanyang Commercial Bank.

Wenzhou

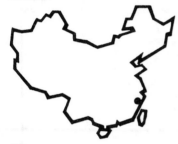

*B*asics

• Population (millions): total 6.11,
urban 0.51, workforce 0.50.
• Area: 172 km^2.
• Climate: subtropical, average temperature 17.9°C, mean annual rainfall
1,700 mm.
• A port trading with Japan and
Southeast Asia since the 12th century.
• Homeland of many overseas Chinese.
• Industries include cattle raising, dairy
farming, leather, food processing,
textiles and shipbuilding.

*I*nfrastructure

• Wenzhou harbour has 20 berths with
passenger and freight connections
throughout Asia. It handles 2.4 million tonnes of cargo a year.

• Rich mineral resources, including
iron, manganese, lead, zinc and
molybdenum.
• Famous for oranges and tangerines,
grown locally for more than 2,000
years.

*D*evelopment Zone, Focus and Plans

• Longwan Economic and Technical
Development Zone covers 18 km^2,
divided into administrative, industrial,
scientific development, entrepot
trade, tourist and residential districts.
Population is expected to reach
100,000 upon completion.
• Planned rail extensions will expand
freight transit throughout southeast
China.
• Airport will be open by the end of
next year.
• Five universities and colleges, plus
29 scientific research institutions.
• Priority to development of extractive industries, particularly alunite
and fluorite deposits, granite and
kaolin, as well as computer-related
electronics, synthetics and dyestuffs.

*F*oreign Investment

• 158 projects earmarked for foreign
cooperation. The first batch were
announced in September 1984.

continued . . .

CITIES OPEN TO FOREIGN INVESTMENT (continued)

Wenzhou

continued . . .

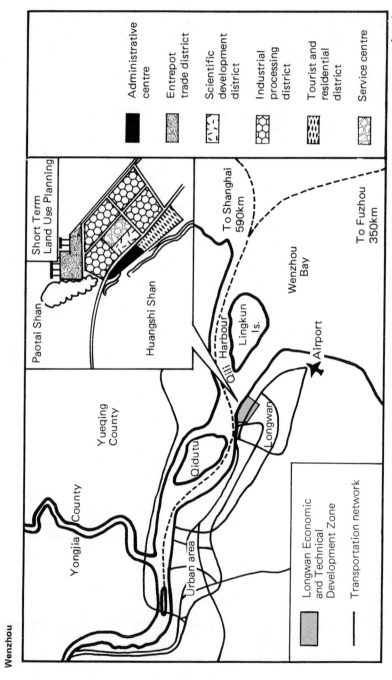

CITIES OPEN TO FOREIGN INVESTMENT (continued)

Wenzhou

*P*rojects for Negotiation

- Total 11, Renovation 6, New 2, Expansion 3.

*I*nvestors' Data

- Wenzhou Committee for Foreign Economic Relations, Zhejiang

Commercial Affairs Office
Officer-in-charge: Lu Shengliang
                    (Mayor)
Address: 13 Chaiqiao Lane,
         Wenzhou, Zhejiang.
Tel: 4681-619
Cable: 1496
- Coordinating bank:
National Commercial Bank

Xiamen SEZ

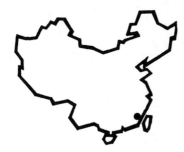

*B*asics

- Population (millions): total 0.98, urban 0.28.
- Area: 2.5 km^2 expanded to 131 km^2.
- Climate: Average temperature $20.9°C$, mean annual rainfall 1200 mm.
- Xiamen was one of the first five Chinese ports opened to trade with the West.

*I*nfrastructure

- A fully modernized international airport operates regular flights to Beijing, Shanghai, Guangzhou, Fuzhou and Hong Kong.
- Present annual handling capacity of the harbour is 4 million tonnes.
- The water supply project to Xiamen Island has been completed; daily supplies have reached 110,000 cubic metres.

- An administration complex, technical training centre, main transformer station and a number of factory buildings have already been completed.

*D*evelopment Zone, Focus and Plans

- The Huli Industrial District, founded in October 1980, comprises 1.2 million m^2 in the first phase, with an adjacent area for residential use.
- Extension work on the airport runway will make it available for jumbo jets operating services to Japan, the Philippines and Singapore.
- Four more harbour berths are under construction; more sites are being surveyed.
- A modern telecommunications system will be in full operation by 1985.
- Completion of power stations at Yungan and Zhanping will directly boost supplies to Xiamen.
- Regional road and rail links are being upgraded.
- Plans focus on technology and knowledge-intensive industries.

*F*oreign Investment

- A total of 110 contracts and agreements have been signed since 1981, representing an overall investment of US$470 million.

continued . . .

CITIES OPEN TO FOREIGN INVESTMENT (continued)

Xiamen SEZ

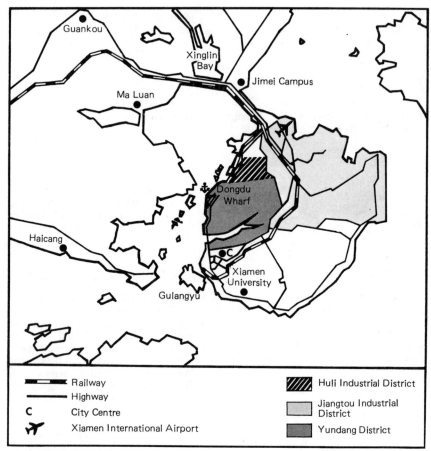

▬▬▬ Railway	▨▨ Huli Industrial District
▬▬▬ Highway	▢ Jiangtou Industrial District
C City Centre	
✈ Xiamen International Airport	▣ Yundang District

• During the first nine months of this year there has been a sharp increase in investors from the US, the UK, France, the FRG, Italy and Japan; 75 contracts have been signed totalling US$253 million.

• Representative offices have been set up by the Hong Kong & Shanghai Banking Corporation, the Chiyu Banking Corporation and the Bank of the Orient.

*P*rojects for Negotiation

• Total 11, Renovation 5, New 5, Expansion 1.

*I*nvestors' Data

• Xiamen Municipal Economic Affairs and Trade Committee
Director: Zhang Lisheng

continued . . .

CITIES OPEN TO FOREIGN INVESTMENT (continued)

Xiamen SEZ

Deputy Director of Foreign
Investment Dept: Zhang Wenguang
Address: 5/F., Administrative Bldg.,
   Huli Industrial District,
   Xiamen SEZ.
Tel: 25002-251, 24024
Cable: 7325 XIAMEN
Telex: 92410 XHID CN
• Xiamen SEZ Huli Industrial District
Management Bureau

Address: 1-2/F., Administrative Bldg.
   Huli Industrial District,
   Xiamen SEZ.
Tel: 25002-310
Cable: 5710 XIAMEN
Telex: 92410 XHID CN
• Coordinating banks:
Chiyu Banking Corp., and the
Hua Chiao Commercial Bank.

Yantai

• The Lancun-Yantai railway links the
city with Beijing, Nanjing, Jinan and
Qingdao.
• Construction of the Longkou power
station will be completed by 1985.
• Domestic and international communications are scheduled to be updated
by 1986.

*B*asics

• Population (millions): total 8.11,
urban 0.68, workforce 0.58.
• Area: 18,900 km^2.
• Climate: Average temperature 10°C,
mean annual rainfall 700 mm.
• Yantai was an important entrepot in
the mid-19th century. In 1976 it
was designated an export-production
base.
• Produces one fourth of China's gold
every year; also rich in other important minerals and heavy metals.
• Largest prawn-producing area in
China.

*I*nfrastructure

• Passenger services to Dalian and
Tianjin. Transportation links are
being developed from the Bohai
Gulf with Japan and Southeast Asia.
Harbour capacity will be doubled
by 1990.

*D*evelopment Zone, Focus and Plans

• The Fulaishan Economic Development Zone covers 10 km^2 in the
western part of Yantai city. It is
planned that 34 high-tech enterprises
will be established, producing textile
items, electronic goods and beverages.
Total investment should reach
US$322 million, of which US$170
million will be foreign funded.
• Immediate plans focus on the further
investment of US$233 million to
import advanced technology for use
in 81 small and medium-sized enterprises by 1987. These will include
electronics, clocks, textiles, wine
making and brewing.
• In total, 265 enterprises throughout
the municipality must be brought up
to date.
• Efforts will be made to attract
another US$73 million to develop
tourist facilities. Yantai will be
linked with Qingdao to become an
international tourist resort.

continued . . .

CITIES OPEN TO FOREIGN INVESTMENT (continued)

Yantai

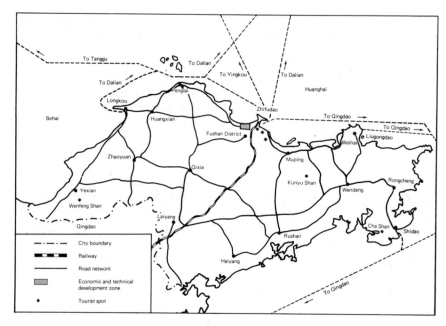

*F*oreign Investment

- In the first eight months of 1984, 69 projects involving foreign investment worth US$37 million were approved, 20% more than the entire total for the period 1972-83.
- Two Japanese companies are involved in brewing and lumber business.
- Yantai's major export destination is Hong Kong. In 1983, Yantai's total exports amounted to US$350 million against imports of just US$70 million.
- Economic cooperation between Yantai and Hong Kong will improve once the Zicheng Trade Corporation (HK) is set up.
- Yantai university will be established as a training centre for technical and managerial skills.

*P*rojects for Negotiation

- Total 12, New 6, Expansion 6.

*I*nvestors' Data

- The Committee of Foreign Economic Relations & Trade of Yantai
  Deputy director: Chi Xuepu
  Address: 16 West Road, Yu Huang Ding, Yantai, China.
  Tel: 4451-5566 557
- Coordinating banks:
  China and South Sea Bank, and the Po Sang Bank

continued . . .

CITIES OPEN TO FOREIGN INVESTMENT (continued)

Zhanjiang

*B*asics

- Population (millions): total 4.63, urban 0.88, workforce 0.36.
- Area: 1,460 km².
- Climate: subtropical, average temperature above 23°C, mean annual rainfall 1,535 mm.
- The deepest port in south China, modernized in 1954, adjacent to the developing offshore oilfields.

*I*nfrastructure

- More than 300 existing factories and enterprises.
- The port has 15 berths, handling more than 11 million tonnes a year.
- Sea links with more than 40 countries.
- Exports totalled US$245 million in 1983, including more than 500,000 tonnes of coal.
- Annual industrial and agricultural output was valued last year at RMB¥700 million.
- Hotels: Xin Jiang Hotel (Cable 6794), Hai Bin Hotel (Tel: 3551, Cable 8832, Telex: 44240 BINTL CN).

*D*evelopment Zone, Focus and Plans

- Zhanjiang Economic and Technical Development Zone is 39.43 m², divided between light and heavy industrial areas.

- A growing base for regional oil exploration. Headquarters of the Nanhai West Oil Company.
- Telephone services are being expanded to Guangzhou. A microwave communications network and telex will be operating by the end of 1985.
- Six new berths are being added to the port facilities to increase handling capacity by next year to 1.85 million tonnes.
- Work is proceeding on airport expansion to take jumbo jets.
- A new road through the middle of the zone is due for completion in the next six months.
- Priority to development of petrochemicals, light industry, commerce and tourism.
- Earmarked to become a major centre of the Chinese petroleum industry.

*F*oreign Investment

- Contracts have been signed with 179 foreign firms, representing an investment of US$175 million.

*P*rojects for Negotiation

- Total 8, Renovation 2, New 6.

*I*nvestors' Data

- Zhanjiang Economic and Technical Development Corporation
  Director: Teng Yifa (Mayor)
  Address: Jiefang Road, Xiashan, Zhanjiang, Guangdong.
  Tel: 4151, Rm 131
  Cable: 8908
- Coordinating bank:
  Kwangtung Provincial Bank

continued . . .

CITIES OPEN TO FOREIGN INVESTMENT (continued)

Zhanjiang

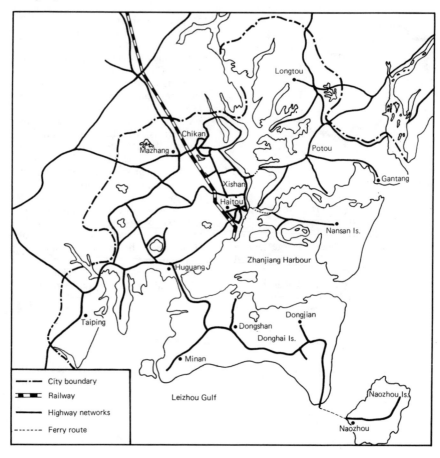

Zhuhai SEZ

*B*asics

- Population: total 32,800, SEZ 9,600 (1982 figures).
- Area: 15 km².
- Climate: average temperature 22.3°C, mean annual rainfall 1,990 mm.
- Situated in the Zhujiang estuary, land-linked to Macao.

continued . . .

CITIES OPEN TO FOREIGN INVESTMENT (continued)

Zhuhai SEZ

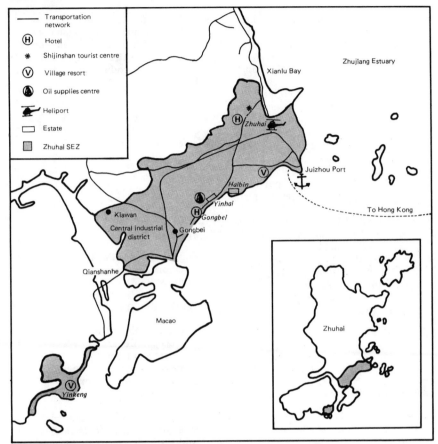

- Reserves include high quality quartz sand suitable for glass making. Rich also in porcelain clay and bauxite.

*I*nfrastructure

- Jiuzhou port with dual-purpose pier: passenger and freight services to Hong Kong, Shekou and Macao.
- 200,000 kw power station recently completed and a water works installed.
- Recent heliport development.

- Restaurants, shopping centres and a joint transportation venture have started operations.
- Part of the construction work on two commercial residential buildings completed.

*D*evelopment Zone, Focus and Plans

- The Zhuhai Special Economic Zone was founded in October 1980. 37% of land use is reserved for industrial purposes, 17% for general commerce and 19% for tourism.

continued . . .

CITIES OPEN TO FOREIGN INVESTMENT (continued)

Zhuhai SEZ

- Zhuhai will be transformed from a sleepy fishing village into a major industrial and agricultural export production base, with a deep-water port designated as one of China's key oil supply bases.
- 6 major foci for foreign cooperation in industrial development have been outlined. They are: building materials, electronics, textiles, everday chemical products, food processing, engineering equipment and machinery & petrochemicals.
- Special emphasis is being put upon tourist activities with 3 resorts planned for development.
- Aluminium and porcelain manufacture are given planning priority to make use of available raw materials.
- The expansion project for Jiuzhou port will provide 3 deep-water berths for oil tankers, 6 berths for support and supply ships plus office and apartment space.

Foreign Investment

- Investment since March 1979 totals US$1.5 billion (1200 contracts). Foreign investment in the first quarter· of 1984 amounted to US$198 million; the figure for the whole of 1983 was just US$1.1 million. 80% of this investment is intended for industrial projects.

Intertrade (Dec 1984), 30-48.

- Agreed projects include a glassware factory, a lumber processing plant, the manufacture of microwave telecommunications equipment, a refrigerator production line and a brewery.

Projects for Negotiation

Total 8, New 8.

Investors' Data

- Zhuguang Trade Co. Ltd.
  Director: Cai Guangcheng
  Address: 34 Shuikengwei Rd.,
  1-5/F., Macao.
  Tel: 71288, 71445

- Guangdong Enterprises Ltd., Zhuhai SEZ Liaison Dept.
  Director: Li Jurong
  Address: 152-154 Connaught Rd.,
  C., 14/Fl., Hong Kong.
  Tel: 5-451939

- The Administration of Zhuhai SEZ
  Director: Liang Guangda (Mayor)
  Address: 127 Xinguangli, Xiangzhou,
  Zhuhai.
  Tel: 22146

- Coordinating bank:
  Nam Tung Bank (Macao)

IMPORTED TECHNOLOGY, 1979-84

	Number of Projects/ Contracts	Value (mn dollars)	Growth Rate (percent)
1979	95	2,484	—
1980	115	1,980	-20.29
1981	73	107	-94.6
1982	102	362	+238.6
1983	212	570	+57.3
1984	336	1,000	+75.4
1985 (Jan-Jun)	318	2,000+	+500

Figures refer only to planned state funds and bank credits. They do not include funds used by local authorities.

Beijing Review, 5 (4 Feb 1985), 30; XNB (1 Aug 1985), 49-50

APPROXIMATE VALUE OF EXPORT LICENSES APPROVED FOR THE TRANSFER OF US HIGH TECHNOLOGY TO CHINA, 1982-85 (bn dollars)

1982	0.5	1984	1.0
1983	0.75	1985 est*	3.0

*This estimate is based on the rate of license approval during the first four months of 1985. US Department of State, *Current Policy No. 725* (Jul 1985), 2. The number of American licenses has increased from 505 in 1981 to 2,257 in 1984. It could reach 4,000 in 1985. *Asian Wall Street Journal Weekly* (10 Jun 1985), 12.

SUMMARY OF JAPANESE FINANCING IN CHINA, 1970-84

Official Development Assistance:

1979 $1.5 billion in development loans for 6 major projects (ports, railways and power projects) 3 percent interest; 30 year term; 10 year grace period;

1984 $2.09 Billion for 7 projects over 7 years (railways, ports, telephone equipment and hydro station) 3.5 percent interest; 3 year term; 10 year grace period;

EX-IM Credits:

1979 $2 billion (coal mines $940 million; $1.06 million oil) 6.25 percent interest, 15 year term;

1984 $2 to 3 billion, energy development projects;

Private Credit:

1979 $6 billion (6 months), $2 billion (4.5 years), $304 million (Baoshan Steel/Daqing oil), and HK$15 billion ($71 million) through PRC bond issue.

Committee on Energy and Commerce, US House of Representatives, *China Economic Development and US Trade Interests* (1985), 58-59.

LABOR SERVICE CONTRACTS, 1981-84

	Number of Contracting Companies	Value (mn)	Number of Contracts	Chinese Employed Abroad (th)
1981	15	520	370	17
1982	28	500	310	31
1983	42	920	460	30
1984	54	1,600	600	47

Beijing Review, 4 (28 Jan 1985), 30.

JOINT VENTURES, 1979-84

Value of foreign investments resulting from signed agreements (bn dollars)	28
Direct investments by foreign businesses (bn dollars)	10
Value of foreign investments used (bn dollars)	16.7
Direct investments by foreign businesses (bn dollars)	4.1
Joint ventures	931
Joint management enterprises	2,212
Firms solely owned by foreign businesses	74
Offshore oil prospecting and exploitation enterprises	31
Contracts on compensation trade signed	1,371

Kaifang, 9 (8 Sep 1985), 2-8, quoted in FBIS-CHI 197 (10 Oct 1985), K4. The number of joint ventures jointly run by Chinese and foreign businessmen reached:

	New Joint Ventures	Total
1979-82	83	83
1983	107	190
1984	741	931
1985 (Jan-Jun)	687	1,618

Hsin Wan Pao (1 Nov 1985), 1. China has decided to extend the term of joint ventures from 30 to 50 years. In some cases, the State Council may permit the contract to run beyond 50 years. These long-term ventures will involve projects requiring high investment, long construction periods, and low profit margins. *Beijing Review*, 1 (6 Jan 1986), 42.

CHINESE VENTURES ABROAD, 1984 yearend

Chinese joint ventures or wholly-owned companies abroad	110
Number of countries with Chinese joint ventures or wholly-owned companies	30*

*Not including Hong Kong and Macao. The PRC has purchased a forest area of 500,000 m^3 of timber in the US, and set up a joint-venture plywood factory in Brazil.

CHINESE SILK EXPORTS, 1978-84 (th tons)

1978	6.1	1982	7.9
1979	7.7	1983	8.6
1980	7.4	1984	8.9
1981	7.2		

The value of exports in 1985 is estimated at $1 billion. China's raw silk exports account for 90 percent of the world's total, and its silk and satin exports are 40 percent of the total. *Beijing Review*, 10 (11 Mar 1985), 29.

CHINA'S FOREIGN TRADE CORPORATIONS

China Council for the Promotion of International Trade

China National Cereals, Oil & Foodstuffs Import & Export Corp.

China National Native Produce & Animal By-Products I/E Corp.

China National Textiles Import & Export Corp.

China Silk Corp.

China National Light Industrial Products Import & Export Corp.

China National Arts & Crafts Import & Export Corp.

China National Chemicals Import & Export Corp.

China National Medicines & Health Products Import & Export Corp.

China National Metals & Minerals Import & Export Corp.

China National Machinery Import & Export Corp.

China National Machinery & Equipment Import & Export Corp.

China National Agricultural Machinery Import & Export Corp.

China National Instruments Import & Export Corp.

China Electronics Import & Export Corp.

China National Packaging Import & Export Corp.

China National Foreign Trade Transportation Corp.

FOREIGN ECONOMIC CONTRACT LAW OF THE PEOPLE'S REPUBLIC OF CHINA
(Adopted at the Tenth Session of the Standing Committee of the Sixth National People's Congress on March 21, 1985)

Chapter 1

General Provisions

Article 1 This law is enacted with a view to protect the lawful rights and interests of the concerned parties to foreign economic contracts and promote the development of China's foreign economic relations.

Article 2 This law applies to economic contracts (hereinafter referred to as contracts), concluded between enterprises or other economic organizations of the People's Republic of China and foreign enterprises, other foreign economic organizations or individuals, but with the exception of the international transport contracts.

Article 3 Contracts should be made in conformity with the principles of equality and mutual benefit, and of achieving unanimity through consultations.

Article 4 Contracts must be made in accordance with the law of the People's Republic of China and without prejudice to the public interests of the People's Republic of China.

continued . . .

FOREIGN ECONOMIC CONTRACT LAW OF THE PEOPLE'S REPUBLIC OF CHINA
(continued)

Article 5 The parties to a contract may choose the law to be applied to the settlement of the disputes arising from the contract. In the absence of such a choise by the parties, the law of the country which has the closest connection with the contract applies. Contracts for Chinese-foreign equity joint venture, Chinese-foreign co-operative enterprise and for Chinese-foreign co-operative exploitation and development of natural resources to be performed within the territory of the People's Republic of China shall be governed by the law of the People's Republic of China. The international practice may apply in case no relevant provision is stipulated in the law of the People's Republic of China.

Article 6 When an international treaty that relates to a contract and which the People's Republic of China has concluded or participated into has provision(s) that differ from the law of the People's Republic of China, the provision(s) of the said treaty shall be applied, but with the exception of clauses to which the People's Republic of China has declared reservation.

Chapter 2

Formation of Contract

Article 7 A contract is formed when the clauses of contract are agreed in written form and signed by the parties. In case one party requests to sign a confirmation letter when the agreement is reached by the means of letter, telegram or telex, the contract is only formed upon the confirmation letter is signed.

Contracts, which are under the provisions of the law and administrative regulations of the People's Republic of China, shall be approved by the competent authorities of the state. They are only formed when the approval is granted.

Article 8 Appendices specified in a contract are integral parts of the contract.

Article 9 Contracts that violate the law or the public interests of society of the People's Republic of China are invalid.

In case that any clauses in a contract violate the law or the public interests of society of the People's Republic of China, the validity of the contract is not derogated if such clauses are cancelled or revised by the parties through consultations.

Article 10 Contracts concluded by means of fraud or under duress are invalid.

Article 11 A party who bears responsibility for the invalidity of the contract is obligated to pay the other party for the loss arising from the invalidity of the contract.

Article 12 Contracts should generally contain the following items:

(1) The corporate or personal names of the contract parties and their nationalities, principal place of business or residence addresses;

(2) Date and place of signature of the contract;

(3) Type of the contract and the kind, scope of the subject matter of the contract;

(4) Technical conditions, quality, standard, specifications and quantities of the subject matter of the contract;

(5) Time limit, place and method of performance;

(6) Terms of price, amount and way of payment, and various additional changes;

(7) Whether the contract could be assigned or conditions for assignment;

(8) Compensation and other liabilities for breach of the contract;

(9) Ways for settlement of disputes in case of disputes arising from the contract;

(10) Languages to be used in the contract and their effectiveness.

Article 13 The limits of risks borne by the parties for the subject matter to be performed should be specified in the contract according to its requirement; and the coverage of insurance for the subject matter should be specified when it is necessary.

Article 14 With regard to a contract that needs to be performed continuously in a rather long period, the parties should set a valid term of the contract and may also set conditions for extension and early termination of the contract.

Article 15 A guarantee clause may be agreed upon in the contract by parties. The guarantor shall undertake responsibility within the agreed scope of guarantee.

Chapter 3

Performance of Contracts and Liabilities For Breach of Contract

Article 16 Contract formed in accordance with law is legally binding. The parties should fulfil their obligations stipulated in the contract. No party should arbitrarily alter or terminate the contract

continued . . .

FOREIGN ECONOMIC CONTRACT LAW OF THE PEOPLE'S REPUBLIC OF CHINA
(continued)

Article 17 A party may suspend performance of his obligations temporarily if it is proved by conclusive evidence that the other party cannot perform his obligations. However, the party who suspends performance should promptly inform the other party. When the other party provides a full guarantee of performance of the contract, the party shall perform the contract. The party who suspends performance of contract, in case of no conclusive evidence for proving the other party is not able to perform contract, shall be responsible for breach of contract.

Article 18 If a party does not perform the contract or its performance of the contractual obligations does not conform to the agreed conditions, that is in breach of contract, and the other party is entitled to demand compensation for losses or to adopt other reasonable remedial measures.

If the losses suffered by the other party still cannot be made up completely after taking remedial measures, the other party retains the right to claim for damages.

Article 19 The liability for damages by a party for breach of contract should be equal to the loss suffered by the other party as a consequence of the breach. However, such damages may not exceed the loss which the party in breach ought to have foreseen at the time of the conclusion of the contract as a possible consequence of the breach of contract.

Article 20 The parties may agree upon in a contract that a certain amount of liquidated damages will be paid to the other party if one party breaches the contract; and may also agree upon a method for calculating the damages arising over such a breach of contract.

The above-mentioned liquidated damages shall be regarded as compensation for the loss caused by breach of contract. However, if the liquidated damages agreed upon in the contract is much more or less than the loss, the parties may request an arbitration body or court to cut or increase it appropriately.

Article 21 In case both parties are in breach of the contract, each shall bear the corresponding liabilities respectively.

Article 22 A party who suffers losses arising from a breach of coutract by the other party should take appropriate measures in time to prevent the loss from aggravating. If he fails to adopt appropriate measures and that leads to aggravate the loss, he shall have no right to claim damages for the aggravated part of the loss.

Article 23 If a party fails to pay on time the due amount agreed upon in the contract or any other due amount related to the contract, the other party is entitled to interest on the amount in arrears. The method for calculating the interest may be specified in the contract.

Article 24 A party should be exempted from his obligations in whole or in part in case he fails to perform all or part of his obligations as a result of force majeure event.

In case a party cannot perform his obligations within the time limit set in the contract due to force majeure event, he should be relieved from the liability for delayed performance during the period of continued influence of the effects of the event. An event of force majeure means the event that the parties could not foresee at the time of conclusion of the contract and its occurrence and consequences cannot be avoided and cannot be overcome.

The scope of force majeure events may be specified in the contract.

Article 25 The party who fails to perform all or part of obligations of the contract because of an event of force majeure should inform the other party in time so as to mitigate the loss which might possibly occur to the other party, and should also provide a certificate issued by the relevant agencies within a reasonable period.

Chapter 4

Assignment of Contract

Article 26 When a party intends to assign all or a part of his contractual rights and obligations to a third party, consent should be obtained from the other party.

Article 27 As for a contract which, as provided by the law or administrative regulations, is formed only after getting approval from the competent authority of the state, the assignment of the rights and obligations of such contract should be subject to the approval from the original approval authority, but with the exception of already approved contracts in which it is otherwise agreed.

Chapter 5

Modification, Cancellation And Termination of Contract

Article 28 A contract may be modified by the parties through consultations.

Article 29 A party is entitled to inform the other party to cancel the contract if one of the following situations occurs:

continued . . .

FOREIGN ECONOMIC CONTRACT LAW OF THE PEOPLE'S REPUBLIC OF CHINA
(continued)

(1) The expected economic interests are infringed seriously for the breach of the contract by the other party;

(2) The other party fails to perform contract within the time limit agreed upon in a contract, and still fails again within a reasonable period of time allowed for delayed performance;

(3) The whole obligations of the contract cannot be performed due to the occurrence of force majeure event;

(4) The conditions agreed upon in the contract for cancellation of the contract have arisen.

Article 30 For a contract containing several independent parts, some of them may be cancelled and the other shall remain to be valid according to the provisions of the previous article.

Article 31 A contract should be terminated if one of the following situations occurs.

(1) The contract has already been performed in accordance with the agreed conditions;

(2) The arbitration body or the court decides to terminate the contract;

(3) The parties agree to terminate the contract through consultations.

Article 32 Notices or agreements for modification or cancellation of the contract should be made in written form.

Article 33 Contracts that under the provisions of the law and administrative regulations of the People's Republic of China, are only formed after getting approval from the competent authority of the state, the significant modification of such contracts should be approved by the original approval authority and the cancellations of such contracts should be filed with the original approval authority.

Article 34 Modification, cancellation or termination of a contract does not deprive the rights of a party to claim for damages.

Article 35 The clauses agreed to in a contract on the settlement of disputes shall not become invalid because of the cancellation or termination of the contract.

Article 36 The clauses agreed to in a contract on settlement of account and winding-up shall not become invalid because of the cancellation or termination of the contract.

Chapter 6

Settlement of Disputes

Article 37 Any disputes arising from contract ought to be settled by parties, if possible, through consultations or mediation of a third party.

In case parties are unwilling to solve dispute through consultation or mediation, or fail to do so, the dispute may, in accordance with the arbitration clause provided in the contract or the written arbitration agreement reached by parties afterwards, be submitted to a Chinese arbitration body or other arbitration body.

Article 38 In case neither arbitration clause provided in the contract nor written arbitration agreement reached afterwards, parties may bring suit in the People's Court.

Chapter 7

Supplementary Provisions

Article 39 The limitation of action for litigation or arbitration concerning the disputes over contract of purchase and sales of goods is four years from the time the party knew or ought to know his rights are infringed. The limitation of action for litigation or arbitration concerning disputes over other contracts shall be separately stipulated by the law.

Article 40 Even the law has new provision, contracts for Chinese-foreign equity joint venture, Chinese-foreign co-operative enterprise and for Chinese-foreign co-operative exploitation and development of natural resources to be performed within the territory of the People's Republic of China, which have already been approved by the competent authority of the state and formed, may still be performed according to the stipulations of the contracts.

Article 41 The contracts formed before the enforcement of this law may be governed by this law in case the parties agree through consultations.

Article 42 Rules for the implementation of this law shall be formulated by the State Council in accordance with this law.

Article 43 This law shall enter into force on July 1, 1985.

(The English version is an unofficial translation, for reference only.)

INCOME TAX PROVISIONS ON PERMANENT REPRESENTATIVE OFFICES OF FOREIGN ENTERPRISES, Approved by the State Council 11 Apr 1985

In accordance with the provisions of Articles 2 and 8 of the industrial and commercial consolidated tax act, Article 1 of the income tax law concerning foreign enterprises and Articles 2 and 4 of the detailed rules and regulations for implementation thereof, and Article 9 of the interim provision of the State Council concerning the administration of permanent representative offices of foreign enterprises, and the relevant provisions of the tax treaties that the Chinese Government has concluded with foreign governments, the following provisions shall be made regarding the collection of taxes from permanent representative offices:

I.   Permanent representative offices, engaged in such activities as conducting market surveys, providing business information and business liaison, consultation and other services on behalf of their home offices, shall be exempted from the industrial and commercial consolidated tax and enterprise income tax, provided they do not receive proceeds for their operations or services as such. Permanent representative offices, appointed by enterprises within Chinese territory to act as agents mainly outside the territory of China, shall be exempted from taxes on the income derived thereof.

II.   The following proceeds and income of permanent representative offices are taxable:

A. commissions, rebates and fees received by permanent representative offices on behalf of their home offices for engaging in business as agents outside the territory of China for other enterprises, or for liaison, negotiation and middleman services within Chinese territory;

B. payments by scheduled installments or in accordance with the volume of commissioned services, made to permanent representative offices by their clients, including their home offices, for conducting market surveys, business liaison, information or consultation services within Chinese territory;

C. commissions, rebates and fees received by permanent representative offices for engaging in business within Chinese territory, as the agents of other enterprises or for liaison, negotiation or middleman services for economic and trade transactions between other enterprises.

III.   Where the amount of commission received by permanent representative offices for general liaison or middleman services is specified in the contracts, the taxes shall be assessed on the amount specified therein. Where the amount is not specified in the contracts and no accurate documentation is available so that the amount of commission cannot be exactly fixed, local tax authorities may, by referring to the general commission rate, determine an appropriate amount of commission on the basis of the business volume realized and assess the taxes accordingly. In cases as mentioned in (a) of Article II of the provisions, where one part of the agency services is performed by their home offices outside the territory of China, permanent representative offices shall declare and present relevant certificates and documents to the local tax authorities for the purpose of assessing the amount of commission taxable in China.

IV.   Where the commissions, rebates and fees received by permanent representative offices for agency or middleman services fall into the categories of taxable items listed in the table of taxable items and tax rates of the industrial and commercial consolidated tax act, the industrial and commercial consolidated tax shall be levied at a reduced rate of five percent. In cases where the enterprise income tax shall be levied, the tax shall be assessed on the taxable income calculated exactly from documents provided by the taxpayer as to costs and expenses; where no such documentation is available, the tax shall be assessed on the taxable income calculated on the basis of an appropriate rate of profit, provisionally determined at fifteen percent of the business proceeds in accordance with the provision of Article 24 of the detailed rules and regulations for the implementation of the income tax law concerning foreign enterprises.

V.   "Enterprise" as used in the above-mentioned provisions encompasses "corporation," "company" and "economic organization."

VI.   The above-mentioned provisions shall be in force as from January 1, 1985.

FBIS-CHI 94 (15 May 1985), K1/2.

REGULATIONS OF THE PEOPLE'S REPUBLIC OF CHINA ON CONTROLLING TECHNOLOGY IMPORT CONTRACTS, Promulgated by the State Council 14 May 1985

Article 1. The regulations are formulated for the purpose of expanding economic and technical cooperation with foreign countries, upgrading China's scientific and technical standards, and stimulating the development of the national economy.

Article 2. Technology imports specified in these regulations mean technological items obtained, through trade or economic and technical cooperation, by companies, enterprises, organizations, or individuals (hereafter referred to as recipients) within the People's Republic of China from companies, enterprises, organizations, or individuals (hereafter referred to as suppliers) outside the People's Republic of China. These items include:

1. Patents, transfers, or permits of other industrial production franchises.
2. Specialized technology such as technological processes, prescriptions, product designs, quality control, as well as management provided in the form of blueprints, technical data, and technical norms.
3. Technical services.

Article 3. Imported technology must be advanced and practical and must be capable of one of the following:

1. Developing and producing new products.
2. Upgrading the quality and performance of products, lowering production costs, and conserving energy or materials.
3. Enabling the comprehensive utilization of China's resources.
4. Expanding the export of products and of increasing foreign exchange earnings.
5. Helping protect the environment.
6. Enhancing safety in production.
7. Helping improve management and operations.
8. Helping upgrade the scientific and technological level.

Article 4. The recipient and the supplier must conclude a written contract on technological imports (hereafter referred to as a contract). Within 30 days after the signing of a contract, the recipient must submit an application for examination and approval by the Ministry of Foreign Economic Relations and Trade of the People's Republic of China or by other organs (hereafter referred to as examination and approval organs) authorized by the ministry; an examination and approval organ shall decide whether to approve an application within 60 days after receiving the application; contracts will go into effect beginning from the day of approval. If an examination and approval organ fails to reach a decision on a contract within the specified examination and approval time limit, the contract shall be construed as approved and will automatically go into effect.

Article 5. The signing of contracts on technological imports should abide by the "Law of the People's Republic of China on Economic Contracts With Foreign Countries" and the relevant provisions of other laws. The following matters should be clearly specified in the contract by both parties:

1. Necessary explanations regarding the contents and scope of the technology to be imported. If the import item involves patents and trademarks, a detailed list of both should be provided.
2. The estimated technological targets to be achieved, as well as the specified time and measures for achieving these targets.
3. Payment, the composition of payment, and payment methods.

Article 6. The supplier must guarantee that he is the legal possessor of the technology being provided. Moreover, he must guarantee that the technology being provided is complete, faultless, and effective and will be able to achieve the targets specified in the contract.

Article 7. The recipient should undertake the commitment to keep secret, within the scope and specified time agreed upon by both sides, the classified portion of the technology provided by the supplier.

Article 8. The deadline of a contract should correspond to the time limit during which the recipient has the right to use the imported technology. The deadline shall not exceed 10 years unless otherwise approved by an examination and approval organ.

continued . . .

REGULATIONS OF THE PEOPLE'S REPUBLIC OF CHINA ON CONTROLLING TECH-
NOLOGY IMPORT CONTRACTS, Promulgated by the State Council 14 May 1985 (continued)

Article 9. The supplier must not force the recipient to accept unreasonable, restrictive requirements; within the special approval of an examination and approval organ, a contract
shall not be permitted to include the following restrictive provisions:

1. A provision that requires the recipient to accept supplementary conditions that are not
   related to the imported technology, including the purchase of unnecessary technology,
   technical services, raw and semifinished materials, equipment, or products.
2. A provision that restricts the freedom of the recipient to purchase raw- and semi-finished
   materials, parts, components, or equipment from different sources.
3. A provision that restricts the recipient from developing and improving the imported
   technology.
4. A provision that restricts the recipient from obtaining similar technology or competitive
   technology of the same category from other sources.
5. Inequitable conditions for improving technology exchanged by both sides.
6. A provision that restricts the quantity, variety, and selling prices of products produced
   by the recipient using the imported technology.
7. A provision that unreasonably restricts sales channels or export markets of the recipient.
8. A provision that forbids the recipient from continuing to use the imported technology
   after the expiration of the contract.
9. A provision that requires the recipient to pay for or to accept responsibility for unused
   patents or patents that have ceased to be in force.

Article 10. Contracts submitted for approval must be accompanied by the following documents:

1. An application for approval.
2. A copy of the contract and a translated version of it.
3. A document verifying the legal status of the two parties signing the contract.

Article 11. The provisions of Articles 4 and 10 of these regulations should be followed in
concluding a contract or extending the deadline of a contract.

Article 12. The Ministry of Foreign Economic Relations and Trade will be responsible for
explaining these regulations and drawing up rules for the implementation of these regulations.

Article 13. These regulations shall go into effect on 14 May 1985.

FBIS-CHI 108 (5 Jun 1985), K8/10.

THE ACCOUNTING REGULATIONS OF THE PEOPLE'S REPUBLIC OF CHINA FOR THE JOINT VENTURES USING CHINESE AND FOREIGN INVESTMENT

(Promulgated on March 4, 1985 by the Ministry of Finance of the People's Republic of China)

Chapter I

General Provisions

Article 1 The present regulations are formulated to
strengthen the accounting work of the joint ventures using Chinese and foreign investment, in accordance with the provisions laid down in "The
Law of the People's Republic of China on Joint
Ventures Using Chinese and Foreign Investment,"
"The Income Tax Law of the People's Republic of

China Concerning Joint Ventures With Chinese
and Foreign Investment" and other relevant laws
and regulations.

Article 2 These regulations are applicable to all
joint ventures using Chinese and foreign investment (hereinafter referred to as joint ventures)
established within the territory of the People's Republic of China.

continued . . .

THE ACCOUNTING REGULATIONS OF THE PEOPLE'S REPUBLIC OF CHINA FOR THE JOINT VENTURES USING CHINESE AND FOREIGN INVESTMENT (continued)

Article 3   The public finance departments or bureaus of provinces, autonomous regions and municipalities directly under the Central Government as well as the business regulatory departments of the State Council shall be permitted to make necessary supplements to these regulations on the basis of complying with these regulations and in the light of specific circumstances, and submit the supplements to the Ministry of Finance for the record.

Article 4   The joint ventures shall work out their own enterprise accounting system in accordance with these regulations and the supplementary provisions made by the relevant public finance department or bureau of their provinces, autonomous regions or municipalities, or by the relevant business regulatory departments of the States Council, and in the light of their specific circumstances and submit their own system to their enterprise regulatory departments, local public finance department and tax authority for the record.

Chapter II

Accounting Office and Accounting Staff

Article 5   A joint venture shall set up a separate accounting office with necessary accounting staff to handle its financial and accounting work.

Article 6   A joint venture of large or medium size shall have a controller to assist the president and to take the responsibility in leading its financial and accounting work. A deputy controller may also be appointed when necessary.

A joint venture of relatively large size shall have an auditor responsible for review and examination of its financial receipts and disbursements, accounting documents, accounting books, accounting statements and other relevant data and those of its subordinate branches.

Article 7   The accounting office and accounting staff of a joint venture shall fulfil their duties and responsibilities with due care, make accurate calculation, reflect faithfully the actual conditions, and supervise strictly over all economic transactions, protect the legitimate rights and interests of all the participants of the joint venture.

Article 8   Accounting staff who are transferred or leaving their posts shall clear their responsibility transfer procedures with those who are assuming their positions, and shall not interrupt the accounting work.

Chapter III

General Principles for Accounting

Article 9   The accounting work of the joint ventures must comply with the laws and regulations of the People's Republic of China.

Article 10   The fiscal year of a joint venture shall run from January 1 to December 31 under the Gregorian calendar.

Article 11   The joint ventures shall adopt the debt and credit double entry book keeping.

Article 12   The accounting documents, accounting books, accounting statements and the other accounting records of a joint venture shall be prepared accurately and promptly according to the transactions actually taken place, with all required routines done and contents complete.

Article 13   All the accounting documents, accounting books and accounting statements prepared by a joint venture must be written in Chinese. A foreign language mutually agreed by the participants of the joint venture may be used concurrently.

Article 14   In principle, a joint venture shall adopt Renminbi as its book keeping base currency. However, a foreign currency may be used as the bookkeeping base currency upon mutual agreement of the participants of a joint venture.

If actual receipts or disbursements of cash, bank deposits, other cash holdings, claims, debts, income and expenses, etc., are made in currencies other than the bookkeeping base currency, record shall also be made in the currencies of actual receipts or disbursements.

Article 15   The joint ventures shall adopt the accrual basis in their accounting. All revenues realized and expenses incurred during the current period shall be recognized in the current period, regardless of whether the receipts or disbursements are made. The revenues or expenses not attributable to the current period shall not be recognized as current revenue or expenses, even if they are currently received or disbursed.

Article 16   The revenues and expenses of a joint venture must be matched in its accounting. All the revenues and relevant cost and expenses of a period shall be recognized in the period and shall not be dislocated, advanced or deferred.

Article 17   All the assets of a joint venture shall be stated at their original costs and the recorded amounts are generally not adjusted whether there is any fluctuation in their market prices.

continued . . .

THE ACCOUNTING REGULATIONS OF THE PEOPLE'S REPUBLIC OF CHINA FOR THE JOINT VENTURES USING CHINESE AND FOREIGN INVESTMENT (continued)

Article 18 A joint venture shall draw clear distinction between capital expenditures and revenue expenditures. All expenditures incurred for the increase of fixed assets and intangible assets are capital expenditures. All expenditures incurred to obtain current revenue are revenue expenditures.

Article 19 Accounting methods adopted by a joint venture shall be consistent from one period to the other and shall not be arbitrarily changed. Changes, if any, shall be approved by the board of directors and submitted to the local tax authority for examination. Disclosure of the changes shall be made in the accounting report.

Chapter IV

Accounting for Paid-in Capital

Article 20 The participants of a joint venture shall contribute their share capital in the amount, ratio and mode of capital contribution within the stipulated time limit as provided in the joint venture contract. The accounting for paid-in capital by a joint venture shall be based on the actual amount contributed by each of its participants.

(1) For investment paid in cash, the amount and date as received or as deposited into the Bank of China or other banks where the joint venture has opened its bank account shall be the basis for recording the capital contribution.

The foreign currency contributed by a foreign participant shall be converted into Renminbi or further converted into a predetermined foreign currency at the exchange rates quoted on the day of the cash payment by the State Administration of Foreign Exchange Control of the People's Republic of China (hereinafter referred to as the State Administration of Foreign Exchange Control). Should the cash Renminbi contributed by a Chinese participant be converted into foreign currency, it shall be converted at the exchange rate quoted by the State Administration of Foreign Exchange Control on the day of the cash payment.

(2) For investment in the form of buildings, machinery, equipment, materials and supplies, the amount shown on the examined and verified itemization list of the assets as agreed upon by each participant and the date of the receipt of the assets shall be the basis of accounting according to the joint venture contract.

(3) For investment in the form of intangible assets, i.e., proprietory technology, patents, trademarks, copyright and other franchises, etc., the amount and date as provided in the agreement or contracts shall be the basis of accounting.

(4) For investment in the form of the right to use sites, the amount and date as provided in the agreement or contract shall be the basis of accounting.

The capital contributed by each participant shall be recorded into the accounts of the joint venture as soon as they are received.

Article 21 The capital amount contributed by the participants of a joint venture shall be validated by Certified Public Accountants registered with the government of the People's Republic of China, who shall render a certificate on capital validation; which shall then be taken by the joint venture as the basis to issue capital contribution certificates to the participants.

Chapter V

Accounting for Cash and Current Accounts

Article 22 A joint venture shall open its deposit accounts in the Bank of China or the other banks within the territory of the People's Republic of China and approved by the State Administration of Foreign Exchange Control or by one of its branches. All foreign exchange receipts must be deposited with the bank in the foreign currency deposit account and all foreign exchange disbursements must be made from the accounts.

Article 23 A joint venture shall set up journals to itemize cash and bank transactions in chronological order. A separate journal shall be set up for each currency if there are several currencies.

Article 24 The accounts receivable, accounts payable and other receivables and payables of a joint venture shall be recorded in separate accounts set up for different currencies. Receivables shall be collected and payables shall be paid in due time and shall be confirmed with the relevant parties periodically. The causes of uncollectible items shall be investigated and the responsibilities thereof shall be determined. Any item proved to be definitely uncollectible through strict management review shall be written off as bad debts after approval is obtained through reporting procedures specified by the board of directors. No "reserve for bad debts" shall be accrued.

Article 25 In a joint venture using Renminbi as bookkeeping base currency, its foreign currency deposits, foreign currency loans and other accounts denominated in foreign currency shall be recorded not only in their original foreign currency of the actual receipts and payments, but also in Renminbi converted from foreign currency at an ascertained exchange rate (using the exchange rate quoted by the State Administration of Foreign Exchange Control).

continued . . .

THE ACCOUNTING REGULATIONS OF THE PEOPLE'S REPUBLIC OF CHINA FOR THE JOINT VENTURES USING CHINESE AND FOREIGN INVESTMENT (continued)

All additions of foreign currency deposits, foreign currency loans and other accounts denominated in foreign currencies shall be recorded in Renminbi converted at their recording exchange rates. while deductions shall be recorded in Renminbi converted at their book exchange rates. Differences in the Renminbi amount resulting from the conversion at different exchange rates shall be recognized as "foreign exchange gains or losses" (hereinafter referred to as "exchange gains or losses").

The recording exchange rates for the conversion of foreign currency to Renminbi may be the rate prevailing on the day of recording the transaction or on the first day of the month, etc. The book exchange rate may be calculated by the first-in first-out method, or by the weighted average methods, etc. However, for the decrease of accounts denominated in a foreign currency, the original recording rate may be used as book rate. Whichever rate is adopted, there shall be no arbitrary change once it is decided. If any change is necessary, it must be approved by the board of directors and disclosed in the accounting report.

The difference in Renminbi resulting from the exchange of different currencies shall also be recognized as exchange gains or losses.

The exchange gains or losses recognized in the account shall be the realized amount. In case of exchange rate fluctuation, the Renminbi balances of the foreign currency accounts shall not be adjusted.

Article 26 In a joint venture using a foreign currency as its bookkeeping base currency, its Renminbi deposits, Renminbi loans and other accounts denominated in Renminbi shall be recorded not only in Renminbi but also in the foreign currency converted from Renminbi at the exchange rate adopted by the enterprise. Difference in the foreign currency amount resulting from the conversion at different exchange rates shall also be recognized as exchange gains or losses as stipulated in Article 25.

A joint venture using a foreign currency as bookkeeping base currency shall compile not only annual accounting statements in the foreign currency but also separate accounting statements in Renminbi translated from foreign currency at the end of a year. However, the joint venture's Renminbi bank deposits, Renminbi bank loans and the other accounts denominated in Renminbi shall still be accounted for in their original Renminbi amounts, and be combined with the other items converted into Renminbi from foreign currency. The differences between the original Renminbi amount of the Renminbi items and their Renminbi amount from currency translation shall not be recognized as foreign exchange gains or losses, but shall be shown on the balance sheet with an additional caption as "currency translation difference."

Chapter VI

Accounting for Inventories

Article 27 The inventories of a joint venture refer to merchandise, materials and supplies, containers, low-value and perishable articles. work in process, semi-finished goods, finished goods, etc., in stock, in processing or in transit.

Article 28 All the inventories of a joint venture shall be recorded at the actual cost.

(1) The actual cost of materials and supplies, containers, low-value and perishable articles purchased from outside shall include the purchase price, transportation expenses, loading and unloading charges, packaging expenses, insurance premium, reasonable loss during transit, selecting and sorting expenses before taken into storage, etc. The cost of imported goods shall further include the custom duties and industrial and commercial consolidated tax, etc.

For merchandise purchased by a commercial or service-trade enterprise, the original purchase price shall be taken as the actual cost for bookkeeping.

(2) The actual cost of self manufactured materials and supplies, containers, low-value and perishable articles, semi-finished goods and finished goods shall include the materials and supplies consumed, wages and relevant expenses incurred during the manufacture process.

(3) The actual cost of materials and supplies, containers, low-value and perishable articles, semi-finished and finished goods completed through outside processing shall include the original cost of the materials and supplies or semi-finished goods consumed, the processing expenses, inward and outward transportation expenses and sundry charges.

The merchandise of the commercial or service-trade enterprises processed under contract with outside units shall be recorded at the purchase price after processing, including the original purchase price of the merchandise before processing, processing expenses and the industrial and commercial consolidated tax attributable.

Article 29 The receipt, issuance, requisition and return of the inventories of a joint venture shall be timely processed through accounting procedures according to the actual quantity and shall be itemized in the subsidiary ledger accounts with established columns for quantities and amounts, so as to strengthen the inventory control. The merchandise, materials, etc., in transit, shall be accounted for through subsidiary ledgers and their condition of arrival shall be inspected at all times. For those goods not arrived in due time, the relevant depart-

continued . . .

THE ACCOUNTING REGULATIONS OF THE PEOPLE'S REPUBLIC OF CHINA FOR THE JOINT VENTURES USING CHINESE AND FOREIGN INVESTMENT (continued)

ment shall be urged to take action. As to those goods that have arrived but not yet been checked or taken into storage, their acceptance test and warehousing procedures shall be carried out in a timely manner.

Article 30   The actual cost or original purchase price of inventories issued or requisitioned from the store of a joint venture may be accounted for by it under one of the following methods; first-in-first-out, shifting average, weighted average, batch actual, etc. Once the accounting method is adopted, no arbitrary change shall be allowed.   In case a change of accounting method is necessary, it shall be submitted to the local tax authority for approval and disclosed in the accounting report.

Article 31   In the joint ventures using planned cost in daily accounting for materials and supplies, finished goods, etc., the planned cost of those issued from stock, shall be adjusted into actual cost at the end of each month.

For the commercial and service-trade enterprises using selling price in daily accounting for merchandise, the cost of goods sold shall be adjusted from selling price to original purchase price at the end of a month.

Article 32   A joint venture shall take physical inventory of its stock periodically, at least once a year. If any overage, shortage, damage, deterioration, etc., is found, the relevant department shall investigate the cause and write out a report. Accounting treatment shall be made as soon as the report is approved through strict management review and the reporting procedures specified by the board of directors. The treatment shall generally be completed before the annual closing of final accounts.

(1)   The inventory shortage (minus inventory overage) and damage (minus salvage) of materials and supplies, work in process, semi-finished goods, finished goods, and merchandise, etc., shall be charged to the current expenses, except the amount, if any, that should be indemnified by the persons in fault.

(2)   The net loss resulting from natural disasters shall be charged to non-operating expenses after deducting the salvage value recoverable and insurance indemnity.

Article 33   If there is any inventory in a join venture to be disposed of at a reduced price due to obsolescence, it shall be reported for approval according to the procedures specified by the board of directors, and the net loss on disposal shall be recognized as loss on sales. If the disposal is not yet done at the end of a year, disclosure shall be made in the annual accounting report for the actual cost per book, the net realizable value and the probable loss thereof.

Article 34   Disclosure shall be made in the annual accounting report of a joint venture on the actual cost per book, net realizable value and probable loss of its inventories of which the net realizable value is lower than the actual cost per book due to the decline of the market price.

Chapter VII

Accounting for Long-term Investment and Long-Term Liabilities

Article 35   The investment of a joint venture in other units shall be accounted for at the amount paid or agreed upon at the time of the investment. and shall be shown in the balance sheet with a separate caption as "long-term investment."

Income and loss derived from long-term investment shall be recognized as non-operating income or non-operating expense.

Article 36   The bank loans borrowed by a joint venture for capital construction during its preparation period or for increasing fixed assets, expanding its business, or making renovation and reform of its equipments after its operation started, shall be accounted for at the amount and on the date of the loan and shall be presented in the balance sheet with a separate caption as "long-term bank loans."

The interest expenses on the long-term bank loans incured during the construction period shall be charged to construction cost and capitalized as a part of the original cost of the fixed assets; but interest expenses incurred after the completion of the construction and the transfer of fixed assets for operation purpose shall be charged to current expenses.

Chapter VIII

Accounting for Fixed Assess

Article 37   A joint venture shall prepare a fixed assets catalogue as the basis of accounting according to the criteria of fixed assets laid down in "The Income Tax Law Concerning Joint Ventures With Chinese and Foreign Investment" and in consideration of its specific circumstances.

Article 38   The fixed assets of a joint venture shall be grouped into five broad categories as follows: Building and structures; machinery and equipment; electronic equipment; transport facilities (trains or ships, if any, shall be grouped separately); and other equipment. The joint venture may further group them into sub-categories according to the need of its management.

continued . . .

THE ACCOUNTING REGULATIONS OF THE PEOPLE'S REPUBLIC OF CHINA FOR THE JOINT VENTURES USING CHINESE AND FOREIGN INVESTMENT (continued)

Article 39 The fixed assets of a joint venture shall be recorded at their original cost.

For fixed assets contributed as investment, the original cost shall be the price of the assets agreed upon by all the participants of the joint venture at the time of investment.

For fixed assets purchased, the original cost shall be the total of the purchase price plus freight, loading and unloading charges, packaging expenses and insurance premium etc. The original cost of the fixed assets that need installation work, shall include installation expenses. The original cost of imported equipment shall further include the custom duties, industrial and commercial consolidated tax, etc., paid as required.

For fixed assets manufactured or constructed by the joint venture itself, the original cost shall be the actual expenditures incurred in the course of manufacture or construction.

Expenditures of a joint venture on technical innovation and reform that result in the increase of the fixed assets value shall be recorded as increments of the original cost of the fixed assets.

Article 40 Depreciation on the fixed assets of a joint venture shall generally be accounted for on an average basis under the straight line method.

(1) Depreciation on fixed assets shall be accounted for on the basis of the original cost and the group depreciation rate of the fixed assets.

Depreciation rate of the fixed assets shall be calculated and determined on the basis of the original cost, estimated residual value and the useful life of the fixed assets.

A joint venture shall determine the specific useful lives and depreciation rates for different groups of fixed assets according to the minimum depreciation period and the estimated residual value of the fixed assets as provided in the "Income Tax Law Concerning Joint Ventures With Chinese and Foreign Investment."

(2) In case where a joint venture needs accelerated depreciation or change of depreciation method for special reasons, application shall be submitted by the joint venture to the tax authority for examination and approval.

(3) Generally, depreciation of the fixed assets of a joint venture shall be accounted for monthly according to the monthly depreciation rates and the monthly beginning balances of the original cost per book of the fixed assets in use. For fixed assets put in use during a month, depreciation shall not be calculated for the month but shall be started

from the next month. For fixed assets reduced or stopped to be used during the month, depreciation shall still be calculated for the month and be stopped from the next month.

(4) For the fixed assets fully depreciated but still useful, depreciation shall no longer be calculated. For the fixed assets discarded in advance, no retroactive depreciation shall be made either.

For the fixed assets declared scrap in advance or transferred out, the difference between the net proceeds obtained from disposal (less liquidation expenses) and the net value of the fixed assets (original cost less accumulated depreciation) shall be recognized as non-operating income or non-operating expenses of a joint venture.

Article 41 For the purchase, sales, disposal, discarding and internal transfer, etc., of the fixed assets, a joint venture must execute accounting routines and set up fixed assets subsidiary ledger for the relevant accounting so as to strengthen the control of fixed assets.

Article 42 Physical inventory must be taken on the fixed assets of a joint venture at least once a year. If any average, shortage or damage of the fixed assets is found, the cause shall be investigated and a report be written out by the relevant department. Accounting treatment shall be made as soon as the report is approved through strict management review and the reporting procedures specified by the board of directors. Generally, this work shall be finished before the annual closing of final accounts.

(1) For fixed assets average, the replacement cost shall be taken as the original cost, the accumulated depreciation shall be estimated and recorded according to the existing usability and wear and tear of the assets, and the difference between the original cost and the accumulated depreciation shall be credited to non-operating income.

(2) For fixed assets shortage, the original cost and accumulated depreciation shall be written off and the excess of original cost over accumulated depreciation shall be charged as non-operating expenses.

(3) For damaged fixed assets, the net loss after the original cost deducted by the accumulated depreciation, recoverable salvage value and the indemnity receivable from the person in fault or from the insurance company, shall be charged as non-operating expenses.

continued . . .

THE ACCOUNTING REGULATIONS OF THE PEOPLE'S REPUBLIC OF CHINA FOR THE JOINT VENTURES USING CHINESE AND FOREIGN INVESTMENT (continued)

Chapter IX

Accounting for Intangible Assests and Other Assets

Article 43 The intangible assets and other assets of a joint venture include proprietary technology, patents, trademarks, copyrights, right to use sites, other franchise and organization expenses, etc.

For intangible assets contributed as investment by the participants of a joint venture, the original cost shall be the value provided in the agreement or contract. The original cost of purchased intangible assets shall be the amount actually paid. Monthly amortization of the intangible assets shall be made over their useful life from the year when they come into use. Those without specified useful life may be amortized over a period of ten years. The amortization period shall not be longer than the duration of a joint venture.

Article 44 The expenses incurred by a joint venture during its preparation period (not including expenditures for acquiring fixed assets and intangible assets and the interest incurred during the construction period to be included in the construction cost) may be accounted for as organization expenses according to the provisions of the agreement and with the consent of all participants, and shall be amortized after the production or operation starts. The annual amortization shall not exceed 20 percent of the expenses.

Article 45 The expenditures incurred by a joint venture on major repair and improvement of the leased-in fixed assets shall be amortized over the period benefited from such expenditures. However, the amortization period shall not be longer than the lease term of the fixed assets.

Chapter X

Accounting for Costs and Expenses

Article 46 The joint ventures shall maintain complete original records, practise norm control, adhere strictly to the procedures of measuring, checking, receiving, issuing, requisitioning and returning of goods and materials, strengthen the control of and accounting for cost and expenses.

Article 47 All expenditures of a joint venture related to production or operation shall be recognized as its cost or expenses.

Materials consumed by a joint venture in the course of production or operation shall be correctly calculated and charged to cost or expenses according to the quantity actually consumed and the price per book.

Wages and salaries of the staff and workers shall be calculated and charged to the cost or expenses according to the provisions in the contract and the decisions of the board of directors on the system of wage standard, wage form, bonus and allowance, etc., as well as the attendance records, time cards and production records. Payment as required on labour insurance, health and welfare benefits and government subsidies, etc., for the Chinese staff and workers, shall also be charged to cost or expenses as the same item as wages and salaries.

All other expenses incurred by a joint venture in the course of production or operation shall be charged to cost or expenses according to the amount actually incurred. The expenses attributable to the current period but not yet paid shall be recognized as accrued expenses and charged to the cost or expenses of the current period; however, the expenses paid but attributable to the current and future periods shall be recognized as deferred charges and amortized to the cost or expenses of the relevant periods.

Article 48 A joint venture shall summarize all the expenses incurred in the course of production or operation according to the specified cost and expense items.

(1) The production cost items of an industrial joint venture shall generally be classified into: Direct materials, direct labour, and manufacturing overhead. A joint venture may set up additional items for fuel and power, outside processing cost, special instruments, etc., according to its actual needs.

Manufacturing overhead refers to those expenses arising from organizing and controlling production by workshop and factory administriative departments, including expenses for salaries and wages, depreciation, repairs and maintenance, materials consumed, labour protection, water and electricity, office supplies, travelling, transportation, insurance and so on.

Selling and general administrative expenses of an industrial joint venture shall be accounted for separately and shall not be included in the production cost of products.

continued . . .

THE ACCOUNTING REGULATIONS OF THE PEOPLE'S REPUBLIC OF CHINA FOR THE JOINT VENTURES USING CHINESE AND FOREIGN INVESTMENT (continued)

Selling expenses refer to those expenses incurred in selling products and attributable to the enterprise, including expenses for transportation, loading and unloading, packaging, insurance, travelling, commission and advertising, as well as salaries and wages and other expenses of specificaly established selling organs, etc.

General and administrative expenses include company headquarters expenses (selaries & wages, etc.), labour union dues, interest expense (less interest income), exchange loss (less exchange gains), expenses of board of directors' meetings, advisory fee, entertainment expenses, taxes (including urban building and land tax, license tax for vehicles and vessels, etc.), amortization of organization expenses, expenses for staff and workers' training, research and development expenses, fee for the use of site, fee for the transfer of technology, amortization of intangible assets and other administrative expenses.

(2) Expenses of the commercial enterprises incurred in the course of operation include purchasing expenses, selling expenses and administrative expenses.

Purchasing expenses include those expenses incurred in the process of merchandise purchase, such as expenses for transportation, loading and unloading, packaging, insurance, reasonable loss during transit, selecting and sorting before warehousing.

Selling expenses include those expenses incurred in the course of merchandise sales and attributable to the joint venture, such as expenses for transportation, loading and unloading, packaging, insurance, travelling, commission, advertising, and salaries and wages and other expenses of sales organ, etc.

Administrative expenses include those expenses incurred in the course of merchandise storage, and the expenses of the enterprise administrative departments, such as expenses for salaries and wages, depreciation, repairs and maintenance, materials consumed, labour protection, office supplies, travelling, transportion, insurance, labour union dues, interest expense (less interest income), exchange loss (less exchange gains), expenses of board of director's meeting, advisory fee, entertainment, tax, fee for the use of site, staff and workers' training and other administrative expenses.

(3) Expenses of the service-trade enterprises incurred in the course of operation include operating expenses and administrative expenses.

The operating expenses include various expenses incurred in business operation and may be summarized separately for different kinds of service.

The administrative expenses include various expenses incurred for the administration of the enterprise.

The joint ventures other than the above mentioned types shall account for their expenses with reference to the above provisions.

Article 49 A joint venture must distinguish the cost and expenses of the current period from that of the ensuing period. Neither accrual nor amortization shall be made arbitrarily. The cost and expenses of different internal departments shall be distinguished from each other and shall not be mixed up. An industrial joint venture shall distinguish the cost of work in process from the cost of finished goods and the cost of one product from that of the other. Neither the cost of work in process nor the cost of finished goods shall be arbitrarily increased or decreased.

Article 50 The joint venture shall select the methods of costing and of expense allocation appropriate to the characteristics of its production and operation, its type of product and its purpose of service.

An industrial joint venture may select one or more than one of the following methods for its cost accounting: Product type costing, process costing, job order costing, product category costing, norm costing and standard costing.

For the enterprises adopting the norm costing or the standard costing in accounting for product cost, the variances between actual cost and norm cost or between actual cost and standard cost shall generally be allocated according to the proportion of the products sold during a month and the products held at the end of the month.

Once the cost accounting method or the cost variance allocation method is adopted, no arbitrary change shall be allowed. If a change is necessary, it shall be approved by the board of directors, reported to the local tax authority for examination and disclosed in the accounting report.

Article 51 The joint ventures shall strengthen the control over cost and expenses, establish responsibility cost system, formulate plans on cost and expenses, control the expenditures at all times in accordance with the plans, evaluate the condition in implementing the plans periodically, analyze the cause of fluctuation in cost and expenses, take appropriate actions to reduce the cost and expenses and to improve the operation and administration of the enterprise.

continued . . .

THE ACCOUNTING REGULATIONS OF THE PEOPLE'S REPUBLIC OF CHINA FOR THE JOINT VENTURES USING CHINESE AND FOREIGN INVESTMENT (continued)

Chapter XI

Accounting for Sales and Profit

Article 52   The sales of merchandise, products and services of a joint venture shall be regarded as realized after merchandise and products are shipped, services are rendered, invoices, bills and the bills of lading issued by shipping agency and all other shipping documents are sent to the buyers or are accepted by the bank for collection.

Under the condition of delivery upon payment, if the sales proceeds are received, invoices and delivery orders are sent to the buyers, sales shall be regarded as realized whether the goods are actually issued or not.

Article 53   All the sales of a joint venture realized in a month shall be recognized in the month, and the relevant cost of the sales and expenses shall be transferred simultaneously. Revenue from sales must be matched with the cost of sales and expenses attributable. It is not allowed to recognize merely the sales revenue and disregard the relevant cost of sales and expenses. On the other hand, it is not allowed to charge the cost of sales and expenses without crediting the relevant revenue from sales.

Article 54   The sales returns of a joint venture occurred in a month shall reduce the sales revenue and cost of sales of the current month, regardless of to which year the returned sales belong.

Sales allowances given to the buyers through negotiation due to unsatisfactory quality of the merchandise or products sold or due to some other reasons shall be deducted from sales revenue of the current month.

Article 55   A joint venture shall account for its profit every month. The joint ventures in agriculture, animal husbandry, aquaculture and other businesses that cannot account for profit monthly shall at least do their accounting for profit at the end of a fiscal year.

Article 56   The elements of the profit of a joint venture are as follows:

(1)   The profit of an industrial joint venture includes profit from sales of the products, profit on other operation, non-operating income and expenses.

Profit from sales of the products refers to the profit derived from the products sold by the joint venture (including finished goods, semi-finished goods and industrial services).

Profit from other operation refers to those profits of a joint venture derived from rendering non-industrial services (such as transportation, etc.) and from sales of purchased merchandise and surplus materials, etc.

Non-operating income and expenses refer to the various gains and losses other than profit from sales of products and from other operations, including income from investment, loss on investment, income on disposal of fixed assets, loss on disposal of fixed assets penalty and fines received, penalty and fines paid, donation contributed, bad debts, extraordinary losses, etc.

(2)   The profit of a commercial enterprise includes profit from sales, profit from other operations and non-operating income and expenses.

Profit from sales refers to the profit derived from selling merchandise.

Profit from other operations refers to those profit derived from operations other than sales of merchandise (such, as occasional repairs, rental, etc.).

Non-operating income and non-operating expenses refer to various non-operating gains and losses other than profit from sales and profit from other operation, including income on investment, loss on investment, income from disposal of fixed assets, loss on disposal of fixed assets, penalty and fines received, penalty and fines paid, donations contributed, bad debts, extraordinary losses, etc.

(3)   Profit of a service-trade enterprise includes net operating income and non-operating income and expenses.

Article 57   The profit distributable by a joint venture shall be the excess of its net profit over income tax payable and the required provisions of reserve fund, staff and workers' bonus and welfare fund and enterprise expansion fund. It shall be distributed to the participants of the joint venture in proportion to their shares of contributed capital if the board of directors decides to make the distribution.

The reserved fund may be used as provisional financial cushion against the possible loss of a joint venture. The staff and workers' bonus and welfare fund shall be restricted to the payment of bonus and collective welfare for staff and workers. The enterprise expansion fund may be used to acquire fixed assets or to increase the working capital in order to expand the production and operation of the joint venture.

Article 58   If a joint venture carries losses from the previous years, the profit of the current year shall first be used to cover the losses. No profit shall be distributed unless the deficit from the previous years is made up.

The profit retained by a joint venture and carried over from the previous years may be distributed together with the distributable profit of the current year, or after the deficit of the current year is made up therefrom.

continued . . .

THE ACCOUNTING REGULATIONS OF THE PEOPLE'S REPUBLIC OF CHINA FOR THE JOINT VENTURES USING CHINESE AND FOREIGN INVESTMENT (continued)

Article 59 A joint venture shall compile a profit distribution programme at the end of a year, based on the profit or losses realized in the year and the retained profit or deficit carried over from the previous years, and submit the programme to the board of directors for discussion and decision. The distribution shall be recorded in the books of account and recognized in the annual final accounts after the decision is made.

Chapter XII

Classification of Accounts and Accounting Statements

Article 60 The rules on the classification of accounts and accounting statements of the joint ventures shall be formulated by the Ministry of Finance of the People's Republic of China, or by the relevant business regulatory departments and sumbitted to the Ministry of Finance for examination and approval.

A joint venture may supplement or omit the stipulated ledger accounts and the stipulated items of the accounting statements according to its specific circumstances, provided that it does not affect the accounting requirements and the sumarization of the indexes in the accounting statements.

Article 61 The accounts of the joint ventures shall generally be classified according to the operation and management needs into four broad categories: Assets, liabilities, capital, profit & loss. Profit and loss accounts may also be classified into income accounts and expenses accounts. For industrial joint ventures, another category may be added for cost accounts. The ledger accounts of a joint venture shall be coded according to their classification.

Article 62 The accounting statements of a joint venture shall include:

  (1) Balance sheet;

  (2) Income statement;

  (3) Statement of changes in financial position;

  (4) Relevant supporting schedules.

A joint venture may add additional information in its accounting statements after it is approved by all its participants, in order to meet the need of the foreign participant's head office in consolidation of financial statements.

Article 63 When a joint venture with subsidiary enterprises combines its accounting statements with those of its subsidiaries, its funds appropriated to and its current accounts with its subsidiaries shall be offset against the corresponding items in the accounting statements of the subsidiaries.

Article 64 On submitting its annual accounting statements, a joint venture shall attach a descriptive overview of its financial condition, primarily explaining:

  (1) condition of production and operation;

  (2) condition of realization and distribution of profit;

  (3) condition of changes in capital and its turnover;

  (4) condition of foreign exchange receipts and disbursements and their equilibrium;

  (5) condition of the payment of industrial and commercial consolidated tax, income tax, fee for the use of site and fee for the transfer of technology;

  (6) condition of overage, shortage, deterioration, spoilage, damage and write-off of different properties and supplies;

  (7) other necessary issues to be explained.

On submitting quarterly statements, the joint venture shall also explain special conditions, if any.

Article 65 The quarterly and annual accounting statements of a joint venture shall be submitted to each participant of the joint venture, local tax authority, the relevant business regulatory department of the joint venture and the public finance department at the same level.

The quarterly accounting statements of a joint venture shall be submitted within 20 days after the end of each quarter, and the annual accounting statements shall be submitted together with the audit report made by the Certified Public Accountants within four months after the end of a year.

Article 66 The accounting statements of a joint venture shall be examined and signed by its president and controller and shall be under the seal of the joint venture.

Chapter XIII

Accounting Documents & Accounting Books

Article 67 A joint venture must acquire or fill out original documents for every transaction occurred. All the original documents must carry faithful contents, evidences of all the required procedures and accurate figures. Original documents from an outside unit must be signed and sealed by the unit. The original documents shall be verified and signed by the head of the department and the person responsible for handling the transcation.

continued . . .

THE ACCOUNTING REGULATIONS OF THE PEOPLE'S REPUBLIC OF CHINA FOR THE JOINT VENTURES USING CHINESE AND FOREIGN INVESTMENT (continued)

A joint venture shall check and inspect the original documents seriously. Any falsified or altered original document, or any fraudulent application or request or other similar events must be rejected and reported to the relevant party. The original documents with incomplete contents, insufficient evidences of required procedures or inaccurate figures shall be returned, amended or refilled. Only the original documents examined and proved correct can be taken as the basis for preparing accounting vouchers.

Article 68 The acounting vouchers of a joint venture include receiving voucher, disbursement voucher, and journal voucher. All vouchers must be filled out with required contents and can be taken as the basis in bookkeeping only after signed by the preparer, the designated verifier and the chief officer of the financial and accounting department. A receiving or disbursement voucher shall also be signed by the cashier.

Each kind of the accounting vouchers shall be filed according to its sequential number and bound into books monthly together with the original documents attached thereto, and shall be kept in safety without any loss or damage. For the important documents concerning claims and debts that need separate safe-keeping, cross reference shall be made on the original documents of the transaction and on the related vouchers.

Article 69 A joint venture shall number sequentially all documents issued to the outside, and retain its duplicate copy (or copies) or the stub. An original of such document with clerical error or withdrawn for cancellation shall be kept together with the duplicate or stub of the same sequential number. If the original copy is missing or unable to be recovered, the reason shall be noted on the duplicate or stub.

Article 70 All the blank forms of important documents, such as check books, cash receipts, delivery orders, etc., shall be registered in a special registration book by the financial and accounting department. Requisition of those blank forms shall be approved by the chief officer or a designated person of the financial and accounting department, and the person making the requisition shall sign the registration book for receiving the forms.

Article 71 A joint venture shall set up three kinds of primary accounting books, namely, journals, general ledger and subsidiary ledgers, as well as appropriate supplementary memorandum books.

All the books shall be kept with complete records, accurate figures, clear description and prompt registration, on the basis of the examined original documents and vouchers or summary of vouchers that are proved correct.

No record in the books of a joint venture shall be scraped, mended, altered or eliminated by correction fluid. When errors are made, they shall be amended by crossing off the error or by preparing additional vouchers according to the nature and circumstances of the error. When crossing method of amendment is used, the person making the correction shall sign on the place of amendment.

Article 72 A joint venture keeping its accounts by electronic computer shall maintain properly its accounting records stored in or printed out by the computer and shall regard such records as accounting books. The tapes, discs, etc., shall be kept and no deletion shall be allowed unless the records in them are printed out in visible form.

Chapter XIV

Audit

Article 73 A joint venture shall engage the Certified Public Accountants registered with the government of the People's Republic of China to audit its annual accounting statements and the books of account of the year and to issue an auditor's report, according to the provisions of "The Income Tax Law Concerning Joint Ventures With Chinese and Foreign Investment."

Article 74 Each participant of a joint venture may audit the accounts of the joint venture. The expenses thereon shall be paid by the participant making the audit. Any problem noted in the audit that needs to be resolved by the joint venture shall be submitted to the joint venture in a timely manner for discussion and resolution.

Article 75 The joint ventures shall furnish the auditors with all the documents, books and other relevant data as needed by them. The auditors shall be responsible for maintaining confidentiality.

Chapter XV

Accounting Files

Article 76 The accounting files of a joint venture, including accounting documents, accounting books, accounting statements, etc., must be appropriately kept within the territory of the People's Republic of China. No loss nor spoilage shall be allowed.

continued . . .

THE ACCOUNTING REGULATIONS OF THE PEOPLE'S REPUBLIC OF CHINA FOR THE JOINT VENTURES USING CHINESE AND FOREIGN INVESTMENT (continued)

Article 77 The annual accounting statements and all other important accounting files relevant to the rights and interests of all the participants of a joint venture, such as joint venture agreement, joint venture contract, articles of association of the joint venture, resolutions of the board of directors, investment appraisal list, certificate on capital validation, auditing report of the certified public accountants, long term economic contracts, etc., must be kept permanently. General accounting documents, accounting books and monthly and quarterly accounting statements shall be kept for at least 15 years.

Article 78 If the accounting files need to be destroyed after the expiration of the retention period, an itemized list of the files to be destroyed shall be prepared and reported to the board of directors, business regulatory department and tax authority for approval. No files can be destroyed unless such list is approved. The list of destroyed accounting files must be kept permanently.

Article 82 The assets of a joint venture left over after the clearance of all its debts shall be distributed among the participants of the joint venture according to the proportion of each participant's investment contribution, unless otherwise provided by the agreement, contract or articles of association of the joint venture.

Article 83 The accounting statements on liquidation and dissolution of a joint venture shall be valid only after an examination is made and a certificate is issued by Certified Public Accountants registered with the government of the People's Republic of China.

Article 84 After the dissolution of a joint venture, its accounting books and all other documents shall be left in the care of the Chinese participant.

Chapter XVI

Dissolution and Liquidation

Article 79 When a joint venture declares dissolution and goes into liquidation on or before the expiration of the joint venture contract, a liquidation committee shall be formed to conduct an overall check of the assets of the joint venture and its claims and debts to prepare a balance sheet and a detailed list of assets, to suggest a basis for the valuation and calculation of the assets and to formulate a plan for liquidation. After the approval is obtained through submitting the liquidation plan to the board of directors for its discussion, the liquidation committee shall make disposal of the assets, collect the claims, pay taxes and clear debts, and resolve all remaining problems appropriately.

Article 80 The liquidation expenses of a joint venture and the remuneration to its liquidation committee members shall be given priority in making payments from the existing assets of the joint venture.

Article 81 The net liquidation income, i.e., the liquidation income in the process of the liquidation of a joint venture less the liquidation expenses and various liquidation losses, shall be dealt with as the profit of the joint venture.

Chapter XVII

Other Provisions

Article 85 The present regulations are formulated by the Ministry of Finance of the People's Republic of China. If there is any change in the laws, regulations and other relevant provisions of the People's Republic of China on which these regulations are based, the new provisions shall govern. If the present regulation need corresponding amendment, it shall be made by the Ministry of Finance of the People's Republic of China.

Article 86 For the joint ventures established in the special economic zones, if there are special provisions in the laws or regulations adopted by the National People's Congress of the People's Republic of China or its Standing Committee, or by the State Council, such provisions shall be followed.

Article 87 The right to interpret these regulations resides in the Ministry of Finance of the People's Republic of China.

Article 88 The present regulations shall be implemented on and after July 1, 1985. ☐

Beijing Review, 27 (8 Jul 1985), v-xvi.

XII FOREIGN AID

CHINESE ECONOMIC AID BY COUNTRIES, 1985

Bangladesh—Beijing has given Bangladesh $500,000 for victims of a cyclone and tidal wave. The Chinese Red Cross Society previously offered $50,000.

Benin—Chinese are helping construct the Lokosa Cotton Mill. It will have 20,000 spindles and 720 looms. The project began in April, 1983.

Botswana—The PRC has given Botswana $100,000 to buy seeds and other goods related to planting. In March, 1985 it announced a donation of 500 tons of maize for famine relief from the drought.

Burma—The No. 1 National Gymnasium is being built on 9,000 square meters of land at Thingangyun outside Rangoon. The gymnasium will seat 10,800. The project was scheduled for completion at the end of 1985. China will also build a 1,000-seat theater in Rangoon.

Central African Republic—China has sent 3,000 freshwater fish to the CAR in accordance with a 1976 economic cooperation agreement. The survival rate of this fish has reached 99.5 percent, and its fry of 1-2 cm grew to 250 grams in four months.

Congo—By the terms of a two-year protocol signed 2 April 1985 China will continue to send medical teams to the Congo. A 40-man team will be provided. Beijing has dispatched eight medical teams to the country since 1967.

Ethiopia—The *Beijing Review*, 21 (27 May 1985), 6-7, lists various donations to African relief, particularly for drought victims in Ethiopia. China provided 120,000 tons of grain to Africa in 1984, and another 50,000 tons to Sudan, Mozambique, Ethiopia, Niger, and Tanzania during the first half of 1985.

Ghana—China has completed the Afife irrigation project ahead of schedule.

Guinea—The PRC sent Guinea 3,000 tons of maize in March, 1985.

Kenya—The Chinese are building a sports complex at Nairobi.

Mauritania—*Le Monde* (1 Apr 1985), 7, describes Chinese aid projects in the country. They include two thermal power stations for Nouakchott, an agricultural mission, and medical teams. A total of 546 Chinese medical personnel have treated 3.2 million people in Mauritania since 1968. A port has been under construction in the capital since 1980, and it is expected to start operations in 1987. The port will have a 580-meter wharf, and warehouses covering 95,000 square meters. The cost for the PRC will amount to $200 million.

Mexico—The Chinese Red Cross Society was to donate $50,000 for victims of the September, 1985 earthquake. The Chinese government promised another $200,000 in cash.

Mozambique—China will provide 645,000 yuan ($230,000) worth of farm machinery, including insurance and freight charges, to Mozambique under an agreement signed in February, 1985. Another accord stipulates that Chinese technicians will help modernize the textile mill in Nampula and provide equipment and spare parts. In January, 1985 Beijing announced the donation of 3,000 tons of maize to help alleviate the effects of the drought.

Nepal—The Pokhara water conservancy and irrigation project was inaugurated 16 June 1985. It was started in November, 1981 and completed in May, 1985. The project includes a 40-km canal system providing year-around irrigation for 1,030 hectares of land and a three-turbine hydropower station with a total capacity of 1,500 kW. The agricultural output of the region is expected to double. The project's cost was 51 million yuan ($18 million). Pokhara is located 200 km west of Katmandu. The PRC has also helped build the Sunkosi Hydropower Station in 1973, with a capacity of 10,050 kW.

Papua New Guinea—An interest-free loan was signed 16 February 1985 providing for the delivery of complete plants and technical assistance.

continued . . .

CHINESE ECONOMIC AID BY COUNTRIES, 1985 (continued)

Rwanda—In January, 1985 the PRC announced a donation of 2,000 tons of maize to Rwanda to help relieve the drought.

Somalia—Beijing provided the Benadir Hospital in Mogadishu with instruments, including 12 reflectors shadowless operating lamps, tower-shaped distillers, and a maternity table. The Hospital was constructed in 1977, and a medical team from Jilin province has worked there. The Chinese-aided Institute for Political Science in a suburb of Mogadishu was completed 20 October 1985. Construction began in 1983. The complex has classroom buildings, a gym, sports ground, auditorium, canteen, and living quarters.

Sri Lanka—China provided a training course in veterinary acupuncture given by four Chinese scientists between 17 December 1984 and 1 February 1985.

Tanzania—The Kiwira coal mine in the Mbeya region is to be ready during 1987-88. Annual production capacity will be 150,000 tons of coal. Reserves are estimated at 35 million tons.

Uganda—The Kibimba rice farm in eastern Uganda had its best harvest in four years. It produced more than 3.5 million kg of rice in 1984, up 47.4 percent over 1983. During the period, the average yield rose from 209 kg to 260 kg per mu (15 mu = 1 acre), or by 24.7 percent. This is a Chinese-aided project.

Vietnam—China claims to have given Vietnam military and other assistance worth $20 billion between 1950 and 1975.

Yemen, People's Democratic Republic—A 207-km highway, linking the eastern provinces with Aden, the capital, has been completed.

Zimbabwe—The PRC has given a garment factory in Chitungwiza, 35 km southeast of Harare, to the country. The factory will mainly manufacture primary and secondary school uniforms.

Press reports.

CHINESE AID DEVELOPMENTS, 1985

ANC—In January, 1985 the Chinese provided the African National Congress with 542 mosquito nets and several boxes of medicine.

Foreign Contracts—The PRC earned $550 million in 1984 through contracting for foreign projects and by providing labor services abroad. This represents an increase of 28.8 percent over 1983. China currently has some 51,000 skilled workers and engineers working overseas, primarily in the Middle East. More than half are building aid projects, and the rest are working on labor service contracts. In 1985 ten countries asked China to provide manpower, including the USSR, Argentina, Iraq, West Germany, and the Congo. Total request exceeded 700,000 personnel.

Medical Teams—Since 1963 Beijing has sent medical teams to 47 countries in Asia and Africa, where they have treated some 70 million patients. Altogether, 1,000 Chinese medical workers have gone abroad.

COMMUNIST ECONOMIC AID TO LESS DEVELOPED COUNTRIES, EXTENSIONS AND DRAWINGS (mn US $)

	Total		USSR		Eastern Europe		China	
	Extended	Drawn	Extended	Drawn	Extended	Drawn	Extended	Drawn
Total	51,240	25,095	30,005	14,050	14,665	6,610	6,575	4,435
1954-74	19,835	9,210	10,080	5,670	5,830	1,900	3,925	1,640
1975	2,925	985	1,970	500	545	270	410	215
1976	2,285	1,235	1,080	475	995	405	205	360
1977	1,180	1,335	435	545	525	505	220	280
1978	4,820	1,215	3,000	485	1,600	425	220	305
1979	4,625	1,130	3,800	580	645	305	175	245
1980	4,400	1,390	2,605	815	1,325	315	470	260
1981	1,405	1,630	600	860	725	485	80	280
1982	1,645	2,165	1,015	1,190	560	650	70	325
1983	3,950	2,425	3,265	1,435	415	680	270	310
1984	4,180	2,370	2,150	1,495	1,500	660	525	215

CIA, *Handbook of Economic Statistics, 1985* (1985), 109.

CHINESE ECONOMIC AID EXTENDED TO THE LESS DEVELOPED COUNTRIES, BY RECIPIENT (mn US $)

	1956-84	1983	1984
Total	6,574	269	526
Africa	3,808	124	379
Algeria	92	...	...
Benin	56	NEGL	12
Burkina	60	...	9
Burundi	58	...	...
Cameroon	103	...	...
Central African Republic	29	15	...
Chad	68	...	...
Congo	199	88	...
Ethiopia	138	...	...
Ghana	42	...	...
Guinea	144	...	...
Kenya	64	...	...
Madagascar	89	...	...
Mali	134	2	5
Mauritania	107	...	20
Mauritius	35	...	...
Niger	58	...	5
Rwanda	56	...	...
Senegal	52	...	NEGL
Sierra Leone	79	...	18
Somalia	168	3	NEGL
Sudan	176	...	37
Tanzania	587	8	158
Togo	46	...	...
Tunisia	97	...	...
Uganda	42	...	...
Zaire	138	...	...
Zambia	345	8	...
Other	546	...	114
East Asia	457	55	25
Burma	240	53	15
Cambodia	92	...	...
Indonesia	47	...	...
Laos	26	...	...
Other	52	2	10

continued . . .

CHINESE ECONOMIC AID EXTENDED TO THE LESS DEVELOPED COUNTRIES, BY RECIPIENT (mn US $) (continued)

	1956-84	1983	1984
Latin America	**227**	**50**	**20**
Chile	65	...	...
Guyana	38	...	...
Peru	42	...	...
Other	82	50	20
Middle East and South Asia	**2,038**	**40**	**102**
Afghanistan	76	...	...
Bangladesh	119	...	...
Egypt	193	...	...
Iraq	45	...	...
Nepal	293	...	NEGL
North Yemen	130	...	...
Pakistan	753	...	102
South Yemen	96	...	...
Sri Lanka	222	NEGL	...
Syria	70	...	...
Other	41	40	...
Europe	**45**	**...**	**...**
Malta	45	...	...

CIA, *Handbook of Economic Statistics, 1985* (1985), 112.

COMMUNIST MILITARY AID TO LESS DEVELOPED COUNTRIES, EXTENSIONS AND DRAWINGS (mn US $)

	Total		USSR		Eastern Europe		China	
	Extended	Drawn	Extended	Drawn	Extended	Drawn	Extended	Drawn
Total	114,515	92,865	94,470	76,465	12,340	10,450	7,710	5,950
1954-74	21,530	15,450	18,910	13,520	2,010	1,450	605	480
1975	3,860	2,410	3,185	2,035	635	275	40	100
1976	6,640	3,560	6,140	3,110	355	350	145	100
1977	10,370	5,245	9,645	4,815	650	355	75	75
1978	3,485	6,720	2,700	6,075	560	550	225	95
1979	9,775	9,085	8,835	8,340	750	645	195	100
1980	16,450	9,020	14,635	8,125	870	635	945	260
1981	12,025	9,830	6,505	8,105	2,560	1,315	2,965	410
1982	15,135	10,880	11,765	8,065	1,795	1,970	1,575	845
1983	5,075	9,780	2,995	7,130	1,310	1,060	770	1,590
1984	10,165	10,880	9,155	7,135	845	1,845	165	1,900

CIA, *Handbook of Economic Statistics, 1985* (1985), 109.

VALUE OF CHINESE ARMS TRANSFERS AND TOTAL IMPORTS AND EXPORTS, 1973-83

Year	Arms Imports Million dollars		Arms Exports Million dollars		Total Imports Million dollars		Total Exports Million dollars		Arms Imports Total Imports Percent	Arms Exports Total Exports Percent
	Current	Constant 1982	Current	Constant 1982	Current	Constant 1982	Current	Constant 1982	Percent	Percent
1973	70	137	230	451	4,625	9,071	5,105	10,013	1.5	4.5
1974	100	180	140	252	6,805	12,274	6,740	12,156	1.5	2.1
1975	110	181	180	297	6,830	11,296	7,130	11,792	1.6	2.5
1976	160	250	140	219	5,575	8,724	7,265	11,368	2.9	1.9
1977	100	147	110	162	6,595	9,747	8,110	11,986	1.5	1.4
1978	80	110	160	220	10,350	14,243	10,175	14,002	0.8	1.6
1979	180	228	130	164	14,490	18,385	13,735	17,427	1.2	0.9
1980	170	198	270	314	19,305	22,482	18,925	22,040	0.9	1.4
1981	120	127	420	447	17,940	19,111	21,495	22,899	0.7	2.0
1982	40	40	1,000	1,000	16,690	16,690	23,435	23,435	0.2	4.3
1983	0	0	1,500	1,439	18,400	17,653	23,985	23,011	0.0	6.3

US Arms Control and Disarmament Agency, *World Military Expenditures and Arms Transfers 1985* (1985), 100.

VALUE OF ARMS TRANSFERS, CUMULATIVE 1979-83, BY MAJOR SUPPLIER AND RECIPIENT COUNTRY (mn current dollars)

RECIPIENT	TOTAL	SOVIET UNION	UNITED STATES	FRANCE	UNITED KINGDOM	WEST GERMANY	ITALY	CZECHO-SLOVAKIA	CHINA	ROMANIA	POLAND	OTHERS
WORLD TOTALS	169,530	56,540	40,375	16,710	9,465	6,630	4,650	3,935	3,455	3,100	1,990	22,680
DEVELOPED*	32,155	5,260	16,240	410	1,750	1,120	135	2,610	-	1,910	480	2,240
DEVELOPING	137,375	51,280	24,135	16,300	7,715	5,510	4,515	1,325	3,455	1,190	1,510	20,440
NATO	18,805	-	12,985 [a]	385	1,070	2,180	310	-	-	-	80	1,795
WARSAW PACT	11,935	6,170	-	50	100	5	-	2,610	-	1,910	480	610
OPEC**	57,065	17,305	6,960	8,960	3,170	1,990	2,455	620	2,050	715	1,120	11,720
AFRICA	28,045	13,910	820	3,000	675	1,415	1,485	605	595	330	430	4,780
ALGERIA**	3,660	3,200	-	30	50	300	-	-	-	-	-	80
ANGOLA	1,730	1,500	-	10	-	-	-	10	-	20	60	130
BENIN	135	120	-	-	-	5	-					10
BOTSWANA	20	10	-	-	5	-	-					5
BURKINA FASO	30	-	-	-	10	10	-					10
BURUNDI	40	20	-	10	-	5	-					5
CAMEROON	130	-	10	40	5	30	5					40

continued . . .

VALUE OF ARMS TRANSFERS, CUMULATIVE 1979-83, BY MAJOR SUPPLIER AND RECIPIENT COUNTRY (mn current dollars) (continued)

SUPPLIER / RECIPIENT	TOTAL	SOVIET UNION	UNITED STATES	FRANCE	UNITED KINGDOM	WEST GERMANY	ITALY	CZECHO-SLOVAKIA	CHINA	ROMANIA	POLAND	OTHERS
CAPE VERDE	40	40	·	·	·	·	·	·	·	·	·	·
CENTRAL AFRICAN REPUBLIC	25	·	·	10	·	·	·	·	10	·	·	5
CHAD	15	·	·	10	·	·	·	·	·	·	·	5
CONGO	130	120	·	·	·	·	·	·	·	·	·	10
EQUATORIAL GUINEA	60	10	·	·	·	·	10	·	·	·	·	40
ETHIOPIA	1,900	1,800	10	·	·	·	20	10	·	·	·	60
GABON**	180	·	·	100	·	·	·	·	10	·	·	70
GAMBIA, THE	·	·	·	·	·	·	·	·	·	·	·	·
GHANA	70	·	·	·	·	50	·	·	·	·	·	20
GUINEA	30	20	·	5	·	·	·	·	5	·	·	·
GUINEA-BISSAU	20	20	·	·	·	·	·	·	·	·	·	·
IVORY COAST	300	·	·	280	·	·	·	·	·	·	·	20
KENYA	450	·	60	110	130	·	30	·	·	·	·	120
LESOTHO	5	·	·	·	·	·	·	·	·	·	·	5
LIBERIA	15	·	10	·	·	·	·	·	·	·	·	5
LIBYA**	12,095	5,800	·	850	40	380	700	575	310	310	230	2,900
MADAGASCAR	150	110	·	10	20	·	·	·	·	·	·	10
MALAWI	40	·	·	5	20	10	·	·	·	·	·	5
MALI	50	40	·	·	·	5	·	·	5	·	·	·

continued ...

VALUE OF ARMS TRANSFERS, CUMULATIVE 1979-83, BY MAJOR SUPPLIER AND RECIPIENT COUNTRY (mn current dollars) (continued)

SUPPLIER / RECIPIENT	TOTAL	SOVIET UNION	UNITED STATES	FRANCE	UNITED KINGDOM	WEST GERMANY	ITALY	CZECHO-SLOVAKIA	CHINA	ROMANIA	POLAND	OTHERS
MAURITANIA	20	·	·	10	·	·	·	·	·	·	·	10
MAURITIUS	·	·	·	·	·	·	·	·	·	·	·	·
MOROCCO	1,785	·	430	950	·	·	50	·	·	·	50	300
MOZAMBIQUE	680	525	·	·	·	5	·	5	·	·	·	150
NIGER	40	·	·	30	·	10	·	·	·	·	·	·
NIGERIA**	1,125	100	20	230	150	300	120	5	·	·	·	200
RWANDA	25	·	·	·	·	5	·	·	10	·	·	10
SAO TOME AND PRINCIPE	5	5	·	·	·	·	·	·	·	·	·	·
SENEGAL	60	·	·	40	·	·	·	·	·	·	·	20
SIERRA LEONE	10	5	·	5	5	·	·	·	·	·	·	·
SOMALIA	580	·	30	5	5	·	410	·	50	·	·	70
SOUTH AFRICA*	25	·	·	·	5	·	·	·	·	·	·	20
SUDAN	640	·	110	10	10	270	10	·	70	·	60	100
TANZANIA	390	270	·	·	10	·	·	·	40	·	·	70
TOGO	60	·	·	50	·	·	·	·	5	·	·	5
TUNISIA	385	·	110	130	5	20	70	·	10	·	·	40
UGANDA	150	10	·	20	20	·	·	·	·	·	·	100
UPPER VOLTA (see BURKINA FASO)												
ZAIRE	210	·	30	50	10	10	50	·	40	·	·	20

continued . . . .

VALUE OF ARMS TRANSFERS, CUMULATIVE 1979-83, BY MAJOR SUPPLIER AND RECIPIENT COUNTRY (mn current dollars) (continued)

SUPPLIER / RECIPIENT	TOTAL	SOVIET UNION	UNITED STATES	FRANCE	UNITED KINGDOM	WEST GERMANY	ITALY	CZECHO-SLOVAKIA	CHINA	ROMANIA	POLAND	OTHERS
ZAMBIA	260	180	-	-	-	-	-	-	10	-	20	50
ZIMBABWE	275	5	-	-	180	-	10	-	20	-	-	60
EAST ASIA	19,040	6,515	7,915	475	495	330	320	30	240	180	-	2,540
BURMA	135	-	10	10	-	30	5	-	-	-	-	80
CHINA												
MAINLAND	520	130	5	100	210	5	-	-	-	-	-	70
TAIWAN	2,525	-	1,700	-	-	-	-	-	-	-	-	825
INDONESIA**	1,360	-	270	200	100	160	5	-	-	-	-	625
JAPAN*	2,560	-	2,500	-	10	40	-	-	-	-	-	10
KAMPUCHEA	190	170	-	-	-	-	-	-	10	-	-	10
KOREA, NORTH	840	210	-	-	-	-	-	-	230	120	-	280
KOREA, SOUTH	2,010	-	1,900	10	5	30	5	-	-	-	-	60
LAOS	190	180	-	-	-	-	-	-	-	-	-	10
MALAYSIA	750	-	180	130	60	10	70	-	-	-	-	300
MONGOLIA	625	625	-	-	-	-	-	-	-	-	-	-
PHILIPPINES	270	-	200	5	10	5	-	-	-	-	-	50
SINGAPORE	445	-	300	10	30	50	5	-	-	-	-	50

continued . . .

VALUE OF ARMS TRANSFERS, CUMULATIVE 1979-83, BY MAJOR SUPPIER AND RECIPIENT COUNTRY (mn current dollars) (continued)

RECIPIENT / SUPPLIER	TOTAL	SOVIET UNION	UNITED STATES	FRANCE	UNITED KINGDOM	WEST GERMANY	ITALY	CZECHO-SLOVAKIA	CHINA	ROMANIA	POLAND	OTHERS
THAILAND	1,320	·	850	10	70	·	230	·	·	·	·	160
VIETNAM	5,300	5,200	·	·	·	·	·	30	·	60	·	10
EUROPE	31,885	6,840	13,145	1,045	935	1,925	380	2,610	·	1,910	560	2,535
NATO EUROPE	15,595	·	11,385	380	425	1,830	290	·	·	·	80	1,205
BELGIUM*	1,660	·	1,300	140	10	180	·	·	·	·	·	30
DENMARK*	785	·	725	·	40	·	10	·	·	·	·	10
FRANCE*	350	·	180	·	140	10	·	·	·	·	·	20
GERMANY, WEST*	2,380	·	1,900	70	60	·	10	·	·	·	·	340
GREECE	1,985	·	900	60	10	300	110	·	·	·	80	525
ITALY*	635	·	600	5	·	10	·	·	·	·	·	20
LUXEMBOURG*	5	·	5	·	·	·	·	·	·	·	·	·
NETHERLANDS*	2,325	·	1,800	5	110	340	10	·	·	·	·	60
NORWAY*	1,045	·	925	·	40	10	·	·	·	·	·	70
PORTUGAL*	260	·	100	·	10	130	·	·	·	·	·	20
TURKEY*	1,865	·	750	10	5	850	150	·	·	·	·	100
UNITED KINGDOM*	2,300	·	2,200	90	·	·	·	·	·	·	·	10

continued . . .

VALUE OF ARMS TRANSFERS, CUMULATIVE 1979-83, BY MAJOR SUPPLIER AND RECIPIENT COUNTRY (mn current dollars) (continued)

RECIPIENT \ SUPPLIER	TOTAL	SOVIET UNION	UNITED STATES	FRANCE	UNITED KINGDOM	WEST GERMANY	ITALY	CZECHO-SLOVAKIA	CHINA	ROMANIA	POLAND	OTHERS
WARSAW PACT	11,935	6,170	-	50	100	5	-	2,610	-	1,910	480	610
BULGARIA	1,105	1,100										5
CZECHOSLOVAKIA*	1,210	1,200								5		5
GERMANY, EAST*	1,980	1,600						20		70	290	-
HUNGARY*	765	650						90		5		20
POLAND*	1,590	1,200		50	100	5		260				130
ROMANIA*	655	420						40		30		10
SOVIET UNION*	4,630	-						2,200		1,800	190	440
OTHER EUROPEAN	4,355	670	1,760	615	410	90	90	-	-	-	-	720
ALBANIA	-											
AUSTRIA*	330		100		40		70			-		120
FINLAND*	430	190	10		200							30
IRELAND*	50		5	20	20							5
MALTA	5											5
SPAIN	1,500		675	550	10	90	5					170
SWEDEN*	520		230	5	130		5					150

continued ....

VALUE OF ARMS TRANSFERS, CUMULATIVE 1979-83, BY MAJOR SUPPLIER AND RECIPIENT COUNTRY (mn current dollars) (continued)

SUPPLIER / RECIPIENT	TOTAL	SOVIET UNION	UNITED STATES	FRANCE	UNITED KINGDOM	WEST GERMANY	ITALY	CZECHO-SLOVAKIA	CHINA	ROMANIA	POLAND	OTHERS
SWITZERLAND*	830	-	700	20	-	-	-	-	-	-	-	110
YUGOSLAVIA	690	480	40	20	10	-	10	-	-	-	-	130
LATIN AMERICA	11,755	3,640	715	1,855	555	1,215	1,090	40	-	-	15	2,630
ARGENTINA	2,480	-	80	360	150	925	180	-	-	-	10	775
BARBADOS	10	-	-	-	10	-	-	-	-	-	-	-
BOLIVIA	205	-	10	-	-	5	-	-	-	-	-	190
BRAZIL	500	-	80	60	260	-	70	-	-	-	-	30
CHILE	1,090	-	10	600	40	10	-	-	-	-	-	430
COLOMBIA	265	-	50	-	10	30	-	-	-	-	5	170
COSTA RICA	-	-	-	-	-	-	-	-	-	-	-	-
CUBA	3,140	3,100	-	-	-	-	-	40	-	-	-	-
DOMINICAN REPUBLIC	20	-	10	-	-	-	-	-	-	-	-	10
ECUADOR**	920	-	40	410	50	-	180	-	-	-	-	240
EL SALVADOR	130	-	90	30	-	-	-	-	-	-	-	10
GUATEMALA	65	-	10	5	-	-	-	-	-	-	-	50
GUYANA	20	-	-	-	10	-	-	-	-	-	-	10
HAITI	10	-	-	-	-	-	-	-	-	-	-	10

continued ...

VALUE OF ARMS TRANSFERS, CUMULATIVE 1979-83, BY MAJOR SUPPLIER AND RECIPIENT COUNTRY (mn current dollars) (continued)

SUPPLIER / RECIPIENT	TOTAL	SOVIET UNION	UNITED STATES	FRANCE	UNITED KINGDOM	WEST GERMANY	ITALY	CZECHO-SLOVAKIA	CHINA	ROMANIA	POLAND	OTHERS
HONDURAS	35	-	20	-	10	-	-	-	-	-	-	5
JAMAICA	-	-	-	-	-	-	-	-	-	-	-	-
MEXICO	320	-	110	20	-	-	-	-	-	-	-	190
NICARAGUA	280	100	-	10	-	-	-	-	-	-	-	170
PANAMA	40	-	30	-	-	-	-	-	-	-	-	10
PARAGUAY	55	-	5	-	-	-	-	-	-	-	-	50
PERU	1,210	440	50	260	-	240	110	-	-	-	-	110
SURINAME	15	-	-	-	5	-	-	-	-	-	-	10
TRINIDAD AND TOBAGO	20	-	-	-	-	-	-	-	-	-	-	20
URUGUAY	145	-	10	70	-	5	-	-	-	-	-	60
VENEZUELA**	780	-	110	30	10	-	550	-	-	-	-	80
MIDDLE EAST	65,355	20,375	14,225	9,695	5,065	1,155	1,255	510	2,135	675	985	9,280
BAHRAIN	120	-	10	40	-	40	10	-	-	-	-	20
CYPRUS	55	-	-	5	-	-	-	-	-	-	-	50
EGYPT	5,645	40	2,400	1,200	575	210	320	-	300	-	50	550
IRAN**	5,365	975	1,200	20	140	5	150	-	230	5	40	2,600
IRAQ**	17,620	7,200	-	3,800	280	140	410	40	1,500	400	850	3,000

continued . . .

VALUE OF ARMS TRANSFERS, CUMULATIVE 1979-83, BY MAJOR SUPPLIER AND RECIPIENT COUNTRY (mn current dollars) (continued)

SUPPLIER / RECIPIENT	TOTAL	SOVIET UNION	UNITED STATES	FRANCE	UNITED KINGDOM	WEST GERMANY	ITALY	CZECHO-SLOVAKIA	CHINA	ROMANIA	POLAND	OTHERS
ISRAEL	3,805	·	3,800	·	·	·	·	·	·	·	·	5
JORDAN	3,430	230	975	1,000	1,100	5	·	·	10	·	·	110
KUWAIT**	450	30	180	·	50	70	110	·	·	·	·	10
LEBANON	395	·	250	90	10	·	10	·	5	·	5	30
OMAN	565	·	80	20	430	·	10	·	5	·	·	20
QATAR**	765	·	10	440	310	·	·	·	·	·	·	5
SAUDI ARABIA**	12,125b	·	5,100	2,500	1,900	525	200	·	·	·	·	1,900
SYRIA	10,530	9,200	·	200	180	40	·	470	90	20	30	300
UNITED ARAB EMIRATES**	620	·	20	350	90	110	30	·	·	·	·	20
YEMEN (ADEN)	1,510	1,500	·	·	·	·	·	·	·	·	·	10
YEMEN (SANAA)	2,355	1,200	200	30	·	10	5	·	·	250	10	650
NORTH AMERICA	3,210	·	1,600	5	645	350	20	·	·	·	·	590
CANADA*	1,770	·	1,600	·	20	110	·	·	·	·	·	40
UNITED STATES*	1,440	·	·	5	625	240	20	·	·	·	·	550
OCEANIA	1,700	10	1,360	·	190	45	10	·	·	·	·	85
AUSTRALIA*	1,530	·	1,300	·	160	40	10	·	·	·	·	20

continued . . .

VALUE OF ARMS TRANSFERS, CUMULATIVE 1979-83, BY MAJOR SUPPLIER AND RECIPIENT COUNTRY (mn current dollars) (continued)

RECIPIENT \ SUPPLIER	TOTAL	SOVIET UNION	UNITED STATES	FRANCE	UNITED KINGDOM	WEST GERMANY	ITALY	CZECHO-SLOVAKIA	CHINA	ROMANIA	POLAND	OTHERS
FIJI	5	·	·	·	·	·	·	·	·	·	·	5
NEW ZEALAND*	95	·	60	·	30	5	·	·	·	·	·	·
PAPUA NEW GUINEA	70	10	·	·	·	·	·	·	·	·	·	60
SOUTH ASIA	8,540	5,250	595	635	905	195	90	140	485	5	·	240
AFGHANISTAN	1,830	1,800	·	·	·	·	·	20	·	·	·	10
BANGLADESH	165	30	5	·	10	·	·	·	90	·	·	30
INDIA	4,695	3,400	40	80	875	5	50	120	·	5	·	120
NEPAL	10	·	·	5	5	·	·	·	·	·	·	·
PAKISTAN	1,830	20	550	550	10	190	40	·	390	·	·	80
SRI LANKA	10	·	·	·	5	·	·	·	5	·	·	·

— None or negligible.   * Developed country.   ** OPEC country.

NOTE: To avoid the appearance of excessive accuracy, all numbers in this table are independently rounded, with greater severity for larger numbers. Therefore, components may not add to totals.

a. Includes transfers to NATO agencies as such and not attributed to any recipient country.

b. Includes some purchases of equipment by the US Army Corps of Engineers from indeterminable supplier countries for use in construction projects in Saudi Arabia and recorded in US accounts as imports to the US.

US Arms Control and disarmament Agency, *World Military Expenditures and Arms Transfers 1985* (1985), 131-34.

NUMBER OF ARMS DELIVERED, CUMULATIVE 1979-83, BY SELECTED SUPPLIER, RECIPIENT DEVELOPING REGION, AND MAJOR WEAPON TYPE

NUMBER OF ARMS DELIVERED, CUMULATIVE 1979-83, BY SELECTED SUPPLIER,[a] RECIPIENT DEVELOPING REGION,[b] AND MAJOR WEAPON TYPE

SUPPLIER / EQUIPMENT TYPE	TOTAL	SOVIET UNION	OTHER WARSAW PACT	UNITED STATES [c]	FRANCE	UNITED KINGDOM	OTHER NATO	CHINA	OTHER DEVELOPED	OTHER DEVELOPING
ALL DEVELOPING RECIPIENTS [b]										
LAND ARMAMENTS										
TANKS	13,654	6,540	1,720	1,829	115	365	305	670	2,050	260
ANTI-AIR ARTILLERY [d]	7,448	2,905	710	193	50	-	150	1,450	1,855	135
FIELD ARTILLERY [e]	20,404	5,545	890	3,874	325	140	4,960	980	3,640	50
ARMORED PERSONNEL CARRIERS	21,281	8,615	290	6,171	1,955	545	930	150	1,485	1,140
NAVAL CRAFT										
MAJOR SURFACE COMBATANTS [f]	139	33	3	27	17	8	42	-	9	-
OTHER SURFACE COMBATANTS [g]	560	127	7	76	34	41	177	23	59	16
SUBMARINES	39	8	-	-	2	-	6	2	21	-
MISSILE ATTACK BOATS	101	46	-	-	12	6	12	12	9	6
AIRCRAFT										
COMBAT AIRCRAFT: SUPERSONIC	3,693	2,070	25	518	250	60	-	320	450	-
COMBAT AIRCRAFT: SUBSONIC	613	205	15	188	80	65	-	-	60	-

continued . . . .

NUMBER OF ARMS DELIVERED, CUMULATIVE 1979-83, BY SELECTED SUPPLIER, RECIPIENT DEVELOPING REGION, AND MAJOR WEAPON TYPE (continued)

SUPPLIER / EQUIPMENT TYPE	TOTAL	SOVIET UNION	OTHER WARSAW PACT	UNITED STATES c	FRANCE	UNITED KINGDOM	OTHER NATO	CHINA	OTHER DEVELOPED	OTHER DEVELOPING
OTHER AIRCRAFT h	2,043	340	325	93	120	55	365	125	335	285
HELICOPTERS	2,145	1,065	165	165	405	20	235	-	60	5
MISSILES										
SURFACE-TO-AIR	21,506	12,280	50	5,011	1,040	870	-	75	1,505	675
AFRICA										
LAND ARMAMENTS										
TANKS	2,445	1,355	155	20	25	80	100	135	565	10
ANTI-AIR ARTILLERY d	2,330	1,500	185	60	5	-	10	205	325	40
FIELD ARTILLERY e	4,453	2,050	305	218	30	40	335	210	1,225	40
ARMORED PERSONNEL CARRIERS	5,828	2,310	75	178	1,265	140	435	5	380	1,040
NAVAL CRAFT										
MAJOR SURFACE COMBATANTS f	41	18	2	-	5	2	14	-	-	-
OTHER SURFACE COMBATANTS g	158	32	-	-	8	9	91	-	15	3

continued . . .

NUMBER OF ARMS DELIVERED, CUMULATIVE 1979-83, BY SELECTED SUPPLIER, RECIPIENT DEVELOPING REGION, AND MAJOR WEAPON TYPE (continued)

NUMBER OF ARMS DELIVERED, CUMULATIVE 1979-83, BY SELECTED SUPPLIER,[a] RECIPIENT DEVELOPING REGION,[b] AND MAJOR WEAPON TYPE (continued)

EQUIPMENT TYPE	TOTAL	SOVIET UNION	OTHER WARSAW PACT	UNITED STATES[c]	FRANCE	UNITED KINGDOM	OTHER NATO	CHINA	OTHER DEVELOPED	OTHER DEVELOPING
SUBMARINES	5	5	-	-	-	-	-	-	-	-
MISSILE ATTACK BOATS	25	16	-	-	9	-	-	-	-	-
AIRCRAFT										
COMBAT AIRCRAFT: SUPERSONIC	734	545	-	24	55	-	-	55	55	-
COMBAT AIRCRAFT: SUBSONIC	176	70	15	6	45	30	-	-	10	-
OTHER AIRCRAFT[h]	628	110	165	3	25	25	205	5	80	10
HELICOPTERS	525	275	75	-	65	-	95	-	10	5
MISSILES										
SURFACE-TO-AIR	5,373	4,170	50	903	-	200	-	-	-	50
EAST ASIA AND OCEANIA										
LAND ARMAMENTS										
TANKS	2,088	865	145	348	-	25	140	50	360	155
ANTI-AIR ARTILLERY[d]	370	250	-	-	-	-	15	25	25	55

continued . . .

NUMBER OF ARMS DELIVERED, CUMULATIVE 1979-83, BY SELECTED SUPPLIER, RECIPIENT DEVELOPING REGION, AND MAJOR WEAPON TYPE (continued)

NUMBER OF ARMS DELIVERED, CUMULATIVE 1979-83, BY SELECTED SUPPLIER,[a] RECIPIENT DEVELOPING REGION,[b] AND MAJOR WEAPON TYPE (continued)

EQUIPMENT TYPE	TOTAL	SOVIET UNION	OTHER WARSAW PACT	UNITED STATES[c]	FRANCE	UNITED KINGDOM	OTHER NATO	CHINA	OTHER DEVELOPED	OTHER DEVELOPING
FIELD ARTILLERY[e]	2,143	875	-	1,123	-	-	110	-	25	10
ARMORED PERSONNEL CARRIERS	1,293	700	-	273	20	240	35	-	25	-
NAVAL CRAFT										
MAJOR SURFACE COMBATANTS[f]	29	4	-	15	-	-	3	-	7	-
OTHER SURFACE COMBATANTS[g]	133	50	-	52	19	-	12	-	-	-
SUBMARINES	2	-	-	-	-	-	2	-	-	-
MISSILE ATTACK BOATS	28	8	-	-	-	-	3	4	9	4
AIRCRAFT										
COMBAT AIRCRAFT: SUPERSONIC	584	300	-	204	-	-	-	40	40	-
COMBAT AIRCRAFT: SUBSONIC	255	55	-	150	-	15	-	-	35	-
OTHER AIRCRAFT[h]	505	105	35	35	35	-	35	70	120	70
HELICOPTERS	461	155	85	131	50	-	30	-	10	-
MISSILES										
SURFACE-TO-AIR	3,157	610	-	1,822	-	145	-	20	20	540

continued . . .

NUMBER OF ARMS DELIVERED, CUMULATIVE 1979-83, BY SELECTED SUPPLIER, RECIPIENT DEVELOPING REGION, AND MAJOR WEAPON TYPE (continued)

LATIN AMERICA

SUPPLIER / EQUIPMENT TYPE	TOTAL	SOVIET UNION	OTHER WARSAW PACT	UNITED STATES [c]	FRANCE	UNITED KINGDOM	OTHER NATO	CHINA	OTHER DEVELOPED	OTHER DEVELOPING
LAND ARMAMENTS										
TANKS	688	325	20	28	20	-	45	-	155	95
ANTI-AIR ARTILLERY [d]	470	235	40	-	-	-	80	-	75	40
FIELD ARTILLERY [e]	1,499	490	115	479	100	-	30	-	285	-
ARMORED PERSONNEL CARRIERS	1,315	185	60	-	75	15	190	-	690	100
NAVAL CRAFT										
MAJOR SURFACE COMBATANTS [f]	50	3	-	7	9	4	25	-	2	-
OTHER SURFACE COMBATANTS [g]	113	29	2	6	5	8	34	-	27	2
SUBMARINES	7	3	-	-	-	-	4	-	-	-
MISSILE ATTACK BOATS	8	8	-	-	-	-	-	-	-	-
AIRCRAFT										
COMBAT AIRCRAFT: SUPERSONIC	247	130	-	12	25	-	-	-	80	-
COMBAT AIRCRAFT: SUBSONIC	62	-	-	32	15	10	-	-	5	-

NUMBER OF ARMS DELIVERED, CUMULATIVE 1979-83, BY SELECTED SUPPLIER, [a] RECIPIENT DEVELOPING REGION, [b] AND MAJOR WEAPON TYPE (continued)

continued . . . .

NUMBER OF ARMS DELIVERED, CUMULATIVE 1979-83, BY SELECTED SUPPLIER, RECIPIENT DEVELOPING REGION, AND MAJOR WEAPON TYPE (continued)

SUPPLIER / EQUIPMENT TYPE	TOTAL	SOVIET UNION	OTHER WARSAW PACT	UNITED STATES c	FRANCE	UNITED KINGDOM	OTHER NATO	CHINA	OTHER DEVELOPED	OTHER DEVELOPING
OTHER AIRCRAFT h	457	45	30	32	45	10	110	-	80	105
HELICOPTERS	385	65	-	55	205	5	30	-	25	-
MISSILES										
SURFACE-TO-AIR	1,125	700	-	-	50	345	-	-	30	-
MIDDLE EAST										
LAND ARMAMENTS										
TANKS	7,708	3,330	1,400	1,333	70	260	20	405	890	-
ANTI-AIR ARTILLERY d	3,798	715	485	133	45	-	45	1,120	1,255	-
FIELD ARTILLERY e	11,319	1,530	470	1,959	195	90	4,365	715	1,995	-
ARMORED PERSONNEL CARRIERS	11,472	4,440	155	5,352	595	125	270	145	390	-
NAVAL CRAFT										
MAJOR SURFACE COMBATANTS f	8	1	1	2	3	1	-	-	-	-
OTHER SURFACE COMBATANTS g	135	13	5	18	2	24	40	6	16	11

continued ...

NUMBER OF ARMS DELIVERED, CUMULATIVE 1979-83, BY SELECTED SUPPLIER, RECIPIENT DEVELOPING REGION, AND MAJOR WEAPON TYPE (continued)

NUMBER OF ARMS DELIVERED, CUMULATIVE 1979-83, BY SELECTED SUPPLIER,[a] RECIPIENT DEVELOPING REGION,[b] AND MAJOR WEAPON TYPE (continued)

EQUIPMENT TYPE	TOTAL	SOVIET UNION	OTHER WARSAW PACT	UNITED STATES[c]	FRANCE	UNITED KINGDOM	OTHER NATO	CHINA	OTHER DEVELOPED	OTHER DEVELOPING
SUBMARINES	4	-	-	-	-	-	-	2	2	-
MISSILE ATTACK BOATS	32	14	-	-	3	6	9	-	-	-
AIRCRAFT										
COMBAT AIRCRAFT: SUPERSONIC	1,597	855	25	272	135	10	-	125	175	-
COMBAT AIRCRAFT: SUBSONIC	115	80	-	-	20	5	-	-	10	-
OTHER AIRCRAFT[h]	302	60	90	22	15	5	15	-	5	90
HELICOPTERS	634	445	5	4	80	10	80	-	10	-
MISSILES										
SURFACE-TO-AIR	10,901	5,890	-	2,286	990	180	-	35	1,435	85

SOUTH ASIA

EQUIPMENT TYPE	TOTAL	SOVIET UNION	OTHER WARSAW PACT	UNITED STATES[c]	FRANCE	UNITED KINGDOM	OTHER NATO	CHINA	OTHER DEVELOPED	OTHER DEVELOPING
LAND ARMAMENTS										
TANKS	765	665	-	100	-	-	-	80	80	-

continued . . .

NUMBER OF ARMS DELIVERED, CUMULATIVE 1979-83, BY SELECTED SUPPLIER, RECIPIENT DEVELOPING REGION, AND MAJOR WEAPON TYPE (continued)

SUPPLIER / EQUIPMENT TYPE	TOTAL	SOVIET UNION	OTHER WARSAW PACT	UNITED STATES[c]	FRANCE	UNITED KINGDOM	OTHER NATO	CHINA	OTHER DEVELOPED	OTHER DEVELOPING
ANTI-AIR ARTILLERY[d]	480	205	-	-	-	-	-	100	175	-
FIELD ARTILLERY[e]	990	600	-	95	-	10	120	55	110	-
ARMORED PERSONNEL CARRIERS	1,373	980	-	368	-	25	-	-	-	-
NAVAL CRAFT										
MAJOR SURFACE COMBATANTS[f]	11	7	-	3	-	1	-	-	-	-
OTHER SURFACE COMBATANTS[g]	20	3	-	-	-	-	-	17	-	-
SUBMARINES	21	-	-	-	2	-	-	-	19	-
MISSILE ATTACK BOATS	8	-	-	-	-	-	-	8	-	-
AIRCRAFT										
COMBAT AIRCRAFT: SUPERSONIC	531	240	-	6	35	50	-	100	100	-
COMBAT AIRCRAFT: SUBSONIC	5	-	-	-	-	5	-	-	-	-
OTHER AIRCRAFT[h]	151	20	5	1	-	15	-	50	50	10
HELICOPTERS	140	125	-	-	5	5	-	-	5	-
MISSILES										
SURFACE-TO-AIR	950	910	-	-	-	-	-	20	20	-

continued . . . .

NUMBER OF ARMS DELIVERED, CUMULATIVE 1979-83, BY SELECTED SUPPLIER,[a] RECIPIENT DEVELOPING REGION,[b] AND MAJOR WEAPON TYPE (continued)

NUMBER OF ARMS DELIVERED, CUMULATIVE 1979-83, BY SELECTED SUPPLIER, RECIPIENT DEVELOPING REGION, AND MAJOR WEAPON TYPE (continued)

a. The suppliers included are the five largest single exporters of major weapons in terms of magnitude of deliveries as well as other countries of the two major alliances.
b. Totals include the "developing" countries, as previously listed in Table beginning on page 240, with the exception of Albania, Greece, Malta, Spain, Turkey, and Yugoslavia.
c. US data are by fiscal years 1978-1982, while other suppliers' data are by calendar years 1978-1982.
d. Air defense artillery includes weapons over 23 mm.
e. Field artillery includes mobile rocket launchers, mortars, and recoiless rifles over 100 mm.
f. Major surface combatants include aircraft carriers, cruisers, destroyers, destroyer escorts, and frigates.
g. Minor surface combatants include motor torpedo boats, subchasers, and minesweepers.
h. Other aircraft include reconnaissance aircraft, trainers, transports, and utility aircraft.

US Arms Control and Disarmament Agency, *World Military Expenditures and Arms Transfers 1985* (1985), 135-38.

MILITARY PERSONNEL FROM THE LESS DEVELOPED COUNTRIES TRAINED IN COMMUNIST COUNTRIES, 1955-84[1] (number of persons)

	Total	USSR	Eastern Europe	China
Total	79,390	63,215	12,410	3,765
Africa	29,130	20,405	5,820	2,905
North Africa	11,345	7,360	3,970	15
Algeria	3,570	2,795	760	15
Libya	7,630	4,490	3,140	...
Morocco	145	75	70	...
Sub-Saharan	17,785	13,045	1,850	2,890
Angola	380	375	5	...
Benin	120	120	NA	...
Congo	1,075	535	125	415
Equatorial Guinea	200	200	...	...
Ethiopia	2,120	1,600	520	NA
Ghana	245	210	35	...
Guinea	1,385	920	105	360
Mali	905	845	10	50
Mozambique	580	400	130	50
Nigeria	835	800	35	...
Somalia	2,635	2,395	210	30
Sudan	610	330	20	260
Tanzania	3,230	2,145	60	1,025
Zambia	685	490	135	60
Other	2,780	1,680	460	640
East Asia	9,300	7,590	1,710	...
Cambodia	30	30	...	...

continued . . .

MILITARY PERSONNEL FROM THE LESS DEVELOPED COUNTRIES TRAINED IN COMMUNIST COUNTRIES, 1955-84[1] (number of persons) (continued)

	Total	USSR	Eastern Europe	China
Indonesia	9,270	7,560	1,710	...
Latin America	**1,320**	**1,040**	**280**	...
Nicaragua	405	125	280	...
Peru	910	910	...	...
Other	5	5	...	...
Middle East	26,790	22,565	3,855	370
Egypt	6,390	5,665	675	50
Iran	875	315	530	30
Iraq	5,310	4,110	1,030	170
North Yemen	4,310	4,310	...	...
South Yemen	1,585	1,395	90	100
Syria	8,115	6,600	1,515	...
Other	205	170	15	20
South Asia	**12,850**	**11,615**	**745**	**490**
Afghanistan	8,380	7,725	655	...
Bangladesh	485	445	...	40
India	3,480	3,390	90	...
Pakistan	490	45	NA	445
Sri Lanka	15	10	...	5

1. Data refer to the minimum number of persons departing for training. Numbers are rounded to nearest five.

CIA, *Handbook of Economic Statistics, 1985* (1985), p. 120.

MILITARY PERSONNEL FROM THE LESS DEVELOPED COUNTRIES TRAINED IN COMMUNIST COUNTRIES, 1984[1] (number of persons)

	Total	USSR	Eastern Europe	China
Total	**5,565**	**3,025**	**2,515**	**25**
Africa	**2,975**	**1,375**	**1,600**	...
North Africa	**450**	**250**	**200**	...
Algeria	250	150	100	...
Libya	200	100	100	...
Sub-Saharan Africa	**2,525**	**1,125**	**1,400**	...
Angola	300	200	100	...
Congo	50	50	...	...
Ethiopia	350	150	200	...
Ghana	30	30	...	...

continued . . .

MILITARY PERSONNEL FROM THE LESS DEVELOPED COUNTRIES TRAINED IN COMMUNIST COUNTRIES, 1984[1] (number of persons) (continued)

	Total	USSR	Eastern Europe	China
Guinea	140	140	...	...
Guinea-Bissau	30	30	...	...
Mali	25	25	...	...
Mozambique	1,200	200	1,000	...
Nigeria	400	300	100	...
East Asia	40	...	15	25
Burma	40	...	15	25
Latin America	1,050	250	800	...
Nicaragua	1,050	250	800	...
Middle East	750	650	100	...
Iraq	600	500	100	...
South Yemen	150	150	...	...
South Asia	750	750	...	...
Afghanistan	500	500	...	...
India	250	250	...	...

1. Data refer to the minimum number of persons departing for training. Numbers are rounded to the nearest five.

CIA, *Handbook of Economic Statistics, 1985* (1985), p. 121.

COMMUNIST ECONOMIC AND MILITARY TECHNICIANS IN LESS DEVELOPED COUNTRIES, BY COUNTRY, 1984[1] (number of persons)

	Economic		Military	
	USSR and Eastern Europe	China	USSR and Eastern Europe	China
Total	125,960	41,755	21,335	535
Africa	83,335	8,305	10,175	380
North Africa	67,315	1,445	3,590	20
Algeria	10,750	500	790	20
Libya	53,800	55	2,800	NA
Mauritania	25	700	...	...
Morocco	2,325	75	...	...
Tunisia	415	115	...	...
Other	...	...	...	...
Sub-Saharan	16,020	6,860	6,585	360
Angola	2,625	10	1,700	...
Ethiopia	2,500	50	2,600	...

continued . . .

COMMUNIST ECONOMIC AND MILITARY TECHNICIANS IN LESS DEVELOPED COUNTRIES, BY COUNTRY, 1984[1] (number of persons) (continued)

	Economic		Military,	
	USSR and Eastern Europe	China	USSR and Eastern Europe	China
Gabon	10	80	...	...
Ghana	60	50	...	...
Guinea	820	100	60	...
Guinea-Bissau	210	75	55	...
Kenya	40	125	...	...
Madagascar	340	600	120	...
Mali	505	250	50	...
Mozambique	3,100	25	1,300	...
Niger	30	70	...	...
Nigeria	4,035	...	10	...
Rwanda	10	400	...	NA
Sao Tome/Principe	5	15	170	...
Senegal	55	100	...	...
Sierra Leone	10	100	...	...
Somalia	5	1,000	...	5
Sudan	100	400	5	55
Tanzania	175	535	65	75
Zambia	345	100	50	20
Other	1,040	2,775	400	205
East Asia	60	180	...	...
Europe	75	300	...	...
Latin America	1,410	140	275	...
Bolivia	55	...	...	...
Brazil	130	...	...	...
Colombia	60	60	...	...
Nicaragua	475	...	160	...
Peru	245	10	115	...
Uruguay	10	...	...	...
Other	435	70	...	...
Middle East	33,110	32,100	8,310	115
Iran	1,785	...	50	...
Iraq	17,700	17,000	1,300	50
North Yemen	550	3,500	510	...
South Yemen	2,325	...	1,100	...
Syria	4,000	15	5,300	...
Other	6,750	11,585	50	65

continued ...

COMMUNIST ECONOMIC AND MILITARY TECHNICIANS IN LESS DEVELOPED COUNTRIES, BY COUNTRY, 1984[1] (number of persons) (continued)

	Economic		Military,	
	USSR and Eastern Europe	China	USSR and Eastern Europe	China
South Asia	**7,970**	**730**	**2,575**	**40**
Afghanistan	5,250	...	2,025	...
Bangladesh	100	100	50	40
India	1,400	...	500	...
Nepal	10	350	...	...
Pakistan	1,150	175	...	...
Sri Lanka	55	100	...	...
Other	5	5	...	...

1. Minimum estimates of number of present for one month or more, rounded to the nearest five.

CIA, *Handbook of Economic Statistics, 1985* (1985), p. 122-23.

ACADEMIC, TECHNICAL, AND MILITARY TRAINEES DEPARTING FROM LESS DEVELOPED COUNTRIES FOR TRAINING IN COMMUNIST COUNTRIES, BY AREA OF DESTINATION[1] (number of persons)

	1979	1980	1981	1982	1983	1984
Total trainees	**19,030**	**20,700**	**19,900**	**22,990**	**26,900**	**29,475**
USSR and Eastern Europe	18,965	20,610	19,750	22,760	26,495	29,065
China	65	90	150	230	405	410
Academic trainees	**13,865**	**13,530**	**12,520**	**12,825**	**14,995**	**16,820**
USSR and Eastern Europe	13,815	13,480	12,465	12,470	14,795	16,695
China	50	50	55	85	200	125
Technical trainees	**2,975**	**3,745**	**4,805**	**5,110**	**5,715**	**5,565**
USSR and Eastern Europe	2,975	3,745	4,805	5,035	5,665	5,540
China	...	...	...	75	50	25
Military trainees	**2,190**	**3,425**	**2,575**	**5,055**	**6,190**	**7,090**
USSR and Eastern Europe	2,175	3,385	2,480	4,985	6,035	6,830
China	15	40	95	70	155	260

. 1. Rounded to the nearest five persons. Data are for persons departing for training and not necessarily those completing training.

CIA, *Handbook of Economic Statistics, 1985* (1985), p. 124.

XIII TRANSPORTATION

TRANSPORTATION, 1984

	Ton-Km (bn)	Passenger-Km (bn)	Percentage Increase Over 1983
Total volume of goods transported by all means	1,451		9.1
Railway freight	724.7		9.0
Truck freight	35.9		7.2
Ships and boats	632.9		9.3
Planes	310.0		34.9
Volume of oil and gas carried by pipelines	57.2		9.2
Cargo handled at major seaports (mn tons)	275.5		10.4
Passengers carried by all means of transportation		357.6	15.5
Railway passengers		204.6	15.2
Road passengers		129.4	17.0
Waterway passengers		15.2	-1.3
Air passengers		8.4	42.4
Per-capita productivity of railway transportation			7.7
Average productivity of each locomotive per day			1.9
Locomotive fuel consumption per 10,000 ton-km			-5.8
Time in port for foreign trade ships (average days):			
1981		10.4	
1982		8.8	
1983		9.9	
1984		8.8	
Average annual productivity per ton of ships under the Ministry of Communications			6.8

Beijing Review, 12 (25 Mar 1985), v.

RAILWAY DEVELOPMENTS, 1984-85

Rail Stock—China has 52,000 km of railways, 11,000 locomotives, and 310,000 freight and passenger cars. In 1984 they carried 1.1 billion passengers and 1.2 billion tons of freight. This amounts to only 50-70 percent of the demand for freight transport, however, and mainline passenger trains frequently carry up to 70 percent more people than there are seats. During 1986-90, the PRC plans to import equipment to modernize factories at Dalian, Zhuzhou, Changchun, and Wuchang. FBIS-CHI 99 (22 May 1985), K14.

Longest Railway Bridge—A 10,282-meter bridge opened in September, 1985 at the border between Shandong and Henan provinces on the Xinxiang-Heze Railroad. This bridge is 3,500 meters longer than the Yangtze River bridge at Nanjing, Jiangsu. XNB (23 Sep 1985), 75-76.

International Railway Transport—Goods shipped by China's international rail service totaled 10.47 million tons in 1985, compared to more than 8 million tons in 1984. The tonnage in 1985 more than doubled that in 1981. The international rail service volume is to grow an average of 10-15 percent during 1986-90. *Beijing Review*, 49 (9 Dec 1985), 10.

Railway Electrification—China built 250 km of electrified lines annually between 1976 and 1980. It laid an average of 500 km each year between 1981 and 1985. This annual figure

continued . . .

RAILWAY DEVELOPMENTS, 1984-85 (continued)

is to double between 1985 and 1990. There are currently only eight electrified trunk lines totaling 3,024 km. Electrified railways include:

Baoji-Chengdu	
(section)	1961
(rest of line)	late 1960s
Yangpingguan-Ankang	mid-1970s
Xiangfan-Chongqing	mid-1970s
Datong-Qinhuangdao	u.c.
Suxian-Shijiazhuang	u.c.
Houma-Yueshan	u.c.
Beijing-Qinhuangdao	1985
Beijing-Guangzhou (section)	c. 1990

China Reconstructs, XXXIV, 7 (Jul 1985), 55.

Local Railways—The PRC has 3,800 km of locally-operated railways, or about 7 percent of China's 52,000 km of track. Henan province has 45 percent of the total, with 15 lines amounting to 1,700 km. Local railroads carried 28.6 million tons of freight in 1984, an increase of 5.4 percent over 1983. Profits rose 25 percent to 35 million yuan. *Beijing Review*, 26 (1 Jul 1985), 7.

Railway Security—In October, 1984 General Secretary Hu Yaobang demanded that order be restored on railway lines. Only a few provinces and regions, such as the Nei Monggol, Guangdong, and Guangxi, have reduced looting, safety violations, and robberies. *Ming Pao* (18 Apr 1985), 5.

Ticket Increases—Prices for railway tickets involving journeys less than 100 km increased 15 May 1985 by 36.8 percent. Tickets for journeys over 100 km remained unchanged. Monthly passenger tickets for suburban trains rose 50 percent. Students and the handicapped still may buy tickets at half price. Freight traffic for distances of 200 km or less will be subject to a surcharge of 4 yuan ($1.40) per ton. The higher prices seek to divert traffic to highways and waterways. *China Daily* (19 May 1985), 3.

Pukou Station—The Pukou Railway Station in Nanjing, Jiangsu has resumed operations after a suspension of 16 years. It was closed in 1968 when the Yangtze River bridge was finished at Nanjing, and the new Nanjing Station started service. The Pukou Station should raise transport capacity in the region by 25 percent. XNB (3 Apr 1985), 25-26.

North Korea—A draft agreement concluded between North and South Korea has proposed the resumption of traffic on the railway severed during the Korean War. FBIS-CHI 131 (9 Jul 1985), D2; New York *Times* (13 Jun 1985), 1, 10.

Locomotive Deals—The US Electric Company will sell China 201 electric locomotives for about $235 million. The locomotives will be delivered between November, 1985 and March, 1986. The China National Machinery Import and Export Corp. will export $2.82 million in locomotive parts to the US. The CMC had previously purchased 220 electric locomotives from GEC in 1983 for $240 million. It has exported locomotive parts to GEC since 1981. FBIS-CHI 80 (25 Apr 1985), B1; *Asian Wall Street Journal Weekly* (29 Apr 1985), 18; New York *Times* (25 Apr 1985), 34. The "50 Hertz" Group (Alsthom-Atlantique and Jeumont-Schneider of France, AEG Telefunken and Siemens AG of West Germany, and Brown Boveri of Switzerland) will supply 150 locomotives to the PRC for about 3 billion FF ($305 million). *Asian Wall Street Journal Weekly* (1 Apr 1985), 6.

New Station—The Japan Overseas Railway Technology Cooperation Association will design and assist in the construction of the No. 2 Beijing Railway Station. The station will have a guesthouse, department store, and a restaurant. FBIS-CHI 96 (17 May 1985), D2.

Locomotive Production—During the past three decades, 11,000 locomotives have been built in China. *China Reconstructs*, XXXIV, 1 (Jan 1985), 37.

continued . . .

RAILWAY DEVELOPMENTS, 1984-85 (continued)

Long Train— A 26-car, extra-long train has gone into service between Nanjing and Qiqihar, Heilongjiang. This is double the length of an ordinary train, and can carry up to 3,000 passengers. XNB (6 Apr 1985), 55-56.

Modernization—Since 1980 the PRC has used Japanese loans totaling 289.02 billion yen and World Bank loans amounting to $450 million to modernize its railways. Japanese loans during 1981-85 have been used for five projects: the double tracking of the Beijing-Qinhuangdao, Yanzhou-Shijiusuo and Hengyang-Guangzhou lines; the double tracking and electrification of the Zhengzhou-Baoji railway; and the construction of the Dayaoshan railway tunnel in Hunan Province. The Beijing-Qinhuangdao railway opened in July 1984, and the other projects will be completed in the next two to three years.

In 1984 China started using World Bank loans, which were granted in two installments and earmarked for the electrification of the Datong-Taiyuan railway, the double tracking and electrification of the Xinxiang-Heze and the Zhengzhou-Wuchang railways, the technical transformation of the Zhuzhou Electric Locomotives Plant and the experimental center of the Academy of Railway Sciences.

The Datong-Taiyuan line will be electrified by the end of 1987. The work on the laying of the railway track of the Xinjiang-Heze line will be completed this month, and the updated section from Heze to Yanzhou will become operational next year. After the construction is completed, the transport capacity of the line is expected to reach 17 million tons in the near future.

Work on the double tracking and electrification of the Zhengzhou-Wuchang railway started this year and is expected to be completed by 1991. The completion of this project will raise the line's annual transport capacity from 35 million tons to 50 million tons, while the daily number of passenger trains running on this line will increase from 16 pairs to 26 pairs.

During the Seventh Five-Year Plan period (1986-90), the World Bank will grant China the third batch of loans worth US$259 million. These funds will be used for four projects involving the updating of the single track and electrified railways and the mechanization of the rail maintenance equipment.

These four projects are: the electrification of the railway from Sichuan Province to Guizhou Province, which will be completed by 1990 and will raise the line's annual transport volume from 9 million tons to 20 million tons; the electrification of the railway from Yingtan in Jiangxi Province to Xiamen in Fujian Province which will be due by 1992 and will increase its annual transport capacity from 6.6 million tons to 14 million tons; the equipping of 10,000 km of rail lines with large maintainers; and the updating of the Xian Railway Signal Factory. *Beijing Review*, 43 (28 Oct 1985), 29.

Shanhaiguan Switchyard—An electric switchyard went into operation at the Shanhaiguan Railway Station in November, 1985. The station, located at the end of the Beijing-Shanhaiguan line, has been able to double its passenger-train handling capacity and increase its freight-train handling capacity 40 percent. *Beijing Review*, 49 (9 Dec 1985), 10.

RAILWAY CONSTRUCTION, 1985

Xinjiang   264 km
More than 1,000 PLA troops are constructing the Northern Xinjiang Railway in the Gobi Desert, 30 km south of Junggar Pendi. Work began 26 April 1985. The line between Urumqi and Usu will be ready in 1988.

Baoshan   80 km
An 80-km railway line opened to traffic at the Baoshan Iron and Steel Complex 1 June 1985. Its annual transport capacity is 3.2 million tons.

Luohe-Fuyang   208 km
Anhui will build a 69-km section of the Luohe-Fuyang Railway. The entire line will run from Luohe through Zhoukou, Henan, Xiangcheng, Shenqui, Jieshou and Taihe counties

continued . . .

RAILWAY CONSTRUCTION, 1985 (continued)

of Anhui to Fuyang county. Its initial transport capacity will be 5 million tons. The grade-2 railway will connect with the Beijing-Guangzhou and the Beijing-Shanghai Railroads.

Wuhu, Anhui-Guixi, Jiangxi   **541 km**
The Anhui-Jiangxi Railway opened 1 June 1985. It links the Nanjing-Wuhu line to the north and the Zhejiang-Jiangxi and Yingtan-Xiamen lines to the south passing through the Huang-shan Mountains and Jingdezhen. It cuts 300 km from the Yingtan-Nanjing route by avoiding Shanghai.

Xinjiang-USSR
A railway will be built from west of Urumqi, Xinjiang to the Soviet Central Asian Railroad.

Zhoukou, Henan-Fuyang, Anhui   **150 km**
This railway to move coal is being financed by Henan province.

Yangquan, Shanxi-Shexian County, Hebei   **190 km**
This line will eventually ship 10 million tons of coal from Shanxi each year.

Guiyang-Shuicheng   **247 km**
This section of the Guiyang-Kunming Railway linking Yunnan and Guizhou provinces completed electrification and opened in December, 1985.

SUBWAYS, 1985

Shanghai—A 62-mile subway will be built in Shanghai beginning in 1986. The project is expected to cost several billion. *Asian Wall Street Journal Weekly* (8 Apr 1985), 11.

Tianjin—A 7.4-km subway line through downtown Tianjin can handle 30,000 passengers a day. It is China's second subway. The first was built in Beijing. *Beijing Review*, 3 (21 Jan 1985), 8.

HIGHWAY PLANS AND IMPROVEMENTS

Construction, 1979-84
     Roads built (th km)   50.9
     Roads asphalted (th km)   36.7
     Highway bridges constructed (th)   1.3

Plans, 1990
     Total length of roads (th km)   1,000
         Expressways and first-grade roads (th km)   2
     Freight transported (bn tons)   7
     Passengers carried by long-distance buses (bn)   7

Status, 1983-84
     Total length of roads, 1984 (th km)   915
     Freight transported, 1983 (bn tons)   0.790
     Passengers carried by long-distance buses, 1983 (bn)   3.39

Construction Plans, 1986-90
     Roads built (th km)   60
     Roads improved (th km)   80
     Bridges constructed   400

A sales tax will be levied on the purchase of vehicles, road tolls will increase, and new tolls on expressways, bridges and tunnels will bring in the revenue for these improvements. FBIS-CHI 173 (6 Sep 1985), K7/8.

MOTOR VEHICLES, 1985

Motor vehicles in China (mn)	2.8
Gasoline consumed by vehicles each year (mn tons)	10+
Percent of total gas consumption	90
Number of vehicles renovated (replacement of cylinder covers, cam shafts, carburetors, and other parts), 1985 yearend (th)	880
Number renovated, 1985 (th)	180
Number of motor vehicles scrapped during the past three years (th)*	145
Number to be scrapped, 1982-91 (th)	500

*Most of these vehicles were imported from East and West Europe in the 1950s and 1960s and have an average of 500,000 km on their odometers. FBIS-CHI 41 (1 Mar 1985), K19.

ROADS AND MOTOR VEHICLES, 1985

Vehicle Surcharges—The PRC began to levy a surcharge on motor vehicles from 1 May 1985. It is 15 percent of the cost of imports and 10 percent on Chinese cars, which presently sell for 20-30,000 yuan. The surcharge is to raise 4 billion yuan over five years for highway construction. China will manufacture 363,000 motor vehicles in 1985. XNB (27 Apr 1985), 39-40.

Fuzhou-Mawei Tunnel—Construction of the Fuzhou-Mawei highway tunnel began 10 May 1985. The tunnel will extend 3,045 meters and the highway will run 5.7 km. *Fujian Ribao* (11 May 1985), 1.

Rural Roads—In 1984 nearly 2 billion tons of cargo was hauled over rural roads, and more than 2.5 billion passengers took buses on rural routes. A road-building campaign was started in 1984, and nearly 15,000 km have been completed since then. Another 12,400 km are under construction. *Beijing Review*, 30 (29 Jul 1985), 7-8.

Local Road Construction—A 30-km road between Chengdu and Guanxian, Sichuan was widened by local residents in a week. Each worker was paid five yuan per day, and part of the wood from trees felled during the project was divided among those who helped widen the road. At the peak, some 200,000 laborers were involved. *National Geographic*, 168, 3 (Sep 1985), 304-05.

Highway Grades—Grade-1 highways total only 0.03 percent of China's 920,000 km of roads. Grade-4 or non-graded highways amount to more than 85 percent of the total. It costs an average of 300,000 yuan per km of grade-3 highway. A single-track railway costs 2 million yuan per km. *Renmin Ribao* (2 Jul 1985).

Automobile and Truck Production—Volkswagen-Shanghai Autoworks plans to increase production from 100,000 vehicles in 1990 to 300,000 in 1995, allowing 30,000 Santanas to be exported each year. Motor vehicle production in China rose 27 percent in 1984 from approximately 237,000 to 300,000. Another 100,000 were imported. Chinese officials approached Japan's Toyota Motor Co. in 1983 to arrange a joint-venture vehicle plant in Shanghai. The Japanese preferred to sell Toyotas to China at a discount. An imported Santana sells for 40,000 yuan, comparable with an imported Japanese automobile before tax, while the Chinese version sells for 25,000 yuan. The State Council has allocated 70 percent of the 76,500 new trucks for the countryside to rural cooperatives and the remainder to individuals. *Far Eastern Economic Review* (23 May 1985), 74-75.

Sino-Korean Bridge—A highway bridge between Changbai County, Jilin and Hyesan, Yanggang Province of the People's Democratic Republic of Korea in October, 1985. The bridge is 148 meters long and 9 wide. *Jilin Ribao* (25 Oct 1985).

Tire Joint Venture—United Tire & Rubber Co. of Canada and Tianjin Rubber Industrial Co., Tianjin International Trust & Investment Co., and Trinity Development Co. of Hong Kong

continued . . .

ROADS AND MOTOR VEHICLES, 1985 (continued)

will establish a joint venture in Tianjin to produce off-the-road tires. The plant will cost $40 million (Canadian) and United Tire will hold a 20-percent share. It will also sell China $14 million in equipment and technology to make the tires. *Asian Wall Street Journal Weekly* (15 Apr 1985), 16.

Transmissions—Eaton Corp. of Cleveland will provide engineering, technical aid, and training for the production of Fuller Roadranger heavy-duty truck transmissions. In about seven years, Eaton will deliver transmissions for assembly in the PRC. *Asian Wall Street Journal Weekly* (11 Feb 1985), 12.

Life Bridge—The Haimen Lift Bridge has opened to traffic near Tianjin Harbor. It is 903.74 meters long and 14 meters wide. Its center span is 64 meters, the longest in the PRC. Its maximum height is 24 meters, accommodating vessels of 5,000 tons and under. *Beijing Review*, 47 (25 Nov 1985), 9.

Ningxia—Over the past several years, Ningxia has built 1,600 km of main highways, 5,000 km of secondary roads, and 655 bridges. There are 10.5 km of road per 100 km^2 of area in the autonomous region, or 1.4 km more than the national average. Ningxia now has 55,300 motor vehicles. Another 1,600 km of roads will be built or reconstructed in the next three years. XNB (1 Mar 1985), 10.

Guangdong Bridges—Since 1979 1,099 highway bridges have been built in Guangdong province. Twenty-two have spans between 100 and 1,000 meters in length. XNB (28 Mar 1985), 51.

Hong Kong Bridge Planned—Work was to begin in December, 1985 on the third bridge between Hong Kong and the PRC. The Korean Shipbuilding and Engineering Corp. will build half the bridge over the Shenzhen River at Lok Ma Chau. The $260 million deal is scheduled to be completed in 1988, and a new road to Guangzhou by 1990. There are existing road crossings at Man Kam To and Shataukok. *South China Morning Post* (20 Nov 1985), 16.

Pakistani Highway—A 420-km highway will be rebuilt to link the Khunjerab Pass with Kashi, in western Xinjiang. FBIS-CHI 224 (20 Nov 1985), F2.

HIGHWAY CONSTRUCTION, 1985

Shaanxi
A highway is being built between Zhenping county, Shaanxi and Hubei and Sichuan provinces. Other highways under construction in Shaanxi will run through the Qinling and Bashan Mountain ranges. Total length will be about 6,000 km.

Yunnan
The province plans to construct 5,000 km of highways and improve another 5,000 km of trunk roads between 1985 and 1987.

Qinghai
A 130-km highway built entirely of salt is nearing completion in the Qaidam Basin. Cement and asphalt do not withstand the corrosion of salt in the Basin, so salt itself must be used. When water is sprayed on the road, the salt dissolves to fill in ruts, then dries in the sun.

Liaoning
Construction of the four-lane, 388-km international-standard expressway between Shenyang and Dalian was to begin in May, 1985. It will cost 2 billion yuan ($0.7 billion) and be ready by 1990. Speed along the road will increase from 60 to 120 kph. The expressway will have the same carrying capacity as the double-track Shenyang-Dalian Railway.

Shanghai
Two expressways will be built in the Shanghai Economic Zone. A 297-km expressway will link Shanghai with Nanjing, Jaingsu, and a 155-km expressway will connect the city with Hangzhou, Zhejiang. The initial four lanes will eventually be expanded to six. Completion is scheduled for 1995.

continued . . .

HIGHWAY CONSTRUCTION, 1985 (continued)

Lhasa
The 86-km highway between the Konggar Airport and Lhasa has been renovated. The highway has been sand and stone, but it has been widened and covered with asphalt. Bridges and tunnels have been constructed.

Xining, Qinghai-Lhasa, Tibet
An 11-year project to renovate the highest highway in the world is nearing completion. It had been sand and stone, but is now asphalt. The 1,943-km highway has handled about 100,000 tons of cargo a year, but in the last two years has increased that total to about 500,000 tons annually.

Hunan-Jiangxi-Fujian
Construction will begin in 1986 on a highway linking southern Hunan with Jiangxi and Fujian provinces. The 1,100-km road will cost an estimated 600 million yuan. When it is completed in 1990, it should be used by about 5,000 vehicles a day.

SHIPPING NEWS, 1984-85

Jiangsu—Shipping routes in Jiangsu province extend 23,500 km. The Jiangsu section of the Grand Canal is being dredged and widened. The Canal runs 1,994 km. XNB (12 Feb 1985), 24.

Hunan—Xiangjiang, Zishui, Yuanjiang and Lishui Rivers and Dongting Lake have been dredged in Hunan province so that 330-ton cargo vessels can navigate on them during the entire year. The province has over 280 rivers with a total of 10,000 km navigable. The nine major river ports, including Changsha, Zhuzhou, and Changde, have increased their annual handling capacity to more than 1 million tons compared to 400-800,000 tons prior to 1979. Changsha handled 750,000 tons of freight in 1984. XNB (9 Jan 1985), 8-9.

Zhangjiagang Port—Zhangjiagang, Jiangsu has become a major container port after Shanghai, Tianjin and Dalian. Three 10,000-DWT berths are to open for foreign vessels late in 1985. XNB (24 Jul 1985), 31.

Dalian Wharf—The Xianglujiao goods wharf in Dalian Harbor has been completed. Investment amounted to 127.69 million yuan, and the annual handling capacity is 960,000 tons. The project includes two deep-water berths, two berths for medium-class vessels, and a pier. FBIS-CHI 194 (7 Oct 1985), S2.

Dandong—Dandong Harbor in Liaoning has opened to foreign vessels. FBIS-CHI 191 (2 Oct 1985), S1.

Zhejiang Canal—A canal 6.97 km long and 70 meters wide is under construction along the Qiantang River in Zhejiang province. When this 70-million-yuan project is completed in 1986, the Grand Canal will be extended some 400 km southward. The Grand Canal now runs 1,800 km from Hangzhou to Beijing. FBIS-CHI 96 (17 May 1985), 02.

Hainan Island—Hainan plans to raise its cargo-handling capacity from 7.6 million tons to 12 million tons by 1990. A deep-water port is being built in two stages at Yangpu Bay in northwest Hainan. The first includes two berths for 10,000-ton-class vessels and three for 5,000-ton-class ships. It will be ready within three years. The port will eventually handle 30- and 50,000-ton-class vessels. The three other ports on the island—Haikou, Basuo, and Sanya—have been expanded since 1983. Hainan has increased its annual freight capacity by 120,000 passengers and 330,000 tons of cargo. The capacity of Basuo Port, western Hainan, will grow from 3.1 to 4 million tons. A dock has been built at Sanya, and a passenger route has started to Hong Kong. FBIS-CHI 173 (6 Sep 1985), P2.

Shuizhuanshui Port—Projects in the Shuizhuanshui port in Hongshengsha in Guangzhou's Huangpu Harbor have been completed. They included two 9-meter-deep 10,000-ton berths, eight 500-ton berths, a passenger and a car ferry, four warehouses, and other structures.

continued . . .

SHIPPING NEWS, 1984-85 (continued)

Annual handling capacity is now 800,000 tons. Cost of port construction was 30 million yuan. FBIS-CHI 188 (27 Sep 1985), P2.

Nantong Port—China will cooperate with the Netherlands in the first port-construction joint venture. The Nantong Port Administration, the Multipurpose Wharf Rotterdam Company, and the Polycalia West Consortium will construct a wharf with eight berths for ocean-going liners of 10,000 tons displacement, 10 berths for Chang Jiang steamers of 5,000 tons displacement, and 12 berths for inland river ships. The total annual cargo-handling capacity of the wharf will be 10 million tons. Total investment will run 400-500 million yuan. The project is scheduled for completion by 1990. FBIS-CHI 64 (3 Apr 1985), G3.

Hubei River Transport—Ten rivers are being dredged and 12 docks built in Hubei province, including work along the Yangtze, Hanjiang, Hanbei, and Neijing Rivers. FBIS-CHI 69 (10 Apr 1985), P2.

Hangzhou—A new harbor has been proposed for Zhapu, north of Hangzhou, to alleviate congestion at Shanghai. A reinforced concrete jetty berth may be erected first, then several 10,000-ton-class berths built along the 16-km coast of Zhapu Harbor in Jiaxing city, Zhejiang. The existing harbor at Zhapu has a handling capacity of 100,000 tons annually. It is the only harbor to the north of the Hangzhou Gulf. Two 25,000-ton-class berths for oil tankers were constructed east of Zhapu nine years ago. There are suggestions to develop Dushan and Baitashan Harbors eventually. XNB (25 Mar 1985), 49.

Ports Open in April—The PRC opened Weihai and Longkou to foreign ships in April, 1985. Both ports are in Shandong. *Beijing Review*, 18 (6 May 1985), 8.

Guangzhou Dock—The first section of a 10,000-ton wharf, the largest in Guangzhou, went into operation in January, 1985. The harbor has only had a wharf for 5,000-ton-class vessels. XNB (31 Jan 1985), 48.

Ports to Open—Lianhuashan port and two wharves at Zhanjiang port, Guangdong will open to foreign ships. A 230-meter wharf in the Zhanjiang Developmental Zone can accommodate three vessels of 1-3,000 tons or five 300-ton ships. Another wharf east of Zhanjiang is being opened for the Western Petroleum Corp. FBIS-CHI 138 (18 Jul 1985), P1.

Coal Terminal—The second phase of the Qinhuangdao coal terminal went into operation in July, 1985. It includes two deep-water berths for vessels up to 50,000 tons and a combined annual handling capacity of 20 million tons of coal. A first phase involved the construction of a berth for 50,000-ton-class ships and another for 20,000-ton-class vessels. Work began in March, 1978 and ended in December, 1983. The berths can handle 10 million tons of coal a year. FBIS-CHI 139 (19 Jul 1985), D1.

Container Berths—Six container berths, built with a loan from the World Bank, were to become operational in 1985. They will increase annual handling capacity by 300,000 containers in Tianjin, by 200,000 in Shanghai, and by 100,000 in Guangzhou. This will raise the number of Chinese container berths to 13, with an aggregate capacity of 850,000 containers holding 5.5 million tons of cargo. FBIS-CHI 191 (2 Oct 1985), K11.

Foshan Harbor—Foshan Harbor in Guangdong will be expanded and opened to foreign trade. The first phase will cost 18 million yuan. The entire project will be ready by 1986. Foshan earned $280 million in exports in 1984. FBIS-CHI 203 (21 Oct 1985), P4.

Xiamen—Xiamen's Dongdu Harbor has planned 23 deep-water berths, increasing its annual handling capacity from 4 to 15 million tons. *Beijing Review*, 49 (9 Dec 1985), 2.

Zhanjiang—Six berths capable of accommodating ships to 35,000 tons went into operation at Zhanjiang port, Guangdong in December, 1985. One berth for grain and five for sundry goods can handle a total of 1,850,000 tons of cargo annually. FBIS-CHI 249 (27 Dec 1985), P2.

Ship Orders—Since 1980 China has received orders for a total of 1.2 million dwt of ships from foreign countries. FBIS-CHI 3 (6 Jan 1986), A3.

continued . . .

SHIPPING NEWS, 1984-85 (continued)

China—The PRC built 15 10,000-ton-class berths with a total handling capacity of 21.95 million tons in 1984. Two 50,000-ton berths were added at Qinhuangdao to move coal.

Tianjin—Tianjin will build wharves and open additional berths along the lower reaches of the Haihe to permit 5,000-ton foreign ships to dock. Barges will transport goods from 10,000-ton vessels. Some 268 loading and unloading machines are to be imported in 1985, and container wharves will begin operations by the end of the year. Tianjin handled 16 million tons of cargo in 1984. A 1.1-billion expansion should raise port capacity to 22.8 million tons by 1991. FBIS-CHI 196 (9 Oct 1985), R6; XNB (10 Jan 1985), 16-17.

Baoshan—A wharf with 10 berths has started operations at the Baoshan Iron and Steel Complex near Shanghai. The center will ultimately produce 6.5 million tons of pig iron, 6.48 million tons of steel, and 4.22 million tons of rolled steel annually.

Shijiusuo—The Shijiusuo coal wharf in Shandong province has begun trial operations. It will be able to handle 15 million tons of exported coal annually. The wharf has two 100,000-ton deep-water berths. A railroad from Yanzhou was completed in late 1984. The coal terminal at Qinhuangdao in Hebei province will add three berths in early 1988. It presently is exporting 50 million tons, and will subsequently be able to ship 80. XNB (29 Jan 1985), 5.

Mawan Harbor—The Nanhai Oil Shenzhen Development and Service Corp. and the Mutual Petroleum Co. of the US have agreed to build four deep-water berths for 50,000-DWT container ships in Mawan Harbor in Shenzhen. They will be constructed in two stages with an investment of $200 million by the American company. The first phase of the two-stage project—two berths and warehouses—will be completed within 18 months. Twelve deep-water berths with a total annual capacity of 11.6 million tons (six for 50,000-ton container ships, three for 35,000-ton container vessels, and three for 10,000-ton cargo ships) are planned for Shenzhen using foreign investment. FBIS-CHI 156 (13 Aug 1985), B2.

Yangtze—There are 803 shipping companies on the Yangtze River. Another 343,000 individuals operate 173,000 boats with a total deadweight tonnage of 2.06 million on the river. Shipping was partially decentralized in 1983. XNB (13 Feb 1985), 27.

Xijiang River Navigation—The Xijiang River is being cleared for navigation. The 2,200-km river runs from Yunnan through Guizhou, Guangxi, and Guangdong to the South China Sea. Its water volume is second only to the Yangtze. The first stage of the project will involve 567 km between Guixian county, Guangxi and Guangzhou, Guangdong. The waterway will be able to accommodate 1,000-ton vessels when the first stage is completed in six years. XNB (2 Mar 1985), 31.

Gezhouba—Before construction of the Gezhouba dam, about 3.4 million tons of cargo passed through the site each year. In 1984 vessels carried more than 66,600 passengers and 5.52 million tons of freight. Before construction, the Three Gorges area was unnavigable when flood waters exceeded 30,000 m^3/sec, or usually one to two weeks a year. The area is now navigable below 50,000 m^3/sec. FBIS-CHI 124 (27 Jun 1985), K10/13.

Double-Hulled Ship—China's first double-hulled passenger ship has been built at the Jiangzhou Shipyard. The vessel has 6,000 h.p. and 1,500 berths. XNB (4 Apr 1985), 12.

SHIPS SCRAPPED IN CHINA, 1984

Number scrapped	
1983	10
1984	163
Gross tonnage scrapped (mn tons)	2.11
Percentage of world total scrapped	12

South China Morning Post (19 Nov 1985), business, 5. The PRC has become the third largest ship-scrapping center in the world.

PORT PLANS

Number of large, medium, and small berths along coast
1985	300
Deep-water berths for ships of 10,000 tons displacement	
1985	150
To be built during 1981-85	54
To be built during 1986-90	100+
1990	300

Annual container transport capacity of coastal ports (th standard containers)
1985	850
1990	1,300

Renmin Ribao (9 Jul 1985).

PORTS, 1984

Vessels entering or leaving Chinese ports (th)	90
Ships handled at ports each day (average)	105
Passengers arriving in and departing from China (mn)	25
Ports opened to foreign ships since 1979	40
Total ports opened to foreign vessels	99

XNB (24 Jan 1985), 20-21.

OCEAN SHIPPING FLEET, 1985 yearend

Total number of ships	608
Combined dead-weight tonnage (mn tons)	12.7

China has added nearly 100 ocean-going ships to its fleet during the last two years. It is currently the ninth largest in the world. The fleet calls at more than 600 ports in 150 countries and regions. It opened 84 new regular shipping routes in 1985. Twenty-five container ships sail to Japan each day, 18 to Hong Kong, and nine to London, Hamburg, and Rotterdam. XNB (28 Oct 1985), 92.

AIRLINE INFORMATION

Aircraft Purchases—China has purchased 21 foreign passenger planes for nearly $1 billion to replace 15 obsolete aircraft. The planes include nine Boeing 373-200s, nine Soviet TU-154s, and three European Airbus A310s. Additional aircraft are needed for the expansion of the CAAC. In 1984 1.25 million persons were unable to book flights for lack of space. *China Daily* (21 Apr 1985), 1. The first two A310-200s will be delivered in June, 1985, and the third will arrive in May 1986. Each A310 can carry 228 passengers. FBIS-CHI 74 (17 Apr 1985), G4/5.

McDonnell Douglas—Shanghai Aviation Industry Corp. and China Aviation Supplies Corp. have signed an agreement with McDonnell Douglas to transfer the technology and permit production and sales of the MD-82 to China. By 1991 25-40 aircraft will have been built in Shanghai. The first will be finished in 1987. FBIS-CHI 72 (15 Apr 1985), B1; *Aviation Week & Space Technology* (22 Apr 1985), 31-32, 34.

Aircraft Scrapped—Fifteen Antonov-24 Soviet passenger planes obtained from the USSR in the 1960s will be replaced by 19 new passenger planes. The CAAC plans to modernize its

continued . . .

AIRLINE INFORMATION (continued)

fleet of some 500 aircraft, and the Antonov's were deemed unreliable after the January 18 crash during a landing at Jinan. *Asian Wall Street Journal Weekly* (4 Feb 1985), 7.

Airliners—The CAAC will purchase eight 36-seat aircraft from Short Bros. Ltd. of Belfast. The planes will be used on feeder routes. *Asian Wall Street Journal Weekly* (11 Mar 1985), 13.

Northwest—Northwest Airlines plans to expand its operations in China beyond Shanghai. It is limited to one flight there each week. Northwest is also allowed to fly to Guangzhou, but has not yet done so. The company will increase cargo to Shanghai during cold-weather months. *Asian Wall Street Journal Weekly* (6 May 1985), 5.

Passengers—The CAAC plans to carry 13 million passengers by 1990. A contract was signed with the Sperry Corp. in May, 1985 to acquire $9 million in computers and software to help handle this volume. FBIS-CHI 98 (21 May 1985), B1.

Heliport—Construction of China's first civilian heliport will soon start at Caochangdi, half way between the city center and the Capital Airport. The first phase includes a terminal, runway, apron and navigation tower. XNB (5 Mar 1985), 29.

Shenzhen—Parsons Lockheed of the US will prepare a feasibility study of an international airport at Shenzhen. A medium-sized facility will be built for Boeing 737s and Tridents at a cost of 200 million yuan. Bidding for the larger project will begin after the airport opens. FBIS-CHI 127 (2 Jul 1985), B2.

Japanese Flights—The CAAC and Japan's airlines provide 6,600 seats each week for passengers traveling between nations. The number will exceed 10,000 in 1986. The CAAC will use recently purchased A-310s and Boeing-737s on some routes. Air freight capacity between countries will grow 70 percent in 1986. *Being Review*, 52 (30 Dec 1985), 27.

China Air Transport—The China Air Transport Co. has started regular flights between Beijing's Nanyuan field and Shenzhen SEZ in Guangdong province. The new airline company began service in December, 1984. This flight is twice a week on British-built Tridents. *Asian Wall Street Journal Weekly* (11 Mar 1985), 13.

British Aerospace Sale—British Aerospace will deliver 10 BAE 146 short-haul jets to China in 1986. The deal is worth $150 million. New York *Times* (25 Apr 1985), 34.

French Sale—Airbus Industrie will provide China with five wide-bodied A-310s for just under $200 million. Two will be delivered in December, 1985 and three in 1986. *Asian Wall Street Journal Weekly* (21 Jan 1985), 4.

Boeing Sales—China recently has bought eight jumbo jets from Boeing: one Boeing-747, two Boeing-767s, and five Boeing-737-200s for $350 million. The CAAC already has 37 Boeing aircraft, including six 747s, two 767s, and nineteen 737s. FBIS-CHI 100 (23 May 1985), B1; New York *Times* (24 Jun 1985), 26.

Aeroflot—China has purchased nine TU-154M three-engine, 160-seat aircraft from Aviaeksport of the Soviet Union.

Xian—An airport capable of handling 2 million persons annually will be constructed outside Xianyang, 30 km northwest of Xian, Shaanxi. Xian plans to purchase five TU-154s from the USSR. Three will be delivered in 1985 and two in 1986. FBIS-CHI 36 (22 Feb 1985), C1.

Yunnan—Yunnan province has agreed to buy two Boeing 737-300 airliners for delivery late in 1985 and early in 1986. Each can seat 149 passengers. This is the first local Chinese airline company to import Boeings from the US. FBIS-CHI 10 (15 Jan 1985), B3.

Third China-Japan Air Route—A third air route between China and Japan was opened 18 April 1985 when a Japanese jetliner landed at Dalian, Liaoning. The two other regular lines are from Tokyo to Shanghai via Nagasaki and from Beijing to Nagasaki via Shanghai. *Beijing Review*, 18 (6 May 1985), 8.

Airports Planned—Two airports to accommodate Boeing 747s, 707s, and 737s will be built in northwestern China during 1985. One will be in Shaanxi and another in Qinghai. *Beijing Review*, 17 (29 Apr 1985), 8.

continued . . .

AIRLINE INFORMATION (continued)

Chongqing– An all-weather airport will be built in Jiangbei county, 25 km from Chongqing, Sichuan. Boeing 707s and 747s will be able to land and take off when the airport is completed by the end of 1987. The first phase of construction will include a 2,600-meter runway. XNB (8 Feb 1985), 7-8.

Haikou—The Haikou Airport on Hainan Island will now accommodate Boeing 737s with a 2,500-meter runway. A new terminal is to be ready by December, 1985. XNB (8 Feb 1985), 31-32.

Airliner Traffic—In 1984 14,000 airliners arrived in and left the PRC. XNB (24 Jan 1985), 21.

Xishuangbanna—An airport will be built in the Xishuangbanna Dai Autonomous Prefecture of Yunnan province by 1987. It will be located 7 km southwest of Yunjinghong, and be able to handle small and medium-sized aircraft. XNB (11 Jan 1985), 48.

Beihai—The construction of the Beihai Airport in the Guangxi Zhuang Autonomous Region began 10 April 1985. It will be able to accommodate Boeing 737s. XNB (11 Apr 1985), 27.

CAAC—CAAC traffic has grown 20 percent annually for the past five years. It increased 50 percent during the first quarter of 1985 compared to the corresponding period in 1984. Domestic load factors are exceeding 80 percent, and nearly 70 percent internationally. Capacity went up 40 percent in 1984 with the addition of 20 domestic routes. The CAAC has 57,000 employees. Its payroll has grown about 10 percent a year. *Aviation Week & Space Technology* (17 Jun 1985), 33-34.

Boeing Sales—China will buy four Boeing 737-300 jumbo jets from Boeing for the new Southwestern Aviation Company. The first plane will arrive in November, 1985 and the rest before June, 1986. FBIS-CHI 137 (17 Jul 1985), B4.

Soviet Deals—A contract to buy 17 TU-154Ms was signed 18 July 1985. The first was to arrive 19 July and the last in 1986. FBIS-CHI 139 (19 Jul 1985), C1. Heilongjiang province has purchased three TU-154-MS aircraft. They will be delivered during the first quarter of 1986. FBIS-SOV 206 (24 Oct 1985), B3.

Guangzhou Airport—Bai Yun (White Cloud) Airport at Guangzhou is near capacity, and an international airport between the city and the Shenzhen and Zhuhai Special Economic Zones is being considered. Some 8,000 passengers use Bai Yun every day, and the number exceeds 10,000 during the peak season. Bai Yun also may get a new international terminal costing 45 million yuan, while the present terminal will only serve domestic flights. The new terminal will be able to handle 15,000 passengers daily. Construction should take two years. *South China Morning Post* (12 Jul 1985), 8.

Xiamen and Changchun—Two ramps will be installed at the Xiamen International Airport. Runways at the Changchun Airport will be reinforced and extended to accommodate Boeing 707s. Floor space at the terminal will more than double. When the expansion is finished in November, 1985 routes will open to Guangzhou, Shanghai, and Dalian. XNB (26 Mar 1985), 31-32.

New Routes—The Civil Aviation Administration of China (CAAC) planned to open seven new domestic routes and one to Singapore in 1985. The seven rutes to mainland cities included:

Shanghai-Lianyungang-Beijing	Mar
Taiyuan-Guangzhou	Mar
Shenyang-Dandong-Dalian-Beijing	Apr
Beijing-Qinhuangdao-Shijiazhuang-Nanjing-Shanghai	Apr
Shenyang-Qinhuangdao-Beijing-Shijiazhuang	Apr
Harbin-Jiamusi	Jul
Harbin-Heihe	Jul
PRC-Singapore	Jun

This will bring the total number of domestic air routes of the CAAC to 83 and international air routes to 24. FBIS-CHI 53 (19 Mar 1985), K27.

CIVIL AVIATION ADMINISTRATION OF CHINA, 1984

Freight (mn ton-km)	920
Freight and mail (th tons)	150
Passengers (mn)	5.54
Passengers carried on international routes and flights to Hong Kong (mn)	1.2
Profit (mn yuan)	317

Routes opened since 1979

Domestic	45
International	12
To Hong Kong	7

XNB (6 Mar 1985), 26.

YUN-8

Maximum range (km)	5,615
Speed (kph)	550
Maximum altitude (m)	10,400
Loading capacity (tons)	20
Number of engines	4

The YUN-8 made a successful test flight 7 May 1985. It can take off and land on grass, sand and dirt runways. The aircraft is made by the Shaanxi Transport Manufacturing Factory. FBIS-CHI 91 (10 May 1985), K5.

TRAVELLER

Weight (kg)	120
Range	450
Maximum speed at 4,500 m (kph)	120

This duck-shaped, one-seater aircraft is the first Chinese plane made of double-layer glass-fiber reinforced plastic. It can take off and land on a runway 40-45 meters long. The aircraft can be disassembled in a half hour. FBIS-CHI 162 (21 Aug 1985), K11.

AIRLINE ACCIDENTS, 1985

18 Jan   A Soviet-built Antonov-24 enroute from Shanghai to Beijing crashes while landing at Jinan Airport. There are 38 fatalities. The CAAC plane was flying in cloudy weather.

24 Aug   A twin-engine bomber similar to the Harbin-5 (Iliushin-28) enters South Korean air space and crashes after running out of fuel. The navigator and a farmer working in the field are killed. The pilot is badly injured and a third crewman is not hurt. South Korean aircraft attempted to escort the Chinese plane to Kunsan Air Base near Iri, south of Seoul, before it crash-landed.

CHINESE AIRFIELDS

Runway Length (in meters)	Runway Surface*			Total
	P	T	N	
4,000 and over	6			6
4,000 - 3,600	2			2
3,600 - 3,000	20	3	1	24
3,000 - 2,700	17			17
2,700 - 2,400	57	1	1	59
2,400 - 2,100	81		3	84
2,100 - 1,800	35	3	11	49
1,800 - 1,500	11	1	11	23
1,500 - 1,200	13	4	13	30
under 1,200	12	1	13	26
under construction				5
seaplane stations				2
heliports				4
highway strips				7
	254	13	53	338

```
*   P  =   Permanent
    T  =   Temporary
    N  =   Natural
```

Most Chinese airfields are east of the 108-degree meridian in the most populous area of the country. The majority of military airfields have runways of 1,800 meters or more, and are generally used in an air defense posture. Defense Intelligence Agency, *Handbook of the Chinese People's Liberation Army* (1985), 66.

XIV INSTITUTIONS

RELIGION, 1985

Christianity

Bishops Consecrated—Li Side, 77 and Jin Luxian, 69, were consecrated in the Xujiahui Cathedral in Shanghai 27 January 1985. The two were nominated by Louis Zhang Jiashu, 92, Head of the Chinese Catholic Bishops College and the Bishop of Shanghai, and elected 7 December 1984. Li Side graduated from the Shanghai Seminary in 1938 and is the Deputy Director of the Administrative Commission of the Shanghai Catholic Church and a member of the National Administrative Commission of the Chinese Catholic Church. Jin Luxian graduated from the Seminary in 1947 as a doctor of theology. He is also a Deputy Director of the Administrative Commission and Head of the Sheshan Catholic Seminary. FBIS-CHI 20 (30 Jan 1985), K27; *China Reconstructs*, XXXIV, 6 (Jun 1985), 50-52.

Printing Facility—The American Bible Society has come to an understanding with the new Chinese Amity Foundation about establishing a modern printing plant in China for Bibles, Testaments and other Christian publications. The Amity Foundation will own and control the plant. Minneapolis *Star and Tribune* (30 Mar 1985), 16A.

Pehtang Cathedral—The largest Roman Catholic cathedral in Beijing will reopen at the end of 1985. The Pehtang Cathedral, built in 1887, was closed during the Cultural Revolution. It will be the third to reopen in Beijing since worship has become easier in recent years. Renovation of the structure will cost $350,000. Minneapolis *Star and Tribune* (14 Jun 1985), 17A; New York *Times* (25 Dec 1985), 1, 4.

Gong Pinmei—Gong Pinmei (Ignatius Kung), appointed the Bishop of the Shanghai Diocese by the Vatican in 1950, was released from prison 3 July 1985. He was born in Shanghai in 1901. Gong was sentenced to life imprisonment for treason in 1960. Louis Zhang became the Bishop of Shanghai after Gong was jailed. FBIS-CHI 129 (5 Jul 1985), K9/10.

Nanjing Church—The oldest Christian Church in Nanjing, Jiangsu, built in 1922, has reopened. More than 600 Christians attended services at St. Paul's Cathedral 28 July 1985. XNB (30 Jul 1985), 29.

Seminaries—A description of 11 theological institutions appears in *China Notes*, XXIII, 2-3 (spring-summer 1985), 341-44. It mentions the Huadong Seminary and the Guangdong Union Theological Seminary, both of which were to open in the autumn of 1985.

Church of the Savior—The Church of the Savior in Beijing has been restored by the Chinese Catholic Church, which is independent of the Vatican. The Church was closed in the 1950s and used as a warehouse by the Red Guards. Fifty-one Catholic churches were reopened in November, 1985 just in Fujian province. New York *Times* (18 Dec 1985), 5.

Buddhism

Mt. Wutai—The Buddhist shrine of Mt. Wutai opened to foreign tourists in March, 1985.

Lapuleng—The 274-year-old Lapuleng Monastery, 260 km southwest of Lanzhou, Gansu, opened to tourists in April, 1985. The lamasery has more than 60,000 Buddhist statues and a valuable collection of scriptures and art. A hotel is available for visitors, and Tibetan yurts will accommodate guests in the summer.

Buddhist Institute—The first Tibetan-language Buddhist Theological Institute has opened at the Taer Monastery in Qinghai. Fifty students have enrolled in a six-year course studying Buddhist religion, culture and philosophy. There are 750,000 Tibetans in Qinghai, making up 19 percent of the population.

Lhasa—A Buddhist nunnery which had been converted into a meeting hall during the Cultural Revolution has reopened with 16 nuns. New York *Times* (17 May 1985), 4.

continued . . .

RELIGION, 1985 (continued)

Rongbo—The world's highest monastery, 17,060 feet up Mount Everest, has been partially repaired at a cost of $35,000, and will open to visitors. The 1,000-year-old Rongbo Monastery once housed 800 Lamaist monks and nuns, but was destroyed during the Cultural Revolution. New York *Times* (7 May 1985), 2.

Sichuan College—The Sichuan College for Buddhist nuns opened in January, 1985 at Chengdu. The first 39 students will take a four-course in Buddhism, the Chinese language, history, foreign languages, and other subjects. *Beijing Review*, 7-8 (18 Feb 1985), 35.

Buddhist Scriptures—*Collections of Buddhist Scriptures* will be published in Chinese in 220 volumes over the next 10 years. The series is based on the *Zhaocheng Jinzang*, a 4,000-volume collection of Buddhist scriptures of the Jin Dynasty (1115-1234). This new publication will include all 4,200 kinds of Buddhist scriptures found in the 23,000 books in China and abroad. *Beijing Review*, 11 (18 Mar 1985), 34.

Kizil Grottoes—Murals of the Kizil Grottoes, halfway between Urumqi and Kashi, Xinjiang, are pictured in *China Reconstructs*, XXXIV, 4 (Apr 1985), 56-61. Begun in the 2nd century, this is China's westernmost grotto complex.

Mt. Emei—The Jindian Temple on Mt. Emei in Sichuan is being rebuilt. The temple was burned down in 1973. The Sichuan government has provided 1.8 million yuan for expenses. Since 1974 it has devoted over 10 million yuan to reconstructuring 23 temples on Mt. Emei, one of the four sacred mountains in China. XNB (7 Oct 1985), 1.

Confucius Research Center—A national research institute to study Confucius was established in Beijing 10 June 1985. Its secretary-general is Sun Kaitai, and membership includes 240 experts. Confucius (551-479 B.C.) was attacked during the Cultural Revolution, but his birthplace at Qufu, Shandong has been restored. XNB (11 Jun 1985), 19-20.

Islam

Islamic Center—China will spend $7 million on its first Islamic cultural center in Yinchuan, Ningxia. It will include a seminary for 200 students, a mosque for 1,000, a library with 1 million volumes, and a 200-bed hospital on 37 acres. About one-third of Ningxia's population are Muslim, and the autonomous region has more than 1,600 mosques. New York *Times* (11 Jul 1985), 6; XNB (17 Sep 1985), 66-67.

Muslim Minorities—In the past year, approximately 1,000 Chinese Muslims were allowed to travel to Mecca. Nine of the 10 Muslim minority nationalities in China are descendants from Mongol, Persian or Turkic ancestors: Kirgiz, Tatars, Uyghurs, Kazakhs, Uzbeks, Salars, Baoans, Tadzhiks, and Dongxiangs. The Hui, who number about 7 million, are Chinese in origin. The total number of Muslims in China exceeds 14 million. *Frankfurter Allgemeine Zeitung* (15 Aug 1985), 3.

Henan—Some 400 mosques have been reopened in Henan province. The provincial government has spent 10 million yuan to restore mosques, including Kaifeng's Dongda Mosque, built during the Northern Song dynasty (960-1127), and the Beida Mosque at Zhengzhou, which dates from the Ming dynasty (1368-1644). A four-year Islamic college is planned for 120 students annually. There are 1 million Muslims in Henan, or one-seventh of China's total. XNB (9 Mar 1985), 14.

Hajj—No Muslim pilgrims from eastern Turkestan were allowed to perform the Hajj between 1964 and 1979. Prior to 1964 only 20-30 traveled to Mecca, but they were carefully selected by authorities. The number was reported to have been over 2,100 in 1985. *Arabia*, 5, 53 (Jan 1986), 74.

BANKING NEWS, 1984-85

American Express—American Express card holders have been able to obtain cash at 97 branches of the Bank of China. An increase in fraudulent transactions has led American Express to reduce these check-cashing services to 37 branches. Check cashing is limited to one transaction every 21 days with a maximum of $1,000 for green cards, and $2,000 for gold and platinum cards. Previously, card holders of all three types could obtain as much as $1,000 per day. *Asian Wall Street Journal Weekly* (14 Jan 1985), 13.

Bank of China Building—The 20-story Bank of China building, designed by I.M. Pei, is scheduled to open in Hong Kong in 1988. See the *Saturday Review* (Mar-Apr 1985), 17.

Provincial Banks—Local banks will be established in Guangdong and Fujian provinces, ending the state monopoly on banking. The People's Bank of China will still provide advice to the provincial banks. *Asian Wall Street Journal Weekly* (3 Jun 1985), 6.

New York Branch—The Bank of China inaugurated a branch in Chinatown, New York, 25 September 1985. It opened its first branch office in the US in Manhattan four years ago, and this is its second. The General Manager is Zhou Zhenxing, 55. FBIS-CHI 188 (27 Sep 1985), B3/4.

President of Bank of China—Wang Deyan was appointed President of the Bank of China in the summer of 1985. Wang was born in August, 1931 in Shanghai. He studied at Qinghua University and the Central Finance and Economic College. He joined the Bank of China after graduation in 1953, and worked at the Hong Kong branch as assistant manager, and subsequently, deputy general manager for 18 years. Wang became a vice-president of the Bank in May, 1984. He studied English for three years at the Beijing Foreign Languages Institute. FBIS-CHI 134 (12 Jul 1985), K2/3; *Cheng Ming*, 4 (1 Apr 1985), 11.

Credit Card Business—The credit card volume of the Bank of China was $60 million in 1984, and should reach $120 million in 1985. MasterCard, American Express, JCB, Federal, Million, Visa, and Diners Club cards are all used in the PRC. *Beijing Review*, 39 (30 Sep 1985), 30.

New Bank Presidents—During 1985 Zhang Xiao was appointed President of the Industrial and Commercial Bank of China. Ma Yongwei has become President of the Agricultural Bank of China. *Beijing Review*, 35 (2 Sep 1985), 8.

World Bank—The World Bank opened a resident mission office in Beijing 25 October 1985. FBIS-CHI 210 (30 Oct 1985), A4.

Banking Reforms—Bank savings have increased an average of 20.2 percent or 38.1 billion yuan annually between 1979 and 1984. Credit has been extended to a broader range of customers and for fixed assets, not merely for use as working capital. New forms of credit have been introduced, including commercial, buyer's, bill-discounted, and consumer credit. Specialized banks have been established, and the management of credit funds decentralized. The insurance business and accounting system have also been decentralized, and an economic information network formed. XNB (18 Nov 1985), 86-87.

First Foreign Branch Bank—The Hongkong & Shanghai Banking Corp., Hong Kong's leading financial institution, has received permission to establish a branch at Shenzhen. It is the first foreign bank allowed to open a branch since 1949. The branch will make loans, accept foreign-currency deposits, issue guarantees, and handle export and import transactions. It will not handle foreign-currency banking. Minneapolis *Star and Tribune* (23 Aug 1985), 7B; *Asian Wall Street Journal Weekly* (10 Jun 1985), 13; FBIS-CHI 164 (23 Aug 1985), K9/10. Regulations were issued 2 April 1985 on foreign banks operating in the Shenzhen, Zhuhai, Shantou, and Xiamen Special Economic Zones. *Beijing Review*, 19 (13 May 1985), 8-9.

Panda Gold Coins—With the shift away from buying Krugerrands, China's one-ounce gold Panda coins are in special demand. They are the first bullion coin to have numismatic value, because their design changes each year. The first minting of 13,000 went on sale in 1982. In 1985 50,000 were minted. When bullion reached $330 an ounce, suggested prices for the Panda coins were $700 for 1982, $475 for 1983, and $348 for 1985. New York *Times*, "Personal Investing '86" (17 Nov 1985), 30.

BANK OF CHINA, 1978, 1984 (yearend)

	1978	1984
Total assets (bn yuan)	38.7	200.3
Domestic offices	58	261
Domestic staff (th)	4	16
Overseas offices	184	286
Overseas staff (th)	6	10
Correspondent relations, 1984		
With head offices and bank branches		3,301
With banks in 150 nations and regions		1,185

Beijing Review, 22 (3 Jun 1985), 23. The *Beijing Review*, 49 (9 Dec 1985), 29, put the number of overseas offices at the end of 1984 at 293 with total assets of $18.3 billion. Its deposits totaled $9.6 billion.

REPRESENTATIVE OFFICES OF MAJOR BANKS OPENED IN CHINA, 1985

17 Apr   Gotabanken of Sweden opens an office at Beijing

6 May   Sumitomo Bank Ltd., Shanghai (This bank already has offices in Beijing and Guangzhou.)

30 May   United Overseas Bank Group of Singapore, Beijing

6 Sep   Spanish External Bank, Beijing

13 Sep   Landerbank of Austria, Beijing

25 Sep   Daiwa Bank Ltd. of Japan, Shanghai

16 Oct   Arab Bank Ltd. of Jordan, Beijing

28 Oct   Gotabanken of Sweden, Shanghai

16 Nov   Nanyang Commercial Bank of Hong Kong, Beijing

5 Dec   Citybank, Shanghai

Amsterdam-Rotterdam Bank N.V. has been granted permission to open a representative office in Beijing. It is the first Dutch bank to open an office in China. *Asian Wall Street Journal Weekly* (29 Jul 1985), 10. The Canadian Imperial Bank of Commerce will establish a correspondent relationship with the Industrial and Commercial Bank of China. It will be the first Canadian bank to form such a relation. *Asian Wall Street Journal Weekly* (22 Jul 1985), 9. Twenty foreign banks opened representative offices in Guangdong province in 1985. This brings the total number to 41 opened there since 1981. They include the Sanwan Bank, the Dai-ichi Kangyo Bank, the Fuji Bank, the Sumitomo Bank, the Mitsubishi, the US International Banking Corp., Banque Nationale de Paris, and Credit Lyonnais. About half are in the Shenzhen Special Economic Zone, and the rest are in Guangzhou and Zhuhai. *Beijing Review*, 8 (24 Feb 1986), 29.

NEW SOCIETIES AND ASSOCIATIONS, 1985

National Association for Factory and Business Administrations 35 Years Old and Under (4 Feb), Beijing; Chairman, Zhang Baoshun

China United Front Theory Research Association (8 Feb), Beijing; President, Yang Jingren

Hunan Society (to promote construction in the province, 11 Mar)

Maoshan Taoist Association (10 Mar), Nanjing

China Association for the Promotion of International Friendship (18 May)

Chinese Tobacco Society (20 May), Beijing

Chinese People's Association for Peace and Disarmament (1 Jun); President, Zhou Peiyuan

China Computer Society (1 Jun), Beijing

Rock Mechanics and Engineering Society (19 Jun), Beijing; there are nearly 10,000 people engaged in this field building dams, tunnels, mines, etc.

China Customs Association (30 Jun), Beijing

Association for Vocational Technical Training (8 Jul), Beijing

China Investment Society (15 Jul), Beijing

United Nations Society (17 Jul), Beijing; President, Wu Xiaoda

Chinese Association of Inventions (16 Oct), Beijing; President, Wu Heng

China Mental Health Association (Sep); Taian; Shandong, President, Chen Xueshi

China Burn Injuries Society, Chongqing (Oct); China's first burn clinic was established in 1958

China Medical Jurisprudence Society, Luoyang, Henan (31 Oct); Chairman, Li Boling

XV SCIENCE

SCIENCE NEWS, 1985

Earthquake Centers—During the last eight years, China has set up six seismic centers at Shanghai, Shenyang, Beijing, Lanzhou, Chengdu, and Kunming. Information is transmitted to computers for analysis. XNB (9 Feb 1985), 16.

Geological Map—China will complete its national geological map with a scale of 1:1,000,000. This project was started in 1949, and the last area to be charted is Gartogfu in western Tibet. XNB (27 Apr 1985), 55.

Ion Microscope—China's first field ion microscope atomic detector has been produced at the Institute of Metal Research at Shenyang. The microscope allows scientists to investigate atomic structures of metals and semiconductors. XNB (9 Jan 1985), 7-8.

Shanghai—There are 299,000 natural scientists working at 710 research institutes and 108 academic organizations in Shanghai. *Beijing Review*, 2 (14 Jan 1985), 25.

Hydrogeological Center—China's first hydrogeological research center has begun operations at Shijiazhuang, Hebei. The UN Development Program and the Chinese Hydrogeological Engineering Research Institute jointly funded the $11 million project. It will study the ground-water resources of the Huanghai Sea and Huihai Sea plain. FBIS-CHI 108 (5 Jun 1985), K20.

Weather Forecasting—The PRC will invest 98.8 million yuan in a medium-range weather forecasting system in the northwestern suburbs of Beijing before 1990. The system will permit forecasts four to six days ahead. *Beijing Review*, 25 (24 Jun 1985), 32.

Science Reorganization—The 119 research institutes of the Chinese Academy of Sciences will gradually lose state funding and enter partnerships with universities and enterprises over the next three to five years. Institutes which invent products and technology may sell them without state interference or taxation. Scientists may share the profits. Researchers also will be permitted to engage in spare-time consultancy services or technological work after meeting their assignments, provided they do not violate the rights and interests of their work units. *Asian Wall Street Journal Weekly* (25 Mar 1985), 4.

Scientific Workers Required in Shanghai—Shanghai will need to train an estimated half million technical workers to make up for the 440,000 expected to retire within the next five years and to fill some 60,000 new jobs. Minneapolis *Star and Tribune* (1 Sep 1985), 10B.

Tibetan Academy—The Tibetan Academy of Social Sciences has opened in Lhasa. It has five institutes for research on the Tibetan language, religion, history, literature, science and economics. There are 59 researchers, 73 percent of whom are Tibetans. *Beijing Review*, 33 (19 Aug 1985), 8.

Prize Winners—Prize winners for science and technology in 1984 included 264 inventions and discoveries approved by the state, or some 52 more than in 1983. Among the first-class awards were those for a new MIG arc-welding technique and a method for propagating woolly-headed crabs in salt water.

Inventions—Cash awards up to 20,000 yuan will now be given for first-class inventions, 10,000 yuan for second-class, 5,000 for third-class, and 2,000 for fourth-class inventions. Since the awards were begun in 1979, more than 900 inventions have been acknowledged. They have yielded a total economic return of 25 billion yuan. *Beijing Review*, 25 (24 Jun 1985), 18-19.

Linear Accelerator—A 90-million-volt linear accelerator for the Beijing electron-positron collider has passed its tests. The accelerator was designed by scientists at the Ministry of the Electronics Industry and the High Energy Physics Institute of the Academy of Sciences. FBIS-CHI 142 (24 Jul 1985), K4.

continued . . .

SCIENCE NEWS, 1985 (continued)

Telescope—The Vatican's observatory at Castel Gandolfo will give its telescope to a Chinese university. The transfer is part of a recent cooperation agreement. New York *Times* (18 Dec 1985), 5.

Snake Island—An island off Dalian, Liaoning is the only place in the world where large numbers of pit vipers live. The island has been a closed snake reserve since August, 1980. Scientists have determined that the numbers of vipers on the 0.63-km island have increased by 1,000 each year since 1982 to the present 13,000. XNB (30 May 1985), 37.

Antarctica—Pictures of the first Chinese expedition to the Antarctic appear in *China Reconstructs*, XXXIV, 8 (Aug 1985), 18-26. A second expedition with 28 Chinese scientists left for the Great Wall Station on George Island 13 November 1985. Thirteen other Chinese will join them later.

Social Science—There are 29 social science research institutes in China. Some 15,000 persons specialize in this area, and over 200 social science societies have been set up. China publishes more than 400 magazines and periodicals on the social sciences, and there are about 15 million copies of books on the social sciences in the country. *Beijing Review*, 48 (2 Dec 1985), 28.

US-CHINESE SCIENCE AND TECHNOLOGY EXCHANGES

Protocol fields: The US-China S&T agreement covers exchanges in the following 23 fields. Further information on these protocols can be obtained from the indicated US Government agencies.

1. Student and Scholar Exchanges: US Information Agency
2. Agriculture: Department of Agriculture
3. Space Technology: National Aeronautics and Space Agency
4. High Energy Physics: Department of Energy (DOE)
5. Metrology and Standards: National Bureau of Standards/Department of Commerce (DOC)
6. Atmospheric Science: National Oceanic and Atmospheric Administration (NOAA)/ DOC
7. Marine and Fishery Science: NOAA/DOC and National Science Foundation (NSF)
8. Medicine and Public Health: Health and Human Services and the National Institutes of Health (NIH)
9. Earthquake Studies: U.S. Geological Survey (USGS) and NSF
10. Earth Sciences: USGS and NSF
11. Environmental Protection: Environmental Protection Agency
12. Basic Sciences: NSF
13. Building Construction and Urban Planning: Department of Housing and Urban Development
14. Nuclear Safety: Nuclear Regulatory Commission, DOE
15. Surface Water Hydrology: USGS
16. Nuclear Physics and Magnetic Fusion: DOE
17. Aeronautical Science and Technology: NASA
18. Transportation: Department of Transportation
19. Managment of Industrial S&T: DOC
20. Basic Biomedical Sciences: NIH
21. Cooperation in S&T Information: National Technical Information Service/DOC
22. Social, Demographic, and Economic Statistics: Bureau of the Census/DOC
23. Direct Reception and Distribution of Landsat Data: NOAA/DOC

continued . . .

US-CHINESE SCIENCE AND TECHNOLOGY EXCHANGES (continued)

Senior US scholars interested in applying for research and study outside the government-to-government programs may contact:

Committee on Scholarly Communication with the People's Republic of China
National Program for Advanced Study and Research in China
2101 Constitution Ave., NW
(202)-334-2718

Key US Government contacts are:

Office of Chinese Affairs
Department of State
Washington, DC 20520
(202)-632-1322

Office of Cooperative S&T Programs
Department of State
Washington, DC 20520
(202)-632-3253

US Department of State, *GIST* (Apr 1985), 2.

CHINESE EARTH-SCIENCE INSTITUTIONS

G	Academia Sinica [Chinese Academy of Science] Division of Earth Sciences Vice President: Ye Duzheng		G	Geology and Paleontology Nanjing Director: Zhao Jinke
	The Academy consists of the following Institutes:		G	Geophysics Beijing Director: Fu Chengyi
G	Desert Studies Lanzhou Director:. Zhu Zhenda		G	Geotectonics Changsha Director: Chen Guoda
G	Geochemistry Guiyang Director: Tu Guangzhi		G	Glaciology and Cryopedology Lanzhou Director: Shi Yafeng
G	Geography Beijing Director: Huang Bingwei		G	Oceanography Qingdao Director: Zeng Chengkui
G	Geography Changchun Director: Huang Xichou		G	Oceanography (South Seas) Guangzhou Director: Qiu Bingjing
G	Geography Chengdu Director: Ding Xizhi		G	Pedology Nanjing Director: Xiong Yi
G	Geography Xinjiang Director: Yue Zhen		C	Remote Sensing Application Beijing Chen Shuping
G	Geology Beijing Director: Zhang Wenyou		G	Rock and Soil Mechanics Wuhan
G	Geology Lanzhou Director: Huang Ruchang		G	Salt Lakes Xining Director: Liu Dagang
G	Geology and Geography Urumchi		C	Surveying Wuhan Director: Fang Jui

continued . . .

CHINESE EARTH-SCIENCE INSTITUTIONS (continued)

H   Soil and Water Conservation
Shaanxi
Director: Zhu Xianmo

G   Vertebrate Paleontology of Paleoanthropology
Beijing
Director: Zhou Minzhen

G   Ministry of Geology and Mineral Resources
(Formerly known as the State Bureau of Geology)
Minister: Sun Daguang

G   Institute of Geology and Mineral Resources
Yichang
Director: Tan Zhangfu

G   Institute of Rock and Mineral Analysis
Beijing
Director: Wang Weiying

G   National Geological Library
Beijing
Director: Deng Geming

G   National Geological Museum
Beijing
Director:. Liu Yongquan

G   Institute of Multipurpose Utilization of Mineral
Resources
Emei
Director: Zheng Youlang

G   State Seismological Bureau
Beijing
Director: An Qiyuan

G   Institute of Seismology
Wuhan
Director: Lee

G   Institute of Geophysics
Beijing
Director: Cheng Zongji

G   Institute of Geology
Beijing
Director: Ma Xingyuan

G   Institute of Engineering Mechanics
Harbin
Director: He Lungjiang

G   Ministry of Coal Industry
Beijing
Minister: Gao Yanquen

G   Institute of Coal Geology and Exploration
Xian
Director: Yuan Yaoting

The Ministry consists of the following units:

G   Academy of Geological Sciences
Beijing
Director: Li Tingdong

G   Composite Geology Research Team
Shanghuxian
Director: Ma Shuzhao

G   Institute of Geology
Beijing
Director: Shen Qihan

G   Institute of Geology of Mineral Deposits
Beijing
Director:. Chen Yuchuen

G   Institute of Geology of Plateau Areas
Chengdu
Director: Liu Zengqian

G   Institute of Geologic Information
Beijing
Director: Feng Zhongguang

G   Institute of Geomechanics
Beijing
Director: Sun Dianqing

H   Institute of Hydrogeology and Engineering
Geology
Zhengding
Director: Zhang Zoughu

G   Institute of Karst
Guilin
Director: Yuan Daoxian

G   Institute of Geology and Mineral Resources
(Sedimentary Rocks)
Chengdu
Director: Liu Baojun

G   Institute of Geology and Mineral Resources
(Volcanic Rocks)
Nanjing
Director: Ye Zhizeng

G   Institute of Geology and Mineral Resources
Shenyang
Director:. Qin Nai

G   Institute of Geology and Mineral Resources
(Quaternary and Precambrian)
Tianjin
Director: Shen Baofeng

G   Institute of Geology and Mineral Resources
Xian
Director: Li Xianxi

continued . . .

CHINESE EARTH-SCIENCE INSTITUTIONS (continued)

G   National Bureau of Oceanography
Beijing

G   National Bureau of Surveying and Cartography
Beijing

G   Ministry of Petroleum Industry
Beijing
Minister: Tang Ke

G   Institute of Petroleum Exploration and
       Development
Beijing
Director: Shen Lisheng

G   Ministry of Nuclear Industry
Beijing
Minister: Jiang Xinxiong

G   Institute of Uranium Geology
Beijing

H   Ministry of Water Resources and Electric Power
Beijing
Minister: Qian Zhengying

     Bureau of Hydrology
Beijing
Director: Chen Jiaqi

C= Cartography
G= Geology
H= Hydrology
R= Minerals and petroleum regulation.

US Geological Survey, *Worldwide Directory of National Earth-Science Agencies and Related International Organizations* (1984), 27-29.

XVI CULTURE AND COMMUNICATIONS

POSTS AND TELECOMMUNICATIONS, 1984

		Percentage Increase Over 1983
Value of transactions (bn yuan)	2.49	12.0
Mail handled:		
Number of letters handled		12.0
Newspapers and magazines distributed		23.0
Long-distance telephone calls		18.9
Number of telephone subscribers in urban areas, yearend		13.3
Number of telegraphs		-3.3

Beijing Review, 12 (25 Mar 1985), v.

CULTURAL FACILITIES, 1984

Feature films produced	144
Full-length new films released	181
Cinemas and film projection teams (th)	178
Performing arts troupes	3,397
Cultural clubs	3,016
Public libraries	2,217
Museums	618
Archives	2,767
Radio stations	161
Hours of broadcasting per day	2,767
Radio transmitting and relay stations	595
Television stations	104
Television transmitting and relay stations, each with a capacity exceeding 1,000 watts	466
Plays shown on Central Television	454
National and provincial newspapers published (bn copies)	18.06
Magazines of all kinds published (bn copies)	2.18
Books and picture books published (bn copies)	6.27

Beijing Review, 12 (25 Mar 1985), vii-viii.

PUBLISHING, 1985

Scholarly Publishing—Each month the Chinese duplicate and distribute the contents of more than 1,800 foreign scholarly periodicals in English, Russian, Japanese and other languages to universities and colleges, research institutes, and persons engaged in research. Extensive information on Chinese publishing appears in Harry Campbell, "The present revival of scholarly publishing in China," *Scholarly Publishing* (Apr 1985), 223-37.

Tabloids—The proliferation of spicy Chinese tabloids is described in the *Asian Wall Street Journal Weekly* (3 Jun 1985), 6. One tabloid with an article on Jiang Qing, Mao's widow, reportedly sold a million copies and made a profit of about 30,000 yuan ($10,570).

Underground Writers—John Minford identifies several young underground writers in China who have gradually achieved some official recognition and been allowed to travel in the *Far Eastern Economic Review* (8 Aug 1985), 30-32. They include Bei Dao, the pen-name

continued . . .

PUBLISHING, 1985 (continued)

for the poet and short-story writer Zhao Zhenkai, 36; Yang Lian, a member of the new Misty School of poets; the abstract artist Yan li; Ma Desheng, a founder of the Xingxing group of artists; Gao Xingjian, the author of the plays *The Bus Stop* and *The Primitives*; and Chen Kaige, director of the film *Yellow Land*, who has been influenced by traditional Chinese landscape painting. On renewed interest in Chinese classics, see pages 32-33.

Translations—The "Chinese Literature Today" issue of *Renditions*, 19-20 (spring and autumn 1983) includes drama, poetry, literary and art criticism, and fiction by Chen Yingzhen, Xi Xi, and Zhao Zhenkai, in a dual-language edition.

Price of Newspapers and Magazines—The price of newspapers will not be allowed to exceed 8 fen and of journals and magazines 0.20 yuan. It is expected that a number of publications run by the people and localities will have to shut down because of the continuing increase in the cost of paper and the new limit on their retail price. *Hongqi* will still be sold for 0.26 yuan. *Cheng Ming*, 96 (1 Oct 1985), 6-10.

Fourth Writers' Congress—Information on the Fourth Writers' Congress appears in *Chinese Literature* (autumn 1985), 177-81. The Chinese Writers' Association now has 2,525 members.

Media—May Seto has written "Modernization and the Media" in the *China Business Review*, 12, 5 (Sep-Oct 1985), 10-13.

Remuneration for Authors—The basic fee for Chinese authors ranges between 15 and 20 yuan per 1,000 characters. About a third of book publishing is involved with educational materials for primary, secondary and higher schools and for radio and television educational institutions. There are 406 publishers in China. They issued some 40,000 titles in 1984. Hong Kong *Standard* (5 Nov 1985), 5.

Spiritual Pollution—During the campaign against "spiritual pollution" in 1984, Li Ping's novel *When Sunset Disappears* was criticized for betraying the principles of Marxism. The author had given a Kuomintang General human qualities. Dai Houying's *People, Ah, People* was condemned for showing Chinese socialism inhumane. Just months before, in a more liberal period, these themes had been encouraged. *Asian Wall Street Journal Weekly* (25 Feb 1985), 10.

Writers—Chinese writers and trends are discussed in Harrison E. Salisbury, "On the Literary Road: American Writers in China," New York *Times Book Review* (20 Jan 1985), 3, 24-25.

Book Imports—The China National Publications Import and Export Corp., which handles 85 percent of China's book imports, acquired 100,000 books in 1984, primarily dealing with science and technology. Allocations for books amounted to $38 million in 1984, almost six times that in 1977, and the allocation will rise to $55 million in 1985. There will be 18 book exhibits in over 25 cities during 1985, and the PRC will hold its first international book fair in Beijing in mid-1986 to show 40,000 titles. *China Daily* (19 May 1985), 1.

US Books for Exhibits—Some 1,200 books from 67 American academic publishers will be displayed at Beijing, Shanghai, Guangzhou, Chengdu, Fuzhou, and Urumqi beginning in November, 1985. The USIA will also produce and send 12,000 catalogues listing each book title. New York *Times* (14 Jun 1985), 22.

The Literary History of the Bouyei Nationality—Over 2.1 million Bouyeis live in Guizhou, Sichuan, and Yunnan provinces.

World Directory of Industry and Commerce—1986—This new publication will allow foreign firms to advertise and list their goods and services for Chinese buyers. A Japanese edition with some 1,100 firms was to be published in the fall of 1985. American and German editions are under consideration.

Selected Works of Li Dazhao—This collection, with 437 articles by one of the first Chinese Marxists Li Dazhao (1889-1927), is the most complete compilation of his works ever published.

Tibetan-Chinese Dictionary—The late Zhang Yixun has compiled a dictionary with some 53,000 Tibetan words.

continued . . .

PUBLISHING, 1985 (continued)

Science of Law—This volume of the Encyclopedia Sinica has contributions by 200 editors and specialists.

Almanac of China's Economy 1984—This was to appear in an English and a Chinese edition.

Encyclopedia of Literature—This edition is in Chinese.

Ye Wenfu—The Army poet Ye Wenfu, who was criticized in 1981 during a campaign against liberalism and Bai Hua, was published in the February issue of *Shikan* (*Journal of Poems*).

Selected Works of Liu Shaoqi—The second volume contains 38 important documents, including 25 which have not previously been published.

Concise Encyclopedia Britannica—The Chinese edition will contain 71,000 entries in 10 volumes. The entire series is to be ready by September, 1986.

Selected Works of Mao Zedong—The fifth volume of the *Works* has been withdrawn from circulation. It contains speeches and writings from September, 1949 through 1957, but Mao mentioned during the long interval between the publication of volumes 4 and 5 that he did not want it issued. Deng Xiaoping was, nonetheless, appointed editor in 1975, then removed from the job by the Gang of Four at the end of the year. The *Works* were published hurriedly in 1976 by Hua Guofeng, Wang Dongxing, and others. *Ta Kung Pao* (Hong Kong, 1 Feb 1985), 3.

Collection of Laws of the People's Republic of China, 1979-1984—This collection contains the 34 laws passed by the National People's Congress and its Standing Committee during the six years and other documents.

Kanjur—A new edition of the *Kanjur*, the 1,100-volume collection of Lamaist scriptures, will be issued in Tibet.

Folktales of the Lisu Nationality—This 10-volume edition has stories of a nationality in Yunnan province numbering 480,000.

Medicinal Book of China's Nationalities—This five-volume series describes some 800 medicinal herbs.

The Literature and Art Series of Tibet—This will appear in 21 volumes.

Zhou Enlai—A Profile—Reviewed in the *Beijing Review*, 1 (6 Jan 1986), 48-50, with a chapter on pages 16-29.

Sequel to *A Dream in the Red Mansion*—Zhang Zhi, 57, of Puyang, Henan, has written a sequel to the 18th-century novel by Cao Queqin, *A Dream in the Red Mansion*. Gao E, a friend of Cao's, produced a 40-chapter continuation of the 80-chapter novel. This lastest continuation will be published in 1 million copies.

Population Yearbook—Tian Xueyuan has been named the editor-in-chief of the first Chinese population yearbook, which should appear in late 1985.

History of China's Livestock and Poultry—This six-volume set was compiled from an eight-year survey of China's livestock and poultry beginning in 1976.

The Last Winter—This novel by Ma Yunpeng describing the Beiping-Tianjin campaign has been praised as healthy, progressive, and instructive for youth.

Contemporary China—Deng Liqun, a Secretary and Director of the Propaganda Department of the Central Committee, will be the chief editor of this series. One part will be comprehensive, a second part will deal with departments and trades, and the third will cover provinces, municipalities and autonomous regions. The last volume will appear in 1989.

Jin Ping Mei—A revised, abridged edition of *Jin Ping Mei*, a novel banned in China for more than 30 years, was to be published. The novel first appeared during the reign of Emperor Wan Li in the Ming dynasty. FBIS-CHI 55 (21 Mar 1985), K24.

Tourist Guides to China—An estimated 300-400,000 English-language China guidebooks will be sold in 1985. *Asian Wall Street Journal Weekly* (4 Feb 1985), 6.

Pergamon Agency—Britain's Pergamon Press has set up an agency in Beijing. It is the first foreign agency of this type to open an office in China. XNB (2 Aug 1985), 37.

continued . . .

PUBLISHING, 1985 (continued)

Textbooks—Macmillan and the Higher Education Press of China signed an agreement in October, 1985 to publish English textbooks for non-English-speaking countries. The British firm will compile the text *Modern English* on the basis of a Chinese syllabus for science and engineering students, and Chinese linguists will make final changes. The Chinese publisher will issue the books in the PRC, and Macmillan will publish them for the rest of the world. The texts and additional materials for teachers will appear between 1986 and 1989. XNB (9 Oct 1985), 6.

The Collection of Ancient and Contemporary Books—This encyclopedia was first edited during the reign of Emperor Kangxi (1662-1722), with additions during the reign of Emperor Yunzheng (1723-35). All 80 volumes should be published by 1988.

Literary Quantity—More than 200 novels, 1,500 novellas, 10,000 short stories, and 50,000 poems were published in China in 1985. XNB (5 Nov 1985), 30.

1983—An excerpt from Liang Heng and Judith Shapiro's *Intellectual Freedom in China After Mao, With a Focus on 1983* (1984) appears in the *Index on Censorship*, 13, 6 (Dec 1984), 6, 32. They list 10 major events during the year, such as greater independence for performing artists; the discussion of Marxist humanism and socialist alienation during the 100th anniversary of the death of Karl Marx; the model individual Zhang Haidi, introduced to encourage young people to overcome disillusionment; and the brief campaign against "spiritual pollution." More recent information may be found in the *Index on Censorship, 14*, 5 (Oct 1985), 35-37, and "China: How Much Freedom?" *New York Review of Books*, XXXII, 16 (24 Oct 1985), 14-16.

CHILDREN'S PRESS

Magazines for children	83
Newspapers for children	46
Combined circulation (mn)	50
By types:	
Total	129
News	50
Scholastic	27
Science-oriented	19
Specializing in fine arts, music, sports and recreation	13

Beijing Review, 24 (17 Jun 1985), 31.

REGULATIONS OF THE CHINESE WRITERS' ASSOCIATION, Adopted in Principle by the Fourth Congress of the Association 5 Jan 1985 and Revised by the Second Meeting of the Presidium of the Association 29 Mar 1985

General Rules

Article 1. The Chinese Writers Association is a specialized mass group of writers of all the nationalities of China united on a voluntary basis.

Article 2. Under the leadership of the CPC, the Chinese Writers Association takes Marxism-Leninism-Mao Zedong Thought as a guide, upholds the direction of making literature and art serve the people and serve socialism, carries the guideline of "letting a hundred flowers bloom and a hundred schools of thought contend," shows full respect for the laws governing literature and art, promotes democracy in literature and art, guarantees freedom in creation, and unites and organizes writers of all nationalities of the country in carrying out creative labor and developing and enlivening socialist literature with Chinese characteristics in a struggle to strengthen the building of socialist spiritual civilization and realize socialist modernization.

continued . . .

REGULATIONS OF THE CHINESE WRITERS' ASSOCIATION (continued)

Article 3. The Chinese Writers Association encourages writers to study hard, to get deeply involved with life, to emancipate the mind, to show the courage to create the new, to promote diversity in subject matter, and literary form and the free competition of various styles and schools of art, and to continuously improve the ideological and artistic levels of literary creations. It cites and gives awards for fine creations.

Article 4. The Chinese Writers Association organizes and stimulates activities involving literary comments and studies; promotes and encourages free discussion among holders of different viewpoints and different schools of thought; realistically guarantees the right to make criticisms and counter-criticisms; and works toward the healthy development of socialist literature.

Article 5. The Chinese Writers Association energetically unearths and trains new forces involved in literary writing and criticism and strives to enlarge the socialist literary ranks.

Article 6. The Chinese Writers Association shows respect for the traditions and features of the literature of various minority nationalities, energetically trains writers of minority nationalities, encourages the development of the literature of various minority nationalities, and strengthens literary exchanges among various nationalities.

Article 7. The Chinese Writers Association maintains extensive contacts with various mass literary societies and magazines devoted to enlivening socialist literature and renders them help where necessary and possible.

Article 8. The Chinese Writers Association widely unites all patriotic writers of all nationalities of the country, including those of Taiwan Province, Hong Kong, and Macao and those among Overseas Chinese and continuously seeks to expand and strengthen the patriotic literary united front.

Article 9. In line with the principles laid down in the Constitution, the Chinese Writers Association upholds the democratic rights and legitimate economic rights and interests of its members, safeguards its members' personal freedom and their freedom to carry out literary activities.

Article 10. The Chinese Writers Association energetically promotes literary exchanges between China and other countries, introduces Chinese literature to foreign countries, participates in international literary activities, and strengthens friendly relations with writers all over the world in an effort to promote the cause of world peace.

Members

Article 11. All those people who subscribe to this association's regulations and who have had literary works, theory-related comments, research-related works, and translations measuring up to set standards published, or have outstanding records of involvement in literary editing, teaching, and organizational efforts, can become members upon application by the person concerned through the recommendation of two members of the association or any of its local branches, subject to investigation and approval by the Secretariat of the association.

Article 12. The members of this association have the obligation to observe its regulations, pay membership fees and participate in its various activities; have the right to vote and stand for election and the right to dismiss the leaders of this association falling short of its requirements; and have the right to put forth criticisms and views to the association, the right to enjoy its welfare facilities, and other rights. The members of this association have the freedom to give up membership.

Article 13. The members of this association have the right to demand its protection where their personal freedom, fruits of labor, copyright, and other economic rights and interests are encroached upon, while this association has the duty to defend them and even lodge a complaint with the procuratorial and judicial organs.

Article 14. If a member of this association commits a serious offense against its regulations or forfeits his citizenship because of his crime, his membership is suspended or revoked, subject to approval by the Presidium of the association.

continued . . .

REGULATIONS OF THE CHINESE WRITERS' ASSOCIATION (continued)

Organization

Article 15. The organ with supreme power of this association is its congress whose deputies are separately elected by its members in various parts of the country. During the closing period of the congress, the council undertakes to carry out its functions. During the closing period of the council, the Presidium takes charge of the association's work as a standing body in charge.

Article 16. The congress of the association meets every 3 years, as convened by the council. Where necessary, the council is allowed to advance or postpone the date of its convention, the convocation of the congress not to be delayed for more than 1 year.

Article 17. The council is made up of councillors elected at the congress, who undertake to carry out the decisions of the congress. The council meets once every year, as called by the Presidium. Where necessary, the Presidium is allowed to advance or postpone the date of its convention, the date of its convocation not to be delayed for more than 1 and 1/2 years.

Article 18. The Presidium is made up of a chairman and some vice chairmen and members elected at the council. It undertakes to carry out the decisions of the congress and the council. The meeting of the Presidium is called by its chairman in case of need. A meeting is held at least every 6 months.

Article 19. The Presidium recommends a number of people to form a Secretariat, which undertakes to take care of the association's routine work. Various work organs are set up in case of need.

Article 20. A number of advisers are recommended by the congress or employed by the Presidium. The advisers can attend council and Presidium meetings as observers playing an advisory and stimulating role in the business of the writers association.

Article 21. This association renders guidance and help for its branches set up in various provinces, autonomous regions, and municipalities directly under the central government, in regard to the guidelines for literary work and relevant business matters.

In light of local conditions, the branches of this association in various areas separately formulate their own regulations and recruit their own members.

The members of this association who live in different areas can at the same time join the local branches.

Operating Funds

Article 22. The sources of this association's funds are: (1) state subsidies; (2) income from various cultural enterprises and undertakings launched by this association; (3) social contributions; (4) membership fees.

This association energetically serves the welfare of writers, setting up sites for writing, giving needy writers allowances for trips taken in connection with writing, providing extra allowances for living expenses for writers who are old and weak and often ill, or who are plagued by some other particular problems.

Supplementary Article

Article 23. The right to revise this association's regulations belongs to its congress.

Renmin Ribao (6 Apr 1985), 3, translated in FBIS-CHI 70 (11 Apr 1985), K10/13.

FILM NEWS, 1985

Film Industry Problems—Six films attracted more than 1 million movie-goers in Beijing in 1984. Five films attracted over a half million viewers each in Chongqing, but only one did so during the first six months of 1985. A theater in Tianjin sold just one ticket for *A General*

continued . . .

FILM NEWS, 1985 (continued)

and an Orphan. A survey of major Chinese cities indicated that the movie audience fell 25-30 percent in the first quarter of 1985 compared to the corresponding period in 1984. Film revenue for distributors dropped 35 percent. The reasons may be declining quality and television in more Chinese homes. *Beijing Review,* 29 (22 Jul 1985), 29.

Dunhuang—China and Japan will coproduce the movie *Dunhuang,* based on the novel by Yasushi Inoue written in 1959. Kinji Fukasaku will direct the film. The movie will be made in Gansu and should be released in 1987. Previous Sino-Japanese coproductions have included *The Game Yet to Finish* and *Roof Tile of Tenbyo.* XNB (6 Jul 1985), 52-53.

Xiangshi Inn—This film by director Dong Kena, 56, portrays a young woman trying to modernize an inn in a mountain village in Hunan. The former manager of the inn sabotages her efforts with the support of the county Party secretary. The young woman finally leaves in despair. The movie was previewed in July, 1985 but not distributed. New York *Times* (2 Oct 1985), 34.

Films Produced—China produced 144 feature films in 1984, including more than 60 with contemporary themes. They included:

Wreaths—A story about China's war with Vietnam.

Life—A movie on a young school teacher in the countryside.

Breakthrough from Zero—A documentary.

Don't Waste Your Youth—A documentary.

100 Days in Hong Kong—A documentary.

Alarm—A documentary on economic crime.

Bus Ride—A short film on problems of urban transportation.

Invisible Shackles—A documentary exposing prejudice against women.

Sun Yat-sen—A two-part color feature on Sun Yat-sen will be made by the Zhujiang Film Studio in Guangzhou.

Marco Polo—This five-hour color film in four parts is a condensation of the tv series produced jointly by Italy and China in 1981.

Gesser Khan—A joint-venture film of the Tibetan folk epic will be made by the Qinghai Film Service Company and the Kwun Lun Film Production Company Ltd. of Hong Kong.

Four Generations Under One Roof—This 28-episode television serial was rebroadcast in August, 1985. It is based on a novel by Lao She, and recounts the lives of people living on a lane in Peiping during the Japanese occupation.

Dubbing—More than 100 foreign films are dubbed into standard Chinese each year, and several are dubbed into Cantonese and other dialects. Some 469 films were dubbed in minority languages in 1984. Minority languages are broadcast over one loudspeaker and the original language is broadcast over another. The audience sits in the appropriate section of the outdoor theater to hear the dialect or language they understand. *Beijing Review,* 16 (22 Apr 1985), 31.

Women Directors—There are more than 30 women film directors in China. Seven of the 15 best films of 1984 selected by the Ministry of Culture were directed by women, including Shi Xiaohua (*Bubbling Spring*), Wang Ruwei (*Sunset River*), and Lu Xiaoya (*Girl in the Red Shirt*). XNB (31 Oct 1985), 34.

Documentaries—About 100 newsreels and documentaries have been sold abroad in the last two years. They have provided almost 40 percent of China's film export revenue. XNB (27 Apr 1985), 41.

Spheric-Screen Cinema—China's first spheric-screen cinema opened in Fuzhou, Fujian in February, 1985. The theater was installed through a joint venture with US Domes America Inc. Beijing, Shanghai, Hangzhou, and Wenzhou are planning similar theaters. The first Chinese spheric-screen film, *Navigation Channels of the Huangpu River,* was recently shot in Shanghai. XNB (18 Feb 1985), 54-55.

Trial Balloon—*The Yin & the Yankee* (1983) documents attempts by publisher Malcolm Forbes ("The difference between men and boys is the price of their toys.") to be allowed

continued . . .

FILM NEWS, 1985 (continued)

free-flight balloon rides in China. Forbes and others traveled between Xian and Beijing in 1982, and the film shows his party racing through villages on Harley-Davidsons waving wildly at bewildered peasants along roads, complaining that they are being forced to drive their motorcycles too slowly, and having very little luck dealing with security officials about free flights near military installations. There are several nicely photographed scenes and lots of fun in the movie. Forbes also led the first and last group to motorcycle across the USSR several years ago.

Hong Kong People in Shenzhen—This film, jointly produced by the Beijing Film Studio and Hong Kong's Tung Luen Motion Picture Ltd., is being made by several children of China's leaders. The female lead, Li Juanjuan, is the wife of the fifth son of Premier Zhao Ziyang. The son of State Councillor Gu Mu is a scriptwriter, and Ling Zi, the daughter of Ye Jianying, is its director. *South China Morning Post* (26 Sep 1985), 18.

Film Surveys—Recent Chinese films are discussed in *China Reconstructs*, XXXIV, 2 (Feb 1985), 8-13.

China Film Association—The CFA has 4,000 members in 21 local branches. Xia Yan is the Chairman of the Association. FBIS-CHI 79 (24 Apr 1985), K17.

HUNDRED FLOWERS FILM AWARDS, 23 May 1985

Best Feature Film—"Wreaths at the Foot of the Mountain"

Other Winners—"Life;" "Girl in a Red Skirt"

Best Male Leading Actor—Lu Xiaohe, 40, for "Wreaths at the Foot of the Mountain"

Best Male Supporting Actor—He Wei, 29, for "Wreaths at the Foot of the Mountain"

Best Female Actress—Wu Yufang, 20, for her role in "Life"

Best Female Supporting Actress—Wang Yumei, 50, for "Wreaths at the Foot of the Mountain"

These awards are presented by *Popular Cinema*. More than a million readers voted in this year's poll XNB (24 May 1985), 40-41; (25 May 1985), 51. The Hundred Flowers Award was begun in 1962, suspended in 1966 when the film magazine was shut down, and resumed in 1980. A second film prize, the Golden Rooster Award, was started in 1981. Academics and professionals select the winners. The Ministry of Culture presents a third award for best films. *China Reconstructs*, XXXIV, 2 (Feb 1985), 14-15.

TELEVISION PROGRAMMING, 1985

Foreign Programming—China will allow foreign companies to produce programs for Central Television. Yue-Sai Kan, who produces a weekly program on Asia for American cable, will prepare a half-hour series of "mini-documentaries" on foreign art, politics, business and life styles called "One World" for CTV. Mrs. Kan will receive the first $1 million in revenues before expenses from the three-and-one-half minutes of commercials per half hour, and the remaining profits will be divided 50-50 with the Chinese.

CBS is selling companies 32 minutes of commercial time on CTV over a one-year period for $300,000. CBS programs will be from American tv with dubbing in Chinese. CCTV has chosen the made-for-tv movies "Muggable Mary," about a woman police decoy, and "Quarterback Princess," describing a girl who goes out for her high-school football team. *Asian Wall Street Journal Weekly* (28 Jan 1985), 20; New York *Times* (17 Jan 1985), 22.

continued . . .

TELEVISION PROGRAMMING, 1985 (continued)

Shanghai Television—There are three channels in Shanghai: entertainment (STV), educational, and network. Broadcasts occur only mornings and evenings. The salary of broadcasters on the most popular program is $40 a month. "World Outlook" is a news program, and "Friends of Living" relates life styles. There are 60 million viewers in the Shanghai area. PM Magazine (18 Feb 1985).

Taiwanese Novel Filmed—The Chinese are filming their first novel by a Taiwanese author, Bai Xianyong. The tv film is based on *Azalea, As Red As Blood*, and describes the unhappy life and suicide in Taiwan of a retired soldier from Hunan. Two other novels from Taiwan, Yao Yiwei's *Red Nose* and Lin Haiyin's *Old Days in Southern Beijing*, have been adapted for movies and the stage. XNB (11 Mar 1985), 1.

First Tibetan TV Film—Narration by a Wife was the first tv movie directed and performed by Tibetans. Its screenwriter and director was Qamba Yundan, 37, an actor in at least 20 films and plays since 1962. The first tv play was dubbed into the Tibetan language three years ago. XNB (23 Feb 1985), 77.

Television—Molly E. Wyman has written "The Lure of Television" in the *China Business Review*, 5 (Sep-Oct 1985), 14-19. It includes a table on foreign participation at China's major television production facilities (16-17).

Programs from the US—Several American television programs for Chinese viewing are mentioned in the *New Yorker* (1 Apr 1985), 30-31.

TELEVISION PLAYS PRODUCED, 1983-85

1983	400
1984	800
1985 est.	1,300+

Beijing Review, 48 (2 Dec 1985), 8.

BEST TELEVISION PLAYS, 1984

Best Serial—The Snowstorm Came Tonight

The serial also won awards for the best director, videotaping, male supporting role, music and sound.

Best Television Plays—The Enlightenment of News; Into the Distance

Into the Distance also won awards for the best screenplay, male lead, female supporting role, and lighting.

The awards are known as the Sky Flier. There was no award in 1984 for female lead, and no second prizes were given. The PRC began to produce tv plays in 1980. In 1981 one hundred were produced. The number rose to 800 in 1984, and 1,300 are planned for 1985. XNB (17 Jun 1985), 30.

ENGLISH-LANGUAGE BROADCASTS OF RADIO BEIJING

	GMT	Local Standard Time	Metre Bands	kHz
NORTH AMERICA (EAST COAST)	00:00-01:00	19:00-20:00 (E.S.T.)	19,19	15385,15520
	11:00-12:00	06:00-07:00 (E.S.T.)	25	11860
	12:00-13:00	07:00-08:00 (E.S.T.)	49,31	6160,9820
NORTH AMERICA (WEST COAST)	03:00-04:00	19:00-20:00 (P.S.T.)	25,19,16	11970, 15520,17795
	04:00-05:00	20:00-21:00 (P.S.T.)	25, 16	11970, 17795
THE SOUTH PACIFIC	08:30-09:30	18:30-19:30 (Aust. E.S.T.) 20:30-21:30 (N.Z.S.T.)	30, 25, 19	9700, 11755, 15195
	09:30-10:30	19:30-20:30 (Aust. E.S.T.) 21:30-22:30 (N.Z.S.T.)	30, 25, 19	9700, 11755, 15195
SOUTHEAST ASIA	12:00-13:00	19:00-20:00 (Western Indonesia, Bangkok) 20:00-21:00 (Singapore) 20:00-21:00 (Ho Chi Minh City, Manila) 18:30-19:30 (Rangoon)	223, 25, 19, 25	1341, 11600, 15280 11755
	13:00-14:00	20:00-21:00 (Western Indonesia, Bangkok) 21:00-22:00 (Singapore) 21:00-22:00 (Ho Chi Minh City, Manila)	223, 25, 19, 25	1341, 11600, 15280 11755
SOUTH ASIA	14:00-15:00	19:30-20:30 (Delhi, Colombo) 19:00-20:00 (Rawalpindi) 20:00-21:00 (Dacca) 19:40-20:40 (Kathmandu)	25, 19	11600, 15165

continued . . . .

ENGLISH-LANGUAGE BROADCASTS OF RADIO BEIJING (continued)

	GMT	Local Standard Time	Metre Bands	kHz
	15:00-16:00	20:30-21:30 (Delhi, Colombo)	25, 19	11600, 15165
		20:00-21:00 (Rawalpindi)		
		21:00-22:00 (Dacca)		
		20:40-21:40 (Kathmandu)		
EAST AND SOUTH AFRICA	16:00-17:00	18:00-19:00 (Cape Town, Harare)	25, 19, 19	11600, 15095, 15165
		19:00-20:00 (Dar-es-Salaam)		
	17:00-18:00	19:00-20:00 (Cape Town, Harare)	25, 19, 19	11600, 15095, 15165
		20:00-21:00 (Dar-es-Salaam)		
WEST AND NORTH AFRICA	19:30-20:30	18:45-19:45 (Monrovia)	31, 26, 25	9440, 11515, 11905
		19:30 20:30 (Accra, Freetown)		
		20:30-21:30 (Lagos)		
		21:30-22:30 (Cairo)		
	20:30-21:30	19:45-20:45 (Monrovia)	31, 26, 25	9440, 11515, 11905
		20:30-21:30 (Accra, Freetown)		
		21:30-22:30 (Lagos)		
		22:30-23:30 (Cairo)		
EUROPE	19:00-20:00	20:00-21:00 (London, Stockholm, Paris)	30, 26	9860, 11500
	21:00-22:00	22:00-23:00 (London, Stockholm, Paris)	30, 26	9860, 11500

Exact dates for these programs will be announced on the air.

Beijing Review, 24 (17 Jun 1985), 36.

TV SATELLITE RECEIVING STATIONS

There are now 53 stations in China. More than 1,000 will be constructed within the next two years. The PRC will purchase two foreign telecommunications satellites for launch in 1987. China planned to orbit its first domestically made tv satellite at the end of 1985. Broadcast time will increase more than eight times to 172 hours a week, and reception will grow from 30 to 64 percent of the country.

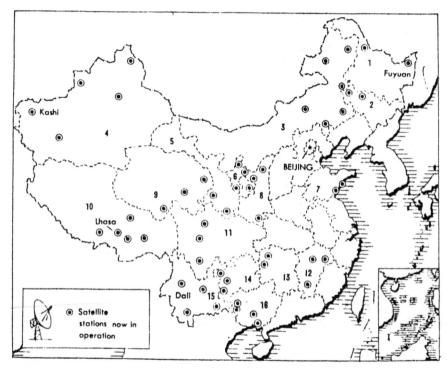

1. Heilongjong Province
2. Jiln Province
3. Inner Mongolia Autonomous Region
4. Xinjiang Uygur Autonomous Region
5. Gansu Province
6. Ningxia Hui Autonomous Region
7. Shandong Province
8. Shaanxi Province
9. Qinghai Province
10. Tibet Autonomous Region
11. Sichuan Province
12. Jiangxi Province
13. Hunan Province
14. Guizhou Province
15. Yunnan Province
16. Guangxi Zhuang Autonomous Region

Beijing Review, 39 (30 Sep 1985), 9.

THEATER, MUSIC, AND DANCE, 1984

John Denver Concert—John Denver has been negotiating with the Chinese to arrange a televised concert. Denver sang for Deng Xiaoping at the Kennedy Center in Washington in 1979 and for Premier Zhao Ziyang in New York in 1984. His "Take Me Home, Country Roads" is a favorite English-language pop song in the PRC. The Chinese have suggested an indoor location for a concert, but Denver wants a well-known outdoor site. He had hoped to perform on 1 September 1985, but now foresees a concert in the spring of 1986. He has not been able to find a sponsor or network for the show. CBS, "Nightwatch" (17 Jul 1985); Minneapolis *Star and Tribune* (5 Jul 1985), 6C.

Salaries—The monthly salary of a musician in a Chinese orchestra averages about $22. Musicians must supplement this low wage by tutoring or playing in a pop musical group. New York *Times* (4 Sep 1985), 22.

Rock—The British duo "Wham," the first major Western rock group to visit the PRC, performed at the Workers' Stadium in Beijing and Guangzhou in April, 1985. Hits include "Wake Me Up Before You Go-Go." Back-up dancers wore black leather outfits. *Time* (22 Apr 1985), 31. Deng Pufang, the son of Deng Xiaoping, promoted a rock concert in March, 1985 at the 19,000-seat Capital Gymnasium in Beijing. Composed of foreign musicians, the band played a combination of rock, reggae, and African tunes. So far, *yaogunye* ("shake-roll music") has been confined to major cities. New York *Times* (26 Feb 1985), 22.

Guan Sushaung—It has been revealed that Guan Sushaung, a famous actress of the Beijing opera, made a profit of 70,000 yuan during a tour of Sichuan with the opera troupe, but had only 7,000 net profit left when she returned to Yunnan province. *Renmin Ribao* (15 Apr 1985).

Huang Zuolin—Biographical information on the theater director Huang Zuolin may be found in *Chinese Literature* (spring 1985), 203-09.

Wu Xiaobang—A biography of Wu Xiaobang, dancer and choreographer, appears in *Chinese Literature* (summer 1985), 216-23.

Uygur Culture—Colin Mackerras has published "Uygur Performing Arts in Contemporary China," *China Quarterly*, 101 (Mar 1985), 58-77.

Beijing Opera—Kenneth Rea notes that Beijing opera has been losing its audience to television and disco. He reviews Wu Zuguang's *The Three Beatings of Tao Sanchun*, the revival of a 1962 Beijing opera, currently starring Wang Yuzheng. Manchester *Guardian* (24 Jul 1985), 9.

Cultural Restraints—Zhang Xing, perhaps the most popular male singer in China, has been arrested in Shanghai for "seducing and philandering with many women under the guise of courting them." Zhang had a best-selling record, "I'm Saying Goodbye to You," in the fall. The magazine *Democracy and Law* published two letters in September claiming that he put money above everything else. Zhang earned about 100 yuan per concert compared to 10-30 ($3.12-$9.37) for most singers. The popular play *Wo Men* (We), about seven teenagers who survived the Cultural Revolution, has been canceled in Beijing. A five-day writers' workshop in the capital ended with officials asking for more "self-restraint" and use of literature to serve socialism. Minneapolis *Star and Tribune* (29 Nov 1985), 8B; Washington *Post* (23 Nov 1985), A15.

Cultural Relations—The PRC has 104 cultural relations agreements with 136 countries. Fifty-eight Chinese have won awards in international music competitions since 1980. XNB (30 Jan 1985), 17.

Shakespeare—Shanghai will hold a month-long Shakespeare festival in April, 1986. His works were banned during the Cultural Revolution (1966-76), but *The Merchant of Venice* and *Macbeth* were staged in 1980. The festival will include productions of *Hamlet, Othello, King Lear, The Tempest, Much Ado About Nothing, Twelfth Night,* and *The Merchant of Venice.* Associated Press (4 Dec 1985).

Acrobats—*Der Spiegel*, 46 (11 Nov 1985), 264, 267, describes the Vienna performance of acrobats from schools in Beijing and Anhui.

ART NEWS, 1985

Revolutionary Kitsch—Porcelain, bamboo, plastic and metal objects, including figurines, buttons, fans, clocks and other revolutionary trinkets, were displayed in 1985 at the Galerie-70 in West Berlin. *Der Spiegel*, 20 (13 May 1985), 242-43. A more sophisticated show featuring 126 "Treasures from the Forbidden City" was part of the Horizonte-Festival in West Berlin. See *Der Spiegel*, 19 (6 May 1985), 202-03.

German Paintings—The first exhibition of 19th-century German paintings in the PRC was held in Shanghai in September and Beijing in October, 1985. It included 74 landscapes, portraits, and still lifes in the Classical, Romantic, Realist, Naturalist, and Impressionist styles. XNB (3 Sep 1985), 37.

Photography—Photographs of China by Hiroji Kubota appear in *Life* (Dec 1985), 150-56. An exhibition of photos of the PRC was held at the New York International Center of Photography late in 1985, and would then tour Boston, Miami, and seven other cities in North America.

According to a survey by the Chinese Photographers' Association, there are 5 million cameras in use by professional photographers, and 2 million produced for the domestic market in 1985. Two universities have recently opened photographic courses, and six more planned to offer photographic specialties in the fall. At Beijing's Photo Studio, the demand for color prints has increased from 150,000 at the beginning of the year to 320,000 in April, 1985. XNB (9 May 1985), 42-43.

Valuables Returned—Since 1979 the government has searched 60,000 households in Beijing and found 25,909 pictures and calligraphy, 113,659 books, and 4,748 art objects in crates and warehouses which had been taken during the Cultural Revolution. Some 2,830,000 valuables worth 69.9 million yuan (more than DM70 million) have been returned. Confiscated objects are being displayed in the Beijing suburb of Chongwen so their owners can identify and reclaim them. *Der Spiegel*, 14 (1 Apr 1985), 132-33.

Art Exhibits—Issues of the *Worldwide Art Catalogue Bulletin* review shows of Chinese art and provide catalogue information.

Central Art Institute—Jamey Gambrell mentions several Chinese painters and shows a few works in "A Visit to the Central Art Institute in Beijing," *Art in America*, 73, 3 (Mar 1985), 133-37. No prints were available at the painting Academy. Also see Hal Foster, "China is Near," in the same issue, 126-32.

Albertina Collection—The China Art Gallery in Beijing displayed 74 works from the Albertina in Vienna 12 September-2 October 1985. XNB (13 Sep 1985), 38.

TELEPHONES PER 100 PERSONS

Sweden	85
US	79
USSR	10
China	0.5

Report of the Commission for Worldwide Telecommunications Development (1985).

TELEPHONE NEWS, 1985

ITT—ITT has agreed to a joint venture in Shanghai for the production of more than 2 million equivalent lines over 10 years. *ITT Annual Report* (1985), 6.

Alcatel—CIT Alcatel SA will provide 100,000 new lines to Beijing by 1987, with 28,000 put in during 1985. The capital currently has 140,000 telephone lines for a population of 9.5 million. Alcatel will also provide 2,000 switchboards for domestic long-distance calls. *Asian Wall Street Journal Weekly* (15 Apr 1985), 16. Only 5 percent of Beijing's citizens have phones. FBIS-CHI 71 (12 Apr 1985), G1.

continued . . .

TELEPHONE NEWS, 1985 (continued)

Belgian-Joint Venture—As a result of an agreement signed in July, 1983, the Shanghai Bell Telephone Equipment Manufacturing Company, a Sino-Belgian joint venture, will install 30,000 lines in 1985 with imported parts, and 70,000 in 1986. The annual output of lines will reach 300,000 by 1988. FBIS-CHI 75 (18 Apr 1985), G3.

Plans—The PRC will increase the number of inner-city telephones by 3 million and the number of long-distance lines by 60,000 during the Seventh Five Year Plan (1986-90). The main structure of the Shanghai Postal and Telecommunications Center and the Beijing International Postal and Telecommunications Bureau will be completed by the end of 1985. FBIS-CHI 185 (24 Sep 1985), K16/17.

Telephone Exchange Venture—A Sino-US joint venture to manufacture program-controlled digital telephone exchanges was begun 16 October 1985. It will build 150,000 units and 20,000 m^2 of multi-layer printed electronic circuit boards each year. XNB (17 Oct 1985), 52.

New Telephone Office—The Dongdan Telephone Office started operations in Beijing 11 December 1985. It has 40,000 channels and urban and suburban direct-dial equipment. Floor space is 25,000 m^2. *Beijing Review*, 52 (30 Dec 1985), 9.

NEW AND RESUMED CHINESE JOURNALS, MAGAZINES AND NEWSPAPERS, 1985

China Electronics		W	Jan	1—
China Pictorial	Overseas edition.	M	Jan	1—
China Reconstructs	Overseas edition.	M	Jan	1—
Read Extensively (Bolan Qunshu)	This is a magazine.	M	Jan	5—
Open Door (Kaifeng)	This is a magazine.	M	Jan	8—
Sports Enthusiasts (Tiyu Aihaozhe)	This is a publication of the All-China Sports Federation and Hong Kong's International Sports Co.		Jan	20—
Mainland and Taiwan Monthly (Dalu Taiwan Yuekan)		M	Feb—	
China	Ding Ling edits this new monthly.	M	Feb—	
Science and Technology Review	Resumed in 1980, but publication interrupted for technical reasons.		Feb—	
Chinese Writers (Zhongguo Zuojia)	Feng Mu edits this literary journal.	BM	Feb	11—
Divine Sword (Shen Jian)	This deals with national defense.			
Information News on Transferring Military Industrial Technology to Civil Circles (Jungong Jishu Zhuan Minyong Xinsi Bao)	This is a newspaper of the National Published by the Defense Technology Information Committee.		Mar	15—
International Business News (Guoji Shangbao)	This is an economic newspaper in Chinese.	BW	Apr	1—
Chinese Patents and Trademarks	This Hong Kong magazine is edited by Liu Gushu.		Apr—	
Voice of the Masses (Qunyan)	This magazine will discuss political and and academic issues.	M	Apr—	

continued . . .

NEW AND RESUMED CHINESE JOURNALS, MAGAZINES AND NEWSPAPERS, 1985
(continued)

Machinery of the Special Economic Zone (Tequ Jixie)	This is published in Fujian.		May—
Journal of Traditional Medicine (Zhong Yi Bao)	This newsletter appears every 10 days.		
China Daily	A business weekly will be added to the China Daily for North American readers.		Jun 19—
Literary and Art Gazette (Wenyi Bao)	This will change from a monthly magazine to a four-page weekly paper. Xie Yongwang will be the editor-in-chief.	W	
People's Daily (Renmin Ribao)	An overseas edition will be printed in old-fashioned characters rather than the simplified forms adopted in 1949.	D	Jul 1—
Chess and Bridge Weekly		W	Jul 2—
China Labor and Personnel Newspaper		W	Jul—
Kexue	This has resumed publication after 25 years. Its editor-in-chief is Zhou Guangzhao.		
Forum on Science and Technology	This is a magazine.	BM	Oct—
Electronics for China	This is the first magazine in a series called Modern Technology and Equipment.	M	Oct—
Industry Prospects	On Shanghai's economic and technological developments, this monthly appears in Chinese and English editions.	M	Nov 7—
Literature for Chinese Blind Children	This is the first Chinese magazine in Braille for blind children.	BM	Nov—

M = monthly; W = weekly; D = daily; BW = bi-weekly; BM = bi-monthly
Compiled from press reports.

THE PRESS, 1985

Xinhua News Agency—The *Asian Wall Street Journal Weekly* (8 Apr 1985), 10, carries an article about the Xinhua News Agency in Hong Kong. Its director, Xu Jiatun, 69, is a member of the Central Committee and former First Secretary of Jiangsu province. His chief deputy is Li Chuwen, once a Protestant clergyman from Shanghai. Geng Yan, the daughter of former Defense Minister Geng Biao, and Qiao Zonghuai, son of the late Foreign Minister Qiao Guanhua, are employees of the Agency. Xinhua has 5,000 employees throughout the world, including 1,000 correspondents and editors inside the PRC and 300 overseas. The Agency has directed the Chinese Communist Party in Hong Kong.

Brian Eads describes changes at the Hong Kong branch of Xinhua as the removal of the "East River Gang" in the *Spectator* (26 Oct 1985), 11-12, 14. This group had a guerrilla base for operations against the Japanese near a tributary of the Pearl River in Guangdong province.

Neibu Cankao—Michael Schoenhals assembles information on *Neibu Cankao* (Internal Reference) in "Elite Information in China," *Problems of Communism*, XXXIV, 5 (Sep-Oct 1985), 65-71. This is the most important controlled-circulation bulletin in the PRC. Schoenhals believes it began publication in 1951 and has a circulation of 1-2,000.

continued . . .

THE PRESS, 1985 (continued)

Director of *Renmin Ribao*—Qian Liren, 63, the former Director of the International Liaison Department of the Central Committee, has been appointed the Director of the newspaper *Renmin Ribao*. *Wen Wei Po* (17 Dec 1985), 2, with his biography.

MUSEUMS, 1984-85

Museums—China opened 150 museums in 1984. The total has reached 700. *Beijing Review*, 29 (22 Jul 1985), 8.

Literary Museum—The Museum of Modern Chinese Literature opened in Beijing in 1985. Its collection contains more than 60,000 printed volumes, 200 manuscripts, letters and diaries, calligraphy, more than 1,700 photographs and portraits, and phonograph records and video-tapes on modern Chinese writers and poets from the May 4th Movement in 1919. The museum has the collections of Mao Dun and Ba Jin. *Za rubezhom*, 16 (12-18 Apr 1985), 23.

XVII HEALTH, EDUCATION AND WELFARE

MEDICAL NEWS, 1985

Private Physicians—There are more than 80,000 private physicians in China, an increase of 63 percent over the previous year. *Beijing Review*, 17 (29 Apr 1985), 8.

Heart Disease—Prior to 1976 the death rate among acute cardial infarction patients sent to a hospital was 25 percent. It has now dropped to about 12 percent. XNB (1 Jun 1985), 20-21.

Anti-Cancer Drug—A new anti-cancer drug has been made at the Shanghai Materica Medica Institute. The drug, aclacinomycin a, is said to have one-tenth the toxicity of the conventional drug adriamycin. XNB (27 May 1985), 36.

Mental Illness—In 1974 the Chinese Institute of Mental Health started a survey of the Haidian District of Beijing. It found that the most common mental illness in the district was schizophrenia (about 2 cases per 1,000 people). Some 77 percent of the 341 cases in Haidian were judged serious. Two-thirds of the patients had case histories of more than five years, and 20 percent had been ill for 10 or more years. A survey taken three months after a home-care mental-health program was begun showed that 65 percent of the 211 chronic schizophrenics exhibited a marked improvement. *China Reconstructs*, XXXIV, 5 (May 1985), 58-59, 61. "Schizophrenia" is a term sometimes applied to political dissidents in Communist countries. Some of these figures may represent dissidents.

Medical Fees—In the countryside, peasants must pay a small fee to use clinics and half the cost of drugs or an operation. "Heart of the Dragon" (PBS, part 3, 20 May 1985).

Alpha Interferon—Chinese scientists have genetically engineered human alpha interferon. Professor Hou Yunde of the National Center for Preventative Medicine's Virology Institute and Associate Professor Liu Xinyuan of the Academy of Sciences' Biochemistry Institute in Shanghai have led a group to produce interferon since 1979. The first natural white cell interferon of clinical grade was made in the PRC in 1981, and the interferon gene was cloned from a white cell in 1982. By 1984 the interferon was produced and purified to a homogeneity for clinical use. The interferon will be used to treat some viral diseases and malignant tumors. XNB (14 Feb 1985), 28-29.

Henan Medical College—The Zhang Zhongjing College of Traditional Chinese Medicine opened in February, 1985 at Nanyang, Henan. Its first 150 students will enroll in three-year courses in the fall of 1985. XNB (7 Feb 1985), 37-38.

Opium—Opium is said to be available among mountain tribes living in Yunnan along the border with Burma. In the past year, at least six persons have reportedly been shot for trafficking in opium. New York *Times* (20 May 1985), 6.

Heart Research—Hoechst AG and the Shanghai Institute of the Pharmaceutical Industry have signed a 10-year pact to exchange scientists and technology. The program will try to develop medicines for the heart and the circulatory system. *Asian Wall Street Journal Weekly* (4 May 1985), 11.

Tampons—Tambrands Inc. of Lake Success, New York will form a joint venture to make tampons and sanitary pads in the PRC for domestic use and export. Tambrands will own 60 percent of the venture, and will provide equipment, technology and funding. The company will be in Liaoning. *Asian Wall Street Journal Weekly* (28 Jan 1985), 20.

Artificial Limb Research Institute—An artificial limb research institute will be built in Beijing. It is to cost 4.8 million yuan ($2 million) and be completed in 1986. There are 49 artificial limb factories in the PRC. XNB (2 Jan 1985), 18-19.

Retarded Children—A survey of 220,000 children throughout China found that about 3 percent were mentally retarded. Another survey determined that there were more than 6,000 mentally retarded children in Beijing and its suburbs. The Beijing Blind Children's School has 150 students. It was begun in 1982. *Beijing Review*, 11 (18 Mar 1985), 20, 22.

continued . . .

MEDICAL NEWS, 1985 (continued)

Peasant Doctors—There are 3.2 million barefoot doctors in the countryside. XNB (8 Feb 1985), 21.

Blindness—China claims that about 5 million persons are blind, or appxoximately half the average of 1 percent in developing countries. The discrepancy may be one of definition, however, and by World Health Organization standards, the actual number could be closer to 10 million. New York *Times* (9 Jun 1985), 8.

Name Restored—The Capital Hospital in Beijing was renamed the Union Medical College Hospital in June, 1985. This was the name given it by the China Medical Board, which had been set up by the Rockefeller Foundation in 1914. The facility was called the Anti-Imperialist Hospital between 1967 and 1972. It currently has 700 beds, 28 clinical departments, and four research institutes. The hospital will begin a five-year $46 million expansion from 1986, increasing the number of beds to 1,200. Its medical school will be known as the Beijing Union Medical College. New York *Times* (9 Jun 1985), 8.

Top Killers—A 1983 survey of 28 cities in China showed that 21.4 percent of fatalities were from heart diseases, 21.3 percent from cerebral diseases, and 20.5 percent from malignant tumors. These three diseases were fifth, sixth and seventh in 1957. They were the top three killers in May, 1985. Approximately 26 percent of all deaths in Shanghai result from cancer. Since 1980 the incidence has been around 14,000 annually, 10,000 of which are fatal. About 55 per 100,000 men and 23 per 100,000 women are diagnosed with stomach cancer each year. *Beijing Review*, 39 (30 Sep 1985), 10. .

Children's Health—A 1983 survey of 179,000 children found 98.6 percent of those 14 and younger to be healthy. The share of unhealthy children among those 2 and younger averaged 1 percent. The rate rose to 1.6 percent among 14-year-olds, primarily from illnesses contracted as they aged and from an increase in the number of deaf-mutes. *Beijing Review*, 42 (21 Oct 1985), 22.

Red Cross Society—The Chinese Red Cross Society has a membership of 1.4 million, with branches in 26 provinces, municipalities and autonomous regions. The Society was founded in 1904 and reorganized in 1950. A national Red Cross training center is being built. XNB (25 Jan 1985), 28.

Cell Biology Lab—China and the Federal Republic of Germany have built the first guest laboratory of cell biology in the PRC. The Shanghai Institute of Cell Biology Academic Sinica and the Max Planck Society have cooperated in this research venture. XNB (5 Apr 1985), 46-47.

Plague—In 1984 China did not have a single plague patient for the first time since plague was discovered in the country. FBIS-CHI 122 (25 Jun 1985), K17.

Prenatal Anemia—The Shanghai Children's Hospital now has a method of diagnosing Mediterranean anemia before birth. The method analyzes the gene cells of the infant, its parents and their families. The incidence of the disease is about 0.66 percent in the PRC, and, as yet, there is no cure. XNB (24 May 1985), 31.

Pacemakers—Cardio-Pace Medical Inc. of Roseville, Minnesota, has signed the first US-Chinese medical-electronics joint venture. The firm will receive an initial payment of $500,000 from the Chinese for its heart pacemaker technology. The Qinling Semiconductor Factory in Baoji, Shaanxi, will be renamed the Qinming Medical Co. and manufacture about 1,000 pacemakers in 1986, increasing to 5,000 units annually within three years. Estimated revenues have been put at $1 million during the first year, and $5-$6 million by the third. Cardio-Pace will contribute 49 percent of the $1.5 million needed to begin operations, and the Chinese will retain 51 percent of the venture. The pacemakers sell for about $2,000 in the US and are expected to cost $1,500 in the PRC. Minneapolis *Star and Tribune* (18 Dec 1985), 1M, 6M.

Inoculations—China plans to inoculate 85 percent of the children in its 2,490 cities and counties by 1990 against six diseases, including measles, whooping cough, tuberculosis, diphtheria, and tetanus. The target has only been met in 214 cities and counties as of the end of 1985. *Beijing Review*, 51 (23 Dec 1985), 8.

HEALTH SUMMARY, 1984

		Percentage Increase Over 1983
Hospitals (mn)	0.670	
Number of hospital beds, yearend (mn)	2.168	2.8
Professional health workers (mn)	3.341	2.7
Doctors	1.377	1.8
Physicians of traditional Chinese and Western medicine	0.715	
Doctors in private practice (th)	80+	
Nurses (mn)	0.616	3.4
Average per 1,000 persons:		
Doctors	1.33	
Hospital beds	2.07	

The incidence of 15 acute infectious diseases, including hepatitis, diphtheria, whooping cough, measles and poliomyelitus, dropped 20 percent in 1984 from 1983. *Beijing Review*, 12 (25 Mar 1985), viii; 20 (20 May 1985), 8-9. The number of hospitals was incorrectly listed in CHIFFA/8, p. 326, as 2.11 million in 1983. This was the number of hospital beds.

TRADITIONAL CHINESE MEDICINE, 1985

Number of practitioners of traditional Chinese medicine (th)	310
Colleges	25
Students (th)	20
Hospitals (th)	1+
Research institutes	48
Persons taking college-level correspondence courses sponsored by *Health News* (th)	90+
Circulation of *Zhongyi Zhazhi* (*Journal of Traditional Chinese Medicine*) (th)*	150

Zhongyi Zhazhi began publication in 1955. An English edition appeared in 1981. FBIS-CHI 11 (16 Jan 1985), K14/15; 12 (17 Jan 1985), K9.

EDUCATIONAL NEWS, 1984-85

School Reforms—Middle school entrance exams were eliminated in Beijing for the 1985-86 academic year. Local primary students have had to take two tests in the past to obtain their graduation certificates and to determine whether they would enter middle school. The graduation examinations will continue, but promotion to middle school will be based on academic achievement. The age to enter primary schools will be lowered from seven to six years and three months for urban children and to six years and nine months for suburban and rural children in the Beijing system.

In 1984 China enrolled 24,729,300 students in 853,700 primary schools. Some 13,025,300 primary school graduates enrolled in 93,700 ordinary middle schools. *Beijing Review*, 18 (6 May 1985), 9-10.

Student Exchange with GDR—China signed an agreement 26 September 1985 on the exchange of students. It is the first such agreement between the countries since 1965. FBIS-CHI 195 (8 Oct 1985), H4.

continued . . .

EDUCATIONAL NEWS, 1984-85 (continued)

First Patent College—China opened its first patent training college in Shanghai 3 September 1985. It will teach 30 subjects. Fifty persons will study for a half year at the college. XNB (4 Sep 1985), 34.

Fujian Vocational Colleges—Fujian province has established a Fuzhou branch of the Beijing Posts and Telecommunications College and the Nanping Vocational College. There are 11 vocational colleges in the province, including four in Fuzhou. FBIS-CHI 74 (17 Apr 1985), 01.

Lianhe University—The Lianhe United University has been established in Beijing. It is composed of 12 branches of other higher educational institutions in Beijing. They form the University's School of Liberal Arts and Sciences, the School of Economic Management, the School of Arts and Law, the School for Teachers in Professional Studies and Technology, the School for Teachers of Foreign Languages, the School for Tourism, the school of Automation Engineering, the School of Electronic Engineering, the School of Mechanical Engineering, the School of Light Industrial Engineering, the School of Textile Engineering, and the School of Chinese Medicine and Pharmacology. FBIS-CHI 69 (10 Apr 1985), R3.

Beijing University—There are currently 12,000 students at Beijing University. "Student Life at Beijing University," *China Reconstructs*, XXXIV, 5 (May 1985), 7-11.

First University in Tibet—Tibet's first university opened at Lhasa 20 July 1985. It will enroll 220 students in 1985 for teacher training. Within the next few years, enrollment will rise to 1,600. Ciwang Zunmei, 39, is its President. XNB (22 Jul 1985), 43.

Yantai University—Yantai University in northeast Shandong was established 20 October 1985. Shen Keqi has been appointed its President. FBIS-CHI 204 (22 Oct 1985), K10.

Design Courses—The Suzhou and Zhejiang Silk Engineering Colleges, the Northwest and Tianjin Textile Engineering Colleges, and the East China Textile Engineering College and Shanghai Textile Industry Institute are now offering design courses. Some 20,000 garments are designed every year in Shanghai. In 1984 the city sold 60 million garments on the local market and exported another 70 million. XNB (10 Apr 1985), 19.

Vocational School Graduates—An analysis of vocational school graduates since 1949 has found their ratio to university graduates to have been 1.7:1. This ratio does not meet China's needs for economic and technical development. *Frankfurter Allgemeine Zeitung* (5 Aug 1985), 10.

Enrollment of Overseas Chinese—Seven Chinese colleges will enroll students from Hong Kong, Macao and Taiwan and Overseas Chinese. They are Beijing, Qinghua, Fudan, Zhongshan (Sun Yat-sen), and Shenzhen Universities, the Sun Yat-sen Medical College, and the South China Institute of Technology. *Beijing Review*, 20 (20 May 1985), 8.

College Course for the Disabled—The first spare-time college course for the disabled began in Beijing in April, 1985. The four-year course includes Chinese, logic, English, and philosophy. Over 25 percent of Beijing's 120,000 disabled are aged 18 to 35, and need advanced education. China's universities enrolled 20 disabled students in regular courses in 1983 and another 301 in 1984. XNB (4 Apr 1985), 47-48.

Nine-Year Schooling—China will gradually introduce nine-year education. During the next six years, junior middle school education will become universal in cities and coastal areas, and within 10 years in the countryside. Primary-school education is universal in most cities and towns, and 95 percent of the school-age children in rural areas attend school. About two-thirds of the primary-school graduates now go to junior middle school. XNB (29 May 1985), 28.

Post-Graduates—China enrolled 44,000 post-graduates in 1985, bringing their total to 600,000. The number of undergraduates reached a record 1.68 million. *Beijing Review*, 51 (23 Dec 1985), 6.

Law Students—The five institutes of political science and law and the 31 law departments in other universities graduate approximately 3,000 Chinese law students annually. There are

continued . . .

EDUCATIONAL NEWS, 1984-85 (continued)

currently some 14,300 law students in China, or 1.2 percent of the nation's total university and college enrollment. They are instructed by 1,800 teachers. The 12 universities with law departments under the Ministry of Education are Beijing, Nankai, Sichuan, Lanzhou, Sun Yat-sen and the Chinese People's University, and at the provincial level, Heilongjiang, Hangzhou, Shenzhen, Xinjiang, Yunnan and the Overseas Chinese University. *Beijing Review*, 18 (6 May 1985), 22-23.

Nationalities University—The Beijing University of Nationalities near the Summer Palace opened 1 April 1985. He Luo has been named its President. FBIS-CHI 82 (29 Apr 1985), R2.

Vocational Education—The PRC plans to channel more junior middle school graduates into technical schools. In 1984 there were only 3.7 million vocational and technical school students compared to 45.54 million in regular middle schools. FBIS-CHI 102 (28 May 1985), K4.

Military Training—Students attending 52 colleges and 102 high schools will begin military training in September, 1985. It will be compulsory for first- and second-year students. Beijing University, Qinghua University, and other key institutions will conduct training before it is extended to all college and high school students in China. FBIS-CHI 103 (29 May 1985), K16.

Tibet—Some 73.74 million yuan has been allocated for education in Tibet in 1985. This amounts to almost 10 percent of Tibet's budget, and nearly 10 percent more than was allocated in 1984. *Beijing Review*, 16 (22 Apr 1985), 8.

Research on Japan—There are about 70 institutes and research units in the PRC devoted to the study of Japan. A comprehensive history of Japan is being compiled at Liaoning University in collaboration with Nankai University. FBIS-CHI 161 (20 Aug 1985), D2.

Proliferation of Universities—The *China News Analysis*, 1290 (1 Aug 1985) describes the proliferation of new universities during the past few years. Ministries, regions, counties and rural communes have started universities and colleges. One correspondence university has an enrollment of 650,000 and in Henan, a single individual operates three "universities." In January, 1985 103 non-governmental universities advertised in a Beijing newspaper. Ninety-seven universities were established in 1984, bringing the total to 902. Another 40 were under construction in 1985.

Charters—C. Montgomery Broaded examines the dimensions of Chinese educational policy using content analysis of the *People's Daily* in 1971, 1975, and 1978 in "Higher Educational Charters in Mainland China," *Issues & Studies*, 21, 2 (Feb 1985), 53-79.

Non-Governmental University—The first Chinese non-governmental university for minority people has opened in Beijing. The school, sponsored by Beijing's Society of Minorities Folk Art and Literature and funded by donations and private and state loans, offers courses in fine arts, law, industrial management and political science. *Beijing Review*, 17 (29 Apr 1985), 8.

University for the Elderly—China's first university for the elderly opened in the Beijing suburb of Haidian in March, 1985. About 400 pensioners are studying painting, history, calligraphy and the Beijing opera. *Der Spiegel*, 35 (26 Aug 1985), 111, 113.

Unqualified Teachers—Many junior middle schools may stop teaching foreign languages because of a shortage of qualified teachers. Half of the 8 million primary and middle school teachers do not have formal professional training. Some of these schools cannot offer courses in biology, music, geography or the fine arts. China needs an estimated 1 million teachers for primary schools, where the current ratio of teachers to students is 1:50 in large cities and 1:40 throughout the country. At least 750,000 teachers are needed for junior middle schools and 300,000 for senior middle schools during 1986-90. The PRC has 240 teachers colleges and 1,000 normal schools with a total enrollment of some 300,000. *Beijing Review*, 50 (16 Dec 1985), 9-10.

ENROLLMENT, 1983-84

	1983	1984
Institutions of higher learning		
Students newly enrolled	391,000	475,000
Students graduated	335,000	287,000
Total enrollment	1,207,000	1,396,000
Post-graduates		
Newly enrolled	16,000	23,000
Total enrolled	37,000	57,000
Adult educational institutions including television and radio college courses, correspondence courses, evening schools and part-time colleges for workers, peasants, managerial personnel and middle-school teachers		
Students newly enrolled	413,000	474,000
Students graduated		164,000
Total enrollment	926,000	1,292,000
Secondary schools		
Enrollment in senior middle school	6,290,000	6,898,000
Enrollment in junior middle school	37,687,000	38,643,000
Enrollment in secondary technical schools	1,143,000	1,322,000
Enrollment in agricultural middle schools and vocational middle schools	1,220,000	1,745,000
Enrollment in workers training schools	525,000	639,000
Enrollment in adult middle schools		5,160,000
Enrollment in adult secondary technical schools		827,000
Primary schools		
Total enrollment	135,780,000	135,570,000

Beijing Review, 12 (25 Mar 1985), vii; CHIFFA/8, 336.

ENROLLMENT IN HIGHER EDUCATIONAL INSTITUTIONS

Enrollment (th)	
1984	475
1985	520
1990	700
Number of colleges	902
Additional number planned	40

XNB (25 Jan 1985), 13.

POSTGRADUATE STUDENTS

Enrollment (th)	
1984	39.7*
1985	64.3
Number studying three years for	
Master's degrees	29.3
Doctoral candidates	3.143

*Calculated. XNB (15 Feb 1985), 14-15; *Beijing Review*, 30 (29 Jul 1985), 8.

STUDENTS AND TEACHERS, 1984 (mn)

	Students	Teachers
Regular middle schools	45.54	2.55[1]
Primary schools	135.57	5.36[2]
Students per teacher[3]		
Middle schools	17.9	
Primary schools	25.3	

1. Including 540,000 teachers in schools operated by local people.
2. Including 2.95 million teachers in schools run by local people.
3. Calculated.

Renmin Ribao (12 May 1985).

LIVING STANDARDS AND WELFARE, 1984

		Percentage Increase Over 1983
Peasant Households Surveyed		
Average annual per-capita net income	355.3	14.7
From productive activities	313.0	
From cash and articles remitted or brought back by family members working away from home and relief funds issued by the state	42.3	
Average per-capita living expenses (yuan)	273.4	10.1
Households of Workers and Staff Surveyed		
Average annual per-capita income for living expenses (yuan)	608.0	15.5
Increase in real income, considering the rise in the cost of living index (percent)		12.5
Savings		
Urban and rural savings deposits in individual banks, yearend (bn yuan)	121.47	36.1
Employment and Wages		
New jobs provided in urban areas (mn)	3.53	
Workers and staff, yearend (mn)	118.240	2.7
Self-employed workers in cities and towns (mn)	2.96	28.1
Total annual wages of workers and staff (bn yuan)	111.23	19.0
Bonuses and wages paid for above-quota piece work (bn yuan)	17.92	48.1
Average annual cash wage for workers and staff (yuan)	961	16.3
Percentage growth when the cost of living increase is included		13.2
Housing		
Housing completed by state-run and collective enterprises in cities and towns (mn sq m)	100	
Housing built by peasants (mn sq m)	600	
Welfare		
Elderly, disabled, widowed and orphaned who had no other means of support assisted by rural collectives (mn persons)	2.711	50.0

continued . . .

LIVING STANDARDS AND WELFARE, 1984 (continued)

		Percentage Increase
Homes for the aged in rural areas (th)	21	
Persons housed (th)	241	50.0
Number of social and children's welfare institutes		
In cities and towns	1,198	
Persons given assistance (th)	70	

Aid was granted to 2,43 million poor village families to help develop production, and 1.3 million of these families were able to escape their poverty.

Based on a sample survey of 31,435 peasant families in 600 counties of 28 provinces, municipalities, and autonomous regions. Based on a sample survey of 12,050 worker and staff households in 82 cities across China. *Beijing Review*, 12 (25 Mar 1985), viii.

STANDARDS OF LIVING, 1978, 1984[1]

	1978	1984
Per-capita real income (yuan)	137[2]	355
Per-capita urban living expenses (yuan)[3]	316	608
Average per-capita consumption (kg)		
Grain	195.5	230
Edible vegetable oil	1.6	4
Pork	7.5	12.5
Bank savings		
Total (bn yuan, yearend)	21.1	121.5
Average per-capita savings (yuan)		
Urban residents	75	320
Rural residents	7	50

1. These figures are based on sample surveys of households.
2. Calculated. The 355 yuan represents a 160-percent increase over 1978, or a 100-percent increase when price rises are considered.
3. A survey of more than 10,000 urban families in 82 cities indicated a 92.4-percent increase over 1978, or a 60.5-percent rise if price rises are included.

Beijing Review, 16 (22 Apr 1985), 16.

SALES OF PRIVATE HOUSING, 1983-84

Housing (floor space) sold to private buyers (mn m^2)

1983	0.99*
1984	1.9

* Calculated.

Housing has been allocated to families by their employer or the local housing administration. Housing was first sold to individuals in Changzhou, Jiangsu; Shengzhou, Henan; Shashi, Hubei; and Siping, Jilin. Housing sales began in Beijing in 1982, but only to Overseas Chinese. Some 1,000 new apartments were sold in Shanghai in 1984. Purchasers generally pay one-third of an apartment's cost, and the rest is subsidized by the state and local employers. Prices average 500 yuan per square meter in Beijing. As of 1 January 1985, all organizations there were ordered to offer 20 percent of their new housing to individuals. Each urban resident had an average of 4.8 square meters of living space at the end of 1984, and the goal is 8 square meters by the end of the century. One-third of China's households, or 7.5 million families, still live in overcrowded facilities. Some 2 million urban young couples reach marriageable age each year, putting great strains on the housing market. *Beijing Review*, 25 (24 Jun 1985), 6-7.

HOUSING, 1979-84

State investment in urban housing construction (bn yuan)	86.5
Area built (mn m^2)	580
Households which have occupied the new housing (mn)	40
Average cost per m^2 (yuan)	149

An apartment of 50 m^2 costs 9,000 yuan. An individual buyer pays one-third of the cost, and the remainder is paid by the unit where the person works. XNB (14 Jan 1985), 30

URBAN HOUSING SHORTAGE

Per-capita housing space (m^2)

1978	3.53
1982	4.4
2000 plan	8.0
Families with insufficient living space (mn)	7.49
Increase, 1978-82 (th)	600
Percent of urban households	33
Families without living quarters (mn)	1.99
Increase, 1978-82 (th)	680
Percent of urban households	10

To alleviate the housing shortage, the Chinese are considering raising rents; selling part or all of government-built apartments (over 900 million m^2); and replacing the allotment of living quarters by work units to employees by sales according to income. Low-income families would continue to be subsidized, middle-income families would pay a greater share of the rents, and high-income and Overseas Chinese would pay the full cost of housing. *Renmin Ribao* (10 Jun 1985), 5.

SAVINGS DEPOSITS IN URBAN AND RURAL AREAS, 1952-84 yearend (bn yuan)

1952	0.86	1963	4.57	1974	13.65
1953	1.23	1964	5.55	1975	14.96
1954	1.59	1965	6.52	1976	15.91
1955	1.99	1966	7.23	1977	18.16
1956	2.67	1967	7.39	1978	21.06
1957	3.52	1968	7.83	1979	28.10
1958	5.52	1969	7.59	1980	39.95
1959	6.83	1970	7.95	1981	52.37
1960	6.63	1971	9.03	1982	67.54
1961	5.54	1972	10.52	1983	89.27
1962	4.11	1973	12.12	1984	121.47

Statistical Yearbook of China 1981 (1982), 410; *Asian Wall Street Journal Weekly* (4 Feb 1985), 7; *Beijing Review,* 19 (9 May 1983), xi; 12 (25 Mar 1985), viii. The average account is 117 yuan ($41.74), equal to about four months peasant wages and just over two months wages for workers and staff in 1984.

ANNUAL AVERAGE PER-CAPITA DISPOSABLE CASH INCOME, 1952-84 (yuan)

	Peasants	Workers and Staff
1952	62	148
1957	79	205
1965	100	237
1975	124	324
1978	134	316
1979	160	406

continued . . .

ANNUAL AVERAGE PER-CAPITA DISPOSABLE CASH INCOME, 1952-84 (continued)

	Peasants	Workers and Staff
1980	191	444
1981	223	463
1982	270	500
1983	309.8	526
1984	355.3	608

Keith Griffin, ed., *Institutional Reform and Economic Development in the Chinese Country-side* (1985), 295, to 1981, and annual state statistical reports, 1982-84.

PER-CAPITA CONSUMPTION OF CONSUMER GOODS, Selected Years (jin)

	Grain	Vegetable Oil	Pork
1956	408	5.13	NA
1957	NA	NA	10.15
1961	317	2.75	2.82
1962	NA	2.17	4.43
1963	329	2.25	NA
1978	190	3.19	15.34
1982	450	7.07	23.51

Guangming Ribao (30 Nov 1985). 1 jin = o.5 kg.

NUMBER OF SELECTED CONSUMER GOODS PER 100 FAMILIES AND NUMBER OF PERSONS PER COMMODITY, 1983

	Commodities in China	Commodities per 100 Families	Chinese per Commodity[1]
Air conditioners (th)	80	0.035^2	
Refrigerators (th)	434	0.19	
Watches (mn)	258	113^2	4
Sewing machines (mn)	82.63	37	
Bicycles (mn)	150	65.7^2	
Urban areas			2.5
Rural areas			10.8

1. This means that there were watches for one person in four, for example.
2. Calculated. *The China Investment Guide 1984/85* (1984), 224-25.

COMPARISONS OF PUBLIC FACILITIES IN BEIJING AND TOKYO

	Beijing*	Tokyo
Population	5,340,000	11,680,000
Agricultural workers (percent)	12.5	1.2
Hotels:	484	4,045
Large	36	
Small and medium	448	
Restaurants	2,020	175,000
Laundries and dry cleaners	255	13,000
Hairdressing salons	1,226	11,000
Swimming pools	118	2,800
Cinemas	18	NA
Public Auditoriums	63	NA
Large halls	1,337	NA

* Beijing and suburbs.

Renmin Ribao (17 Feb 1985).

GUIDE TO PROVINCES AND AUTONOMOUS REGIONS IN THE PEOPLE'S REPUBLIC OF CHINA

GANSU PROVINCE

Party Secretary: Li Ziqi

Area (th sq km): 450 The province is named after the first character in the names of two ancient cities: Ganzhou (now Zhangyi) and Suzhou (now Jiuquan)

Population (mn): 19.2 Some 7.6 percent of the population are from the Hui, Tibetan, Dongxiang, Mongolian, Tu, Yugur, Baoan, and other minority nationalities.

Population Density (inhabitants per square km): 44

Urban (percent): 11 Rural (percent): 89

Capital: Lanzhou This city is on the Yellow River in the Longxi Basin.

Other Major City: Jiayuguan

Topography: Gansu adjoins the Loess, Inner Mongolia, and Qinghai-Tibet plateaus, averaging 1,000-3,000 meters in elevation. The eastern part, composed of the undulating Loess Plateau, is drained by the Huanghe River and its tributaries, the Weihe and Taohe, and has potential for the development of hydropower. The Bailong River valley south of the Qinling range has a warm, humid climate for lush plant growth. The Qilian Mountain Area on the Gansu-Qinghai border generally exceeds 4,000 meters above sea level. There are the Heihe, Shule and other inland rivers in the Gansu Corridor between the Qilian range and the Longshou and Heli mountains. Although the greater part of the Corridor is deserts and semi-deserts with an arid climate, there are contiguous oases which have the benefits of the melt-water from the Qilian Mountains for the development of farming and animal husbandry. A natural passage from the heartland of China to Xinjiang and Central Asia in ancient times, the Gansu Corridor is crossed by the Lanzhou-Xinjiang Railway.

Major Rivers: Huanghe, Weihe, Taohe, Bailong, Heihe, Shule

Gansu means "the corridor west of the river," with the corridor running northwest from the Yellow River between the Qilian Mountains and the Mongolian Plateau. Sites in the province include the White Pagoda Mountain, Five Springs and Yan Tan Parks. A three-hour boat trip down the Yellow River reaches the Buddhist caves at Bilingsi dating from 513 A.D. Other Buddhist caves and cliff carvings may be seen at three sites at Dunhuang.

Cultivated Area (mn mu): 53.22

Grain Production, 1984 (mn tons): 5.55

Major Crops and Livestock: wheat, maize, millet, cotton, linseed, Bailan melons, sheep, pigs, cattle, and horses

Major Industries: coal, oil (Yumen and Changqing fields), petrochemicals, non-ferrous metals, electric power, woolen textiles, mining

Industrial Output Value, 1984 (bn yuan)   9.8
Increase Over 1983 (percent)   11.2

Retail Sales, 1984 (mn yuan):
In Collective Commerce   1,590
In Individual Commerce   199.24

Minerals: China's leading nickel producer; lead, zinc, copper, troilite, cement, limestone, antimony, mercury, iron, chromium, tungsten

Railways: Tianshui-Lanzhou; Sanzhou-Xinjiang; Baotou-Lanzhou; Lanzhou-Qinghai

continued . . .

GUIDE TO PROVINCES AND AUTONOMOUS REGIONS IN THE PEOPLE'S REPUBLIC OF CHINA (continued)

GANSU PROVINCE

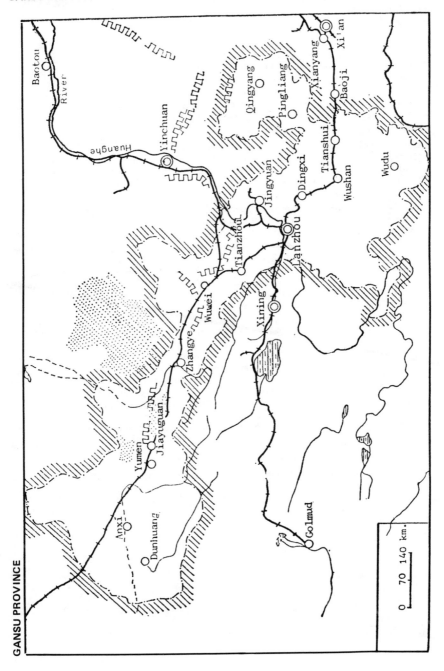

GUIDE TO PROVINCES AND AUTONOMOUS REGIONS IN THE PEOPLE'S REPUBLIC OF CHINA (continued)

GUANGXI ZHUANG AUTONOMOUS REGION

Established: 1958

Party Secretary: Chen Huiguang

Area (th sq km): 230

The name of the autonomous region means "wide west." The Taiping Rebellion of 1850 originated at Jintiancun. Rebels took Hankou (Wuhan), Nanjing, but were defeated at Beijing in 1864.

Population (mn): 34.7 More than 90 percent of the Zhuangs (11.6 million), China.s largest minority nationality, live in Guangxi. Other nationalities include the Han (21.6 million), Yao, Miao, Don, Mulam, Maonan, Hui, Kinh, Yi, Shui, Gelo

Urban (percent): 11 Rural (percent): 89

Capital: Nanning The capital is on the north bank of the Yong River. Tourist attractions include South Lake (Nanhu), where the Dragon Boat Festival is held annually on the fifth day of the fifth lunar month (around June 15), White Dragon Lake and the Old Fort in the People's Park, Xijiao Park. Excursions take visitors to the Yiling Cave, about 12 miles from Nanning.

Other Major Cities: Beihai (seaport), Liuzhou (largest industrial center in the region), Giulin (meaning "osmanthus groves"), Wuzhou (located at the confluence of the Xijiang and the Guijiang)

Topography: Some 70 percent of the region is mountainous, 20 percent rivers and 10 percent farmland. Guangxi is known for its picturesque mountains and rivers. High on four sides and low in the middle, it is called the Guangxi Basin topographically. Its northwestern portion is part of the Yunnan-Guizhou Plateau and its northern portion is locked in the Jiuwandashan, Damiao and Tianping mountains. The northeastern portion is part of the Nanling Mountain Area, comprising the Yuechengling, Haiyang, Dupangling and Mengzhuling ranges which extend southwestward parallel to each other. In the south are the Yunkaidashan, Liuwandashan, Shiwandashan and Daqingshan mountains. Most of the mountains are 1,000-1,500 meters above sea level. In the Guangxi Basin, there is an arc-shaped range, of which the highest mountain chain is the Dayao Mountains. The central part of the basin contains vast areas of flatland with fertile soil and is the major grain and sugar-cane grower of the region. The southern half also contains wide areas of hilly land interspersed with orchards and rice fields. Limestone predominates over more than half of Guangxi. The Guilin-Yangshuo area has a karst topography where the age-old erosion of the limestone has given shape to numerous exotic pinnacles and spires, bizarre sink-holes and caverns, and picturesque hills and subterranean streams.

Major Rivers: Zhujiang, Nanpan, Hongshui, Qianjiang, Xunjiang, Yujiang, Liujiang, Guijiang

Grain Production, 1984 (mn tons): 13.50

Major Crops: rice, maize, sweet potatoes, wheat, beans, peas, sugar cane, peanuts, tobacco, ramie, jute, rapeseed, hemp, rubber, aniseed, fennel oil and cassia bark, Shatian pomeloes (grapefruit from Rongxian), longans (a pulpy fruit from Yulin), lichees (Lingshan). There are two to three crops annually here.

Major Industries: fishing (Beibu Bay), pearls (bays around Hepu), oil (Beibu Bay)

The Tiandong oilfield covers 340 sq km in the Bose Basin of Guangxi. It is the only major oilfield discovered in southern China. Production should begin shortly.

Total Value of Industrial and Agricultural Output, 1984 (bn yuan)   19.82
   Increase Over 1983 (percent)   4.83

Total Income (bn yuan)   12.34

Minerals: Guangxi leads China in reserves of manganese and rock crystal; tin bauxite (Pingguo, Tianyang)

Railways: Hunan-Guangxi; Litang-Zhanjiang

continued . . .

GUIDE TO PROVINCES AND AUTONOMOUS REGIONS IN THE PEOPLE'S REPUBLIC OF CHINA (continued)

GUANGXI ZHUANG AUTONOMOUS REGION

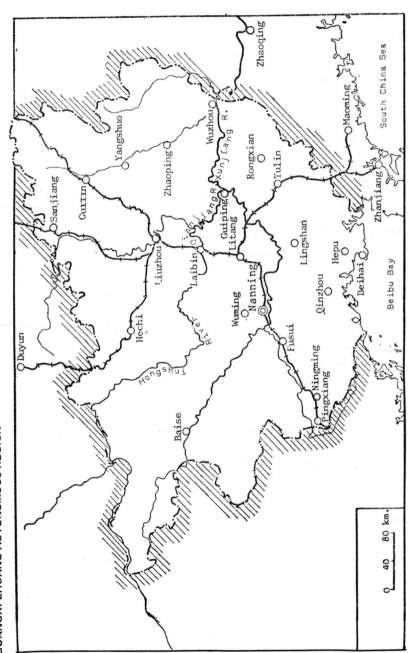

GUIDE TO PROVINCES AND AUTONOMOUS REGIONS IN THE PEOPLE'S REPUBLIC OF CHINA (continued)

HEILONGJIANG PROVINCE

Party Secretary: Sun Weiben (16 Nov 1985)

Area (th sq km): 460

Population (mn): 32.04 Most of the population lives in the Songnen Plain and the mining and industrial cities. Approximately 1.4 million persons belong to the Manchu, Korean, Hui, Mongolian, Daur, Hezhen, Oroqen and Ewenki minority nationalities.

Urban (percent): 31.5 Rural (percent): 68.5

Capital: Harbin The city's name is Manchu for "a place for drying fish nets in the sun." Sites in this capital of 2 million include Sun Island in the Songhua River, Stalin, Zhaolin, and Children's Parks, and the Zoo on Hexing Road.

Topography: Lesser Hinggan and Yilehuli Mountain Areas in the north (generally over 1,000 meters, rounded hills and broad valleys, active volcanoes in the Hinggan Mountains); Songnen Plain (fertile black earth from the Songhua and Nenjiang Rivers); Sanjiang Plain (swamps and marshes formed by silt from the Heilong, Songhua and Wusuli Rivers, wastelands); Southeast Mountain Area south of the Songhua, with the Zhangguangcailing and Laoyeling Mountains

Major Rivers: Heilong, Songhua, Wusuli, Nenjiang, Suifen

Major Lakes: Greater and Lesser Xingkai, Jingbo, Wudalianchi

Cultivated Area (mn mu): 130

In the early 1980s there were some 71 million mu of wasteland and 78 million mu of barren mountain areas and steppes to be reclaimed.

Major Crops: soya beans, maize, wheat, millet, sorghum, sugar-beets, flax, sunflowers, ginseng

Total Agricultural Output Value, 1984 (bn yuan)	11.27
Increase Over 1983 (percent)	7.4
Grain Production, 1984 (bn jin)	35
(mn tons)	17.50

Forest cover (percent): 49

Major Industries: coal, oil (Daqing in the Songliao Basin has 6,000 producing wells), timber, machinery, sugar, bast fiber, chemicals, paper

Total Value of Industrial and Agricultural Output, 1984 (bn yuan)	43.77
Increase Over 1983 (percent)	9.3
Total Industrial Output Value, 1984 (bn yuan)	32.0
Increase Over 1983 (percent)	10.0
Retail Sales of Social Commodities, 1984 (bn yuan)	14.49

Coal Deposits: Hegang, Jixi, Shuangyashan

Minerals: copper, aluminum, bismuth, cobalt, lead, zinc, silver, and molybdenum

continued . . .

GUIDE TO PROVINCES AND AUTONOMOUS REGIONS IN THE PEOPLE'S REPUBLIC OF CHINA (continued)

HEILONGJIANG PROVINCE

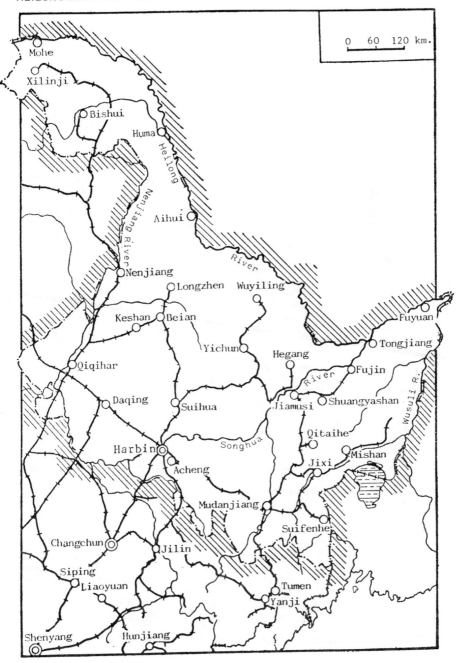

GUIDE TO PROVINCES AND AUTONOMOUS REGIONS IN THE PEOPLE'S REPUBLIC OF CHINA (continued)

HENAN PROVINCE

Party Secretary: Yang Xizong

Area (th sq km): 160 Henan means "south of the river" (Huanghe). It was a political and cultural center of ancient China.

Population (mn): 68

Urban (percent): 12.3 Rural (percent): 87.7

Capital: Zhengzhou The city is on the Jinshui River. One may wish to visit the Provincial Museum, and take excursions to Anyang, the first capital of the Shang dynasty (1711-1066 B.C.) and Kaifeng, an important city of the Northern Song dynasty.

Other Major Cities: Luoyang, Kaifeng (formerly Bianlaing or Bianjing), Pingdingshan, Xinxiang, Anyang

Topography: Henan's terrain slopes from west to east. It is bisected from north to south by the Beijing-Guangzhou Railway, which is flanked on the west by hills and mountains and on the east by a vast plain. On its northwestern border is the Taihang range. The western mountain area includes the eastern extensions of the mountains. Extending east from the Waifang Mountains is Songshan, one of the country's five sacred mountains, whose main peak towers 1,440 meters above sea level. The low, flat Nanyang Basin in the southwest has always been a natural passage between north and south. On the southern border is the Tongbai range, which stretches east to adjoin the Dabie Mountains. The wide plain east of the Beijing-Guangzhou Railway is part of the North China Plain and the principal farming area of the province. The Huanghe River, which has burst over its dykes and changed its course many times, has left broken dykes and sand dunes in the north of the plain. Of the province's total area, mountains make up 26 percent, hills 18 percent and plains 56 percent.

The Huanghe and Huaihe rivers are Henan's main waterways. The Huanghe River runs through the northern part of Henan from west to east for 700 kilometers. It is narrow and flows swiftly west of Mengjin, where a key water conservancy project has been built over the Sanmenxia Gorge. East of Mengjin it flows slowly across a vast expanse of flatland, where its silt-choked bed rises higher than its banks. The Huaihe River flows through southern Henan from west to east for 300 kilometers, draining an area 43 percent of its total catchment area.

Major Rivers: Huanghe (flows through northern Henan past the Sanmenxia Gorge project at Mengjin), Huaihe (flows 300 km through southern Henan)

Cultivated Area (mn mu): 107.08

Grain production, 1984 (mn tons): 29.20

Wheat (mn tons)

1984	16.8
1985	15.95
1986 planned	17.5

Major Crops: wheat, maize, soya beans, rapeseed, tobacco, sesame, cotton, jute, dogbane, peanuts, sweet potatoes

Major Industries: mining machinery, aluminum, chemical fertilizer, cotton textiles, electric power, tractors, ball-bearings, coal

Total Value of Industrial and Agricultural Output (constant 1980 prices, bn yuan)	49.1551
Increase Over 1983 (percent)	11.6
(current prices, bn yuan)	51.7771
National Income, 1984 (bn yuan)	30.5101

Minerals: iron, titanium, dolomite, porphyry, natural soda, graphite, talcum, sulphur, coal, oil and natural gas (Nanyang Basin and areas east of Puyang), bauxite (reserves of 270 million tons), gold, silver, molybdenum

Oil: The Zhongyuan oilfield covers about 4,000 sq km in Henan and Shandong provinces. It consists of six smaller fields: Wenliu, Fucheng, Wenminzhai, Weicheng, Gyoyunji, and Qiakou.

Coal Deposits: Pingdingshan, Jiaozuo, Hebi, Yima, Xinmi, Yongcheng

Railways: Beijing-Guangzhou; Longhai; Jiaozuo-Zhicheng

continued . . .

GUIDE TO PROVINCES AND AUTONOMOUS REGIONS IN THE PEOPLE'S REPUBLIC OF CHINA (continued)

HENAN PROVINCE

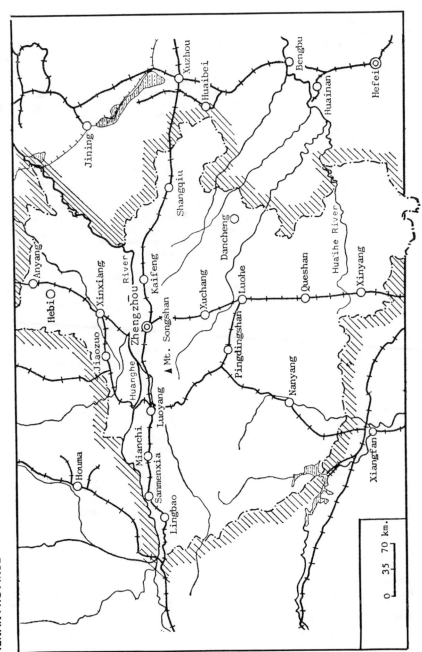

GUIDE TO PROVINCES AND AUTONOMOUS REGIONS IN THE PEOPLE'S REPUBLIC OF CHINA (continued)

HUNAN PROVINCE

Party Secretary: Mao Zhiyong
Area (th sq km): 210
Population (mn): 55.6
Urban (percent): 9.4 Rural (percent): 90.6
Capital: Changsha The population of the capital is 1 million. The city has expanded in recent years, particularly to the south, where factories and apartments have been built. Most of the city is on the east bank of the Xiang Jiang River. The west bank, about 20 percent of Changsha, is residential and the center of cultural and educational facilities. Both sections are linked by a bridge over Orange Island. A 2,000-year-old female corpse is displayed at an exhibition of funerary objects from the Han period at the Changsha Museum. Mao Zedong attended the Hunan No. 1 Teachers' Training School in the city during 1913-18, and his birthplace is 53 miles away at Shaoshan.

Other Major Cities: Zhuzhou, Hengyang, Xiangtan, Shaoyang, Lengshuijiang

Topography: With mountains in the east, south and west, the land generally slopes from the south towards the north in the shape of a horsehoof-like basin. Topographically, it may be divided into five parts. 1. The Dongting Lake Plain in the northeast, contiguous to the Jianghan Plain of Hubei and with numerous rivers and lakes, is known as a "land of fish and rice." 2. The Central Hunan Hilly and Basin Area has wide areas of low hills and mounds and basins and valleys. Hengyang is the largest of the basins. The scenic Hengshan Mountain, whose main peak is 1,290 meters above sea level, is one of China's five sacred mountains. 3. The Nanling Mountain Area, rising mostly more than 1,000 meters on the southern border, is the watershed of the Changjiang and Zhujieng river systems and the climatic divide between central and southern China. 4. The Eastern Hunan Mountain Area is the watershed of the Xiangjiang and Ganjiang basins. 5. The Western Hunan Mountain Area, mostly exceeding 1,000 meters in elevation, comprises mainly the Wuling and Xuefeng mountains. Extending for more than 300 kilometers, the Xuefeng range is the natural and economic divide between the western and eastern parts of the province.

Major Rivers: Xiangjiang, Zishui, Yuanjiang, Lishui

Major Lake: Dongting, the second largest freshwater lake in China accepts the floodwaters of the Changjiang and the four major rivers. Hunan means "south of the lake" (Dongting).

Cultivated Area (mn mu): 51.37, with nearly 80 percent paddy fields

Grain Production (mn tons):		
	1984	26.10
	1985 est	24.25

One-third of the grain production came from the area around Lake Dongting in 1984.

Major Crops: rice (over 80 percent of the total grain crop), wheat, oil-bearing crops, bast fibers, tea, cotton, ramie (which produces a silk-like fiber), tea- and tung-oil; pigs for export, fish, lotus seeds and roots from Dongting Lake, tangerines and oranges from Xupu, Hengdong, and Changsha

Major Industries: spruce from the Xuefeng and Nanling Mountains, coal, non-ferrous metals, chemical fertilizer, iron and steel, embroidery (Changsha), Porcelain (Liling), bambooware, fireworks, feather goods

Minerals: Hunan's reserves of tungsten (Nanling Mountains) and antimony (Xikuangshan mine at Xinhua) rank first in the world. Deposits of bismuth and realgar rank first in China, and those of zinc (Shuikoushan mine at Changning), lead, mercury, kaolin, and graphite are second in the PRC. Manganese, phosphorous, diamonds, and sulphur are also present.

Total Value of Industrial and Agricultural Output, 1984 (bn yuan)	42.399
Increase over 1983 (percent)	10.5
National Income (bn yuan)	24.557

Average Net Annual Income (yuan):		
	Peasants	348.2
	Urban Workers and Staff	922
Total Social Retail Sales, 1984 (bn yuan)		14.208

Railways: Beijing-Guangzhou; Zhejiang-Jiangxi; Hunan-Guizhou; Hunan-Guangxi; Zhicheng-Liuzhou

continued . . .

GUIDE TO PROVINCES AND AUTONOMOUS REGIONS IN THE PEOPLE'S REPUBLIC OF CHINA (continued)

HUNAN PROVINCE

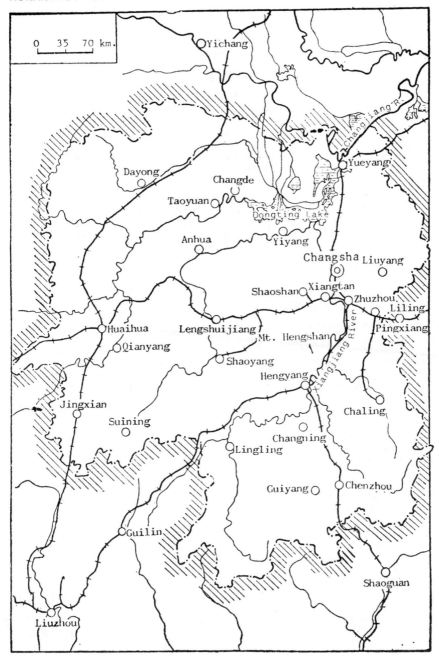

GUIDE TO PROVINCES AND AUTONOMOUS REGIONS IN THE PEOPLE'S REPUBLIC OF CHINA (continued)

SHAANXI PROVINCE

Area (th sq km): 190+

Population (mn): 28.31 Most of the population resides in the Hanshui Valley and Weihe Plain.

Population Density (inhabitants per square km): 143
Urban (percent): 18.4 Rural (percent): 81.6

Capital: Xian This is the largest city in northwest China. It was formerly Chang An ("everlasting peace") when it served as the capital of the Zhou dynasty. The tomb and funeral vault of Qin Shih Huang Di, the first Emperor of a unified China (221 B.C.), guarded by an army of 6,000 terra-cotta warriors, is located outside the city. The vault was discovered in 1974 a mile east of the tomb. Sites in and around Xian include the Bell Tower (1384), Drum Tower (1375), Little and Big Goose Pagodas, neolithic village of Ban Po (found in 1954 six miles from Xian), and the Temple of Great Good Will.

Topography: Northern Shaanxi Plateau (loess, sparse vegetation, stony mountains, erosion); Guangzhong Plateau or Weihe Plain of Guanzhong Basin (30-30 km wide and 300 km long, fertile); Southern Shaanxi Mountain Area or Qinba Mountain Area, including the Qinling and Daba Mountains and the Hanshui Valley (The Qinling range is the major watershed of the Huanghe and Changjiang River Valleys. Mount Taibai is 3,767 meters, and the Huashan Mountain in the east is one of China's sacred mountains. The Daba range is the boundary between the Hanzhong and Sichuan Basins.) Shaanxi means "west of the pass" (Tong Guan).

Major Rivers: Huanghe, Weihe, Hanshui, Wuding, Yanhe, Luohe, Beiluo and Jinghe

Mountain Ranges: Qinling, Daba

Cultivated Area (mn mu): 57.58

Grain Production, 1984 (mn tons): 10.24

Major Crops and Livestock: Northern Shaanxi: millet, broom corn millet, sheet; Guanzhong Plain: wheat, cotton, cattle, and donkeys; Southern Shaanxi: maize, rice, peas, beans, oranges, tangerines, tea, tung-oil, lacquer, bamboo, medicinal herbs, rapeseed

Major Industries: machine-building, textiles, mining, coal, chemicals, petroleum, building materials, electric power

Major Industrial Centers: Xian (accounts for about 45 percent of the province's total industrial output), Baoji, Tongchuan

Minerals: coal, molybdenum, mercury, gold, sulphur, asbestos, barite, fluorite, lead, zinc, nickel, aluminum, phosphorus, iron, silver, limestone

Railways: Longhai-Baoji-Chengdu; Xianyang-Tongchuan; Yangpingguan-Ankang; Xiangfan-Chongqing

Highways (th km): 38

Yanan and other areas in northern Shaanxi were the headquarters of the Central Committee of the Chinese Communist Party from October, 1935 to 1948.

continued . . .

GUIDE TO PROVINCES AND AUTONOMOUS REGIONS IN THE PEOPLE'S REPUBLIC
OF CHINA (continued)

SHAANXI PROVINCE

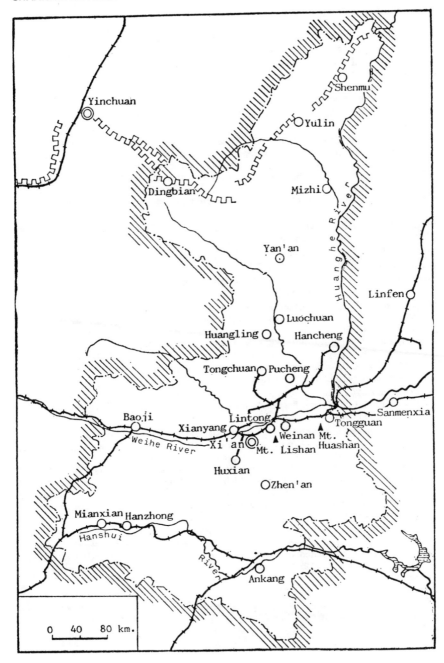

GUIDE TO PROVINCES AND AUTONOMOUS REGIONS IN THE PEOPLE'S REPUBLIC OF CHINA (continued)

SHANXI PROVINCE

Area (th sq km): 156

Population (mn): 24.76

Urban (percent): 13.6 Rural (percent): 86.4

Capital: Taiyuan Sites include the Shanxi Provincial Museum, Temple for Worshipping Goodness, and the Temple of Great Mercy. Outside Taiyuan are located the Scented Forest and White Cloud Monasteries, God of War Temple, Temple of the Jin Minister, Jin Ci Temple at the base of the Xuanweng Mountains, and the Pagodas of the Monastery of Endless Happiness. The Fen River flows through the city.

Other Major City: Datong; the Yungang Grottoes with Buddhist images carved in the rock faces are nearby.

Topography: Shanxi Plateau (loess); Central Shanxi Basin, with Datong, Xinxian, Taiyuan, Linfen, and Yuncheng Valleys running north to south (fertile); Eastern Shanxi Mountain Area, including the Taihang, Hengshan, Wutai, Taiyue and Zhongtiao Mountains, interspersed with the Changzhi, Pingding, Jincheng and Shouyang Basins; Western Shanxi Tableland, with the Luliang Mountains (loess, severe erosion in the form of gullies). The name Shanxi means west of the (Taihang) mountains. Mountains cover 67.5 percent of the province.

Major Rivers: Huanghe and its tributaries, the Fenhe, Sushi, Qinhe; Haihe and its tributaries, the Sanggan, Hutuo and Zhanghe

Cultivated Area (mn mu): 58.86

Grain Production, 1984 (mn tons): 8.72

Major Crops: maize, wheat, sorghum, rice, cotton, oil-bearing crops, pears and dates; animal husbandry in northwestern Shanxi

Major Industries: coal, machine-building (hoisting, metallurgical, and textile machines), electric power, chemicals, textiles, iron and steel, building materials, non-ferrous metals There are 10,000 enterprises in the province. The thermal power plants Datong No. 2 (cap. 2,400 MW), Shentou (5,950 MW in three stations of 1,350, 2,200, and 2,400 MW), Zhangze (800 MW), Taiyuan No. 1 (180 MW, to be expanded to 780 MW), Taiyuan No. 2 (220 MW, to be expanded to 620 MW), and the Niangziguan (400 MW, to double its current capacity) are under construction.

Minerals: coal (203.5 billion tons of verified reserves, or about a quarter of China's total), bauxite (340 million tons of reserves), iron, copper, aluminum, refractory clay, limestone, gypsum, and iron

Coal Fields: Datong and Ningwu in the north; Xishan and Huoxi in central Shanxi; and Qinshui in the southeast and Hedong in the west (37 percent of the province, or 57,000 square km, is on top of coal fields). Approximately 45 percent of the coal seams range from 1.3 to 3.4 meters. They have a slope of 5-10 degrees, and have few faults. In 1980 there were 230 mines, 22 percent of which were mechanized. Miners numbered 408,800 in 1980. Coking coal for the Baoshan Iron and Steel Complex will come from Gujiao. Currently 85 percent of the province's freight volume is coal, and 70 percent of the freight transported by road is coal.

Railways: Beijing-Baotou; Datong-Puzhou (electrification and double-tracking completed in 1985); Shijiazhuang-Taiyuan; Taiyuan-Jiaozuo; Changzhi-Jiaozuo (electrification and double-tracking completed in 1985); Taiyuan-Shijiazhuang (electrification and double-tracking completed in 1982, increasing shipping capacity from 21 to 46 million tons annually.

Highways (th km): 31.9

Road construction within the next year or two will increase annual capacity from 9.09 million tons in 1983 to over 20 million.

continued . . .

GUIDE TO PROVINCES AND AUTONOMOUS REGIONS IN THE PEOPLE'S REPUBLIC
OF CHINA (continued)

SHANXI PROVINCE

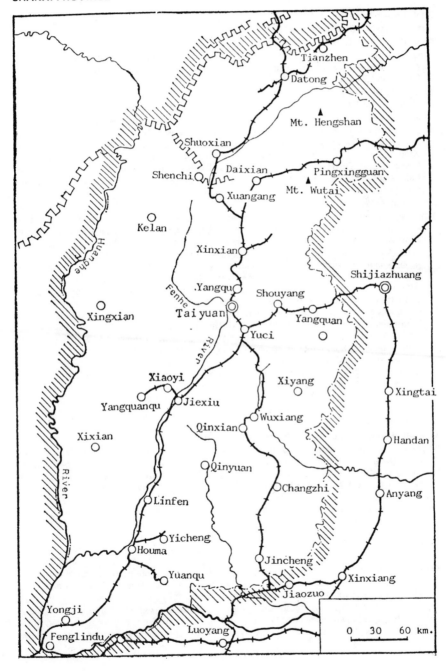

GUIDE TO PROVINCES AND AUTONOMOUS REGIONS IN THE PEOPLE'S REPUBLIC OF CHINA (continued)

XINJIANG UYGUR AUTONOMOUS REGION

Established: 1 October 1955

Party Secretary: Song Hanliang (31 Oct 1985)

Area (th sq km): 1,600

Population (mn): 13.44 Approximately 6.1 million are Uygurs, 5.4 million Hans, and the rest Kazakhs, Mongolians, Huis, Xibes, Kirgiz, Uzbeks, Tadzhiks, Russians, Manchus, Daurs, and Tatars

Population Density (inhabitants per square km): 8.2
    Urban (percent): 22   Rural (percent): 78

Capital: Urumqi ("fine pasture" in Mongolian; called Dihua until 1953). There is a nine-tiered pagoda on Red Hill (Hongshan) on the east bank of the Urumqi River. Nearby are the Lake of Heaven and the Valley of the White Poplars. Major Buddhist cave shrines in Xinjiang include the Shanshan Caves about 100 km east of Turpan; the Thousand Budda Caves outside Turpan; the Yanqi Caves near Bosten; the Kumtura Caves near Kuqa; the Baicheng Caves west of Kuqa; the Xihe Caves southwest of Kuqa; and the Wensu Caves north of Aksu.

Other Major Cities: Kashi, Yining, Shihezi

Topography: Xinjiang is divided into five topographical zones: 1. The Tianshan Mountain Area, mostly 3,000-5,000 meters above sea level, consists of several ranges running parallel from west to east across the middle part of the region. The Tianshan range divides Xinjiang into two vastly different natural geographical regions, northern and southern Xinjiang. The numerous intermontane basins and valleys are important farming-pastoral areas. The area around the Hami and Turpan basins is customarily called eastern Xinjiang. 2. The Altai range lies in the north and northeast. 3. In the south are the Karakorum, Kunlun and Altun mountains and the Pamirs. 4. The Junggar Basin between the Tianshan and Altai ranges has the Curbantunggut Desert in the middle. 5. The Tarim Basin south of the Tianshan range makes up more than half of the region's total area and has the Taklimakan Desert in the middle. Deserts make up about 22 percent of the area of Xinjiang. Mount Qogir, towering 8,611 meters above sea level over the China-Pakistan border, is the highest peak in the region. Aydingkol Lake in the Turpan Depression with its surface 154.43 meters below sea level is the lowest point in China. The Turpan Basin is about 150 km southeast of Urumqi. It is the hottest place in the PRC, with temperatures reaching 48-49 degrees Centigrade in the summer. Rainfall averages 16.6 mm a year.

Major Rivers: Tarim, Ili, Ertix, Manas

Largest Lake: Lop Nur

Cultivated Area (mn mu): 48   Arable Land (mn ha): 3.2

Major Crops: wheat, cotton, maize, rice, silkworm cocoons, grapes (Turpan), Hami melons (Shanshan), sheep, horses (Ili). Grain production amounts to 400-450 kg per person. There are 750 million mu (50.7 mn ha) of grasslands, about 25 percent of China's total, capable of grazing about 62 million animals. Xinjiang has some 10 million hectares of wasteland.

Total Agricultural Output Value, 1984 (bn yuan)	4.55
Grains (mn tons)	4.87
Cotton (th tons)	185
Meat (th tons)	185
Cattle, 1985 (mn head)	30.25

Major Industries: coal, electric power, chemicals, textiles, metallurgy, building materials, cotton and woolen textiles, sugar, salt, household articles, timber (Tianshan and Altai Mountains), petroleum. There are more than 4,300 enterprises in Xinjiang.

Minerals: coal, oil shale, iron, gold, silver, non-ferrous metals, salt, mirabilite, sulphur, mica, asbestos, quartz, and jade. Xinjiang has 118 types of minerals, and leads the PRC in reserves of beryllium, soda-nitre, muscovite, feldspar, pottery clay, serpentinite, lithium,

continued . . .

GUIDE TO PROVINCES AND AUTONOMOUS REGIONS IN THE PEOPLE'S REPUBLIC
OF CHINA (continued)

XINJIANG UYGUR AUTONOMOUS REGION

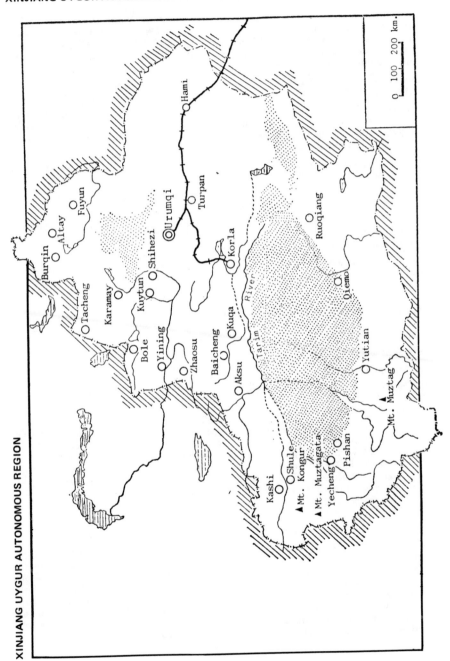

XINJIANG UYGUR AUTONOMOUS REGION

GUIDE TO PROVINCES AND AUTONOMOUS REGIONS IN THE PEOPLE'S REPUBLIC OF CHINA (continued)

XINJIANG UYGUR AUTONOMOUS REGION (continued)

white mica and albite. Sixty minerals are now being mined. Verified oil reserves amount to 700 million tons. The Karamay (Uygur for "black hill") is in the northwestern edge of the Junggar Basin, which covers 130,000 sq km in Xinjiang. Some 20 smaller fields operate in the Karamay field. Coal reserves are estimated at 1,600 billion tons, or approximately one-third of China's total.

Water Resources: Glaciers in Xinjiang have 500 billion cubic meters of water. Lakes and rivers hold 90 billion cubic meters, and subterranean water is estimated at 20 billion.

Railways: Lanzhou-Xinjiang; Southern and Northern Xinjiang Railways under construction In the first phase of the 3,561-km railway from the east China coast to Urumqi, Xinjiang, a 240-km line will be built between Urumqi and Usu. When completed in 1988, the railway will be extended westward to join the Soviet system.

Highways: China will upgrade the highway linking Kashi in southern Xinjiang with the Kunjirap Daban Pass to facilitate exporting through Pakistan.

Education: There are 2.95 million students attending 14 universities and colleges, 2,325 middle and secondary technical schools, and 8,253 primary schools.

Construction: Since 1955, 18,000 km of roads, 1,400 km of railways, 487 reservoirs, and 180,000 km of irrigation canals have been built. Some 1.47 million hectares of farmland have been reclaimed.

Gross Industrial and Agricultural Output Value, 1984 (bn yuan)	10.538
Total Industrial Output Value, 1984 (bn yuan)	5.987

XIZANG (TIBET) AUTONOMOUS REGION

Established: 1965

Party Secretary: Wu Jinghua

Area (th sq km): 1,200

Population, 1984 yearend (mn): 1.9668. Some 1.78 million are Tibetan, and about 200,000 are Hui, Menba, Lhoba, Dulong, Nu, and Han
Urban (percent): 15 Rural (percent): 65

Capital: Lhasa Sites here include the Potala Palace (composed of the White and Red Palaces, 1645-93), Norbulingka Palace (formerly the summer palace of the Dalai Lama) and Park, and the Jokhan Monastery in the city, and the Drepung (1416, six miles north of Lhasa) and Sera (1419, 3.5 miles north of Lhasa) Monasteries in the suburbs. Lhasa is more than 12,000 feet above sea level, and visitors may require oxygen getting adjusted to the thin air. Persons with high blood pressure, heart conditions, or colds are usually not allowed to visit the city. Entry for foreigners has generally been restricted to June, July, and August.

Other Major City: Xigaze with the Zhaxilhumbo (Tashi-Lhunpo) Monastery

Topography: The Himalayas in the south of Tibet have an average of 6,000 meters, the highest range on the earth. Their main peak, 8,848-meter Mount Qomolangma on the Sino-Nepalese border, is the summit of the globe. In the north are the Kunlun range and its branch, the Tanggula Mountains; in the middle the Gangdise range; and in the east the Hengduan range with numerous canyons and imposing mountains. North of the Gangdise range and south of the Kunlun range is the vast Northern Tibet Plateau. The Southern Tibet Valleys between the Gangdise and the Himalayas, crossed by the Yarlungzangbo River from west to east, are the principal farming and pastoral area of Tibet.

continued . . .

GUIDE TO PROVINCES AND AUTONOMOUS REGIONS IN THE PEOPLE'S REPUBLIC OF CHINA (continued)

XIZANG (TIBET) AUTONOMOUS REGION

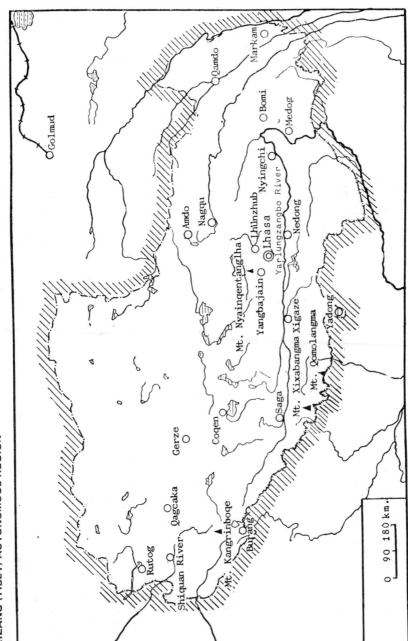

GUIDE TO PROVINCES AND AUTONOMOUS REGIONS IN THE PEOPLE'S REPUBLIC OF CHINA (continued)

XIZANG (TIBET) AUTONOMOUS REGION (continued)

Major Rivers; Yarlungzangbo, Nujiang, Lancang, Jinsha

Large Salt Lake: Nam Co
More than one-third of China's lakes are in Tibet. They cover some 27,000 square km on the Tibetan Plateau, or approximately one-third of the total lake area in the PRC. Namcuo is the highest in China, located 4,718 meters above sea level. Celincuo, the second highest, is 4,530 meters above sea level. There are more than 30,000 geothermal spots.

Cultivated Area (mn mu): 3.45

Major Crops and Livestock: qingko (highland barley), wheat, peas, rapeseed, yaks, goats, sheep

There are 800 million mu of grasslands.

Total Agricultural Output Value, 1984 (mn yuan)	638.18
Increase Over 1983 (percent)	16.78
Agricultural Production, 1984:	
Grains (th tons)	494
Livestock, 1984 yearend (mn head)	21.68

Major Industries: coal, machinery, mining, food, paper, forestry, electric power (Tibet ranks second in hydropower potential in China), woolens, hide-processing, medicinal musk, caterpillar fungus, fritillary bulbs. There are 296 factories in Tibet. Forty-three projects costing a total of 400 million yuan ($140 million) have been started since a conference on the development of Tibet in 1984. Several new projects are shown in *China Reconstructs,* XXXIV, 9 (Sep 1985), 40-43. To improve the economy of the region, Tibetans have been exempted from taxes for 15 years. Private ownership of farmland is now allowed, and 30-year leases on grazing lands have been negotiated with peasants.

Total Value of Industrial and Agricultural Output, 1984 (mn yuan)	984.87
Total Industrial Output Value, 1984 (mn yuan)	168.32
Increase Over 1983 (percent)	7.49
National Income (mn yuan)	909.91
Per-Capita National Income (yuan)	466.83
Average Annual Net Income of Peasant and Herdsman (yuan)	317
Total Retail Sales (mn yuan)	1,057.59
Total Bank Deposits (mn yuan)	154.61
Urban	126.22
Rural	28.39

Minerals: chromium, iron, copper, lead, zinc, salt mica, gypsum, borax

Energy: About 600 geothermal fields have been located in Tibet. Potential geothermal generating capacity has been estimated over 800 MW. The first geothermal well was sunk in 1975 at Yangbajain at the foot of Nianqing Tanggula Mountain. it was subsequently expanded to a station with four generators totaling 10 MW. A second station in Langjiu of the Ari Prefecture in western Tibet is to begin operation shortly. Its capacity will be 1,000 KW. Wind energy was first exploited in Tibet in 1982. There are 15 wind generators with a capacity of 2 KW and 210 with a capacity of 100 W in the Naqu district of northern Tibet. Surveys have indicated that water resources total 200 million KW, or 30 percent of China's total water reserves. By the end of June, 1985 Tibet had more than 700 small and medium-sized hydropower stations with a combined capacity of 113,000 KW.

Highways: Sichuan-Tibet; Qinghai-Tibet; Xinjiang-Tibet, Yunnan-Tibet; China-Nepal
The total length of highways open to traffic reached 21,611 km, with freight attaining 802,500 tons.

continued . . .

GUIDE TO PROVINCES AND AUTONOMOUS REGIONS IN THE PEOPLE'S REPUBLIC OF CHINA (continued)

XIZANG (TIBET) AUTONOMOUS REGION (continued)

Air Routes: Lhasa-Galmud; Lhasa-Chengdu

Railway: Qinghai-Tibet Railway under construction

Administration: Xizang has 75 counties and 2,065 townships. Tibetans make up 59.1 percent of the 57,485 local government workers.

Medical Institutions: There are 928 medical institutions with 4,738 hospital beds.

Educational Institutions: Xizang has three colleges with a total enrollment of 1,370 students, 13 vocational and technical schools, 56 middle schools, and 2,475 primary schools.

Maps and some information are from the China Handbook Series, *Geography* (1983). Descriptions of other provinces and regions in China will appear in subsequent volumes of CHIFFA.

XIZANG (TIBET) AUTONOMOUS REGION

Beijing Review, 34 (26 Aug 1985), 17.

HUNAN PROVINCE

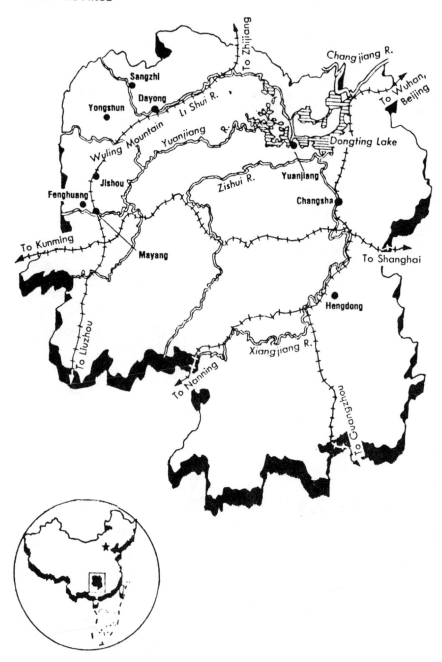

BEIHAI

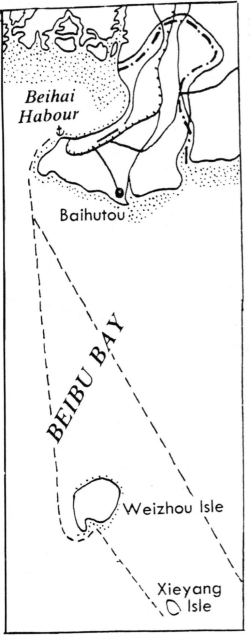

Beihai Habour

Baihutou

BEIBU BAY

Weizhou Isle

Xieyang Isle

Located at 109°06' east longitude and 21°29' north latitude on the north-eastern shore of the Beibu Bay, Beihai is the southernmost port city of the Guangxi Zhuang Autonomous Region. It is surrounded by the South China Sea on three sides and is linked to Hepu County to the northeast. Its 275 km^2 territory includes Weizhou and Xieyang isles, both located 20 nautical miles offshore to the south.

The city enjoys a maritime monsoon climate typical of the subtropical area, with an average temperature of 22.6 degrees Celsius (it ranges from 2 degrees Celsius to 37 degrees Celsius), and an average relative humidity reading of 81 percent. Yearly precipitation averages 1,636 mm and the rainy season comes between April and September.

Forests cover 19 percent of Beihai's land area. Main crops on the 27,145 hectares of farmland include peanuts, sugarcane, litches and jackfruit.

The 1982 national census put Beihai's population at 168,442 and 67 percent percent of them live in the city districts.

Beihai is the native place of many Chinese now living overseas. Some 10,000 people there are returned overseas Chinese and compatriots from Hongkong, Taiwan and Macao.

DALIAN

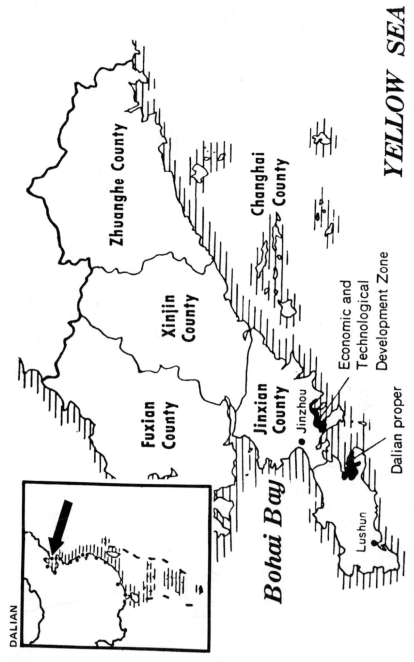

FUZHOU

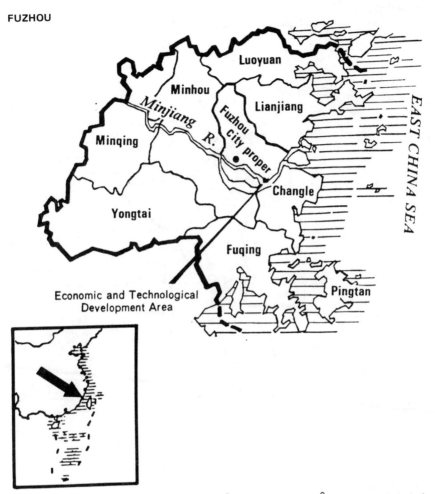

Fuzhou, in Fujian Province, is located at 26°N latitude and 119°E longitude. It includes eight counties and five districts, covering 11,900 km² which are home to 4.75 million people.

Fuzhou has a subtropical monsoon climate. Its temperature averages 19.6°C. with 1,300 mm of rainfall annually.

Verified reserves of 30 minerals include alum, pyrophyllite, laolinite, silica ore and granite, plus metal ores such as manganese, lead, molybdenum and zinc. Fuzhou also has geothermal energy potential and uranium deposits. The tidal and wind power along its coastline is worth developing. The untapped water resources near the city are estimated at 1 million kilowatts.

The farmers around Fuzhou grow lichee, olives, longan, citrus and other fruits. The area is also rich in farm and sideline products.

Fuzhou has 1,281 km of coastline with 40,000 hectares of beaches. It is a good place to develop the cultivation of shell fish, prawns and crabs.

Out of 70,000 hectares of surrounding mountains, 45.8 percent are covered with China fir, *nanmu,* camphor and other valuable trees.

Beijing Review, 6 (11 Feb 1985),

HANGZHOU

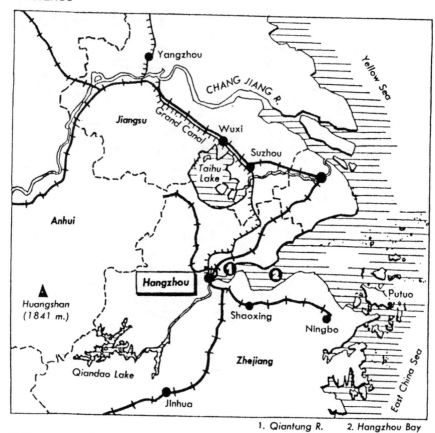

1. Qiantung R.   2. Hangzhou Bay

LIANYUNGANG

The city is situated on the southern coast of the Shandong Peninsula, midway up China's coastline. It has an area of 6,265 km², with the city proper spreading over 850 km². The population is 2.93 million, of whom 430,000 live in the city proper. Lianyungang includes the city proper and three counties under its jurisdiction.

The city enjoys the oceanic climate of the southern temperate zone. The annual temperature averages 14 degrees Celsius (57 Fahrenheit). Annual rainfall averages 1,000 mm (39 inches).

Lianyungang has a varied topography. In the northwest, there are small mountains and hills, while in the east a plain abuts the coastal line. A solitary mountain peak just up from the plain. The coastline is 119.1 km long, and there are seven small islands.

There are 40 kinds of confirmed metallic and non-metallic mining deposits in Lianyungang. City economic enterprises include farming, forestry, livestock breeding and fishing. Many plants grown in the north and south of China are found here. It has abundant freshwater resources.

Of the city's total industrial output value, light industry accounts for 61.5 percent and heavy industry represents 38.5 percent. There are 1,200 industrial enterprises producing 500 varieties of major products. During the last few years, industrial output value has increased 11 percent per year.

Beijing Review, 17 (29 Apr 1985), 25.

NINGBO

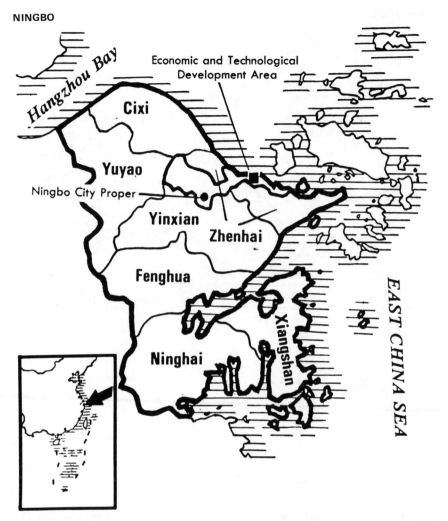

Ningbo, just south of Shanghai in the center of China's coastline, is the second largest city in Zhejiang Province and one of the 10 cities of the Shanghai Economic Zone. It has under its jurisdiction four districts and seven counties which cover 9,397 km^2, 403 km^2 of which are urban areas. It has a population of 4.81 million, with 600,000 living in the urban districts.

The city has a subtropical maritime monsoon climate which is mild, warm and humid, with plenty of rainfall. The average annual temperature is 16.5 degrees C.

Ningbo farmers grow large crops of rice, cotton and aquatic products. The area also has rich mineral resources such as fluorite, lead, zinc, pyrophyllite and quartz.

Tremendous achievements have been made in the city's economic development. Its gross industrial and agricultural output value reached 7.46 billion yuan in 1983, showing an average annual increase of 8.85 percent since 1949 and a 114 percent increase over 1978.

Beijing Review, 9 (4 Mar 1985), 26.

QINHUANGDAO

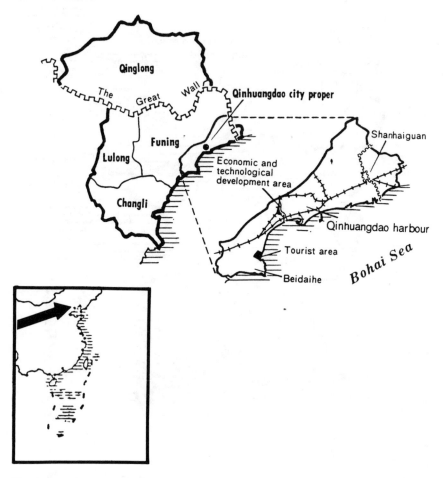

Situated on the coast of eastern Hebei Province, the city of Qinhuangdao includes three districts and four counties. It covers a total area of 7,721 km² and has 113 km of coastline. The three urban districts, with a total area of 363 km², are in a belt along the coastline.

Qinhuangdao has a total population of 2.23 million, with 410,000 residents living in the urban districts, mainly concentrated in the harbor district where the city government is located. The Shanhaiguan district is 19 km to the northeast and the Beidaihe district is 18 kilometres to the southwest.

The city enjoys the oceanic climate of the northern temperate zone. The annual temperature averages 10.1 degrees Celsius, and in July the average temperature is 23 degrees. In January the average temperature is 4 to 5 degrees. The average humidity is 62 per unit.

Mountains and hills rise in the north part of the city, where fruit and Chinese medicinal herbs are grown. As one of the major fishing centers in north China, the aquatic products include prawns, sea cucumbers and jellyfish. Non-metallic mining dominates the mining scene. There are an estimated 600 million tons of quartz reserves and 220 million tons of limestone reserves. The city also has sizable deposits of granite and marble, as well as mining potential for coal, iron, lead, zinc, gold, silver and graphite.

Beijing Review, 52 (24 Dec 1984), 23, 27.

SHANGHAI'S ADMINISTRATIVE DIVISIONS

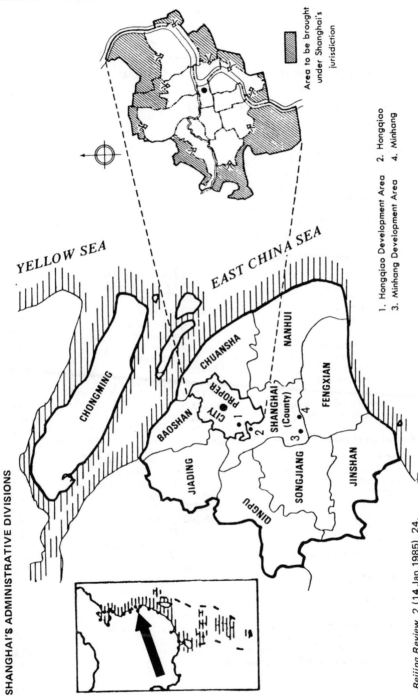

Area to be brought under Shanghai's jurisdiction

1. Hongqiao Development Area   2. Hongqiao
3. Minhang Development Area   4. Minhang

YELLOW SEA

EAST CHINA SEA

CHONGMING

BAOSHAN

JIADING

CHUANSHA

NANHUI

CITY PROPER

SHANGHAI (County)

FENGXIAN

QINGPU

SONGJIANG

JINSHAN

SHANGHAI'S ADMINISTRATIVE DIVISIONS

SHANGHAI STATISTICS

		Increase Over 1983
Total production value (bn yuan)	37.8	9.8
Increase in output value of tertiary industry (percent)		14.5
Per capita production output value (yuan)	3,148	
National income (bn yuan)	33	8.8
Industrial and agricultural output value (bn yuan)	79.3	10.2

Industry

Industrial output value (bn yuan)	76.65	10
(including 2.21 billion yuan of output value of industries operated by rural villages)		
Industries owned by collectives		21.1
Publicly-owned industries		7.9
Industries in other economic forms		15.2
Output value of light industry (bn yuan)	41.66	10.4
Output value of heavy industry (bn yuan)	32.78	8.8

Production of major light industrial products:

Cotton yarn	2.178	million bales	0.4
Cloth	1.52	billion meters	- 3.6
Chemical fibers	176,000	tons	11.9
Detergents	86,000	tons	10.2
Wristwatches	10.995	million	0.5
Bicycles	5.622	million	8.1
Sewing machines	2.94	million	3.2
Television sets	2.231	million	18.1
Color TV sets	244,000		62.7
Cassette recorders	1.453	million	51.4
Cameras	443,000		20.2
Household washing machines	616,000		93.5
Household refrigerators	34,000		120

Production of major heavy industrial products:

Steel	5.49	million tons	7.3
Rolled steel	4.47	million tons	5.5
Electricity	24.5	billion kilowatt hours	9.2
Sulfuric acid	379,000	tons	7.7
Caustic soda	263,000	tons	3.2
Plastics	175,000	tons	2.8
Cement	2.37	million tons	6.3
Plate glass	1.94	million standard cases	1.4
Power generating equipment	1.23	million kilowatts	60.8
Motor vehicles	8,958		10.3
Steel merchant ships	345,000	tons	3.9

Agriculture

Agricultural output value (bn yuan)	2.63	18.2
(excluding the output value of village industries)		
Output value of crop cultivation		21.9
Output value of sideline production		200

continued . . .

SHANGHAI STATISTICS (continued)

Production of major farm products:

Grain	4.99	billion jin	20.5
Cotton	2,069,000	dan	35.2
Rapeseeds	2,303,000	dan	13.7
Marketed vegetables	33.61	million dan	48.7
Pigs raised	5,484,000	head	-8.1
Milk	250	million jin	23.4
Marketed eggs	130	million jin	11.3
Aquatic products	240,000	metric tons	10.6
Seawater products	166,000	metric tons	6.0
Freshwater products	38,000	metric tons	36.5

		Increase Over 1983
Total power capacity of farm machinery in suburban areas (yearend, mn h.p.)	3.31	5.4
Large and medium-sized tractors (th)	13	
Small and walking tractors (th)	33	
Farm trucks (th)	5.6	

Capital Investment

Investment in fixed assets of state-owned units (mn yuan)	6.9	
Capital construction investment	4.7	9.1
Projects financed by other than capital construction funds	2.2	

In 1984 2.93 billion yuan, or 62.4 percent of the total capital construction investment, was spent on the first phase of the Shanghai Baoshan Iron and Steel Complex, the second phase of the Shanghai Petrochemical General Plant, and the second phase of the Shanghai Gongqing Wharf. The last two projects were completed and put into operation.

Transportation

Volume of goods transported (mn tons)	230	6.8
Railway freight (mn tons)	48.41	4.6
Road freight (mn tons)	86.4	7.3
Waterway freight (mn tons)	95.79	7.5
Air freight (th tons)	26	26.2
Cargo handled in Shanghai harbor (mn tons)	101	9.5

For the first time, Shanghai harbor handled more than 100 million tons of cargo.

Railway, waterway, highway, and civil aviation passengers (mn)	31.5	11.5
Average daily passenger transportation (th)		
1983	77	
1984	86	

Posts and Telecommunications

Transactions (mn yuan)	130	13.6
Number of letters		11.5
Newspapers and magazines distributed		5.1
Long-distance telephone calls		19.0

continued . . .

SHANGHAI STATISTICS (continued)

Domestic Trade

		Increase Over 1983
Total value of retail sales (bn yuan)	12.96	21.7
If goods sold by peasants to non-peasant residents are included	13.24	
Retail sales at state-owned enterprises (bn yuan)		19.2
Retail sales at collectively-owned enterprises, including supply and marketing cooperatives		23.7

Foreign Trade and Tourism

		Increase Over 1983
Joint venture contracts signed	53	180
Value (mn dollars)	440	400
Number of technologies imported from abroad	372	33.8
Value of contracts (mn dollars)	410	90.8
Exports (bn dollars)	3.59	- 1.7
Value of exports made in Shanghai (bn dollars)	2.83	
Percent of total exports	78.8	
Foreign tourists, Overseas Chinese, and compatriots from Hong Kong, Macao and Taiwan (th)	532	20.9
Income from tourism (mn yuan)	290	39.6

Science, Education and Culture

		Increase Over 1983
Major research results in science and technology	1,585	120

		Absolute Increase Over 1983
Students (th)		
Kindergartens	35	19
Primary	830	37
Adult secondary	620	
Secondary specialized		9
Vocational middle		14
Ordinary secondary		- 29
Secondary	610	5
Higher educational institutions	90	11
Adult higher educational institutions	150	
Graduate students	5.6	1.930
Feature films produced	19	
Radio programs broadcast daily (hours)	103.5	
Public libraries, including branch libraries	45	

		Percentage Increase
Newspapers published (bn copies)	1.96	8.3
Magazines published (mn copies)	310	23.5
Books published (mn copies)	540	15.5

Health

Professional health workers (th)	102
Doctors (th)	48
Hospital beds (th)	53
Per 10,000 urban residents:	
Doctors	40
Hospital beds	44

continued . . .

SHANGHAI STATISTICS (continued)

Wages

		Percentage Increase
Total annual wages of workers and staff (bn yuan)	5.36	24.9
Average annual wage (yuan)	1,105	23.2
State-owned units	1,137	
Collectively-owned units	994	
Number of workers and staff at state-run and urban collective units (mn)	4.866	
Number of individual laborers (th)	85	

Population

Total population (mn)	12.05
Population in the urban areas of the municipality (as redefined 1 Sep 1984) (mn)	6.8

Savings

Total (bn yuan)	5.6	21.7
Urban residents	5.0	
Rural residents	0.6	

Jiefang Ribao (16 Feb 1985).

Shanghai has been empowered to approve its own imports of technology up to $30 million. FBIS-CHI 17 (25 Jan 1985), AI. Shanghai handles 20 percent of China's exports and produces one-ninth of its industrial goods. The municipality hopes to double its GNP by 1990 from about 70 billion yuan in 1980. The contribution of service industries to Shanghai's total output is to increase from 21 percent in 1984 to 30 percent in 1990 and eventually to 50 percent in the year 2000. Shanghai has recently established 40 trading centers to increase domestic trade with other provinces. A financial district will be set up in Shanghai to attract foreign capital. The municipality also plans to issue bonds in Japan. *Asian Wall Street Journal Weekly* (25 Mar 1985), 2. Starting in 1985, Shanghai will remit only 77 percent of its revenue to Beijing, down from 90 percent. The additional money will be used to develop the city. Shanghai hopes to attract $4 billion in foreign investment between 1986 and 1990. During the six years prior to 1984, foreign investment totaled only $1 billion. Between 1979 and 1983, just 21 foreign companies signed joint-venture agreements with Shanghai, compared to some 1,500 contracts with the Shenzhen Special Economic Zone. The city wants similar privileges so that it can tax foreign investors only 15 percent of profits rather than the normal rate in China of 30-50 percent. *Asian Wall Street Journal Weekly* (25 Mar 1985), 3. Shanghai's 1,700 state-owned factories account for 62 percent of the total output value. FBIS-CHI 105 (31 May 1985), K16/17.

SHENZHEN AND SHENZHEN SPECIAL ECONOMIC ZONE

Beijing Review, 49 (3 Dec 1984), 19. Five industrial areas—Shekou, Shangbu, Bagualing, Shuibei, and Shahe—have been established in the Shenzhen Special Zone. Total industrial output of the zone was 1.8 billion yuan in 1984, an increase of 2,900 percent over 1979, before the Shenzhen SEZ was established. There are now over 600 factories in the zone. It has absorbed more than $600 million in foreign investment, or one-seventh of the total foreign funds invested directly in China during the last five years. *Yangcheng Wanbao* (10 Aug 1985).

continued . . .

SHENZHEN AND SHENZHEN SPECIAL ECONOMIC ZONE (continued)

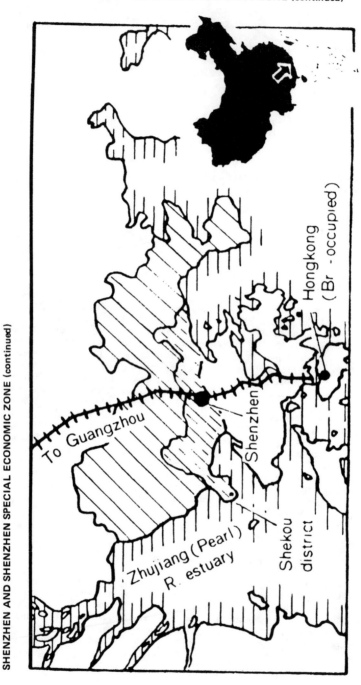

SOUTHERN FUJIAN

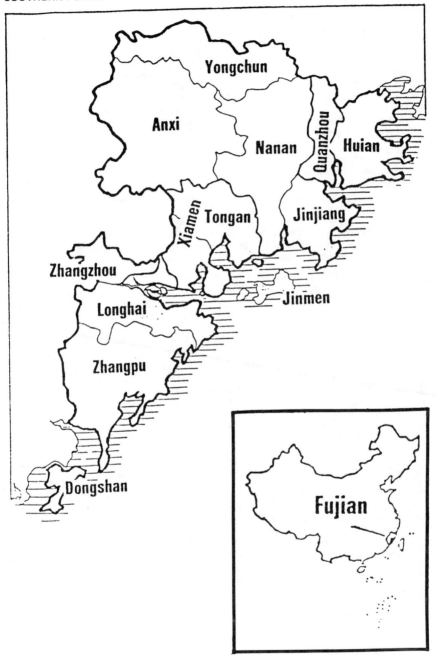

WENZHOU

Territory and Population—Located at 119°04′:−121°12′ east longitude and 27°04′−28°38′ north latitude. Wenzhou has a total territory of 11,784 km² and a population of 6.2 million, 520,000 of whom live in the 183 km² city proper. The city's jurisdiction covers two districts and nine counties.

Climate and Topography—The marine monsoon climate gives Wenzhou a mild climate the year round, with plentiful rainfall. The annual temperature averages 17.9 degrees Celsius, and annual precipitation stands at 1,700 mm.

The city's eastern sector is all flat, fertile land crisscrossed by rivers and canals, and the western, southern and northern parts are mountainous and hilly land. Many isles dot the sea off Wenzhou's 355-km coastline.

Resources and Production—Thanks to its ideal natural conditions farming, forestry, animal husbandry and fishing have been extensively developed in Wenzhou. Paddy-rice, jute, essence and other cash crops are produced in large quantities. The area is one of China's major orange and tangerine exporters and a high-yielding sugar producer.

Wenzhou's aquiculture is highly developed, producing several dozen products. Its rivers and reservoirs, rich in nutrients, abound in freshwater fish.

Gradually Wenzhou is changing itself from a commercial and handicraft city into one with modern industries such as machine-building and ship-building. Today it turns out 1,000 industrial products and its industrial output has been growing at an average annual rate of 10 percent over the last few years.

Beijing Review, 16 (22 Apr 1985), 23.

WUHAN

Wuhan, the capital of Hubei Province, is located at the confluence of the Changjiang (Yangtze) River and the Hanshui River in central China. A hub of communications since ancient times, it is, in fact, a name given collectively to three separate cities—Wuchang, Hankou and Hanyang. The three cities are naturally divided by the two rivers. With an aggregate population of 3.3 million, Wuhan constitutes the political, economic and cultural center of Hubei Province.

Wuhan developed into a business and handicraft city during the Tang and Song dynasties (618-1279). By the 15th century, it has become one of China's four major commercial metropolises.

Before the War of Resistance Against Japan (1937-45) broke out, Wuhan's domestic and foreign trade volume was second only to Shanghai. It had 52 navigation routes, leading not only to small inland ports along the Changjiang and Hanshui but also to Japan and Germany. In the pre-war years, up to 10,000 Chinese and foreign ships berthed at Hankou port annually. The city of 1 million people had 200 Chinese and foreign financial institutions, making it China's second most important financial center after Shanghai and the key banking city of the interior.

The war, however, deprived Wuhan of its importance as a financial and trading center.

Wuhan's economy picked up after 1949. Today it has become an important industrial center—its annual industrial output value ranks fourth in China. However, because the commodity economy was ignored for years, Wuhan has still not regained its role as a trading center.

Beijing Review, 28 (15 Jul 1985), 24-25.

continued . . .

WUHAN (continued)

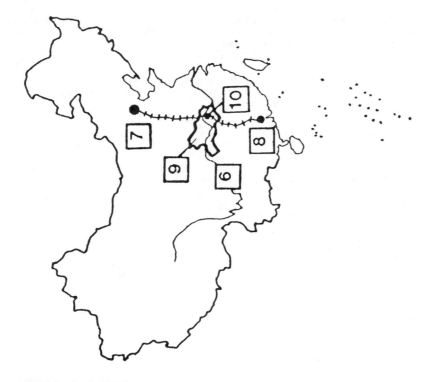

WUHAN (continued)

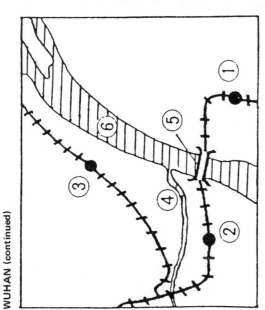

1. Wuchang
2. Hanyang
3. Hankou
4. Hanshui River
5. Changjiang River Bridge
6. Changjiang River
7. Beijing
8. Guangzhou
9. Hubei Province
10. Wuhan

ZHANJIANG

Area and Population—Zhanjiang is located in the northeast part of the Leizhou Peninsula in Guangdong Province at 110°07—110°38E longitude and 20°52—21°27N latitude. It covers 12,471 km² and has a population of 4.62 million. The city proper covers 80 km² with a population of 880,000, of which 300,000 live in the urban area and 580,000 in the suburban area.

Zhanjiang city is divided into three districts: Xiashan, Chikan and Potou and the suburbs. It has five counties under its administration, Xuwen, Haikang, Suixi, Lianjiang and Wuchuan. The city government is in Chikan.

Topography and climate—Zhanjiang has a subtropical oceanic climate, with abundant rainfall and high temperature. The average temperature exceeds 23°C. with a low of 2.8°C. and a high of 38°C. The average rainfall is 1,534.6 mm per year. Most of the rain falls between April and September.

The city's topography combines tableland and flatland. It has 1,300 km of winding coastline. There are numerous islands, bays and coral reefs.

Industry and natural resources—There are 1,012 industrial enterprises in the city producing machinery, chemicals, electric power, ships, foodstuffs, sugar, textiles, electronics and household electric appliances.

Zhanjiang's main natural resources are arenaceous quartz, volcanic ash, silica and ilmenite.

Culture, education and health work—Zhanjiang city has 5 colleges, 12 secondary technical schools and 2,353 middle schools and primary schools, with about 830,000 students and pupils. The city also has 15 scientific institutes and 6,400 technicians.

There are 553 hospitals and health departments with 12,000 doctors nurses.

Beijing Review, 12 (25 Mar 1985), 22.

ZHUHAI, 1984

	1984	Increase over 1983 (percent)
Total output value of industry and agriculture (mn yuan)	408	107
Financial revenue (mn yuan)	148	135
Projects built with foreign funds	604	141
Imported funds (mn dollars)	370	570
Total investment (mn dollars)	125	333
Capital construction investment (mn yuan)	340	151
Tourism income (mn yuan)	240	1,400

Beijing Review, 13 (1 Apr 1985), 23.

ZHUHAI SPECIAL ECONOMIC ZONE

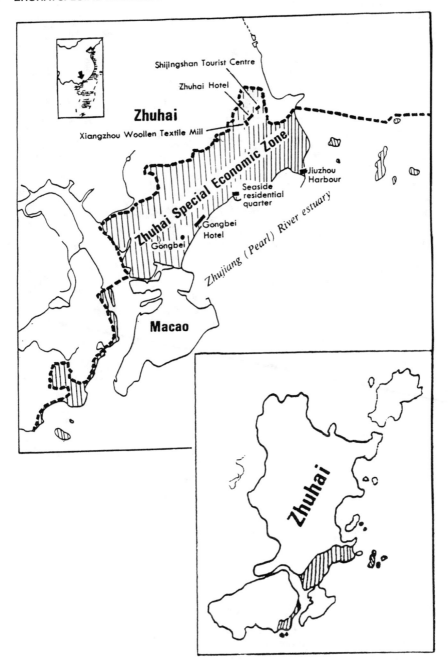

GUIZHOU

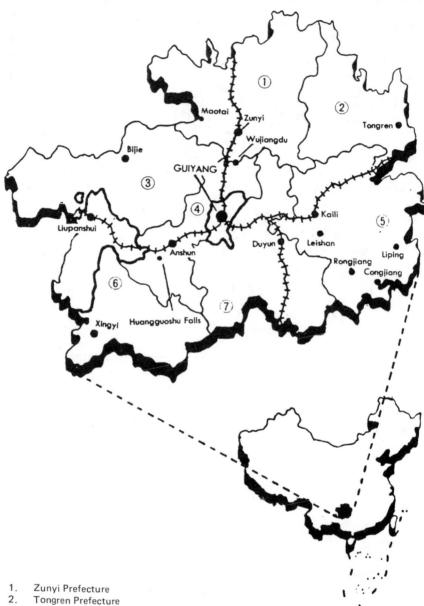

1. Zunyi Prefecture
2. Tongren Prefecture
3. Bijie Prefecture
4. Anshun Prefecture
5. Qiandongnan Miao and Dong Autonomous Prefecture
6. Qianxinan Bouyei and Miao Autonomous Prefecture
7. Qiannan Bouyei and Miao Autonomous Prefecture

Beijing Review, 32 (12 Aug 1985), 25.

XIX SPECIAL TOPICS

1985 CALENDAR OF EVENTS

January

1   The daily two-hour lunch break for urban workers is halved to an hour.

1   *Renmin Ribao* carries the speech by Deng Xiaoping to the Third Plenary Session of the CCPCC Advisory Commission 22 October 1984 in which he says of critics: "I am afraid that some of our old comrades have this fear: after a generation of socialism and communism, it is unacceptable to spout some capitalism. It cannot harm us. It cannot harm us."

1   *Renmin Ribao* quotes Zhao Ziyang that plans to decontrol prices had caused anxiety in China, but prices were still the key to the economic reforms. "Some of our comrades, good-hearted people, are a bit afraid; they fear the reform, especially the price reform," Zhao said. "China cannot reform the economic structure without a price reform."

5   The Fourth Congress of the Chinese Writers Association ends in Beijing. The meeting is characterized by calls for greater creative freedom. Ba Qin is reelected Chairman of the Association.

6   The government reports that archeologists have unearthed over 23,000 bamboo strips bearing inscriptions from the Han dynasty (206 B.C.-220 A.D.). They were found in Gansu province and record events from 9 B.C. to 111 A.D. during the reign of Emperors Wuti and Anti. The find included the first known wanted poster, ordering the apprehension of a maid who had fled the mansion of a relative of royalty.

15   *Renmin Ribao* commemorates the 50th anniversary of the accession of Mao Zedong to Chinese Communist Party leadership. It notes that Mao was allowed to commit "leftist errors" after 1949 because the people were not mentally prepared to believe he could make mistakes. The newspaper remarks that Mao saved the Party by defeating the rival faction at the Politburo meeting at Zunyi, Guizhou in January, 1935. His role between 1935 and 1949 gave him such prestige that it was impossible to think he could be seriously wrong.

26   An accident at the No. 8 Mine at Pingdingshan stops production for nine days. Miners were using an experimental production drill to attain a record output when the accident occurred.

23   Beijing says that its forces have counter-attacked against Vietnam within the past few days following a series of provocations. Vietnam had reported that Chinese troops occupied hills inside the country and bombarded the area with over 500,000 shells and mortar rounds.

February

1   *Honggi* (*Red Flag*) asserts that Marxism cannot solve all the problems facing China and must "march with the times." It criticizes Mao's tenet of "destruction first and construction in its wake."

2   *Pravda* claims that large quantities of Chinese-made arms have been seized from Afghan rebels. The weapons included ground-to-air launchers and rockets and anti-aircraft guns. The newspaper accuses the Chinese of training Afghans in camps in Pakistan.

9   Beijing protests the decision of the Reagan Administration to withhold a $23 million contribution to the United Nations Fund for Population Activities because of its opposition to birth control. China accuses the US of interfering with its internal affairs, and claims that there are no forced abortions in the PRC.

10   Li Ning is named the best athlete of 1984 in a mail poll of 1.6 million people. The gymnast won three gold medals, two silver, and a bronze at the 1984 Olympics in Los Angeles.

1985 CALENDAR OF EVENTS (continued)

18   China calls the seizure of the Khmer Rouge headquarters on the Phnom Malai Mountain Range along the Thai-Cambodian border militarily insignificant. It says that Vietnam will never achieve its "vicious aim of perpetual occupation" of the country.

20   The PRC formally opens its first Antarctic research station and invites Taiwan to participate in scientific studies.

20   Hu Yaobang says in a speech published today that Communists had wasted 20 years since coming to power in 1949 because of "radical leftist nonsense" linked to the ideas of Mao Zedong. Hu was apparently referring to the period from the Great Leap Forward in 1958 to the Cultural Revolution between 1966 and 1976. The speech was delivered 19 January to 400 graduates of a high-level Party training course but withheld from publication for two months. Deng Xiaoping had said much the same in an October, 1984 speech which was not published until December. Deng remarked that China had been impoverished and backward for 300 years because it had closed its door to the world. Even though it began relations with the USSR and Eastern Europe in 1949, even by 1960 "we did not make any progress."

20   The Year of the Rat becomes the Year of the Ox. A televised lottery attracts an audience estimated at 200 million. Prizes for some of the 30 million ticket-holders include refrigerators, tv sets, furniture, and a motorcycle. Chinese newspapers subsequently condemn the lottery as a "disgusting show" similar to race-track gambling in pre-Communist China. Such events supposedly discouraged work and convinced people they could become rich by chance.

28   It is reported that three performers for cultural groups have been sentenced to prison as spies for Taiwan. Xin Peiwen, 46, an actor in an Army cultural troupe, receives 10 years. Su Mao, 27, a musician with the Central Ballet Company, gets seven, and Li Qiang, 39, an actor with the Experimental Opera Troupe, is given three years imprisonment.

March

3   Zhang Chengxian, a member of the Standing Committee of the National People's Congress, leads a delegation to the USSR at the invitation of the Supreme Soviet. The 10-day visit by an NPC delegation is the first in over two decades, and follows the December, 1984 trip to Beijing by First Feputy Minister Ivan Arkhipov.

4-9   President Li Xiannian visits Burma.

4   The Chinese press says that cliff carvings of the 13th-century conqueror Kublai Khan (1215-94) have been found on the northern bank of the Yangtze near Luzhou, Sichuan. The carvings depicted the Khan flanked by two bodyguards and a Chinese general kneeling to his left.

6   The finals of a beauty pageant are held in Guangzhou, Guangdong. More than 600 contestants compete to become Miss and Mr. Guangzhou (Canton).

7   Deng Xiaoping remarks that China would continue its flexible economic policies, but changes were intended to enhance socialism and achieve communism. He warns the young against becoming "captives of capitalist ideas."

11   President Li Xiannian visits Thailand. Bangkok had hoped that the five-day visit would result in increased Chinese activity against the Vietnamese in Kampuchea.

13   The State Council calls for an immediate stop to illegal price increases. Certain departments and enterprises have sold scarce commodities at exorbitant prices, while others have abused the concept of "negotiable prices." Restaurants are forbidden to raise prices indiscriminately, and individuals may not resell train or ship tickets at higher prices or resell ration coupons.

15   The new General Secretary of the Communist Party of the Soviet Union Mikhail Gorbachev states in his inaugural speech that the USSR would like a "genuine improvement in relations with the Chinese People's Republic." During his meeting

continued . . .

1985 CALENDAR OF EVENTS (continued)

	with Gorbachev after the funeral of Konstantin Chernenko, Chinese Vice-Premier Li Peng refers to the USSR as a "socialist country."
21	The 10th meeting of the Sixth National People's Congress Standing Committee ends in Beijing. Chen Muhua is appointed President of the People's Bank of China and Zheng Tuobin the Minister of Foreign Economic Relations and Trade.
22	The crew of a PLA Navy torpedo boat on a training mission defects to South Korea. The vessel and its crew are returned to China 28 March.
24	Yi Xigong, who was arrested in 1982 and sentenced to two and a half years in a camp for his relations with an American woman, arrives in San Francisco to marry Lisa Wichser. He had been expelled from Beijing as a "CIA agent."
25	*Renmin Ribao* publishes the text of Central Committee Document No. 1 of 1985 entitled "Ten Policies of the CCP Central Committee and the State Council for Further Invigorating the Rural Economy."
27	The passenger ferry Hongxing No. 283 capsizes during a storm off the Junan district of Shunde county, Guangdong. Some 156 persons, including 13 crew members, are saved immediately, and rescuers continue to search for another 72.
27	The Third Session of the Sixth National People's Congress begins in Beijing. Zhao Ziyang reports that the total value of industrial and agricultural growth was 14.2 percent in 1984, straining energy and transport systems. He calls for a target of 7 percent in 1985, with industry to grow by 8 percent and agriculture by 6 percent. A number of criticisms voiced by delegates to the Congress are mentioned in the *Far Eastern Economic Review* (18 Apr 1985), 12-13.

April

10	Hu Yaobang tells Australian and New Zealand reporters that Washington has agreed to exclude nuclear-armed ships from the port call planned for Shanghai in 1985. The US had refused New Zealand such assurances, resulting in the withdrawal by Washington from a joint naval exercise and, in effect, suspension of its participation in the ANZUS Pact. An American spokesman declined to comment on Hu's remarks.
11	Radio Beijing reports that consortia from France, Canada, and Monaco have started to build an 88-story skyscraper in the Shenzhen Special Economic Zone. The structure will be 26 stories higher than the tallest building in Hong Kong. It will have a restaurant on the top floor and a heliport on the roof. The cost will run about $450 million.
12-24	General Secretary Hu Yaobang tours Australia, New Zealand, Western Samoa, Fiji, and Papua New Guinea. Hu says that China wants no military role in the South Pacific.
17	Deng Xiaoping calls the Vietnamese occupation of Kampuchea/Cambodia the "easiest" of the three major obstacles to the normalization of relations between the USSR and China. He says that Beijing would not oppose a Soviet naval base at Cam Ranh Bay if Moscow were able to persuade Hanoi to withdraw from Kampuchea.
18	An earthquake registering 6.3 Richter hits Luquan county and Dongchuan city, about 100 km north of Kunming, Yunnan. Twenty-two are killed and over 300 injured.
18	An American and five North Koreans are among 10 people who die in a fire at the new 15-story Swan Hotel in Harbin. The fire engulfed the upper stories shortly after midnight. Richard S. Ondrik, 34, an American representing Energy Projects Southeast Asia Ltd. of Hong Kong, is arrested and charged with criminal negligence. He is sentenced to 18 months in jail and fined $52,000 in August, 1985, but subsequently released.
21-29	Peng Zhen, Chairman of the Standing Committee of the National People's Congress, visits Tokyo, Osaka, Kobe and Kyoto during his trip to Japan. He urges leaders to expand ties with Third World countries.

continued . . .

1895 CALENDAR OF EVENTS (continued)

25 Hundreds of Chinese occupy the steps of the Communist Party headquarters in Beijing to demand permission to return to the capital from Shaanxi. They had been sent to the countryside in 1968 as Red Guards and rural workers. Some 20,000 persons still remain in the province, or about half of those originally sent. Authorities call the demonstration "completely wrong," and the protest ends 30 April.

28 *Renmin Ribao* announces that 1,000 young officials have been chosen from all over China to comprise a "third echelon" of provincial and ministerial leadership. Other tens of thousands have been selected for eventual promotion to lower-level posts in counties and prefectures. The "first echelon" refers to revolutionary leaders such as Mao Zedong, Zhou Enlai, and Deng. The "second echelon" is made up of people who have been promoted since 1949, such as Hu Yaobang and Zhao Ziyang.

May

8 China joins the African Development Bank (ADB) and the African Development Fund (ADF).

10 Prices of meat, fish and eggs and some 1,800 non-staple items rise by an average of more than 50 percent. The increases attempt to eliminate state subsidies for foods. Each person will be given about $2.65 a month to help offset the price hikes.

10 During a visit to China by PLO Chairman Yasir Arafat, Premier Zhao Ziyang criticizes Israel for failing to recognize the legitimate rights of the Palestinian people and for refusing to return Arab lands. Zhao says "their mistaken stand is the greatest obstacle to a peaceful settlement of the Mideast problem."

15 China says it will release Hanson Huang, 34, a Hong Kong-born, Harvard-trained lawyer who disappeared in the PRC in January, 1982 during a visit to Beijing. He had been sentenced to 15 years for spying, but was released purportedly because of his model behavior and "willingness to serve Chinese modernization."

18 It is reported that the first completely hollow *dagoba* has been found in Shenyang, Liaoning province. *Dagobas* contain the relics or ashes of Buddhas or Buddhist saints. The 13-story, 33-meter-high hollow *dagoba*, called the Tawan *dagoba*, may have been constructed around 1100 A.D. The structure contains murals of the Liao dynasty (916-1125).

18-24 The visit by three US destroyers to Shanghai as a symbol of bilateral military cooperation is postponed. It would have been the first US Navy port call to the PRC.

19 Violence erupts after China is eliminated from World Cup competition in soccer by Hong Kong (2-1) at the Workers' Stadium in Beijing. An estimated 5,000 Chinese youths hurl bottles and garbage at the visiting team, then rough up a number of diplomats and a reporter outside the Stadium. Thirty police are beaten, some 130 fans arrested, and three eventually receive public trials. The coach of the Chinese Football Association, Zeng Xuelin, subsequently resigns, and the entire team is disbanded.

20 People caught spitting in Beijing's public places will be made to clean up after themselves and pay a fine of 50 fen.

23 China announces that it will negotiate with Portugal to reclaim Macao. It will model the colony on the basis of "one country, two systems," similar to the future promised Hong Kong after 1997. Portugal offered to return Macao to China in 1974, but Beijing refused, apparently occupied with the Cultural Revolution. This announcement was made during a week-long visit by the President of Portugal Antonio Ramalho Eanes beginning 20 May.

29 China announces plans to allow more autonomy for universities, colleges, and private schools, and to expand technical and vocational training. Nine years of schooling will become universal in large cities and coastal areas by 1990, and throughout China by 1995. Various institutions will have more control over admissions, administrative appointments, curriculum, and scientific research. Free

continued . . .

1985 CALENDAR OF EVENTS (continued)

tuition will be replaced by some stipends and scholarships, and other students will be encouraged to find part-time employment. The percentage of students taking vocational training will increase from 32 to 50 by 1990.

29   Xinhua reports that Beijing's highest skyscraper has been finished. The China International Trust and Investment Corp. (CITIC) has constructed a 31-story, 101-meter-high office building for 65 million yuan. Work started in April, 1982.

June

1   A 5-percent industrial and commercial consolidated tax is imposed on all foreign, Hong Kong and Macao corporations doing business in the PRC and other economic organizations. Taxable items include commissions, rebates, and fees for conducting market surveys and providing business information as well as performing liaison, consultation and other services for clients in China. Foreign firms and other organizations must register to do business in the PRC. Enterprises were required to pay a 15-percent income tax as of 1 January 1985.

2-19   Premier Zhao Ziyang visits Britain, the Federal Republic of Germany, and the Netherlands. He seeks broader trade and political ties between the PRC and Western Europe.

10   The retired Australian aircraft carrier *Melbourne* arrives in Guangzhou's Huangpu port, where it will be turned into scrap.

26   The Foreign Ministry accuses the Vietnamese of 90 "acts of aggression" during the first half of June. Shelling occurred daily, including incidents involving more than 10,000 rounds.

26   The Chinese ocean-liner *Jianzhen* arrives in Kobe, Japan. It is the first Chinese liner to visit the country in 35 years. The *Jianzhen* goes to Osaka 28 June.

30   Bo Yibo, Deputy Chairman of the Central Commission for Guiding Party Consolidation, warns against "spiritual pollution" and "money worship" corrupting some Chinese. The warning appears in all major newspapers.

July

1   The length of the lunch break at all government offices is extended from one hour to an hour and a half between 1 June and 30 September of each year. The change is supposed to allow workers to rest longer during the summer heat.

5-10   Talks are successfully conducted on opening the ports of Heihe and Blagoveshchensk for Sino-Soviet trade. The volume of trade between Heilongjiang and the Soviet Far East was to increase 43 percent in 1985 over 1984.

5-20   Taylor Wang, 44, a Chinese-American astronaut, visits China. Wang was born in Shanghai, educated in the US, and now works at a jet-propulsion laboratory in California. He was on the 17th flight of the *Challenger* space-shuttle in 1985.

9-16   Deputy Prime Minister Yao Yilin visits the USSR to sign the 1986-90 trade agreement. The 1986-90 trade agreement between the USSR and the PRC is signed 10 July. Trade during the five-year period will total some 12 billion rubles, reaching 3 billion by 1990. The Soviets will assist the Chinese in building seven new facilities and reconstructing 17 others in such fields as ferrous and non-ferrous metallurgy, machine building, power engineering, and the coal and chemical industries.

12   The No. 3 coal mine of the Guangdong Meitian Mining Administration explodes. Out of 109 miners, 53 are killed and three are missing.

20   The *China Daily* reports 275 deaths from torrential rains in Guizhou and Sichuan provinces during July. Two dams with a total water capacity of 52,000 cubic meters broke 2 July at Qiandongnan, killing 47. Landslides and flooding left another 64 dead in Liupanshui, Guizhou. By the second week of August the death toll had reached 500 after a series of storms throughout the PRC. Some 14,000 were left homeless in Yunnan province alone.

22   President Li Xiannian visits the US. He travels to Niagara Falls, Washington, D.C., Chicago, Los Angeles, and Honolulu. He is the first Chinese Communist head of

continued . . .

1985 CALENDAR OF EVENTS (continued)

    state to come to the US. On 23 July Li and President Reagan sign an agreement to allow the sale of American nuclear reactors and technology to China. The pact had been stalled since April, 1984, when President Reagan initialed the agreement during his visit to the PRC. It was subsequently discovered that Chinese nuclear specialists were seen at the Kahuta Plant in Pakistan where a nuclear device is thought under construction. The US Department of State claims that it now has sufficient assurances from the Chinese to prevent the transfer of nuclear technology.

27   An Indonesian trade mission arrives in Beijing to resume commercial contacts. Relations were suspended by Indonesia in 1967 following an abortive Communist coup in 1965.

29   The Ministry of Public Health announces that an Argentine tourist, Oscar Messina, 34, has died of AIDS, the acquired immune deficiency syndrome. It calls for a quarantine to stop the spread of the disease. This is the first case ever reported in in the PRC.

August

7   The Ministry of Civil Affairs puts the death toll at 177 from the typhoon which swept across Zhejiang province 30 July. Some 1,400 ships sank or were badly damaged, 20,000 homes were destroyed, and about 1,400 people were injured.

11   *Renmin Ribao* says that a conference of foreign investors at Lanzhou called to develop western China has resulted in 162 agreements worth $1.27 billion.

13   An American businessman, Richard S. Ondrik, 34, receives 18 months in jail after being found guilty of criminal negligence in the fire at the Swan Hotel in Harbin, Heilongjiang 19 April. A deputy chief of security at the Hotel, Jiang Guoyun, was sentenced to two years and a hotel floor attendant, Gu Su, got three months in jail for having left their posts. Ondrik has sought to appeal the verdict.

14   A gas explosion at the Renziping coal mine in Qinzhou, southern Guangxi causes a 300-meter tunnel to collapse. Twenty-one miners are killed. It is the worst gas explosion in Guangxi coal mines since 1955.

18   Ferry No. 423, traveling southwards from Sanlian wharf of scenic Taiyang Dao, capsizes near the main channel in the center of the Songhua Jiang at Harbin with 234 passengers aboard. Only 60 survive. Exceeding the boat's capacity of 148 persons, the absence of the helmsman from his post, and fighting among some passengers were deemed the causes of the disaster.

21   The Chinese Ministry of Education reports that the first Soviet students in Beijing in more than 20 years left the University dormitory in shambles when they went home in July. Some of the 19 students apparently disliked the constant surveillance and limited access to information.

22   Xinhua criticizes the visit by Japanese Prime Minister Yasuhiro Nakasone and most members of his cabinet to a shrine for Japan's war dead. The visit coincided with the 40th anniversary of Japan's surrender in World War II. The Xinhua News Agency said that China hoped the Japanese would "bow to the historical facts and take an unequivocal stand on that appalling war of aggression and on where the guilt and responsibility lie." It linked General Tojo, who was among those honored by the visit to the shrine, to the Nanjing Massacre in December, 1937, during which the Japanese reportedly killed some 300,000 Chinese.

23   An earthquake registers 7.4 Richter in the Xinjiang Uygur region. At least 60 people are killed and more than 100 injured. Aftershocks, which injure another 125, register above 5 on the Richter scale.

24   A Chinese light bomber twin-jet Harbin-5 (based on the Soviet IL-28) crash-lands south of Seoul after running out of fuel. The pilot requests political asylum in Taiwan, but the radio operator says he wants to return to the PRC.

continued . . .

1985 CALENDAR OF EVENTS (continued)

September

1   New limits are imposed on access to Tibet for foreign reporters and observers. The government is dissatisfied with the stories reporters have filed about the region.

4   China welcomes the resignation of Pol Pot as head of the Khmer Rouge. Ma Yuzhen of the Foreign Ministry adds that the move will enhance unity among anti-Vietnamese rebels forces. A Western diplomat reports that Chinese leaders recently attended a screening of *The Killing Fields,* a movie about the seizure of power by the Khmer Rouge in 1975, and that they were shocked by what they saw.

7-15   The Second National Workers' Games are held at the Beijing Workers' Stadium. Almost 5,000 participants from 32 teams compete in track and field, football (soccer), basketball, volleyball, table tennis, swimming, cycling, and *wu shu.* Athletes broke 298 records. About 40 million Chinese participate regularly in sports. There are 244 stadia and gymnasiums, 168,000 sporting grounds, and 2,000 swimming pools in the PRC. Over 400,000 teams have been organized.

9   The Soviet radio station which has broadcast anti-Chinese programs to the PRC for six years ends its transmissions.

11   Three Iranian naval vessels seize the Chinese cargo ship *Jinjiang,* which had been sailing from Thailand to Kuwait with 13,000 tons of corn, while it is passing through the Hormuz Strait. The ship is searched and force to the Iranian port of Bandar-e 'Abbas.

12   An earthquake registering 6.8 Richter hits the western part of Xinjiang around Wuqia and Shufu counties. An earthquake of 7.4 magnitude hit the same area in late August.

14   *Wen Wei Po* of Hong Kong reports that China and Portugal are preparing for talks on the future of Macao. China plans to employ the same "one country, two systems" principle there that it will use in Hong Kong after 1997. Macao has been a Portuguese enclave for 428 years.

16   *Hongqi (Red Flag)* says the ranks of the Communist Party are filled with corruption, arrogance, cynicism, moral degeneracy, crime and greed. It calls for improvement within three years. The editorial coincides with a meeting of the Central Committee at which a large number of Party veterans are retired to make way for younger leaders.

22   Sixty-four persons are named to the Central Committee, including 29 new full members and 35 alternate (non-voting) members. The average age of these new appointees is just over 50, and 76 percent have college educations. Another 27 alternate members were promoted to full membership in the Central Committee, bringing the total to 210 full members and 123 alternates. Those 64 who have retired from the Central Committee were in the 70s and 80s. Among those promoted to the Central Committee are Deputy Foreign Minister Qian Qichen; Air Force Commander Wang Hai; Hu Jintao, 42, the youngest provincial Party leader (Guizhou) ever appointed in the PRC; Wan Shaofan (f), the Party Secretary of Jiangxi province and the first woman to head a provincial organization; and Ye Xuanping, the Governor of Guangdong and son of Marshal Ye Jianying. During a special Party conference, fifty-six mew members were named to the Central Advisory Commission, Party elders, and 31 of the Central Discipline Inspection Commission. Ten of the Politburo's 24 members have been retired, including Ye Jianying, 88.

23   Chen Yun tells deputies to a national Party conference to reject capitalism and follow Marxist theory. "There are now some people, including some party members, who have forsaken the socialist and communist ideal and turned their backs on serving the people," he remarks. Chen claims that it was a mistake to downgrade ideological and propaganda departments and this had led to speculation, bribery and other crimes for personal gain.

continued . . .

1985 CALENDAR OF EVENTS (continued)

24   The International Atomic Energy Agency announces that the PRC has agreed to permit the inspection of some of its non-military nuclear facilities. Inspectors will try to discover whether any nuclear material is being diverted for military purposes.

26-5 Oct   Party General Secretary Hu Yaobang retraces a portion of the Long March, which was taken by Communists from southeast to the northwest China during 1934-35, to observe the anniversary.

30   Foreign Minister Wu Xueqian tells the 40th UN General Assembly that the USSR and US should halt their arms race in outer space immediately. He calls on the powers to pledge not to be the first to use nuclear weapons. Xu says NATO and the Warsaw Pact should agree to reduce sharply conventional forces. He calls on the Conference on Disarmament in Geneva to speed negotiations to ban the production, deployment, and use of chemical weapons.

October

2   China and the USSR agree to exchange visits of their Foreign Ministers. It would be the first exchange in more than 20 years.

15   US Vice-President George Bush ends three days of talks with Chinese leaders. Deng Xiaoping is said to have told Bush that relations were "normal on the whole," but the most important problem continued to be the Taiwan question. When this is settled, Deng claimed, Chinese-American relations will flow smoothly in every field. Beijing has accused Washington of violating the spirit of a 1982 agreement, which promised a gradual reduction in weapons sales to Taipei, by selling Taiwan an estimated $760 million in arms during 1985, only marginally down from the $780 in 1984. The Chinese have been concerned about trade protectionism in the US, but Bush commented later that prospects for trade were encouraging. Bush also apparently raised the question of human rights in the PRC. The Vice-President won two of three doubles sets against Vice-Premier and Politburo member Wan Li, 69.

18   The Bolshoi Ballet performs in Beijing for the first time in 20 years. The company arrived in Shanghai 10 October and gave four performances prior to coming to the capital.

31   Xinhua News Agency reports that some 30,000 persons and 2 million animals have been stranded in northwest China since a blizzard hit the area 17 October. The Qinghai-Tibetan Plateau is covered with 20 inches of snow.

November

2   *Renmin Ribao* announces that China will convert to the metric system 1 January 1986. The system will be introduced gradually in the packaging and pricing of food.

8   *Renmin Ribao* reports that Navy divers saved 15 coal miners trapped in a flooded shaft in northern Shanxi. Seven miners are still missing.

23   Retired CIA analyst Larry Wu-Tai Chin, 63, is charged with having spied for the PRC for more than 30 years. Chin is said to have been paid over $140,000 for information he supplied while working in the US Consulate in Hong Kong and in the CIA's Foreign Broadcast Information Service. He allegedly also provided classified materials after retiring in 1981.

26   An iron bar holding overhead lights falls on one of nine Chinese clay warriors being exhibited at Dublin Hall. They were part of the terra-cotta army which guarded the tomb of China's first emperor. A clay soldier loses an arm. The next day scaffolding falls, decapitating one of two ancient warhorses in the exhibition. Dublin is the last stop for these art treasures in a worldwide tour.

28   A special session of the Communist Youth League meets in Beijing following two recent student marches in Tiananmen Square 18 September and 20 November and protests in at least three other cities since September. The marches have been

continued . . .

1985 CALENDAR OF EVENTS (continued)

aimed against Japan, but it is believed they actually represent opposition to Deng Xiaoping's "open door" policy of broadening China's foreign relations. A series of rallies will be held in December throughout China to observe the 50th anniversary of the student uprising in the capital that persuaded Chiang Kai-shek to join the Communist Party in a united front against Japan. Last week, veterans of the 1935 uprising attended a forum at Beijing University to urge students to end their marches and agitation. They told the students that foreign contacts will ultimately strengthen China's economy.

December

7   The temperature reaches -15.1 Centigrade, the lowest reading since 1915. Nearly 260 buses refuse to start. The Beijing subway is jammed, and entrances are closed to regulate the flow of passengers.

10   A rally of about 4,000 students is held in Beijing to support the "open door" policies of Deng Xiaoping. It is Deng's response to a series of demonstrations against Japan and against his broadening of foreign relations. The rally includes a speech by Nie Weiping, who was called a hero at a student rally 20 November for defeating a Japanese player in a recent chess championship. Nie calls for student support of the modernization program, which includes the import of foreign technology.

19   An official reports that about 1,500 students had protested housing PLA Army units at the Agricultural University in Beijing. They also had demonstrated against poor food and security on campus.

19   A twin-engine Aeroflot Antonov-24 on a flight between Chita and North Korea is seized by "an armed criminal" and told to fly to South Korea. The plane apparently runs low on fuel and lands at Gannan, Heilongjiang province, where passengers and crew are returned to the USSR two days later.

22   Some 200-300 students stage a protest march in Tiananmen Square in Beijing to demonstrate against atmospheric testing of nuclear weapons in the Xinjiang Autonomous Region. Many protesters are Uygurs from Xinjiang who are attending the Central College of Nationalities. About a thousand people demonstrated in Urumqi 12 December against testing at Lop Nor.

24   The principal dam of the Tianshengqiao Hydroelectric power station under construction in Guangxi collapses, burying 55 workers. Forty-eight people die in the accident. A leak in the dam was either ignored or not noticed by construction workers.

SPACE NEWS, 1985

Ground Station—China has developed a mobile ground station able to communicate through satellites with other ground stations. FBIS-CHI 120 (21 Jun 1985), K20.

Orders—The PRC will accept orders for space equipment, including satellites, ground stations, and launch vehicles. *China Daily* (13 Jun 1985), 1.

Space Facilities—Facilities and hardware at the Shuang Cheng Tzu launch site in the Gobi Desert appear in *Aviation Week Space Technology* (8 Apr 1985), 52-53.

17th Satellite—A Long March-2 rocket launched the 17th Chinese satellite 21 October 1985. The satellite was recovered five days later. The Long March-2, a two-stage liquid rocket capable of putting a two-ton satellite into near-earth orbit, and the Long March-3, which has launched a telecommunications satellite into geostationary orbit, will be used to launch foreign satellites. They will be orbited from Jiuquan, Gansu (near-earth) and Xichang, Sichuan (geostationary). Early-stage support services are also available to customers. *Beijing Review*, 45 (11 Nov 1985), 30.

continued . . .

SPACE NEWS, 1985 (continued)

French Agreement– China and France signed an agreement 21 June 1985 for cooperation in building ground observation satellite platforms, satellite monitoring equipment, and carrier-rocket parts. Minneapolis *Star and Tribune* (22 Jun 1985), 10A.

Space Revelations in 1984–The Chinese made several revelations about their space program during 1984. For example they announced that they had flown a puppy in space in 1967. The puppy, named Xiao Bao (Little Leopard), apparently flew on a suborbital rocket and was successfully recovered. They also reported that there had been a major explosion at one of their launch pads on January 28, 1978 which resulted in at least seven people being seriously injured, and a dozen or more people receiving burns to their hair, eyebrows, and faces. In addition, they honored as a martyr a young engineer who helped develop the first geostationary satellite, but died after six or seven years of suffering the health effects of exposure to radiation during experiments related to that task. Finally, they announced that they have outfitted two ships to provide tracking services for satellite launches. Marcia S. Smith, *Space Activities of the United States, Soviet Union and Other Launching Countries/ Organizations: 1957-1984* (1985), CRS-107.

Launch Plans–The PRC has announced that it will compete with the US and European countries to launch satellites for other nations. China has not yet decided how much to charge or how to market the service. FBIS-CHI 34 (20 Feb 1985), K11; London *Financial Times* (13 Jun 1985), 24.

Altitude-Control System–Jiaotong University in Shanghai has developed a solar-battery-powered system to control satellite altitude. The system works more reliably than the air jets which had been used. *Ta Kung Pao* (11 Apr 1985), 7.

CHINESE SPACE LAUNCHES, 1970-84

Spacecraft Name	Launch Date	Launch Site	Comments
China 1	04/24/70	SCt *	Engineering test. "East is Red" song played until 05/20/70.
China 2	03/03/71	SCt	Housekeeping test and possible science.
China 3	07/26/75	SCt	Science? Reconnaissance? Not recovered.
China 4	11/26/75	SCt	Possible reconnaissance test. Recovered.
China 5	12/16/75	SCt	Like China 3.
China 6	08/30/76	SCt	Possible electronics intelligence gathering test and/or science. Not recovered.
China 7	12/07/76	SCt	Possible reconnaissance test. Recovered.
China 8	01/26/78	SCt	Possible reconnaissance test. Recovered.
China 9-11	09/19/81	SCt	Triple scientific payload for space physics experiments.
China 12	09/09/82	SCt	Possible reconnaissance test. Recovered.
China 13	08/19/83	SCt	Possible reconnaissance test. Recovered.
China 14	01/29/84	Chengdu	Possible failure of new upper stage.
China 15	04/08/84	Chengdu	First Chinese geostationary communications satellite.
China 16	09/12/84	SCt	Possible reconnaissance test. Recovered.
China 17	10/21/85	SCt	Possible reconnaissance test. Recovered.

* SCt = Shuang Cheng-tzu

Marcia S. Smith, *Space Activities of the United States, Soviet Union and Other Launching Countries/Organizations: 1957-1984* (CRS 85-45 SPR, 1985), 108. Also see P.S. Clark, "The Chinese Space Programme," *Journal of the British Interplanetary Society*, 37 (1984), 195-206.

TOURISM, 1984

		Percentage Increase Over 1983
Visitors from 162 countries and regions for tourism (mn)	12.85	35.6
Foreign tourists (mn)	1.13	30.0
Overseas Chinese and compatriots from Hong Kong and Macao	11.72	36.2
Foreign exchange earned through tourism (bn dollars)	1.13	20.2

Beijing Review, 12 (25 Mar 1985), vii.

HOTELS AND TOURISM, 1985

Shearson-Lehman Hotel Project—A 25-story hotel will be put up on the site of Beijing's Friendship Store. The first five stories will be occupied by the new store. Shearson-Lehman Bros. will arrange financing of $150 million and run the project. A separate apartment and office complex will be constructed in the Sanlitun district in northeast Beijing. The firm will split profits 50-50 with the Chinese, and then pay management.

Tianjin—The Commonwealth Bank of Australia Ltd. will provide a $15 million loan to aid construction of the 450-room First Hyatt Hotel in Tianjin. The project is to be finished early in 1986.

Sauna—Beijing's first public sauna has opened at the public bathhouse at Zhushikou, south of Tiananmen Square. The price of a bath and sauna is 2.5 yuan ($0.90).

Tourist Institute—A tourist institute of the Beijing Joint University was established 4 April 1985. It has guide and tourist management departments with specialties for English and Japanese guides and in hotel management. The institute plans to add specialties in accounting and cuisine. It offers one- and three-year courses.

Tours—Kit Salter describes typical tour stops in "Windows on a Changing China," *Focus*, 35, 1 (Jan 1985), 12-21.

Huating Hotel—The Sheraton Corp. has agreed to manage the Huating Hotel in Shanghai. It is scheduled to open in April, 1986. Sheraton took over management of the 1,007-room Great Wall Sheraton Hotel-Beijing in March, 1985. The hotel in Shanghai will be built with a $70 million investment by the Corp. *Beijing Review*, 45 (11 Nov 1985), 31.

Scenic Wonders—A nation-wide poll has named the top 10 scenic wonders in China. They are:

> The Great Wall
> Sun Moon Lake, Taiwan
> Guilin (karst formations)
> West Lake, Hangzhou
> The Forbidden City, Beijing
> Suzhou
> Huangshan Mountain
> The Yangtze River Gorges
> Chengde (mountain resort)
> Emperor Qin Shi Huang's terra-cotta warriors at Xian

Hangzhou—In 1984 over 13 million Chinese tourists and more than 180,000 foreign tourists visited Hangzhou, the capital of Zhejiang province. There are now 591 hotels in the city. Hangzhou has more than 100 sites of historic interest, about 40 of which have opened to the public after recent renovation.

Guilin—A tour of Guilin is described in the *Christian Science Monitor* (11 Oct 1985), B6-7, B12.

continued . . .

HOTELS AND TOURISM, 1985 (continued)

Urumqi—The foundation stone for the Huanqiu Hotel in Urumqi, Xinjiang was laid in October, 1985. The hotel will be a joint venture between the Urumqi City Economic Development General Company and Hong Kong's Jiahua Enterprises Ltd.

Shanxi—Shanxi province hopes to attract 1.5 million foreign tourists by the year 2000. Some 124,000 visited Shanxi in 1984. Foreign companies have signed joint ventures for 10 tourist hotels with 9,300 beds. The hotels will cost $349 million. The terra-cotta army of Qin Shihuang is located near Xian.

Beijing—Over 657,000 foreign tourists and Chinese from Hong Kong, Taiwan, and Macao visited Beijing in 1984, representing an increase of 29.1 percent over 1983. Beijing has some 50 tourist hotels with 13,000 double rooms. Nine hotels with 3,000 rooms were finished in 1984.

Dalian Golf Club—A golf club covering 600,000 m^2 is to be built at Dalian, Liaoning by June, 1985. Three local Chinese companies will cooperate with the Toko Trading Company and the Taisei Engineering and Construction Company of Japan. There is already a course designed by Arnold Palmer at the Zhongshan hot springs in Guangdong, and an 18-hole course opened in May, 1985 at Tangjiawan in the Zhuhai Special Economic Zone. The Japan Golf Promotion Corp. is spending $11.8 million to built an 18-hold golf course near the Ming Tombs, 25 miles north of Beijing.

Sichuan—Sichuan province will open several areas to tourists, including the Jiouzhai Valley, a mountain resort; Zigong county, the "home of the dinosaurs;" Changning county, known for its bamboo groves; and the stone forests in Xingwen county.

Xian—Xian, Shaanxi expects 180,000 foreign tourists in 1985. By 1990 the city will receive 600,000. FBIS-CHI 36 (22 Feb 1985), C1.

Holiday Inns—Holiday Inns, Inc. currently has 12 hotel projects under negotiation in the PRC. *Asian Wall Street Journal Weekly* (29 Apr 1985), 12.

Ice Sculptures—*L'Express* (8-14 Feb 1985), 162-66, features photographs of ice sculpture at the annual Harbin festival. The event was suspended in 1966, but resumed in 1978.

Inner Mongolia—A 20-story hotel is planned for Hohhot, the capital of Inner Mongolia. The hotel will have 500 beds. Completion is scheduled for the end of 1985. XNB (3 May 1985), 28-29.

Beijing—Restrictions on foreigners visiting certain areas around Beijing were lifted 1 April 1985. The areas which were opened included seven counties and districts: Daxing, Tongxian, Shunyi, Pinggu, Miyun, Fengtai and Yanshan. Parts of seven other areas were opened to foreigners: Fangshan, Yanqing, Changping, Huairou, Haidian, Shijingshan and Mentougou. It is not necessary to obtain permits to visit these places.

Hotel for the Handicapped—The Kanghui Hotel in southeastern Beijing opened 24 May 1985. The establishment can accommodate 120 handicapped persons, and has special facilities for tourists who require wheel chairs.

Beijing-Guangzhou Hotel—An agreement has been signed with Japan's Kumagai Gumi Group to build a $100 million hotel, office and exhibition complex in Beijing. The 53-story Beijing-Guangzhou Hotel is the tallest in the capital. It will be located in the Chaoyang District. Completion is scheduled for 1988.

Lhasa—The Tibet Hotel in Lhasa is under construction. It consists of three ivory-colored buildings and two villas with 1,100 beds.

Miyun Amusement Park—The Miyun International Amusement Park has opened near the Miyun Reservoir in Beijing. The roller coaster attains speeds of 100 km per hour over its 1,060-meter course.

Great Wall—A second section of the Great Wall of China is to open to tourists 1 October 1985. The portion is located at Mutianyu, 60 km northeast of Beijing. The only section which had been open previously was at Badaling, 80 km north of the capital. *Le Devoir* (10 Aug 1985), 30. It is also possible, however, to visit the Wall at Shanhaiguan, 125 miles east

continued . . .

HOTELS AND TOURISM, 1985 (continued)

of Beijing, where it runs into the sea. It was here that Wu Sangui opened the gate to the Man-chus. The trip by train from Beijing is five to seven hours. New York *Times* (8 Sep 1985), 12xx, 29xx.

Gunsu— The Qilian Mountains in Gansu were opened to foreign tourists and climbers in July, 1985. There is a 5,548-meter unconquered peak in the area.

Mt. Luofo—The Mount Luofo Development Corp. has invested 30 million yuan to open the mountain to tourism. It covers 250 km^2 on the northeastern edge of the Pearl River delta.

Huangshan—Tian-Bo China Investment Ltd. of Canada will put up $15 million (Canadian) to build a 300-room hotel at Huangshan, Anhui.

Domestic Tourism—During 1984 over 200 million persons took tours lasting at least one day. About 80 million visited Beijing, and the sacred mountains of Taishan, Huashan, and Emei each had more than a million visitors. Some 1.6 million went to Changde and Beidaihe, and 600,000 people took tours organized by Shanghai travel agencies. Over 10 million people visited Hangzhou, including 186,000 foreigners. *China News Analysis*, 1288 (1 Jul 1985), 7. This issue is devoted to tourism in the PRC.

Xilihu—Photos of the new vacation village at Xilihu, 32 km northwest of Shenzhen appear in *China Reconstructs*, XXXIV, 7 (Jul 1985), 39-43.

Ming Tombs—China will restore the mausoleums of the 13 Ming dynasty emperors north of Beijing. The dynasty lasted from 1368 to 1644. The first tomb scheduled for restoration will be that of Emperor Mu Zong, who ruled from 1567 to 1572. Hotels and recreational facili-ties will be built. More than 4 million persons visited the tombs in 1984.

Club Med—The Xiaomeisha Village of Club Med will include a three-story hotel complex, nine-hole golf course, sauna, amphitheater, and restaurant. The $5.5 million project is probably going to open in 1986. See the *Asian Wall Street Journal* (28 Jan 1985), 1, 22.

Slot Machines—Slot machines were installed in the PRC three years ago, removed because authorities felt they encouraged gambling, and have now reappeared in Guangzhou. The machines take 20-fen pieces, and anyone over 18 can play.

Women's Hotels—Construction will begin in 1985 on two 600-room hotels in Beijing for visiting women's delegations from abroad. The hotels are to open in late 1986.

Caves—The Waterfall Cliff Cavern at Zhongshan, Guangxi has opened to tourists. The lime-stone cave has 11 chambers running 4,500 meters into the hill. The largest is 100 meters high. The Lingquan Cavern in Jiande County also opened in March, 1985.

Zhaoqing—The Xinghu Amusement Park, covering 200,000 square meters, has opened at Zhaoqing, Guangdong province. The Songtao Hotel there now has 205 rooms, and the Qixing-yuan shopping center cost $9 million. Hong Kong firms financed the Zhaoqing complex.

Dalian— Work has started on a 500-room, $100 million (HK) hotel in the development zone of Dalian. It will be built jointly by the Qingda Economic and Trade Company of Daqing and the Wah Kong Construction Co., Ltd. of Hong Kong.

Lhasa—A Tibetan-style hotel has opened on Bargor Street in Lhasa. The Xueyu Hotel is one of three hotels, each with over 200 beds. The structure was financed locally.

Shenyang Restaurant—The Yushan Restaurant, which serves Imperial dishes, opened just before 1 January 1985 in Shenyang. It is an expansion of the Yingbin Restaurant. Another restaurant serving Imperial cuisine has started up in Beijing's Yanjing Hotel. The Tong Ren Tang Imperial Dining Hall adds tonic Chinese medicines to its dishes. The menu includes chicken with longan and abalone with deer antler.

Kublai Khan Race Course—Construction has begun on China's first horse-racing course in Kublai Khan Equestrian Park in northeast Beijing. There will be polo games, horse and camel rides, and horse races. The 1,000-meter race course will have a stadium for 7,000. The cost of the project will be $1.5 million.

continued . . .

HOTELS AND TOURISM, 1985 (continued)

China Hotel, Guangzhou—The 19-story China Hotel in Guangzhou earned a profit the first year of its operation, and repaid $20 million in capital and interest on a total investment of $100 million. The hotel opened in 1984. It has 1,200 rooms and a staff of 3,000.

Jingan—The Chemical Bank of the US has granted a $5 million loan for construction of the Jingan Sheraton, a joint venture in Shanghai.

Areas Opened in Tibet—The Tibetan Autonomous Region will open all of its high peaks and areas along the Yaluzangbu, Lujiang and Lancang Rivers for mountaineering, hiking, motor-cycling, and horseback riding before 1988. In the autumn of 1985 an American team planned to scale the 19,190-foot Mount Kailas, known as the "throne of the Buddhas," and located in western Tibet. The border between China and Nepal reopened in 1985, permitting travellers to Tibet to avoid a long trip across the PRC.

Old Dragon Head Resort—The Asbee Corp. of Edina, Minnesota will design and build the Old Dragon Head Resort Village at the head of the Great Wall in Qinhuangdao. It will have 250 villa-type apartments, a 500-room hotel, a 100,000-square-foot shopping center, and an amusement park. Qinhuangdao attracted 1.8 million tourists in 1984, including 60,000 foreigners.

Great Wall Hotel—The second phase of construction of the Great Wall Hotel in Beijing was to start in 1985. The hotel is a joint venture between the E-S Pacific Development and Construction Co. Ltd. and the China International Travel Service with an investment of $75 million. The Chinese own 51 percent, and the term of the joint venture has been extended from 10 to 14 years. The 1,007-room hotel has had trouble maintaining high occupancy and its four-star rating. See the *Beijing Review*, 17 (29 Apr 1985), 31, and the New York *Times* (24 Mar 1985), F13.

Imbalance in Occupancy—During 1984 the Chinese hotels in Hangzhou, Zhejiang had occupancy rates of 120-152 percent, with people sleeping in halls and storage rooms almost every night. The rate at the five hotels catering to foreigners was only 42.8 percent. It rose to 81.9 percent after they began to register Chinese tourists. Many cities continue to build first-class accommodations. Some 24,000 new rooms are planned for Beijing. Shanghai will add 20,000 rooms in the next three years, and Xian has signed contracts for luxury hotels amounting to $350 million. Beijing currently has about 13,000 rooms for foreigners and is able to take in 800,000 annually. Only 509,000 visited the capital in 1983. Experts have predicted that Beijing will have 38,000 rooms capable of accommodating more than 3 million overseas tourists by 1990, but the actual number expected will not exceed 1.65 million. There are approximately 6 million hotel rooms in the PRC, with 300,000 in Beijing. Some 700-800,000 non-residents are in the capital every day, but the new luxury hotels are not easing the burden.

Bowling—A four-lane bowling alley opened 1 March 1985 at the Nationalities Palace of Culture in Beijing. The Japanese businessman Ryonosuke Hasebe donated the equipment. The lanes are open Tuesday, Thursday and Saturday evenings.

Bets—Bets International of Santa Monica, California plans to invest up to $500 million in hotel construction in the PRC within the next seven years. Contracts have been signed for a $20 million hotel in Dalian with the Lashufang Industrial Development Co. and for a $10 million hotel with the Service Company of Yantai, Shandong. Agreements for another hotel and a restaurant have been reached.

Taipingyang Hotel—Contracts have been signed between the Kogyo Bank and the Aoki Development Co. of Japan and the Bank of China and the Minhang Hongqiao Development Co. in Shanghai to build the $60 million five-star Taipingyang (Pacific) Hotel.

Yangtze—Barbara Goldsmith describes river tours in "7 Days on the Yangtze," New York *Times Magazine* (17 Mar 1985), pt. 2, 86-87, 109-12.

Diving Resort—China's first diving resort opened in July, 1985 in Sanya on Hainan Island. The resort will have a four-story hotel and four villas.

continued . . .

HOTELS AND TOURISM (continued)

Jingan Hilton—The 43-story, 800-room Jingan Hilton in Shanghai is under construction. The project is a joint venture between the Shanghai Jinjiang Co. and the Cindic Hotel Investment Co. Ltd. of Hong Kong. This will be a five-star accommodation.

Haitain—Work has started on the Haitain Hotel on Hainan Island. Three Japanese firms are participating in the $35 million project. The 13-story hotel should open in 1987.

Xingcheng—Xingcheng, Liaoning on Bohai Bay will be turned into a major tourist resort over the coming five years. Its 14-km coastline will have four beaches. More than 4 million Chinese and foreign tourists were expected in 1985. The city has hot springs and Ming dynasty buildings.

Grand-View Garden—The first phase of the Grand-View Garden is nearing completion in southwest Beijing. The garden will resemble the one in Cao Xueqin's *A Dream of Red Mansions*. The entire project will cost about 20 million yuan ($7.14 million) and should be ready by the end of 1986. Narrow garden paths will lead to various scenes from the novel.

Dalian—A 21.5-square-km tourist zone will be built 15 km along Liangshui Bay 60 km northeast of Dalian. It will feature complex geological formations, a rotating restaurant, an underwater crystal palace, beach, villas, and mountain garden. The zone will fully open in 1988.

Karsts—Photographs of karst formations appear in "Exploring the Karst Caverns of Guizhou," *China Reconstructs*, XXXIV, 9 (Sep 1985), 18-24.

Accommodations in Beijing—Beijing's existing and planned hotels, apartments, and office space are described in a table in the *China Business Review*, 12, 4 (Jul-Aug 1985), 39-41.

Bao Zhaolong Hotel—The 270-room Bao Zhaolong (Pao Sui Loong) Hotel was inaugurated 25 October 1985. The hotel is named after the father of Yue-kong Pao, Chairman of the Hong Kong Worldwide Shipping Group. It is located in eastern Beijing.

Aviation Hotel—The CAAC and a Hong Kong engineering firm reached an agreement in December, 1985 to build an aviation hotel in Beijing. Completion is scheduled for 1987.

Chinese Delegations to the US—More than 300 Chinese delegations visited the US every month in 1984. *Time* (18 Mar 1985), 40.

Prices—Louis Kraar mentions that apartments rent for $6,000 a month in advance in "China After Marx: Open for Business," *Fortune* (18 Feb 1985), 28-33. An office costs about $250,000 a year. A spartan room at the Beijing Hotel runs $50 a day, and a light meal without drinks may cost $9.

Club Med—Club Med will open two facilities at the Imperial Palace in Beijing. ABC News, Nightline (1 Jan 1986).

Chinese Delegations to the US—Every month 150 scientific or commercial delegations from China visit the US US Department of State, *Current Policy No. 725* (Jul 1985), 2.

MING TOMBS

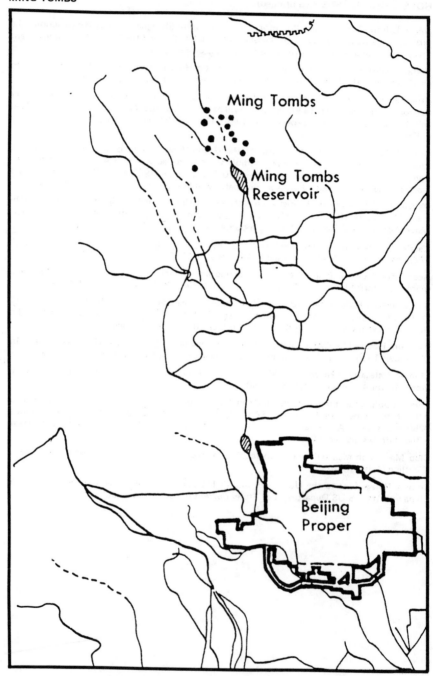

NEW AREAS OPEN TO FOREIGNERS, 1 Feb 1985

Another 154 areas in China were opened to foreigners 1 February 1985. The list brings to 257 the number of cities and counties open to foreigners. The new opening falls into two categories. The 67 areas in Category A require no permit to visit. The 87 areas in Category B require special permit. Names of new open cities and counties, grouped by province and autonomous region, follow:

Category A

Hebei Province: Shijiazhuang City, Chengde City, Zhuoxian County

Inner Mongolia Autonomous Region: Baotou City, Hohhot City

Liaoning Province: Anshan City, Fushun City, Dandong City, Jinzhou City

Jilin Province: Jilin City, Yanji City

Heilongjiang Province: Qiqihar City, Daqing City

Jiangsu Province: Lianyungang City, Nantong City, Changzhou City, Yangzhou City

Zhejiang Province: Ningbo City, Wenzhou City, Shaoxing City

Anhui Province: Hefei City, Wuhu City, Huangshan City, Bangbu City, Tunxi City, Jiuhua-shan Tourist Resort

Jiangxi Province: Nanchang City, Jiujiang City, Jingdezhen City

Fujian Province: Fuzhou City, Xiamen City, Quanzhou City, Zhangzhou City

Shandong Province: Yantai City, Tai'an City, Weifang City, Zibo City, Jining City

Henan Province: Anyang City

Hubei Province: Yichang City, Shashi City, Xiangfan City, Jiangling County

Hunnan Province: Hengyang City, Yueyang City, Xiangtan City

Guangdong Province: Shenzhen City, Zhuhai City, Shantou City, Haikou City, Zhanjiang Zhongshan City, Jiangmen City, Shaoguan City, Huizhou City

Guangxi Zhuang Autonomous Region: Beihai City, Liuzhou City, Wuzhou City

Sichuan Province: Leshan City, Emei County

Guizhou Province: Guiyang City, Anshun City

Shaanxi Province: Yan'an City

Gansu Province: Lanzhou City

Qinghai Province: Xining City

Ningxia Hui Autonomous Region: Yinchuan City

Xinjiang Uygur Autonomous Region: Urumqi City

Category B

Hebei Province: Baoding City, Tangshan City, Handan City

Shanxi Province: Linfen City, Yuncheng City

Inner Mongolia Autonomous Region: Dongsheng City, Abagnar Qi (Xilin Hot), Butna Qi (Zalantun City), Tongliao City

Jilin Province: Siping City, Liaoyuan City, Tonghua City, Baicheng City

Heilongjiang Province: Jixi City, Hegang City, Wudalianchi City, Qitaihe City, Heihe City, Suifenhe City, Tongjiang County

Jiangxi Province: Ganzhou City

Henan Province: Nanyang City

Hubei Province: Huangshi City, Jingmen City, Suizhou City, Shiyan City, Ezhou City

Anhui Province: Huainan City, Huaibei City, Tongling City, Chuzhou City, Chaohu City Shexian County, Xiuning County, Fengyang County, Jingxian County

Guizhou Province: Zunyi City, Kaili City, Liupanshui City, Shibing County, Qingzhen County, Zhenyuan County

Shaanxi Province: Baoji City, Hancheng City

Gansu Province: Yongjing County

Guangdong Province: Chaozhou City, Maoming City, Meixian City, Xingning County, Feng-shun County, Dapu County, Huiyang County, Boluo County, Huidong County, Heyuan

continued . . .

NEW AREAS OPEN TO FOREIGNERS, 1 Feb 1985 (continued)

County, Dongwan County, Lufeng County, Haifeng County, Gaoyao County, Xinxing County, Yunfu County, Sihui County, Qiongshan County, Wenchang County, Ding'an County, Qionghai County, Wanning County, Tunchang County, Chengmai County, Danxian County, Linggao County, Baoting County, Baisha County, Qiongzhong County, Lingshui County, Sanya City, Ledong County, Dongfang County, Changjiang Fengkai County, Huaiji County, Deqing County, Luoding County

Guangxi Zhuang Autonomous Region: Luchuan County, Beilu County, Rongxian County, Guixian County.

China Daily (16 Feb 1985), 2, and JPRS-CPS-85-031 (1 Apr 1985), 1-3. Four more areas opened to travel without permits in September, 1985: Yingtan, Jiangxi; Chaozhou city and Gaoyao county, Guangdong; and Yingkou, Liaoning. Exit-entry visas can now be issued to foreigners in Beijing, Tianjin, Shanghai, Hangzhou, Fuzhou, Xiamen, Guilin, Kunming and Xian. XNB (27 Sep 1985), 19.

WOMEN'S DELEGATIONS, 1949-84

Number of invitations to women's delegations in 119 countries to visit China	557
Percentage from developing countries	75
Chinese women's delegations to 86 countries	117
Number of women's organizations in 120 countries and regions and non-governmental organizations in some 40 countries having ties with the All-China Women's Federation	230

The invitations were extended by and the delegations sent from the All-China Women's Federation. *Beijing Review*, 9 (4 Mar 1985), 17-18. The Federation is currently promoting the Five-Good Family Campaign. The requirements for a "Five-Good Family" are: diligent work and study; consideration for the family members as well as neighbors; careful family planning and attention to children's education; observance of law and discipline; and courteous public behavior.

NUCLEAR EXPLOSIONS, 1945-84

	Number	Percent
Total	1,507	100.0
US	756	50.2
USSR	556	36.9
France	127	8.4
United Kingdom	38	2.5
People's Republic of China	29	1.9
India	1	0.1

Based on information in Center for Defense Information, *Defense Monitor*, XIV, 5 (1985), 5.

CHINESE WOMEN

Employment rate of China's working-age population (percent), 1982	86.7
Percentage of women in China's work force, 1983 yearend (excluding farmers)	36.5
Percentage of working women performing manual labor, 1982	83.0

Distribution of employment (per 100 working women):

Farm workers	77
Factory workers	13
Workers in the service sector	4
Technicians, government functionaries and managers	5.5

Number of women in school and illiterates per 1,000:

Age Group	University	Secondary school	Primary school	Illiterate
20-29	5	400	291	304
30-39	6	191	386	417
40-49	10	94	238	658
50-59	6	26	98	870
60 and over	1	8	37	954

Number of divorced women in China, Jul 1982 (th)	820

Average age of women marrying for the first time (years)

1949	18.6
1982	22.7

In 1949 half of the women were married under the age of 18. In 1982, half were under the age of 23, and 4.4 percent were between 15 and 19 years old.

Number of women 25 years and older who are unmarried (mn)	2.3*
Average life expectancy (years)	69

The average life expectancy for men is 66 years.

Infant mortality rate (percent)

Pre-1949	c. 20
1985	3

Women who die in childbirth (per 10,000 women who give birth)

Pre-1949	150
1985	5

Beijing Review, 37 (16 Sep 1985), 28-29. The *Christian Science Monitor* (4 Apr 1985), 25-27, describes a film by Carma Hinton and Richard Gordon, "Small Happiness: Women of a Chinese Village," prepared during a visit to Zhang Zhuang, 400 miles southwest of Beijing, in 1982.

CRIME, 1984-85

Work of the Procuratorate—During 1984 procuratorial organs in the PRC approved the arrests of over 420,000 persons and decided to prosecute 520,000, including cases from 1983. Some 14,000 persons were arrested for economic crimes in 1984, 15,000 prosecuted, and over 90 million yuan recovered. FBIS-CHI 81 (26 Apr 1985), K1/6.

Guangdong—Courts in Guangdong province sentenced 30,207 for crimes in 1984, including 17,482 cases for serious crimes such as rape, murder, arson, robbery and bombings. About 2,600 were sentenced for serious economic offenses, such as bribery, corruption and smuggling. *China Daily* (21 May 1985), 3.

continued . . .

CRIME, 1984-85 (continued)

Shanghai Jail—More than 60 percent of the 3,700 inmates in the Shanghai prison are men and women under 35 whose educations and families were uprooted by the Cultural Revolution. New York *Times* (5 Feb 1985), 4.

Crimes in Beijing—Some 5,825 criminal cases were reported in Beijing in 1984, representing a rate of 6.2 per 10,000 inhabitants. Criminal cases fell 46.6 percent in 1984 compared to 1983, the lowest rate in 18 years. Beijing's civil dispute cases dropped 43 percent in 1984 compared to 1982, even though the population grew by 274,000 to 9.14 million persons. Civil disputes include marriage, family, debt, support of the elderly, street fighting, and petty theft. Family and marriage problems account for almost half of the civil cases. XNB (16 Feb 1985), 25; (10 Apr 1985), 18-19.

Beijing Prisoners—There are 1,900 prisoners in the Beijing jail. XNB (31 Jan 1985), 13.

Forestry Laws—In 1984 more than 5,100 people were arrested or sentenced to jail for violating forestry laws. Some 1,900 cadres were dismissed or disciplined by the Party for breaking forestry laws. *Beijing Review*, 28 (15 Jul 1985), 9.

Sanchahe—The crime rate in Sanchahe, Jilin province was 1.5 per thousand before 1981. In 1984 it had dropped to 0.7 per thousand. The change is attributed to mobilizing citizens and publicizing the laws. *Beijing Review*, 31 (5 Aug 1985), 27.

Profiteering—The biggest case of profiteering from foreign trade apparently occurred in Hainan when officials imported 75,000 Japanese vehicles worth $600-$900 million and sold them for three to four times their cost. *Asian Wall Street Journal Weekly* (22 Jul 1985), 14; *Chiushih Nientai*, 187 (Hong Kong, 1 Aug 1985), 50-51; New York *Times* (12 Nov 1985), D12.

Major Crimes—Serious crimes such as rape, murder, arson and robbery made up 10-15 percent of the approximately 500,000 crimes reported in 1984. More than 70 percent were thefts or minor offenses. *Beijing Review*, 34 (26 Aug 1985), 8.

Abducted Children—There have been reports that children visiting the PRC with family or friends have been kidnapped and set up as beggars in Shenzhen and Guangzhou. Their fingers and toes are cut off or they are disfigured to make them look more pathetic. FBIS-CHI 156 (13 Aug 1985), W7.

Criminal Cases—Between April, 1984 and February 1985 people's courts at all levels and special courts tried more than 310,000 criminal cases and sentenced over 470,000 persons who committed various crimes, including over 140,000 cases of murder, rape, robbery, arson, explosion, criminal gang activity, major larceny, kidnapping, and forced prostitution. These major crimes involved more than 230,000 persons or 49 percent of the total number of criminals. FBIS-CHI 80 (25 Apr 1985), K3.

Crime Rates—In 1984 the number of criminal cases reported to public security authorities was 510,000, a drop of 15.7 percent from the number in 1983. This is close to the crime rate of about 0.04 percent during the 1950s. When a campaign against major crimes was launched in August 1983, the rate was 7.1 per 10,000 persons, or 0.071 percent. In 1984 76.9 percent of all criminal cases and over 90 percent of the major cases were resolved. *China Daily* (18 Apr 1985), 1.

Gambling Arrests—Some 34,000 persons were arrested in Shanghai during the first 10 months of 1984 for gambling. *Asian Wall Street Journal Weekly* (11 Mar 1985), 13.

Illegal Enterprises—Ren Zhonglin, the Director of the State Administration for Industry and Commerce, has estimated that there are at least 16,000 illegal enterprises in the PRC. *Asian Wall Street Journal Weekly* (18 Mar 1985), 6.

Penal System—The *China News Analysis*, 1279 (15 Feb 1985) discusses the Chinese penal system of maximum security prisons, labor camps, and reform schools.

Rehabilitation—China's crime rate has dropped from 7 to 5 per 10,000 people between 1982 and 1985. Between 1949 and 1984 the PRC has rehabilitated more than 13,000 criminals. Today only 6-7 percent of former inmates commit crimes after release from jail. *Beijing Review*, 50 (16 Dec 1985), 21-23.

Crime Rate, 1984—The crime rate in China dropped to five per 10,000 people in 1984 (0.05 percent). *Beijing Review*, 52 (30 Dec 1985), 17.

CRIME RATES IN TIBET

Rates (per 100,000 inhabitants)
Tibet	
1981	5.9
1984	3.7
China, 1984	5.1
Farming and pastoral areas of Tibet, 1984	2.0
Number of cases in Tibet	
1981	1,090
1982	873
1983	788
1984	742
1985 Jan-Jun	311

XNB (29 Jul 1985), 86-87.

POLLUTION AND ECOLOGY

Garbage—The average amount of garbage in Beijing, Shanghai, Tianjin, and 24 other major cities has increase by 9.6 percent annually over the past three years. *Beijing Review*, 7-8 (18 Feb 1985), 10.

Offshore Dumping—As of 1 April 1985 no one will be allowed to dump any kind of waste at sea without the prior permission of the State Administration of Oceanography. Pollutants include mercury and cadmium compounds, oil products, and radioactive wastes. Chinese and foreign vessels were prohibited from dumping sludge at sea in a January, 1984 law. New York *Times* (17 Mar 1985), 10.

Pollution from Factories—Li Peng, Director of the Environmental Protection Committee under the State Council, has attributed about 40 percent of China's industrial pollution to the mismanagement of industry by local governments and departments. *China Daily* (29 Jan 1985), 1.

Protection Measures—Environmental protection measures planned for 1985 include a requirement that every province, autonomous region, and municipality must maintain smoke and dust under control (a "white-smoke" law) in at least one district of their capitals, clear one lake or river of pollution, and keep traffic noise within 70 decibles in the main thoroughfares of cities with populations exceeding 1 million. XNB (27 Mar 1985), 42-43.

Daily Pollution—Each day more than 70 million tons of waste and polluted water are produced in China. *China Daily* (28 Jun 1985), 1.

Industrial Pollution—Every year China produces over 400 million tons of industrial wastes and tailings. Only 20 percent are treated for further use. Waste dumps cover about 60,000 hectares of land and exceed 5.6 billion tons. XNB (29 Apr 1985), 86-87.

Thermal Power Plants—Coal-fired power plants account for about 90 percent of China's thermal power stations, and prior to 1975 there was virtually no treatment of their residue. In the last decade, thermal plants have reduced dust pollution below 10 percent. XNB (14 Jun 1985), 22.

Suzhou River—Shanghai has approved a project to reduce the pollution of the Suzhou River. A 29.9-km pipeline will be laid to block the flow of pollutants and to empty treated water into the Changjiang River. Forty-four drainage systems will also be constructed. The second stage of the project will reduce pollution in the sources of the Huangpu River and improve pipelines which carry waste water in western and southern Shanghai. The project will cost more than 1 billion yuan. *Beijing Review*, 35 (2 Sep 1985), 32.

Desert Encroachment—Desert encroachment threatens 29,000 square miles of arid and semiarid regions in north China within the next 15 years. The land has been misused by overgrazing, poor planning, overcultivation, and the inefficient development of water resources. *China Daily* (14 Sep 1985).

TOTAL AREA COVERED AND AFFECTED BY NATURAL DISASTERS (mn mu)

	Area covered by natural disaster	Area affected by natural disaster	Area affected as percent of area covered by disaster	Flood		Drought	
				Area covered by disaster	Area affected by disaster	Area covered by disaster	Area affected by disaster
1952	1.23	0.66	54.1	0.42	0.28	0.64	0.39
1957	4.37	2.25	51.4	1.21	0.90	2.58	1.11
1965	3.12	1.68	53.9	0.84	0.42	2.04	1.22
1978	7.62	3.27	42.9	0.43	0.14	6.03	2.70
1979	5.91	2.27	38.4	1.01	0.43	3.70	1.40
1980	6.68	3.35	50.1	1.37	0.75	3.92	1.87
1981	5.97	2.81	47.1	1.29	0.60	3.85	1.82
1982	4.97	2.42	48.7	1.25	0.67	3.10	1.50
1983	5.21	2.43	46.6	1.82	0.86	2.41	1.14
1984	4.78	2.29	47.9	1.59	0.81	2.37	1.05

State Statistical Bureau, *China: A Statistical Survey in 1985* (1985), 42.

WORLD SPORTS RECORDS BROKEN AND WORLD CHAMPIONSHIPS WON

	World records broken or surpassed			World championships won		
	Number of events	Number of times	Number of record-breaking athletes	Number of events	Number of championships	Number of athletes
1956-1983	107	268	234	53	122	139
1957	3	3	3			
1965	28	41	66	5	5	9
1978	3	3	6	4	4	4
1979	12	26	32	12	12	20
1980	7	15	17	3	3	3
1981	8	18	15	25	25	53
1982	11	15	16	12	13	31
1983	13	18	25	37	39	50
1984	12	17	17	33	37	46

Numbers of events and winning/record-breaking athletes do not include duplicated successes in a single year. Thus the total given is smaller than the sum of figures given for each year.

State Statistical Bureau, *China: A Statistics Survey in 1985* (1985), 112.

MAIN RANGES AND MOUNTAINS IN CHINA

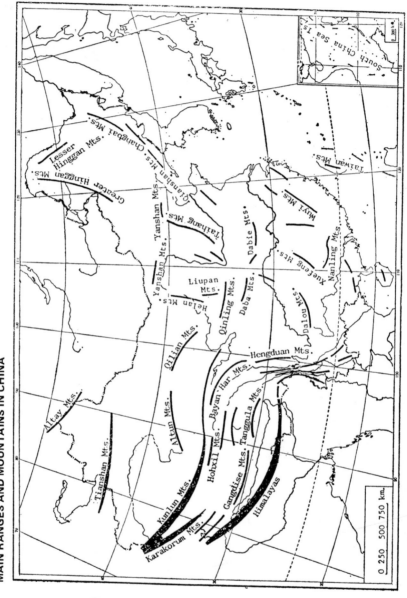

continued . . .

MAIN RANGES AND MOUNTAINS IN CHINA

MAIN RANGES AND MOUNTAINS IN CHINA (continued)

Name	Position	Sea-level eleva-tion (in metres)	Remarks
Hima-layas	extending from China's Tibet to Pakistan, India, Nepal, Sikkim and Bhutan	Great Hima-layas average 6,000	See separate paragraph.
Mount Qomolangma	on Sino-Nepalese border	8,848.13	See separate paragraph.
Gangdise Mountains	across south-western Tibet	the main peak, Mount Kang-renboqi, 6,656	Watershed between inland drainage system and Indian Ocean drainage system. Parallel with the Himalayas and bounded by Nyainqen-tanglha Mountains in the east.
Tanggula Mountains	stretching from north-eastern Tibet to Qinghai-Tibet border	averagely 6,000. The main peak, Mount Gela-dandong, 6,621	Extending southeast to join with Hengduan Mountains (Yunling and Nushan Mountains). Source of the Nujiang, Lancang and Changjiang rivers. With many glaciers.
Nyain-qentang-lha Mountains	Tibet	5,000-6,000. The main peak, Mount Nyain-qentanglha, 7,111	Bordering on Gangdise range in the west and extending southeast to join with Hengduan Mountains. Watershed between the Yarlung-zangbo and Nujiang rivers.

continued . . .

MAIN RANGES AND MOUNTAINS IN CHINA (continued)

Name	Position	Sea-level elevation (in metres)	Remarks
Hengduan Mountains	western Sichuan and Yunnan and eastern Tibet	2,000-6,000. Mount Yulong 5,596	See separate paragraph.
Karakorum Mountains	extending from southwestern Xinjiang to northeastern Kashmir and eastward to northern Tibet	average elevation 6,000. The main peak, Qogir, 8,611	400 km. long. With many snowcapped peaks and giant glaciers. Mount Qogir, the world's second highest, is the boundary mountain between China and Pakistan.
Kunlun Mountains	between Xinjiang and Tibet	6,000. The main peak, Mount Muztag, 7,723	See separate paragraph.
Hohxil Mountains	straddling northeastern Tibet and southwestern Qinghai	5,000. Mount Gangzhari 6,305	Southern offshoot of Kunlun Mountains. Extending eastward to adjoin Bayanhar Mountains. Snowcapped all year round. The Qumar, northern source of the Changjiang, originates here.
Bayanhar Mountains	central Qinghai	5,000-6,000. The main peak, Mount Bayanhar, 5,267	Southern offshoot of Kunlun Mountains. Source of the Huanghe River. Watershed between the Changjiang and Huanghe.

continued . . .

MAIN RANGES AND MOUNTAINS IN CHINA (continued)

Name	Position	Sea-level elevation (in metres)	Remarks
Anye-maqen (Jishi) Mountains	southeastern Qinghai	4,000-5,000. Mount Maqengangri 6,282	Central offshoot of Kunlun Mountains. The Huanghe River skirts its southeastern side.
Tianshan Mountains	across central Xinjiang	3,000-5,000	See separate paragraph.
Altay Mountains	northern Xinjiang	1,000-3,500. The main peak, Mount Youyi, 4,374	Extending northwest to USSR and southeast to Mongolia. With dense forests and rich metal deposits. Its intermontane valleys suitable for farming and stockbreeding.
Altun Mountains	southeastern Xinjiang	3,500-4,000. The main peak, Mount Altun, 5,798	Extending to Qinghai-Gansu border, between Qaidam and Tarim basins.
Qilian Mountains	astride western Gansu and northeastern Qinghai	average height, over 4,000. The main peak, Mount Qilian, 5,547	Extending northwest to Altun Mountains and southeast to Qinling range and Liupan Mountain for 1,000 km. With many intermontane valleys. Watershed between the Huanghe River and inland drainage system. Glaciers cover an area of 1,300 sq. km.

continued . . .

MAIN RANGES AND MOUNTAINS IN CHINA (continued)

Name	Position	Sea-level elevation (in metres)	Remarks
Qinling Mountains	stretching from Gansu-Qinghai border in the west to central Henan in the east	2,000-3,000. The main peak, Mount Taibai, 3,767	See separate paragraph.
Daba (Bashan) Mountains	straddling Sichuan-Gansu-Shaanxi-Hubei border	2,000-2,500. The main peak, Mount Dashennongjia (in Hubei), 3,053	Running from northwest to southeast and including Skyscraping Mountain, Mount Micang and Mount Wudang. Dividing line between Sichuan and Hanzhong basins.
Yinshan Mountains	central Inner Mongolia	1,000-2,000	See separate paragraph.
Greater Hinggan (West Hinggan) Mountains	northeastern Inner Mongolia	1,500. The main peak, Mount Huanggangliang, 2,029	See separate paragraph.
Lesser Hinggan (East Hinggan) Mountains	northern Heilongjiang	600-1,000	400 km. long. With dense Korean pine and spruce forests and an abundance of fur-bearing animals.

continued ...

MAIN RANGES AND MOUNTAINS IN CHINA (continued)

Name	Position	Sea-level elevation (in metres)	Remarks
Chang-bai Moun-tains	extending from east-ern Liao-ning, Jilin and Hei-longjiang provinces to the northeast-ern section of the Sino-Korean border	mostly 1,000-2,000. The main peak, Mount Baitou, 2,750	Running northeast-south-west. Composed of sev-eral parallel mountain chains: Wanda, Taiping-ling, Laoyeling, Zhang-guangcailing, Jilinha-daling and Laoling. With dense forests and rich mineral deposits.
Taihang Moun-tains	astride Shanxi Plateau and Hebei Plain	1,500-2,000. The main peak, Mount Lesser Wutai, 2,870	Running northeast-south-west. Rich in coal.
Dabie Moun-tains	Henan-Hubei-Anhui border	1,000. The main peak (in Hu-bei), Mount Tiantangzhai, 1,729	Adjoining Tongbai Mountains in the west and Huoshan Mountains in the east. Running northwest-southeast. Wa-tershed between the Changjiang and the Huaihe rivers.
Wuyi Moun-tains	Jiangxi-Fujian border	1,000-1,500. The main peak, Mount Huang-gang, 2,158	Running northeast-south-west. Watershed between the Ganjiang and Min-jiang rivers. Mount Wu-yi, in Chongan County, Fujian, is the most fa-mous mountain in the province, known for its Wuyi Tea.

continued . . .

MAIN RANGES AND MOUNTAINS IN CHINA (continued)

Name	Position	Sea-level elevation (in metres)	Remarks
Wuling Mountains	northwestern Hunan	1,000	Extending to Hubei-Guizhou border. Watershed between the Wujiang, Yuanjiang and Lishui rivers.
Nanling Mountains	Hunan-Jiangxi-Guangdong-Guangxi border	averaging 1,000. Yuechengling Mountain (Mount Zhenbaoding) 2,123	See separate paragraph.

China Handbook Series: Geography (1983), 18-24.

URBAN WATER SHORTAGE

Urban water consumption (bn m^3)	
1985	57.2
2000 plan	130
Capacity of reservoirs (bn m^3)	400+

A bureau has been established to protect China's seven major rivers: the Yangtze, Yellow, Huai, Hai, Songhuajiang, Liao, and the Zhujiang. They provide water for 80 percent of China's population and 70 percent of its industrial production. *China Daily* (28 Jun 1985), 1. China consumes some 300 billion m^3 of water annually, with 24 percent from underground sources. Underground water is estimated at 870 billion m^3. It is believed that China has used only 8.5 percent of its underground resources. FBIS-CHI 132 (10 Jul 1985), K15/16.

Only a little more than 20 percent of China's industrial water is recycled. Some 86 percent of its cities lack sewerage treatment plants. Today 188 cities are short of more than 10 million tons of water each day, and in 40 cities the situation is worse. At the end of 1984, a daily supply of 39.07 million tons of running water was available to 89.02 million persons, or 83 percent of China's urban residents. Industrial enterprises generate another 65.6 million tons of water a day for their own use. By 1990 China's cities may need an additional 15 million tons of water a day, and by 2000, 88 million tons daily. The PRC has 270 million m^3 of water resources, making it sixth in the world, but this amounts to only 25 percent of the world per-capita average.

China will try to ease the shortage by moving water over long distances. In 1980 and 1982, water from the Huanghe (Yellow) River was twice diverted to Tianjin, an industrial city in north China. Later came projects of diverting water from the Luanhe River to Tianjin, the Biliu River to Dalian, a port city in the northeast, and the Luanhe River to Tangshan, a coal city in north China. All initially eased shortages in these cities. More such projects are now in the planning stage, including the diversion of Songhua River water to cities in the Liaohe River region. Luanhe River water to Qinhuangdao, a port city in north China; and Huanghe River water to Qingdao in Shandong Province. When the diversion of the

continued . . .

URBAN WATER SHORTAGE (continued)

Huanghe to Qingdao is completed, the city's daily supply will rise from its present 150,000 tons to 700,000 tons. Attempts are also being made to divert water from the Changjiang (Yangtze) River to the north.

Beijing Review, 26 (1 Jul 1985), 4.

ANIMALS IN CHINA

Pere David Deer—Twenty-two Pere David deer, named after a Lazarist priest and naturalist who traveled around China in the nineteenth century, have been returned to their native habitat from a preserve in Woburn Abbey, northwest of London. This rare species, called Sibuxiang by the Chinese, once roamed northeast of China, but has been extinct in the wild for hundreds of years. Some were put in the imperial hunting park, Nanhaize, by the Manchus in the seventeenth century. The last deer were apparently eaten by foreign troops who occupied the capital during the Boxer Rebellion in 1900. A few deer had been sent to England in 1894. The Chinese have built a walled area at Nanhaizi for these new deer. A lake has been drained and refilled, and grass and trees planted in the park. The cost of transporting the animals to the PRC is being shared by the Marquis of Tavistock, who owns Woburn Abbey, and some naturalists. New York *Times* (26 Aug 1985), 3.

Nature Reserves—China has established 274 nature reserves over 16.26 million hectares, or almost 2 percent of its territory. There are plans to increase this number to 500 by the end of the century. *Beijing Review,* 43 (28 Oct 1985), 8.

Panda Farm—A second farm to study giant pandas has been completed at the Baishuijiang Nature Reserve in Gansu province. There are an estimated 1,000 wild pandas in the PRC. Since the arrow bamboo on which they feed began dying two years ago, 55 giant pandas have died. Minneapolis *Star and Tribune* (25 Oct 1985), 10A.

Birds—China has 1,186 kinds of birds. About 14 percent of all the world's species are found in the PRC. *Beijing Review,* 15 (15 Apr 1985), 9.

Bird Zoo—China's first zoo for birds will be built in Shenyang, Liaoning. The Bainiao (Hundred Birds) Park will have 180 species. The park will open in 1988. *Beijing Review,* 20 (20 May 1985), 8; XNB (29 Apr 1985), 64.

Zoos—China has 171 zoos and animal exhibitions in parks. More than 100 million persons visit these places each year. By the end of 1983, the PRC had exchanged 1,717 animals of 262 species with foreign countries. There are 194 animals in the zoos in Beijing and Shanghai. XNB (28 Oct 1985), 24.

FIRES, 1984 and Jan-Jun 1985

	1984	Jan-Jun 1985
Fires (th)	33+	18.185
Fire damage (mn dollars)	160.1	159.5
Fatalities	2,080	1,246
Injuries	2,698	NA
Percentage change from 1983		
Fires	−9.2	
Losses	−21.2	

These statistics do not include forest fires, mine pit fires, and blazes at Army installations. XNB (7 Mar 1985), 42; (29 Jul 1985), 48-49. During the past two years, forest fires have consumed 0.1 percent of China's forests. The figure was 1.96 percent in the late 1970s. XNB (12 Aug 1985), 23.

OBITUARIES, 1985

Chen Shu—journalist, a founder of the Xinhua international service, Vice-President, Chinese Translators' Association, 75, 14 Jun

Du Xinyuan—former Secretary of the Sichuan Provincial Party Committee, Chairman, Standing Committee Provincial People's Congress, 78, 18 Dec

Dun Xingyuan—former Deputy Commander of PLA Armed Forces, 72, 25 Jan*

Fan Rouyu—Marxist theoretician, 73, 20 Jun

Ge Zhixu—chief engineer of the Fujian Provincial Building Corp., Deputy Secretary General of the Fujian Provincial CPPCC Committee, 70, 20 Oct

Geng Changsuo—agricultural model worker, Vice-Chairman, Fifth Provincial People's Standing Committee, 85, 26 Nov

Guo Xilan—Chairman, Xizang Regional Advisory Commission, First Deputy Chairman of the Xizang government, former Secretary of the Xizang Regional CPC Committee, 66, 21 Aug

Guo Yingqiu—historian, honorary President of the China People's University, 76, 29 Oct

Han Quanhua—State Councillor, 82, 30 Jan

Han Youtong (f)—jurist, member of the Standing Committee, Sixth CPPCC National Committee, Deputy Head of the Civil Court of the Supreme People's Court, 77, 13 Mar

Hu Feng—literary and art critic, poet and translator, arrested in 1955 as the ringleader of an anti-Party clique and not rehabilitated until 1980, 83, 8 Jun

Hu Jiabin—former Deputy Minister in charge of the State Nationalities Affairs Commission, 77, 12 Feb

Hua Luogeng—mathematician, Deputy Chairman, CPPCC National Committee, Deputy Chairman, China Association for Science and Technology, 74, 12 Jun, in Tokyo

Jiang Junchen—economist, 81, 5 Nov*

Ji Tiezhong—former Deputy Minister of the Petroleum Industry, 69, 23 Apr

Li Bozhao (f)—Deputy Chairman, Chinese Dramatists' Association, wrote the opera *Long March,* the stage play *Mother,* and the novel *A Woman Communist,* wife of Politburo member Yang Shangkun, 74, 17 Apr

Li Chaoran—former Director of the Policy Research Office of the Jiangsu government, 70, 14 Oct

Li Daigeng—former Deputy Minister of the Power Industry and of the Ministry of Water Resources and Electric Power, 67, 8 Jan

Li Jitai—former Deputy Commander and Commander of the Beijing Military Region's Air Force, 66, 22 Jan;

Li Zezhong—former Deputy Political Commissar of the Kunming Military Region, 67, 25 Oct

Li Xin—former advisor to the PLA artillery, 78, 26 May

Li Yanlu—exemplary CPC member, 90, 18 Jun

Liu Douquan—member of the Sixth CPPCC National Committee, adviser to the Standing Committee of the CC of the Revolutionary Committee of the Chinese Kuomintang, 22 Jul

Liu Shuzhou—former Deputy Chairman, China Association for Science and Technology, 74, 22 Mar

Liu Simu—adviser to the Institute of World History of the Chinese Academy of Social Sciences, specialist on international relations after World War II, 81, 20 Feb

Liu Yin—member of the Standing Committee, Sixth CPPCC National Committee, Permanent Deputy Minister of the former Ministry of the Fourth Machine-Building Industry, 75, 26 May

continued . . .

OBITUARIES, 1985 (continued)

Ma Bi—member of the Standing Committee, Sixth CPPCC National Committee, member of the Standing Committee of the Kuomintang Revolutionary CC, 15 Oct*

Ma Lianjue—former Deputy Secretary General of the State Council, 63, 22 Feb

Ma Shuliang—Party official in the Ministry of the Coal Industry, 80, 8 Feb

Qian Junrui—economist, former Director of the Institute of World Economy and Politics, 77, 25 May

Qian Zhongyuan—painter, Honorary President of the Jiangsu Chinese Painting Academy, 11 Sep*

Shi Guanghua—Secretary, Discipline Inspection Committee and Standing Committee member of the Nei Monggol Autonomous Region, 64, 10 Oct

Shi Liang (f)—lawyer, co-founder of the China Democratic League, first Minister of Justice of the PRC, 85, 6 Sep

Tao Li—former Deputy Secretary of the Party committee of the Ministry of Health, 11 Jun*

Wang Chaobei—adviser to the China National Metals and Minerals Import and Export Corp. under the former Ministry of Foreign Economic Relations, 82, 1 Oct

Wang Kejun—member of the Standing Committee, Sixth CPPCC National Committee, 77, 1 Jun

Wang Kunlun—Vice-Chairman, CPPCC National Committee, historian, Chairman, CC of the Revolutionary Committee of the Chinese Kuomintang, 83, 23 Aug

Wang Xuewen—economist and educator, 22 Feb

Wu Wenzao—member of the Standing Committee of the CC, China Association for Promoting Democracy, sociologist and ethnologist, 84, 24 Sep

Wu Yifang—President, Jinling Women's College in Nanjing (1928-51), first Chinese woman to serve as a college president in China, 93, 10 Nov

Xia Nai—archaeologist, rptd 30 Jun

Xiao Hua-former Chief Political Commissar of the PLA (1949-64), 69, rptd 12 Aug

Xie Ming—former Deputy Political Commissar of the PLA Political College, 70, 21 Apr

Xiong Yi—soil specialist, 30 Jan*

Xu Shiyou—former Politburo member, former Deputy Minister of National Defense and concurrently Commander of the Nanjing Military Region (1954-73), former Commander, Guangzhou Military Region, who provided sanctuary for Deng Xiaoping in 1976, Deputy Chairman, CPC Central Advisory Commission, 80, 22 Oct

Yang Lingde—member of the Sixth National CPPCC Committee, Deputy Chairman of the Nei Monggol CPPCC Committee, 81, 21 Oct

Yang Shixian—honorary President of Nankai University, chemist and educator, 19 Feb

Yu Huiyong—former Minister of Culture, 1975-76(?), suicide prior to sentencing, rptd 25 Apr

Zeng Xianjiu—surgeon, head of Surgery Department at Beijing Xiehe Hospital, 30 May

Zhang Tianyi—writer of children's books, 11 May*

Zhang Wenyou—a founder of the science of tectonics in China and a developer of the Daqing oilfield, 75, 11 Feb

Zhou Chunquan—First Deputy Director of the former Armed Strength Inspection Department of the PLA, 80, 28 Jul

* Date of memorial service.
PLA=People's Liberation Army
CPC=Chinese Communist Party
CPPCC=Chinese People's Political Consultative

KEY WORKS ON THE PEOPLE'S REPUBLIC OF CHINA

Elizabeth J. Perry and Christine Wong, eds., *The Political Economy of Post-Mao China*. Cambridge, MA: Harvard UP, 1985. xvi, 331, $14. This is an imaginative, intelligent study which suggests Deng's reforms are unpopular and will fail. No time frame is indicated for a partial reversion to the Maoist model, and concentration on various problems may have obscured the apparent overall success of these reforms. Nonetheless, the collection of essays offers an excellent summary of developments in China since 1978.

Keith Griffin, ed., *Institutional Reform and Economic Development in the Chinese Countryside*. Armonk, NY: M.E. Sharpe, 1985. x, 336, $37.50/$18.95 paper. This is how a field study should be done. Most of the material was obtained by seven contributors during a three-week field trip to rural China in 1982. It asks intelligent questions and provides a significant finding: there exists a theoretical and empirical basis to believe that the Deng reforms have led to greater rural equality, that is, they are failing. Some of the data were updated in 1983. The main problem, of course, is that it is difficult to say anything about China after visiting 14 work units in three weeks. This is well worth reading, but there should be a follow-up in two or three years.

David S.G. Goodman, ed., *Groups and Politics in the People's Republic of China*. Cardiff, Wales: Univ. of Cardiff Press, 1984. vi, 218, £12.50. Goodman has edited an absorbing collection of papers analyzing China on the basis of various group theories. Sometimes the categories appear too broad (the book is organized in categories such as the military, intellectuals, peasants). Sometimes they seem too narrow. For example, Gerald Segal distinguishes among services/field armies, steel/electronics, generations/region, etc, and apparently does not consider the military as a group in Chinese politics. It is probable that Deng Xiaoping and other Chinese leaders do have an abstract concept of "the military" which they consider in their decisions. In another article, categories such as the "liberal" and "institutional" approach to reform may not be so easily distinguished (pp. 47-48). Advocates of each approach have called for institutional restructuring and greater economic efficiency. One also gets the impression that the authors are covering rather safe territory, since most people already accept factions and group theory in politics.

William L. Parish, ed., *Chinese Rural Development: The Great Transformation*. Armonk, NY: M.E. Sharpe, 1985. viii, 278, $35/$14.95 paper. Contributors analyze the new responsibility systems, providing information on loans, quotas, prices, etc. They adopt a "rational peasant" model (peasants respond predictably to incentives) in explaining the behavior of farmers, but they do not indicate whether the peasants are "rational" in the long- or short-term. For example, it is "rational" to want to minimize risks by accepting the communes and socialism, and it is also "rational" to want to maximize income by accepting private farming and the Deng reforms. One author points out that the gap in consumption between cities and rural areas has barely changed in three decades despite the rhetoric about favoring peasants over city dwellers. Other contributors offer interesting observations of life at the village and county levels.

Thomas E. Stolper, *China, Taiwan, and the Offshore Islands*. Armonk, NY: M. E. Sharpe. xiv, 170, $30. Stolper provides an intelligent, careful study of this key issue from September, 1954 to January-March, 1955 and August to October, 1958. He contends that Beijing did not plan to capture the small, coastal islands of Quemoy and the Tachens, but rather hoped to prevent any change in the status of Taiwan which put it outside the Mainland's reach. The problem with this approach is that the Chinese should have realized their actions would provoke greater determination in Washington to conclude a mutual defense treaty with Taiwan, resulting in a much tougher stand. The book is also important for its use of declassified sources. The study already has appeared in journal format bearing this title (XV, 1-2 [spring-summer 1985]).

Gerald Segal and William T. Tow, eds., *Chinese Defense Policy*. Champaign, Illinois: Univ. of Illinois Press, 1984. xxii, 286, $29.95. *Chinese Defense Policy* includes excellent summaries

continued . . .

KEY WORKS ON THE PEOPLE'S REPUBLIC OF CHINA (continued)

of the services, deficiencies, capabilities of the PLA and the effect of the military on Chinese foreign policy. The tone is optimistic. There is very little new in this volume, and some hedging: "China may not be in the first rank of military power, but neither is it fifth rate." Nevertheless, it offers a great deal of reliable information on the PLA.

James D. Seymour, ed., *China Rights Annual 1.* Armonk, NY: M.E. Sharpe, 1985. 197, $25. The first volume in this series covers October, 1983-September, 1984. It results from the SPEARhead project and its bulletin on human rights in East Asia. Information has been extracted from a wide variety of sources (primarily official Chinese sources, however) on aspects of human rights, such as women, religion, the handicapped, and punishment. Consequently, there is a great deal of valuable information here, even for people who have no particular interest in human rights. The major problem involves imposing the Western concept of "human rights" on the Chinese setting. One hopes this publication will continue.

Anita Chan, Stanley Rosen, and Jonathan Unger, eds., *On Socialist Democracy and the Chinese Legal System: The Li Yizhe Debates.* Armonk, NY: M.E. Sharpe, 1985. 311, $35/ $14.95 paper. Ki Yizhe, termed "China's only Marxist," was the pen name for the dissidents Li Zhengtian, Chen Yiyang, and Wang Xizhe. They authored the important manifest "On Socialist Democracy" in 1974 and other works. The reader is left wondering whether these people are indeed representative and somewhat puzzled why they wrote the manifesto. The editors suggest that the three hoped to reform the Chinese legal system, but did these Chinese dissidents so fundamentally misunderstand the system to believe they could change it, and completely fail to anticipate the legal response to their actions? The editors sensibly point out that Zhao Ziyang used Li Yizhe to attack the ultra-left in Guangdong in the late 1970s.

Albert Keidel, ed., *China Macroeconomic Newsletter* and the *China Projection Report.* Washington, D.C.: Rock Creek Research, 2607 24th Street, N.W. 20008. $185 for the 24 newsletters, and $175 for the semi-annual projection report/$335 for both. The *Newsletter* for 16 August 1985 was eight pages and included five tables in a mimeographed format. One observation notes that the volume of Chinese imports are tied closely to exports, but in general, the analysis is both good and extremely optimistic about China's growth potentials. The *Newsletter* with brief summaries can be read in about five minutes.

Alan Samagalski and Michael Buckley, *China: A Travel Survival Kit.* South Yarra, Victoria, Australia and Berkeley, CA: Lonely Planet, 1984. 820, $14.95 paper. This guide has been put together by an Australian free-lance journalist and a folk musician, with help from numerous travelers to China who have provided notes and letters about their experiences. In addition to giving the usual information on attractions and history, the guide offers many personal insights into such things as haggling at certain markets, where you will encounter bad railway connections, opportunities for hitch-hiking, and "nightlife" in Tianjin. The book resembles *The South American Handbook* in being helpful to visitors, especially young travelers who wish to spend something less than $250 a day. This is highly recommended.

World Bank, *China: Long-Term Development Issues and Options.* Baltimore: Johns Hopkins Press, 1985. xiv, 183, $29.95 cloth/$14.95 paper. This World Bank report should be read by everyone interested in China. It offers three scenarios in several areas of development to the year 2000: quadrupled gross value of industrial and agricultural output, moderate growth and balanced growth. The suggestions to improve economic efficiency and development are reasonable and helpful, if sometimes obvious: "To offset the likely slow growth in textile exports, China should more rapidly expand exports of other manufactures, including machinery and metal products . . ." (p. 104). This report uses data from the 1982 census not available for the previous edition, and includes statistics provided exclusively to the World Bank. The authors may err in generally 1) treating issues as economic rather than political decisions; 2) viewing problems from a national rather than from a local or individual perspective; and 3) assuming people benefit more from a rational and efficient economic

continued . . .

KEY WORKS ON THE PEOPLE'S REPUBLIC OF CHINA (continued)

system. By the year 2000, all of these assumptions may have turned out wrong. This is a very good value and a sophisticated analysis of data.

Bill Brugger, ed., *Chinese Marxism in Flux, 1978-84: Essays on Epistemology, Ideology and Political Economy*. Armonk, NY: M.E. Sharpe, 1985. 218, $30/$14.95 paper.

Michael S. Duke, ed., *Contemporary Chinese Literature: An Anthology of Post-Mao Fiction and Poetry*. Armonk, NY: M.E. Sharpe, 1985. 137, $35/$14.95 paper.

China issue, *Annals of the American Academy of Political and Social Science,* 476 (Nov 1984).

Cary Wolinsky, "Sichuan: Where China Changes Course," *National Geographic,* 168, 3 (Sep 1985), 280-317.

Committee on Energy and Commerce, US House of Representatives, *China's Economic Development and US Trade Interests*. Washington, D.C.: GPO, 1985. vi, 154.

Calvin Trillin, "American Chronicles: Zei-da-man," *New Yorker,* (7 Oct 1985), 61-94.

Lillian Craig Harris, "China's Foreign Policy Toward the Third World," *The Washington Papers,* 112 (1985). xii, 121.

Jeffrey R. Taylor, *Estimating Input-Output Tables From Scarce Data: Experiences of the US Census Bureau's Center for International Research*. Washington, D.C.: Bureau of the Census, 1984. 10.

Louis Kraar, "China After Marx: Open for Business," *Fortune* (18 Feb 1985), 28-33.

William DeB. Mills, "Content Analysis of Communist Documents," *Studies in Comparative Communism,* XVIII, 1 (spring 1985), 81-92, with bibliography in the footnotes.

China issue, *Time* (23 Sep 1985), 42-56.

China issue, *Current History,* 84, 503 (Sep 1985).

Nine P. Halpern, "Learning From Abroad: Chinese Views of the East European Economic Experience, January 1977-June 1981," *Modern China,* 11, 1 (Jan 1985), 77-109.

Modern Chinese Literature, 1, 1 (Sep 1984). This new journal is issued by the Center for the Study of Modern Chinese Literature of San Francisco State University.

Stevan Harrell, "Why Do the Chinese Work So Hard?" *Modern China,* 11, 2 (Apr 1985), 203-26.

Stanley Rosen, "Recentralization, Decentralization, and Rationalization: Deng Xiaoping's Bifurcated Educational Policy," *Modern China,* 11, 3 (Jul 1985), 301-46.

Susan Witty, "Barbarians on Wheels," *GEO,* 7 (Jan 1985), 36-45, 96-97, on bicycling through China.

Jean C. Robinson, "Of Women and Washing Machines: Employment, Housework, and the Reproduction of Motherhood in Socialist China," *China Quarterly,* 101 (Mar 1985), 32-57.

"Der alte Teng, er lebe 10 000 Jahre," *Der Spiegel,* 23 (3 Jun 1985), 132-40. This discusses peasant life in Shang Nian, 40 km northeast of Beijing.

continued . . .

KEY WORKS ON THE PEOPLE'S REPUBLIC OF CHINA (continued)

"The Economic Contract Law of the People's Republic of China" issue, *Chinese Law and Government,* XVIII, 1 (spring 1985).

Interview with Fan Rongkang, chief commentator of Remnin Ribao, on economic reforms, *Der Spiegel,* 17 (22 Apr 1985), 121-27.

Interview with Chinese sociologist Fei Xiaotong, *Der Spiegel,* 23 (3 Jun 1985), 140-46.

Wu Duo, "A Tentative Analysis of the Phenomenon of Beggary in Urban Shanghai Today," *Chinese Sociology and Anthropology,* XVII, 2 (winter 1984-85), 53-65, a translation of an article in *Shehui,* 1 (1981), 42-45. Wu notes that beggars were earning 5 or more yuan *a day* in Shanghai, while the average *monthly* urban wage was about 65 yuan.

"Die Sowjetunion und Asien" issue, *Osteuropa,* 34, 9 (Sep 1984).

Committee on Energy and Commerce, US House of Representatives, *Nuclear Energy Cooperation with China.* Washington, D.C.: GPO, 1984. iv, 219.

Committee on Foreign Affairs, US House of Representatives, *United States-China Relations.* Washington, D.C.: GPO, 1984. iv, 248.

Committee on Foreign Relations, US Senate, *United States-China Relations: Today's Realities and Prospects for the Future.* Washington, D.C.: GPO, 1984. iv, 73.

Robert Shaplen, "A Reporter at Large: Vietnam," *New Yorker* (22 Apr 1985), pt. 1, 104-25; (29 Apr 1985), pt. 2, 92-15, with information on Sino-Vietnamese relations.

Sotheby's, *Important Chinese Export Porcelain from the Mottahedeh Collection* (NY, 30 Jan 1985); *Chinese Decorative Arts and Snuff Bottles* (London, 2 May 1985); *Fine Chinese Paintings* (NY, 3 Jun 1985); *Fine Chinese Ceramics and Works of Art* (NY, 5 Jun 1985).

Denis Fred Simon, "Chinese-Style S&T Modernization: A Comparison of PRC and Taiwan Approaches," *Studies in Comparative Communism,* XVII, 2 (summer 1984), 87-109.

William deB. Mills, "Leadership Change in China's Provinces," *Problems of Communism,* XXXIV, 3 (May-Jun 1985), 24-40.

A. Tom Grunfeld, "In Search of Equality: Relations Bwtween China's Ethnic Minorities and the Majority Han," *Bulletin of Concerned Asian Scholars,* 17, 1 (1985), 54-67.

Fang Shan, "The Development of Small Towns in Mainland China," *Issues & Studies,* 21, 2 (Feb 1985), 80-99.

K.C. Yeh, "Review of Studies on Mainland China's Economy," *Issues & Studies,* 21, 5 (May 1985), 32-55.

Committee on Energy and Commerce, US House of Representatives, *China's New Patent Law and Other Recent Legal Developments.* Washington, D.C.: GPO, 1984. vi, 67.

R. David Arkush, "'If Man Works Hard the Land Will Not Be Lazy:' Entrepreneurial Values in North Chinese Peasant Proverbs," *Modern China,* 10, 4 (Oct 1984), 461-79.

Major (P) Michael J. Speltz, "Chinese Territorial Claims on the Soviet Far East," *Military Review,* LXV, 8 (Aug 1985), 63-73.

continued . . .

KEY WORKS ON THE PEOPLE'S REPUBLIC OF CHINA (continued)

Lewis M. Stern, "The Overseas Chinese in the Socialist Republic of Vietnam, 1979-82," *Asian Survey,* XXV, 5 (May 1985), 521-36.

Jeffrey R. Taylor, *Employment and Unemployment in China: Results from 10-Percent Sample Tabulation of 1982 Population Census.* Washington, D.C.: Bureau of the Census, FER No. 23, 1985, 47.

Wojtek Zafanolli, "A Brief Outline of China's Second Economy," *Asian Survey,* XXV, 7 (Jul 1985), 715-36.

Eberhard Sandschneider, "Political Succession in the People's Republic of China," *Asian Survey,* XXV, 6 (Jun 1985), 638-58.

Kitaiskaia narodnaia respublika v 1981 godu: politika, ekonomika, ideologiia. Moscow: Nauka, 1985. 269. 1R 60k.

Vaclav Smil, "China's Food," *Scientific American,* 253, 6 (Dec 1985), 116-24.

John F. Burns, "China On the Move: Will the Changes Last?" New York *Times Magazine* (8 Dec 1985), 38-42, 86-94.

Joint Economic Committee, US Congress, *Allocation of Resources in the Soviet Union and China—1984.* Washington, D.C.: GPO, 1985. vi, 259.

Jean C. Robinson, "Of Women and Washing Machines: Employment, Housework, and the Reproduction of Motherhood in Socialist China," *China Quarterly,* 101 (Mar 1985), 32-57.

CIA, *Beijing Street Guide.* Washington, D.C.: CIA, 1985. 241.

"Man of the Year: Deng Xiaoping" issue, *Time* (6 Jan 1986), 24-65.

US General Accounting Office, *Nuclear Agreement: Cooperation Between the United States and the People's Republic of China.* Washington, D.C.: GAO, NSIAD-86-21BR, 1985. 12.

Donald C. Clarke, "Political Power and Authority in Recent Chinese Literature," *China Quarterly,* 102 (Jun 1985), 234-52.

Elizabeth J. Perry, "Rural Violence in Socialist China," *China Quarterly,* 103 (Sep 1985), 414-40.

ACADEMIC INTERNATIONAL PRESS

THE RUSSIAN SERIES

1 S.F. Platonov *History of Russia* Out of Print
2 *The Nicky-Sunny Letters, Correspondence of Nicholas and Alexandra, 1914-1917*
3 Ken Shen Weigh *Russo-Chinese Diplomacy, 1689-1924* Out of Print
4 Gaston Cahen *Relations of Russia with China . . . 1689-1730* Out of Print
5 M.N. Pokrovsky *Brief History of Russia* 2 Volumes Out of Print
6 M.N. Pokrovsky *History of Russia from Earliest Times . . .* Out of Print
7 Robert J. Kerner *Bohemia in the Eighteenth Century*
8 *Memoirs of Prince Adam Czartoryski and His Correspondence with Alexander I* 2 vols.
9 S.F. Platonov *Moscow and the West*
10 S.F. Platonov *Boris Godunov*
11 Boris Nikolajewsky *Aseff the Spy*
12 Francis Dvornik *Les Legendes de Constantin et de Methode vues de Byzance*
13 Francis Dvornik *Les Slaves, Byzance et Rome au XIe Siecle*
14 A. Leroy-Beaulieu *Un Homme d'Etat Russe (Nicolas Miliutine) . . .*
15 Nicholas Berdyaev *Leontiev* (In English)
16 V.O. Kliuchevskii *Istoriia soslovii v Rossii*
17 *Tehran Yalta Potsdam. The Soviet Protocols*
18 *The Chronicle of Novgorod*
19 Paul N. Miliukov *Outlines of Russian Culture* Vol. III (2 vols.)
20 P.A. Zaionchkovsky *The Abolition of Serfdom in Russia*
21 V.V. Vinogradov *Russkii iazyk. Grammaticheskoe uchenie o slove*
22 P.A. Zaionchkovsky *The Russian Autocracy under Alexander III*
23 A.E. Presniakov *Emperor Nicholas I of Russia. The Apogee of Autocracy*
24 V.I. Semevskii *Krestianskii vopros v Rossii v XVIII i pervoi polovine XIX veka* Out of Print
25 S.S. Oldenburg *Last Tsar! Nicholas II, His Reign and His Russia* 4 volumes
26 Carl von Clausewitz *The Campaign of 1812 in Russia*
27 M.K. Liubavskii *Obrazovanie osnovnoi gosudarstvennoi territorii velikorusskoi narodnosti. Zaselenie i obedinenie tsentra*
28 S.F. Platonov *Ivan the Terrible* Paper
29 Paul N. Miliukov *Iz istorii russkoi intelligentsii. Sbornik Statei i etiudov*
30 A.E. Presniakov *The Tsardom of Muscovy* Paper
31 M. Gorky, J. Stalin et al., *History of the Civil War in Russia* 2 vols. Out of Print
32 R.G. Skrynnikov *Ivan the Terrible*
33 P.A. Zaionchkovsky *The Russian Autocracy in Crisis, 1878-1882*
34 Joseph T. Fuhrmann *Tsar Alexis. His Reign and His Russia*
35 R.G. Skrynnikov *Boris Godunov*
43 Nicholas Zernov *Three Russian Prophets: Khomiakov, Dostoevsky, Soloviev* Out of Print
44 Paul N. Miliukov *The Russian Revolution* 3 vols.
45 Anton I. Denikin *The White Army* Out of Print
55 M.V. Rodzianko *The Reign of Rasputin—An Empire's Collapse. Memoirs* Out of Print
56 *The Memoirs of Alexander Iswolsky*

THE CENTRAL AND EAST EUROPEAN SERIES

1 Louis Eisenmann *Le Compromis Austro-Hongrois de 1867*
3 Francis Dvornik *The Making of Central and Eastern Europe* 2nd edition
4 Feodor F. Zigel *Lectures on Slavonic Law*
10 Doros Alastos *Venizelos—Patriot, Statesman, Revolutionary*
20 Paul Teleki *The Evolution of Hungary and its Place in European History*

FORUM ASIATICA

1 M.I. Sladkovsky *China and Japan—Past and Present*

THE ACADEMIC INTERNATIONAL REFERENCE SERIES

The Modern Encyclopedia of Russian and Soviet History 50 vols. 1976-
The Modern Encyclopedia of Russian and Soviet Literatures 50 vols. 1977-
Soviet Armed Forces Review Annual 1977-
USSR Facts & Figures Annual 1977-
Military-Naval Encyclopedia of Russia and the Soviet Union 50 vols. 1978-
China Facts & Figures Annual 1978-
Encyclopedia USA. The Encyclopedia of the United States of America Past & Present 50 vols. 1983-
The International Military Encyclopedia 50 vols.
Sports Encyclopedia North America 50 vols. 1986-

SPECIAL WORKS

S.M. Soloviev *History of Russia* 50 vols.
SAFRA Papers 1985-